CONSERVATION CLASSICS

Nancy P. Pittman, Series Editor

With the Conservation Classics, ISLAND PRESS inaugurates a new series to again make available books that helped launch the conservation movement in America. When first published, these books offered provocative alternatives which challenged established methods and patterns of development.

Today, they offer practical solutions to contemporary challenges in such areas as multiple-use forestry, desertification and soil erosion, and sustainable agriculture. These new editions include valuable introductions from the leaders of today's conservation movement.

The inaugural titles in the series are:

BREAKING NEW GROUND
by Gifford Pinchot

Introduction by George T. Frampton, Jr.

PLOWMAN'S FOLLY
and
A SECOND LOOK
by Edward H. Faulkner

Introduction by Paul B. Sears

TREE CROPS
A Permanent Agriculture
by J. Russell Smith

Introduction by Wendell Berry

ISLAND PRESS
WASHINGTON, D.C. COVELO, CALIFORNIA

GIFFORD PINCHOT

Breaking New Ground

ISLAND PRESS

Washington, D.C. □ Covelo, California

Library of Congress Cataloging-in-Publication Data

Pinchot, Gifford, 1865-1946.
Breaking new ground.

(Conservation classics)
Reprint. Originally published: New York : Harcourt, Brace, and Co., 1947.
Includes index.
1. Pinchot, Gifford, 1865-1946. 2. Politicians--United States--Biography. 3. Conservationists--United States--Biography. 4. Conservation of natural resources--United States--History. I. Title. II. Series.
E664.P62A3 1987 333.75'092'4 [B] 87-82038
ISBN 0-933280-42-4 (pbk.)
ISBN 0-933280-50-5 (cloth)

Manufactured in the United States of America
10 9 8 7 6 5 4 3 2 1

Dedication

To the men and women of the Forest Service, whose courage, devotion, and intelligence have made it and kept it the best organization in the Government of the United States

Acknowledgments

My warm thanks and appreciation for their generous assistance in completing this book are due to more men and women than I have space to name. First of them all is Herbert A. Smith of the Forest Service, foremost authority on the history of Forestry in America and my close personal friend for over half a century. Next is Raphael Zon, also of the Service, who took up the work after Herbert had been called to his reward, and without whose help this volume would be unfinished still.

After these come John Lydenberg and Professor R. P. Holdsworth, whose co-operation was of outstanding value. And in addition, many members of the Service have written their memoirs for me. Others too numerous to mention have given much help in many ways, including Lyle F. Watts, Chief of the Forest Service, Earl W. Loveridge, Assistant Chief, Mrs. Edna F. Crocker, Miss Edith Simonson, and Mrs. Herbert A. Smith.

Note

It is a fixed habit among persons of literary experience to insert ellipsis marks whenever they fail to include the whole of a passage they quote. Now to me quotations interrupted by dots make hard reading. Accordingly, this is to notify you that this book contains many condensed quotations unmarred by rows of dots. I have done my best to keep the sense unchanged. I trust this meets with your approval.

Quotations not otherwise identified come from my diary or my letters home.

Contents

Introduction

It may come as something of a shock to our current generation of committed environmentalists to discover that the modern conservation movement sprang from a highly developed philosophy of *intensive use*, that is, exploitation, of our natural resources.

The influence of John Muir notwithstanding, this country's early concept of "conservation" was a product of the Progressive Era's enlightened utilitarianism, which held that the greatest good could be derived for the public by scientifically and intensively managing resources such as forests, for a productive use such as lumber, in a manner that would ensure their continued productivity for many generations to come. This was indeed an enlightened concept.

One of the principal architects of this vision was Gifford Pinchot, America's publicly-declared first forester and a tireless promoter of the early conservation ideal. He was a key figure in a small group of men who convinced two Presidents to create and vastly expand the "Forest Reserve" on Federal land in the West. As a confidante of Theodore Roosevelt and founder and first Chief of the U.S. Forest Service, Pinchot translated his philosophy for the "National Forests" into a public policy that continues to this day.

For nearly half a century, Pinchot's philosophy of wise and productive use of our National Forests served the nation well. Only a tiny percentage of the country's demand for timber was taken from the National Forests. Conflicting demands between logging and other forest uses, such as recreation, hunting and fishing, the need for clean water, habitat protection, and preservation of wilderness and scenic beauty, had not yet become troubling. The government agency that Pinchot created to manage the National Forests was able to carry out its mandate of good stewardship of the public's forestland in exemplary fashion. Indeed, the Forest Service gained a reputation for professionalism, competence and integrity that was the envy of other government agencies. For fifty years, Pinchot's "conservationist" program for managing the National Forests *worked* to balance a variety of national interests and competing demands for these resources.

More recent decades, however, have exposed the outlines of a conundrum that has always existed between the two integrally related goals of Progressive conservation: highly productive *use*, on the one hand; and *preservation* of the forests for future generations, on the other. Today, our National Forests comprise nearly 10 percent of the nation's land base, and controversy over the relative priorities to be accorded these goals has called into question the fundamental validity of Pinchot's original vision. The re-publication of *Breaking New Ground*, Gifford Pinchot's personal memoir of how he brought "Forestry and Conservation to America" is a timely restatement of Pinchot's original philosophy of conservation. It is particularly interesting to see the extent to which Pinchot's ideas about conservation were influenced by the broader Progressive movement.

One of the tenets of turn-of-the-century Progressivism was "scientific management;" the belief that government policymakers could develop "positive scientific methods" to eliminate waste and to maximize the benefits of natural resources for both present and future generations. It was a time of tremendous optimism about the future. Pinchot believed deeply in the social and economic reforms of the Progressive era. The idea that scientific timbering of forests could be comfortably accommodated with their long-term preservation as a productive resource was naturally embraced by the Bull Moose Republican Progressive. The Progressive basis for his philosophy, that resources should be used "for the greatest good of the greatest number in the long run" is a statement that cannot be improved upon.

Pinchot also sought to imbue forest conservation, perhaps inaccurately, with the trust-busting aspects of the Progressive movement. Pinchot's aim was to break up the monopoly of ownership of the large lumber and electric power companies, who were recklessly exploiting the timberlands, and to disperse the resources for the benefit of the "little man" by placing as much of the nation's forests as possible under rational government stewardship. (In reality, of course, it was not only the large companies, but the "little men" throughout the West who were clamoring the loudest for unregulated access to the forests.)

Conservation for Gifford Pinchot was in many ways a moral crusade. He was a leader of extraordinary charisma: handsome, tall, and very thin, with a sharply chiseled jawline that radiated certainty. His early staff of dedicated foresters were created 'in his own image.' And his memoir demonstrates how much the Forest Service's present-day forest management policy has been shaped by its first Chief.

* * *

By any standards, Pinchot was a remarkable man who is remembered as much for his two outstanding terms as governor of Pennsylvania as for his zeal in bringing scientific forestry to America. From one of America's patrician families, "he astounded his own Republican Party by appointing women and blacks to office." He also "reminded coal miners that though he supported their cause, he wouldn't tolerate their violence." He was a teetotaler, spoke French like a native, and had serious presidential ambitions.

This memoir, completed shortly before Pinchot died in 1946, covers only a portion of his life, beginning in 1889 with Pinchot's post-college education in European forestry and ending in early 1910 with his dismissal by Roosevelt's successor, William Howard Taft. Pinchot had picked a public fight with the new administration's Secretary of the Interior, Richard Ballinger, whom he accused of corruption in the matter of some Alaskan coal leases. (Known as the Pinchot-Ballinger controversy, serious scholars are still debating who was in the right.) The reader should be warned that *Breaking New Ground* covers even that portion of Pinchot's career somewhat selectively. For Pinchot was wont to take offense easily, to claim his own with ususual alacrity, and to apportion credit to others in sparing fashion.

After his dismissal by Taft, Pinchot began a kind of "second life" in liberal Republican politics in Pennsylvania. He married for the first time at the age of almost fifty, after pining for twenty years over a dead sweetheart. He ran for the Senate twice, losing both times. (His wife, with Pinchot's encouragement, also ran for Congress and lost.) He served two terms as a crusading, anti-corruption, public works-oriented Governor. But little of that subsequent life is recounted here. Indeed, *Breaking New Ground* is by no stretch of the imagination an intimate biography. If Pinchot was ever a man beset by internal doubts, there is no hint of it here. Rather, this volume reveals him to be a man consumed by a public passion and almost messianic reformist crusade. And if it reveals him to be a proud, self-righteous and stubborn man, given to promoting himself as well as the ideas he held so dear, *Breaking New Ground* also serves to remind us of the sheer force of his personality, the keenness of his intellect, his astonishing energy, and the enormous impact this one man had on the management of the country's natural resources, an impact that has been felt throughout the twentieth century.

Readers may find particular interest in Pinchot's account of the year he spent in Germany and France studying forestry after his graduation from Yale in 1889. The lesson Pinchot drew from the European forestry model—that scientific timbering of forests could be comfortably accommodated with their long-term preservation as a productive resource, was the basis of his future philosophy. Pinchot returned to this country thirteen months later to find that the notion of prudent management of forests in this country—by private landowners or the government—was unheard of. Even as late as the 1880's, America's stock of forests still seemed endless; more of a hindrance than a precious resource. Lumber companies practiced what had come to be known as "cut and run" forestry, taking the best trees and leaving behind a scattered slash which hindered regeneration of the forest, encouraged rapid erosion and often gave rise to sweeping forest fires that destroyed thousands of square miles of virgin timber. The silviculture methods that were practiced of necessity in Europe—cutting selectively on a planned basis so that a forest could produce an "even flow" of timber for fifty to a hundred years until each section was completely regenerated and could be harvested again—were barely known and had never been attempted in America.

As early as 1864, George Perkins Marsh had warned in *Man and Nature* that "we are, even now, breaking up the floor and wainscotting and doors and window frames of our dwelling." A few concerned citizens had formed the American Forestry Association in 1875. Congress authorized creation of a small Division of Forestry within the Department of Agriculture. But these efforts were more symbolic than practical. As Pinchot himself describes the situation, "When the Gay Nineties began, the common word for our forests was 'inexhaustible.' To waste timber was a virtue not a crime. There would always be plenty of timber and everything else in America for everybody, world without end. The lumbermen, whose industry was then the third greatest in this country, regarded forest devastation as normal, and second growth [regeneration of cut-over forests] as a delusion of fools. . . . As for sustained yield, no such idea had ever entered their heads." Of course, there were no forestry schools—and no jobs for foresters—anywhere in this country.

* * *

It was Pinchot's father, James, a wealthy Republican of Victorian mien but liberal social views, who first sparked Gifford's interest in conserving the country's forestlands. James Pinchot, a second generation Frenchman, whose flourishing New York dry goods business had allowed him to retire to a French-style chateau in Pennsylvania, owned several hundred acres of prime forest which he harvested with a Frenchman's frugality. Not only did he urge his son, Gifford, to consider forestry as a profession, he and other members of the Pinchot family later helped to found the Yale School of Forestry.

But in 1889, the only possibility of training for Gifford was abroad. There Gifford came under the tutelage of Sir Dietrich Brandis, the German authority on silviculture. Brandis encouraged him to attend the French Forest School at Nancy during the winter of 1889–90 and arranged several month-long apprenticeships with other leading European foresters. But after thirteen months, the budding young forester decided it was time to return to America and begin his career in earnest—his newfound mission to bring the science of European forestry to the United States.

The forestry Pinchot sought to transplant to America was a science designed to ensure a continuing flow of timber (and a perpetual cash flow). "Forestry is tree-farming," Pinchot wrote, "handling trees so that one crop follows another." This scientific program of intensive use was seen as an essential reform to combat the undisciplined, unscientific exploitation to which forests were being subjected at that time: what Pinchot himself called "the most rapid and extensive forest destruction ever known," a "gigantic and lamentable massacre of trees." Pinchot and his contemporaries feared that if such forest destruction continued unabated, the country might soon experience a "timber famine." The idea of a disciplined program of timber harvesting seemed, in the context of the day, a radical and reformist solution to the problem of rampant forest destruction.

Immediately upon his return, Gifford Pinchot, using his father's contacts, arranged a series of interviews with an illustrious constellation of figures in the "forest movement," ranging from Charles S. Sargent, founder of *Garden and Forest* magazine, to Dr. Bernard Fernow, the head of the Agriculture Department's Forestry Division, to the secretaries of Agriculture and the Interior, and even the Vice President! After two exciting inspection trips to the West, one with Fernow, Pinchot decided to reject advice that he pursue an advanced degree, and turned down an offer of an assistantship with Fernow in favor of putting his new-found expertise into practical application. That opportunity came early in 1892.

The great landscape architect, Frederick Law Olmstead, a friend of James Pinchot, was creating for George W. Vanderbilt what was to be the most elaborate country estate in America on seven thousand acres near Asheville, North Carolina. It was to include an arboretum, a model farm, and a forestry demonstration project, which Vanderbilt asked Gifford Pinchot to supervise. Pinchot immediately set to work mapping the forest, preparing a six-year working plan, undertaking selective cutting, and training the logging crews. In addition to planning and running the Biltmore Forest (which showed a profit of $1,200 the first year), Pinchot prepared an exhibition on forestry for Vanderbilt for the Chicago World's Fair, opened an office as a "Consulting Forester" on Fourth Avenue in New York City, undertook a heavy schedule of writing and speaking to proselytize his views, and began to attract clients. Despite this early success, however, Pinchot despaired that "except for Biltmore, there were times when I seemed to be getting very little done in the way of practical forestry."

In the meantime, a little-noticed bill passed by Congress in 1891 authorized the President to designate Forest Reserves on public lands. Soon after its passage, Benjamin Harrison set aside over thirteen million acres of western forestland. But no law specified how or for what purpose these lands were to be managed. In 1896, the Secretary of Interior asked the National Academy of Sciences to appoint a Forest Commission to advise on the use of the reserves. This prestigious Commission was chaired by the legendary Charles Sargent, famous botanist and former Chairman of the New York State Forest Commission which originated the Adirondack Forest Preserve. Gifford Pinchot, at age thirty-one, became the Commission's youngest member.

The very existence of the Commission was due in large part to the efforts of a small group of men, of whom Sargent was the most prominent, who had been agitating since the late 1880's for withdrawal of all the federally-owned forests in the West, temporary use of the Army to protect them, and development of a long-range plan to administer and preserve these lands. But Pinchot was vigorously opposed to this scheme, fearing that any new reserves would, as he put it, "be taken out of circulation and locked up," rather than being available for the intensive productive forestry of the European model, which he favored. Internal struggles within the Commission almost caused Pinchot to file a minority report, but at the last minute he demurred. The ultimate report, though not to Pinchot's liking, had spectacular results: President Cleveland, without notice to Congress, and only ten days before going out of office in February, 1897, acted on the Commission's advice and unilaterally created twenty-one million acres of additional Forest Reserves.

The following year, Pinchot went off to the West as Special Agent of the Interior Department's General Land Office to examine the new almost forty million acres of Forest Reserves which they administered. In 1898, when Dr. Fernow retired from the Agriculture Department's Division of Forestry, Pinchot was asked to take his place. Finally in a position of some power, Pinchot rapidly began to build up the budget and staff of the Division, which grew from 11 to 179 people by 1901. But the Division had one problem: it had no forests to administer. The Forest Reserves were under the Interior Department's General Land Office. Thus, Pinchot was consigned to publicizing and pamphleteering to convince the public that forests that were scientifically and intensively managed for lumber production would be in the best interests of the country.

There was politicking, too. For Pinchot soon began a campaign to have the Forest Reserves transferred to the Agriculture Department and put under his own sway. Among those to whom he appealed were western interests, arguing that they would benefit from productive but careful use of federal forestlands. Pinchot made little headway under President McKinley. But when McKinley was assassinated in 1901, he was replaced by a President who shared Pinchot's utilitarian conservation ideas and his reform mentality. Indeed, Roosevelt was already a friend of Pinchot's from the mid-1890's, when T.R. nominated him to the Sportsman's Boone and Crockett Club, which Roosevelt helped to found.

Finally in 1905, with Roosevelt's help, Pinchot succeeded in winning approval from Congress for the transfer of authority over what had now grown (with further set-asides) to eighty-six million acres of federal forests. The Forest Reserves would henceforth be called the National Forests and would be managed by a U.S. Forest Service, of which Pinchot was the first Chief. Indeed, the charter of the new Service and its initial management guidelines were contained in a letter to himself from the Secretary of Agriculture which Pinchot wrote. The charter stressed that the forests were to be devoted to their "most productive use for the permanent good of the whole people," that "all the resources of forest reserves are for *use*, and this use must be brought about in a thoroughly prompt and businesslike manner, under such restrictions only as will insure the permanence of these resources," and that the "water, wood, and forage of the reserves [must be] conserved and wisely used for the benefit of the home builder first of all." Pinchot could say proudly in 1946 that "in the four decades between [1905–1946] this letter has set the standard for the Service, and it is still being quoted as the essence of Forest Service policy."

* * *

However, since the early 1950's, the average annual timber harvest from our National Forests has been approximately ten times what it was before World War II. Much of the productive timberland in these forests has already been clear-cut. Our National Forest System is crisscrossed by 340,000 miles of roads. That is eight time the mileage of the interstate highway system. In the mid-1930's, the National Forests contained about 150 million acres of roadless areas. Today, there is less than a third that amount outside areas that have been formally designated as Wilderness. Beginning in the 1980's, the Forest Service embarked on a long-range plan to *double* the annual timber cut, and proposed to build another 580,000 miles of new logging roads.

Today, many environmentalists regard Pinchot's reformist program of intensive forestry, as it is being applied by the U.S. Forest Service, as the engine of destruction of that same public forestland that Pinchot set out to protect and sustain. Indeed, the Wilderness movement arose in the 1930's partly in response to what was perceived as an overzealous application of Pinchot's original forest reforms.

From the environmentalist perspective of today, Pinchot's unabashed optimism contained the naive assumption that over the long run we could really "have it all"; that it was really possible to exploit our forests for short-term production of lumber and *also* preserve them indefinitely;

that scientific principles could help us avoid making difficult political decisions and trade-offs between the different uses to which public forests might be dedicated; that rationalism and efficiency might make it unnecessary to solve the problem of generational equity by choosing between exploitation and preservation. (This is not to say that Pinchot did not clearly perceive the underlying conflict between use of natural resources and their long-term preservation. But he believed they could be wrapped together into a single program.)

If the environmentalist position is correct—that the original program of converting most of our public forestland to an intensively managed and regulated forest is not the right prescription for today—are we to conclude that Pinchot's original vision of setting aside public forestlands for intensive use was wrong? Perhaps not for its time. It must be remembered that the very creation of the National Forest System, in which Pinchot played such a central role, was a mighty victory for the protection of our natural heritage. That victory required the kind of broad political consensus that, possibly, only the Progressive utilitarian movement could have forged.

Or, have his ideas been misappropriated by the Forest Service over time? Again, I think the answer is no. Over and over, Pinchot made the point that the "first great fact about conservation is that it stands for *development*." He goes on to say, "There has been a fundamental misconception that conservation means nothing but the husbanding of resources for future generations. There could be no more serious mistake." Pinchot's epic fight with John Muir (whom he both admired and thought demented) over the damming of Yosemite's Hetch Hetchy Valley to supply drinking water for San Francisco, and his resistance to seeing forestland "locked up" in new National Parks, clearly demonstrates his preference for exploitation. Pinchot believed that provision of wood products for immediate use must be the predominant goal of forest management. So the current accelerated program to extend "intensive management," i.e., tree farming, to as much of the National Forests as possible, is simply the realization of Pinchot's dream.

What Pinchot could not have foreseen was the tremendous competition that is occurring today from all segments of society for our publicly-owned forest resources: not just for timber (and the jobs dependent upon cutting it), but also for recreation (the National Forests support twice as many recreation visitations every year as our National Parks), for protection of municipal watersheds, for wildlife habitat, for wilderness and scenic beauty, and crucially, for the rapidly shrinking opportunity to protect a few of the last remaining fragments of a million years of nature's evolving hand, intact from human development.

Nor could Pinchot have contemplated the rise of the science of ecology, along with the modern understanding of an ecological system as an interrelated, interdependent whole. Pinchot looked at forests primarily as a source of wood fiber, not as delicately-balanced systems that, if disturbed, might be unalterably damaged. We understand better than in 1900 that many areas of our public forestland simply cannot be tree-farmed. Pushing intensive logging operations into fragile watersheds can cause erosion that destroys streams. Roadbuilding and clearcutting with modern technology in higher elevations or in areas with thin soil can destroy the ecosystem and prevent, or at least impede, regeneration of the forests.

Pinchot made no fundamental distinction between public and privately-owned forestland. Indeed, he wanted eventually to extend his program of forest conservation to private forests, by suasion or government regulation. For our National Forests contain only twenty percent of the commercially viable timberland in this country. But in the past few years, a very different vision has begun to be articulated for their future management. This vision holds that *public* forestland ought to be managed primarily to provide those public benefits that private land is never going to provide for in a market economy: recreation, clean water, biological diversity, scientific study, protection of fragile natural ecosystems, and preservation of wilderness.

Doubtless in 1905 it would have seemed a heresy to Pinchot to suggest that our federal forests should be managed for timber production only when necessary to supplement the supply available from private forestland; that logging should be restricted to areas where reforestation can be ecologically assured; and that non-disturbing uses which preserve the forests for future generations should be given equal or possibly greater weight than logging. But the modern science of ecology is leading us in this direction.

And modern economics are far different than they were in 1905. In many areas greater economic values are now received from recreation and tourism, and from the availability of clean water values that are often diminished by logging. It has long been imbedded in our law that the National Forests should be managed for "multiple uses"—not only timber and range, but also recreation, clean water, sport and commercial hunting and fishing, protection of wildlife habitat, biological diversity, and scientific research. Not fully recognizing that these uses often conflict, the Forest Service has continued to emphasize timber production. However, it may be that in the future the greatest economic as well as ecological benefits can be derived for the country by managing the National Forests primarily for multiple uses other than timber. One wonders how the brilliant and committed forester and reformer Gifford Pinchot would react to this new definition of "the greatest good for the greatest number in the long run."

George T. Frampton, Jr.
President, The Wilderness Society
Washington, D.C.
July 1987

On Writing History

This is my personal story of how Forestry and Conservation came to America. It is the story of an eyewitness, an account of events in which I had a part, written to tell not only what happened but also why and how it happened. Unless the circumstances of the times are set forth, and in particular the condition of public opinion, a true picture of what it took to bring Forestry and Conservation to America is hard to get. And for drawing that picture personal experience beats documentary history all hollow.

A document may represent a fact, or it may represent the concealment of a fact. It may arise from the free and original action of the signer, or it may have been forced upon the signer, or forced from the signer, in any one of a thousand ways—or for any one of a thousand reasons. It may be honest or it may be false. Its face value may be its true value or the exact opposite.

Documents have their place, of course. Obviously history could not be written without them. But my respect for history written from documents alone, after the men who lived it and made it have passed away, is distinctly qualified. I have been in on, or have known about, the making of too many documents not to know how often they tell but part of the real story, or even distort it altogether. More than once I have been present when high Government officials, confronted with documents bearing their own signatures, found, too late for correction, that what they had signed was directly opposed to their actual intentions or beliefs. And I have lived through many events of which historical accounts, written from documents, do not bear even a distant family resemblance to the essential truth.

Liddell Hart, the brilliant historian of the First World War, remarks, after twenty years of historical work, that "Nothing can deceive like a document." He adds that pure documentary history seems to him akin to mythology. And an American historian, Henry F. Pringle, relying upon documents, attributes the Conservation policy, which was

Theodore Roosevelt's greatest contribution to the world, mainly to Taft, the man who betrayed it and thereby lost his second term.

History written from personal recollection, fortified by documents, impresses me more and more as I grow older. There are many portions of the American story of Forestry and Conservation which never will be rightly understood unless the men who had a part in them supply the background of facts actually experienced, which alone can explain what the documents really mean.

Statements in books and in the press may be blind guides to actual happenings or to the state of public opinion. Ever since newspapers began, news has been colored by the mental bias of owners, reporters, writers, or editors, and that hardly less by omissions than by false statements. So also the facts have been colored in the eyes of historians who have accepted the occasional utterances of advanced thinkers as accurately representing the public mind.

It is easy enough, by running your eye across the literature of the generations, to find quotable references to the value of the forest in America and the importance of protecting it. And it is equally easy to draw the conclusion that these isolated appeals sprang from or represented a widespread interest in the forest—a general concern which, at least in my opinion, until the early days of the present century wasn't there at all.

Take, for example, George P. Marsh's epoch-making book, *Man and Nature,* afterward called *The Earth as Modified by Human Action,* published in 1864. Unquestionably it started a few people thinking. But did it indicate any general public interest in Forestry in America at the time of the Civil War?

Marsh was one man, and his book one book. Let us check it against an encyclopedia, written to furnish many men with information in which they took an interest and which they were likely to want.

The several volumes of the *New American Encyclopedia—a Popular Dictionary of General Knowledge,* published in 1862, still occupy a shelf in our library. Under the word "Forest," it offers one entry and only one, and that refers to Forest County, Pennsylvania. There is no such heading as Forestry and nothing whatever about that subject except an article under the heading "Arboriculture." And that deals exclusively with tree planting.

How unsafe it would be to assume, from Marsh's great book, that

Forestry occupied any appreciable space in the American mind of Civil War times!

The common statement that actions or events cannot be properly appraised until after generations have passed has always seemed to me pure nonsense. If it means anything, it means that actions and events cannot be understood until there is nobody left alive who knows the inside causes which produced them, or the true conditions which gave them their meaning.

This is not a formal history, decorated and delayed by references to authorities. As to nearly every statement it contains, you will have to take it or leave it on my say-so.

About many parts of the story of Forestry in America from 1885 to 1910, I am the only living witness. That is another reason why you must take my word or leave it.

In order to tell the story accurately, I have judged it necessary, here and there, to include quotations that are friendly, or overfriendly, to myself. That I take pride in them it would be futile to deny. Yet however much I may love angling for trout, angling for credit is a form of sport with which I have little sympathy. The task I have set myself requires me to tell the truth, let the credit fall where it may. This book would be useless on any other basis.

But I am eager to give credit where credit is due—credit to as fine a body of men and women as ever gave their very best to a great cause, the members of the Forest Service of the United States, whose character and capacity accomplished what all but they believed to be impossible.

All of which is submitted as a reason why I have tried to write down some of the things I know of my own knowledge about the origin and growth, the struggles, the losses, and the victories, of Forestry and Conservation in America.

GIFFORD PINCHOT

August 1, 1946

PINCHOT AND ROOSEVELT

This photograph, taken on the Inland Waterways Commission trip down the Mississippi River in October, 1907, shows Pinchot in the middle of the story he tells on p. 330.

PART I
CHOOSING A LIFEWORK

1. *Through Yale to Nancy*

"How would you like to be a forester?" asked my foresighted Father one fortunate morning in the summer of 1885, just before I went to college. It was an amazing question for that day and generation—how amazing I didn't begin to understand at the time. When it was asked, not a single American had made Forestry his profession. Not an acre of timberland was being handled under the principles of Forestry anywhere in America.

Outside the tropics, American forests were the richest and most productive on earth, and the best able to repay good management. But nobody had begun to manage any part of them with an eye to the future. On the contrary, the greatest, the swiftest, the most efficient, and the most appalling wave of forest destruction in human history was then swelling to its climax in the United States; and the American people were glad of it. Nobody knew how much timberland we had left, and hardly anybody cared. More than 99 per cent of our people regarded forest perpetuation, if they thought about it at all, as needless and even ridiculous.

So far as the natural resources were concerned, we were still a nation of pioneers. The world was all before us, and there would always be plenty of everything for everybody.

Public opinion held the forests in particular to be inexhaustible and in the way. What to do with the timber? Get rid of it, of course.

Only a meager handful of men and women had any concern for the future of the forests. They spoke of Forestry, but they thought only of forest preservation, forest influences, and tree planting. The actual practice of Forestry—forest management for continuous production—if they had ever grasped what it meant, was something far outside the field of practical affairs.

At a time when the few who considered Forestry at all were discoursing, deploring, and denouncing, and nothing more, my Father, with his remarkable power of observation and his equally remarkable prophetic outlook, looked ahead farther and more wisely than the rest. While they talked, he compared the forest conditions on two continents and clothed his thoughts with action.

He had seen foresters and their work, and the results of their work, in France and elsewhere in Europe. He was fond of quoting the great saying of one of his heroes, Bernard Palissy, the inspired potter, naturalist, and philosopher, who died in the Bastille, that neglect of the forest was "not merely a blunder, but a calamity and a curse for France."

Without being himself a forester, my Father understood the relation between forests and national welfare, as another of his heroes, Colbert, minister of Louis XIV, had understood it three centuries before. He was sure that Forestry must come to America, he was convinced of the prodigious service it could render, he was confident that foresters would be needed, and he believed the time was ripe.

My Father was the first American, so far as I know, to ask his young hopeful the question with which this chapter begins. He saw what nobody else had seen, that here was a career waiting for somebody's son.

Looking back over more than sixty years, his clear vision and far-seeing action seem to me most remarkable. And equally so was his refusal to be shaken by the cold water thrown on his plan by most of his friends and substantially all the leaders of the forest movement. He was sure he was right, in spite of the general judgment against him, and because he was sure, so was I.

My Father's foresight and tenacity were responsible, in the last analysis, for bringing Forestry to this continent. That being true, he was and is fairly entitled to be called the Father of Forestry in America.

Forestry was a brand-new idea to me. I had no more conception of what it meant to be a forester than the man in the moon. Just what a forester did, since he no longer wore green cap and leather jerkin and shot cloth-yard arrows at the King's deer, was beyond my ken. But at least a forester worked in the woods and with the woods—and I loved the woods and everything about them.

As a boy it was my firm intention to be a naturalist. Camping was my delight. My pin-fire shotgun was my treasure. I had heard a panther scream in the Adirondack woods the summer my Father gave me my first rod and taught me to cast my first fly. The broken butt of that rod is in my rack to this very day.

Of course a youngster with such a background would want to be a forester. Whatever Forestry might be, I was for it.

Until that moment I had been undecided between medicine and the ministry. My Father's suggestion settled the question in favor of Forestry. There were not many tracks in that trail, and that was all the more reason for taking a chance. So simply my happy adventure began.

But how to start on my adventure—how to become a forester—was not so simple. There were no schools of Forestry in America, nor even any school where Forestry could be studied, so far as I could learn. And even if there had been, for the time being I had other fish to fry. I proposed to follow the family tradition and go to Yale. Once there, I would look around and pick up what Forestry I could. And what I could pick up turned out to be little enough.

Whoever turned his mind toward Forestry in those days thought little about the forest itself and more about its influences, and about its influence on rainfall first of all. So I took a course in meteorology, which has to do with weather and climate. And another in botany, which has to do with the vegetable kingdom—trees are unquestionably vegetable. And another in geology, for forests grow out of the earth. Also I took a course in astronomy, for it is the sun which makes trees grow. All of which was as it should be, because science underlies the forester's knowledge of the woods. So far I was headed right.

But as for Forestry itself, there wasn't even a suspicion of it at Yale. The time for teaching Forestry as a profession was years away.

Under such circumstances, with little more knowledge of what I was after than a cat has about catalysts, and with the thousand pressing interests of the undergraduate busily blocking off the future, I set out to become a professional forester.

In those days undergraduate life at Yale was strenuous enough to block off any future. Forestry was forgotten when, in a Freshman-Sophomore rush, half a dozen Sophomores got hold of my arms and pulled me across the famous Yale Fence. Half a dozen more detained my raiment, so that I came out of that rush tastefully, if not lavishly, attired in a pair of shoes and a leather belt. My Father, on a surprise visit to his serious-minded son, turned up just as a delighted Junior was covering me up with a linen duster.

My family gave me some books on Forestry, and I searched the Yale Library for others. Marsh's great work, *The Earth as Modified by Human Action,* led me along the path a little way. Charles S. Sargent's monumental volume on American Forests in the Tenth Census contained much information on distribution and botanical relationships, but nothing at all about forest management.

The publications of the Department of Agriculture and the American Forest Congress set me no forrarder. Indeed only one book that came my way at Yale actually discussed the application of Forestry to the forest, and that was published in Paris three years before I was born—Jules Clavé's *Studies in Forest Economy.*

But if there was little or nothing to be learned at Yale about the practice of Forestry, there was some information to be had about forests. William H. Brewer, Professor of Agriculture in the Sheffield Scientific School, had published a highly intelligent mapping and description of the distribution of American forests in Walker's *Statistical Atlas of the Ninth Census,* thus antedating Sargent by ten years. I found that Brewer knew far more about forests at home and Forestry abroad than any other man at Yale.

Dear old Professor Brewer, that wise and kindly compendium of universal information, was among the very last of the great men who took all learning for their province. There appeared to be no subject upon which he was not ready to lecture, or give a whole course of lectures, at a moment's notice—forests among the rest. His service to Forestry in America should never be forgotten.

Four busy and happy years at Yale passed like a watch in the night. "We had a good time and studied, some—Fol de rol de rol rol rol." What with my work as a Class Deacon, Class committees, athletics, writing for the *Yale Literary Magazine,* the Grand Street Mission, and a thousand other matters, my studies got no more than half my time. And that was well enough. What I learned outside the classroom was worth at least as much as what I learned inside it.

As a sample of my economic views in college, I submit my indignation over Government regulation of railroad rates: "The railroads own the tracks and the cars, don't they? Then why shouldn't they charge what they please?" Which wasn't exactly a good start for a forester and a man who was to become and remain a Theodore Roosevelt Progressive.

The truth is that I had not yet begun to think. Like most of the glorious class of '89, I was too much absorbed and fascinated by living to do much thinking. I had a lively and deep-seated desire to be of use in the world, and occasional questionings as to whether I could serve best as a minister, a doctor, or a forester. But the why of things interested me little.

Action was what I craved. The fact that Forestry was new and strange and promised action probably had as much to do with my final choice of it as my love for the woods.

During the winter of my senior year (1888-89) I went to Washington to check my plan to be a forester against the Government forest authorities.

Dr. George B. Loring, then recently retired as United States Commissioner of Agriculture (we call them Secretaries now), and one of the leaders in advocating forest preservation, thought there was little chance to find work in Forestry, and little need for it anyhow, because "there was no centralized monarchical power," and because the country was so vast and second growth so rapid.

Dr. Bernard E. Fernow, a trained German forester, Chief of the Forestry Division, and as such head of the Government's forest work and of the forest movement in America, advised me not to take up Forestry as my profession, but only as second fiddle to something else. A few days later he wrote, "The wiser plan would be to so direct your studies that they will be useful in other directions also. The study of the sciences underlying forestry will also fit you for landscape gardening, nursery business, botanist's work, etc."

Dr. Fernow, a tall, vigorous, and very active man, spoke naturally with the voice of authority. He saw the American situation through European eyes, and one of his fundamental ideas was that under existing conditions Forestry was impracticable in the United States.

Other opinions agreed with Washington. Professor Charles S. Sargent, head of the Arnold Arboretum at Harvard and publisher of *Garden and Forest,* the foremost advocate of forest preservation, took the same position. So did my Grandfather Eno, who had made a great fortune for himself and offered me the chance to do likewise. It was pretty unanimous.

Nevertheless and notwithstanding, my Father strongly advised me to stick to my guns. With his support I did stick to them. As I wrote him: "In spite of the unfavorable opinions of those who know, it appears to me that there must be a future for Forestry in this country."

At the end of the course at Yale I had a little new knowledge, many friends who were to last through life, and associations worth more than any riches. And I was more than ever determined to be a forester, although I had yet to learn just what it was I had started to become.

Being a convert to Forestry, I was eager to bear witness to my faith. Out of a clear sky came the chance. At Commencement, after Mark Twain, in a speech since become famous, had discussed macerated spiders, pulverized lizards, and other abominations which doctors fed to their patients in the not-so-long-ago, and after other notables had said their say before the Alumni meeting, a member of the graduation class by the name of Pinchot, sitting with his Father in a modest place, was called upon.

I had carefully prepared myself to talk, not on Forestry, but on some subject long since forgotten. But on the spur of the moment I dropped it, my future profession welled up inside me and took its place, and I made to the exalted graduates of Yale (in June of 1889) my first public statement on the importance of Forestry to the United States—and my first public declaration that I had chosen it for my lifework.

I had chosen Forestry, but still I did not know exactly what it was I had chosen. So in the fall, when the will to work came back to me after the strenuous senior year at Yale, in spite of an offer to be Secretary of the Yale Y.M.C.A. for a year, another from the University of Chicago, and still another to study in the Forestry Division at Washington, I went abroad to find out. It was my simple intention, after having done so, to buy a few books and come home—proof enough that I was still lost in the fog.

There was then in Paris a Universal Exposition, which included a special exhibit of Waters and Forests. I was on my way to see it when good fortune overtook me. What set my feet in the path was the kindness of an Englishman to an American youngster who had no possible claim upon him.

I had heard that Forestry was practiced in British India, and it occurred to me that I might get some publications on the subject if I went to India House in London and asked for them. The publications I got, but I got also what was worth infinitely more. Mr. W. N.

Sturt, a high official of the Indian Civil Administration, was good enough not only to see and talk with the seeker for light, but also to take an interest in him.

Mr. Sturt got me a letter from his Chief, Sir Charles Bernard, to Sir Dietrich Brandis, founder of Forestry in British India; and another to Sir William Schlich, head of the Forest School at Cooper's Hill, where foresters were trained for the British Indian Service. Like Brandis, Schlich was a German—a man of great experience and learning, a trained forester who had succeeded Brandis as Inspector General of Forests to the Government of India.

Schlich received me most kindly; listened to my story; regretted that under the rules he could not take me as a student at Cooper's Hill; and advised me to strike for the creation of National Forests (this was before there were any in America). Also he gave me an autographed copy of Volume I of his *Manual of Forestry* (I have just been running over that well-thumbed book once more), and sent me with his blessing on my pilgrimage to Sir Dietrich Brandis at Bonn-on-the-Rhine.

"As I learn more of Forestry, I see more and more the need of it in the United States, and the great difficulty of carrying it into effect." So I wrote home after seeing Schlich. Sir William had done nothing to conceal the hard going ahead.

In Paris (and how glad I was to be in Paris again!) I revisited the Jardin des Plantes (where as a boy I had studied insects and snakes), saw Louis Pasteur inoculate an American friend of mine for mad-dog bite, was given letters to the French forest authorities by Whitelaw Reid, an old friend of my Father's and our Minister to France (Ambassadors came later), and met M. Daubrée, head of the French Forest Service, who in turn put me in touch with the head of the French Forest School.

I recall being introduced, also, to William M. Evarts, then a big figure in American public life, and escorting some of my French and American friends to see Buffalo Bill, the great American Scout, who was taking Paris by storm. To him I had been made known years before by William Tecumseh Sherman, General of the Army and close friend of the Pinchots. The tree the latter planted at Milford is still the finest Maple on our place. As to Buffalo Bill, for him I came to have strong liking and high respect. He remained my friend until he died.

In between many distractions I studied the Forest Exhibit; was impressed, bewildered, and discouraged by its complexity and extent; recovered and made no end of notes upon it; and went up in a captive balloon with my best girl of that period, who happened to be in Paris with her mother.

From the Eiffel Tower, then the tallest structure ever built by human hands, I looked down upon Passy, where as a small boy I had seen streets still filled with debris, and houses cut in two, by the German bombardment of 1870; upon the Gardens of the Tuileries, whose palace was burned by the Communards after the siege; upon Saint Cloud, where I watched some of these same Communards waiting in a prison yard for their trial and the blank wall; upon the Mare d'Auteuil, where, like Peter Ibbetson, I followed the dragon flies; and upon the Arc de Triomphe, in sight of which so much of my childhood had been spent.

Meanwhile, by another great piece of luck, I forgathered with a young French forester named Edouard Blanc, and told him my story. He insisted that I could get little or nothing by going to a forest school just to look it over, and that I would have to spend a year in study to do anything worth while. He said that my best chance was at the *Ecole nationale forestière* at Nancy in Lorraine, and added that now was my last chance, for after this year the course there would require three years' preliminary work in Paris.

Edouard Blanc's talk was convincing. So at the end of a hectic stay I departed for Bonn with the consciousness that I had certainly put in my time, and the determination to go to Nancy unless Brandis said no.

Those were great days, as I look back upon them. I was on my own and on my way. The world was all before me. I was having a lot more fun than I realized while I was having it.

En route to the Valley of Decision, I saw again the Cathedral at Cologne, which all my life has seemed to me the most impressive building ever raised by human hands, and the hawks that lived and nested among its pinnacles. Arrived at Bonn, I put on my best bib and tucker at the Inn of the Golden Star, and at the appointed hour presented myself, with no little trepidation, before Sir Dietrich Brandis.

He was a tall, spare, austere, and formal man, a perfect Prussian in appearance, who concealed immense kindliness and helpfulness behind an old-fashioned manner of great courtliness and severity. Like Umslopagaas in Rider Haggard's story, there was a deep hole in the middle of his forehead, made, however, not by a battle ax, but by a surgical operation.

My first impression of him I never had reason to change. "Dr. Brandis is splendid. Energy, power, thought, determination—all these and much more. He was more than kind. He was inspiring."

Dr. Brandis, as I always think of him (like most big men, he was much bigger than his title), was originally a botanist. He had been knighted by the British Government for his service in organizing the forests and introducing systematic forest management in Burma and India, beginning in 1856. Measured by any standard of achievement, he was the first of living foresters.

But what came first with me, he had done great work as a forest pioneer, had made Forestry to be where there was none before. In a word, he had accomplished on the other side of the world what I might hope to have a hand in doing in America.

To Dr. Brandis the American forest problem was neither new nor strange. He knew far more about it than I did. He was acquainted, for example, with Franklin B. Hough, first Government forest officer in America, and for years had corresponded with him.

It was almost the luckiest day in my life when Dr. Brandis took charge of my training—and so it was also, later on, for the long succession of young American forest students who followed me to his door. To them, as to me, he was guide, teacher, example, and friend.

In a few words I laid my problem before him. He asked me many questions, seemed pleased to know that I could chop and plow, and decided on the spot that I should go to the French Forest School, as I had planned. He also gave me a letter to the Director, M. Puton. I remember to this day the queer broken-backed steel pen he wrote it with, and the table at which he sat.

And I shall never forget how, when I said (to make a good impression), "I don't mind getting up to take an early train," he snapped, "Of course you'll take the first one."

I did take it in the cold gray dawn of the morning after. Taking the first train is no bad plan.

2. *At the French Forest School*

I was glad the choice fell on the French Forest School because my Grandfather Pinchot was French. He was a soldier of Napoleon, at nineteen captain of a company on its way to join the Army when Waterloo was fought. After the return of the Bourbons he was driven out of France for taking part in a plan to get his leader off the island of St. Helena on an American vessel. He escaped to England in a fishing boat, and in 1816 with his father and mother came to Milford, Pennsylvania, where the Pinchots have been ever since. I could speak French about as well as English.

At Nancy I presented my letters and was accepted as a foreign student by Director Puton on November 13, 1889—thirteen always was my lucky number—found rooms in the house of le Père et la Mère Babel, just outside the school gate, bought the necessary books, went to work, and cabled home for permission to stay, all in the order named.

L'Ecole nationale forestière was an enclosure of dull gray buildings, whose only cheerful spot was the garden of the Director. The latter was a precise little man, a high authority on forest law, whom I remember chiefly for his genuine kindness. He opened to me all the doors there were. If I got nothing out of Nancy it would be my own fault.

The work at the Forest School was almost entirely in the form of lectures of an hour and a half each, with occasional excursions in the woods and some reading on the side. My courses were three:

Silviculture, which deals with trees and forests and what they are, how they grow, and how they are protected, handled, harvested, and reproduced.

Forest Organization—the economic side of Forestry—dealing with the forest capital, rent, interest, sustained yield, and in general with how to get out of the forest the most of whatever it is you want.

Forest Law—which, since it was purely French and based on the *Code Napoléon,* I thought of very little use. Today I am not so sure. I have had to spend no little time on American forest laws since then.

In general the professors could hardly have been kinder; partly, perhaps, because I was the first American to come to Nancy; and perhaps also because they saw I wanted to learn. They gave me much help, counsel, and forest lore that was not in the regular courses.

The Assistant Director, Lucien Boppe, who taught silviculture, was by far the most pervasive personality in the school. Short, stocky, with immense vitality and a great contempt for mere professors, he had learned in the woods what he taught in the lecture room. He made a tremendous impression on me.

Professor Boppe's lectures made Forestry visible. I followed his excursions in the woods with delight. We measured single trees and whole stands, marked trees to be cut in thinnings, and otherwise practiced the duties of a forester. Such work was far more valuable than any reading.

"Patience," insisted this impatient man, "is the master quality of the forester." But his whole teaching went to prove that the master quality of the forester is not patience but what he called *"le coup d'œil forestier"*—the forester's eye, which sees what it looks at in the woods.

"When you get home to America you must manage a forest and make it pay," said Boppe. I never lost sight of his advice.

But if the professors were admirable, the French forest students were distinctly otherwise. Many of them looked with contempt on the profession they had chosen, and most of them were far more interested in their light-o'-loves than in their work. Their resort in the evening was a low-class music hall. I went to one students' ball, and that was enough.

One French student, however, was a notable exception. He was Joseph Hulot, who lived with his mother in the charming little château of Sainte Cécile on the outskirts of Nancy. In spite of being a baron he was really interested in Forestry. He was simple, straight, eager, and clean. We spent many days together in the forest, and we struck up a friendship that lasted until his death.

Nancy was used to foreign students. For many years the foresters for the British Indian Service had been trained there. In my time the outlanders were mixed peoples, mostly from Eastern Europe. The one Russian, Nesteroff, was different from the rest. He worked. Many years later I met him again in Moscow and saw something of Russian Forestry under his kind and understanding eye.

Because Joseph Hulot and I tramped the woods in all weathers, many of the French and most of the foreign students thought we had lost our minds. I wrote home: "That any human being should ever think of walking abroad when it is snowing is a thing which has not entered into their conception of civilized man. I have been lucky enough to find another fellow, a Frenchman, fool enough to love the woods as I do, and who is not so miserably afraid that he may be a little too hot or a little too cold or may get a little tired, as the rest of these scarecrows are."

As to living quarters, I had fallen on my feet. The Babels did everything they knew how to make the stranger happy. But they could never reconcile themselves to my crazy notion that I must sleep with the windows open, nor understand my neglect to *"faire la noce"* (raise Cain) with the other students.

Every morning le Père Babel brought me my breakfast. Part of the time I went to Le Rocher de Cancale for the rest of my meals, part of the time I cooked them myself. Broiled tenderloin à la Pinchot is not to be sneezed at, and neither is the humble prune, if you soak it long enough.

Among my few amusements were fencing bouts with the bully of the school. Joseph and his family, two or three professors, three or four students, and the Presbyterian minister, M. Cleisz, under whom I sat, made up my circle.

Nancy itself was a pleasant town. I liked it well. There was the Librairie Husson-Lemoine, where I bought such books as my courses demanded and where a fierce-eyed older sister watched like a dragon in black alpaca over the safety of a plump little, meek little younger sister. The town was full of wicked students. There was the conscientious shoemaker who made my woods shoes too big because they would grow smaller with use, which they did. And there were also drugstores. A generation later M. Coué, the world-famous author of "Every day in every way I am getting better and better," recognized me in New York as the American student who used to come into his pharmacy at Nancy so many years before. It was a delightful meeting.

Saturdays, if the weather was good, all the budding foresters at Nancy went into the woods. I went anyhow. Fridays, having no lectures, I spent in the National Forest of Haye and the Communal Forest of Vandoeuvres; on the latter I was writing a report for Dr. Brandis. I was learning more about Forestry from the forests than from lectures and books.

Usually I went alone, but often with Joseph, who knew all the forest guards, wood choppers, and peasants for miles around. We ate our lunches with them and saw the inside of practical forest questions through the eyes of the men who did the work with their hands. I was on the job at last.

The Forests of Haye and Vandoeuvres are (or were, for they stood near Verdun, and I suppose the two World Wars have left little of them) hardwood forests, managed on the system of coppice (sprouts cut once every thirty years) under standards (seedling trees cut once in 150 years). They gave me my first concrete understanding of the forest as a crop, and I became deeply interested not only in how the crop was grown, but also in how it was harvested and reproduced.

Work in these woods was assured for every year, and would be, barring accidents, world without end. The forest supported a permanent population of trained men—expert woodsmen who handed down their knowledge from father to son—and not only a permanent population but also permanent forest industries, supported and guaranteed by a fixed annual supply of trees ready for the ax.

The French wood choppers' axes were wretched, ill-balanced, goose-necked abominations, made by the local blacksmith. Just to demonstrate the difference, I wrote home for some American axes. But the choppers declined to use the newfangled tools, even though they came from Collinsville, near Simsbury, Connecticut, where I was born. They warned me that the bits would break in cold weather, like their own. Custom, as is not unusual, was stronger than common sense. So I presented my axes to the museum of the School and let it go at that.

These forests, the first I ever looked over that were managed by professional foresters, lay on a level plateau above the town of Nancy. They were divided at regular intervals by perfectly straight paths and roads at right angles to each other, and they were protected to a degree we in America knew nothing about. There was, for example, a serious penalty for building any fire in the woods for any purpose, except that wood choppers might do so on spots picked out in advance by the forest guards.

This was the kind of forest I had read about, where peasants carried away every scrap of dead wood, and where branches down to the size of a pencil could be made into fagots and actually sold. And unfortunately this also was what the advocates of Forestry back home were recommending for America—for America, where settlers were still rolling saw logs into piles and burning them to get them out of the way.

But I was learning better. Lectures, books, work in the woods, and talks with every forester I could reach, all the way from Sir Dietrich Brandis and the head of the French Forest Service down to the forest guards and the men who swung the ax—all these were helping to open my eyes. This was what I came for.

"Forestry," I wrote home, in the somewhat florid style of my age, "promises about all that my fondest dreams had hoped in the way of pleasant work, and I become more and more convinced of the imperative need of Government control [of cutting] in the United States"—a conviction which has grown steadily with the years and was never so strong as now.

My head, of course, was full of questions. How soon could I learn what a competent forester must know? And where and how was I going to use what I was learning after I had learned it? Could I get a job in the Adirondacks, where the New York State Forest Preserve had been established, or in the South? And what were the conditions I would meet in the field?

My country was to me practically an unknown land. Fortunately I realized it. "I see more and more how foolish I have been not to get more fully acquainted with the facts at home when I had the chance. The whole question of a Forest Administration must turn on a thorough knowledge not only of the forests but also of the laws and the people, and I am without either." Which was horse sense. And I went on to ask for a copy of *The American Citizen's Manual.*

I had never been West even so far as Niagara, which every living soul I met in Europe had heard of and wanted to know about. They all inquired whether I had seen it and what it was like; and every time I admitted I never had and didn't know, I lost caste visibly. One of the very first things I did when I got home was to go and see that majestic falling flood. I didn't propose to be caught that way again.

Like most exiles, the longer I was away from America the higher grew my pride in the Land of the Free, and the more interest I took in American affairs. As a citizen, I read the *Weekly Tribune* and the *Nation,* which was then the weekly *New York Evening Post.* They took opposite sides on nearly every question and often left me guessing. As a forester, I studied *Garden and Forest* and the *Mississippi*

Valley Lumberman, and those two differed no less than the others. I was learning, but the road was by no means easy.

For the Christmas holidays of 1889-90 I joined my old friend, James B. Reynolds, Yale '84, in Paris. On Christmas Day we two and nine other Americans played a team of French boys a very one-sided game of football in the Bois de Boulogne. On our side was the tradition of Yale Elevens which had been scored on only once in my four years. We ate them up.

From Paris I went again to see Dr. Brandis in Bonn. He was convinced that "Nothing general can be done until some State or large individual owner makes the experiment and proves for America what is so well established in Europe, that forest management will pay." On this point Boppe and Brandis were agreed. No wonder their opinion was my lodestar for many years.

The winter passed in hard work at Nancy. In the spring of 1890, thanks again to Dr. Brandis, I spent a month with Forstmeister Meister, the forester in charge of the Sihlwald, the city forest of Zurich in Switzerland. Meister was not only a forester of international note, but also what every forester should be, a good citizen in all that the name implies. Among other things he was head of the Liberal Party in Switzerland; President of the biggest Swiss newspaper; head of the Swiss Fish Cultural Society and *Anglers' Journal;* Representative at Berne for the City of Zurich; Brigadier General in the Swiss Army; and in his spare time he was writing a book.

The Sihlwald, which Dr. Brandis considered the most instructive forest in Europe, had been under regular forest management since before Columbus discovered America. Its production in wood and money was almost beyond belief.

The Forstmeister gave me every chance to learn the lessons of the Sihlwald, and much of his own time besides. We were friends from the beginning, and until he answered the last roll call. I owe him a great debt.

I lived in the little inn next to the Forsthaus, where the Forstmeister and Frau Meister made me, and many an American forest student after me, so warmly welcome. On a visit to Zurich, where Elias Landolt, the greatest forester in Switzerland, showed a kindly interest in the struggling American student and the problems he was about to face, I found one day the Tauchnitz edition of Mark Twain's *A Connecticut Yankee in King Arthur's Court.* The two small volumes smelled and tasted of home. I stayed up all night to finish them. Since then I suppose I have read that story no less than forty times, and *Huckleberry Finn* even oftener.

When I got back to Nancy, after a marvelous time in the Sihlwald, the winter courses were finished and the spring field work was about to begin. The French students were getting ready to study forest management in the Vosges and the control of torrents in the Alps of Southern France. The Silver Fir forests of the Vosges and the dams and forest planting to control erosion in the Alps both gave me much new light—but not on Forestry alone.

In the Vosges the living conditions of the peasants interested me profoundly. I remember, for example, one house in a little village where we stopped to eat our lunches. The floor was of beaten earth, the fireplace a sort of sandbox in the middle of the floor. There was no chimney—only a hole in the roof. And yet the man who lived there was a leader among his equals.

In the Vosges, again, I made a discovery—namely, that you can walk past a vicious dog in safety if you keep on going without change of pace or manner, precisely as though he were not there at all. I tried it first on a big shaggy mongrel. Thank Heaven, it worked. It has continued to work on a certain kind of antagonist from that day to this.

In the Alps we visited the Grande Chartreuse and its forests, and spent a night in the monastery. I was deeply impressed by the magnificent mountain highway over which we drove to reach it. That drive may have had something to do with the 13,400 miles of good hard roads we built in Pennsylvania during my last term as Governor.

My work in France ended in the French Alps, but not my work in Europe. The excursion with Dr. Brandis was still to come.

3. *The Brandis Excursion*

Dr. Brandis was a man of strong convictions, great religious faith, an unshakable belief in his own purposes, and a complete willingness to make any sacrifice necessary to carry them out. And what he required of himself he expected of others. "What's the use?" had no appeal for him.

A courteous and even ceremonious gentleman of the old school, yet practical as a pickax, Dr. Brandis never forgot that he was a scientist as well as an administrator—not always, in the hurly-burly of public life, an easy thing to do. In his declining years he turned again to botany, the love of his youth. But he never ceased to be a forester, and never lost his interest in spreading his gospel in other lands.

Dr. Brandis' interest in Forestry did not stop with the forest. Forestry he regarded simply as one means to the general good. It was his chief concern, but he was hardly less devoted to political and social problems. His breadth of sympathy was remarkable. He was, for example, a vigorous champion of Christian missions, and in particular of American missionaries in Burma, where he had seen them at work; he was widely known in German labor circles; he had founded a workingmen's club in Bonn; and for years he gave one night a week to it.

To Dr. Brandis I owe more than I can ever tell. I doubt whether any other man in Europe could have been as wise a guide. Moreover, he could scarcely have taken more trouble with me if I had been his own son. As I look back, I think he saw in this long-legged youngster a possible instrument for bringing Forestry to a new continent.

At Nancy I wrote to him continually, and he to me. After I came home I sent him news and many questions about what was doing and needed to be done in American Forestry, and I never went abroad without going to see him. So long as he lived we never lost touch.

As I think it all over, I believe the greatest service Dr. Brandis did for me, and for the rest of his American students, was to inspire in us the same profound respect for Forestry as a profession that he held himself. Without that, groping in the murk of American public indifference, we would have been lost indeed.

The systems of forest management introduced in India by Dr. Brandis were, curiously enough, rather French than German. Admirable as German Forestry certainly was, there was about it too much artificial finish, too much striving for detailed perfection, too much danger that executive aggressiveness would be trained away, to fit it for use where Forestry was young.

Dr. Brandis never let his pupils forget a great truth which most German foresters had never grasped—that in the long run Forestry cannot succeed unless the people who live in and near the forest are for it and not against it. That was the keynote of his work in India.

And when the pinch came, the application of that same truth was what saved the National Forests in America.

All in all, Brandis' services to American Forestry were so great that President Theodore Roosevelt sent him his photograph with this well-deserved inscription: "In high appreciation of the work of Sir Dietrich Brandis for the cause of forestry in the United States." I never saw a man more pleased with anything than Dr. Brandis was with that picture.

It was Dr. Brandis' yearly custom to take the English students from Cooper's Hill for a summer excursion through the most interesting forests of Germany and Switzerland. He was good enough to say I could join the tour when my work at Nancy was over.

It was a great chance, and I had to be ready to use it. What German I once knew had almost been forgotten. So I engaged a young medical student at Nancy to talk German with me when I walked for exercise. That brought my German back to a usable level.

Although retired and in his sixty-sixth year, Dr. Brandis still retained most of his famous energy and endurance. More than one British Indian forester has told me that on his inspection tours Brandis would walk down the forest officers of one district after another, leaving a train of worn-out men behind him. One down, t'other come on. He was one of the very few great trampers I have known that turned their toes out as they walked.

On my first day with the Cooper's Hill boys, Dr. Brandis' turned-out toes walked us through the forest for eight hours straight, without a bite to eat and without once sitting down, to the intense disgust of most of the English students. Their examinations had been passed, their positions in India were already secure. Why should they break their backs any further? But it seemed to me that we youngsters ought to be able to stand it if the Doctor could.

A number of these young Englishmen were very fine fellows indeed, and some were hard workers. For a few days, while Dr. Brandis was looking after one of them who had been taken sick, he asked me to step into his shoes. Said my diary: "Great sport being in command. Fellows are very nice, making no kick about anything." Which was less the rule than the exception.

My revived German often won me the chance to ride in the carriage (automobiles were still far below the horizon) with Dr. Brandis and the local forest officers, and listen to their expert discussions. All of these men were eager to tell about their own woodlands, and many of them were deeply interested in the American forest problem. It amounted almost to a liberal education.

At Dr. Brandis' suggestion, my Father had sent me a number of very large photographs of American forests. These pictures certainly paid their way. Wherever I showed them, as I did to every forester I could, they put me in position to hear discussions and learn facts that never would have been open to me without them.

In particular they got me the chance to talk with a number of the best foresters in Europe about what ought to be done in America. Most of these hard-working prints I gave away when the Brandis excursion was over, but one or two of them are with me yet.

Nothing could have been more useful to a lot of foresters in the egg than this tour through some of the best-managed forests on earth. Even if we were not able to see everything we looked at, at least we built up some mental picture of what a forest under good management actually looked like—a standard against which to check our future work.

We saw natural reproduction of Oak in the Spessart Forest in Prussia; planted Spruce in Saxony; Scotch Pine in many places; Silver Fir and Spruce in the Bavarian Black Forest; and last, and best of all, the mixture of hardwoods and conifers in the Sihlwald. To see Forstmeister Meister again was a great delight.

We measured sample plots and single trees, learned to estimate stands of various kinds and densities, made miniature working plans for compartments, worked at crude lumbering, wrote endless notes on everything we saw and did, and some of us, at least, crowded almost a year of learning into those few weeks. It was certainly the chance of a lifetime.

When the trip was done, I was done too. Nevertheless I went by myself to Vienna to see the great Wienerwald, one of the famous forests of the world; but my time was too short and my steam pressure too low to get more than a glimpse of it.

All this was very simple and straightforward, as I have told it to you; but throughout my training two puzzling questions would not down: First, how long would it take to get ready for my work; and second, just what kind of work should I try to do when I got home?

Sargent, when I put the matter of my training up to him, wrote me that I must take two years in study and one in travel before I would be ready for work at home. Loring and Fernow were of the same general opinion.

Every European forester I could lay my hands on I asked for his answer to this same question. They gave me, most kindly, their opinion—that my training must be thorough and long—all but one. The head of the Department of Forests and Waters in France, many official forest leaders in Germany and Switzerland, and the great names of that day in scientific Forestry (Buehler, Ebermayer, Hartig, and Gayer in Germany; Puton, Boppe, and Henry in France; Meister in Switzerland)—all these authorities, except Meister alone, turned out to be as wrong as the wise men at home.

The authorities were wrong because they thought an intensive, all-inclusive European training would be necessary to deal with American forests; and that European remedies would meet American needs. They imagined that economic and political practicabilities, national habits of thought, and the conditions of success in Forestry were substantially the same on the two sides of the Atlantic—that the same training and the same measures would have the same results in Europe and America.

It was curious—or perhaps not so very curious after all—that Dr. Brandis should have made this mistake. He was a man of vast experience, a statesman as well as a forester, and a liberal one at that. And he himself had never had a formal training in Forestry. But he was also a teacher of Forestry, with a teacher's reliance on study. And I suppose he was no more free from the shackles of his later experience than the rest of us.

Dr. Brandis had done his work under an autocracy. But America was not an autocracy. What went in America wasn't somebody's say-so. It was the widespread, slow-moving pressure of public opinion. And so the one man who saw the situation in America most nearly as it turned out to be was the one man who best understood how things get done in a democracy—Forstmeister Meister.

Forstmeister Meister was a citizen of the most democratic country in Europe. (Even the bookkeeper in the Sihlwald was elected by popular vote.) The Swiss people recognized that the private ownership of timberland carried with it a definite responsibility to the public. Through their Government they exercised the right to prevent forest destruction by private owners, and they do so still, in common with nearly every other civilized nation. Such democratic control of lumbering in the public interest is the one step most vitally needed to stop the forest butchery now so common and so dangerous in the United States.

The Forstmeister brought together all the qualities a pioneer public forester must have to succeed in a country like ours—practical skill in the woods, business common sense, close touch with public opinion, and an understanding of how and why things get done in government and politics in a democracy.

In the spring, before I had made the excursions with the French Forest School and the English forest students, Meister had told me that in his judgment I was far enough along already to organize a forest administration in the United States if I got the chance. You can imagine how that made a young beginner feel his oats. And when on top of that he advised me to go home and get to work after finishing the summer's tour with Dr. Brandis (which was exactly what I wanted to do), of course I was sure he was right.

I intended to be a practicing forester all my life, yet I thought I could spare but thirteen months to get ready for my lifework. So I covered all the ground I could in the time I had for preparation. Today, with the long perspective behind me instead of ahead, I am still convinced that my decision was right. A forester thoroughly trained in scientific forestry, if he had attempted to apply his knowledge to American forests in those early days, would have been doomed to fail.

But, if I were a young man today and had to make a similar decision, it would be to get as thorough training as I could in the sciences underlying forestry. With millions of acres of National and State Forests permanently dedicated to timber growing, with Government control of cutting on private forest lands certain to come, thorough training is a necessity and every bit of knowledge can find a ready application.

So much for my first question. As to my second—what kind of work should I try to do when I got home—my letters from men of light and leading in America were anything but encouraging. They continued to regard Forestry as more or less an iridescent dream. But my neck was stiff and my heart was hard. The glooms of the elder statesmen slid off me like water off a duck. My barometer was set fair for Forestry.

A month or two before sailing home, I wrote to my Father, asking him in substance what I was to do when I got back. How much of a gamble Forestry then was his answer made plain:

"It seems to me that you may fairly depend upon this, that in a very short time there will be something to do in this country for the man best prepared to decide upon Forestry matters. I cannot tell, but I feel all this, that the subject will soon have to be seriously considered and generally considered, and that you will have a chance somewhere. Don't fret about just how it is to come around."

The event proved him exactly right, but not to fret was easier said than done.

For my last bit of training Dr. Brandis sent me to stay with a Prussian Oberfoerster at Neupfalz, just back of Bingen-on-the-Rhine, and not so far from where our men crossed that great river shortly before Germany's surrender in 1945. There I put in a month studying the details of forest administration—the keeping of accounts and records, the making of reports, and so forth and so on. Fortunately I managed also to see something of forest management on the ground. Otherwise it was mainly time wasted, except for what I learned about the training of Prussian foresters and the Prussian point of view.

I shall never forget the old peasant who rose to his feet from his stone-breaking, as the Oberfoerster came striding along, and stood silent, head bent, cap in both hands, while that official stalked by without the slightest sign that he knew the peasant was on earth. And I remember also the shocked amazement of the whole family, male and female, when I declined to join in their Saturday night drinking bouts. Any way but their way was unthinkable.

In December the time I had allowed myself was up. I came home on a German freight boat which succeeded in making the passage in thirteen days and a half. We had head gales all the way. Even the paper on which I wrote a description of European forest policy, to be read at the annual meeting of the American Forestry Association, had to be held from sliding off the table.

4. *When I Got Home*

When I got home at the end of 1890 the situation, if I had known it, was enough to discourage Sisyphus himself. Mercifully the worst of it was hidden from me. The widest opportunity for Forestry on this round earth was here, and the clear promise of the greatest returns in national safety and well-being. But there was no Forestry. Instead of it the most rapid and extensive forest destruction ever known was in full swing.

That gigantic and lamentable massacre of trees had a reason behind it, of course. Without wood, and plenty of it, the people of the United States could never have reached the pinnacle of comfort, progress, and power they occupied before this century began.

The Nation was obsessed, when I got home, by a fury of development. The American Colossus was fiercely intent on appropriating and exploiting the riches of the richest of all continents—grasping with both hands, reaping where he had not sown, wasting what he thought would last forever. New railroads were opening new territory. The exploiters were pushing farther and farther into the wilderness. The man who could get his hands on the biggest slice of natural resources was the best citizen. Wealth and virtue were supposed to trot in double harness.

East and West the same spirit was general. Today, when the frontier is alleged to be gone and Conservation is a household word, it is hard even for a man who swam against it to realize how strong and how wrong the stream of public opinion was then.

Something like half of our forests had passed into private ownership. Get timber by hook or by crook, get it quick and cut it quick—that was the rule of the citizen. Get rid of it quick—that was the rule of the Government for the vast timberlands it still controlled. And it has been got rid of both by the Government and by private owners with amazing efficiency and startling speed.

When I got home the Federal public land laws were more than liberal, and the states were more spendthrift still. Maine and Pennsylvania had sold great areas for a shilling an acre, and North Carolina, for ten cents an acre, had disposed of some of the finest hardwood stands in the East. The richest Government timberlands could be bought for $2.50 an acre.

Settlers and miners took what timber they needed from the Public Domain, freely and for nothing. "Miners" was held to mean even great mining corporations, and some of them took many millions of feet of Government timber every year, for which they did not pay.

Not only was standing timber given away, but so were hundreds of millions of acres of timbered land. Whole principalities went in grants to states and railroads in the certain knowledge that the forests upon them would be destroyed. The land grant of the Northern Pacific Railroad, for example, included almost forty million acres—more than the total area of Pennsylvania and New Jersey, with Rhode Island and the District of Columbia thrown in.

But while Government timber could be given away, or could be sold with the land, under the law it could not be sold apart from the land, which would have made Forestry possible. Men who needed timber, but not land, often found no way to get it but to steal it.

Stealing Government timber, accordingly, became a common and perfectly normal occupation, freely and openly pursued by the most respectable members of the community. High officials and great business men, teachers and even here and there a preacher, rich and poor, big and little, they all sat in on the timber-stealing game together. And few thought the worse of any man because of what he stole.

Of the value of Government timber stolen, little more than 1 per cent was being recovered from the thieves. Here and there prosecution of some politically undesirable thief broke the rule, but by and large Government officials made little or no objection to the stealing of Government timber, provided the papers were in order.

Forest fires raged unchecked. According to the estimates of the day, they were destroying as much timber as was cut. Fires in the woods were regarded as acts of God, beyond human control. They helped to clear the land, and there would always be plenty of timber.

Major John Wesley Powell, the distinguished head of the United States Geological Survey, told in print how he had set fire to a great alpine tree just to see it burn. His account of how that fire caught other trees and then went roaring off through the Western mountains gave no slightest indication of regret. It was interesting, and that was all.

It is also worth recalling that while a very partial survey showed twelve million acres of forest burned over in the United States in 1891, with scant attention paid to that vast loss, in Germany one fire of less than six thousand acres was still a timely topic of discussion when I went over the ground, ninety years after it happened.

Curiously enough, waste and destruction had not always been rampant throughout America. Long before the white man came, certain tribes of Algonquin Indians had learned the wisdom of dividing their tribal hunting grounds into family-size parcels in which none but family members had the right to hunt or fish. These family parcels descended from father to son. In them the game was kept account of, closed years for certain kinds were sometimes established, and killing was strictly regulated within the limits of natural increase.

Centuries before the Conservation policy was born, here was Conservation practice at its best. The natural resources on which these Indians depended for their very life, as you and I depend on natural resources for ours, were being handled with foresight and intelligence. So far as game was concerned, their future was secure.

It seems almost impossible that the early settlers should have escaped all knowledge of this native wisdom. But if they failed to learn foresight from the Indians, they did bring European traditions of forest preservation with them to America. After they landed, moreover, the forest was at first their main dependence. Out of it came much of their food, their only means of warmth, most of their shelter, the greater part of the raw materials of their simple industries. Out of it came the means of life.

But out of it came also the threat of death. The forest harbored hostile Indians. It stood in the road of progress. The heaviest job of work the settlers had to do was to clear the forest away.

After a time the practical facts of their lives drove the pioneers to regard the unending forest as their enemy. And so in truth it was. Small wonder they came to feel that the thing to do with the forest was to get rid of it. Small wonder they transmitted that feeling to their descendants.

It is true that for a time fear of timber shortage turned their colonial minds toward forest preservation. What worlds of wood lay beyond the reach of their feeble means of transportation could give them no help. With half a continent of rich forest before them, they enacted not a little colonial legislation to regulate the cutting of trees.

Even the indirect influences of the forest had their defenders. In 1753 Lewis Evans wrote in his *Brief Account of Pennsylvania:* "When the country was cover'd with Woods, and the Swamps with Brush, the Rain that fell was detained by These Interruptions, and so had time to insinuate into the Earth, and contribute to the Springs and Runs. But now the Country is clear'd, the Rain as fast as it falls, is hurried into the Rivers, and washes away the Earth and Soil of our Naked Fields."

Noah Webster (1758-1843), whose dictionary is with us yet, strongly urged upon his fellow-countrymen the need of forest preservation. And there were others. But these were passing phases, and when they passed, hostility to the forest remained.

At long last, however, the reaction began. Any great evil eventually gives rise to protest. Slavery did; the liquor trade did; the concentration of political power in the hands of the overrich did; the lack of security for millions is doing so now. Very slowly and ineffectively protesting flashes of public sentiment against forest devastation began to appear. But the early action they led to, whatever else it may have been, was not Forestry.

Let us pass over the earliest legislation. In 1872 Congress created the Yellowstone National Park, not, however, as a forest for the production of timber, but as a park in which cutting, and therefore Forestry, were forbidden. Next year came the Timber Culture Act, under which title to homesteads on the public lands could be secured by the planting of trees, the vast majority of which died, however, soon after the settler had got his title.

Also in 1873, the American Association for the Advancement of Science addressed to President Grant a memorial which, in 1876, the Centennial year, led to the appointment of Franklin B. Hough, in the Department of Agriculture, to collect statistics and distribute information at a salary of $2,000 a year. Five years later, in 1881, the little organization he built up became the Forestry Division, the germ of the present United States Forest Service.

In the same year of 1876 my Father took me to the Centennial Exposition at Philadelphia, held to celebrate the hundredth birthday of the richest forest country on earth. It contained no forest exhibit of any sort or kind except from the single State of Michigan.

Also in 1876, the American Forestry Council called a National Forestry Convention at Cape May Point, hired a special train, and secured a total attendance of three persons, of whom Hough was one, and John Gifford another.

Likewise in the Centennial year, the State of Colorado had put forest protection into its constitution, but had done nothing about it thereafter. A number of other states had Forest Commissions. Not one had any Forestry.

In 1885 New York State created the Adirondack State Forest Preserve, not for Forestry, but to "preserve" the forest and the water supply. The exclusion of Forestry from the Preserve was made certain, in 1891, by an amendment to the State Constitution which forbade the cutting of any tree. That indefensible provision is still in force.

The American, the Pennsylvania, the Connecticut Forestry Associations, and doubtless others also, had contributed a good deal of discussion in halls, but no action in the woods. Praise of forest protection in Europe and demand that something should be done in America had filled many an editorial column, but with rare and doubtful exceptions had neither guided nor controlled a single ax. While forest devastation was going like a runaway locomotive, forest protection was pursuing it like a manpower handcar, and falling farther behind with every mile.

I realize that an examination of the record as to state legislation, Forestry Associations, and newspaper propaganda may appear to controvert this view. But here again the printed record tells but a fraction of the truth. When the test of action is applied, it shows again that Forestry in words and Forestry in the woods are two entirely different things. They are not even kissing kin.

To sum it all up, when I came home not a single acre of Government, state, or private timberland was under systematic forest management anywhere on the most richly timbered of all continents. The American people had no understanding either of what Forestry was or of the bitter need for it.

When the Gay Nineties began, the common word for our forests was "inexhaustible." To waste timber was a virtue and not a crime. There would always be plenty of timber and everything else in America for everybody, world without end.

The lumbermen, whose industry was then the third greatest in this country, regarded forest devastation as normal and second growth as a delusion of fools, whom they cursed on the rare occasions when they happened to think of them. And as for sustained yield, no such idea had ever entered their heads.

The few friends the forest had were spoken of, when they were spoken of at all, as impractical theorists, fanatics, or "denudatics," more or less touched in the head. What talk there was about forest protection was no more to the average American than the buzzing of a mosquito, and just about as irritating. Let these agitators run along and roll their hoops.

Then how about the future and posterity? Well, what did posterity ever do for us? Then why worry about it? Many and many a time was I given that answer.

The handful of forward-looking men and women who had established the Forestry Associations were working with genuine moral enthusiasm, great self-sacrifice, and admirable persistence, but unfortunately with very little result. They deserved much credit for their unselfish devotion. And without question they were of real use in spreading a doctrine which they called Forestry but which in fact was forest preservation—a very different thing.

Among the few who looked farther ahead than their fellows there was talk about the forest and its effect on climate and floods, rainfall and run-off, springs and erosion; a good deal of discussion about forest planting, ornamental planting, and even gardening; but very little about the forest as a permanent producer of timber.

One good lady said to me, "So you are a forester! How very nice! Then you can tell me just what I ought to do about my roses." And she was no rare exception.

The report of the New York Forest Commission for 1886 faithfully represented the attitude of the microscopic minority who were equipped to consider the forest question: "At the present time it would be equally as vain to endeavor to employ the methods of European forest science for our State purposes as it would be to try to find the ideal European educated forester in the North Woods."

Nevertheless, the friends of the forest continually denounced American timberland owners for not doing what was being done abroad. They pointed out that even small twigs and dead branches were utilized in Germany and France, and demanded to know why that should not be done at home. No wonder they were scorned.

They were utterly right in their purpose, but utterly wrong in their method. Individually they were among our best and most enlightened people—devoted and untiring—but they forgot that you cannot beat something with nothing. They tried to stop the advance of one of the greatest, most necessary, and most thriving and driving of industries simply by explaining to each other how wrong and ruthless it was.

Their eyes were closed to the economic motive behind true Forestry. They hated to see a tree cut down. So do I, and the chances are that you do too. But you cannot practice Forestry without it. Naturally the lumber juggernaut rolled over them—rolled over them and went on its forest-devastating and home-building way without even paying them the tribute of serious attention.

Such were the facts when I came home. In spite of all the efforts of all the lovers of the forest—Webster, Emerson, Marsh, Warder, Hough, Schurz, Lundy, Rothrock, Fernow, and the rest—men and women who deserve far more credit than they ever got for their public-spirited efforts to save a great natural resource; in spite of the meetings and the writings and the attempted legislation, in the year 1891 there was not, I repeat, a single acre of forest under Forestry anywhere in the United States.

5. *The Job Ahead*

From the point of view of a fledgling forester, the situation when I got back left something to be desired. Unaware of the worst of it, I proceeded cheerfully to tackle the dragon Devastation in his own home cave.

Under the circumstances I had to play a lone hand. I could not join the denudatics, because they were marching up a blind alley. I could not join the lumbermen, because forest destruction was their daily bread. There was nothing left for me but to blaze my own trail.

The job was not to stop the ax, but to regulate its use. For that the whole stream of public thinking about the forest had to be shifted into a new channel—that of the few forest preservers no less than that of the many forest destroyers. A nation utterly absorbed in the present had to be brought to consider the future. The ingrained habit of mind of the best part of a hundred million people about a fundamental necessity of human life had to be changed.

I don't mean that I saw all this as clearly then as I do now. But at least I knew that I stood at the beginning of a long, long trail. It was probably just as well that I did not realize how rough and rocky that trail was going to be.

There were two possible ways of going at it. One was to urge, beg, and implore; to preach at, call upon, and beseech the American people to stop forest destruction and practice Forestry; and denounce them if they didn't. This was the method chosen by the Forestry Associations, by the Forestry Division, and by the friends of the forest generally.

This method got onto the platform and into the papers, but it never got into the woods. It had been followed for at least a quarter of a century, and still there was not a single case of systematic forest management in America to show for it.

The other plan was to put Forestry into actual practice in the woods, prove that it could be done by doing it, prove that it was practicable by making it work.

My good luck led me to choose action instead of exhortation. Indeed, I could hardly have done otherwise, for Dr. Brandis was never tired of urging me to prove the value of Forestry by practicing Forestry in the forest. The method of practical demonstration was literally "what the Doctor ordered."

And it was a happy chance that the thing now turned out to be possible. It had not been possible when Major George Haven Putnam started out to become a professional forester, soon after the Civil War. He was too far ahead of his time and was obliged to turn to other pursuits.

A scattering of European-trained foresters had come to the United States, but none of them (not even Dr. Fernow) had been able to put Forestry into practice. As an American, however, I thought I might succeed where they had failed.

For whatever it was worth, I had the field pretty well to myself. Thanks to my Father's suggestion, I was the first American to make Forestry his profession.

It is true that I was no more than half-trained. I had, however, some acquaintance with forest management in action, learned mainly in the woods; what common sense the Lord had given me; a consuming desire to get acquainted at first-hand with the actual forest situation in America; and my own, my Father's, and my Mother's belief in the usefulness of what I was trying to do.

And what was it that I was to introduce and demonstrate, if I could? What was this thing called Forestry, which America needed (and still needs) so desperately? What was this Forestry, without which our future could not be safe, about which there had been such a flood of talk and such a drought of action?

When I came home Forestry was so little understood in America that before long I set out to write, but never wrote, a book which would answer that question. Here is my answer, as I sensed it then and know it now, my answer not only as of half a century ago, but likewise as of today.

Forestry is Tree Farming. Forestry is handling trees so that one crop follows another. To grow trees as a crop is Forestry.

Trees may be grown as a crop just as corn may be grown as a crop. The farmer gets crop after crop of corn, oats, wheat, cotton, tobacco, and hay from his farm. The forester gets crop after crop of logs, cordwood, shingles, poles, or railroad ties from his forest, and even some return from regulated grazing.

Because the plants he grows ripen in a single season, the farmer usually gets a crop every year from the land he farms. The forester, because the plants he grows—his trees—mature only after many seasons, may get his crop from the same acre only once in thirty or fifty or a hundred years, or even longer.

But what the forester gets is a crop—his crop, although he may not live to see it harvested. It takes more time and less attention to grow a crop in the forest than it does on the farm. That is the main difference.

Farmer and forester alike get a lot of other products on the side. Good farming yields also such things as butter, eggs, apples, calves. Good Forestry, in addition to lumber, firewood, and other produce, yields such services as regulation of stream flow, protection against erosion, and some influence on climate.

Farming cannot go on unless crop succeeds crop. No more can Forestry. A farm crop may reproduce itself, or it may have to be sown or planted. Just so with trees.

Each succeeding crop of trees may come up, like each succeeding crop of hay, either from seed sown by the preceding generation or by sprouts from the old roots. Or young trees may have to be planted, just as each crop of tobacco has to be set out.

Different kinds of trees must be handled in different ways, just as winter wheat cannot be handled like spring wheat, or corn like oats, or hogs like cattle. And as fodder corn is treated differently from field corn, so trees handled to produce cordwood or telephone poles must have different treatment from those handled to yield lumber or protection.

A well-handled farm gets more and more productive as the years pass. So does a well-handled forest.

On a badly handled farm, contrariwise, production decreases, the soil washes or blows away, floods are encouraged, and not only the farmer, but also the public interest, suffers loss. The same is true in general of a badly handled forest, except that damage to the public interest is wider and worse.

The purpose of Forestry, then, is to make the forest produce the largest possible amount of whatever crop or service will be most useful, and keep on producing it for generation after generation of men and trees. And the more you think about the services of the forest, the more you understand them, the more essential they appear. It is true indeed that the forest, rightly handled—given the chance—is, next to the earth itself, the most useful servant of man.

Of all this not even a respectable fraction of the American people were otherwise than in complete and completely satisfied ignorance when I came home. It had not dawned upon them that timber can be cut without forest destruction, or that the forest can be made to produce crop after crop for the service of men.

When I brought home my little sheaf of knowledge, the prospect for Forestry in America was, as I have tried to tell you, meager, to say the least. It was far more meager than I was able, luckily for me, to realize or even suspect.

At any rate the slate was clean. But I must find and sharpen my own pencil before I could begin to write.

To start with I had to know something about the people, the country, and the trees. And of the three the first was the most important.

I was born a Connecticut Yankee. American ways of thinking were native to me. But, as my diary said, I had a lot to learn about our people; that was beyond dispute. As to the country, I had never been west of the Alleghenies. And I knew hardly anything about American trees as a forester should know them. But then neither did anybody else.

The first thing was to get in touch with the men who had been thinking about the forest question. The next was to find a toehold somehow, somewhere, and begin to use what I had learned.

Two days after landing I saw William A. Stiles, editor of *Garden and Forest,* in his office in the Tribune Building. The glimpse he gave me of internal politics among the friends of Forestry was an eye opener. Charles S. Sargent's distrust and dislike of the American Forestry Association, and of Fernow, whom he regarded as "devoured with jealousies," was especially important.

Stiles was a slow-spoken, emaciated Jerseyman, a politician turned philanthropist, with uncommon knowledge of what American Forestry should mean, and where it ought to be headed. Then and later I gathered much wisdom and encouragement from him, as he sat in his shirt sleeves with his feet on the desk, an old paper shade over his eyes, and let his broad common sense illumine whatever he happened to be talking about. It was a most serious loss when he died and *Garden and Forest* died with him.

Within the next two weeks I saw and conferred with many or most of the leaders of the forest movement from Boston to Washington.

Abner L. Train, Secretary of the Adirondack Commission, was in favor of forest management in the North Woods, but not too soon. Morris K. Jessup, who gave the great collection of wood specimens in the American Museum of Natural History, urged me to take up his agitation for saving the Adirondacks. He held a position very common in those days—strong for what he called Forestry, but equally strong against cutting any trees.

Sargent's position was not encouraging. He was against my accepting Fernow's offer of the position of Assistant Chief in the Forestry Division, and generally glum. "Sooner or later," he said, "I am satisfied that we shall have in this country a practical system of forest control. Whether you or I are going to live to see it is another matter." He convinced me that he was neither "thoroughly up to the situation nor in touch with the movement."

My friend Dick Welling took me to see Carl Schurz, a man of the broadest vision, the only Secretary of the Interior who had sensed the forest problem and tried to get action. He too saw great difficulties in the way of Forestry, and was disgusted with the condition of state and national forest legislation.

At the end of the two weeks I read parts of my paper on "Government Forestry Abroad" to a joint meeting of the American Forestry Association and the American Economic Association in Washington. From the other papers and the discussions I learned a lot, but not about how to practice Forestry on this continent.

Edward A. Bowers, former Inspector of Public Lands, future Assistant Commissioner of the General Land Office, and one of the most devoted and effective friends of the forest in America, described

"The Present Condition of the Forests on the Public Lands." It was the paper of a man who knew his business, and it was as alarming as it was competent.

Bowers declared that although 38,000,000 acres had been entered under the Timber Culture Act (taken up by settlers on condition that they plant trees), not over 50,000 acres had been successfully covered with young tree plantations. His paper was a complete demonstration that the laws relating to public timber, as administered, were utterly inadequate. "From this statement of the condition of the public timber lands of the United States but one conclusion can be drawn; that is, a new departure in the management by the Government of its forest property *is imperative.*"

Dr. Fernow discussed "The Practicability of an American Forest Administration." "The title of the paper assigned to me," he said, "should have been made, by preference, to read: 'The difficulties attending the introduction of forest management in the United States,' for the negative elements in the problem are still so numerous as to make a positive result, at first sight, at least doubtful."

Then followed a catalogue of the obstacles in the way. Government control over private timberland owners, Dr. Fernow said, "is not only unsatisfactory and distasteful, but as it means reduction of private gain, unjust." Which was about as wrong as it could be. As for a national forest administration: "Personal considerations and considerations of expediency offer such obstacles to the enactment of thorough legislation as that proposed, that there is little hope for it."

The conclusion of Dr. Fernow's argument against the possibility of introducing Forestry in America was this: "It takes a giant, or rather two giants combined, strengthened by the courage of conviction that this is an urgent matter to be acted upon, to carry through the flood of legislative streams any measure involving radical changes in the existing land policy. It is the tremendous momentum of bad habits, unfair usage, and personal politics, that must be overcome, to make a rational forest policy possible."

Dr. Fernow forgot, I think, that unless the leader of a cause believes he can win, or at the very least makes his followers believe it, his chance of victory is small indeed.

In my own paper I had the sense to say that "Forest management in America must be worked out along lines which the conditions of our life will prescribe. It can never be a technical imitation of that of any other country." And I added, "It is an admirable training to become thoroughly at home in the details of the most complete forest organization, but it is a far more practically useful thing in the United States to be able to do without it."

Furthermore, I pointed out the contrast between German Forestry, so greatly admired by our forest reformers, in which everything is regulated down to the minutest detail, and Swiss Forestry, in which the forest officer is allowed to use his head. "As an example set by a republic to a republic," my paper said about Forestry in Switzerland, "I believe that the advocates of forest reform in America can set before themselves no better model and take encouragement from no worthier source."

"We are surrounded," I said in conclusion, "by the calamitous results of the course that we are now pursuing. In fact, it seems as though there were no civilized or semicivilized country in either hemisphere which cannot stand to us as an example or a warning. To this great truth they bear witness with united voice: The care of the forests is the duty of the nation."

That was the frozen truth, and it is an even colder and truer fact today, when forest destruction is so much more dangerous to the nation's life than it was when I came home.

All things considered, it wasn't such a bad paper. The Economic Association thought it was worth printing—fifty-odd pages of it—and so did *Garden and Forest,* although it dealt with organizations and objectives that were at least a generation beyond our reach. Good or bad, however, it was, except for my talk at Yale and a description of the Sihlwald which appeared in *Garden and Forest* while I was still abroad, my opening move in the great game of bringing Forestry to America.

That meeting was worth a lot to me. It was my first contact with most of the little band of devoted and indomitable defenders of the forest who made up the American Forestry Association. Among them were Dr. J. T. Rothrock of Pennsylvania and Warren Higley of the Adirondack League Club, who wanted the Club's forest lands properly handled.

Fernow was cordial and helpful, although firm in the belief that Forestry was still impracticable in America. He introduced me to many men I needed to know, and assured me that the job as his assistant was still open if I wanted it.

Old Jerry Rusk, Secretary of Agriculture; Arnold Hague and Henry Gannett of the Geological Survey; James G. Blaine, leader of the Republican party and its candidate for President; Levi P. Morton, Vice-President of the United States, and many others gave me more or less, and more or less useful, advice.

Best of all, General Sherman, not long retired from command of the Army, made me see that I must know my country better before I began to give it free advice. He recognized the need for Forestry, but doubted the possibility of getting legislation right away. And so my diary says: "Scheme for immediate work on legislation busted." Which doubtless saved me much useless effort.

Instead I turned to the forest as seen from a railroad car window, and began "to know many of the trees by shape." That is perhaps as good a way as any to show how far I was from ready for the work I planned to do.

Within another week, in spite of all discouragements, I had decided, on my Father's suggestion, to write a book on Forestry for the schools (which I never did), was commended editorially by the New York *Tribune* on the choice of my profession (I suspect Stiles had a hand in that), and found my first job.

Phelps, Dodge & Company, one of whose partners was D. Willis James, a member of the New York State Forest Commission which recommended the Adirondack Forest Preserve, and all of whom were heirs to a long tradition of wealth, respectability, and good works, owned mines and timberlands from New Jersey to Georgia and Michigan to Arizona. After a long talk, the firm decided that I should make a preliminary examination of their White Pine and Hemlock lands in Pennsylvania and report on what could be done to introduce Forestry upon them. It was great luck. The next day, January 7, 1891, I was in the woods.

Members of the firm in New York might think Forestry worth considering, but not so their lumbermen on the job. My work lay in Monroe County, and also in Pike County, where five generations of Pinchots have lived, where they are still living, and where I am writing this veracious tale. In both places the woodsmen's story was the same. The White Pine would never seed itself again (which it was doing abundantly before their very eyes), and if it did come up, the Buckwheat (second growth) Pine would never amount to anything. And there was too much fire. Which last nobody could deny.

This was my first contact with American lumbermen and the lumber woods—all new and fiercely interesting. It was also my first attempt to apply what I had learned in Europe to an American forest problem. And it seemed likely to work if I could get it applied. I was beginning to feel my feet under me, even if I was a good deal like an Eskimo trying to teach a man from the Desert of Sahara to catch seals.

So far as I know, what I wrote my clients after this trip was the first practical report on the application of Forestry to a particular forest ever made in America. Most unfortunately I cannot find a copy. But I have my report on another week's examination made in November 1893, of other White Pine lands of Phelps, Dodge & Company, but this time in central Pennsylvania.

Although second-growth White Pine was then everywhere regarded as worthless, the annual rings told a different story. "The second growth," said my report, "where it stands thickly, promises to be at least as valuable per acre as the former crop at an equal age, and on the same scale of prices. In my judgment not only is it possible to bring the Pine back, but it will be impossible, in the long run, it keep it out from most of the situations where it once stood."

Nevertheless, I pointed out, the lumbermen would in this region have an overwhelming pecuniary advantage over the forester for the present, and I did not recommend the immediate introduction of Forestry.

I was paid for the Phelps, Dodge report of 1891, but I suspect the firm got less out of it than I did. On the next job I worked for nothing, met my own expenses, and was heartily glad of the chance.

Dr. Fernow had been asked to examine a body of hardwood timber in the overflow lands of the Mississippi in eastern Arkansas. Very kindly he invited me to go along. Here was an open door to learning a little more about the United States.

On the way West I made careful notes of everything I could see from the car window. At Memphis I had my first glimpse of the Father of Waters, and in the Arkansas bottoms, which were then a refuge for criminals, my first contact with an outlaw community, my first look at the hardwoods of the Mississippi Valley, and my first taste of sowbelly and saleratus biscuit. The emblem of this civilization was the frying pan.

For miles on end Fernow and I rode our horses through the great flatwoods of superb Oak timber—miles of the richest alluvial soil, where there wasn't a stone to throw at a dog, and the cotton in the little clearings grew higher than I could reach from the saddle. Everything was new and strange. Every fence in the scanty settlements was plastered with signs of Ague Buster, and the people looked as if they needed it.

The Arkansas lumberjacks were tough, but very willing to talk. I got new light on logging and sawing, learned some of the mysteries of whisky staves and quartered Oak, collected a fine specimen of Hackberry (I have it yet), ate my first 'possum and found it good, and played a low trick on my family at home.

Chained in the yard of the house where we stayed in Jonesboro was a young bear by the name of Betsy. Betsy and I struck up a vivid affection, stimulated, if not created, by sundry bottles of molasses and water. It was love at first sight.

So I wrote home about the nice people I had met, and in particular and in detail about how much I liked Betsy. Then, when I judged the family were sufficiently keyed up over the prospect of an Arkansas flatwoods daughter-in-law, I sent them a photograph of Betsy and me very close together, with the molasses bottle in full flood. It achieved an instant and unconditional success.

After ten days in the woods, Dr. Fernow and I followed the Mississippi down to New Orleans, where I bought me a .32 Marlin rifle that I certainly did not need. At Mobile we stayed with Dr. Charles Mohr, and there I had my first sight of the Longleaf Pine.

Dr. Mohr was a lover of nature, a botanist who knew about trees. In his blue dressing gown, velvet skullcap, spectacles, and white beard, the good old man opened his heart and his home to us, and won me completely from the first. "Simple as a child, and certainly wiser than any serpent."

The differences between Fernow and me which later helped to keep me from joining him in the Forestry Division began to develop on this trip. His bent was to lecture rather than to lead, and he was unhealthily apt to take up real or imaginary offenses. My diary says: "Am getting pretty weary of Fernow. Hear nothing from him but endless self-appreciation at the expense of others. Runs everybody down with tiresome uniformity." It seemed that Sargent was right.

When Fernow directed one of his tirades against Dr. Mohr in the very room the kindly white-haired elder had given us, I was so disgusted that our association very nearly ended then and there. That incident settled my opinion of Fernow as a man, and colored all my future contacts with him.

From Mobile Dr. Mohr took me with him into northern Alabama, near the German colony of Cullman, to help measure, estimate, and report on a tract of timber. There I saw the mixed forests of the Piedmont Plateau and ran into such mud as I had never imagined. In one mudhole I had to keep our wagon from capsizing by hauling hard on a rope fast to the top.

From Cullman I went north; stopped to see George Vanderbilt's place near Asheville, North Carolina, which later turned out to be the wisest thing I could have done; found the Asheville mud the worst yet, but the property "just right for forest management on a rather intensive plan, and the reproduction of both conifers and deciduous trees excellent;" ran out of money; tried to trade my rifle for a Pullman ticket; failed; but got home anyhow.

It was an eye opener of a trip, and it did the beginner much good. I had seen new kinds of trees, I had touched new kinds of people, and I had gained a new conception of what the United States was like. My real preparation had begun.

PART II
ON THE TRAIL

6. *A Tenderfoot Goes West*

The report to Phelps Dodge & Company on their Pennsylvania lands made in 1891 must have been fairly satisfactory, for in March of that year, Mr. Dodge suggested that I should look over certain lands of theirs in southern Arizona, with a view to planting trees. No pay, but expenses and the chance to see the country and come home by way of the Pacific Coast and the Canadian Pacific Railroad.

It was a lot more than I was worth, in the first place, and besides it gave me just the chance I was after to shake hands with the U.S.A. And on the way to Chicago I stopped to see Niagara. Once again I was having the time of my life.

Sagebrush, prairie dogs, flat-topped buttes, hills covered with Piñon and Cedar; irrigation ditches, mountains that looked as if you could almost throw a stone and hit them, yet were miles away; log cabins, corrals, and the bones of cattle along the track—all these helped to make up my first picture of the West. The forests came afterward.

It was not the West of today. The tourist was still unknown in the land, ten-gallon hats were not, and the bad man of latter-day legend, or something somewhat like him, was still alive. The whole round, until I got home again, was full of wonder and delight.

From Bisbee, Arizona, site of the Phelps Dodge Copper Queen Mine, I drove alone to the Copper Queen Ranch in the Sulphur Spring Valley, where lay the lands I was to study. The Apache Indians were just then raiding in the Chiricahua Mountains across the valley, and my peace of mind was by no means enhanced when four horsemen in single file, rifles across their saddles, appeared from behind a butte above the road. But they disappeared as they had come, and I reached my destination safely, keeping my own arms handy the while.

The Sulphur Spring Valley, with its desert vegetation of mesquite and sagebrush, was a hard proposition. Water there was in fair supply, but it was twenty feet underground. The annual rainfall was only about ten inches, evaporation was enormous, and the constant winds made it worse. Records covering less than a year showed temperature changes in a few hours from freezing to 100 degrees. Nevertheless I thought there was a chance.

The trees of the higher lands about the valley might give me some information. Since the Apaches blocked off the Chiricahuas, I climbed the snow-covered Huachucas instead with one Charlie McNally, who told the tenderfoot about "the first man I ever saw murdered." I met a lot of new trees—not one, I thought, good for the valley. But, said my report, my own scanty acquirements in Forestry made my judgment of small account.

It was a good trip, nevertheless. I saw a lot of new country; collected specimens for Fernow; got caught out overnight in the mountains; was snuggled up to by an orphan litter of little pigs while sleeping in the barnyard of a ranch; killed a hawk, flying, with my 45-70 rifle; and enjoyed myself exceedingly. Then I headed for northern Arizona.

From Phoenix I drove all night in a four-horse stage, with highly disreputable companions of both sexes, over the famous Black Canyon Road. My seat was on the box with the driver. One jolt out of many threw me clear off it. I lit sprawling on the side of a cut; which was lucky, for much of the road skirted a precipice.

After drinking from the Hassayampa River, which is supposed to make a tenderfoot into an old-timer (it failed notably in my case), measuring tree growth all the way, I came to Flagstaff, under the shadow of the San Francisco Mountains, and within two or three days' drive of the Grand Canyon of the Colorado, which was what I had come to see.

I had letters to the Riordans of the Arizona Timber Company, and they could not have been kinder. They started me off for the Canyon in a buckboard, with the Riordan office boy, one Doran, and a pair of Riordan mules fresh from the lumber woods.

The mules were fine mules, beyond question, but it was evident that Doran and I didn't speak their language. Before we were out of sight of town, we had worn out a black-snake whip on them in a futile effort to get them out of a walk. Finally I cut me a stick of *Quercus engelmanni* (though I didn't know it at the moment), split it halfway down, and by hitting the same spot every time succeeded in making an impression.

But it was too late. The next water was too far ahead. We made a dry camp that night on the edge of the magnificent forest of Western Yellow Pine, and another of the same (and for the same reason) the next night. Toward evening of the third day we reached John Hance's, hobbled and turned loose our mules, and walked from his solitary little cabin up to the Grand Canyon's rim.

Awe-struck and silent, I strove to grasp the vastness and the beauty of the greatest sight this world has to offer. Meanwhile Doran stood beside me and kept repeating, "My, ain't it pretty?" I wanted to throw him in.

Next day Doran and I made it from the rim down to the Colorado River and back on foot. It was a most impressive and somewhat hazardous trip, partly through the gorge of a plunging tributary stream. Ropes hanging down certain otherwise unclimbable waterfalls had not been tested since the year before, for we were the first that season. The stream was high and the ropes were under water. We stripped and threw our clothes ahead before we tried them, and the worst that happened to us was a thorough soaking.

The vast dark river, in its fearful chasm of black rock, was tremendous and appalling in the gloom of a gathering storm. We did not linger to admire, for the rain might fill the narrow creek bed down which we had come and keep us in the Canyon all night.

Halfway to the top flowers were blossoming, but a snowstorm was raging when we reached the rim. With storm clouds sailing through it, with snow clouds partly veiling it, the Canyon was beyond imagination.

"A man can only wonder. At sunset it is magnificently beautiful, and by moonlight magnificently terrible. But the great power of it lies in its serenity. It is absolute peace."

The snowstorm lasted two days, during which those wretched mules, hobbles and all, started for Flagstaff, ninety miles away, and I acquired a firsthand knowledge of no small part of the great Coconino Forest trying to find them. However, what they made me learn about that pure stand of Western Yellow Pine was of much use later on.

Between times John Hance impressed on us the important fact that he was the best shot, the best walker, the best boatman and swimmer, the best rider, and had the best horses and the best mines "of any man that ever saw or read of Arizony."

Years later I learned that Hance had started a register of visitors. Mine was the first name on the list. He spelled it "Pinchob."

After Flagstaff came Los Angeles, where I was mighty glad to get my trunk again and a good wash. It wasn't so easy then to be happy though dirty as it has since become.

The region around Los Angeles was full of Eucalypts—magnificent gray-green trees standing in fence rows mainly, and most impressive. If they would grow in the Sulphur Spring Valley even half as well as they did in the San Gabriel Valley, my problem was solved.

The Santa Monica Forest Experiment Station buoyed up my spirits still further. There State Forester Lyon pointed out and I measured a *Eucalyptus gunni* less than three years old that was 45 feet 4 inches high by the little Nancy dendrometer.

But in spite of Lyon's help and the best I could do, the Sulphur Spring problem was not solved. So far as I know it remains unsolved to this day. The Eucalypts, which were the backbone of my hope, did not pan out.

After Santa Monica, Abbott Kinney, a leader in the forest movement of California, showed me the effects of floods in the San Gabriel Valley and introduced me to the erosion problem of the West. And I may add that the erosion problem of the West has since moved east and occupied the land from coast to coast. Already one-third of the fertile soil of the United States has gone down the streams. Either we shall control erosion, or it will drive us out, as it has driven out more than one nation already. There is no middle way.

From "South of Tehachapi" I headed for the Tulare Grove of Big Trees on the Marble Fork of King's River. My road to them was by way of the Kaweah Co-operative Colony, a little group of economic enthusiasts long since dispersed.

As I rode my hired horse through the California foothills, glorious in the lap of spring, I was enchanted. Every fence post seemed to hold a meadow lark, and great blankets of the richest colors kept the hillsides warm.

Nearer the mountains I got a shot at a cinnamon bear, three hundred yards away downhill, and missed her. Today I'm not so sorry, for she had a cub along.

In the Sierras, where the snow in places was twenty feet deep, the timber was magnificent. "But who shall describe the Sequoias? Their beauty is far more wonderful than their size. When the black marks of fire are sprinkled on the wonderfully deep richer ocher of the bark, the effect is brilliant beyond words."

These highly decorative but equally undesirable fires bulked large in the minds of the Kaweah colonists, most of whom were Eastern tenderfeet. One of them told me they had saved the Big Trees from burning up twenty-nine times in the last five years. Which might naturally have raised the question, Who saved them during the remaining three or four thousand years of their age?

The colonists had named the biggest Sequoia for Karl Marx. Today that might entitle them to be called Bolsheviks. Under whatever name, they were very kind to one stranger I could mention.

Forty-six years later I saw that tree again. This second time I traveled to it not on makeshift snowshoes improvised out of barrel staves but by automobile. The vast Sequoia itself had shared the change. It was no longer Socialist, but had taken the name of a great soldier and citizen, General Sherman. Unlike that other General Sherman tree, planted by himself on our place at Milford, it was said to be the largest tree on earth.

Next, from Berenda I rode in to the Mariposa Grove, and spent the day mainly with its biggest tree, that superb and decrepit veteran, the Grizzly Giant. "I took lunch with him and then measured him and a lot more. Entirely apart from the Big Trees, that Sierra Forest was tremendously worth seeing."

It was all of that, and a whale of a lot more. My diary goes into little detail, and a description written today would merely reproduce later impressions. But the glory and dignity of that supernal forest I shall never forget.

And then the Yosemite. One of the great mistakes of a long and misspent life is that I saw the Yosemite Valley only after the Grand Canyon had dulled my sense of wonder. "Everything is tame after that."

A bitter controversy was then raging as to whether California, to which the Yosemite Valley had been granted by the United States, was protecting its beauty and the beauty of the Mariposa Grove or destroying it. One of the State Commissioners, for example, recommended the systematic cutting of all young trees in the Valley. That, as Frederick Law Olmsted wisely observed, would have been "a calamity to the civilized world."

I went to the Yosemite as a forester to see for myself, and I concluded that "the simple and effective remedy lies in the preparation of a plan of management for the Valley which will embrace, not one, but a number of years. No such plan at present exists, nor is there, so far as I know, anyone connected with the management of the Valley competent to prepare one."

The Yosemite Fall, with its 1,700 feet of drop, was worth crossing the continent to see. As the wind waved the falling water back and forth across the face of the great cliff, it left me nearly stunned with amazement. And stunned with water, too, when, like the boy I was, I ran under it, and it beat upon me at the end of more than a quarter of a mile of fall. Such a maelstrom of wind and water I was never in before or since. It was a great experience.

There is too much to tell; about the trip on foot up to Glacier Point; about my talks with Galen Clark, the veteran guardian of Yosemite; about the old trapper who complained to me that the country was getting all settled up—his nearest neighbor only twenty miles away; about getting acquainted with magnificent new kinds of Firs and Pines, as a forester should know them; about all the impacts of an incomparable forest, the glorious Sierras, and all the rest of a flamboyant frontier on a young and hungry mind.

When I came to the railroad from Yosemite, civilization reached for me again. My clothes began to worry me. "Looked like an awful wreck with holes in my shoes and clothes, and a general appearance of dirt and dilapidation." It bothered me then. It wouldn't now. But anyhow it was cheap at the price.

After Yosemite, San Francisco, where irrigation in the hinterland made forest preservation a live issue; Cazadero, where the glorious Redwood forest of the famous Bohemian Club Grove bade fair to exhaust what power of admiration I had left; and Mount Shasta, fairest of all the snow peaks the United States has to show, if you leave it to me.

At Portland, as elsewhere in western Oregon and Washington, lumbering was the all-important industry. Here were great sawmills cutting Douglas-fir. Here was my first acquaintance with the titanic logging of the Pacific Coast. Back of Castle Rock (where the hotel rate, as in so many places then, was $1.00 a day—two bits for a meal and two bits for a bed), was "the most magnificent timber I ever saw, barring the Redwoods of the two kinds. Lots of trees three hundred feet high, many eight feet in diameter six feet from the ground. And the trip cost $7.00 too. But it was worth it."

It was here that I first ran across the belief that forest fires can be prevented only by annual burning of the leaf litter on the ground. But hardly anybody thought they could be prevented at all.

By the time I reached Tacoma, the trip was beginning to wear me out. Solitary travel had lost its charm and I was burning to get home. I was seeing too fast too many things in which I was furiously interested.

The next day, however, found me in touch with the Land Department of the Northern Pacific Railroad, and visiting the St. Paul and Tacoma two-band sawmill, with a capacity of 150,000 board feet a day. The next at Wilkinson, among the Douglas-firs. "Up at 3 A.M., and went with a small kid to see the most splendid forest I ever looked at. Then took a 7 A.M. train to Tacoma. Read a good deal of *Paradise Lost* today."

In Stanley Park at Vancouver I finally found the great Tideland Spruce, and never shall I forget it—fifteen feet in diameter and more beautiful than an army with banners.

Then on the Canadian Pacific through the canyon of the Frazer River, which is just a vast tumbling trout stream with salmon for trout, and on through the main range of the Rocky Mountains. After that, back home. How utterly dwarfed and insignificant the hardwoods of the East did seem after I had soaked myself in the immeasurable evergreen forests of the West!

When the trip was over I was pretty well all in. "Footless, useless, selfish, dumb, and generally of no use to anybody. Not able to talk or act like anything but an ass. Disgusted with myself most thoroughly." I didn't know enough to know what was the matter with me.

This first Western trip could hardly have been more useful. I was like a cat let out of a bandbox. Whereas I had been blind, now I began to see. But still I had not begun to practice Forestry. That, however, was on the way.

In my first six months at home I had seen something of the forest in thirty-one states and Canada, even if only from the train, and had actually been in the woods in nine of them. Not such a bad start, although my apprenticeship was far from ended.

Apprentice or not, my new profession attracted attention. Invitations came to speak at Massachusetts Agricultural College, at a Forestry convention in South Carolina, and to write for the annual report of the Minnesota State Geological Association. Notice of my new departure was even taken in Kate Field's syndicated Washington column, where she wrote: "It's about time that forestry became a profession, and it's infinitely to his credit that young Gifford Pinchot has set an honorable example." It was not young Gifford Pinchot, however, to whom the credit belonged, but to his Father, without whose sagacious foresight the first American forester would have borne some other name.

Father and Forestry, in 1892, secured my election to the Century Club of New York, which my Father had joined thirty years before. Doubtless it was mainly because I was my Father's son, but also because I represented a new cause and a new profession. In any case it was not for the love of my bright eyes.

Off and on throughout the year 1891, whenever there was nothing more pressing, I was working on the book about Forestry which my Father had suggested. Fernow, Sargent, and Dr. Brandis all thought well of it, and I even had one offer to collaborate. Progress on it was mighty slow, however, and what with other things coming along it was seven years before it finally appeared as *A Primer of Forestry,* Part I.

Also I had several conferences with George Vanderbilt and Frederick Law Olmsted about putting Forestry into practice on George's great new estate at Biltmore in North Carolina. What came of that will appear in the next chapter.

7. *Forestry Comes to America*

Richard M. Hunt, at that time the foremost American architect, and Frederick Law Olmsted, first and greatest of American landscape architects, were engaged, in the early nineties, in creating for George W. Vanderbilt near Asheville, North Carolina, what was intended to be the most beautiful and elaborate country estate in America.

Mr. Olmsted was to me one of the men of the century. He was a quiet-spoken little lame man with a most magnificent head and one of the best minds I have ever had the good luck to encounter. His knowledge was far wider than his profession. He knew the territory of the United States as few men knew it, and he was full of stories of early days. For instance:

Riding into Sacramento, California, one day in the early fifties, Mr. Olmsted noticed a single figure standing out in the open plaza. The figure in the plaza was amusing himself by taking pot shots with a pistol at every man he saw. Presently a man walked straight out to the shooter, who was shouting, raging drunk, and took his gun away.

The man who did this bravest thing was a gambler who had given clothes taken from smallpox victims to peaceful and harmless Digger Indians—a form of murder as low and contemptible as the gambler's courage was high and fine.

That story did me a lot of good. It shed a light on human nature that has helped me ever since not to underestimate people I don't like.

Biltmore House, the center of the Vanderbilt estate, not yet completed when I saw it first, was a magnificent château of Indiana limestone. With the terrace and stables it was a thousand feet in length. Its setting was superb, the view from it breath-taking, and as a feudal castle it would have been beyond criticism, and perhaps beyond praise.

But in the United States of the nineteenth century and among the one-room cabins of the Appalachian mountaineers, it did not belong. The contrast was a devastating commentary on the injustice of concentrated wealth. Even in the early nineties I had sense enough to see that.

The Biltmore Estate was to include a model farm, a great arboretum, a vast game preserve, and, if Mr. Olmsted's recommendations were carried out, the first example of practical forest management in the United States. The conception was, of course, Mr. Olmsted's, but it was George Vanderbilt who put it through.

George was a lover of art and of the great outdoors, a slim, simple, and rather shy young man, too much and too long sheltered by female relatives, enormously rich, unmarried, but without racing stables or chorus girls in his cosmos. Biltmore was his heart's delight. To his very great credit, considering his associations and his bringing up, he had a real sense of social responsibility and was eager to do more than merely live on his money.

G.W.V. was thus a shining contrast to many of his friends, whose ideal of life was to exist without work. I wondered then, and I continue to wonder, at the invincible stupidity of the young men with money who believe they can have a good time in this world just by trying to have a good time.

The man who merely hunts amusement soon finds that his life is given over to escaping from boredom. Sooner or later dullness pursues him like a fury. Gilded idlers are just plain fools. I have worked hard all my life, if I do say it, I have earned my living, although I never had to, and I have had more fun than any ten of them. No man can be really happy without a job. All of which is respectfully submitted.

It was Mr. Olmsted who was responsible for the plan to make Biltmore Estate the nest egg for practical Forestry in America. I was able to discuss the matter with him because I had already made myself familiar with the needs and conditions at Biltmore. Moreover, my Father and Mr. Olmsted were old friends. Both facts doubtless had much to do with my being invited to take charge of Biltmore Forest. It happened on December 6, 1891, just under a year after I got home.

Work in the woods looked better to me than work in any office. Accordingly I notified Dr. Fernow that I would not go into the Forestry Division as his assistant, a plan to which neither of us was committed, but take to the forest instead. His reply referred to the work at Biltmore as "an impracticable fad."

I agreed to make working plans for the management of Biltmore Forest and the larger area afterwards called Pisgah Forest, and to carry them out, with such assistance as might be necessary. Part of my contract, also, was to prepare an exhibit of Biltmore Forest for the Chicago World's Fair of 1893. I was to give whatever time was necessary, beginning in February 1892, and to get $2,500 a year and subsistence while on the job.

Here was my chance. Biltmore could be made to prove what America did not yet understand, that trees could be cut and the forest preserved at one and the same time. I was eager, confident, and happy as a clam at high tide.

But to me, as I set down at the time, what was worth almost more than the opportunity to work was the fact that Mr. Olmsted took my profession seriously, and took with equal seriousness the assumption which he made that I was able to practice it. I have never forgotten what it meant to a youngster just getting started to be treated to some extent as an equal, and I shall always hold myself deep in his debt for what he did for me.

Thus Biltmore Forest became the beginning of practical Forestry in America. It was the first piece of woodland in the United States to be put under a regular system of forest management whose object was to pay the owner while improving the forest. As Dr. Fernow wrote me on July 20, 1893, "forest management has not been put into operation on any other area in this country except Biltmore."

Biltmore Estate covered a little over 7,000 acres of rolling hills and bottom lands on both sides of the French Broad River. Half of it was woodland. It had been put together from small impoverished farms, the forest on which had been burned, slashed, and overgrazed until it was little more than the shadow of its former self. In Europe I had seen nothing like it, but millions of acres east of the Mississippi were its brothers and sisters.

I wrote to Dr. Brandis that "if forest management is successful in producing a profit off this land it will do so on almost any land in this part of the country. In a word, the more I know of the conditions the more thoroughly satisfied I am that if Biltmore Forest is a success I need not fear to undertake the management of any piece of forest land that I have seen in the United States."

Fernow, on the other hand, wrote me "if you can 'make forestry *profitable*' under the conditions at Biltmore within the next ten years, I shall consider you the wisest forester and financier of the age." Which could scarcely be called encouraging.

Biltmore Forest lay in Western North Carolina on the great continental tableland between the Blue Ridge and the Allegheny Mountains. Its general altitude was a little over 2,000 feet. It was made up mainly of Oaks and other broadleaf trees, most of them very young, with Pines scattered among them by single trees, or here and there by pure stands in old fields. Of the broadleaf trees, the White Oak was in all respects first. Next, but less valuable in quality, came the Black, Scarlet, and Spanish Oaks. And next came the Shortleaf Pine and Chestnut, with some Yellow-poplar.

The forest was exceptionally rich in kinds of trees. Indeed this general region is the richest in species in the whole United States. Reproduction was, for the most part, good. But the Biltmore stands were broken and irregular, and varied greatly in density, size, and condition. The soil was poor, and the percentage of valuable kinds in the mixture greatly reduced. The better trees had been cut out, and the worse remained to perpetuate their kind. Worse still, old spreading trees, mostly unsound, were endangering or suppressing the next generation.

My work in Biltmore Forest began February 3, 1892. First of all I had to get acquainted. So I set out to describe the forest, using squares of 5.7 acres into which a topographical survey had divided the Estate. When that was done, I had a complete card catalogue description of the whole forest, and I knew it like the back of my hand. But as I look back now, I think the description by such small sections, in spite of the praise it received from European authorities, was largely a waste of time.

So far as future management was concerned, the forest was mainly of two kinds. In one of them trees of all ages were more or less completely present in all parts. In the other, one age class predominated, usually composed of saplings and low poles, over which the remaining old trees spread their widening crowns.

What was needed before a permanent working plan could be prepared was to harvest the old trees that were going back themselves and at the same time shading out the young growth. A series of improvement cuttings would remove these older trees, leaving the young growth to develop.

No improvement cutting could be made where the young trees were very far from thick enough to protect the soil, and none that would cost more than it would bring in. A period of six years was tentatively set for carrying out the improvement cuttings and beginning the permanent working plan.

Besides the improvement cuttings, which would bring about a more valuable mixture of species and a healthier and more uniform forest, cattle had to be excluded, and fire must be kept out. I got my first taste of fire fighting on Biltmore Forest. It wasn't much of a fire, but the smoke and the heat, the aching muscles and stinging eyes, gave me some realizing sense of the enormous labor and acute physical suffering that fire fighters must sometimes undergo.

Based on the detailed description of squares above mentioned, the forest was next divided into compartments, ninety-two of them, of about forty-two acres each, and these were grouped in three blocks, as the larger units of management. On this foundation improvement cuttings were laid out for the first period of six years.

During the first year, while woods crews were being trained and we were getting our feet under us, the cost of the improvement cuttings had to be kept down. The roads were bad—how permanently bad you will perhaps realize when I tell you that the deed for one of the farms George bought gave a certain corner of the boundary as "at a mud hole in the road." In wet weather they were awful. Therefore the haul had to be short. Yet the cost of hauling had to be more or less equalized from year to year. Also we must cut first where improvement cuttings were needed most.

Work was begun at a point near Biltmore Village where the old trees were numerous enough and the younger growth vigorous enough to justify cutting and to make it pay. The quality of the old trees and the lack of a sawmill within hauling distance forced us to cut nothing but cordwood and railroad ties, for which the brickworks at Biltmore Village and the branch line to Biltmore House gave a steady and profitable market.

The old way of lumbering at Biltmore, and everywhere else, was to cut out of the way all the young growth that would interfere with cheap and easy logging, and leave desolation and a firetrap behind. It was no easy matter to break this habit and train the loggers to respect all small trees of valuable species, no matter how much they stood in the way of chopper or sawyer.

To fell timber where it would do the least harm to the future of the forest was a new idea and required an entirely novel point of view. It had to be drilled first into young Whitney, son of an Adirondack woodsman, who was my assistant; next into the foremen, and then they had to drill it into their crews.

Whitney was a simple soul, but he had his lucid moments. One day after we had ridden together for an hour or two in silence he broke out, "Say, there's a lot of good reading in the Bible, ain't there?" And in that he was everlastingly right.

By keeping at it, we found that large trees surrounded by a dense growth of smaller trees could be logged with surprisingly little injury to the young growth, and that the added cost of taking care was small out of all proportion to the result. To establish this fact, which at first no lumbermen would admit, was of immense importance to the success of Forestry in America.

Before any trees were cut they were first carefully chosen by myself or my assistant. Each tree was then blazed breast high and at the ground, and each blaze stamped with the marking hatchet. The stump of every tree felled had to show the Circle V brand of the hatchet.

Each marked tree was notched with an ax, under the direction of the foreman, and then thrown by the loggers as nearly as might be where it would do the least harm to young growth. A sound straight tree can be thrown in any direction (when the wind isn't blowing), a sound leaning tree anywhere in a half-circle, but you must throw an unsound tree where you can. There's generally plenty of choice.

Each trunk was then sawed into cordwood lengths, and the sawyers went on to the next, leaving the splitting by wedge and mallet to another gang, which also cut the tops into cordwood and unsalable piles of brush. The wood was next piled and measured, hauled by mule teams to a sidetrack on the railroad which connected Biltmore Village with the site of Biltmore House, and there loaded on cars and shipped.

With my only technical advisers 3,000 miles away across the ocean, it is not surprising that after many a hard day in the woods I spent anxious hours over my French and German textbooks, when I ought to have been in bed. But it was hard to get much light from the writings of men who had never seen a forest such as I had to handle.

We were very careful not to cut too heavily at first. There was no previous cutting like this to check against anywhere in this country. Moreover, the thinness of the forest, and the unpredictable amount of damage to young growth which might be done by the old trees in falling, kept us on the anxious seat. In the end our mistake was in cutting too lightly, but at least it was a mistake on the right side.

The lumbering for saw logs, which came a little later and in denser forest, was more complicated. Trees to be cut had to be selected with even greater care, roads had to be built and kept roughly in order from the rollways to the sawmill. After the better parts of the trunks had been cut into logs and as much of the rest as possible into shingle bolts, logs and bolts were skidded by mules to the roads, loaded on wagons, and hauled to the mill. We used drays or go-devils in the skidding.

The mill was a small portable circular with a 52-inch saw, run by a twenty horsepower steam engine. Considering the quality of the logs and the mill, the lumber was excellent. From the saw it went to the lumberyard, where it was stacked in piles until called for. After the available logs about the mill had been sawed up the engine was used to run a shingle mill, and when all the bolts had been disposed of the whole plant was moved to another site.

The lumber was Oak, Pine, and Poplar. Pine and Poplar shingles were sawed out of slabs and defective logs as well as from shingle bolts, so that the waste, always very large in a portable circular mill, was kept down. After the lumbering, we cut cordwood from what was left on the ground.

At Biltmore, in those days, labor was cheap. Wages ran from 90 cents to $1.00 a day. Mule hire was 75 cents. Wood delivered on the cars brought $2.00 a cord, Oak lumber from $8.00 to $25.00 a thousand, Pine from $4.00 to $14.00, and railroad ties 30 cents apiece.

Because we had a ready market for our cordwood and sawed lumber, the first year's work showed a balance of $1,220.56 on the side of practical Forestry—conservative lumbering that left a growing forest behind it. To that extent we made it pay.

Thus the balance sheet of Biltmore Forest for the first full calendar year (1893) was at least hopeful. If the 6,708 cords of wood on hand, for which we were getting $2.00 on cars, had been credited at $1.50 instead of $1.00, the balance would have covered also my salary and expenses, with something left over. It could have been worse.

The first year at Biltmore I lived on the Estate in the Brick House, which was kept open for George's convenience and mine. While I was a fair camp cook, I was perfectly green at housekeeping. But when the bill came in for sixteen dozen eggs and a gallon of cream in one week, even I could understand that 192 eggs in seven days exceeded the capacity for eggs of two men and one ancient colored cook. Just how many of Martha's children and grandchildren and children-in-law were being fed on the food we were supposed to eat I never learned—but certainly plenty.

At the Brick House I fell violently in love with a fiery little black gelding by the name of Punch. He taught me most of what I know about riding bucking horses. To begin with Punch won more bouts than I did, but not in the end. After I could pick my handkerchief off the ground while he was putting on his act, I looked for other fields to conquer. When, however, a bucking mule bolted into the stable with my arms and legs both around its neck, it appeared that I wasn't so good after all.

As I look back on my Biltmore incarnation, more than half a lifetime ago, I wonder at the vitality that drove me, after a hard day in the woods, to ride a bucking horse just for the fun of it. Well, if you like that sort of thing, that's the sort of thing you like. Them was the happy days.

The plan of the Biltmore Estate, of which the Brick House was a temporary part, might fairly be described as high, wide, and handsome. In addition to Biltmore House, the most remarkable of its kind in America, and the Biltmore Dairies, which supplied milk for Asheville, and Biltmore Village for workers, a model of its kind, and a private railroad, and half a dozen other enterprises—in addition to all these there was the Biltmore Nursery and Arboretum.

The Arboretum plan was not merely to make a botanical collection, but to show the value of the trees as elements both in scenery and in practical Forestry. About three hundred "Forest Acres" were to be planted, each to a single kind of tree. For them I collected tree seeds from nearly all the temperate regions of the globe. Part of my job also were forest plantations, mostly of White Pine, on old fields in various parts of the Estate.

The Biltmore Arboretum, under the competent leadership of Dr. Charles W. Beadle, became the most complete in existence in the forest flora of the Southeastern United States. But it was far more. In it were gathered more kinds of woody plants than in Kew, the most celebrated botanical garden and arboretum on earth. They came not only from almost the entire United States but from nearly all the rest of the temperate world also.

Unfortunately, after reaching such supremacy and arousing the expectations of botanists and foresters the world over, the Biltmore Arboretum was allowed to drop. Mr. Olmsted and I urged G.W.V. to make permanent provision for it, but to no avail.

Out of all the vast expenditure at Biltmore, the great and lasting contribution of what the natives called "Vanderbilt's Folly" came from Biltmore Forest. Its demonstration that forest management was something more than an "impracticable fad" was permanently worth while.

Forestry at Biltmore had no relation to that ancient and deceitful saying, "Plant a tree for every one cut down." Nearly two and a half centuries ago, in the Colony of New York, Lord Bellemont knew better than that. He urged the passage of an act "obliging everybody who cuts down a tree to plant four or five young trees in its stead."

Therein he was ahead, both in time and in theory, of Governor Cadwallader Colden, also of New York, who in 1723 recommended that "white pines be planted one for each tree cut down or dying." Five trees are five times better than one.

To find this hoary superstition embalmed far back in American history is of very real interest. Every now and then I hear it still. And perhaps this is as good a place as any to say that, so far as I have ever seen or heard, there is no such practice in Forestry anywhere in the world, there never has been, and there never could be.

A forest crop ready for the ax may number a hundred, two hundred, or possibly three hundred trees to the acre. To replant that acre after clean cutting would require not less than fifteen hundred young trees—and more often two, three, or four thousand.

One seedling set out for each mature tree cut down, or even two for one, might result in an open park of branching shade trees. It never could reproduce an old forest of clean trunks fit for saw logs and lumber.

Nevertheless, this quack prescription remains even yet the easy wisdom of too many good friends of the forest, who firmly believe that it covers the whole duty of the forester and summarizes the practice of Forestry in Germany and France. Biltmore Forest knew better.

Biltmore Forest made also another, although an indirect, contribution to the progress of Forestry in America that thoroughly deserves to be remembered.

Professor Joseph A. Holmes, at that time State Geologist of North Carolina, was one of the best men I ever ran across. He and I were holding a session on things in general and Forestry in particular around the fire at the Brick House one night in the winter of '92 or '93, I'm not sure which. In the course of it he suggested that the Federal Government ought to buy a big tract of timberland in the Southern Appalachians and practice Forestry on it.

It was a great plan, and neither he nor I ever let it drop. Nearly twenty years later the Weeks Law was passed, Holmes's dream came true, and today Eastern and Middle Western National Forests which cover eighteen millions of acres owe their origin to his brilliant suggestion.

The first real chance to get the facts about Biltmore Forest to the people was at the Chicago World's Fair of 1893. To prepare that exhibit was part of my contract. But such exhibits were among the extremely numerous things that I knew little or nothing about. So in May, three months after taking charge at Biltmore, I went abroad, partly to find out, partly to submit my plans for handling Biltmore Forest to Dr. Schlich, Dr. Brandis, Forstmeister Meister, Professor Landolt, and many others, who one and all approved them.

The Biltmore Forest Exhibit at Chicago was, so far as I know, the first exhibit of practical Forestry ever made in the United States. It showed by greatly enlarged photographs what the forest was like, and what had already been done to improve it while making it pay. It showed by models of well-managed European forests, prepared under the eye of Professor Hartig, what was planned for the future. And it showed by maps the division of the forest into compartments, the succession of cuttings, the lines of transportation, and other practical details.

A pamphlet, written in the sweat of my brow for free distribution at the exhibit, described the work in words and pictures, gave the figures of receipts and expenditures for the first year, and showed a small balance to the credit of Forestry.

Friendly comment came not only from visitors to the Fair, and from friends of Forestry all over America, but also, and most cordially, from the newspapers, to thousands of which the pamphlet had been sent. Forestry was gaining ground not only in the woods but also in print and conversation.

8. *In the Carolina Mountains*

The plan for Biltmore included from the start not only the Estate around Biltmore House, but also a great game preserve and camping ground in the higher mountains. When I got back from abroad in August of '92, my first job, after casting an eye over what had been done to Biltmore Forest in my absence and finding it good, was to look over the Pink Beds, a magnificent tract of 20,000 acres in the main range of the Appalachians that George was thinking of buying. It was a great bowl with mountains for the rim, and in the middle, in their seasons, the white and rosy blossoms of impenetrable thickets of the Laurel and Rhododendron which gave the place its name.

It was my business to spy out the ground. With me went a real estate agent in a derby hat, whose memory I treasure. His name was Plumadore. I never saw him without his celluloid collar, in bed or out.

The second night we spent in a cabin far back in the mountains. In the room where we slept there were three beds, with at least two people in each. The third bed was a trundle bed, trundled out from under one of the other beds for the children.

When bedtime came, the men turned in first. Then, lamp put out, the women took their turn. These arrangements were taken for granted, because every isolated cabin of necessity took in such strangers as might happen along. There was no place else for them to go.

At the end of the third day's ride we ran into heavy rain. Plumadore lost his way, night came on, and we had to make a wet and hungry camp on a little knoll in a swamp, where a small jar of vaseline out of my saddlebags helped us start a fire. We fed his horse and my mule with chestnut leaves, the while Plumadore beguiled the time with the cheerful story of an enormous rattlesnake he said had been killed on that very spot.

At daylight I went ahead on foot (leaving Plumadore to bring the riding stock, I can't remember why), made a preliminary breakfast on blackberries in a clearing, and another at the house of one King, a local preacher whom afterward I came to know very well, and in whose little church I spoke on a later Sunday.

After soaking all night in the woods I felt pretty sticky, and I asked the old man where I could get a real allover wash. He took me to a pool in a stream hard by, and as he sat on the bank and watched me apply the soap, pensively remarked: "I ain't had a bathe in twelve year."

The forest in the Pink Beds country was superb, where fire had not destroyed or depressed it. It was a virgin stand of Yellow-poplar, Oak, Hemlock, Hickory, Black Walnut, and Beech. But fire and cattle together had left a superb body of seed-bearing trees almost entirely without successors. As to young growth, practically there wasn't any.

Poplar was the chief lumber tree, with the Oaks and Chestnut next. I figured a sustained yield for all merchantable species of about a million feet a year, but I knew so little about how to secure the necessary natural reproduction that I advised no cutting at that time. As a game preserve and outing ground, however, the Pink Beds left practically nothing to be desired.

I had hardly parted from Plumadore and his celluloid collar before Whitney and I were off to look over two even larger tracts, together of more than 150,000 acres. This time I proposed to sleep in no more overpopulated cabins. In the local tongue, I taken my camp outfit along.

George Vanderbilt was the proud possessor of two sawbuck pack-saddles and a pair of magnificent gray mules. Mules I knew from much experience, mostly unpleasant, but I had never cinched a pack-saddle on a single one. I had never even seen a pack put on; the diamond hitch was a name to me, and it was nothing more.

That, however, was a difficulty but not an objection. Whitney and I tied our packs on the mules somehow or other, and with a Negro handy man and cook along, set out for a look at lands on Pigeon River and in the Great Smokies. But the way those packs skinned up those mules has been on my conscience ever since.

Apparently no pack outfit had been seen in the Great Smokies since the Civil War. So they took us for revenuers, United States Treasury agents, who would naturally be looking for the colorless blockade whisky (never moonshine) which was common everywhere and led to many a killing. In view of what these people often did to the revenuers, I can assure you the situation was highly uncomfortable until I got it straightened out.

Appalachian mountaineers of those days had opinions and were willing to back them. Their usual argument was the old Kentucky single-shot, muzzle-loading rifle, as often as not an ancient flintlock altered to caps. It had a long and heavy octagon barrel and a slim, curving, curly maple or walnut stock, with a brass box for bullet patches let in. The men who carried them certainly could bring the squirrels down out of the tops of the tallest trees. I've been sorry ever since that I hadn't collected one of those primeval weapons to hang on a pair of antlers at home.

The mountaineers were highly religious on Sunday, but not noticeably so on the other six days of the week. They spoke with a drawl, but there was no drawl in their action when action began. Their courage and fighting quality left nothing to be desired.

Feuds and rattlesnakes abounded. The orthodox defense against the former was to "lay way" the other fellow; against the latter to tie your trousers around your ankles and stuff them full of leaves. By and large, it was a good place to watch your step.

Once in the Great Smokies, stopping at a lumber camp while I looked the country over, I noticed that a hole had been blown with a shotgun in the door. Naturally I was curious. It appeared that a native whose cabin was in plain sight a couple of hundred yards away was in the habit of getting drunk on blockade whisky. There was nothing remarkable in that, but what was perhaps less usual was his cheerful custom, when lit up, of sitting on his porch with his old rifle and taking pot shots at anyone who came in sight.

The loggers stood it with only moderate resentment, for his shooting was poor. But when he transferred the scene of hostilities to the camp itself, that was something else again. On one such occasion the foreman grabbed a sawed-off shotgun and would have abated the nuisance then and there if the rifleman hadn't slipped out and slammed the door behind him. Hence the hole in the door.

The morning after I learned of these amenities I noticed a man watching the camp, half hidden in the edge of the woods. Inquiry developed the fact that he was wanted for murder. The presence of strangers made him shy. But I managed to scrape acquaintance, and we spent a pleasant day together, mostly fishing. He seemed a harmless sort of fellow, in spite of the gun stuck in his belt. Somebody must have picked on him pretty hard.

Watching your step in the literal sense was not easy in a forest as exciting in its variety and beauty as this one. Biltmore Forest had nearly seventy different kinds of trees. The higher lands of Pisgah Forest, some of which rose into the region of Spruce and Balsam, had many more. The whole effect was enough to keep, and it did keep, a certain northern-bred forester in a state of continuous wonder and exclamation.

High mountains, long smooth slopes running steeply down to clear swift streams that watered rich coves full of great trees, Yellow-poplar, Red Oak, Cherry, Walnut, and a host of others. Here the Northern and Southern forests met and mingled. Nowhere else in America were there so many kinds of trees, nowhere else in the East mountains so high, forests so gorgeous, trees so huge as in this Southern Appalachian region. Small wonder that it caught and held the interest of G.W.V.

All these desirables, however, lay in a region whose people knew nothing of game preserves and but little of property rights. On the contrary, they regarded this country as their country, their common. And that was not surprising, for they needed everything usable in it—pasture, fish, and game—to supplement the very meager living they were able to scratch from the soil of their little clearings, which often were no clearings at all, but mere "deadenings," filled with the whitening skeletons of trees killed by girdling.

By immemorial custom and by law, the cattle and the long-legged hogs ran free over ridge and slope and bottom. You had to fence them out, not to fence them in. They were kept some sort of track of by feeding the razorbacks a little corn now and then, and by hanging bells on the necks of the cattle.

There were no game laws in the North Carolina of that day. How much you could kill, how much you could catch, and when, depended on how well you could shoot and fish—and when your time off came around.

Oscar King Davis (friend of Theodore Roosevelt, famous newspaper correspondent, and "O.K." to his friends) said that years afterward, when my conscience had come alive, I walked into his Washington office one day looking glum. He asked me what was the matter. According to him I replied, "Down in the Old North State I caught a trout out of season in a posted stream on Sunday with a worm." Which is about the limit.

Now I fish with a barbless dry fly and put back more trout than go into my creel. Then I caught eighty little trout in a single day for no better reason than a frying pan.

The lives of these mountain people were literally as cribbed, cabined, and confined as the country in which they had their being was spacious, rich, and beautiful. They dwelt and slept mostly in one-room cabins, and they lived very far from high.

An open fireplace was cookstove and furnace, with a kettle hanging from a crane. Glass was rare, and windows were closed by solid board shutters. Homespun was the common wear.

There was, of course, nothing approaching sanitation, shoes were little worn around home, and hookworm was everywhere. So were typhoid fever and tuberculosis. Queer diseases, it seemed, for mountain people who lived mostly in the open air.

They had no newspapers and few books except the Bible. But a sentence written by one of them I shall never forget. Riding a saddle mule one day between Biltmore and the Pink Beds and meditating generally on the state of the nation, I came to a little house with a fence around it and a tombstone inside the fence. I rode over to look at it. On the stone, under a man's name, was this, "He left this country better than he found it." No man ever earned a finer epitaph.

The distance and the difficulties of the country in which these mountain people lived had kept them strictly to themselves for generations. In ancestry they were purebred English, and their language had the pith and vigor of Shakespeare's time. A bag was still a poke, a comical person was an antic, a sweetheart was a donna, and when a man gave notice of a meeting by word of mouth he norated. Their virtues and their vices, too, had the robustness of Shakespeare.

Many of them I grew to know, like, and respect, but my special pal was a little man named Jimmy Case. Jimmy and I covered many a long mile with our packs on our backs, and made many a camp together where night found us.

Jimmy had never set foot outside his beloved mountains. He could neither read nor write, but no truer gentleman ever stepped. Our friendship was unbroken until the great scourge of his people carried him away.

There were black bear in that country, and Jimmy Case built me a cabin far back on a ridge where the black bear "used to use." It had a chimney, a fireplace, a half-portion door, and half the floor was raised to sleep on. I called it Cheap Enough. It cost me $9.50.

One time Jimmy and a few of his friends were out on a coon hunt, and I with them. Headquarters, Cheap Enough. In the bright afternoon one of us noticed a gray squirrel on the ground acting very queerly. It paid us no slightest attention, as we gathered near, but kept on barking viciously, jumping from side to side, and always coming closer to the foot of a certain tree, as though a string were pulling it.

What was pulling it, however, was no string but a rattlesnake, coiled against that tree, head up, eyes blazing, and rattle going strong.

Was the snake charming the squirrel? Would the squirrel have been drawn within reach of its fangs? We all thought so then, and I think so now, although the final proof is missing. The proceedings were violently interrupted, and it was the snake that died.

Vanderbilt's chief caretaker was a man named Sorrels, who had been a warden in the North Carolina Penitentiary. Sorrels was an A-1 rifle shot. He and I went together to a dinner the people around the Pink Beds had made up their minds to give me after we got acquainted. But when we arrived, the banquet was still walking around. Before the dinner could be given the chickens had to be killed. We undertook to shoot their heads off. Have you ever tried to hit the head of a walking chicken with a rifle bullet? We did it because we had to. No hit, no dinner!

When at last all was ready, the women put the food on the table and we men sat down to eat. The women waited. Grace was said, and the host waved his hand: "You set handy. He'p yourself!"

No banquet in my honor has ever pleased me more.

It was in the Pink Beds (in May 1894) that I spent my first night alone in the woods. Later the habit got me, and I never let a chance go by. You see more and learn more when no one else is there. But this was the first time, and I was miles from anywhere.

I built my fire, cooked my supper, and was sitting in the mouth of my little tent when a big buck rabbit undertook to drive me out of the country. He cocked his ears at me, pounded the ground with his hind feet, looked as fierce as a rabbit can, and generally did what it takes to scare another buck rabbit. Finally he had to give it up. I turned in. But not to sleep.

When you are alone in the woods at night all sounds are magnified. In the stillness you can hear a little noise a long way off. Small creatures move. The trees creak. In winter they crack. Dry leaves rustle. A pine cone falling on a dead log sounds like artillery. On that first night alone in the forest everything was new and strange.

After a long time I dozed off. In the middle of the night a sound dragged me half awake with a start. My fire was almost out.

Thud! Thud! Something was coming! My heart was in my throat. For the only time in my life the hair was rising on my head in pure fright. (It isn't a pleasant feeling, and don't you think it is.) Whatever made those steps was coming—coming nearer and nearer!

And then I woke up the rest of the way. It couldn't be a bear because bears make no noise. It had to be a cow—it was a cow—and what I did to that cow with stones and clubs was a shame. She went out of there on the gallop.

After that I worked out a 25-pound kit, including a change of underclothes, rubber sheet, small blanket, aluminum cooking outfit, and grub enough for a week. And of course my .22-caliber Wasp Stevens rifle. In the woods it was never out of my reach.

It was on another solitary trip of mine in the Pink Beds that Fritz Olmsted, once coxswain of the Yale crew, walked into my camp. He was no forester then, but an engineer engaged in surveying the lands George expected to buy. I cooked him a mess of trout so small that we ate them heads and all, and talked Forestry to him to such effect that he changed his profession, and in later years became one of the mainstays of the Forest Service. His country owes him very much.

And Fritz was not the only convert. As the story of Biltmore Forest got about, young men began to ask about Forestry as a career. Most of these youngsters I discouraged on the ground that if a boy had the stuff in him to make a good forester he would keep at it anyhow. I told them Forestry meant hardship and hard work, much responsibility and small pay, which was the cold fact. They could come and study at Biltmore at their own expense, but they must count on a year or two in Europe before their training would be complete.

Although I was not conducting a forest school at Biltmore, applications from aspiring forest students became so numerous that a form letter was required to answer them. Meantime Biltmore Forest had broken into the news abroad, and trained foresters from France, Germany, and Switzerland asked about openings. These also I discouraged, but much more vigorously, for they knew nothing about American conditions. Work for foresters was scarce, and what there was must be used to train young Americans.

When the Biltmore Forest enterprise was on its feet and going strong, and the work in Pisgah Forest was in the offing, I began to chafe at carrying the growing routine alone. Besides, the work in my New York office (of which more hereafter) and elsewhere was increasing even faster than the work in North Carolina. It was evident that I was going to need help, and George a resident forester. But no American foresters were to be had—there weren't any. All I could do was to try for the best available foreigner.

As usual, I turned to Dr. Brandis, and asked him to recommend a man to work under my eye. He chose a highly trained and energetic young German named Alvin Schenck, whom I had come to know on the Cooper's Hill excursion. But even Schenck had very much to learn.

Schenck came in the spring of 1895. I did my best to break him in, but never quite succeeded. Being a German with official training, he had far less understanding of the mountaineers than he had of the mountains and the woods. He thought of them as peasants. They thought of themselves as independent American citizens—and, of course, they were right.

The Prussian point of view dies hard. After two years it prevailed with me, and after four years with Vanderbilt, who let Schenck go in 1899.

Meantime Schenck had established the Biltmore Forest School. He began to take forest students in 1896, opened the school in 1897, and kept it going until 1913, whereby he made a genuine contribution to Forestry in America. Among the young men who came to him in '96 and '97 were Overton Price and Fritz Olmsted, of whom this story will have much, and much good, to tell.

9. *Pisgah Forest*

In the spring of 1894 I made the first of several trips to look over a tract of eighty-odd thousand acres adjacent to the Pink Beds, which George Vanderbilt was thinking of buying. It was a superb region of sharp ridges, steep slopes, and narrow valleys. In its coves Chestnut (the most numerous species), Red Oak, White Oak, and Yellow-poplar were the principal lumber trees. The high percentage of mature timber offered a fine chance for profitable Forestry.

I recommended the purchase. "To say that I am delighted with the whole area is to put it mildly." Early in 1895 G.W.V. took it over and named it Pisgah Forest.

The total amount of Yellow-poplar in the whole tract I estimated at 40,000,000 feet. On Big Creek, in a deep valley directly under Mt. Pisgah, the highest peak in the Vanderbilt purchase, 8,000,000 feet of it grew in a heavy stand of mature trees already going downhill. Under them were many young seedlings, where light enough reached the ground. Much study convinced me that good natural reproduction would follow fairly heavy cutting in this Big Creek stand, if damage from cattle and fire, which was conspicuous throughout the whole tract, could be kept down.

It was, you will perhaps remember, the common belief of the woodsmen of those days that whatever trees they were logging would never grow lumber again. In spite of much young growth scattered about, not seldom in small pure stands, none of the lumbermen I knew in western North Carolina believed that Yellow-poplar, once cut, would ever come back. But I thought I knew better, and the event proved I was right.

In January of 1895 I recommended cutting the Big Creek Poplar under Forestry. In June, after prolonged consideration, George decided to go ahead. Logging was to begin in the fall, a splash dam was to be built, and the logs were to be driven down Big Creek, Mills River, and the French Broad to Asheville, and there sawed at the mill of the French Broad Lumber Company, which was bought for that purpose.

I figured that between 3,000,000 and 4,000,000 feet of Poplar could be cut the first season. Actually about 3,000,000 feet was cut. In addition, as an experiment, we girdled a number of Chestnut trees to make them light enough to be driven with the Poplar a year later, and, I believe, a few Red Oaks also.

The estimated cost of rough lumber at the mill would be about $8.75 per thousand. Prices at Asheville ran from $10.00 for culls, $16.50 for No. 1 common, $24.50 for 1-inch firsts and seconds, up to $28.50 for 4-inch squares.

The product of Biltmore Forest, although sold at competitive prices, was taken almost entirely by the Estate. Big Creek's product was to be sold in the open market. So far as I knew then, or know today, Big Creek was the first successful attempt in America to secure the natural reproduction of a particular tree by commercial lumbering under forest management.

When it was undertaken, I knew little more about the conditions necessary for reproducing the Yellow-poplar than a frog knows about football. My observation was all I had to go on, but it was easy to make sure that this tree was intolerant of shade. I could see that.

Natural reproduction was good in the little openings of the forests, where already numerous seedlings from one to two or three years old gave promise of a good crop of young trees, as soon as the light conditions were made right. And when they were made right, the trees certainly lived up to their promise. Most fortunately, too, for planting a single acre would have cost the price of ten to twenty acres of fully stocked forest.

Here was a marvelous opening. As I wrote Dr. Brandis, there was nothing that I wanted so much as to undertake the management of a large tract of forest for revenue. And that in spite of the business depression then going on.

While the work at Big Creek was getting started in the autumn of 1895 a great piece of luck befell me. Bernhardt Ribbentrop, Dr. Brandis' successor as Inspector General of Forests to the Government of India, recently retired, came through the United States on his way to Germany, made us a visit at Milford, and then traveled to North Carolina to see the work at Biltmore and on Big Creek. He had already supplied seed of many Indian forest trees for the Biltmore Forest Acres.

Of the work at Biltmore Ribbentrop said, in his German-English, "a wonderful good operation—a perfect piece of work." Next to Dr. Brandis himself there was no one whose opinion I would have valued more.

Ribbentrop was the original of Rudyard Kipling's head forester Müller in the Mowgli story "In the Rukh"—a big bluff German, famous for his reckless courage, the slayer of more than fifty tigers killed on foot, and the father of a daughter who had no small list of tigers of her own. He took an eager and most generous interest in what was going on, went vigorously into the conditions and plans of our Big Creek lumbering and the reproduction of the Yellow-poplar, and in the end gave us his full approval and his blessing.

It was an immense satisfaction to me to know that one of the most experienced foresters in the world, whose bailiwick had extended from equatorial ungles to timber line on the highest mountains on earth, thought we were doing the right thing.

Ribbentrop was even willing to come to the United States as adviser in Forestry to the Department of Agriculture. But though no forester of anything like his experience had ever studied the forest problem of the United States, his promising proposition was promptly nipped in the bud by Secretary J. Sterling Morton, the inventor of Arbor Day, who knew something about tree planting but certainly nothing about Forestry.

Of the many stories about India that Ribbentrop told Schenck and me, here is the one I remember best. One day at the head of a line of elephants carrying his camp equipment, Ribbentrop was marching on foot up the stony bed of a dry stream when a king cobra, probably the most dangerous snake in the world, lifted high its head straight in front of him.

Ribbentrop carried a shotgun, which is a whole lot better than a rifle when you are dealing with snakes. Here was his chance to find out what truth there was in the story that the hamadryad, whose bite can kill an elephant, would attack a man. So he walked steadily forward with his gun at the ready.

The king cobra stayed where he was—just kept on swinging his head from side to side. The distance between man and snake grew steadily less until even Ribbentrop had enough. Remembering the lightning speed with which a hamadryad can move, and how hard it is to hit any snake in rapid motion, he ended the tension by blowing off its head.

The word to start on Big Creek came so late that it nearly rushed us off our feet. This was no case of applying a maturely considered system. On the contrary, we had to reach our decisions, make our plans, perfect our methods, build our dam, and train our men as we went along. We did it, and not so badly for a first attempt. But it could have been better.

Work began in October. With much searching of our souls the Poplar trees to be felled were carefully chosen and marked, breast high and on the stump, with the Circle V stamp. Then they were thrown with great care not to smash the long smooth trunks or destroy the young poplars already on the ground, the logs were skidded to the rollways on the bank of Big Creek below the dam, and the brush was disposed of.

As I wrote Dr. Brandis, I was disappointed because so much damage was done by the logging. However, after a thorough inspection, I was forced to conclude that it was a good job after all, considering the difficulties of working with new men, the size of the timber, and the necessity of getting every tree down without breaking it.

When we were ready for the drive, the drive went through. The logs held in our boom on the French Broad were sawed, and well sawed, in our mill, and the lumber sold. The first year showed a profit. Unfortunately, later years did not. Whether the fact that I had turned to other work had anything to do with it, I cannot say. But if the financial side of this first American attempt on a commercial scale to reproduce the forest and make it pay from the very start left something to be desired, in the long run it was a shining success.

Forty years afterward, when Professor Holmes's Appalachian National Forest plan and George Vanderbilt's farsighted purchase of the land had brought Pisgah Forest into the hands of the Government (Overton Price and I had something to do with that), I tramped down from Pisgah Ridge through the old Big Creek operation. The Poplar reproduction we had tried for was there in great abundance. I was profoundly delighted, as I had a right to be, with the stand of young Poplar that dated from our marking and cutting. It proved that our method was right.

While the Big Creek operation was going on, the work at Biltmore was not neglected. As I wrote my Father in June 1895, "Altogether the forest work here was never so promising." Floating cordwood from the Estate to the boom on the French Broad was a success, our plantations were flourishing, and the work generally was making good.

10. *Consulting Forester*

My arrangement with George Vanderbilt left me free to take on additional work. Because the Biltmore enterprise was going so well, because it presented no acute problems and required so little attention, by 1893 I found myself growing impatient for fresh fields and pastures new.

So in December of that year I opened an office in the United Charities Building on Fourth Avenue at 22nd Street, New York City, and put "Consulting Forester" on the door. Here I would satisfy the demands of the gigantic multitudes that were clamoring for someone to consult about their forests. And as a matter of fact, what with one thing and another, I was kept busy as a bee.

The owners of various tracts of forest land asked for advice. At the request of Seth Low, President of Columbia University, I prepared an outline of a two-year postgraduate course in Forestry which was never started; with Dr. Britton, Director of the New York Botanical

Garden, I worked over, fortunately to no avail, a plan for a forest school of which I was to be the head; the Cotton States Exposition at Atlanta invited me to act on the Jury on Forestry, which had no Forestry to consider; and my unfinished *Primer of Forestry,* with constant writing and speaking on forest questions, filled in the chinks. Yet, except for Biltmore, there were times when I seemed to be getting very little done in the way of practical Forestry.

Much or most of this work paid me nothing but experience, yet from the beginning I took in something in the neighborhood of $3,500 a year. That sounds well, and indeed it was far more than I had any right to expect. I was earning a decent living, and to that extent at least, I was making Forestry pay.

But Forestry would never make me wealthy. My Grandfather, Amos R. Eno, starting from nothing, had become one of the very rich men of New York. He thought highly of business, but very little of Forestry. In 1894 he tried for the second time to get me to drop it. This time he offered me a place in his office, a salary of $2,500 to begin with, and the practical certainty of a fortune. It was a generous proposal, but with my Father's strong approval I turned it down.

The New York Constitutional Convention of 1894 proposed an amendment to prevent any timber on the State Forest Preserve from ever being sold, removed, or destroyed. That amendment was born of well-founded distrust of the politicians in Albany and the Commission in charge. It vetoed selling out to the lumbermen (which had its advantages), but it vetoed Forestry as well. Nevertheless the people approved it overwhelmingly.

On the question of Forestry on the Forest Preserve my acquaintance with the Adirondacks gave me some right to speak. In a talk to a meeting of the New York Farmers, an organization of wealthy amateur agriculturists whose milk, in the words of the ancient wheeze, cost them as much per quart as their champagne, I said that the people of New York, when they adopted the amendment, in effect made this confession:

"For ten years we have been trying to provide suitable protection and management for the state forest preserves. At the end of that time we find ourselves reduced to the conclusion that the very best thing we can do is to give up all hope of a sound and profitable management, and simply content ourselves with putting it out of the power of the guardians of the forest to do it any harm."

And be it noted, the Amendment against Forestry is still in effect today.

Those horny-handed sons of the soil in swallow-tailed coats had no more idea of what Forestry was or was able to do than the rest of the population. I found it necessary to tell them what it wasn't. I said, and told the truth, that "Forestry has nothing whatever to do with the planting of roadside trees, that parks and gardens are foreign to its nature, that it has no connection with the decoration of country places, that scenery is altogether outside its province, and that it is no more possible to learn Forestry in an arboretum than to learn surgery in a drug store."

In 1895 the State of New Jersey employed me as Consulting Forester to the Geological Survey, to report on the forests of southern New Jersey. Professor J. C. Smock, head of the Survey, was genuinely interested and helped all he could. The result was to give me some acquaintance with the growth and reproduction, and the difficult fire problem, of those sandy woodlands.

I was amazed to find the Pitch Pine sprouting from the stump, like a broadleaf tree; I wondered at the swarming young growth of the White Cedar—sometimes 100,000 seedlings to the acre; and I walked underneath a crown fire driven by the wind through the tops of the trees before it caught along the ground. That was worth seeing.

Later on, in 1900, the Survey printed a report entitled "Silvicultural Notes on the White Cedar," by Gifford Pinchot, State Forester. I was proud of that.

Forestry was by no means all that my New York office brought me. Through Jim Reynolds, I became an active member of the University Settlement in Delancey Street. There I came into operating contact with the other half and learned something of how it lived and thought and why, whereby my original conservative opinions were greatly changed, to my very marked advantage.

Furthermore, I shared with Jim a lively interest in the Citizens Union and its fight against rotten New York politics and politicians, and made my first in half a century of open-air campaign speeches. And was thus early introduced to the heckler, whom I later found to be far less formidable than he sounds. Says my diary of November

2, 1895, "Tried to speak from cart opposite Tammany Hall. Crowd would not let us."

This was my first taste of politics. It taught me things I needed to know. Later on, doing what I could against the enemies of Forestry and Conservation, and against the control of government by Big Money, I was to be soaked in politics, often up to my ears and not seldom over my head. In the end I came to realize that you may gain almost as much ground by making and losing a good fight for a good cause as if you had won it.

Soon after I began the practice of Forestry it became evident that G. Pinchot alone could not carry the whole load. There was more work to be done than one man could do. So I went over in my mind all the men I thought might fill the bill, and in the end decided to try for Henry Solon Graves as the best man in sight. He was teaching, in the winter of 1892-93, in King's School, at Stamford, Connecticut.

As Class Deacons at Yale he and I had become close friends. He had beaten me for quarterback on the Yale eleven when I was a senior and he a mere freshman. What was more, I knew him to be absolutely straight and entirely fearless. He was able, steadfast, untiring, he had unusual capacity to get along with people, and what he began he would surely finish.

Graves thought it over, gave up his teaching, studied awhile at Biltmore, worked for a time under Professor Sargent at Harvard, and after a year and a half of field studies in this country went to Dr. Brandis, as I had done. The professional equipment he brought home was far ahead of mine, and by the time he was back there was plenty of opportunity to use it.

One of the luckiest things that ever happened to me or to the cause was Harry's decision to adopt Forestry as his profession. He was the second American to do so. Throughout the years he has been a strong pillar in the growing structure of practical forest management in the United States.

I grew to depend on Harry Graves in every way. His remarkable capacity for detail and careful and intelligent work was just what was needed to balance my less accurate mental habits. To him more than to any other individual, as the years went by, was due the high credit for setting up the standards of training, ethics, and performance which have given the profession of Forestry so high a place in American life.

One of the first studies which Graves and I undertook was concerned with the management of White Pine, the most important commercial timber tree of those days. It resulted in the first professional forester's account of the growth of a North American tree. Its purpose was to enable forest students (who were beginning to appear), lumbermen, and others, to ascertain the volume of individual White Pine trees and of whole stands, in cubic feet and in board feet, more easily and accurately than had hitherto been possible, and to predict the yield at any desired number of years.

The study grew out of a fund of $1,000 subscribed by D. Willis James, William E. Dodge, and James W. Pinchot, my Father. Graves, with the help of P. F. Nash, Jr., a volunteer, did the field work, most of it on the Dodge lands in Pennsylvania, where he reported one magnificent Pine 351 years old, 42 inches through, and 155 feet high. Its 114 linear feet of merchantable logs scaled 3,335 square feet of boards one inch thick. I doubt whether the mate of this patriarch can be found alive today.

The White Pine appeared in 1896. It kept in mind both the forest and its owner—did not forget interest, taxes, and other expenses in relation to forest production. It also proved two points which the lumbermen of that day uniformly denied: that the White Pine was coming back; and that the new growth would in time produce good lumber like the old. The annual rings in the young trees were going through the same cycles of growth as their elders before them.

I still think it was a workmanlike job, but very technical for its time, as was not unnatural in view of the youth and inexperience of its authors. Incidentally, it made nobody rich. Before long, the annual royalties on the sale of it came in postage stamps because they were too small for checks.

Nevertheless *The White Pine* did arouse favorable comment. One overenthusiastic young American studying in Germany even reported a lively interest in the book there and a desire that it might be translated. Fernow, on the other hand, possibly influenced by the fact that the Forestry Division was preparing a bulletin on the same tree, roasted it thoroughly in a review in *Garden and Forest.* There was nothing unexpected in that.

11. *Ne-Ha-Sa-Ne*

While the foregoing preliminaries were taking place, Forestry, except at Biltmore, seemed to be achieving little practical progress. Yet the situation was better than it appeared. The pioneer work at Biltmore began to raise a family, which was precisely what I had hoped it might do.

On a visit to George Vanderbilt, his brother-in-law, Dr. W. Seward Webb, saw the work at Biltmore and was impressed by it. He was the owner of a superb tract of 40,000 acres in the Adirondacks in Hamilton County, New York, which he named Ne-Ha-Sa-Ne Park. October of 1892 found me there making an examination with a view to the practice of sound forest management.

With Fitz-Greene Halleck (namesake of the poet), an old friend of mine and a fine woodsman, I carried my pack through many enchanting miles of autumn forest, put in a gorgeous week, and as a result was able to make Dr. Webb a report which led before long to Forestry on many thousands of Adirondack acres.

Ne-Ha-Sa-Ne Park was a typical northern hardwood forest of Beech, Birch, and Maple, with a scattering of White Pine and Hemlock, and an important percentage of Spruce, commercially the most important tree. An actual count showed thirty-one Spruce trees and forty-two trees of all other kinds on the average acre.

This forest was admirably adapted for forest management and needed it. Everywhere mature trees overshadowed and held back the younger growth, and so made it possible to cut and yet increase the annual production of wood from year to year.

Under the dense cover of their older neighbors the annual rings of small suppressed trees told the story. The first fifty or a hundred rings had usually grown so close together that I could not count them, even with a glass. Of the few I could count, one Hemlock stump 17 inches in diameter was 292 years old. A Spruce stump 4.5 inches across, evidently stunted by older hardwoods, showed 128 rings. Two others, growing where light came through, were twice as big and only half as old.

For a few years the forest would yield slightly more under ordinary lumbering than it would under forest management. After that time the revenue from forest management would surpass that from lumbering, and would go on increasing indefinitely. Not only would forest management on Ne-Ha-Sa-Ne Park pay, but it would pay at once.

The primary objects of the management would be, first, "A steady annual return (sustained yield) which ought to yield a fair rate of interest on the investment," and second, "to increase the value of the forest by favoring the better kinds of trees (especially Spruce), so that the market value of the land, as well as the return from the lumber, would increase steadily from year to year." I have no apology to make for any of that.

Dr. Webb agreed, with great public spirit and practical wisdom, to back a study of the Adirondack Spruce. He was to contribute the cost of the field work. I made myself responsible for planning and supervision and for preparing the results for publication. But the chief credit for the Spruce study, for it and for what came out of it, belongs to Harry Graves. The whole undertaking had for its object the "preservation and proper management of Spruce lands in the northeastern United States," by providing for a second and successive crops. It led straight to the practice of Forestry at Ne-Ha-Sa-Ne, and from there the ripples kept on spreading.

The first field work for the Spruce study was done in the winter of 1896-97, and done on snowshoes. Snowshoes were nothing new in my young life, but the volunteers who came to help us in this early work, Bender and Farnam, and others later, were strange to the winter woods and had to be broken in. The job of teaching them was a short horse and soon curried, for they loved the work and simply ate it up.

Other volunteers came to help us in the summer of '97—Will Walcott, Mosle, Leupp, Woodruff, and Walter McClintock, whose later study of the Blackfoot Indians gave him a wide reputation. And with these Tom Sherrard, afterward a respected veteran of the Forest Service, and Fritz Olmsted, one of the shining figures of American Forestry, who, like Sherrard, has gone where good foresters go, taking his many sheaves with him.

Under the plan worked out for logging the older Spruce, the younger trees must be left uninjured for another crop. At the same time, the lumberman must not lose his profit, which meant that logging under Forestry must cost very little more than logging in the old way. We had to make Forestry pay, and pay it did.

In general, all Spruce trees twelve inches in diameter and over were to be cut, except, and this was vital, such as were needed for seed. To that end every tree to be cut must first be selected and marked by the forester in charge, or under his eye, with due allowance for actual conditions where each tree stood. In Forestry every rule must be applied with judgment, and nearly every rule has its exceptions. Unless you are a forester, the rules laid down for the cutting at Ne-Ha-Sa-Ne, though few and simple, may be tedious for you to read. If so, skip them. They are included here because they make a landmark in the story of American Forestry.

Cutting Rules for Ne-Ha-Sa-Ne Forest

"1. Only trees marked by the forester must be cut, and each tree marked must be cut unless a reason satisfactory to the forester can be given for leaving it.

"2. No timber outside the line of a road shall be used for corduroy, culverts, or other road purposes, until all timber cut for the clearing of the road has been utilized; and when more timber is necessary, all available trees of other kinds within reach must be used before any Spruce is taken.

"3. All lumber roads must be marked out by the contractor with the co-operation and assistance of the forester.

"4. As a protection against fire, all tops must be cut or lopped so that the thin branches will be brought in contact with the ground by the weight of the winter's snow.

"5. Extreme care must be taken to prevent fire. No fire must ever be lighted where it can get into a rotten log or into the duff.

"6. Great care must be taken not to injure young growth in felling timber, or to bark valuable young trees in skidding.

"7. Felled trees must be cut into logs at once, to release young growth crushed by their fall, unless a reason satisfactory to the forester can be given for some other course.

"8. Any young growth bent over by felled trees must be released and allowed to straighten without delay.

"9. Provision for carrying out these regulations should be made in all contracts with lumbermen, and fines should be imposed by the contracts for failure to comply with them."

These cutting rules proved out. With one notable exception, all cutting under Forestry in the Adirondacks since that day has followed their lines, of course with changes and improvements as foresters came to know more about the forest.

The Spruce study made possible by Dr. Webb not only led to Forestry at Ne-Ha-Sa-Ne but also resulted in *The Adirondack Spruce,* published in the fall of 1898, after I had given up my consulting work to join the Forestry Division in Washington. It was a little book of 150 pages, with rounded corners to slip in your pocket; and it was also the first American book (unless you count the Biltmore pamphlet) that told you how to go about forest management in the lumber woods.

The Adirondack Spruce was a working plan for a particular forest, whereas *The White Pine* was not. The latter was written in the general hope that someone would make use of the new knowledge it contained. It was a random shot, like shooting at a herd of deer, and therefore almost sure to miss, as every rifleman knows. But *The Adirondack Spruce* was like a shot at a particular spot on a particular deer, and that, as every rifleman knows, is almost sure to score. And score it did.

It was intended to help lumbermen and forest owners get better returns from their investments in eastern Spruce lands, through selective lumbering and successive crops, than they could by destructive logging without regard to the future. It dealt with the forest strictly as a factory of wood—a factory which must be kept going for the benefit of the owner. Lumbering must keep it in order and speed it up instead of leaving it a dismantled wreck.

Between its modest green covers *The Adirondack Spruce* gave tables of growth, volume, and yield, so that the owner of Adirondack Spruce lands could tell not only what he had now, but what he would have in ten, twenty, or thirty years if he cut his Spruce down to ten, twelve, or fourteen inches in diameter. The more he cut now the less he would get at the next cutting, or the longer he would have to wait for the same yield.

Since practical Forestry was so little understood, *The Adirondack Spruce* was filled with simple explanations about the forest and the essence of sound forest practice. It included a discussion of forest management for sustained yield, the great object of foresters the world over, under which forest industries can count on about the same amount of material every year, together with the reasons why it was not practicable in the Adirondacks at that time.

As yet Forestry in America was very young. It could not transplant the practices of older countries. It must develop its own methods in the light of American conditions. Rules, practices, and policies devised without reference to American forests could not then, and usually cannot now, be made to fit American needs. *The Adirondack Spruce* was strictly American.

Practical Forestry at Ne-Ha-Sa-Ne had hardly got into its swing before it moved on to additional thousands of acres of adjoining land owned by the Honorable William C. Whitney, Secretary of the Navy under President Cleveland. It was to be lumbered jointly by Mr. Whitney and Pat Moynehan under a working plan Graves and I prepared and supervised.

Mr. Whitney was a brilliant New York business politician, of a most winning personality. Pat Moynehan, a vigorous, keen, driving Irish lumber boss, with eyes in his head, a mind of his own, and that mind open, was among the very first of American lumbermen to give Forestry his blessing. Moynehan's blessing, however, did not wear well. Before long his own interest as a lumbering contractor got the better of him, and he violated the provisions of his contract to such a degree that Gene Bruce, afterward Chief Lumberman for the Forest Service, beat him up severely as an inducement to follow the rules.

Among other things, the Whitney-Moynehan rules called for cutting low stumps, even when deep snow had to be shoveled out of the way. Damn foolishness, said the lumbermen. Try it, said Graves and I. They did try it, and it repaid its cost many times over by saving a foot or two of the best lumber in the tree. Maybe the foresters were not such impractical theorists after all. A little later the top-lopping provisions of the Webb-Whitney contracts were enacted into the law of the State of New York.

Thirty-six years after logging under Forestry on the Whitney tract began, a study by the United States Forest Service in 1935 found the forest to contain as much Spruce stumpage ready for the ax as Graves and I said it would. The first trained foresters to tackle the Adirondack problem were justified by their works, and I for one am proud of it. Score another point for Forestry.

PART III
PUBLIC AWAKENING

12. *The Public Lands*

What you have been reading tells mainly of forests in private ownership. By far the larger question in those days, however, and the chance for swifter progress, had to do with the public lands of the United States, whose forested portions covered areas to be measured not in thousands but in millions of acres.

These public forests held this enormous attraction for a forester—they were under one and only one ownership and control. In contrast with the slow process of inching along from private owner to private owner, which I knew so well, Congress by a single act could open the way for the practice of Forestry upon these enormous stretches of public forest lands. No wonder they caught and held my keen interest and attention.

Substantially the whole vast land surface of the United States, except the territory of the thirteen original states and Texas, was once Federal public land—the Public Domain. When our continental expansion was over, the Nation owned the best part of two billion acres—a domain richer in soil, water, forage, timber, and minerals than any other similar area on earth.

The woodland of the Public Domain, some of it the richest on any continent, some of it little more than desert, was opened to private appropriation under a variety of land laws. Some of these laws were good, but all of them were badly and, more often than not, corruptly administered. Yet upon these laws and their administration depended the future of Forestry, and very much besides, in by far the larger part of America.

Under the Pre-emption Act of 1841 not more than 160 acres of nonmineral land could be taken by a settler, who must live on it and pay for it at $1.50 an acre.

The Homestead Act of 1862, signed by Abraham Lincoln, the best and most important land law ever passed, put settlement in the place of revenue. Under it any citizen could earn 160 acres of the Public Domain by living on it for five years, making certain improvements, and paying fees of about sixteen dollars. Or he might commute his entry—that is, get title by paying for the land a minimum of $1.25 per acre, but not until fourteen months after entry. That unlocked the door to many abuses.

The Mineral Land Act of 1866 opened the mineral lands of the Public Domain to exploration and development.

The Desert Land Act of 1877 provided that any land, except timber and mineral land, that would not produce crops without irrigation might be reclaimed by "conducting water upon it" and paying for it $1.25 per acre.

In many parts of the West there was no legal way to get timberlands that were neither desert nor agricultural, or timber apart from the land. Yet timber was absolutely necessary. So in 1878 Congress passed the Timber and Stone Act, under which not more than 160 acres of nonmineral land chiefly valuable for timber and stone could be sold to one person at not less than $2.50 per acre. The applicant had to swear that he had not "directly or indirectly, made any agreement or contract, in any way or manner, with any person or persons whatsoever," by which title would pass, in whole or in part, to any person except himself.

The purpose of all four of these land laws was highly praiseworthy, but the way they worked out could hardly have been worse. That was because the General Land Office in Washington, under the Department of the Interior, and the local Land Offices under it were dripping with politics. They early adopted the general idea that their business was not to safeguard the Public Domain, but to pass Government lands into private hands as fast as possible, without regard to actual compliance with the law, so long as the papers were in order.

Congress, moreover, under political pressure from land fraud profiteers, declined to appropriate money enough for special agents to go-look-see whether the law had actually been complied with on the ground as well as on paper. Stealing public lands became a regular business.

The rest of this book will mean more to you if you know, as you may already, that the public lands were surveyed "on the rectangular system devised by a committee appointed by the Continental Congress." Of that committee Thomas Jefferson was chairman. Under his system the land was divided into townships 6 miles square, each township into 36 sections 1 mile square, each section into quarter sections of 160 acres, and these again into 40-acre quarter-quarters.

The numbering of the townships and their subdivisions was such that any 40-acre tract on the whole vast Public Domain, if already surveyed, could be located with certainty and at once. No system was ever better.

But the actual surveys on the ground were often worse than a joke. Under one method of cheating, for example, in timberless country the survey contractor, instead of hauling in corner posts, marked his corners by nothing more expensive than a match lighted and stuck in the ground. Having thus created a landmark which was something less than permanent, he proceeded to swear that he had set at each corner a stick of the best available timber, "charred at the end as the law directs."

The best way to discredit a good system or a good law, or to perpetuate a bad one, is not to enforce it. And certainly the public-land laws, good or bad, were not enforced. Fraud enveloped them like a blanket.

To illustrate: The law required a dwelling on a homestead claim. So the claimant would build a toy house, swear to the existence of a dwelling on his claim "14 by 16 in size," but omit to mention that the said dwelling was 14 by 16 inches instead of 14 by 16 feet.

Under the mining laws alleged mineral lands were taken up for every imaginable purpose except mining. The largest single land piracy of this kind was perhaps the Yard group of claims in California, which covered a mere quarter of a million acres. It would appear that Nature, with a foresight as remarkable as it was considerate, had deposited her mineral treasures, millenniums before, along the precise line the Western Pacific Railroad survey was to follow across the Sierras millenniums afterward. In the words of a favorite philosophical observation, Ain't Nature Wonderful!

On one of the Desert Land claims I remember in Montana, the alleged irrigation ditch consisted of a single plowed furrow that started on a steep and rounded hillside as dry as a shingle. Yet the witnesses swore, with pure hearts and easy minds, that they had seen water running in the ditch. How come? Because the claimant had transported his water (in a barrel) and his witnesses in the same wagon, and while they watched he poured it in.

To get from the Government, under the Timber and Stone Act, quarter sections of the heaviest forests on earth at $2.50 an acre, lumber companies took whole trainloads of schoolteachers and others on acquisition bent, often from distant states, on free trips to the Redwood forests of California. Each claimant then swore, as the Act required, that a particular quarter section was taken for his or her own use and not for the benefit of anyone else. At the very same time he or she signed a paper transferring title to the lumber company which had organized the excursion. Thereupon the company completed the proof by paying $2.50 per acre to the local Land Office, which, of course, was well aware of the fraud.

Fraud was just as common in taking up lands granted by the Government to the states. For example, to get possession of good dry land on the pretext that it was swampland belonging to the state, oath would be made by the claimant, and made with all exactness, that he had gone over his claim in a boat. But no mention was made of one small detail—namely, that while the claimant was sitting in the boat, the boat was sitting in a wagon, being hauled over the good dry land, the same with intent to deceive.

Funny? Yes, but mighty tragic too. For the vast common heritage of land fit for and intended for American homes was falling, in huge quantities, into the crooked, mercenary, and speculative hands of companies, corporations, and monopolies.

Enormous areas of the Public Domain, moreover, in alternate sections of a square mile each, were presented "in aid" to railroad and wagonroad companies. So huge were these free grants that by 1909 twice as much land had been given away in land grants as had been taken up under the Homestead Act.

Thus the natural resources, with whose conservation and wise distribution and use the whole future of the Nation was bound up, were passing under the control of men who developed and destroyed them with one and only one object in mind—their own personal profit. And to all intents and purposes the Government of all the people did nothing about it.

It is not easy now to realize the atmosphere toward the end of the last century. While millions of acres did go to bona fide homemakers, irrigators, miners, and others, frauds on a gigantic scale were being perpetrated in the regular course of business, and few men thought the worse of another because he was stealing from the Government. The condition of respectability was that you must not be caught and convicted. And convictions were mighty hard to get.

When enormous holdings of land were put together by fraudulent means, local monopolies flourished and the people suffered. Indeed land monopolies in the West far surpassed anything that existed in the East. And with land monopoly went political control to a degree the East knew nothing about, except in a few great cities. Out in the Great Open Spaces where Men were Men the domination of concentrated wealth over mere human beings was something to make you shudder. I saw it and fought it, and I know.

If the public-land laws and their administration had been less soaked in politics that stank to Heaven, and therefore more workable, much of this orgy of stealing could, and perhaps would, have been avoided. Under the law Government timber, for example, could not be bought apart from the land. A settler without timber on his claim must nevertheless build a house for his family, put up his fences, and keep his fire burning. Timber he had to have, but usually there was no legal way he could get it. More often than not he had to steal it or let his family suffer.

So of course he did steal it, although he never thought of it that way. And if you and I had been in his place, you and I would have stolen it too, and small blame to us. But no such justification applied to the men who stole not to shelter their families and develop their homesteads, but at wholesale and for profit, and for that alone.

Large-scale lumber operations took millions of feet of Government timber without the shadow of right. In many cases a claim or title to a quarter section (160 acres) or a quarter-quarter (40 acres) was stretched for miles. That is how the term "rubber forty" was added to the language of the lumberjack.

It is true that here and there a Government official, in high place or low, fought the timber and land thieves and speculators as best he could—men like Commissioner Sparks of the General Land Office and Secretary Schurz of the Interior Department, and an occasional brave and honest special agent. But they were the rare exceptions.

While as yet I had no direct responsibility for any part of the Public Domain, I could not escape a deep and justified concern over the theft and destruction of the public timber and timberlands. To deal with such questions would inevitably, I felt sure, become part of my job as a forester, since Uncle Sam was beyond comparison the greatest timberland owner of them all.

13. *Early Forest Legislation*

To the little group of forest reformers in the last quarter of the eighteen hundreds, the destruction of public timber was Public Enemy No. 1. For all practical purposes Forestry on private timberlands was still far below the horizon.

Beginning about 1870, an increasing number of bills about the public timberlands appeared in Congress. In general they were either for some system of forest protection or for a commission to make a plan.

In 1876 Congress authorized the Commissioner of Agriculture "to appoint a competent person" to study the forest situation. Franklin B. Hough was chosen. Out of his work grew the Forestry Division.

In 1888 the American Forestry Association presented a bill, drawn by Dr. Fernow, then head of the Forestry Division, for reserving and administering the public timberlands. Like so much of the forest legislation proposed about that time, it was based on an amazing ignorance of actual conditions in the West. It would have prevented any miner or settler from taking up a claim near the headwaters of any stream; it would have required four men burdened with heavy executive duties to inspect personally the whole of the forested public lands at least once every year; and it would have authorized the President "to employ the land and naval forces of the United States for the protection of the forest lands of the United States"—a somewhat unusual occupation for the Navy.

But Fernow's bill did give the President power to proclaim forest reservations, or it would have if it had passed. There was no little good in it, and it was the ancestor of many bills that followed.

In an address before the American and Pennsylvania Forestry Associations in Philadelphia, October 15, 1889, Carl Schurz, Secretary of the Interior under President Hayes, gave a true picture of the times. After declaring that the destruction of the forests would be the murder of our future prosperity, he described "a public opinion, looking with indifference on this wanton, barbarous, disgraceful vandalism;

a spendthrift people recklessly wasting its heritage; a Government careless of the future and unmindful of a pressing duty." And he added: "But I found myself standing almost solitary and alone. Deaf was Congress, and deaf the people seemed to be."

This he said on almost the very day I sailed for Europe to study Forestry.

In 1891 the most important legislation in the history of Forestry in America slipped through Congress without question and without debate. It was an amendment to the Act of March 3, 1891, "For the repeal of the Timber and Stone Act and for other purposes," and it authorized the creation of Forest Reserves. This was the beginning and basis of our whole National Forest system.

Secretary Noble of the Interior Department, and Edward A. Bowers, at that time a Special Agent in the General Land Office, who suggested it, deserve the credit for this fundamental legislation. Under it President Harrison, at the instance of Arnold Hague of the Geological Survey, set aside the Yellowstone Park Timberland Reserve of over a million and a quarter acres. This was the first Federal Forest Reservation, the seed from which the National Forests grew.

When the first Forest Reserve was created, lumbering was one of the greatest of our great businesses. Only Agriculture produced more wealth than the industries which depended upon the forest for their raw materials. But no one knew even approximately how many acres there were in the timberlands which were making this enormous contribution to American prosperity. What appears to be certain, however, is that the forests were being burned even faster than they were being cut.

The Noble-Bowers Amendment, vitally important though it was, did not provide for the practice of Forestry on the Forest Reserves. It did not even set up a form of administration. It gave the Reserves no protection, and they had none, except as an occasional Agent might be spared from the meager force of the Land Office. It merely set the land aside and withdrew it, legally at least, from every form of use by the people of the West or by the Government.

The law of 1891 did save the title and did put the question of the public timberlands where doing something about them was merely a matter of time. For the situation it created was clearly impossible. Under it no timber could be cut, no forage could be grazed, no minerals could be mined, nor any road built, in any Forest Reserve. Legally at least, no man could even set foot upon a single one of them.

Don't forget that the attitude of the Western people toward the public timber was natural and inevitable. Without lumber there could be no development. So they took what they had to have, and public opinion sustained them. As a result, penalties for stealing Government timber were practically unknown. It was almost impossible to get convictions because the law did not fit the facts.

Congressman McRae, of Arkansas, in 1893 introduced a bill which, as rewritten by the House Committee on Public Lands, wisely avoided irritating and attackable details. It merely authorized the Secretary of the Interior to "establish such service as shall be required" on the Forest Reserves. It did not require settlers, miners, water users, and others to take out licenses; and it did not mention grazing at all, perhaps because grazing was the best-organized interest of the West.

Because on the whole it was reasonable, the McRae Bill passed both Houses and failed only in Conference. In 1896 it passed the House again, but unfortunately that was the end of it. However, the forest law we have today is largely built upon it.

14. *Toward a Forest Commission*

The story you have been reading tells something of the long and costly failure of American Forestry to make its way into the Public Domain, and of its actual beginning on private lands. But while it was unrolling its slow length (for slow it seemed to me), Forestry on the national timberlands was getting ready to be born.

Early in 1889 an editorial in Sargent's *Garden and Forest* proposed three things: temporary withdrawal of all public forest-bearing lands from sale or entry; temporary use of the Army to protect them; and the appointment by the President of a commission to report to Congress a plan of administration and control.

The first suggestion was politically impossible, the second practically unworkable, but the third, in the end, put Government forestry on the map. It was a long shot into the bull's eye, and for it Sargent deserves immense credit, in spite of what came after.

The whole plan was vigorously pushed by *Garden and Forest,* was approved by the American Forestry Association, among others, and was strongly supported by the *Century Magazine* and by many newspapers.

Early in 1894 a forestry congress held in Albany (at which I read a paper on "Forester and Lumberman in the Adirondacks") strenuously urged upon the President and Congress the pressing necessity for an immediate and thorough inquiry "with a view to establishing a systematic and permanent policy concerning the National Forests."

Nothing came of it all, however, until on December 16, 1894, at Sargent's suggestion, Stiles, Robert Underwood Johnson of the *Century Magazine,* and I met him at the old Brevoort House on Fifth Avenue in New York. In the long talk that followed we agreed on the details of a proposed bill to appoint a Commission to report on the public timberlands. That started something.

The next day I worked the details we had agreed on into the outline of a bill. This outline authorized the President to appoint a commission of three men who should study the public timberlands on the ground, learn their condition and extent, ascertain their relation to the public welfare, recommend what areas should be kept in forest, and prepare a plan for the general management of the public forests in accordance with the principles of Forestry.

On the same day Johnson and I took that outline before a committee of the New York Chamber of Commerce, and on January 3, 1895, the Chamber itself passed a resolution which recommended our commission plan to the House and Senate in Washington. A copy was sent to each Member of Congress, with the usual result—nothing.

Half a year later I read a paper on "The National Timberlands" before the New York Board of Trade and Transportation, in which I said, "The key to the whole situation lies in the fact that this earnest desire for better things among the men in power results in nothing, and has for years been wasted, because the special knowledge of what to do, and how to do it, was not at hand."

Thereupon the Board also gave us its support, and suggested an appeal (which we never got around to) to some two thousand similar bodies all over the United States.

The Commission plan was gathering strength. But, unfortunately, so was Sargent's plan for military control of the Forest Reserves. I fell for it to some extent myself. It included military instruction in Forestry at West Point, an experimental forest, control of the Federal

Forest Reservations by Army officers, and an enlisted body of forest guards.

The whole plan rested partly on the failure of Sargent the botanist to realize that Forestry is not botany, but something vastly different; and still more on his autocratic habit of mind and inability to understand that out in the woods mere orders do not go. Forestry is about as far from the brass hat point of view as you can get.

With all of this and much besides, it had been for me a busy winter. I thought I had a vacation coming. So toward the end of April, 1895 my Mother and I sailed for Liverpool. At Bonn and in the woods I had long talks with Dr. Brandis about my forest problems; saw Harry Graves, who was studying under Oberförster Gericke at Hambach bei Jülich; consulted with several German foresters; and was back in New York in a little over a month.

Promptly on arrival I wrote Sargent that I wanted to see him about the Forest Commission right away. On June 5, Stiles and I met at Sargent's home in Brookline, just outside of Boston, in the midst of magnificent rhododendrons and azaleas. Dr. Wolcott Gibbs, head of the National Academy of Sciences, the most distinguished body of scientific men in America, was there too.

Dr. Gibbs pointed out that the National Academy had been incorporated by Congress with the specific duty "that it shall, whenever called upon by any Department of the Government, investigate, examine, experiment, and report upon any subject of science or art." That provision would meet both the need for action and the need for haste.

The Gibbs plan was not only the easiest and the shortest road to what we were working for, but also the best. A National Academy Commission would be made up of scientific men with free and open minds, and not of politicians with political debts to constituents determined to keep on with their looting.

But if this plan were to go through, some Department of the Government had to call on the Academy. Without question the Department of the Interior, which had charge of the public lands, ought to do the calling. So Bowers, who had done such good work in securing the law of 1891, undertook to put the Gibbs plan before Hoke Smith, Secretary of that Department.

Fortunately for us, Hoke Smith, a big, smooth-faced, powerful, confident man of real capacity, had something of President Cleveland's own determination to go through with whatever he started. Fortunately again, he came from Georgia, whose politicians were little interested in Western lands.

In November, at Bowers' suggestion, Hoke Smith agreed to call on the National Academy for a report, and thereby rendered a service to the cause of American Forestry whose results are with us yet. But he didn't say when. Delay followed delay.

Johnson went to Washington to hurry things up. I got William C. Whitney to write Hoke Smith, and I asked Johnson for a letter to Cleveland for the same purpose. Bowers, with such help as Johnson and I could give him, drafted the letter to Gibbs for Hoke Smith to sign. He did a good job, but when at length the letter was signed, it bore no earlier date than February 15, 1896.

Meantime, Sargent had evidently abandoned the idea that Smith would act, for he proceeded to lay out a long trip to the West for the coming summer, on which, he said, he was counting on me as a companion. "I hope nothing will prevent your going with me on this journey."

15. *The Forest Commission Is Born*

The letter of February 15 from Hoke Smith to Wolcott Gibbs was well worth waiting for. It asked the National Academy of Sciences to answer three vital questions:

"(1) Is it desirable and practicable to preserve from fire and to maintain permanently as forested lands those portions of the public domain now bearing wood growth, for the supply of timber?

"(2) How far does the influence of the forest upon climate, soil, and water conditions make desirable a policy of forest conservation in regions where the public domain is principally situated?

"(3) What specific legislation should be enacted to remedy the evils now confessedly existing?"

And it concluded with this important paragraph:

"As I believe that a speedy change in the existing policy is urgent, I request that you will give an early consideration to this matter, and favor me with such statements and recommendations as may be laid before Congress for action during this session."

"During this session"—most desirable, of course, but unfortunately it couldn't be done. Sargent and Gibbs, and I with them, believed that before reporting the Commission would have to get into the Western woods. And while it was in the woods, the present session would end. Moreover, Cleveland would go out of office on March 4, 1897, and nobody could tell where the next Administration would stand. Obviously the time to report was soon.

To Hoke Smith's letter I drafted an answer, but how much of it Dr. Gibbs used in his acceptance of March 2, I do not recall. His letter made this highly satisfactory statement:

"No subject upon which the Academy has been asked before by the Government for advice compares with it in scope, and it is the opinion of thoughtful men that no other economic problem confronting the Government of the United States equals in importance that offered by the present condition and future fate of the forests of western North America."

Furthermore, Dr. Gibbs set down these three questions for the Commission to answer:

"1st: The question of the ultimate ownership of the forests now belonging to the Government; that is, what portions of the forest on the Public Domain shall be allowed to pass, either in part or entirely, from Government control into private hands." That meant Forest Reserves.

"2nd: How shall the Government forests be administered so that the inhabitants of adjacent regions may draw their necessary forest supplies from them without affecting their permanency." That meant use.

"3rd: What provision is possible and necessary to secure for the Government a continuous, intelligent and honest management of the forests of the Public Domain, including those reservations already made, or which may be made in the future." That meant Forestry.

It was a good letter. It stated the case and put the Commission's job squarely before us.

Gibbs then proceeded to name the seven men who formed the Forest Commission of the National Academy of Sciences, better known afterward as the National Forest Commission. There was not a politician in the lot. No such body of men could have been secured except through the Academy.

Charles S. Sargent, Professor of Arboriculture in Harvard University, and Director of the Harvard Botanic Garden and the Arnold Arboretum, was Chairman.

Sargent was already one of the great figures in the story of American Forestry. A rich man with a mission, master in his own surroundings and his own field, he was a natural autocrat. Tall, strong, and gruff, with great energy and determination, he made a sort of fetish of being shabbily dressed. Perhaps, like most of the rest of us, he was more comfortable that way.

Sargent was first and always a botanist, interested in trees mainly from the botanist's standpoint, and with little or no conception of the forest as a forester sees it. Yet he gave eminent service to Forestry, through forest botany, by his work at the Arnold Arboretum, and by his magnificent *Silva of North America.*

Sargent had been Chairman of the New York State Forest Commission which originated the Adirondack Forest Preserve. He had planned the Jessup Collection of North American Woods, the most remarkable of its kind in the world, and his superb volume on *American Forest Trees,* published in the Tenth Census, was the last word of its time on forest distribution. It played an important part in arousing the public sentiment upon which the epoch-making work of the National Forest Commission was based.

These were achievements of the first rank. Yet I think his greatest service to Forestry—but one—was made through *Garden and Forest,* a weekly journal, "conducted by Charles S. Sargent" from 1888 to 1897, and founded and supported by him, which distributed more information about American forests and forest trees than all other periodicals combined. It throws an interesting sidelight on Sargent that the name of its editor, William A. Stiles, who had far more to do with its usefulness than Sargent himself, appeared nowhere in the publication.

After Sargent, the first member appointed by Dr. Gibbs was General Henry L. Abbot, a distinguished Army engineer and the foremost authority in America on the physics and hydraulics of streams. But in dealing with forest questions he was a little like a cat in a strange garret.

Next came Alexander Agassiz, Curator of the Harvard Museum of Comparative Zoology, which his distinguished father had founded. He had little interest and less part in the work of the Commission, and attended but a single meeting.

The fourth member, Professor William H. Brewer of Yale, was my teacher friend of college days. His part in the American forest movement has never been given the recognition it deserves. His sound conception of what Forestry was all about gave his unflagging readiness to help great usefulness in many places.

Brewer knew the West, much of which he had explored. Mt. Brewer commemorates his early work in California. He was a strong man, in body as well as mind, with a remarkable knowledge of our country, and he was the first man I came in contact with who had a clear understanding of what this great land of ours amounts to. There was practically nothing outside the sphere of his interest. He was full of knowledge and wisdom, kindliness and common sense.

The fifth was Wolcott Gibbs, member ex officio, very distinguished chemist and physicist, who took little part in the work of the Commission. His great service was in suggesting and appointing it.

Arnold Hague was the sixth. A geologist and geological explorer, he was a man of understanding and genuine ability, somewhat blunted by ease in his later years, but his contribution to the work of the Commission was invaluable.

Hague had a wide and useful personal acquaintance with the West. He was really interested in Forestry, understood Congress, and knew everybody worth knowing in Washington. It was Hague I consulted with most on most of the affairs of the Forest Commission. Hague and Brewer were easily the best men on it.

The last man on the Commission, and the only one who was not a member of the National Academy, was Gifford Pinchot, whom Dr. Gibbs described as having "a very high reputation as an arboriculturalist." This seven-syllable compliment was much appreciated, but with some question as to the nature of the beast. What is an arboriculturalist, anyhow?

I was the solitary forester on the National Forest Commission, and the youngest member. The others were on the average more than twice my age. Brewer and Hague, who also were Yale men, had both graduated from college before I was born.

The members of the Commission all served without pay, but at Gibbs's request, with Hoke Smith's backing, Congress appropriated $25,000 for expenses, not all of which was spent.

The appointment of the Commission was very well received. Its high character was recognized and praised, and in general the stage was set, East and West, for public approval of its report when it should come along.

Even my name was approved. One overenthusiastic Pennsylvania paper described me as "probably quite the most widely known practical forester in the world," to which utterly baseless assertion other papers proceeded to give the lie by referring to me as Pinchon, Pinghot, and Phingshot.

16. *A Great Chance Lost*

Hoke Smith had asked for an early report. Sargent, in spite of what he himself had written about the need for haste, began by wasting a precious seven weeks. The first meeting of the Commission was not called until April 21, and nothing was done then except to elect me as Secretary and delegate Hague and the Secretary as a committee to make a preliminary report and recommendation.

At the meeting of May 16 our committee reported. It submitted lists and descriptions of proposed Forest Reserves, reports on bills in Congress, maps of timbered public land, many documents from the General Land Office, and personal suggestions from Lieutenant George P. Ahern, afterwards head of the Philippine Forest Service, Dr. C. Hart Merriam, head of the Biological Survey, and F. V. Coville, Botanist of the Department of Agriculture.

Dr. Charles D. Walcott, Director of the United States Geological Survey, had supplied our committee with much valuable material and the Commission with office room in Washington. Without the Survey, then and later, the Commission would have been up a very tall tree.

Letters and petitions were loaned to us by the President, relating to a persistent attack on the Cascade Reserve by Senator Mitchell and others of the Oregon delegation in Congress, acting as the spokesmen of big sheep owners and others. But, as the result of a conversation Hague had with the President, we reported no danger to the Cascade Reservation from executive action.

Cleveland was the uncompromising friend of Forestry from first to last. In his first message to Congress three years before he had said, "The time has come when efficient measures should be taken for the preservation of our forests from indiscriminate and remediless destruction."

Most important of all, the President had told Hague that he wanted the Commission's report on a plan of forest management by November first, so that it might be possible for him to examine it, and refer to it in his annual message. Nothing could have been better. That was an opening it were folly to neglect.

What came next was almost as valuable—perhaps even more so. After speaking with enthusiasm of the personnel of the Commission, and after saying that he desired to co-operate in its work, Cleveland, as quoted in our committee report, made the following specific suggestions:

"Take up the organization of a forest service first and then the question of more reserves.

"Let the plan be one that looks small, and at first costs little, and yet has in it the elements of growth; let it avoid points liable to attack by reaching its object, if possible, along other lines. To that end, the bills necessary to carry out the plan should be prepared in consultation with someone thoroughly familiar with the temper of Congress."

It was good counsel, if ever good counsel was offered. Cleveland was in the very middle of right. He knew his Congress and he knew Government organization. If the Commission had had the good sense to follow his advice, much trouble for many years would have been avoided, and great stretches of land now in private hands would still be public forest.

Hague and I made our own suggestions for the work of the Commission: study the silvicultural and economic character of the forest; its powers and rate of reproduction; the rate of growth of its various species; the productive power and commercial value of the forest; its adaptability for management, and the kind of management to be applied; the sources of demand and means of transportation; the danger and preventability of fires; the character of the forest floor and other matters pertaining to the water supply; and many other similar facts.

That is, get ready for practical Forestry. To that end employ as many trained assistants to the Commission as the funds might justify. And we went on to point out that while it would be "impossible to apply refined methods of management in these forests for many years to come, such data were needed for the discussion of even the broadest lines of policy, which often depend on matters of this nature."

Furthermore, we added, such information would be "indispensable when the Commission is called upon to justify its recommendations, and to answer the question of what a forest service will do when it is constituted, and how the reserves are to be used." Hague knew his Congress.

Finally our report recommended that the Commission should proceed to study selected forest regions on the ground; base its recommendations only on its own personal work; report the outline of a rational forest policy by November first; and prepare a draft of legislation with the help of someone who knew Congress, as the President advised.

Looking back across half a century, it was a workmanlike document, that report of Hague's and mine, and its conclusions were fully confirmed by the subsequent history of the Commission and the Forest Service—all of them, that is, except its bias in favor of Army-officer control. That, however, was the commonly accepted judgment of the time.

Getting the Commission's report into Cleveland's hands in time to use it in his Annual Message to Congress of 1896, as he had asked us to do, was the key to the whole situation. Yet the Commission, under Sargent's leadership, deliberately threw it away. We were certain of the President's support if only we had followed the President's sound advice. Cleveland, as was his habit, had hit the nail squarely on the head. What he had said to Hague was horse sense of the first water, and worth more than any diamonds. But the Commission knew too little to know it.

Sargent was a dominating chairman, he was against the Cleveland plan, and most of the members present were unwilling to oppose him. If he had been less autocratic and more willing to take advice, if the rest of us had had the good sense to see the light, and the nerve to follow it—ah well . . .

The rest of us, however, had a lot to learn as well as Sargent, and the great opportunity knocked but once and it returned no more. Cleveland was out of office before our plan of management for the public forests was finished And Sargent not only refused to follow Cleveland, but he also refused to follow Hague's advice and mine about studying the forests as a forester would.

My diary's comment: "Sargent opposed to all real forest work, and utterly without a plan, or capacity to decide on plans submitted. Meeting a distinct fizzle."

Of course I did not see all this then as clearly as I see it now. Nevertheless Sargent's unwillingness to act seemed to me so wrong and such a pity that, with the advice of Brewer and Hague, I wrote him within the week a strong letter of protest, and sent copies to all the other members of the Commission. There was to be no other meeting before we took to the field.

My protest wasn't against the neglect of Cleveland's good advice, the full value of which I knew too little about Washington to understand, but against Sargent's refusal to deal with the forest problem from the forester's point of view. Without such economic and silvicultural studies as a forester would make, my letter said, and told the truth, the three questions Hoke Smith had asked and the three problems set in Dr. Gibbs's letter of acceptance, problems stated in language which Sargent must have approved, could none of them be met.

Furthermore, justification in the eyes of Congress of the forest policy and legislation the Commission would recommend, the answer to attacks which would be encountered, and the description of the work a forest service would have to perform, all imperatively demanded information of the kind we were asking authority to collect.

Moreover, Hoke Smith wanted an early report on the proposed Forest Reserve in Montana, the chief argument for which was its fitness for prompt and paying forest management. And the attack on the Cascade Reserve required a plan of utilization to meet it. Neither could be supplied without the work of foresters.

So my letter asked for one man trained in Forestry to help me, and pointed out that we had money enough for that purpose. Finally, I added that investigations of the kind in question were fully practicable under the actual circumstances of great areas and restricted time, and that "a scientific treatment of the questions before the Commission required much information which can be gathered in no other way."

It was a good position and a sound argument, as the sequel proved, it was vigorously supported by Brewer and Hague, but on Sargent it had not the least effect.

Sargent's reply was conciliatory but evasive. "It is still a question in my mind whether such a technical matter can be made workable in our report, and whether it would not at the very end of it . . . weaken our position.

"My whole idea is to go slow and feel our way—not to attempt too much, and to take plenty of time."

Plenty of time and no Forestry. So I had to find another way. If I could do nothing to speed up our report, at least I could see to it that some of the facts on which to base a workable forest policy were provided. And they had to be forester's facts and not mere botanical observations. Although Hoke Smith was for it, Sargent refused to authorize the employment of another trained forester. All right, then, I would do it at my own expense.

Moreover, since the time was all too short, I proposed to start for the woods in June. This also, as I wrote Sargent, I would do at my own expense, for our appropriation became available only on July 1. And I proposed to take another forester with me.

17. *Hunting Forest Reserves*

Harry Graves, keen and reliable observer, full of mental and physical energy and initiative, and far better trained than I, was, of course, the man I wanted. He and I started for the Northern Rockies on June 1, 1896, several weeks ahead of the Commission.

The jumping-off place for Graves and me, at two o'clock in the morning, was Blackfoot, Montana, where Billy Jackson met us at the train. Billy was one of the finest frontiersmen I have ever known, himself a Blackfoot Indian, one of Reno's scouts at the battle of the Little Big Horn, and a wonderful storyteller.

Harry and I were tenderfeet, of course, and tenderfeet had to be shown. Billy had brought a horse for each of us. I shall never forget the wild ride he led us from the railroad to his ranch, mostly before daylight, and the fragrance of the Balm of Gilead trees along Cut Bank Creek as the dawn came on.

From Jackson's ranch we went on into the St. Mary's country, where the main range of the Rockies reaches a summit of beauty and wildness I am incompetent to describe. There Walter McClintock of Pittsburgh, afterward adopted by Chief Mad Wolf into the Blackfoot tribe, came to join us. In and about the two St. Mary's Lakes we spent three wonderful weeks.

Harry and I studied the trees, the forest, and the effects of fire. We made valuation surveys, discussed what we found, photographed the forest and the mountains, and climbed some of the lesser peaks. We learned the lay of the land, and why this was the place for a Forest Reserve.

But that is not all we did. Because I was drawing no salary and paying my own expenses, I took time out for a little hunt. With my last cartridge I killed a Bighorn ram on Kootenai Mountain. What happened to the other shells is a military secret.

With Harry I had another thrill—the thrill of a lifetime. We had seen a grizzly without getting a shot. One day we heard shuffling and scratching out of sight in a steep gully where a dead horse lay. Here was our chance!

Rifles at our shoulders, hearts in our throats, we crept forward. And then—

There in the gully were a couple of wretched grouse, scuffling in the leaves and dry earth. And away flew our feathered grizzly, with the dust in the light behind him.

Bear or no bear, our examination of the Blackfoot region resulted in the creation of the Flathead Forest Reserve, part of which later became Glacier National Park. That job done, we crossed the Continental Divide and had a look at the superb forest (likewise soon to be reserved) on the lower South Fork of the Flathead River, and from there went in to Swan Lake.

From Swan Lake, Graves left for Michigan to make a forest-working plan for the Cleveland Cliffs Iron Company, while I, with Jack Monroe, the best man I have ever carried my pack beside in the woods, and Jack's bear dogs, started on foot up the valley of Swan River between the Kootenai Mountains on the east and the Mission Range on the west. The Lewis and Clark Forest Reserve came out of that trip.

To me it was a fairy land, in spite of the mosquitoes, which were so bad that I wore gloves, a flour sack across my shoulders, and a handkerchief over my ears and neck. The only chance we had to sleep was when the cold of the short July nights moderated their zeal. But the country more than made up for everything.

Jack and I had a look at the forest on both sides of the river, ran out of grub and starved awhile, recuperated on the venison and bear meat my rifle provided, and slept when the clouds of mosquitoes would let us. There is a freedom in the pathless woods, if you are there on your own feet and on your own resources. It was a gorgeous trip—the best I ever made on foot. You see more when you go alone, but no solitary trip I ever made was as much fun as this one with Jack Monroe.

The country was new both to Jack and to me. Huge Western Larches, my favorite among all American trees, and Western Yellow Pines and Douglas-firs made us good company. Green above but blackened at the base, they told the story of great forest fires. I was seeing this forest in about as intimate a way as it was possible to see it. In these glorious surroundings new facts in Forestry called for notice and explanation at almost every mile. Life was good along Swan River in them thar days.

Early one evening, just as I had finished cleaning the skull of my bear (my only bear), a startling thought brought me up standing. My family was about to be notified that I had been drowned!

How was that possible? Why, like this. Jack and I had stopped one day with a hospitable old trapper, to whom we told our plan to cross Swan River. He said we'd be drowned if we tried it. We said we'd try it anyhow. We did try it, and got over dry shod on a tremendous jam of uprooted trees.

Soon afterwards Jack's bear dogs, all five of them, took after a deer and left us. Only two returned. The other three, undoubtedly, had followed our back trail to the old trapper, who must have concluded that Swan River had got the other four of us.

The trapper was, we knew, going in to Kalispell a few days after we left him. There he would report, of course, that Jack and I had ceased to be. And that would have been all right except for one thing. I had arranged to meet the Forest Commission at Belton, not far from Kalispell, on a certain day, and this trip was going to make me several days late.

The Commission, having got word of the trapper's story, would wire home to the effect that it had used up one Secretary and needed a new one. And my Mother and Father would have every reason to believe it.

We had to beat that telegram.

And beat it we did, by the skin of our teeth. At nightfall we swam our guns, packs, and clothes on a raft ahead of us across Swan River, which was a rifle-shot wide and in flood from the melting snow, and in the next twenty-six hours made fifty-two miles, mostly without a trail, lifting our feet over down logs without end. That tramp took us across the Divide into the Clearwater drainage, into a superb stand of Yellow Pine, and into the old cutting of the Big Blackfoot Lumber Company—a power in the land in those days.

At length we reached the railroad at Drummond and sent the wire home. And it was lucky we did. For although the Commission was even later than I was, the trapper had gone into town and someone else had sent the bad news East. But my message just did get there first.

18. *The Commission Goes West*

At long last I met the Commission—Sargent, Brewer, Hague, and Abbot—at Belton, Montana, on July 16. To my great delight, John Muir was with them. In his late fifties, tall, thin, cordial, and a most fascinating talker, I took to him at once. It amazed me to learn that he never carried even a fishhook with him on his solitary explorations. He said fishing wasted too much time.

Next with the Commission to Columbia Falls, down Clark's Fork of the Columbia, and past Lake Pend Oreille to Bonner's Ferry. I had never seen such desolation by fire. On the other hand, the Western Larch was acting so finely in resisting the fire when it had the least chance, and in covering the ground again, that it was a pleasure to see it.

Back at Missoula, we found Lieutenant George P. Ahern, of the Twenty-fifth Infantry, whose knowledge of the country and interest in the forests were invaluable to us. Ahern had been lecturing on Forestry at the State College in Bozeman, beginning in 1894. It was, I understand, the first systematic instruction in Forestry given in America. Of Ahern I wrote home, "It would be impossible to select a better companion for a mountain trip."

The Commission rode up the Bitterroot Valley by train as far as the town of Hamilton, and then, like the King of France, rode down again, and headed for the Coast. But Ahern and Graves (back from the Cleveland Cliffs working plan, whom the Commission still refused to employ) and I crossed the Bitterroot Mountains at the Lost Horse Pass with a pack outfit, and spent three weeks in the Clearwater country (this time in Idaho), which in consequence soon became the Bitterroot Forest Reserve. Then back into Montana by the Nez Perce Pass and to Missoula again.

On the trip our two packers, who had taken us for regulation Eastern tenderfeet, were not happy because we had required them to work, and we had barely escaped trouble. As I came down next morning early to take the train for Portland, one of them was waiting for me in the hotel lobby. The only reason somebody escaped a licking was that the firewater which incited him to warlike deeds had also put him to sleep.

Next with the Commission I went by train up the great valley of the Willamette, across the Umpqua and Rogue Rivers, and to Ashland, where I had another fruitless talk with Sargent on the policy we ought to follow.

Sargent, as I wrote home, was curiously deficient in ability to see things about a forest. In the words of the old proverb, he couldn't see the forest for the trees—the individual, botanical trees. "Sargent doesn't fish or hunt or know anything about the mountains." It was hard to understand him. But in spite of our disagreements on policy my personal relations with Sargent during this trip were entirely cordial. With the other members of the Commission they were never anything else.

From Ashland, late in August, we went by wagon in to Klamath Lake, where I had some fishing that I hardly dare tell about. In one afternoon and evening at Pelican Bay my 4-ounce Chubb lancewood rod accounted for three trout, one of 3½ pounds, one of 8, and the last of 9½ pounds. It took me one hour and forty-seven minutes to get that fellow, and it was black dark when I finally had him in the boat.

From Pelican Bay we drove to Crater Lake, through the wonderful forests of the Cascade Range, while John Muir and Professor Brewer made the journey short with talk that was worth crossing the continent to hear.

Crater Lake seemed to me like a wonder of the world. A great body of the clearest water miles across, fed by springs, surrounded on all sides by high cliffs, set in majestic forest, and at that time without a visible sign of human occupation. It was already in the Cascade Range Forest Reserve.

Meanwhile Graves was in the Cascades, to see parts of the Reserve we had missed, study the rate of growth of the Douglas-fir, that most wonderful tree, and make himself familiar with the effect of sheep grazing on the forest. He and I knew—none better—that the facts we were collecting were few and far between over against what remained to be learned. But it was original, firsthand information; in comparison with what was already known it loomed large; and it gave us firm ground on which to plant our feet in our constantly defeated yet constantly renewed effort to make Sargent see something of the problem as we foresters saw it.

From Oregon I headed for the California Sierras, where Colonel S. B. M. Young, from his camp at Wawona, sent me with a pack outfit to the Tuolumne Meadows, from which enchanting spot I made my solitary way to the top of Mt. Dana and saw the glorious chain of the Sierras tumbling like granite waves from south to north, and wearing about its middle a girdle of green trees. There are some sights you never forget.

From the Meadows my way led down Bloody Canyon and by wagon past the alkali waters of Mono Lake. In one day the mules I drove behind made seventy miles. Then to the little town of Independence, where I hired a horse to take me and my pack up the long grade to and through the Keersarge Pass, and a man on another horse to lead him home. (Years afterward a pass and a peak were named for me just here or hereabouts.) At Bullfrog Lake I made my first camp, and the next day, pack on back, started down King's River.

There were no adventures to give a single exclamation point to my ten days' solitary promenade. Not a California grizzly showed his face. (Worse luck, they are all gone now.) I missed a coyote with my rifle and killed a rattlesnake with a stick; watched my footing as a man should when alone; ate like a wolf and slept like a log; learned something more every day about the forest, from timber line to chaparral; and enjoyed every minute. Those were good days.

At Millville, outside the Sierra Forest Reserve, I ran into the gigantic and gigantically wasteful lumbering of the great Sequoias, many of whose trunks were so huge they had to be blown apart before they could be handled. I resented then, and I still resent, the practice of making vine stakes hardly bigger than walking sticks out of these greatest of living things.

All in all, it was a journey beyond my power to describe—from bare rocks and snowdrifts and glacial lakes and wind-twisted Pines and Cedars at timber line down to magnificent huge Sequoias and Sugar and Ponderosa Pines and Firs and Incense Cedars, down again to Digger Pines and out into the chaparral, and so at last to the vines and orchards of the San Joaquin Valley around Visalia.

From Los Angeles the Commission took a look at the San Bernardino Mountains, already reserved, and the San Jacintos, which were to be. Next came Flagstaff, and the great Coconino Forest, still to be saved, at least in part. At the Grand Canyon, by this time, a sort of tent hotel offered a place to sleep and eat.

While the others drove through the woods to a "scenic point" and back again, with John Muir I spent an unforgettable day on the rim of the prodigious chasm, letting it soak in. I remember that at first we mistook for rocks the waves of rapids in the mud-laden Colorado, a mile below us. And when we came across a tarantula he wouldn't let me kill it. He said it had as much right there as we did.

Muir was a storyteller in a million. For weeks I had been trying to make him tell me the tale of his adventure with a dog and an Alaskan glacier, afterward printed under the title of *Stickeen*. If I could get him alone at a campfire— We had left from our lunches a hard-boiled egg and one small sandwich apiece, and water enough in our canteens. Why go back to the hotel?

That, it developed, suited Muir as much as it did me. So we made our beds of Cedar boughs in a thick stand that kept the wind away, and there he talked until midnight. It was such an evening as I have never had before or since.

That night it froze, but the fire kept us from freezing. In the early morning we sneaked back like guilty schoolboys, well knowing that we must reckon with the other members of the Commission, who probably imagined we had fallen over a cliff. They had done just that, and they told us what they thought of us with clarity and conviction.

Then eastward on the Santa Fe over the Arizona Plateau. Next evening in New Mexico, as Dr. Hague, Mrs. Hague, and I were peacefully reading in our Pullman, the train stopped. Shots rang out. Probably some cowboys celebrating. But in a moment the brakeman rushed in, wildly excited. His lantern had been shot out of his hand.

Then more shots; then for a long time nothing. Finally a young policeman from the White Mountain Apache Reservation said he was going to find out. He had his forty-five, I had my rifle, but all my shells were in a trunk in the baggage car. (You may well believe that taught me a lesson.) Still like an idiot I volunteered to go along.

In the day coaches ahead every living soul was sitting on the floor, which was good judgment. By the time we reached the smoker the show was over. A United States Deputy Marshal, whose name would be recorded here if the years had not carried it away, happened to be aboard. He had stepped out on the platform, empty rifle in hand, called to the newsboy to hand him his cartridge belt, jumped off alone into the darkness, loaded up, opened fire, and singlehanded drove the holdups off.

In Colorado we rode to the top of Pike's Peak in a stage, which seemed a scurvy thing to do to that great mountain, saw Cripple Creek in its lurid and disreputable glory, and made a partial acquaintance with the five Colorado Forest Reserves. And, in October, home. Then came the formulation of our results.

PART IV

THE PRESIDENT MAKES THE ISSUE

19. *Cleveland's Thirteen Reserves*

Cleveland had asked for a plan of administration for the reserves by November 1. David R. Francis, ex-Governor of Missouri, who had succeeded Hoke Smith as Secretary of the Interior, wrote to Sargent on October 2 "for the purpose of requesting that you make a report to me concerning the work of your Commission, in order that I may incorporate the same into my annual report and make suitable recommendations in connection therewith." Opportunity was at the door again.

Hague and I were, as you know, strongly in favor of giving Cleveland, Hoke Smith, and Francis what they all wanted: first, and promptly, a plan for handling what Reserves we had, and then recommendations for more Reserves. That summer I had seen far more of the Western forests, and the people who lived in and near them, than any other member of the Commission, and far more intimately. And the cross sections I had made of actual and future Reserves, to a total of more than 14,000,000 acres, strongly confirmed my desire.

At Hague's home in Newport, on October 24, 1896 (that date is worth remembering), in the only full meeting of the Commission ever held, the members agreed without dissent to recommend the creation of a number of new Reserves and the Mount Rainier and Grand Canyon National Parks. Sargent presented his plan of action, in accordance with which, and against my opposition, it was decided to jettison Cleveland's advice, turn down Francis's request, and make no try for legislation at the coming session of Congress. So the die was cast.

There remained the chance to make a strong public statement, at the time when the new Reserves were created, that they were not to be taken out of circulation and locked up. Congress and the Western people were entitled to that. I did my best for it, failed, and came very near making a minority report, but unfortunately decided against it.

The Commission's refusal to make such a statement was a blunder of the first water. What made it all the worse was that strong Western sentiment could have been brought to the support of the Reserves if we had tried to arouse it.

Sargent's characteristic proposal, made at the same meeting, to recruit forest officers only from West Point, the Commission wisely turned down. General Abbot read us his and Sargent's "Proposed System of Forest Administration." That also was military, of course, and to it there was strong opposition. Later on, however, the Commission voted to transmit to Professor Gibbs a bill for military protection of the Reserves, without benefit of foresters.

The Sargent-Abbot plan was not only military, but it provided for the appointment of isolated forest superintendents with no central bureau to unify their work. Such an organization could not, as I said in a written protest, "grow into a forest service without new laws, and progress in that direction can only be achieved hereafter at the cost of reversing the existing policy and reopening the whole question by the attempt to pass new legislation."

I was doing a lot of protesting, but not without constructive suggestions. In this instance I went on to submit an outline of organization which had a strong family resemblance to that eventually recommended in the Commission's report.

After Sargent had put forward his plan and I my protest, I wrote Dr. Brandis to ask, "What are the primary essentials of a government forest service, first, as to principles and, second, as to actual organization? The latter half of this question relates to the number, residence, and duties of the superior officers only, on the smallest effective footing."

Dr. Brandis's reply was completely characteristic of his generous willingness to take pains. It covered no less than twenty large pages written in his own hand, and divided into eleven topics by headings in red ink. The writing of it spread over four days, as the dates showed. Said he:

"The main point which I wish to impress upon you, is that any organization which it may be possible to establish must be developed *gradually* from comparatively small beginnings." Just what Cleveland also had advised.

After pointing out certain difficulties and prescribing "a healthy feeling of professional pride and confidence," and *esprit de corps,* as the only safeguard, Dr. Brandis went on:

"The indispensable condition for the growth of such a spirit is a thorough professional training, both practical and theoretical. The growth of that spirit may be furthered by a free interchange of experiences and opinions upon professional matters. It has been explained that all operations in a State [meaning Government] Forest must be governed by a well-considered working plan. The main provisions of this working plan must be the result of free personal discussion between all officers concerned. These discussions must be open to all foresters who may be able to attend. There must be no secrecy in professional matters, everything must be aboveboard and open to all competent to understand it."

I suspect that not only the unequaled morale of the Forest Service but also the existence of the Society of American Foresters may have had their points of departure in that remarkable letter.

While the Sargent-Abbot plan got nowhere, what did get action was a draft of a report to Professor Gibbs, presented by Sargent on January 29, 1897, recommending the creation of thirteen new Forest Reserves, the descriptions of which I had worked out and sent him a few days before. Gibbs sent it to Secretary Francis, who promptly approved the Commission's recommendation and transmitted it to the President with the suggestion that "the birth of the Father of our Country could be no more appropriately commemorated than by the promulgation by yourself of proclamations establishing these grand forest reserves."

So on Washington's Birthday, February 22, 1897, Cleveland, who was going out of office in ten days, did the only thing the Commission had made it possible for him to do, and created the 21,279,840 acres of additional Forest Reserves we had recommended.

1. Black Hills Reserve in South Dakota	967,680
2. Big Horn Reserve in Wyoming	1,198,080
3. Teton Forest Reserve in Wyoming	829,440
4. Flathead Forest Reserve in Montana	1,382,400
5. Lewis and Clarke Forest Reserve in Montana	2,926,080
6. Priest River Forest Reserve in Idaho and Washington	645,120
7. Bitterroot Forest Reserve in Montana and Idaho	4,147,200

8. Washington Forest Reserve in Washington	3,594,240
9. Olympic Forest Reserve in Washington	2,188,800
10. Mount Rainier Forest Reserve in Washington	1,267,200
11. Stanislaus Forest Reserve in California	691,200
12. San Jacinto Forest Reserve in California	737,280
13. Uinta Forest Reserve in Utah	705,120
Total estimated area	21,279,840

Thus, by the irony of fate, Sargent's greatest and most vital contribution to the forest movement in America came through his inexcusable mishandling of the National Forest Commission.

If the Commission had reported its plan for managing the Reserves at the time it recommended the new Reserves, how many Senators and Congressmen who were driven into bitter and lasting hostility would have been friendly, because they would have had no excuse to be otherwise? How many newspapers, associations, interests, would have been with us, or at least not against us, who can tell? How many millions of acres now denuded would be green with growing trees? The whole forest movement paid dearly for Sargent's contrariness, however sound to him the reasons that lay back of it.

The area of then existing Forest Reserves was 17,564,800 acres. At one stroke Cleveland more than doubled it. Then followed the most remarkable storm in the whole history of Forestry in America, with the single exception of the Ballinger case, of which more hereafter.

Remember that Cleveland's move was without notice and altogether unexpected. Sargent had done his persistent and highly effective best to avoid and prevent any public knowledge of what the Commission was for, or what it was doing, or even that it had been appointed. The first mention of the Commission in *Garden and Forest,* Sargent's own journal, was a note on the last page of the issue of February 24, 1897, more than a year after Hoke Smith's request. Apparently Sargent was completely unaware of how things are done in a democracy.

So far as I know, not a single session of the Commission was reported for the papers, not a single public meeting was held during the Commission's Western trip, and what information local newspaper men dug out of Sargent was meager and not always exact.

The net result was entire ignorance, in Congress and throughout the West, that the Commission wanted Forestry practiced on the public forests, wanted all their resources put to use, wanted tnem to contribute their full share to the development and prosperity of the West. And in particular the public had been kept deliberately from any inkling that the Commission intended to double and more than double the area of existing Reserves.

The creation of thirteen new Reserves in seven States came like a thunderclap. And since under existing interpretations of law no use whatever could be made of the resources of the old Reserves, or of the new, since even to set foot upon them was illegal, the only possible conclusion was that this vast area was to be locked up, settlers were to be kept out, and all development permanently prevented. No wonder the West rose up.

20. *The War Is On*

Sharply the war broke out. On February 28, six days after Cleveland's action, Senator Clark of Wyoming offered an amendment to the Sundry Civil Appropriation Bill to nullify the Cleveland proclamations and restore the Reserves to the Public Domain. The Reserves were set aside, he remarked with some fervor, "without consultation, so far as I have been able to inform myself, with any Senator or any Representative in Congress from any of the States affected by the order."

The miner, said Clark, was compelled "to pause with pick in air, the settler shall not burn a stick of timber to light his hearth." And all this had come about at the behest of scientific gentlemen who had never been near at least one of the Reserves they recommended (which was too true to be comfortable).

"I honor them," said the Senator, with no little sarcasm, "I honor them for their knowledge; they are an ornament to the country; I read their reports with admiration; but they belong to that class of scientific gentlemen who think more of the forest tree than they do of the roof tree, and we have a whole lot of people in the West who think as much of their roof tree as the people of any other part of this Nation." And he went on to press his amendment because "It involves substantially the development of that whole Western country."

Stewart of Nevada, Pettigrew of South Dakota, and Carter of Montana, ex-Commissioner of the General Land Office, joined in protest, ignoring repeated statements that the people in the West themselves were in favor of wise forest preservation.

The Western Senators who joined in this debate became, most of them, the permanent enemies of the Forest Reserves. Stupid tactics drove them into opposition at the very start. For that reason, and afterward for other reasons also, they stayed in opposition, and we had to fight them for years.

The Clark Amendment passed the Senate the day it was introduced. Next day a wire from Secretary Francis hurried me to Washington, where Allison of Iowa and Gorman of Maryland had been doing what they could to help our cause in the fight the Commission's own blunder had brought upon us.

The Senate had gone wrong, but there was still a chance in the House, and if the House should vote our way, a chance in conference also. Congressman John F. Lacey of Iowa, always a good, true, and active friend of the forest, introduced a substitute for the Senate amendment which would have given us substantially everything we actually did get at the end of a grueling fight. The Lacey Amendment authorized the Secretary of the Interior *"in his discretion, to make sales of timber on any forest reservations, now or hereafter proclaimed, for mining and domestic purposes, under such regulations as he may prescribe, and to make all needful rules and regulations in furtherance of the purposes of said reserves, for the management and protection of the same."*

This provision is in all essentials the same as the law under which the National Forests are handled today. It would have opened wide the door to sound forest administration and the practice of Forestry. In addition the Lacey Amendment ordered the elimination of lands more valuable for agriculture, and made the Reserves free to mineral development.

The debate in the House occupied parts of two days at the very end of the session, when time was at a premium. The opponents of the Lacey Amendment, like the friends of the Clark Amendment, made three points against the Cleveland Reserves—all use prevented, no notice or consultation, and no adequate examination on the ground.

Frank W. Mondell of Wyoming, afterward Speaker of the House, made a fiery attack on the President and the Commission which fairly represented the feeling of the West. Said he: "The gentlemen of the forestry commission have laid themselves open to the severest censure by fair-minded men everywhere in that they conducted by a sneaking still hunt a so-called investigation of the regions they proposed to have set up as forest reservations."

And he also represented Western sentiment when he went on:

"If these reservations are again opened, the citizens of the Western states will be pleased to co-operate with the National Government in the selection of forest reserves in proper locations and of the proper size after Congress shall have enacted suitable laws for their control. Then will be time enough to enlarge the forest reserve acreage." Which was exactly in line with Cleveland's historic advice.

Lacey's Amendment was attacked by members from the West, who were directly concerned, and supported by members from the East, who were not. In the fight for the National Forests we were to see much more of that same partition.

Speaking in support of his amendment, Judge Lacey made a phrase which fitted the looting of the public lands as wallpaper fits the wall. Said he, "There is nothing so sacred as an abuse."

There is nothing so adamant against change, nothing that excites such indignation when attacked, as a wrong way of doing things that people have got used to. Illegal privilege and maladministration entrenched in time are far harder to break through than the Maginot Line.

One other matter of immense significance, unnoted at the time, was brought out in this debate. Judge Lacey put into the *Record* a permit to the Anaconda Mining Company, granted in 1895 and continued in 1896, to cut 14,250,000 feet of timber from public lands in Ravalli County, Montana, free of charge, but subject to "conditions, restrictions, and limitations herein set forth, and such additional rules and regulations as may hereafter be promulgated."

And if cutting could be regulated on the Public Domain, why not on the Forest Reserves? So far as I can see, there was not a word in the law of 1891 or in the President's proclamations that stood in the way. It was just one more case of the same old standpat Land Office guiding principle, "We've always done it that way."

Those were hectic days for me, while the Reserves were on the brink. I saw Senators, many Senators, kept Secretary Francis posted at short intervals, and met constantly with Hague, Brewer, Abbot, and

Sargent. Also I went and put our case to Uncle Joe Cannon of Illinois, afterwards Speaker, and at that time Chairman of the House Committee on Appropriations.

Uncle Joe had learned of Cleveland's anger over the Senate amendment, he had defended the Lacey Amendment on the floor, and he was with us—not, as he told me with engaging frankness while we walked through Capitol corridors, because he gave a damn for the Forest Reserves, but because he wanted to save his Sundry Civil Bill. And he added, with that delicacy of language for which he was famous, that it might be possible to do something "if we didn't have a Senate of nits and lice."

After the Lacey Amendment, that wise and moderate draft of legislation, had passed the House, it went, with the rest of the Sundry Civil Bill, to conference, where the differences between the two Houses were ironed out. Somehow or other I got a chance to make a statement before the Conference Committee, the first of many before Committees of Congress, and there did my best for the Lacey Amendment.

When Sargent heard of it, he wrote me in his excessively fine and almost illegible hand: "It is more dangerous to talk than to keep silence. Of course what you may say personally is all right, but the Committee [meaning the Commission] ought not to be further put on record as endorsing the House Amendment.

"It is the worst thing that has happened yet."

So spake Sargent. Yet the Lacey Amendment, I repeat, was to all intents and purposes the same as the legislation under which the National Forests have been so well and wisely administered since the year 1905.

The conferees were overwhelmingly against the Clark Amendment. The temper of the Senate made it clear that the Lacey Amendment was equally impossible. So the conferees compromised on the last clause of that amendment, which gave the President power to keep or cancel all or any part of any Reserve. It must have seemed to them the surest way to save both the bill and the Forest Reserves.

Cleveland, however, must have found in this provision some danger to the Forest Reserves, some attack on his dignity, or some other serious fault. What his specific reason was I do not know. But that he had it there is no doubt. For when the Sundry Civil Bill, by far the most important of all appropriation bills, was presented to him at the Capitol on March 4, 1897, it is said that he dashed it to the floor. In any case he refused to sign it, and the bill, with its amendment, died.

And so after Cleveland pocket-vetoed Uncle Joe's pet bill, I saw McKinley inaugurated and came on home, well knowing that the worst of our troubles were still ahead of us.

21. *Laying the Foundation*

Cleveland's veto was by far the biggest thing any President had yet done for Forestry. It put Forestry on the front page all over America, and made it, for the first time, a generally recognized national question. From that time on the man in the street had an idea there might be something in it.

Cleveland deserves immense credit, for his courageous action led directly to the beginning of Government Forestry in the woods. During all this contention I had occasion to see him more than once. His firmness, his directness, and his common sense were as obvious as his bulk. He was the kind of man who does things for himself, but for that very reason not the most capable executive.

I remember being ushered into the old Cabinet room one day to find the President of these United States, with Congress, as he himself had said, very much "on his hands," adding up columns of figures before he signed some official document. It seemed to me a supererogatory work of supererogation, if you know what I mean.

While the Sundry Civil Bill died on Cleveland's last day in office, the Forest Reserve question remained very much alive. Our fight would have to be made all over again in the new Congress, which McKinley called in extra session for March 15, 1897. Meanwhile, forty million acres of Forest Reserves had neither management, utilization, nor protection, and the Commission, a full year after its appointment, had not yet decided what to do about it.

In the new Congress the attack on the Reserves flared up furiously. The prospect looked hopeless when help came from a source that had helped us mightily already. Charles D. Walcott, Director of the United States Geological Survey, was the man who actually saved our bacon. Partly because he believed in the Reserve policy, partly because of what there was in it for the Geological Survey (no one could blame him for that), he led us out of the wilderness Sargent's obstinacy had led us into.

It happened like this. Cornelius N. Bliss of New York, who had succeeded Francis as Secretary of the Interior, was also Treasurer of the Republican National Committee, and far from blind to political considerations. The Homestake Mining Company, not only the greatest gold miner but also the greatest political power in South Dakota, sent Judge Moody, its counsel, to see the new Secretary. Bliss assured Moody that the Homestake could go right on cutting mining timber in the new Black Hills Forest Reserve, free and for nothing, just as it had before. A complete revolution in Homestake-made local public sentiment trod on the heels of that assurance and opened the way.

Walcott, a man of first-class ability, who knew Congress like the back of his hand, must have known of this shift. He was familiar with the work of the Commission and believed in it, and he began to consider what he could do to keep it from being destroyed.

Casually meeting Fernow, says Walcott, as I put it in my diary, "I asked him if anything could be done to prevent such action. He said he feared not, as the opponents of any Forestry policy on the part of the Government were in full control, and that the person attempting it would undoubtedly be censured, if not driven from the Government service."

That, however, did not stop Walcott. He saw Senator Richard F. Pettigrew, Free Silver Republican of South Dakota, who had violently attacked Cleveland's proclamations. But Pettigrew must have decided to change his mind when the Homestake did. So Walcott, after several conferences, convinced him that Forest Reserves were good for the West, and in the latter part of March at Pettigrew's request drafted a bill which, in addition to saving the forest situation, provided for the survey of the Reserves by the Geological Survey.

Pettigrew introduced Walcott's draft as an amendment to the new Sundry Civil Bill. Drawn on the basis of the McRae Bill, it was intended to get everything possible out of a thoroughly bad situation, and in the end it succeeded.

On March 29 Walcott had a conference with Bliss, who was with him in wanting to save the Cleveland Reserves, but doubtful of the outcome. Nevertheless Bliss put the forest question up to the President. To quote further Walcott's own account, "On Friday, April 2, I was called to the White House, and on arrival was ushered into the

Cabinet Room, where President McKinley was seated with the members of his Cabinet. He explained to me that Secretary Bliss had told him of the proposed legislation, and asked me to explain it to him and to the Cabinet. I did so, and before leaving was assured that it met with his approval."

At this meeting, I believe the first full meeting of McKinley's Cabinet, according to press dispatches, "the only question of public importance discussed was the question of rescinding the order of former President Cleveland setting apart thirteen forest reservations in the West."

While Walcott followed up the Pettigrew Amendment from one committee to another, the President sent for Senator Allison, Chairman of the Committee on Appropriations, and, says Walcott, "explained to him the importance of securing the forestry legislation and thus putting at rest a bitter controversy. The President told me that he had also consulted with other leaders in the Senate and House."

Bliss, uneasy about the outlook, wired the members of the National Forest Commission to meet him on April 5 "for hearing on forest reservations." On that day the Commission (except Gibbs and Agassiz) met first with Walcott, for advice, and then with Bliss, Commissioner Hermann of the General Land Office, and Senator Wilson of Washington.

The question before the meeting was a simple one—save the Cleveland Reserves or lose them. Should the Commission agree to suspend the proclamations and open the Reserves to entry for a year in order to save the bulk of their area, or take the chance of losing the whole lot? Half a loaf or no bread.

My diary says: "Sargent and Abbot against suspension and McRae (Pettigrew) Amendment to Sundry Civil Bill, the rest for." Bliss was for it too. The result proved that he was right.

Then, on the same day, we went and put our case to the new President. As McKinley, quiet and unruffled, came into the Cabinet Room where we waited, almost the first thing he said was: "Everybody who comes here brings a crisis along."

We laid our crisis before him in detail and at length, for nearly an hour, and with good effect. "President strong for the Reserves. He impressed me very favorably." Which was not unnatural, under the circumstances.

The same day we talked with McKinley, the Commission had a

conference with Pettigrew. Nothing came of it, for Sargent and the Senator did not agree. That same day also, says my diary, I saw "Walcott with Hague, and at my suggestion he [Walcott] made changes in amendment to exclude mineral lands from recession [restoration to the public domain] after survey, permit Secretary to utilize forests, etc."

The next day Pettigrew reintroduced his amendment with these changes. I have a copy of that edition, in which further changes were made in my handwriting. The one essential alteration provided that when the Secretary gave timber and stone free of charge to bona fide settlers, miners, residents, and prospectors, those terms "shall be confined to apply strictly to individual parties, and nothing herein shall be construed to extend the meaning of said terms to firms, companies, or corporations."

Whether this sound suggestion was mine or another's, I do not recall, and it doesn't matter. It appeared in the Pettigrew Amendment, edition of April 8, but you will not be surprised to learn that it was cut out somewhere on the road to final passage. The Homestake was a corporation.

The changes before the Pettigrew Amendment became part of the Act of June 4, 1897, are too complicated to follow here. In its final form, it provided for surveying the Reserves, suspension of the Cleveland Reserves until March 1, 1898, and authority for the Secretary of the Interior to protect and administer the reserved public forests, as many a law never applied had done already for the timbered parts of the Public Domain.

Except for the Act of 1891, the Pettigrew Amendment to the Sundry Civil Act of June 4, 1897, was and still is the most important Federal forest legislation ever enacted. It did two essential things: it opened the Forest Reserves to use; and it cleared the road to sound administration, including the practice of Forestry. Unfortunately the Interior Department, with its tradition of political toadeating and executive incompetence, was incapable of employing the powers the act gave it.

The amendment began with an appropriation of $150,000 to the United States Geological Survey for surveying the Forest Reserves, and went on to authorize the President "to revoke, modify, or suspend any and all" proclamations creating such reserves. Then it provided that the orders and proclamations of February 22, in the States of Wyoming, Utah, Montana, Washington, Idaho, and South Dakota, be "suspended, and the lands embraced therein restored to the Public Domain the same as though said orders and proclamations had not been issued" until March 1, 1898. But not in California. California was always the friend of Forestry. After March 1, what land had not been taken up would again become Forest Reserve. As a matter of fact, the area lost was comparatively small.

The amendment then set forth the conditions under which the public Forest Reserves should be established and administered.

"No public forest reservation shall be established except to improve and protect the forest within the reservation, or for the purpose of securing favorable conditions of water flow, and to furnish a continuous supply of timber for the use and necessities of citizens of the United States." And it was not the intention of the act to include lands more valuable for their minerals or for agriculture than for forest purposes.

The Secretary of the Interior was given charge of the Reserves, "and he may make such rules and regulations and establish such service as will insure the objects of such reservations, namely, to regulate their occupancy and use and to preserve the forests therein from destruction."

That was the milk in the coconut. It made forest protection and forest management possible, and it is still today, almost fifty years afterward, the law under which the National Forests are administered and Forestry is practiced upon them.

Specifically, the Secretary was authorized to sell "the dead, matured, or large growth of trees" on the Forest Reserves, after the trees had been "marked and designated." Another door wide open to the forester.

But not even Congress, partner of the Interior Department in much shabby politics, was willing to trust that Department in full. The timber marked "shall be cut and removed under the supervision of some person appointed for that purpose by the Secretary of the Interior, not interested in the purchase and removal of such timber nor in the employment of the purchaser thereof." Which should have gone without saying.

Provision followed for the free use of Forest Reserve timber and stone at the Secretary's discretion, "by bona fide settlers, miners, residents, and prospectors for minerals, for firewood, fencing, buildings, mining, prospecting, and other domestic purposes"—firms, companies, and corporations not ruled out.

Wagon roads and other improvements could be built, schools and churches could be maintained, and "all waters on such reservations may be used for domestic, mining, milling, or irrigation purposes," under state and national laws.

Also the legal fence against setting foot on the Reserves was done away: "Nor shall anything herein prohibit any person from entering upon such forest reservations for all proper and lawful purposes, including that of prospecting, locating, and developing the mineral resources thereof."

Excellent. What was needed above all things was local approval and support of the Reserves, and use was the key to that.

The men who wrote and passed the rider of June 4, 1897, were taking no chances. They intended to see that all the resources of the Forest Reserves were open to use, and what they tried to do they actually accomplished.

One additional clause, however, should have been left out. That was the lieu-land clause, under which "the settler or owner" of a claim or patent in a Forest Reserve might relinquish the tract to the Government and "select in lieu thereof a tract of vacant land open to settlement not exceeding in area the tract covered by his claim or patent."

Settler *or owner*. When this lieu-land provision first appeared, only the settler was given the right of exchange. No one could object to that. But when the Sundry Civil Bill came back from the Senate to the House, Judge Lacey moved that Section 8 of the McRae Bill, which had been introduced again on March 15, be incorporated. That is how the words "or owner" got in.

These two words "or owner" cost the Government millions upon millions of acres of its best lands. What induced McRae to adopt them or Judge Lacey to insert them I can only surmise. What they meant was that any lumber company, mining company, railroad company, cattle outfit, or any other large owners could get rid of their cut-over land, their worked-out claims, the valueless portions of their land grants, or any other land they had no use for, and take in exchange an equal area of the most valuable nonmineral land they could find anywhere on the Public Domain.

But we of the Forest Commission had small reason to blame

Judge Lacey or anybody else. For in Section 4 of the first bill advocated in our report we ourselves used the very words "settlers or owners" in precisely the same connection. "Let him that is without sin cast the first stone." What the poor and honest settler got out of the lieu-land law was small indeed compared to the immense booty of the richest and most powerful corporations of the West.

We who were working for the Pettigrew Amendment knew this lieu-land provision to be dangerous, but how dangerous it was we had, and we could have had, no idea. Many of the then boundary lines of the Forest Reserves were, and could have been, nothing but shots in the dark. Many of them had not even been surveyed. As to how much worthless or unsuitable land was included, one man's guess was almost as good as another's.

But even if we had known the worst, still it was better to lose a part than to lose everything. We stretched our influence to the utmost in getting what we got. We saved the Reserves, we cleared the way for Forestry and the Forest Service, and I for one think we did better—far better, considering the Sargent blunders—than we had any reasonable right to expect.

22. *Too Late and Too Little*

While the fate of the Reserves was being settled in the long fight for the Pettigrew Amendment, the Commission was finding much difficulty in formulating its recommendations. Sargent was still sticking to military control; Brewer, Hague, and I were not.

My diary of March 20 says: "Forest Commission meeting at Century Club [in New York] all day. One of the hardest day's work I ever did. But we got a great many concessions from Sargent's original plan." And at other meetings the civil war went on.

At long last, on May 1, 1897, six months after Cleveland had asked to have it ready, the Report of the National Forest Commission "on the inauguration of a rational forest policy for the forested lands of the United States" was transmitted to the Secretary of the Interior. In strict accordance with the then going conception of Forestry, it began with a discussion of the influence of forests on stream flow based on European data, for which Abbot was doubtless responsible, and a description of forest administration in foreign countries written by G.P. After that it got down to the actual conditions on the Forest Reserves, including fire, sheep, and timber stealing.

Then it said what should have been said half a year before:

"These great bodies of reserved lands cannot be withdrawn from all occupation and use. They must be made to perform their part in the economy of the Nation. Unless the reserved lands of the public domain are made to contribute to the welfare and prosperity of the country, they should be thrown open to settlement and the whole system of reserved forests abandoned."

And land more valuable for other uses than for forests should be excluded from the Reserves, whose timber and mineral resources should all be opened to use. If the Commission had been wise enough to make, and make public, such statements as these on November 1, 1896, instead of May 1, 1897, the attack in the Senate would have been impossible, the Reserves would not have had to be saved by the skin of their teeth, and in all likelihood they would not have been subjected to the political mismanagement of the Land Office for seven critical years. Hindsight is a whole lot better than foresight.

Next in the Report came the proposed system of forest administration. "Silviculture in Western North America [it said] will only be really successful under sustained Government control [which can] only be secured by a permanent Government administration composed of officers of the highest character, entirely devoted to duty."

Government control of cutting on all timberland, private as well as public, is still today, as it was then, the one most indispensable step toward assuring a supply of forest products for the future in the United States. That supply is in far greater danger now than it was when the Forest Commission made its report.

As to temporary organization, "Each important Forest Reserve should be placed at once in charge of an officer of the Army," detailed during the fire season only, to report to the Secretary of the Interior, and a United States Commissioner should be stationed near by to deal with transgressors. The officer in charge should issue passes to persons desirous of entering or crossing the Reserve (an utterly unworkable requirement), sheep should be wholly excluded (another equally unworkable), and cattle owned by actual settlers should be admitted in moderate numbers.

As to permanent organization, "The fundamental principle of any government system of forest management should be the retention of the fee of forest lands, and the sale of forest products from them at reasonable prices, under regulations looking to the perpetual reproduction of the forest." That was right as rain.

But not the following statement, that many of the duties of forest officers "are essentially military in character and should be regulated for the present on military principles." That was pure Sargent, and as out of place as a dog in a church. The safety of forests depends on local co-operation, and you can't get frontier people to co-operate on military principles.

The Report did recommend, however, a service with permanent tenure of office, chosen by civil service examination. It was to include a Director of Forests in the Department of the Interior, four Inspectors, each in charge of the Reserves in one of four forest departments, twenty-six Head Foresters, each in charge of from half a million acres to a million and a half acres, two hundred Rangers, and necessary assistants along the line.

As to unreserved forest lands, the laws now in force, said the Commission, "have debased the public conscience and deprived the Government of millions of dollars." There was no exaggeration in that. And all public lands more valuable as timberlands than for other purposes should be withdrawn from disposal.

Coming as it did after the fight in Congress was practically over, the Commission's Report amounted, to all intents and purposes, to nothing more than so much waste paper. So far as I can tell there is not a word in the Pettigrew Amendment of June 4, 1897, that priceless piece of legislation, that would have been left out, not a word left out that would have been put in, if the Report of the National Forest Commission, dated May 1, 1897, had never been made at all.

Who was it said that nine-tenths of wisdom is to be wise in time?

Hoke Smith had asked the National Academy three specific questions. Our answer to the first was that it was not only desirable but essential to protect the forested lands of the Public Domain and practicable to reduce the ravages of fire, but "not with the present methods and machinery of the Government."

To the second question we replied that forests are in fact necessary to prevent destructive floods and corresponding periods of low water.

In answer to the third question the Commission submitted a series of five bills intended to provide for military control of the Reserves until a bureau of public forests could be organized in the Interior Department, for a board to select new Reserves, and for lieu-land selections. They provided also for the practice of Forestry on the Reserves, and for opening all their resources to regulated use. Since they never had the slightest chance of passing, there is no need for further detail.

When the National Forest Commission Report was finished, I had a difficult question to settle. Should I sign it, with all its faults, and thus subscribe to many propositions with which I thoroughly disagreed, or should I make a minority report? After much heart searching I decided to sign. I should have been alone in refusing, and anyhow, as I set forth in a long letter to Walcott, what would have been the use? "Since the fate of the forest legislation already before Congress will not be affected by the Report, no practical object would have been served by dissenting from it beyond protecting my own professional position. Under the circumstances I preferred to wait until the latter was specifically attacked." Looking back over so much fighting and so many years, I am glad to think I was right.

The National Forest Commission deserved well of its country. It was the means of bringing the public timberlands to national attention as they had never been brought before. It had set a marker that would remain. Never again would the forest sink to the negligible position it had occupied in the public estimation of days gone by. And for that Sargent was mainly responsible. His perversity had added one more, and the greatest of all, to the brilliant list of his services to Forestry in America.

Finally, its work being ended, the National Forest Commission was discharged by Dr. Gibbs in a brief notice dated June 23, 1897. It had worked hard, it had made mistakes, but its very mistakes had turned out to be of enormous use.

23. *Confidential Forest Agent*

As the time came for organizing a service on the Reserves under the Act of June 4, 1897, members of the Commission met Secretary Bliss more than once. Sargent was still for the Army. Others urged a nonpartisan, nonpolitical service under the merit system. Bliss had his own idea. Said he, "There are just as good men in the Republican Party as there are Democrats." I was there when he said it.

Yes, and just as worthless political rejects, just as incompetent mental, moral, and physical cripples. Down went our shanty, and down went the administration of the Forest Reserves to a depth I would find it hard to believe if I had not seen it myself.

The Cleveland Reserves outside California were suspended and opened to private appropriation till March 1, 1898. Before then the forest question would be up again in Congress. Further and more detailed facts would be needed to meet the next attack. There being no one else in sight to round them up, I decided to go and get them myself. I went, but as an officer of the Government, and not as a private citizen.

The day after the Act of June 4 opened the way to Forestry on the Forest Reserves, Secretary Bliss asked me to make an examination and report on the Reserves as a Special Agent of the Land Office at $1,200 a year. I hesitated, for I had learned something about Special Agents, and I had little desire to be numbered among them. A few days later, thanks to Walcott and Hague, I was offered the same work under the title of Confidential Forest Agent, at $10 per day and expenses. Bliss approved the instructions I wrote out for myself, and I accepted.

I was to examine and report upon the suspended Reserves, their condition and needs, their forests, and their relations to lumbering, agriculture, mining, grazing, commerce, and settlement. I was to draw up a set of principles to govern future increase and decrease in the Reserves and apply them to individual cases. Finally, I was to report a practicable plan for the establishment of a Forest Service, with specific recommendations for individual Reserves—recommendations which the report of the Commission had not contained.

Before and after taking this job I had long consultations with Henry Gannett, Geographer of the Geological Survey, to whom Walcott had turned over the mapping and description of the Forest Reserves. Henry and I had taken to each other from the first day the work of the National Forest Commission threw us together. He was a man of decided opinions and strong antagonisms, brusque in manner but with a golden heart. He knew more geography than I did, I knew more Forestry than he did, and so we worked together like Damon and Pythias, if those worthies ever did any work.

About this time Secretary Bliss asked Congress to give him the funds left over from the National Forest Commission's appropriation for his own forest work, and in addition $100,000 for a Forest Service. If he got it, Walcott told me, I was to have charge. Perhaps it was just as well he didn't. The Angel Gabriel himself could hardly have done a good job with the derelicts Bliss appointed at the recommendation of Joe Cannon and other politicians.

On July 10, 1897, I left for the West. My brother Amos, to my great satisfaction, went along. At Blackfoot, Montana, we picked up Jack Monroe and proceeded to look over the Priest Lake Forest Reserve in Idaho, where stood, according to the report of the Commission, the "most valuable body of timber in the interior of the Continent."

It wasn't exactly an armchair job. Out of six days in the Priest Lake country my diary says we were up at 3:30 in the morning on three of them, on another at 4:00. The other two not stated.

Between the railroad and the lower lake we passed through a superb old forest of Western White Pine (locally called Silver Pine) mixed with Western Larch, most of which has now gone the way of all flesh. As we rowed the length of the lower lake (Kaniksu), through the thoroughfare, and into the upper lake (Priest Lake), the fire devastation of the old forest between the Priest Mountains to the east and the Pend Oreille range to the west was sickening. As my report said: "Except for one area of 1,600 acres on the Lower West Fork [of Priest River], there is probably not a body of one thousand acres on the whole reserve which has not been more or less seriously injured by fire."

Larch supplied most of the young growth. Then as always I was immensely impressed with its gallant resistance to fire. Western Yellow Pine, Douglas-fir, Western Cedar, and Lodgepole Pine, whose specialty is seeding up old burns, made up most of the rest of the forest.

In addition to the enormous damage from fire two incidents left an impression. One happened when I stepped out on the shore from our camp early one morning. Some fool, camped across the narrow lake, took a shot at me with his rifle and missed me narrowly. He was like other pestilent greenhorns in the woods who shoot at a motion or a noise. I rowed across and gave him my opinion free of charge.

The same day, while I was photographing the lake and its forests from an open burn, a mule-deer buck walked out of the brush and stood looking at me. My rifle, as it should have been, was leaning against the tripod of my camera within reach of my hand. I picked it up, killed the buck, leaned the rifle against the tripod again, took the photograph, and then walked over to my game.

It took Jack and me hours to tote that buck back to camp. His horns were in the velvet. I buried an antler in the coals of our camp fire, roasted it like a potato, and found it better than good. Have you ever tried roast horn?

July is no time to kill a deer in these days of game laws and game wardens. But in those days, back in the wilderness, we killed meat when we needed it.

From Priest Lake to Spokane, where Will Cowles, whom I had known at Yale, owned and directed the Spokane *Spokesman-Review*. To him I went with my story that the Forest Reserves were made to be used, not just to look at; asked for his help; and got it. Next day appeared a long interview in his paper and an editorial backing up my point of view.

Will Cowles was one of the first Western editors, outside of California, to take up the defense of the Cleveland Forest Reserves, and one of the most influential.

From Spokane to Wenatchee and up the Columbia River to Lake Chelan. As we went up it, the lake, many times longer than it is wide, lay first like a wide still river in open ranch country, then between forests of Western Yellow Pine along the rising shores. Engelmann Spruce and Douglas-fir, very badly burned, grew on the higher slopes. Higher again, subalpine groups and groves and single trees of Hemlock and White Bark Pine ended the story.

After three days Jack, Amos, and I made camp at Bridge Creek in the midst of the glorious rugged peaks of the Cascade Range, with great white mufflers of glaciers around their necks. From there our packer, Merritt E. Field, a first-class mountain man, and I made a trip with horses into the valleys of the Twisp and then the Methow, where we found the sign of a frontier xenodochium (if you know what I mean) nailed to a tree, "Spuds and sourdough 25 cents a gorge."

Next to Early Winters Creek, peppered with rattlesnakes, of which I killed a couple (thirty-one miles that day with a pack outfit, which isn't bad); Rainy Pass; and back to Bridge Creek, as usual taking photographs all the way.

At Bridge Creek Amos and Jack had been joined by F. H. Newell and Henry Gannett, and those two old-timers had drunk up every bit of coffee we had in camp. We loved them none the less for that. Next day we took them to the summit, and they went on down to Marblemount and the coast.

The rest of us went on to Horse Shoe Basin, where Amos and I each collected a mountain goat. Then through the Cascade Pass down to the Skagit River and Leach's ranch. We were back in the settlements again where there were fences, and so we took the chance to hang the salted skins and scalps of our goats on a fence to dry. But it was poor judgment. A cow carried off the scalp of mine for the salt that was in it, and I never could find out what she did with it.

After that to Seattle, where long conferences with Judge Thomas Burke helped me to understand public opinion in the State of Washington, and convinced him that the Forest Reserve policy was wise and right. Judge Burke took me to see the editor of the *Post Intelligencer,* commonly known as the *P. I.* He, as my diary puts it, "came to the right view," and gave me a chance to tell about it in an interview in his paper.

While Amos started East, I went into the western slope of the Washington Reserve again, took my pack, spent the night alone in the forest near Columbia Peak, and climbed it next morning. But it was too smoky from forest fires to see much. Then after two more days on foot in the woods, to Seattle again.

I had now seen something of both the east and the west slopes of the huge Washington Forest Reserve. You may say, if you like, that it was ridiculous to report on a Reserve of three and one-half million acres, bigger than the whole State of Connecticut, after spending a mere couple of weeks in and around it. And so it was from the standpoint of today.

But remember that this was, so far as I know, the first time any forester had ever looked this region over, and the same was true of most of the country I saw that summer. The information I got was scanty enough, but what there was of it was pure gain.

My next job was to have a look at the Olympic Reserve, also in the State of Washington, which rejoices in the heaviest rainfall in the United States. I suppose there is nowhere, except in the Redwood belt of California, a more magnificent body of woodland. From Lake Crescent with Al Blackwood, a first-class woodsman, I made a trip to see the supermagnificent forest on Section 16, Township 30, Range 9 West. So thick was the undergrowth, so formidable the down timber, and so dense the forest, that it took us from ten in the morning until seven in the evening to make less than five miles.

And no wonder. Many of the trees were 275 feet in height, and not a few of them were 10 or 12 feet through breast high, or even more. Douglas-fir, Western Cedar, Sitka Spruce, and Western Hemlock were the principal kinds. The Douglas-fir, which made up nearly half the forest, would average 200 feet high and 6 feet in diameter, with 100 feet of clear trunk. Near a settler's cabin I measured a Fir foot log across a stream. It was 134 feet long, 26 inches through at the butt, and 18 inches at the top. In 134 feet it had lost only 8 inches in diameter.

The overpowering sense of bigness which emanated from that gigantic forest I can never forget. One of the photographs I took of it, duly enlarged, hung on my wall for years. I saw it many times a day, and always with wonder and delight. A windfall in timber like that was something to work through.

But the most significant thing I found, and to me it was an amazing discovery, was that every part of the Reserve I saw appeared to have been cleared by fire within the last few centuries. The mineral soil under the humus, wherever it was exposed about the roots of windfalls, was overlaid by a layer of charcoal and ashes. Continuous stretches of miles without a break were covered with a uniform growth of Douglas-fir from two to five feet in diameter, entirely unscarred by fire. Among them numerous rotting stumps of much larger trees did bear the marks of burning. "I did not see a single young seedling of Douglas-fir under the forest cover, nor a single opening made by fire which did not contain them."

Fire conditioned and controlled the forest in the Olympics. Fires burned not only in the summer, but, believe it or not, in the rain-soaked winter also. They burned far down into the deep layer of humus, and into fallen logs, especially Hemlock logs, and often survived the pouring rains. I was told that on the trail from Wineton to Beaver a fire which began in August 1896, survived the winter in this way, and was still burning in February 1897.

Next to fire, the thing that surprised me most was the incredible reproduction of the Western Hemlock. Its seedlings stood in crowded rows on nearly every fallen log. Others sent their rootlets down from the tops of broken stubs, over the rotting wood to the humus and the mineral soil sometimes twenty or thirty feet beneath. When their supports disintegrate, the young Hemlocks are left to stand on their leg-like roots, propped high above the ground, until at length the separate roots unite into a single stem. To all appearances it is like an ordinary tree trunk grown up from the ground instead of down from the sky, except that it is a little thicker and less regular near the base.

At Lake Crescent, to my great delight, Dr. C. Hart Merriam turned up, and we went together by way of the Soleduck Hot Springs to the Hoh River Divide, from which the view of Mt. Olympus was beyond description. I never saw the classic original, but if the gods of ancient Greece had anything approaching this peak to live on, they were certainly in luck.

From this camp Blackwood and I went on foot down the Bogachiel River. It was a great trip. I believed then, and I may have been right, that white men had never passed that way before. At any rate, for three days we saw no trace of humans, but only wolf tracks and the deep-worn trails of the Olympic elk.

Although it was only the end of August, one night it rained so hard that Blackwood and I had to pile our fire of driftwood high and wide to keep it from being drowned out, while we sat in our leaky brushwood lean-to, hoping against hope that the heat would dry us faster than the rain could wet us down. I tell you again, them was the happy days.

Finally, through the settled portions of the Soleduck Valley to the little settlement of Sappho, from which, just the week before, a mountain lion had carried off a child. It was the only case I ever knew of, outside the nature fakers, and on the very spot it was extremely real.

And so off to Blackfoot, Montana, where I "slept in the freight house by courtesy of the night operator." In those days I always had my bedroll along.

Being on a per diem basis, paid only when I worked, I had a right to take time off and go a-hunting. Accordingly, deep in the St. Mary's country, in the heart of the Flathead Forest Reserve, I joined Amos and Henry L. Stimson at their camp at the foot of Mt. Going-to-the-Sun. Harry Stimson, once Secretary of State, twice Secretary of War, and Theodore Roosevelt's candidate for Governor of New York, is the only man I ever knew to watch for grizzlies alone at night with a single-shot rifle.

With Amos and Jack Monroe I saw a good deal of the Reserve on foot, sleeping out in the snow a night or two without blankets, got a better knowledge of the region and its forests, and generally enjoyed myself.

This glorious part of the Rockies is to my mind the finest mountain scenery in the United States. From there I reported to the Secretary of the Interior: "Public sentiment in the regions I have visited is far more ready to support the reservations than I had ventured to hope. An explanation of the true situation has always, with a single exception, resulted in expressions of hearty approval on the part of the persons with whom I have talked." However stilted my official language, the fact was mighty comforting after the furious attacks in Congress so short a time before.

Toward the end of September Amos, Jack, and I left the Stimson party, and one of us nearly left this sinful world for good. On the second night of our return trip, hungry and thirsty and good and tired, we reached Fox's ranch house just at sundown. Fox we had left with Stimson, but we counted on finding his wife, a gray-haired Blackfoot Indian woman, at home and hospitable, for the grub we started with was used up.

We knocked. No answer. We tried the door. Locked. We called. Silence.

This was getting serious, for we had to eat. So I started to break in through a window. And at that precise moment Mrs. Fox, who was inside with a young squaw and a loaded rifle, waiting to pot the first man who should show his nose, recognized Jack's voice. In consequence of which nobody got shot, and we three, full to the neck, threw down our blankets under the stars and slept the sleep of the righteous.

Back at the railroad and at the job again, Jack and I set out for a look at the eastern slope of the Lewis and Clarke Reserve. We had already, as you may recall, seen something of its western slope along Swan River and elsewhere.

Our way lay across Birch Creek Pass, over the Teton River, and into the North Fork of Sun River, through forests of Engelmann

Spruce, Lodgepole Pine, and Douglas-fir, with Alpine Fir on the ridges, through great burns along the North Fork, and so to the open country and the hot springs where the North and Middle Forks join hands. Before we were far along it began to snow and rain. But with our tent and a fire we were dry and warm part of the time anyhow. And that was good enough.

Next to the Black Hills Reserve, where I found Harry Graves waiting at Custer. We climbed Harney Peak and a number of other high spots; very inappropriately spent a Sunday in Hell Canyon; established by original investigation the highly important biological fact that prairie dog is a whole lot better eating than rabbit, cottontail or jack; and got a good cross section of the Hills in cold and snow.

Not uncommonly, according to our guess, 50 per cent of the merchantable timber was unsound, and beetle damage was serious—how serious we did not begin to appreciate.

From Spearfish Harry left for the Bear Lodge Mountains. I went on to Rapid City for a conference with Land Office officials, of whom Myron Willsie, a United States Deputy Mining Surveyor, "was most interesting about the Homestake lode locations for timber," which were fraudulent, of course.

Thus fortified, at Deadwood I had a talk with Moody and Grier, Counsel and Superintendent of the Homestake Mine, Carpenter, Superintendent of the next largest concern, and one or two others. At the end of three hours, says my diary, "they had arrived, in words at least, at my own position regarding the Reserve, including the desirability of including all the area of the Black Hills."

From Custer on November 5 I reported to the Secretary "a general change of opinion in regard to the Reserve, both among the ranchers and among those interested in mining. So far I have talked with no one who was not strongly in favor of preserving the timber." That was better than good.

In the late fall I got home again and took up with my Father a letter I had received from Dr. Brandis in August. Said the Doctor: "Sargent wrote to me on 19th July in exceedingly severe terms. He says: 'When I made him [Pinchot] secretary (an unprecedented thing, as only members of the Academy serve on such Commissions) I did so in the expectation that he would eventually be able to take a prominent place in National Forestry. He has gone over now to the politicians, accepting some sort of position under the Secretary of the Interior, without consulting his friends in the Academy about it, and his usefulness, I fear, is nearly at an end.'

"This expression of Sargent's views," Dr. Brandis continued, "has greatly grieved me. Sargent has fought the battle of Forestry in the United States for more than 20 years; if ever Forestry is to be a reality in your country, his work in publishing the *Silva,* and otherwise, will always be recognized as having laid the foundation of an accurate knowledge of American trees." Which nobody can deny, however little of a jolly good fellow Sargent may have been.

After much consideration I wrote Sargent what seems to me now an overmild rebuttal and sent a copy to Dr. Brandis:

"My action in connection with the Government has the entire approval of a majority of the working members of the Commission, and in their view it has been in direct accord with the main features of policy recommended in the Commission's report. It was undertaken after full consultation with Professor Brewer and Mr. Hague. Both of these gentlemen have been good enough to send me their views on the subject, in writing.

"In consonance, therefore, with the wish expressed by Dr. Brandis, I am hopeful that the present misunderstanding may not continue."

Whether Sargent ever answered my letter I cannot recall. At least there is no such reply in my files.

Among the things I owed Sargent (and I owed him very much) was my chance to work as a member of the National Forest Commission, and, because of that, as Confidential Forest Agent. Together they amounted to a liberal education for the job that lay ahead. They taught me something about the Western forests on the ground, and something about the big men and the little men who used or abused them. The powers and principalities which controlled the politics and the people of the West began to emerge from the general landscape.

Principalities like the Homestake Mine in the Black Hills, the Anaconda Mine in the Rockies, Marcus Daly's feudal overlordship of the Bitterroot Valley, and Miller and Lux's vast holdings of flocks and herds and control of grazing lands on the Pacific slope—these and others showed their hands or their teeth. So did powers like the Northern and Southern Pacific and the Great Northern Railroads, the irrigation interests of California, and the great cattle and sheep stock growers' associations.

My contact with newspapers like the St. Paul *Dispatch,* the Spokane *Spokesman-Review,* Seattle *P. I.,* Portland *Oregonian,* San Francisco *Chronicle,* and Los Angeles *Times* gave me some inkling of how public opinion is created or directed. Indeed not a single item of knowledge or experience that I managed to scrape together in the West during those two years but came good, as they say where I was born, in the work of the Forest Service later on.

In Washington meantime I met two Presidents in the White House on a working basis; became acquainted with the leaders of both House and Senate; found out at least something about how legislation comes to pass, the bearing of public sentiment upon it, and the jargon in which it is written; and began drawing bills myself.

Also I got to know essential facts about the administration of the public land laws; had the devastating effect of spoils politics on the public interest rubbed into my hair; saw how trying to bull things through may cost more than it comes to; learned to keep my temper and be thankful for half a loaf; was forced to form opinions and express them on nationwide questions of real importance; and had to make plans for handling millions of acres of public forest, and defend them when made.

All the while I was thrown into close contact with older men, outside of politics, who not only knew the United States from one end to the other but whose experience in dealing with public men and public questions made their example a sort of terrestrial guiding star. Take it by and large, it was a chance in a million—and the luckiest of all chances that it came to me.

PART V
SPADE WORK

24. *The Old Forestry Division*

The year of the Spanish War—1898—opened with more work ahead than ever. Graves and I were completing *The Adirondack Spruce.* Forest management on Seward Webb's tract at Ne-Ha-Sa-Ne in the Adirondacks was in full swing, and negotiations were under way for applying practical Forestry on the 68,000 acres of the William C. Whitney tract, also in the Adirondacks. Similar negotiations were pending with the American Pulp and Paper Company, the International Paper Company, and the Atchison, Topeka, and Santa Fe Railroad.

A plan for a two-year study of forest fires was in hand, and an ambitious scheme for a description of the forests of the whole world in co-operation with the National Geographic Congress of 1899; field work and a report as State Forester of New Jersey were staring me in the eye; and a number of papers were on the fire.

Meantime the Forestry Division at Washington was in trouble with Congress. Year after year it had walked around the outskirts of Forestry, like Joshua around the walls of Jericho. But Joshua got inside. The old Division never did. It had never put, or been the means of putting, a single acre of forest under forest management anywhere in the United States.

Dr. Fernow's opinion of the practicability of Forestry was set forth in a paper read by him at a meeting of the Forestry Congress, October 18, 1893, more than a year after the work at Biltmore began. Said he, "The main reliance for a conservative forest policy as far as Government action is concerned lies with the individual states."

In his ninth annual report Dr. Fernow said that the Division was "instituted to preach, not practice." And he added that it "is, then, a bureau of information."

Of the forty-three bulletins and circulars issued while Dr. Fernow was head of the Division, nineteen dealt with the uses of timber after it had been cut, but not one gave practical directions for applying forest management to American timberlands before they were cut.

The old Division saw too many lions in the path. It held that before it could manage a forest growth intelligently it must know first of all the biology, or life history, of all the kinds of trees which compose it.

All of which was true enough from the point of view of elaborate German forestry, but emphatically not true under pioneer conditions in America. Forestry in the land of the ingenious Yankee could be built on a whole lot less information than that. I was born in Connecticut myself.

Knowledge of trees is the basis of Forestry, Heaven knows, and the more we have of it the better. But it must be used as a help to practice Forestry, not as an excuse for sidetracking it. What America needed to hear was not why Forestry couldn't be practiced, but how it could.

Besides the dearth of practical Forestry, another thing that hurt the old Division was its experiments in making rain. It is only fair to say that Congress ordered them much against Dr. Fernow's will. When the rain makers shot off bombs attached to balloons over the Staked Plains of Texas, nobody cared—not even the moisture in the atmosphere. But when their explosions shattered nearly all the window glass in Alexandria, just across from Washington, that put the Division on the Congressional spot.

The growing impatience up on the Hill also exploded. It wrote into the agricultural appropriation bill of 1898 a clause which in effect demanded to know what the Division had done to justify its existence, and why it should not be abolished. That was the show down.

For not only the patience of Congress, but also the patience of Fernow's chief, Secretary Wilson, was exhausted. As he told me himself, he was just about to ask for Dr. Fernow's resignation, when, in the nick of time, Cornell University decided to open a forest school and invited the Doctor to take charge. Fernow accepted and thereby beat the gun.

Whether it was the failure of the old Division to get practical Forestry going in the United States; whether it was the fact that Forestry had started on private lands without the help of the Division; or whether some other reason was the moving cause—I cannot say. But the fact is that the time of the old Division was up.

And that was a pity, for the history of the old Division ran back for a quarter of a century.

In 1873 the American Society for the Advancement of Science, on the initiative of Dr. Franklin B. Hough, addressed a memorial to President Grant in the interest of forest preservation. In 1876 Congress appropriated $2,000 for the salary of "a man of approved attainments and practically well acquainted with the methods of statistical inquiry," but not, you will observe, with Forestry. Dr. Hough was selected, and so became the first Federal forest officer.

In 1880 the Division of Forestry, in the Department of Agriculture, was created. Three years later Dr. N. H. Egleston, one of those failures in life whom the spoils system is constantly catapulting into responsible positions, replaced Dr. Hough.

After three years of innocuous desuetude, Dr. Egleston in turn was replaced on March 15, 1886, by Dr. Fernow, a graduate of the Prussian Forest School at Muenden, for a time a member of the Prussian State Forest Department, a founder of the American Forestry Association, and its secretary for many years.

By position and activity Dr. Fernow was a leader in the American forest movement. He was also one of the principal reasons why, before Biltmore Forest, there was no forest management in America. Oberfoerster Paulus, when I was studying under him in Prussia, gave me the very interesting information that Dr. Fernow, before he came to America, had never had charge of any practical forest management in the woods.

Dr. Fernow being on his way to Cornell, someone must be found to take his place. Wilson consulted Walcott, and Walcott suggested Pinchot. Wilson agreed, and Walcott carried the offer to me.

I refused on the spot. There were too many different jobs already on hand. Moreover, I thought small—very small—of the Division, which was slowly losing out. And besides I wanted to work in the woods instead of pent up in an office. Walcott asked me to see Wilson.

My diary of May 11, 1898, has this to say:

"To see Secretary Wilson, who said if I would take the Forestry Division I could run it to suit myself. I could appoint my own assistants, do what kind of work I chose, and not fear any interference from him. Said I could also run the Adirondack work. Said he would keep the place open three years for me. Could not have said more."

"Forestry," said the Secretary, "is still in the Dark Ages." I thought so too, and I made it clear that if I took the job I would strike first of all to get Forestry out of the dark and into the woods.

I had been practicing Forestry at Biltmore, in the Adirondacks, and elsewhere, without waiting to learn all about all the trees I was working with. I was for the American way as against the German way. So was the Secretary. We were agreed all along the line.

Still I hesitated. The bad taste of the Division's circumlaboration (which means what I mean, whether it is English or not) was strong in my mouth. Congress, which paid the piper and could call the tune, was openly skeptical or worse. But everybody I consulted in Washington said I ought to pitch in and have a try at bringing the Government's forest work to life.

So did my Father and Professor Brewer. So did Harry Graves, and what was more, he agreed to come with me as Assistant Chief. Nothing could be better than that.

In a week I threw off my prejudice, came to my senses, and realized that here was the chance of a lifetime. Gladly I accepted Secretary Wilson's offer, and went eagerly to work to get ready for my new job. I was blind not to do so the very minute the offer was made.

But the position of Chief of the Forestry Division was under the classified civil service. Before I could hold it I had to pass an examination. Since there was nobody else under the Government who could do it, I was asked to make out the questions for myself to answer. Before, however, I got a chance to answer my own questions, which were stiff enough in all conscience, President McKinley, at Secretary Wilson's request, covered me into the civil service without any examination at all.

Friday, July 1, 1898, was a red-letter day for me. On that day I became chief of the little old Forestry Division. I was highly enthusiastic and deeply pleased. Yet the prospect was something less than brilliant.

So far as the Division's standing was concerned, our way was all to make. We had few friends. As yet we were not even important enough to have active enemies.

Where public opinion was favorable, it was ineffective. Where it was effective, it was unfavorable. The timberland owners, whose attitude was most important of all, held us in amused toleration or open contempt. But for the most part the great public knew nothing about us and cared less. For all practical purposes the old Division wasn't there at all.

Five days after I started in, Secretary Wilson, to my great satisfaction, gave me the title of Forester, instead of Chief of Division. In Washington chiefs of division were thick as leaves in Vallombrosa. Foresters were not. I was a forester in fact before that happy day. I have since been a Governor, every now and then, but I am a forester all the time—have been, and shall be, all my working life.

25. *Freshman Year*

My first year in the new Division of Forestry was worth more to me than all the treasures of all the pirates of history, from Captain Kidd to the present day. It was, in a phrase my Father loved to quote, a halcyon and vociferous time, and no mistake.

My chief, Tama Jim Wilson, came from Tama County, Iowa. He was a grand man to work for. He knew enough, as plenty of executives do not, to give a man his head—let him alone, so long as he stayed on the right track. He kept his promise of a free hand in letter and in spirit. Without his backing we could never have done our work and won our fight as we did. I owe him a great debt, and none the less because years afterward we fell out over the Ballinger controversy. Peace to his ashes.

As for the new Forester, he knew almost nothing of Government work and nothing at all about the work of a Government executive. I had to learn the game before I could play it. It might have been hard sledding if it had been less furiously interesting. But if anybody, except T.R. himself, has ever had more fun than I have out of working for Uncle Sam, I have still to come across him.

When I joined up, the Division had all of ten people in it. I made the population eleven. It was a microscopic and mixed outfit—some good, some not so good.

There was George B. Sudworth, dendrologist, highly trained in the botanical knowledge of trees, a competent and industrious public servant entirely devoted to his work. His long, honorable, and useful career blossoms and smells sweet in the silent dust.

There was a Russian forester by the name of Mlodziansky, a plump and irascible little man who developed the quaint idea that office hours from nine to four applied to field work also. He didn't last long after that.

Turner Speller, the Negro messenger, a leader among his people, was a man of high probity and good will, with a deeply religious, serene, and very kindly nature. As the years passed he and I became real friends.

Filibert Roth, who, with Sudworth, was the best man Fernow had, went with him to Cornell. What was left of us were facing five or six hundred million acres of timberland, and the job of doing something about it.

Like myself, every member of the Division held his place under civil service regulations. But an earnest job hunter could generally find a loophole if you let him try hard enough. Relying on Secretary Wilson's promise, I refused to join the hunt for political loopholes, and before long the word spread that the Division was barren job-hunting ground. After that I had no trouble.

The first questing Congressman who dropped in after I took charge was a Mr. White of North Carolina. In spite of his name, White was not white, but colored. He wanted Turner's job for some constituent. It seemed to me as good a time as any to make a stand. So I told him he couldn't have Turner's job.

He said if he didn't get it he would abolish the Division. I told him to go ahead and turn loose his wolf. We parted the worst of friends. But the Division continued in business and Turner stayed.

That set the pace. I can honestly say that in my eleven and a half years in the forest work of the Government I never appointed, refused to appoint, promoted, demoted, transferred, or dismissed a single person on political grounds. Which was one reason why that work reached and held the high standard it did.

The Division had two rooms high up in the east wing of the old red brick Agricultural Building, long since torn down. One of them, a little hall-bedroom effect, was my office. In the second the other ten members of the force had to live and move and have their being.

There was no stenographer. The very small mail I answered by writing the letters out in longhand and then getting them copied on the typewriter. I was hardly warm in my seat when the young person who performed this necessary task heard me speak of a trip to Chicago. She invited me to take her along, "in any capacity."

That was not what I enlisted for. The young person was plenty old enough to know better, and of course I ought to have fired her out of hand. But she was under the political protection of Senator X, and I was a new, unsettled, and very minor official. So I transferred the letter copying to somebody else and let her sit in front of her typewriter day in and day out, without anything whatever to do. She stood it for three weeks and then removed herself to parts permanently unknown.

The incoming correspondence of the Division was a barometer worth reading. It wanted to know about anything but practical Forestry—about shade trees, ornamental shrubs, how to preserve elms from decay, and how to raise mushrooms. That was what such of the great public as had heard about it at all still thought the Forestry Division was for, after nearly twenty years.

Beyond the will to make good, the equipment of the Division was just about nil. There wasn't even a single marking hatchet—clear proof that the Division wasn't thinking about practical Forestry, for with that tool the forester marks the trees to cut or leave standing. The marking hatchet carries Forestry into the woods.

What equipment there was consisted of one tape measure from which, if you put it around a tree, you could read off the diameter; one pair of calipers that could be unfolded out of a cane; and one increment borer, by which instrument the student could sample the growth of a standing tree much as a careful buyer cuts a plug out of a watermelon.

And when we came to work up in the office the tree measurements we took in the field, I had to send to New York for my own comptometer. The Division was too poor for such luxuries. We had less than one cent to spend for every dollar available to the rest of the Department—no great war chest with which to open the campaign for saving a million or so square miles of unsaved forest.

26. *A Bid to the Lumbermen*

Over against the new Division's poverty of appropriations, equipment, personnel, and public appreciation, the world was all before us where to choose. I could pick my own trail, and there was no question which trail to pick.

The business of foresters is to manage forests, as the business of farmers is to manage farms. The business of the new Division was to to break away from exhortation, indirection, and inhibition, and get down to the brass tacks of spreading the gospel of practical Forestry by creating practical examples in the woods.

On the face of the facts the odds were just about impossible. The forests in which the new Division proposed to bring about the practice of Forestry covered more land than all the states east of the Mississippi River, with another state or two thrown in. In comparison with that continental sweep the forests already under management were less than flyspecks on a map. To take on that job with the force we had—two foresters and a dendrologist—must have seemed like a new Children's Crusade.

Some of these vast forests belonged to the Nation—were part of the Public Domain. A very few belonged to some of the states. But most of them were in private hands. And they were being destroyed faster than timberlands had ever been destroyed before in all the long history of forest devastation.

The Government forests—43,000,000 acres of Forest Reserves, and several times more millions of unreserved public timberland—were all in charge of the Interior Department, which had not a single forester to look after them.

All the Government foresters, the whole two of them, were in the Department of Agriculture, with not a single acre of Government forest in their charge. Forests and foresters were in completely separate watertight compartments.

It was a fantastic situation. Obviously to bring Uncle Sam's forests and foresters together was nothing more than common sense. Brought together they were going to be, if I had any luck, and when they were I proposed to be the forester in charge. But until then the Government Forest Reserves seemed to be out of my reach.

Privately owned timberlands were not. They ran to something like half a billion acres—two-thirds of all the forests in America—and the most valuable and accessible at that. Their owners, or some of them, could practice Forestry if they chose. If we could make a go of Forestry at Biltmore and Ne-Ha-Sa-Ne, why not in other places also? So I let it be known that the Division was prepared to help private owners harvest their timber with a view to a second crop.

Circular 21, which made public the Division's offer to help farmers, lumbermen, and other private timberland owners apply Forestry to their holdings, came out on October 15, 1898. The Division had come of age. This was our major offensive. The offer included whatever was needed to get Forestry going—working plans for conservative lumbering, with full directions for practical work, and assistance on the ground.

Help was free to the owners of woodlots. Owners of larger tracts paid the expenses of our men in the field, but not their salaries, and the cost of local assistants. Timberland owners who accepted the terms of Circular 21 must and did put up good money to show they meant business. And what they put up was just so much added to our appropriation.

The same offer could have been made by the Division ten years before. If made, it would certainly have brought the beginnings of Forestry to America. But the great chance was lost, and Forestry came to America in another way.

The new Division did not wait till Circular 21 was in print. We cast our bread upon the waters by word of mouth, and the demand for help to practice Forestry came back to us with a rush. Within four months after I took office, applications had been made for help in handling nearly a million acres in nineteen states.

To deal with that huge job, after Mlodziansky was gone and until Graves came, I was a lone forester, but with no time to be lonesome. In addition, and most important, there was the fight in Congress to prevent the further suspension of the Forest Reserves, which you know about already. Co-operation with the Geological Survey in revising the Reserve boundaries, also, was vitally necessary to supply the forester's point of view; and the report on my examination of the Forest Reserves as Confidential Agent of the General Land Office the previous summer had to be written up. No time hung heavy on my hands.

As the months passed, our little force grew, but the work grew faster. By the end of the year successful forest management under Circular 21 was in actual operation on 108,000 acres, for the Whitney-Moynehan work was transferred to the Division.

It wasn't gilt-edged, wiredrawn German Forestry by any means. It wasn't even what we could have made it with more men and more time. But it did pay, it did stop forest devastation, and it did provide for a second crop.

It may have been only a little egg, but the Division was entitled to cackle. For here was the beginning of practical and paying Forestry on an important scale among lumbermen in America. This was what all the friends of Forestry had been talking around and about for many years without result. This was the biggest forward step that had ever been taken in the actual practice of American Forestry.

It was bigger than Biltmore, and far more significant, for the lumbermen controlled thousands of acres for every one included in any forest estate. But it could not have been started with such a rush except for the foundations laid at Biltmore, thanks to George Vanderbilt, and at Ne-Ha-Sa-Ne, thanks to Seward Webb, before either Graves or I came into the Division. We had learned our job in the Appalachians and the Adirondacks, and we were doing what we had trained ourselves to do. That was why we were able to make it stick.

By June 30, 1899, the end of my first year in the Division, 123 lumbermen, farmers, and others had asked for help in starting Forestry on a million and a half acres of timberland in thirty-five states. Forty-eight applications were for large tracts, seventy-five for farm woodlots.

With the men we had we managed, in that first year, to take a look at something more than four hundred thousand acres in nineteen states, but we couldn't begin to meet the demand. There were at that time only eight or ten American foresters—nothing like enough for the work in sight even if I could have got them all. We had turned on the water and were like to be drowned.

Large oaks from little acorns grow. It is worth noting that the whole cost of getting practical Forestry into the lumber woods for the fiscal year 1898-99 was $4,133.35 to the Government, and $2,239.23 to the private owners. Seeing that the Congressional seed graft in that same year absorbed $130,000, and that the old Forestry Division had already cost the Government a quarter of a million dollars without producing any forest management whatsoever, it was certainly cheap at the price.

As our enterprise widened, so also grew our little force of foresters. Harry Graves came in October of '98. He was a host in himself. Ned Griffith joined in the same month, Ralph Hosmer in the next. All three had studied Forestry abroad. So had Tom Sherrard, who came a little later. Alfred Gaskill, George Schwartz, and William W. Ashe had not. Just the same they pulled their weight.

In the spring of '99 Jim Toumey gave up his professorship in the University of Arizona to head the Section of Economic Tree Planting. In June came Overton Price. He took over the work under Circular 21 when Graves went to Yale.

To say that Price was my right hand is a feeble understatement. He had more to do with the good organization and high efficiency of the Government forest work than ever I had. Most of the credit for it that came to me rightly belongs to him.

Within a year after the change from exhortation to work in the woods the mailing list grew from 1,200 to 6,000 names, including 2,000 newspapers. That might have had some connection with a very marked increase in public co-operation and interest in the work of the Division.

There came also a momentous change for the better in the attitude of the West toward the Forest Reserves. Such shifts in public opinion are sometimes hard to explain. Perhaps reaction from a previous state of overindignation and the enormous spread of forest fires in the fall of 1898 may have had something to do with this one.

Every man in the Division was on his toes. We were all young together, all eager, all proud of the Division, and all fiercely determined that its attack on forest devastation must win. We were ready to fight it out on this line if it took the rest of our lives. With such a cause and such a spirit we couldn't lose.

But although Forestry could be started on what little we knew about the growth and habits of American forest trees, we had to know much more to keep Forestry spreading, and for that we needed men. Only a meager scattering of even the more important timber trees had ever been glanced at, much less studied, from the forester's point of view.

One of our first jobs was to go and find out about what we named the Silvics of our trees, by which we meant their behavior as they grew in the forest. We needed to know their rate of growth in height and diameter; the amount of wood or lumber produced by a tree or an acre; the coming of seed years; the tolerance of young seedlings for shade and sunlight; and all the other facts, necessary but then unknown, about the reproduction and growth of dozens and dozens of important forest trees. We had to learn that we might practice.

Instead of the old Division's vague and pointless scheme to plant trees and then wait to find out what they would have to teach after a generation had gone by, we looked for and found trees, long planted, that were ready to tell us now. Before the year was over we were prepared to give tree planters practical advice on the ground.

The new Division had already studied a number of our most important commercial trees, and had notably advanced tree planting, especially in the almost treeless Western plains. It had studied the relation of forests to stream flow, water supply, evaporation, erosion, and irrigation; it had laid a firm basis for the regulation of grazing in the Western Forest Reserves in a way fair both to the cattle and sheep owners and to the users of wood and water.

We began an extensive study of forest fires and their history, reaching from Washington and Montana to Florida and Georgia, with the sound idea of finding out how much they were costing the Nation. But after we had reached a tentative figure of $20,000,000 a year, more pressing work crowded it aside, and nothing more important ever came of it. The same thing happened to historical studies of the forest movement in several of the states. Our general direction was right, but I made mistakes aplenty.

Today I am not much troubled about that. In his introduction to *Personal Recollections of Joan of Arc,* one of the great books of our time, Mark Twain has a paragraph which may be paraphrased like this, "To arrive at a just estimate of work accomplished one must judge it by the conditions which existed at the time, not by the conditions of today." Judged by that standard, I have few apologies to make.

But mistakes or no mistakes, I was having the time of my life. Forestry was in the woods (some woods, anyhow), God in his Heaven, and most things, except the Interior Department and the Forest Reserves, right with the world.

Early in 1899 an application under Circular 21 from the Adirondack League Club for its lands at Tahawus (where, nearly three years later, Theodore Roosevelt was to get the news that McKinley had been shot) gave me a glorious winter trip in the woods.

This trip led also to better acquaintance with T.R., to whom, two years before, I owed my election to the Boone and Crockett, the club of big game hunters he had founded. It happened because Grant LaFarge, son of the famous painter, with whom I planned to write, but never wrote, a book on Adirondack trees, was T.R.'s close friend. He and I spent the night with the Roosevelts in Albany on our way to Tahawus. We arrived just as the Executive Mansion was under ferocious attack from a band of invisible Indians, and the Governor of the Empire State was helping a houseful of children to escape by lowering them out of a second-story window on a rope.

After all the children had been saved from the Indians, I laid before the Governor my plan for a single-headed New York Forest Commission instead of the spineless many-headed Commission of those days, and he approved it entirely. Also he highly approved Grant's plan and mine for a winter ascent of Mt. Marcy, the highest peak in the State. That was exactly in his line.

Incidentally T.R. and I did a little wrestling, at which he beat me; and some boxing, during which I had the honor of knocking the future President of the United States off his very solid pins.

From Albany Grant and I headed for the North Woods. After we left the train, my diary says: "Delightful drive to Tahawus. Overturned on the way." In the deep snow it didn't matter.

After the serious work of looking over the forest was finished, with a couple of men who called themselves guides we snowshoed to a cabin at Lake Colden on the trail to Marcy, taking pictures for the proposed book all the way. Every tree was a monument of snow. The temperature was far below zero, and well I knew it, for I was wearing just what I wore in the woods in summer, plus sweater, cap, and mittens.

Next morning we started for the mountain. Lake Tear of the Clouds, source of the Hudson River, from which the actual climb began, was just below timber line and under something like twenty feet of snow. More was falling, and it was blowing like the devil, although we were still in the lee of the peak. While we ate a bite and planned the attack, we built a fire, which promptly melted itself down out of sight.

When we were ready for the climb, one of the "guides" elected to stay with the vanishing fire, which by that time amounted to a hole in the snow with a little steam coming out of it. The other "guide" kept on with Grant and me till we reached the edge of the timber.

Right there he developed a highly opportune pain in his leg. And that was as far as he went.

We left our snowshoes stuck in the snow at timber line. Outside the shelter of the trees the wind was really terrific. Beyond the timber the slope was covered with glare ice, but thin enough so that we could make hand and knee holds by breaking through it. It was impossible to travel upright, and without the holds in the ice there would have been no small chance of being blown over the cliff on our right.

Grant, who was lighter than I, soon found he could make no headway against the furious gale, and very wisely gave it up. I crawled on slowly, holding my head down in the squalls, and stopping every minute or two to rub my face against freezing.

It seemed to take a little eternity, but at last I could make out the signal at the top. After several trials I managed to stand up against the snow-filled blizzard long enough to take two exposures of the signal (both of them, incidentally, on the same plate), and then thankfully crawled down again.

Back at Lake Tear we found that the man who stayed there had, like a fool, stood around with the thongs of his snowshoes tightly tied. One of his feet was very badly frozen. The other man's pain in the leg was no longer needed and was gone. My own ears and neck were frost-bitten in spite of my sealskin cap, and my upper lip through my mustache. But nothing to matter.

How cold it was on Marcy I have no means of knowing. At the nearest Weather Bureau Station, 3,000 feet nearer sea level, that same day the thermometer went down to 23 degrees below zero.

By morning the thawed foot of the careless one had turned blue and split open in cracks you could lay a pencil in. Nevertheless he walked out, which certainly showed sand. He was laid up for over a year. Hard luck and no mistake.

This was the famous blizzard of February 1899. Trains were still stalled when we got back to Albany, and at Washington the snow was thirty inches deep on the level in the streets.

27. *Building a Profession*

American Forestry being in its infancy, we could get the facts we had to have only by sending men into the woods to look and see and measure and count. Therefore the Division must get together and train a force capable of gathering the information we needed and later of practicing Forestry in the woods. And it had to be done on a shoestring.

Of course any number of foresters from abroad were ready to come over. But my experience with Schenck and Mlodziansky was not encouraging. I was perfectly certain it would be worse than useless to fill the gap with imported Europeans, even if we had had the money to import them, and in that I was perfectly right. To do the work we had to do, a man must know about forests, of course, but he must also know about how people think, and how things are done in America. In a very real sense, that came first.

So I began to pick up youngsters, one here, one there, who were willing to work for the chance to learn and a very little besides. Treadwell Cleveland was the first. He came in January 1899. Smith Riley, who grew to be District Forester at Denver, with millions of acres of National Forests in his charge, was the second.

In the spring of '99 I gave notice, by a speech at Yale and in other ways, that a limited number of college students who had definitely made up their minds to take up Forestry as a profession could get $25 a month and their expenses in the field ($40 and no expenses in Washington), and a chance to find out what Forestry really meant. But only on condition that they could convince us they had the earnestness, the physical hardiness, and the love of the woods to fit them for the job.

Almost in the twinkling of an eye we had more applicants than we could use. And these green college boys had snap and punch. It was a delight to watch them dive in.

In 1899, the first year in which the position was open, the applicants had numbered only 35. Of the 123 people who made up the Division on July 1, 1900, 61 were Student Assistants, chosen from 232 applicants. Most of the applications were from the larger universities.

Harvard and Yale alone accounted for 100. The total from the Atlantic States was 177. California, however, furnished 16 applicants, and the Prairie States a goodly contingent.

The relatively small number for whom we had places made it possible to pick and choose—to skim the cream. And if, among the sixty-one whom we accepted, any cherished the illusion that they had won a chance for a pleasant summer camping trip at Government expense, they soon got over it.

These boys, wherever they worked, were the wonder of the natives for the hours they put in and the way they drove themselves. That men on Uncle Sam's pay roll should work so hard was beyond local understanding. In some places, where they lived in the same camps with lumberjacks, they outdid even these seasoned veterans.

Eaten by black flies and midges in the Northeast, by mosquitoes in the Northwest, by ticks and jiggers in the South, soaked and frozen and roasted by turns, as every woodsman must be, the Student Assistants fared hard and worked hard. A few of them failed to stand the gaff, but the rest of them took their medicine, did their work, and did it well.

What the boys were up against is well told in some of their diaries. One field party, for instance, upon completion of its summer work in the Black Hills, was sent in the fall to the overflow lands of the Mississippi River in Missouri to collect data upon 80,000 acres belonging to the Deering Harvester Company.

The forest consisted mainly of heavily mixed hardwoods with a dense undergrowth of bamboo cane from three to ten feet in height. The land was as flat as the top of a table. Four-fifths of the area was covered with backwater from six inches to six feet in depth. Not seldom there was a thin skim of ice in the early morning. The men were wet nine-tenths of the time.

There were no roads or trails. Compasses had to be used in going to and from work. On dark days wolves would follow the survey crews and burst into howling at intervals. But the work was done, and well done, in time to get home for Christmas. That was the spirit that made the Forest Service. No wonder I was strong for the Student Assistants.

Thus the hardening work and the physical test of the field parties weeded out the less stouthearted and provided us with a small but exceedingly promising body of young men. For a hastily assembled and largely improvised organization they could show a pretty imposing list of things done.

But many of them certainly were green. The stories about our tenderfeet were endless. The leader of one field party in the East got hopelessly lost by adopting the south instead of the north end of the compass needle. Another in the West kept his horse from grazing in the only time he had to graze by tying him up at night because he said he wanted him to rest. I saw that same man hold a box of oats under that same horse's nose so the poor beast wouldn't have to take the trouble of bending his neck.

Another, rifle in hand, came rushing breathless into a lumber camp. "There's a bear on the ridge!"

"Yep," replied the foreman, "I thought I'd have to tie up that old black sow when you came round."

In time the men got over their greenness, but the stories never grew old. They had a habit of turning up years afterward in Congressional debates, but always dated up to the minute.

Nevertheless and notwithstanding, as a whole the Student Assistants were magnificent. They furnished some of the very best leaders the Forest Service has had. Their work not only produced much useful information, but it pleased the lumbermen and brought us much practical assistance. And they gave me an abiding faith in young men.

Another device to meet the shortage of men was the appointment of Collaborators. In universities, state agricultural colleges, and elsewhere were men who had accumulated much solid information on the forest problem which the Division needed. Most of them were very willing to help. In this way we were able to tie in with us experts of established reputation in Forestry, lumbering, or tree planting. The Collaborators were not residents of Washington. They were given the enormous salary of $300 a year, and, what was far more attractive to them, the chance of publishing under Government auspices what they had learned and wanted to tell. It was a good plan, and it worked.

In 1900 the number of Collaborators was fifteen. Ten more were appointed in 1901. Among them were such outstanding scientists as Professor Nathaniel E. Shaler of Harvard, famous geologist and geographer, Professor William R. Dudley of Stanford University, whose study of the California Big Trees became classic, Professor George E. Bessey, botanist of the University of Nebraska, and others of similar caliber. These men served also as advisers on occasion. Their appointment stimulated interest in Forestry generally, and in our work.

But while these scientific men were of very material help in giving us more knowledge of American forests, they were not foresters; and it was foresters that we had to have if we were to show forest owners, private or public, how to apply Forestry. Here lay our greatest handicap.

On July 1, 1901, when the Division became a Bureau, it numbered what was to us the imposing total of 179 people. Of these 81 were Student Assistants. About 25 were Collaborators. We had thus emerged from the narrowest part of the bottleneck that had threatened to keep us too few to be effective.

It was mainly to help our budding foresters that the Society of American Foresters was formed. The first meeting was held in November 1900, in my little office in the old Department building. Present at the meeting besides myself were Graves, Price, Allen, Hall, Hosmer, and Sherrard. Seven in all, but enough.

The purpose of the Society was "to further the cause of Forestry in America by fostering a spirit of comradeship among foresters; by creating opportunities for a free interchange of views upon Forestry and allied subjects; and by disseminating a knowledge of the purpose and achievements of Forestry."

By and large the Society had no small share not only in educating our men, but also, and that was even more important, in establishing a genuine respect for the profession of Forestry. That would help to induce as many of our hastily equipped leaders as possible to take time, as and when they could, to attend regular professional courses before settling down to the long pull. And a good many of them did.

The weekly meetings of the Society were held at my home, where the discussion of the evening was regularly followed by a very moderate feast of baked apples, gingerbread, and milk. To some of our men the proceedings were so new and strange that one of them, a Westerner noted for his cool courage, actually fainted when the time came for him to speak. But he made his talk just the same.

These meetings brought our boys into touch with many men of distinction in fields of science related to Forestry. Men like Charles D. Walcott, Arnold Hague, F. H. Newell, Henry Gannett, J. A. Holmes, Frederick V. Coville, and Edward A. Bowers came and spoke. They were early associate members of the Society. And so were General C. C. Andrews of Minnesota, Colonel William F. Fox of New York, James Wilson, Secretary of Agriculture, and Theodore Roosevelt.

Later on, T.R., as President of the United States, addressed the members of the Society at 1615 Rhode Island Avenue. It was a rare and most inspiring proof of his interest in Forestry, for Presidents seldom, if ever, address meetings in private houses. T.R.'s speech did very much to stimulate the spirit of devotion to their work among the men who heard him.

In such ways the little group of members of the Society was welded together into what was later to become the vital core of the Forest Service—vital in loyalty to all that the Service stood for, and with the highest morale to be found anywhere under the Government of the United States.

And this was true not only for members of the Society, but of all the men and women who in the early days crowded to bursting our two rooms (in addition to my own small office) in the main building of the Department of Agriculture and overflowed into some borrowed space.

We were alive and on our way. We had come through our first crisis. After the perils of launching, our ship was afloat and right side up. We were ready to go places—provided Congress would kindly provide the necessary wherewithal. And Congress did.

We did get more money to do more work. But without competent direction a field party of green youngsters trying to gather the facts for a working plan would be like the crew of a rudderless ship. The number of available leaders was small indeed; and the preparation of some of them for leadership was smaller still.

The place to develop such leadership naturally should have been the forest schools. Professional education in Forestry, however, was only just beginning. In 1898 the New York State College of Forestry had been established at Cornell University with a four-year undergraduate professional course directed by Dr. Fernow. The State provided a demonstration forest of 30,000 acres in the Adirondacks for the use of the College, and as an example in public Forestry. This tract was, however, so inexcusably mishandled by the College (as I myself saw on the ground) that its appropriations were refused and the College was closed in 1903.

Also in 1897 the Biltmore Forest School, under Dr. C. A. Schenck, had offered a course of one year of theoretical and practical instruction. It had little academic standing and was discontinued in 1913.

We in the Division of Forestry fully recognized the necessity for professional education in Forestry in this country. But we had small confidence in the leadership of Dr. Fernow or Dr. Schenck. We distrusted them and their German lack of faith in American Forestry. What we wanted was American foresters trained by Americans in American ways for the work ahead in American forests.

Harry Graves and I talked it over at great length. Somehow the Division must have the trained foresters it needed. In the end we saw just one way out. Since the kind of forest school that would meet our need did not exist, such a school must be established. And Yale was the place for it. We were both enthusiastic Yale men.

After talking it over with my Father and Mother, it appeared that they also were enthusiastic about the plan, and that the Pinchot family could and would supply the funds to start the school. President Hadley of Yale likewise gave his hearty approval, and in the autumn of 1900 the Yale Forest School began. The first endowment from the Pinchots was in the sum of $150,000, later increased to $300,000.

We decided, I think very wisely, on a two-year postgraduate course in order to get the right type of men. As quarters for the school, the University provided the former home of Professor Othniel C. Marsh, famous paleontologist and president of the National Academy of Sciences. I still treasure the magnifying glass he gave a certain small boy.

Later on, a summer session for first-year students was opened at our place at Milford, Pennsylvania. My Father built Forest Hall in the village, a stone office near our home, a mess hall, and numerous wooden buildings for the Milford Summer School of Forestry.

Trained men were so vitally necessary that I was willing to let Graves and Toumey, who were the backbone of our little Division, leave it and go to Yale. Graves became the first Dean of the School. To his character, wisdom, and intelligence the high standard and achievement of the Yale School of Forestry were directly due.

Of the original endowment of the Yale Forest School Graves recently had this to say: "It is impossible to measure the significance of these gifts in the initiation and furtherance of Forestry in the United States." My Father and Mother would have been proud could they have heard him.

Toumey succeeded Graves as Dean when the latter took over the Forest Service in 1910. As for me, I became a member of the Governing Board and for a time gave lectures on forest organization, Government Forestry at home and abroad, and other topics, as one of the professors of the school. But I fear my service was far less than my title implied.

The Yale Forest School did what was expected of it. It supplied the men we needed in the early days. It furnished many of the leaders of the United States Forest Service. From 1905 to 1940 without a break, the heads of the Forest Service were founders or graduates of the Yale School.

For many years the Yale School set the standard for forest education in this country. The School also supplied many teachers for the new forest schools which soon began to spring up in large numbers throughout the country.

In 1900, when the academic year opened, the school at Cornell had an enrollment of twenty-four and Biltmore nine. Yale had seven. In 1946 we have some six thousand American-trained professional foresters in the United States.

28. *First Congressional Appropriation*

As that first year ended, thanks to Student Assistants, Collaborators, and others who did much work for the little we could pay them, and did it gladly, the new Division numbered five times more workers than at its beginning. We had been eleven. We were now sixty-one. And on the same appropriation.

But other years were to follow. After the new work in the woods had struck its gait, the first big hurdle to cross was the lack of funds. Our appropriation for the first year was fixed before I was appointed. But the Division was hungry for money enough in the second year to do the work that was demanded of it.

In its first ten years (1877-86) the appropriation for what was now the Division of Forestry had grown from $2,000 to $10,000. In the next ten years it grew to $33,520. Then it dropped back to $28,520, where I found it. In the ten years that followed, under the new policy of work in the woods, it multiplied more than a hundred times.

We could not begin to do the work demanded of us with only $28,520. So the Secretary approved my estimate for an increase to $69,920 in the fiscal year 1899-1900. But getting any such increase through the House and Senate was going to be something else again. And that was a job for which I was poorly equipped.

In spite of my title of Forester, I was nothing but a green young Division Chief. My personal way with Congress was yet to make. And legislation, and especially getting appropriations, is more largely personal than most people think.

Beyond those I had met through the National Forest Commission and its work, I knew few men of influence, and still less knew me. On the other hand, the new policies of the Division were undeniably making good, and the Government forest work was on its way as it never had been before. We had an argument, at least.

As I rode back and forth to the office on my bicycle, which was the common conveyance of those days, I could think of nothing but the appropriation. Would it be increased? Or wouldn't it? More money meant a chance to take the chance that was opening before us. No more meant a dangerous check.

When the hour came to appear before the House Committee on Agriculture, I was as twittery as a high school graduate just before his commencement oration. But I stood up and told my story as well as I knew how, with deep conviction of the need for Forestry, and entire faith in the plans I had for meeting it.

The members of the Committee asked a few questions, but I thought they seemed to show a lack of interest. Which was natural enough. To them the Division of Forestry was just another Division. To me it was the center of the world.

At that time the House Committee on Agriculture, and not the Committee on Appropriations, was responsible for the Agricultural Appropriation Bill. James W. Wadsworth of New York, its Chairman, was willing to help. He was one of the Geneseo Wadsworths, some of whom were my friends. He was also a man of real intelligence, deeply interested in farming, and ready to go as far as he could get his Committee to go with him in pushing Forestry ahead. Credit for the progress of the Division, and its successors, the Bureau of Forestry and the Forest Service, lies in no small part on his doorstep.

John Sharp Williams of Mississippi (afterward Senator), senior member on the Democratic side, was even more friendly. He was a spirited, cultivated, and particularly well-read Southern gentleman, who had great influence with the Committee and the House. He had lived much abroad, and when he found I could talk French with him he counted it to me for righteousness and backed me up on every possible occasion.

After the hearing was over Mr. Wadsworth wouldn't tell me what was going to happen. Perhaps he couldn't. I was on pins and needles for many days—could hardly have been more so if a jury had been weighing my case on a capital charge. And I shall never forget the enormous relief when the House Committee finally voted an increase to $48,520—an increase of $20,000 over the previous petrified sum.

But how about the Senate? Redfield Proctor of Vermont was Chairman of the Senate Committee on Agriculture and Forestry. I had no lines to him. But as it turned out, I had no better friend on the Hill, and no more effective one. He was a tall, powerful, slow-spoken, notably kindly New Englander of conspicuous ability, stick-to-itiveness, and common sense.

He was also a famous fisherman. To him, later on, I owed my membership in the Tobique Salmon Club, where I found that a 5-ounce trout rod was weapon enough. The best description of him I ever saw was a cartoon which showed him seated by a stream reading a treatise entitled *How to Get What You Go After,* but carefully keeping his hook in the water. Getting what he went after had grown to be a habit.

These House and Senate hearings, and others after them, taught me that the only way to deal with an appropriation committee, or any other committee of Congress, is to tell the whole story from the start. If a committee gets the impression that you are concealing anything, your goose is cooked. Conceal nothing, good or bad—better, have nothing to conceal. And if you don't know, say so.

And don't ask for an increase in your own salary. I asked for none in mine. Members of appropriation committees have two phobias—officials who try to get their pay raised, and bureau or cabinet chiefs who try to get more power just because they want more power.

To meet the charge of grasping for power I could show that the demands on the Division were many times greater than its present resources could possibly fill. It was a good defense as well as the spearpoint of my attack. Also the Committee knew that a pay increase meant little to me. That helped.

Senator Proctor's Committee went along with the House increase. So did the Senate, and it was ours. The new policy of working at Forestry, instead of merely talking about it, was making good with Congress as it had already made good in the woods.

That whole year I was seldom in any place more than three days together, and I suppose I must have been away from Washington a good half of it. I was still learning the United States. But the new ideas were on the job, and our attack on forest devastation gathered strength without a check.

It was remarkable how fast forest work in and out of the Government gravitated to the Division of Forestry once it had made known its decision to take to the woods.

The Commissioner of Indian Affairs asked for an examination and report on logging and on dead and down timber in the Chippewa Indian Reservation in Minnesota. I had to refuse for lack of men to do the work. The Commissioner of the General Land Office also wanted assistance in drawing the boundaries of Forest Reserves. That I could supply. But I could not meet the requests for help beyond our power to help which came in from local superintendents of Forest Reserves. In view of local hostilities, that they should ask for it was almost beyond belief.

Whenever and wherever I could I gave lectures and published articles. More important, in September 1899, the first edition of my little *Primer of Forestry,* Part I, was issued as a bulletin of the Division to the tune of 10,000 copies. It had taken me seven years from the time I started it to finish this minute volume, and it was going to take five years more to produce the second part. But to me it was worth the trouble for what the writing taught me, and it may have been also to others for what the reading taught them.

The book was well bound and well illustrated—a new thing in Department publications—and the Senate promptly ordered 35,000 copies more. The total circulation of the two volumes, as Farmers' Bulletins and otherwise, eventually ran to a total of 1,300,000 copies.

Far more important, however, than any publication was the good understanding the Division was establishing with the newspapers. They printed hundreds of millions of copies in a year, and their items about our work reached a thousand readers to our bulletins' one. Forestry was beginning to be news.

Likewise we were making Forestry into a real question not only with the newspapers but with the lumbermen, with the Congress, the Cabinet, and the President, and with the general public. "Practical Forestry in the woods, through which alone the forests can be saved" was coming into its own.

In another way the Division was in a strong position. There had been for years enough talk about Forestry to make many people familiar with the word. Now, when we had succeeded in giving that word a new meaning, had made it connote something practical, something the average man could get a grip on and go along with, it was easy to get public approval for what we were trying to do.

Furthermore, we were not in the way of principalities or powers, and we exercised no check on wickedness in high places. We had no control over the forest property of the Government, or of anybody else, except by the voluntary action of the owner. We could say "Please," but we couldn't say "Don't." We could say "Come on," but we could not say "Get out."

We had nothing that anybody was trying to get but ought not to have. We were dealing with ideas and keeping nobody from making dollars. No one had anything of great importance to gain from attacking us. What attacks we had to meet (and there were some) were not matters of life and death. Before the real offensive came we had time to dig in.

But the most important thing of all was that our work in the woods was proving out. Everywhere it was making good, and this year it was better done than the year before. To this day I don't see how on earth we did all this and all the rest on an appropriation of $48,520. The fact remains that we did.

The Division in 1899 was made up of four sections—Working Plans, Economic Tree Planting, Special Investigations, and Office Work. These Divisions were headed, when the year began, by Henry S. Graves, James W. Toumey, George B. Sudworth, and Otto J. J. Luebkert. In the distribution of responsibilities we were already well on the road away from the traditional red tape of those habit-bound days.

There being no one else to do it, editing the publications of the Division (such as I did not write myself) naturally fell to me. I did it at odd times—evenings, on railroad trains, wherever and whenever I could. Clear statement, orderly presentation, no repetitions, and short summaries at the beginning instead of at the end—those were my targets. Editing was a real job.

In the midst of forty other kinds of work, I made every chance I could, and took every chance that came, to work at the Forest Reserves. I made a plan for their management and got it signed by Secretary Wilson, which was easy, but not by Secretary Hitchcock, which would have made it effective. I wrote up examination papers for Forest Rangers on the Reserves and got them approved by Chairman Procter of the Civil Service Commission, but again not by the Interior Department. Too many Congressmen had jobs for too many of their deadhead friends.

That winter, 1899-1900, in the midst of all this work, I found time for a vigorous campaign to transfer the Forest Reserves to the Department of Agriculture—a campaign that was to last for years.

Allison of Iowa, leader of the Senate; Proctor of Vermont, highly respected, and a real friend of mine; Foster of Washington, thanks to whom the St. Paul and Tacoma Lumber Company was co-operating in a study of the Red Fir; Hale of Maine; Wetmore of Rhode Island, who was considering a working plan for timberlands in another state; Warren of Wyoming; Heitfeldt of Idaho; and a number of other Senators took my view and were more or less strongly for the transfer.

So was my friend Congressman James W. Wadsworth, father of a son elected both Senator and Congressman. But Joseph G. Cannon, leader of the House, was vigorously against it. Uncle Joe had some utter incompetents on the Forest Reserve pay roll and knew it. Anyway, from my point of view Uncle Joe was usually wrong.

Secretary Wilson was for the transfer, of course. After some argument so was Secretary Hitchcock, in spite of the best that Binger Hermann, Commissioner of the General Land Office, could do to prevent it. Early in 1900 the question grew large enough to command the personal attention of President McKinley himself.

The position of the White House was that it was for the transfer but would not press it against determined opposition. Determined opposition did develop. Clark of Wyoming, Shoup of Idaho, and others were set wrong. The patronage question in the light of the coming election doubtless had something to do with it. Moreover, the Western Senators had long been in the habit of getting from the Land Office pretty much everything they wanted for their friends. The Department of Agriculture might be less biddable.

In February of 1900 it became evident that my pet project was dead for that year. But for that year only.

When I reported the demise to Secretary Wilson, he advised going after a bigger appropriation. We went after it. We couldn't do the work we were asked to do, or keep up the pace Forestry had struck, without more men in the field, more people in the office. Congress had to be made to see the point, and Congress saw it.

Public interest in Forestry was more than keeping pace with the work in the woods. The number of letters people write to a Government office is a good way to tell how much they are thinking about it and about its work. During the first year the correspondence of the Division doubled. The second year it doubled again. Correspondence, however, tells but a small part of the story.

Taking public and private forests together, toward the end of 1899 examinations on the ground had been made of two million acres. Conservative lumbering was in sight in nearly three-quarters of the states and territories, and for nearly a million and a half acres plans for it were actually begun. The owners of a million more acres asked us to help them keep their timberlands producing wood. Twice the men we had and twice the money could not have compassed anything like all the work they wanted us to do.

At the end of the second twelvemonth, on July 1, 1900, we of the Division numbered 123. The original 11 had multiplied 11 times, with 2 to carry, and our appropriation was $88,520. Our work was going like a house afire. Two years of brass tacks instead of brass lungs—Forestry in the woods instead of propaganda from the office—had put the Division on the map.

The Division was still a little organization, a very little one. But not for us who ate and drank and lived it day and night. For us it was the pivot of the earth and the main current of the stream of time, with all the surge and thunder of the Odyssey.

During the field season of 1900 we were able to put into the field nine parties, all told. Four studied commercial trees, four made working plans, and one planting plans. With them our hands were full.

On July 1, 1901, the Division was promoted. It became the Bureau of Forestry, with a membership of 179 and an appropriation of $185,440.

The readiness with which Congress increased our appropriations was the best evidence that Forestry had proved its importance. The members of the new Bureau could look over their work with real satisfaction. Field work went on all over the country, from Maine to California and from Georgia to Washington. The greatest achievement of the Division was that it had succeeded in turning practical Forestry in the United States from a hopeful experiment into an assured success.

Much progress had been made in giving advice to forest owners in the management of their lands on the principles of practical Forestry. During the life of the Division private owners of some three million acres applied for this advice, which in every case required personal examination on the ground. About 177,000 acres had been put under management.

The greatest demand came from the Department of the Interior of the National Government, which wanted working plans for all the Forest Reserves. Out of what was to us the enormous area of forty-seven million acres, the Division had made a working plan for the Black Hills National Forest Reserve. Several state governments also had applied for help and a working plan for Township 40 in the New York State Forest Preserve had been completed.

Our war had many fronts. My first great purpose was to start practical Forestry going in the woods. My second, to get all Government forest work together in one place, was never out of mind. We lost no time in laying pipe for the transfer of the Forest Reserves to the Department of Agriculture, and we kept at it. In December 1898, the National Board of Trade passed resolutions recommending it. So did the American Forestry Association, that year, the next, and the two next. And so did a long succession of local and national associations until the transfer came to pass in 1905. But many things were to happen before then.

Meanwhile we kept stirring up interest in Forestry among as many people with as many different interests as possible as nearly all over the country as our microscopic funds would reach. We did just that, and interest did spread. Even the National Academy of Sciences was willing to listen to me tell it what the Division had been doing.

Unquestionably our attack was succeeding. But success does not always make friends. The new Division was breaking tradition and forcing people to think. There is no better way to make enemies. And it made plenty for us, both in the Department and outside.

There was contention galore from the start, although on no great scale. Controversies became as common as hen's eggs. If we had depended on foresters alone to meet them, our victories would have been as scarce as hen's teeth. But as our work became known it raised up friends at least as fast as foes, in Congress and out. We were on our way.

29. *Politics in the Woods*

Things were going so well as my second year in the Division began that I could spend most of July and August (1899) in the West. For one thing, I was eager to learn the public-land situation on the ground. As to the Forest Reserves, I was still more eager to go into them, get to know them, and fit myself to handle them when the time came.

The letter of the public-land laws seemed to me on the whole to be wise and right. They were intended to help the small man make a living for himself and his family, and to develop the country. Lincoln's Homestead Act, the Desert Land Act, the Timber and Stone Act, the Mining Acts, etc., were aimed, theoretically at least, in the right direction.

Although written from the standpoint of Eastern men who knew little of the West, in purpose they were generally sound. In the long run it was the East that saved the Western lands for the Western settlers. In practice, thanks to lax, stupid, and wrongheaded administration by the Interior Department, the land laws were easily twisted to the advantage of the big fellows, and Western opinion was satisfied to have it so.

That summer I saw new country and made new contacts, but what helped most was what I learned about the management of the Reserves by the Interior Department and how it affected the people who lived in them and by them.

The management was awful. Division P of the General Land Office at Washington, to which the Department had given the Reserves in charge, knew literally nothing about them or what ought to be done with them. At that time not one man in Division P had ever set foot in a Forest Reserve or had even seen one Forest Reserve tree, unless perhaps from a Pullman car window.

The abysmal ignorance of the Washington office about conditions on the ground was outrageous, pathetic, or comic, whichever you like. Division P ordered one Supervisor to buy a rake for himself and another for his Ranger and rake up the dead wood on the Washington Forest Reserve—a front yard of a mere three and a half million acres, where the fallen trees were often longer than a city block and too thick for a man to see over. And that was no case by itself. Another Supervisor got a similar order for the Lewis and Clarke Reserve. But that was only three million acres.

Said Major F. A. Fenn, a veteran of the Spanish War, who became one of the very best forest officers the West has produced:

"For an officer in the field to question the policy outlined in the regulations on any point no matter how trivial, or to suggest that a change in regulation would be beneficial to the Service or conducive to better administration, was almost equivalent to religious heresy." And when out of his practical experience Major Fenn ventured to suggest certain changes in the regulations, he got this reply: "It is the duty of forest officers to obey their instructions and not to question them."

But if Washington knew nothing about the forests, it did know paper work, politics, and patronage, and the greatest of these was patronage.

Since jobs on the Forest Reserves were for distribution to politicians, Commissioner Binger Hermann of the General Land Office was careful to get his while the getting was good. The average appointee was plenty bad enough, but Binger's personal appointments were horrible. My notes made in the West at the time describe them in the quotations which follow.

One of Binger's brothers-in-law was "an old man absolutely worthless in his position." Another brother-in-law was "ignorant. General report makes him incompetent, and in league with the sheepmen," who were running their herds, legally or illegally, on the Forest Reserves. A third brother-in-law, "an ideally unfit man. Utterly useless in every way," was a Special Agent to report on the Grand Canyon Forest Reserve. He tried to have Gannett and then Fernow and Coville write his report for him. A nephew of Binger, sent from Oregon to handle Reserves in Arizona, and "of very little account," succeeded his father, Binger's brother, "of still less account," who was burned to death by the upsetting of a lamp. The family, you perceive, held on to the job. A son-in-law was a Special Agent. Since my notes make no comment on him, we might hope for the best, except that he was on duty in his and Binger's home town of Roseburg, Oregon, where there were neither forests nor public lands.

Another Roseburg man, an elderly man who had been cashier in a bank, was a close friend of the Commissioner. He frankly admitted he had no knowledge of forest conditions and didn't know one tree from another. But Binger made him Forest Inspector, the most important and responsible post of all.

Other appointees from Oregon ranged from "incompetent but better than the average" to "no good." One man my notes described as "active and energetic" and as "ignorant and worthless," both of which might well have been true. I've known it to happen.

Secretary Bliss had a relative on the force. He came from New Jersey, had once been a preacher, and had compiled two little volumes on the trees and shrubs of Northeastern America, all of which would naturally qualify him to take charge of a Forest Reserve in California, where he was stationed. He was a timid little man, as unable to deal with Sierra Nevada mountaineers as he was to travel the mountains. His explorations went as far as the stage went, and stopped right there. When I saw him he wore a white lawn tie and a shawl around his shoulders.

Political appointees, many of whom had never even seen a Western forest, were sent thousands of miles from all over the Union to handle Western Forest Reserves. Pennsylvania supplied a man for California. So did Michigan. Maryland sent one to Arizona. The Supervisor in South Dakota, "almost purely a politician. Utterly without experience," came from Indiana. Connecticut furnished to Washington State "a perfectly worthless young man."

Moreover, in addition to those who were no good whatever and those who might have been good under good leadership, some were crooks—"altogether a bad egg," "many charges filed against him," "blackmailer," etc.

Influential members of House and Senate shared the loot. Joe Cannon of Illinois had a man named Buntain, "an invalid, incapable and ineffective." He was given charge of Reserves in Arizona and New Mexico. Buntain was in the last stages of consumption. Another of

Uncle Joe Cannon's men was a one-lunger with one leg. When Buntain resigned, another of Uncle Joe's men took his place. This man "made the Forest Reserve a sort of private benevolence, recommending the appointment of many consumptives who had gone to Santa Fe for their health."

To such an extent was the appointment of invalids carried by the Washington office that at one time the Supervisor of the San Francisco Mountains Reserve reported that more than half of his force were unable to perform the ordinary duties of a Ranger.

Two political Supervisors, also in Arizona, indulged in the cheerful but illegal practice of charging a fee for preparing timber sale applications. To them Washington had given conflicting jurisdictions. These rivals not only beat each other up but went around armed, with the laudable intention of killing each other off. Unfortunately nothing came of it.

Men appointed from Western states were not much better than the Eastern incapables. One of them, "utterly useless. Largely responsible for bad work in Black Hills," had Senator Warren and the rest of the Wyoming delegation behind him.

Tom Carter of Montana, a Senator of great influence in public-land matters, and no chicken himself, got a job for his father in Colorado. The ancient, "too old to be of any use," was said to be eighty-two. J. B. Collins, on the other hand, who was Carter's secretary when he was Commissioner of the General Land Office, was "doing excellent work."

Here and there, of course, a good man did get in. Secretary Wilson and Senator Allison recommended B. F. Allen. He was the "best Superintendent in the service," in spite of the fact that he came from Iowa and was sent to Southern California. A Superintendent had several Supervisors under him.

Like Allen, most of the Supervisors were strange to the country they were sent to, and without knowledge of forests anywhere. Also, they had so many papers to attend to and so little help in the office that they were kept indoors just when supervision was most needed in the field. Red tape was doing its perfect work.

Good men like Allen in the better-paid places were scarce, because those jobs were worth going after. Good men among the Rangers were scarce too, not only because of politics, but also because work in the woods was worth \$3 a day, and a good man could get it whenever he chose. But a Ranger had to furnish his own horse and feed himself on the munificent salary of $60 a month.

Lest you should think I have been carried away by prejudice, listen again to the testimony of Major Fenn, universally respected, whose word is beyond impeachment. In 1900 Major Fenn was Chairman of the Idaho Republican State Central Committee. He said:

"Among all the vexatious matters brought to the attention of the Committee, none was more troublesome than the Forest Reserves. Not only was the administration of the Reserves a reproach to good government but the personnel of the Service was such as to disgust the better elements of the people, particularly respectable Republicans jealous of the good name of their party."

Of himself Fenn said: "I went into the forest work primarily to do what I could to labor for cleaner methods in a service which up to that time, at least in Idaho, had been a political catchall into which was cast whatever discarded baggage the dominant party could not deposit elsewhere. The Forest Reserve Service was purely political."

In return for Fenn's good work as Republican State Chairman, Senator Shoup offered him a judgeship in the Philippines at $5,000 a year.

"I promptly told him there was just one place I would accept, that of Forest Superintendent then held by Glendenning, and that I wanted the position for the purpose of proving to the people that the administration of the Reserves could be made respectable and that the Forest Reserve policy of the Republican Party was politically advisable and nationally beneficial."

Glendenning, said Fenn, "was a confirmed drunkard who died of acute alcoholism. He charged and collected $100 as a fee for each of two free-use timber permits, and collected $10 a month from his Rangers out of their meager $60."

When a petition was made by one Gummaer for the elimination of certain townships (rich in timber) from the Priest River Reserve, Glendenning was sent to make an examination on the ground. "During his entire trip that time," said Fenn, "he did not once see any part of the Reserve, but accepted Gummaer's maps and estimates as final, and sent in a bill of $400 for expenses.

"It turned out that the entire bill was due from Glendenning to a man named Jackson, a saloonkeeper, who had furnished champagne and similar necessaries to Glendenning while at Gummaer's house."

Superintendent Glendenning had two Supervisors on the Bitterroot Reserve. One of them "conducted a saloon and although it was notorious that he never was on his Reserve but once during the time he held office, his service reports showed that he regularly 'patrolled out and looked over the Reserve.' As a fact he walked out with scrupulous regularity from the interior of his saloon to the front porch thereof and from that observation point 'looked over' his Reserve, which was in plain view from there."

The reports of the other Supervisor, which were "models in form and elegant chirography, showed the Supervisor most zealous in patrolling his territory 'with saddle horse and pack horse,' for which he was allowed $1.00 a day each when in actual use. What he actually used them for was delivering beef for a butcher," for which he was paid $2.50 per day.

"But it was among the Rangers," went on Major Fenn, "that we had the most striking examples of official inefficiency. Ranger Anderson of Kooskia, later of Stites, Idaho, was a veterinarian, and while he was in the Service regularly drawing $60 per month he did not leave his business and never saw the Reserve. Ranger Beaudette, a jeweler and watch tinker of Kooskia, was Anderson's twin brother so far as the Forest Reserve work was concerned. Ranger Malcolm Glendenning, a son of the Superintendent, pulled down $60 a month from Uncle Sam without interfering with his duties as bookkeeper for Charles Sweeney at a salary of $125 a month at Concord, Idaho."

Out of twenty-five men on the Idaho Reserves when Fenn took charge, twenty-two were unfit, and only three were good enough to keep.

I realize that these details of incompetence and corruption do not make pleasant reading. But they are true, they form an essential part of the story of Forestry in America, and without them much that follows would not be easy to understand.

The orders sent from the chair-warming red-tape worshipers in Washington to the field men were even more incompetent than the men in the field. One such order prevented a Forest Ranger from leaving his District to fight a forest fire over the line. Reports which came to me were full of cases of Rangers found loafing in town or at home while fires were burning on their Districts.

Incompetent Supervisors made bad assignments of Rangers, so that it was often impossible for a Ranger to cover his District, or even to know just what his District was. Under such conditions any Ranger who was not deeply interested in his work did just as little as he could. As a rule the Rangers cut no trails and did no work of any other kind. And here and there a Ranger, originally decent, capable, and industrious, who would have given fine service had it been required of him, went wrong simply because he followed his leader, and his leader was a crook set over him by the spoils system.

When a good man did get in and tried to do his work, the political job holders naturally banded against him and ran him out if they could. He was setting a bad example. Many a worthless Supervisor ordered his Ranger to hold trespassers to strict account, and then notified the trespassers that he had told the Ranger the exact opposite. In the Battlement Mesa Forest Reserve the Supervisor told squatters to drive Rangers off with guns, if they came to interfere with illegal possession of Government land.

One Supervisor's excuse for not pushing a trespass case was that he believed "some of the mill crews would vote right when it came time for election." Trespass cases were frequently canceled for political reasons.

Being mostly city men, the political forest officers stayed in town and out of the woods all they could. The Supervisor of the San Bernardino Forest Reserve, a relative of the famous Mark Hanna (to whom he owed his appointment), spoke his mind to Jim Toumey to the following effect:

"It is far more sensible for me to stay here at the hotel than it would be to go into the mountains. If a fire should break out I can see it at once unless it should be on the other side and the woods over there are of no account anyway. So I stay here where I can have ice and get the news of the outside world." What went with the ice I don't have to tell you.

Take it by and large, the Interior Department's field force on the Forest Reserves was enough to make angels weep. Naturally it aroused strong opposition to the whole Reserve system. However lightly the Western men of those days may have held the land laws, they had high standards of personal courage and hardiness, and they were not lazy. Such men could have nothing but contempt for a service manned by the human rubbish which the Interior Department had cheerfully accepted out of Eastern and Western political scrap heaps and dumped into the Forest Reserves.

Under the Act of June 4, 1897, the Department of the Interior was authorized to make rules and regulations for the use and protection of the Forest Reserves. The first set of these regulations issued through the General Land Office and dated June 30, 1897, was prepared by men familiar with paper work but utterly without experience of Forestry and the woods. They were, of course, impracticable and unworkable. In full accord with Land Office custom, they required local decisions to be made in Washington instead of in the field, and they clogged the use of the Reserves with heavy brakes of red tape.

But even so, they did take the Reserves out of quarantine and open them to use, and that was an immense step in the right direction. Thus they cured, in part at least, the worst complaint the Western people had against the Reserves and brought them much-needed support.

Under these regulations responsible persons might submit petitions for the sale of timber from the Reserves. The petitions must state, among other things, "whether or not the removal of the timber would result injuriously to the objects of forest reservation"—certainly a strange question to put up to Western men or companies if anything more was wanted than a show of compliance with the law.

But this was only a start. If there was any dead timber, the petitioner must "estimate the quantity, in feet, board measure, with the value, and state whether killed by fire or other causes." As to live timber, he was to state the different kinds and estimated quantities of each per acre (in other words, furnish a cruise) and the estimated average diameter of each kind. He was also to estimate the number of trees of each kind per acre above the average diameter and state how many of these the petitioner wanted to buy, their board-foot contents, and their stumpage value.

And again this was only a start. For the regulations required that "before any sale is authorized, the timber will be examined and appraised, and other questions duly investigated, by an official designated for the purpose; and upon his report action will be based." This action had to be taken in Washington.

If after due consideration Washington approved the sale, it had to be advertised for not less than sixty days in a local paper. Then bids must be submitted and sent to Washington for another period of incubation, after which, if any bid was approved in whole or in part a certificate of acceptance was issued by the Commissioner of the

General Land Office. This certificate the bidder must present, after it finally reached him, "to the receiver of public moneys for the land district in which the timber stands," and to him make payment in full within thirty days after notice of the award.

But even then, with the receipt for the stumpage price in hand, cutting could not begin. "Sixty days' notice must be given through the local land office, to the Commissioner of the General Land Office [in Washington] of the proposed date of cutting and removal of the timber, so that an official may be designated to supervise such cutting and removal, as required by law."

If the purchaser needed a sawmill to cut his timber, he must get a temporary permit from the Commissioner of the General Land Office, by whom it "may be granted if not incompatible with the public interests. Thereafter instructions as to disposition of tops, brush, and refuse, to be given through the supervisors in each case, must be strictly complied with, as a condition of said cutting and manufacture." Which would have been all right if the Supervisors had known their business.

If the persevering purchaser survived the foregoing, he must still conform to special instructions "issued for the guidance of officials designated to examine and appraise timber, to supervise its cutting and removal, and for carrying out other requirements connected therewith." Red tape, fed fat on ignorance, was doing its perfect work.

And please note—in all this welter of procrastination, the one thing conspicuously lacking was any provision for perpetuating the forest —for the practice of Forestry on the Forest Reserves.

The reason why the bloated routine you have been following left the Western timber user comparatively cold was obvious. He had neither expectation nor intention of following the Land Office regulations on the ground. Once the papers were signed, the purchaser, as a very general rule, did as he chose, and the devil take the forest.

These regulations were no accident. As time went on they got worse instead of better. Those of April 1900, nearly three years after the first set, required the purchaser of green matured timber to show "on what evidence it is asserted that the trees have attained their full growth [and] that their removal will tend to promote the life and growth of the younger trees." He must also describe the timber as standing green; down not dead; standing dead; and down dead; and tell whether dead timber was killed by fire, windfall, or other cause.

Furthermore, the proposed timber sale must now have the approval of an additional official, the Forest Superintendent, who must send the papers to the Commissioner, and "the Commissioner will then transmit the application, with report and recommendation, to the Secretary of the Interior for action"—to Secretary Hitchcock, who had come to understand that Binger Hermann and his merry men could not be trusted.

This domination of a densely ignorant office over a politically chosen field force did to the forest what you might expect. The Forest Reserves will bear the scars of Interior Department mishandling for generations yet to come. Mistakes can do more harm in a forest than almost anywhere else. A blunder made in a day may take a hundred years to correct.

Apart from the general contempt for the Interior Department's field and office men, public sentiment about the Forest Reserves varied according to the occupations of the people. Irrigated regions were friendly, and California in particular was always the staunch friend of Forestry. I found it so when I reached San Francisco in August of 1899. Here was an open door.

California coast Redwoods are among the most majestic trees on earth. One of them is said to be the tallest tree in the world—364 feet. But little or nothing was known about them as a forester knows trees. So at once I got in touch with the San Francisco Chamber of Commerce, and through it with the Redwood lumbermen. To them I pointed out their need to know more about the growth and reproduction of the Redwood. They agreed. But the Division had no money to do the work.

So the Redwood Association voted to contribute $1,000 to the Division toward a study of the growth and reproduction of their splendid tree. It was the first money ever given by a group of American lumbermen for the progress of Forestry. A great step forward, for which Captain Robert Dollar, of the Dollar Steamship Company, was mainly responsible.

The Big Trees of the Sierras, first cousins to the Redwoods of the coast, are even bigger and even more beautiful than they are huge. They are the grandest of living things.

Many groves of the Big Trees (Sequoias) had passed into private hands and were being cut down, and others were threatened with rapid destruction. The Senate Committee on Public Lands had asked the Division for information about them. So with John Muir and Hart Merriam, head of the Biological Survey, I made a memorable trip to the Calaveras Grove.

If a university could be defined as a log with Mark Hopkins at one end and a student at the other, certainly this little journey was for me in the nature of a liberal education. Never were two more delightful talkers than Muir and Merriam, or with a richer fund of experience to talk about. They had camped and adventured all over the West from Alaska to Mexico; they had seen what they looked at; and they were full of facts I needed in my business.

I could have sat in the front seat of our wagon and listened to them for weeks, while the dust boiled up from the road till it actually hid the front wheel, almost within reach of my hand. There was dust as was dust in the rainless Western summers before anybody ever thought of laying it with oil.

My trip, however, was of little moment compared to the study of the Big Trees made for the Division by Professor William R. Dudley of Stanford University. Dudley was a tower of strength in all forest matters on the Coast, and his report gave the Division a little of the standing it needed with the Senate Committee on Public Lands. That highly important body would have much to say about the proposed transfer of the Forest Reserves.

Another trip I meant to make that summer never came off. I planned to go into the woods with W. T. Radir of Oregon, one of the earliest men in the West to grasp the idea of practical Forestry. He was a land speculator, openly ready to take advantage of the land laws. He was bold, he was able, and he filled me with the pleasant horror a small boy feels about the big bad wolf.

Said Radir to Coville: "You can't tell me anything about the General Land Office. I know just where to go in the General Land Office to get any rotten scheme through." But he was loyal to his friends and upright according to his lights—a perfect example of the going Western attitude toward the Public Domain. I liked him very much, and he was very nearly the cause of my finish.

Radir and I had arranged to look over together certain timberlands in western Oregon, with the idea of practical forest management. But when the time came, something, Government business or whatever, kept me from going with him. Radir went anyhow.

A week or two later he and the other four men of his party were found dead, scattered along the trail for miles. They are supposed to have eaten poisonous canned meat. If I had gone there would have been six dead men instead of five.

30. *The Black Hills*

Soon after I got back to Washington from the West, late in the summer of '99, came a great piece of luck. It came in this wise. Hiram H. Jones, a red-headed young man in the General Land Office, you may remember, had helped Hague and Pinchot prepare their report of May 1896, to the National Forest Commission. He was in fact, though not in title, in charge of the national Forest Reserves. For that reason I had made it my business to keep in touch with him. In the end, holding the hand of Hiram bore good and abundant fruit.

On August 31, 1899, W. A. Richards, Acting Commissioner of the General Land Office, wrote to the Secretary of the Interior recommending that "the said Division of Forestry be requested to favor this office with comprehensive reports upon expert investigations of all related [forest] questions; which shall extend to including a suggested working plan for the harvesting of timber in each of the existing reserves." That letter had H.H.J. in the upper right-hand corner.

Recognition that the Division knew more about the Forest Reserves than the Land Office wasn't control of them by any means. Still it was on the straight road to control. But the main question was how the Secretary of the Interior would react to the Acting Commissioner's recommendation.

Ethan Allen Hitchcock, successor to Cornelius N. Bliss, was a high-minded gentleman with the very best intentions in the world. If you knew him you had to respect him. But he was far from a Heaven-born executive, although he did not, as one of my loving friends of later years once said of me, "rattle around in his job like a shingle nail in a milk can." However much he may have shone as the first American Ambassador to Russia, Government work at home was not his forte.

It took Secretary Hitchcock the months of September, October,

November, and until December 7, 1899, to make up his mind. On that date he transmitted Richards' request for help to the Secretary of Agriculture, "for the good of the forestry service [in the Land Office], if the convenience of your Department will admit of it."

With a note from Secretary Wilson, "Mr. Pinchot, what do you think of this?" Hitchcock's letter came to me. What I thought of it did not take three months to formulate. In a careful letter of December 11 I set forth that, in my opinion, the convenience of Tama Jim's Department most emphatically did admit of doing just what Hitchcock asked. And Tama Jim agreed.

The play had been Pinchot to Jones to Richards to Hitchcock to Wilson to Pinchot. Who would be put out remained to be seen.

Welcome as it was, this new work was not to be entered into lightly or inadvisedly. So I pointed out that the execution of working plans required trained men no less than the making of them, and I suggested four conditions—expenses to be divided, copies of Forest Reserve maps to be furnished, lists of applications for timber to be supplied, and the co-operation of forest officers to be assured.

From and after the time of Hitchcock's letter to Wilson the Division had its hand on every question which affected the Reserves. If we could not get the whole loaf of forest administration, we were anxious to take half a loaf, eager for a slice, pleased to get even a crumb. It was all water on the wheel of the transfer.

Here was the chance to shape the Government's policy in dealing with the Reserves. Here was a step toward the beginning of Forestry upon them. That was something accomplished, something done, to earn a night's repose.

With our little force it was out of the question to do more than make a start on the forty-odd millions of acres of Forest Reserves. But that start must not be delayed. We decided to begin with the Black Hills Forest Reserve, which lay mainly in South Dakota.

The Black Hills, named for their dark forest of Western Yellow Pine, cover an area about the size of Connecticut. A wooded island amid vast treeless plains, the timber of this Reserve was more in demand than that of all the others put together. That was because the Hills had a population of twenty-five to thirty thousand people, who by this time were almost solidly behind the Reserve. They had also good railroad facilities, and an annual production from mining of about $4,000,000 a year.

The Black Hills forest had been burned, and burned again, before and since the white men drove the Sioux Indians out. Except for these fires, the reproduction of the forest would have been sufficient to secure its future. And that was of the first importance to the future also of gold mining, for which the Black Hills were famous the world around.

The mining laws of that day gave even the largest and most prosperous mining outfits an almost unlimited right to cut, free and for nothing, whatever timber they needed from public land. And any right they did not have they usually took, regardless.

First among the mining outfits of the Black Hills was the Homestake Mining Company. It was said to have paid larger dividends than any other gold mine in the world; it employed about 2,000 men; and its monthly pay roll was over $200,000.

After long negotiations with Secretary Bliss, the Homestake people had not only withdrawn their opposition to the Black Hills Forest Reserve, but had agreed to buy from the Government the timber they needed for their mines.

The sale to the Homestake was the first sale of Forest Reserve timber made by the General Land Office. It was known as Case 1; it was for fifteen million board feet at a dollar a thousand; and all the Forestry there was in the contract was a diameter limit of eight inches, which was far too small, and a requirement to pile the brush and cut the tops into cordwood.

Although the Land Office had had charge of the Reserves for more than two years, that was the best it could do. Its duty, under the law, was to handle the Reserves "to furnish a continuous supply of timber for the use and necessities of citizens of the United States," but it was as blissfully ignorant of how to sell stumpage on the Reserves as though Forestry had never been heard of.

Binger Hermann, in his report of 1897, had declared that the Land Office was fully competent to deal with the "question of the preservation of the forests of the United States." This he held to be "the most important matter at present demanding the consideration of this Office." Yet the Land Office was not only incompetent to deal with it, but it understood too little about Forestry even to know that it was incompetent.

Under such conditions, it is not surprising that the Homestake sale, after the manner of the Land Office, dragged along for eighteen months, or until late in 1899. Meanwhile the Homestake had to have timber or shut down.

On the other hand, the Homestake was playing fair. It was willing to cut so as to provide for the future. It was willing also to pay for its stumpage instead of getting it free. Yet the Land Office took a year and a half to allow it to pay, and then the Government sued the Homestake for the timber it had to have to keep on working while waiting for the Land Office to act—sued it for a penalty price of nearly six times the going stumpage rate.

One reason for so much theft of public timber in those days was the heavy punishment inflicted on honesty by Land Office red tape.

Early in January 1900, I sent Edward M. Griffith, a partly trained forester like myself, to the Black Hills to make ready for field work. On May 1 the Black Hills working plan party of Student Assistants under his direction left the town of Spearfish for the Potato Gulch District. It was a fine collection of spirited young colts, some college boys, some farm boys, some neither. Nearly all were green, nearly all enthusiastic, rejoicing in a hard life in the open and in strenuous physical work. Most of them were destined to make successful foresters and leaders.

Because this was the first Forest Reserve working plan, their names deserve to be set down. Under Griffith were R. E. Benedict, A. E. Cohoon, Hugh M. Curran, Coert DuBois, Wesley J. Gardner, William C. Hodge, Jr., Richard P. Imes, W. H. B. Kent, Smith Riley, and two others who turned out to be unsuited for Forestry. Said Riley, "The standards were high from the very first, therefore the weeding out process had not been slow."

The Black Hills working plan was finished but never printed. The only existing copy is incomplete. It contains, for example, nothing about the duties of the Rangers, although several references show that a Ranger system was actually recommended. That there were Rangers in the Black Hills appears from the fact that one of them was fired for turning over his marking hatchet to the lumbermen who were cutting the timber.

Griffith's plan was necessarily rough and incomplete. It did not provide for sustained yield, and in that it was right. Sustained yield would come later. At the moment, other questions were far more pressing. We had first to save the forests from immediate destruction.

The two outstanding immediate problems were fire and bark beetles. Fire was fairly under control. Griffith reported that the season was extremely dry, but "the forest force and the settlers were all unusually cautious, and checked the forest fires at the very start."

The other enemy to the trees, far worse in the Black Hills than fire, was a little beetle, about the size of a grape seed, that dug little galleries between the wood and the bark, and laid its eggs in them. On the basis of actual measurement, Griffith's estimate was that 1,950 feet per acre, board measure, had been "bug killed" on 116,000 acres, which added up to more than 225,000,000 board feet. And even that was not the whole story.

This pernicious insect was known to thousands but then unknown to science. Dr. A. D. Hopkins of the Bureau of Entomology at our request studied it, named it *Dendroctonus ponderosa Hopkins,* and helped us to fight it. It was going to be a hard fight.

Griffith's rules for marking were satisfactory, and so were his rules for cutting, with one significant exception. They provided a heavy penalty for cutting unmarked trees, but they contained practically no directions for saving young growth. Why? I give it up. After all, if the copy we have of his working plan was the final copy, it must have had my approval. In that case I also was to blame.

The Griffith working plan had no immediate effect in changing the cutting practices on the Black Hills Forest Reserve. Nevertheless the indirect result was decidedly good. Better acquaintance with the Forest Reserves and how they were administered began to bear tangible fruit. Take, for example, what happened in the Black Hills the season following our work, and the light it throws on how timber sales were being handled by the Land Office.

As a result of a report made by a Forest Ranger and of my own investigation on the ground, it was discovered that in a timber sale for fifteen million feet the terms of the permit were systematically disregarded. All tops were left unlopped, leaving a perfect fire trap. Trees to be cut were not marked at all. Many logs were unscaled and presumably unpaid for. There was no effective inspection whatever. I brought the facts to the attention of the Secretary of Agriculture, who in turn reported them to the Secretary of the Interior. As a result my recommendations to remedy the situation were eventually carried out, although unfortunately not without great regard for the interests of the offenders. This case (known as the Leppla-McLaughlin case) was typically Land Office except for this—that it was shown up and in the end something was done about it.

31. *Not All Sheep Are Black*

The most ticklish question Secretary Hitchcock had asked our advice about in 1899 was grazing. I was already in touch with the Western sheepmen and irrigators, and I knew it would be a hard nut to crack.

Grazing was the bloody angle, and obviously was to be for years. It was the most important use that had yet been made of the Forest Reserves, and the center of the bitterest controversy.

The woolgrowers were the best-organized interest in the West. When grazing in the Forest Reserves was shut off by order of the Secretary of the Interior in 1897, they raised the West in arms.

The Interior Department asserted that sheep grazing destroyed the forests. Sheepmen contended it did nothing of the kind. Politicians supported the sheepmen. Irrigators supported the Department. Altogether, here were the makings of a high old scrap.

The irrigation ranchers of the Salt River Valley, in Arizona, claimed that sheep grazing on the higher land of the Black Mesa Forest Reserve was responsible for a serious shortage in their water supply. The Arizona Woolgrowers' Association said that was pure bunk.

The quarrel led to an agreement that Frederick V. Coville, Botanist of the Department of Agriculture, and I, with a representative of the irrigators and a representative of the sheepmen, should investigate the question on the ground. Coville was the man who had made (in Oregon) the first study of the effect of Western sheep grazing on the forest, and thereby laid the foundation for grazing control. It would have been impossible to find a better man.

On May 28, 1900, with Albert F. Potter, Secretary of the Eastern Division of the Arizona Woolgrowers' Association, and Professor E. C. (Con) Bunch, of the Salt River Valley Water Users Association, Coville and I left Winslow, Arizona, and put in three weeks that made history for the grazing industry of the West. We had a saddle horse apiece and a chuck wagon, with Alex Nichols as driver and cook.

It was sixty miles from Winslow across the desert to the Mogollon Mesa, the country we were going to examine. On the way our canteens and our water keg gave out, and the only water we came across was a tank, a stagnant pool of terrible green water. Sticking out of it were the horns of rotting carcasses of cattle that had waded in and drunk till they bogged down and died. Other details I omit. We had to drink it or go dry.

I strongly suspected at the time that Potter deliberately set up this test of toughness for us Eastern tenderfeet. But whether he did or not, Coville and I passed it in good shape, although the water was so rank that in camp at nightfall its taste completely hid the taste of strong tea. Why it wasn't poison I don't know. In the desert such corruption seems to be harmless.

The names of the places we saw pretty well tell the story of the trip. Moki Spring, Mud Lake, Lost Camp, Ojo Dan, Show Low, Fishing Camp, Horseshoe, Cienaga, Black Mesa, Thomas Peak, Boneyard, Luna, Blue River, Cannon. It was just as good as it sounds.

Wherever we went Potter had friends, and most of his friends ran sheep. Time and time again they turned over the fattest lamb of the flock. I never ate anything better (except a chop from a fat Bighorn) and never expect to, than that young mutton, cooked a little, and only a very little, on an iron plate thrown on top of the fire.

The Basque and Mexican sheepherders lived on mutton too, but they cut it in small pieces, fried it till it was about as nutritious as so much hay, and washed it down with coffee strong as lye. In spite of their comfortable sheep wagons they led hard solitary lives in the dust and smell of their sheep, and they seldom if ever washed. I never did love a sheepherder.

After leaving Show Low, we camped for several nights not far from the junction of the White River and the Black River, both of them filled with trout. We were out of the heat and the dust of the lowlands, close to the mountain meadows and the pure air of the high peaks. It was a wonderful camp.

Before we went into the White Mountain Apache Indian Reservation we were joined by an escort of a sergeant and three men of the Ninth Cavalry, with two Apache scouts—Sergeant Hague, who had been at Santiago, and Scouts Benito and Ess-Kip-Vai-Gojo, or some such sounds.

From a high point next day we looked down and across the forest to the plain. And as we looked there rose a line of smokes. An Apache was getting ready to hunt deer. And he was setting the woods on fire because the hunter has a better chance under cover of the smoke. It was primeval, but not according to the rules.

Then we climbed the White Mountains, to the top of Thomas Peak, through a trackless forest of dense Spruce. Potter dropped his knife where he sat on a log to rest, and missed it only after the log was a quarter of a mile behind us.

I thought I could go back and find it. Potter was sure I couldn't. So I took a chance, and by good luck I did find it. That fixed my status as a woodsman. Such things have their value. Stories get around. I had to meet the Western men on their own ground or lose out.

Our route took us down the canyon of the Blue River in New Mexico, just on the border of the Apache Reservation. Three separate times the Apaches had broken out and killed every settler along the Blue who wasn't away from home, and each time the blood was hardly dry before a new lot came in and took up the vacant homesteads. The last killing was so recent that we picked up empty cartridges behind the rail fence where—his name has gone with the years—had made his last stand. He had been away when the first two raids came through. The third time the Apaches got him.

Coville and I kept our eyes open wherever we went, with the sheep question uppermost. This trip established what I was sure of already, that overgrazing by sheep does destroy the forest. Not only do sheep eat young seedlings, as I proved to my full satisfaction by finding plenty of them bitten off, contrary to the sheepmen's contention, but their innumerable hoofs also break and trample seedlings into the ground. John Muir called them hoofed locusts, and he was right.

Overgrazing loosens the soil so that heavy rains sweep it from the hillsides where it belongs into the streams where it does not belong, and so to the sea, silting up reservoirs on the way. Sometimes the deposit fills them level with the top of the dam, as on this trip we saw more than once. Through one such silted reservoir the owner had actually been forced to dig a ditch for the water to run in.

From the White Mountains I dropped down to Clifton. Our party scattered, and our trip on the Mogollon Mesa was over. And from

Clifton to Phoenix, with dust storms to give added interest to the journey.

At Phoenix my job was to study from below, where irrigators used the water, the same problem we had just seen from above, where the water came from. I had to see things also with the ranchers' eyes.

One dark night I was driving out through an Indian Reservation to have a look at the diversion dam at the intake on Salt River. The horses were going at a smart trot. Suddenly they both went down.

The driver struggled with the reins to get his horses up. I jumped over the wheel and ran to their heads. On the way a spike of the invisible barbed wire into which they had plunged cut a three-inch gash in my leg. An Indian (bad luck to him) had built a barbed-wire fence right across the main traveled highway. No wonder Lo is sometimes hard to bear.

At our camp in the White Mountains ice had frozen a quarter of an inch thick every night. At Phoenix the thermometer stood at 116 in the shade. It was so hot that sleeping indoors was impossible. There were beds out in the yard of nearly every house. I did the work I came to do and got out of there on the run.

Then to the higher country again, at Flagstaff, to see the effect of sheep grazing in that region and check against it what I had learned in the valley below.

Great stretches of open forest contain much feed that should not be wasted, provided the ranges are not overstocked and provided again (and this is of the first importance) that when reproduction of the forest is needed, grazing stops.

When the young trees are old enough to make it safe, grazing may begin again, but never without careful supervision and control. Exclusion may be necessary for from about a tenth to a fifth of the time it takes to grow a merchantable tree.

Sheep grazing in the forest requires special care. Every sheep owner should have the sole right to his range for a reasonable time and at a reasonable charge, but overgrazing should forfeit his permit and the money he paid for it. And the same if he or his herders are guilty of forest fires.

From some forest regions sheep should be kept out. But northern Arizona is not one of them. When the trip was over and its results digested, Coville and I were convinced that the answer to the grazing difficulties in Arizona was to control sheep grazing on the Mogollon Mesa, and not to shut it out. To regulate grazing is usually far better than to forbid it altogether. And so it was decided.

This was the substance of the report Coville and I made to Secretary Hitchcock. It also laid the basis, later on, for our grazing policy in the National Forests.

In the early days of the grazing trouble, when the protection of the public timberlands was a live political issue, we were faced with this simple choice: Shut out all grazing and lose the Forest Reserves, or let stock in under control and save the Reserves for the Nation. It seemed to me there was but one thing to do. We did it, and because we did it some 175,000,000 acres of National Forests today safeguard the headwaters of most Western rivers, and some Eastern rivers as well.

In those days sheep were ten times worse than cattle, although too many cattle can always make bad trouble. But when strictly limited and controlled, any kind of grazing, even sheep grazing, can go on without great harm to the forests or the plains.

To use a modern instance, overgrazing was largely responsible for the terrible dust storms which so crucified the semiarid West in the spring of 1935. Mrs. Pinchot and I, on our way home from the South Seas in April of that year, flew over parts of New Mexico and Texas in such a storm. Our plane rose to 16,000 feet, and still the dust was above us.

These dust storms cost the Government and the farmers hundreds of millions of dollars, and supplied one more demonstration of what individual greed can do to a great public resource under the gentle impulse of its own sweet will.

On our trip through the sheep-grazing region of the Mogollon Mesa, Potter and I began a friendship that was still strong at the time of his death on New Year's Day, 1944. With our problem plainly before us, we saw and discussed every phase of it, and in the end came to complete agreement and deep mutual respect.

Potter's soft, unemphatic, knowledgeable speech, his thorough mastery of his business, his intimate acquaintance with the country and its people, his quiet, persistent steadiness, his complete fearlessness and fairness, gave him a standing and an influence that were remarkable. I was determined to have him in our work for good.

A little more than a year later (October 1901) I had my way. As head of the Branch of Grazing, Potter was more than able to meet any sheepmen or cattlemen on their own ground. He was the cornerstone upon which we built the whole structure of grazing control.

32. *New York's Problem Child*

Another milestone, or at least a half-milestone, was passed when the New York Forest, Fish, and Game Commission in 1900 asked us for working plans for the State Forest Preserve and the Legislature backed it up with an appropriation of $2,000 for expenses.

Back of this request lay the desire of the Commission to convince the people that the Constitution should be so modified as to permit the practice of Forestry on the Forest Preserve. A very laudable objective, in which Governor Theodore Roosevelt heartily joined. As for me, I have always regarded the sentimental horror of some good citizens at the idea of utilizing the timber of the Forest Preserve under Forestry as unintelligent, misdirected, and shortsighted.

The New York State Forest Preserve, including the Adirondack and Catskill Parks, was not intended originally and cannot now be used, to produce timber for the needs of the people. It corresponds not to a National Forest but to a National Park.

The law of 1885 established the New York State Forest Commission, of which Professor Charles S. Sargent was the first head. The same law also established the New York State Forest Preserve and provided that "the lands now or hereafter constituting the forest preserve shall be forever kept as wild forest lands. They shall not be sold, nor shall they be leased or taken by any corporation, public or private."

One reason for this provision was the scandals which had besmirched the State's handling of its timberlands. In 1798, for example, the State sold the four million acres of the Macomb Patent for eight pence an acre. That was bad enough. But half a century later, in 1855, it sold three whole townships of land to a railroad company for five cents an acre, although a minimum of six shillings (seventy-five cents) was fixed by law. And that was by no means the end of the story.

Let there be no misunderstanding. The Sargent Commission was honest. It did what it could. Nevertheless fraud and theft continued, and the people knew it. In 1890, the Commission suggested paying for new Forest Preserve lands with timber—softwoods not less than twelve inches in diameter—and made this admission and defense:

"Considering the manner in which trees have been heretofore cut, and the devastation that has been wrought by crude and thoughtless methods, this prejudice [against any cutting] is not surprising; nevertheless it is a prejudice. Forestry is not opposed to having trees cut down in the proper way. It is the unwise, improvident, stupid method, or want of method, by which the cutting has heretofore too often been done, that is deplored."

Two years later the Commission recommended the sale of Spruce and Tamarack twelve inches and up and Poplar of any diameter, and in 1893 the Legislature authorized it. At once strenuous protests arose, and a publicity campaign in opposition was started by New York City organizations.

In the same year the Legislature established a new Forest Commission. But the public remained skeptical about any cutting in the Adirondack Park. The New York *Evening Post* reported that fifteen bills were then before the Senate and Assembly, "nearly all of which are directly to the advantage of the timber and land sharks."

In March 1894, a Forest Congress was held at Albany by the American Forestry Association, the New York State Forestry Association, the Adirondack Park Association, and the Genesee Valley Forestry Association. The Forest Congress also refused to approve the new Commission's course.

The Constitutional Convention of 1894 had before it an amendment to prevent cutting on the Forest Preserve. The American Forestry Association, at a summer meeting in New Hampshire, unanimously adopted Fernow's resolution against it. And *Garden and Forest* again made its position clear:

"The absolute prohibition of cutting any wood from the State Preserve means actual and reprehensible waste. Experience has proved, beyond question, that under proper management a forest can yield its products which are indispensable to civilized man, and can even grow in productiveness every year, while its beneficent influences on soil, climate, and water-supply will remain wholly unimpaired."

I wrote in the same vein to Elihu Root, presiding officer of the Convention, and did what I could to the same end. But no protest availed. The Comptroller had just uncovered fraud, bribery, and much illegal cutting in the State forests, and the people voted accordingly. Nevertheless, the new Constitution reasserted the prohibition of timber cutting on the State Preserves, as written in the law of 1885. Thus Forestry on the New York Forest Preserve was shut out by the basic law of the State.

The constitutional provision notwithstanding, sentiment for practicing Forestry in the State forests was not dead. In 1898 Governor Black, in his annual message to the Legislature, foretold that the ban against Forestry would "sometime be changed, for its continuance, except under conditions which ought not long to exist, would be unwise."

Governor Black went on to say, "The knowledge necessary to the proper treatment of the woods must come largely through experiment. It cannot be had unless the means of acquiring it are provided. The best course would be to buy a suitable tract and put it in charge of Cornell University or some similar body not subject to political change."

So the Legislature authorized the purchase of a 30,000-acre tract to be used as an experimental forest by the Cornell Forest School, which was established by the same act. Fernow selected the tract and undertook to show the people of the State how Forestry could be made to serve their interests in the Adirondacks. But the outcome was shortly to prove disastrous. A few years later we were called in to referee this case.

Again in 1900 Governor Theodore Roosevelt, in his annual message, looked forward to the time when the State could trust itself to handle its own forests wisely and honestly. Said he: "We need to have our system of forestry gradually developed and conducted along scientific principles. When this has been done it will be possible to allow marketable lumber to be cut everywhere without damage to the forests."

It was under T.R. as Governor that the Division of Forestry was called in to help the State of New York get ready to practice Forestry "on strictly scientific principles no less than upon principles of the strictest honesty toward the State."

Under the terms of Circular 21, the $2,000 appropriated by the Legislature in 1900 was to be expended by the Superintendent of State Forests "for the payment of the expense of experts furnished by the United States Bureau [Division it was then] of Forestry for estimating standing timber and other information regarding the lands and trees in the forest preserve." The Adirondack Preserve at that time covered an area just short of 1,300,000 acres.

The field work began in June of 1900. Colonel W. F. Fox, the Superintendent, and I agreed that the first working plan should be made for Township 40, Totten and Crossfield Purchase, Hamilton County. Our purpose was to devise a system whereby the forest may be utilized without sacrificing the objects for which the Preserve is held [and] to decide how to make the first cutting so as to insure successive crops within a reasonable time and at a profit to the owner" (in this case the State of New York).

American lumbering methods had been developed to fit American conditions. From the standpoint of low cost and large volume they were admirable, both in the woods and in the mill. From the smallest and roughest beginnings, energy, resourcefulness, business acumen, and common sense had built up one of the greatest of American industries. But what effect it might have on the future of the forest lay wholly outside its reckoning.

There lay our job—to change old habits and combine good logging with good Forestry. It was far too big a job for a handful of youngsters half-trained in Europe for the practice of Forestry under conditions wholly unlike our own. Nevertheless, it was our job—to lead a great, well-established, competent, and successful industry to a new attitude toward the forest. And that we intended to do, whether it was too big for us or not.

The advantage was not wholly with the practical men. When lumberman and forester met in the woods, the lumberman was generally astonished to find how little he knew about the life of the forest—how trees grow and reproduce themselves. The forester, on the other hand, knew little about how to handle a lumber operation. To arrive at a practicable plan the forester and the lumberman must dovetail their functions.

That was why we put the working plan for Township 40 into the joint hands of a forester and a lumberman. The party of twenty-five or thirty was in charge of Ralph Hosmer, a young forester, and Eugene Bruce, a seasoned Adirondack lumberman.

Hosmer came into the Division of Forestry soon after I did, and had absorbed the spirit of those early days. A long career of usefulness in Forestry lay ahead of him. Bruce was a perfect type of the old-time woodsman. Powerful, independent, keen, hardheaded, highly intelligent, honest, loyal, and generous, he was just the man we needed to keep our feet on the ground. He was also a great riverman, a great hunter, and a great shot, and he knew the North Woods from A to Z.

This was the first time forester and lumberman were paired as partners. Hosmer and Bruce made an admirable team. Together they finished the working plan and wrote the bulletin on Township 40. Together they did good work; and both gained by the association. They educated each other.

The plan was made and printed as a Government Bulletin, but it was never applied. It produced no change in New York public sentiment, which has always steadily opposed any form of timber utilization in the Forest Preserve; but it did mark the start of a policy which paid rich returns. By passing a civil service examination Bruce became the first of a long series of official lumbermen in the Forest Service—experts who added their practical knowledge and seasoned experience to the professional training of our young foresters.

The printed working plan for Township 40 told not only results but what we had done to reach them, and why. We were appealing to the public, and that public knew nothing of forest types, valuation surveys, yield and volume tables, or the practice of lumbering. The why and how of marking timber for cutting had to be explained, and the cost; the method of logging had to be set forth—how sawing saves more timber than chopping, and how cutting low stumps may increase the profits of the average lumber job; and much besides.

"Under practical forestry," said the bulletin, "this tract would yield a sustained revenue. A conservative and carefully devised system of lumbering would bring about the right use of the forest resources of the State lands without in any way interfering with the objects for which the Forest Preserve was created, and without injury to its natural beauties.

"The Division of Forestry therefore recommends that the necessary steps be taken to secure the lumbering of Township 40 by conservative methods."

Today the practices we recommended in the management of the forests in Township 40 may look rudimentary and commonplace. In those early days, however, they represented a radical departure from the practices then in use. They have a place in the history of Forestry in America.

In the summer of 1900 I dropped in to see how the boys in Township 40 were getting along. Theirs was a fine camp on the shore of Raquette Lake and the work was going well.

One true story of the North Woods that Gene told me I shall never forget. A man whose name I knew but have forgotten came to hunt deer, and brought his son along. One day he heard a noise in the brush and fired at the noise without stopping to find out what made it. When the father went to look, there his son lay, dead.

That was bad enough—but wait. A few years later the same man, who ought never to have touched a gun again, came back and brought another son along. And then the utterly incredible took place. The father heard a noise again, fired at it without looking, and once more killed a son.

PART VI
PURSUING THE GOAL

33. *T.R.'s First Message*

On September 14, 1901, President McKinley died, shot by an assassin at the Pan-American Exposition in Buffalo, New York. On the same day, Theodore Roosevelt took the oath as President of the United States.

F. H. Newell and I had been consulted by T.R. on questions of Forestry and stream flow while he was still Governor of New York. Newell had long planned and worked for the creation of a United States Reclamation Service. He was anxious that T.R.'s first Message to Congress should help it along. I was equally keen that the Message should say what needed to be said on the question of Forestry. Promptly after his arrival, we made it our business to see the new President.

Our three-cornered conference was more than satisfactory. The new President knew what we were talking about. He was an outdoor man—more, a wilderness hunter. He knew open country, East and West, the forests and the mountains, from much personal experience. It would have been hard to find anywhere a more sympathetic and understanding listener.

We left, two very happy men, authorized to draft for the Message what we thought it ought to say on our twin subjects. It was a Heaven-sent chance.

The men Newell and I asked to work with us were George H. Maxwell, Director of the National Irrigation Association, and (I believe) Dr. W J McGee, head of the Bureau of American Ethnology, whose encyclopedic knowledge of our continent was to help answer many a difficult question in the years to come. All four of us realized how much was at stake. We spent the better part of a week in discussing, formulating, correcting, and recorrecting the very few pages we finally turned in.

CONSERVATION TONIC

J. N. Darling, Des Moines *Register*

T.R. accepted substantially everything we wrote as we wrote it. His Message at once transformed Forestry and irrigation into national issues of continental consequence, and started them toward that high degree of public acceptance they achieved before T.R. left the White House.

The President's Message of December 2, 1901, wisely asserted that "The fundamental idea of forestry is the perpetuation of forests by use. Forest protection is not an end in itself; it is a means to increase and sustain the resources of our country and the industries which depend upon them. The preservation of our forests is an imperative business necessity. We have come to see clearly that whatever destroys the forest, except to make way for agriculture, threatens our well-being.

"The practical usefulness of the national forest reserves to the mining, grazing, irrigation, and other interests of the regions in which the reserves lie," T.R. continued, "has led to a widespread demand by the people of the West for their protection and extension. The forest reserves will inevitably be of still greater use in the future than in the past. Additions should be made to them whenever practicable, and their usefulness should be increased by a thoroughly businesslike management."

The Message then pointed out that responsibility for the Forest Reserves was scattered between the General Land Office (protection), the United States Geological Survey (mapping and description), and the Bureau of Forestry (working plans), which latter was also charged with the general advancement of practical Forestry in the United States.

Then came what was to me the heart and soul of the Message. "These various functions," the President declared, "should be united in the Bureau of Forestry, to which they properly belong. The present diffusion of responsibility is bad from every standpoint. It prevents that effective co-operation between the Government and the men who utilize the resources of the reserves, without which the interests of both must suffer."

Then the new President turned to irrigation. "The water supply itself depends upon the forest. In the arid region it is water, not land, which measures production. The western half of the United States would sustain a population greater than that of our whole country today if the waters that now run to waste were saved and used for irrigation. The forest and water problems are perhaps the most vital internal questions of the United States." That was indeed what I wanted the people to hear.

"The forests alone cannot, however, fully regulate and conserve the waters of the arid region. Great storage works are necessary to equalize the flow of streams and to save the flood waters. Their construction has been conclusively shown to be an undertaking too vast for private effort. Nor can it be best accomplished by the individual States acting alone.

"These irrigation works should be built by the National Government. The lands reclaimed by them should be reserved by the Government for actual settlers, and the cost of construction should so far as possible be repaid by the land reclaimed.

"The reclamation and settlement of the arid lands will enrich every portion of our country, just as the settlement of the Ohio and Mississippi Valleys brought prosperity to the Atlantic States. Our people as a whole will profit, for successful homemaking is but another name for the upbuilding of the Nation."

This first Message of Theodore Roosevelt to the Congress, with his vigorous and consistent support to follow, was the moving power in the establishment of the Reclamation Service. Also it furnished no small part of the foundation upon which the Forest Service was built.

It was indeed a landmark in the development of forestry in the United States. The circumstances under which it was sent to Congress, following the assassination of McKinley, the extraordinarily vigorous personality of the man who sent it, and the space and emphasis it gave to questions purely of the general good—all this ensured for it very special public attention.

If it did not inaugurate national action in Forestry, which had already begun, it certainly did in irrigation. And in Forestry it gave what we were doing, and trying to do, a new standing that was invaluable. From then on all men, in Congress and out, might know that the Administration was behind us.

34. *One Plan That Failed*

The Report of the Secretary of the Interior for 1900-1901 made it clear beyond question that Secretary Hitchcock shared our views on what was needed in Forest Reserve administration, and likewise that the handling of the Reserves by the General Land Office by no means held his confidence. The Reserves, while they remained in the Interior Department, would be carefully supervised by the Secretary himself.

The Report went on to say that men "of high local reputation for character, ability, and knowledge of the woods, in addition to such practical trained experts as may be available, and men thoroughly versed in lumbering and woodcraft, are essential. The time for the introduction of practical forestry on the forest reserves has fully come." To give the Reserves the best practical treatment without delay was of first importance in the interest of the forest and in the interest of the West.

The keynote of Reserve administration should be to increase the value of the Reserves to the public and to perpetuate their forests by wise use. Their usefulness to the agricultural, grazing, and lumber interests of their region was so great, so generally recognized, and so fast increasing that to give them anything short of the best management available was a most serious blow to the prosperity of the West.

Forestry, said the Secretary, dealing with a source of wealth produced by the soil, was properly an agricultural question. "The presence of properly trained foresters in the Agriculture Department, as well as the nature of the subject itself, makes the ultimate transfer, if found to be practicable, of the administration of the reserves to that Department essential to the best interest, both of the Reserves and of the people who use them." Whatever else could be said of Hitchcock, he was not afraid.

An outline of the principles and practice which should govern the administration of the National Forest Reserves "which the Commissioner of the General Land Office has been directed to carry into effect" was printed at the end of the Report. Since this was the outline I had written and given to the Secretary, it was clear that Hitchcock intended the Bureau to take a larger and larger part in shaping the administration of the Reserves, even while they were still in the Interior Department.

What his intentions were is clear from the letter which he wrote to Jim Wadsworth *père* on January 9, 1901:

"It is eminently necessary that the trained foresters of the Government should have charge of all technical Government forest work. In order to bring this about, the following plan has been agreed upon by the Secretary of Agriculture and myself, subject to the action of your Committee:

"The police and patrol of the forest reserves will remain under this Department, together with the routine office work necessary thereto. The investigation and decision of all technical forest questions and the execution of the resulting plans will be in charge of the Forester and his chief assistants, whom I will appoint as special agents without pay, directly responsible to myself."

Good old Secretary Wilson was for it, of course, and it looked as if the plan might go through.

In accordance with Hitchcock's letter to Wadsworth I laid out a plan and submitted carefully thought-out instructions for the Secretary to issue to me. Maybe the plan would have worked out. I thought so then, but I'm not sure now. But it couldn't have been worse than control of the Forest Reserves by the Land Office alone, under which politics-ridden clerks, who knew no more about what they were doing than you and I know about the dark side of the moon, worked their will not only on the Government property but also on the welfare of thousands of settlers.

I kept in close touch with Commissioner Hermann of the General Land Office, prepared the working details of a sort of *modus vivendi* between the two Departments, and secured complete agreement on all of its points, except that the Commissioner wanted applications for timber cutting and grazing made to him, while I thought, and still think, they should have come straight to me.

It seems like a small point now, but it had real importance. By this time I was thoroughly familiar with the unconscionable delays, the complete incompetence, and the thorough misunderstanding of the Reserves and their problems which obtained in the Land Office. I wanted action, and I knew referring anything to the Commissioner meant delay and more delay.

And what is more, I knew Binger Hermann—knew him as a politician with a long beard, fat, smooth, slick, "practical" in the worst sense of the word, with an eye single to the main chance and a deep-rooted conviction that a public office is a private snap. Years afterward, when he was in Congress and running for a second term, he succeeded in getting himself photographed with T.R., who had for him no manner of use. That photograph re-elected him, to T.R.'s great disgust.

The instructions I prepared were to go into effect on February 8, 1901, on which date I was to be appointed as Special Agent and Forester in the Department of the Interior, without pay and without losing my place as Forester in the Department of Agriculture.

When the time came nothing happened. So in June I worked out a more detailed plan which provided that I was to have control of my own people, just as I had in the Department of Agriculture, so that the Honorable Binger couldn't play politics with my work; and that I was to be allowed to go and see the lands I was to be in charge of, contrary to the immemorial habit of the Land Office.

This plan provided, among other things, that all letters concerning the Reserves were to be signed by the Forester, contrary again to the morale-killing custom of the General Land Office (and the rest of the Government too) under which all letters, by whomsoever prepared, were signed only by the head man.

When T.R. became President, Hitchcock took the Forest Reserve question to him. T.R. was strong for bringing the Government forests and the Government foresters together in the Department of Agriculture. But he didn't realize how impossible it might be to do a good job if every letter and order had to wait a month or two for the Commissioner's signature, just as Richards' recommendation was held up three months on Hitchcock's desk. I did, and I was determined not to bite off more than I could chew by undertaking to handle the Forest Reserves with that particular millstone round my neck.

So T.R. jumped on me good and hard, and at the same time gave me just what I wanted. He wrote me (October 18, 1901) the following very characteristic letter:

> I have just had a conversation with Secretary Hitchcock about the Forestry Division in the Land Office. He informs me that he has had an explicit understanding with Mr. Hermann, that Mr. Hermann absolutely and without reservation acquiesces in the Secretary's determination that

if you come over you will have an absolutely free hand, and that what you say as to the policies to be pursued, the men to be appointed, etc., etc., shall be done without question so far as Mr. Hermann is concerned. In other words, you will have exactly the same freedom as though you were the independent head of the bureau. There will not be one shadow of difference. Under these circumstances it seems to me utterly unimportant that you should merely put your initials on a letter instead of signing it yourself. What you and I and the Secretary are after is to get results. It is of no more consequence to you from a personal standpoint that your name should be there than that the Secretary's name should be there, or mine. We all of us have a common object. It seems to me to be to the last degree unwise to refuse to take advantage of the chance to do such excellent work because of anything so unimportant as having your initials on a letter instead of signing it. The condition of affairs is not expected to be permanent. It is expected to be a transition stage, which shall itself develop conditions which will enable us in the future to make a permanent establishment. As long as the Secretary and I are here you will have precisely as much liberty of action, precisely as good a chance to do your work, as if you signed your name instead of your initials. From my point of view it is perfectly obvious that where the matter is really trivial you should not hesitate for a moment in acceding to the Secretary's wishes. He presents what seem to me good reasons against such an entire innovation as having you sign your own name. It would create a precedent that would certainly plague us, and cause in all probability real disorganization of the service.

If you choose, you might show this to Secretary Wilson.

Faithfully yours,

Theodore Roosevelt.

Mr. Gifford Pinchot,
Department of Agriculture.

Next day I answered:

Under the conditions of your letter I am not only willing but glad to take up the work offered me by Secretary Hitchcock. From the beginning I have taken precisely the attitude you describe and have said so to Secretary Hitchcock repeatedly. What I have been after has been to get results. Yesterday morning I told Secretary Hitchcock, with the utmost definiteness, that the reason I was then unwilling to accept his proposal was because, under the circumstances, I did not believe I should be able to get results. With your letter, my position will be in every way stronger than it could possibly have been without it, and I shall go ahead with the hope and intention of getting things done. Your assurance that the condition of affairs is not expected to be permanent is most gratifying, for I had not understood from Secretary Hitchcock that he had any immediate intention of changing the present assignment of work.

I am keenly sorry you should have got the idea that I was sticking on a trivial point. As I have repeatedly assured Secretary Hitchcock, it is of no possible consequence to me, of itself, whether I sign my name or my initials. My whole desire has been to have a free hand. Until today I have not believed that I could control my work if the final decision, involved in the signature, rested with Mr. Hermann. Your letter settles that point permanently. I shall write Secretary Hitchcock today that I am ready to accept.

I did, and again nothing happened. A few days later (October 31, 1901) I sent Hitchcock a "rough outline of the principles and practice which I believe should govern the administration of the National Forest Reserves." Years later, when I did get charge of the Reserves, I followed precisely the road this rough outline prescribed.

The conditions I laid down were clearly not acceptable to the General Land Office. Nothing came out of Hitchcock's original plan to appoint me the Forester in the Department of the Interior without losing my place as Forester in the Department of Agriculture. Instead the Department of the Interior decided to conduct another experiment in putting new wine in old bottles. It was to take the handling of the Reserves out of the Special Service Division (Division P) which had to do with enforcing the land laws and entrust it to a new unit—a Division of Forestry of its own. As this arrangement was clearly of a temporary character, pending the transfer, then why not put some of our own men in charge of the new Division?

Thanks to the influence of the President, with what help I could give, that plan went through. Filibert Roth was induced to leave his professorship at Cornell, where his relations with Fernow were none too satisfactory, and take over the new Division. Four of our best men went with him. Smith Riley and W. H. B. Kent were assigned to help Roth as Head Rangers, E. T. Allen as Inspector, and H. J. Tompkins as Forest Expert.

Roth and his little group of assistants did their best to bring honest and effective forest administration to the Reserves in the Land Office. For nearly a year they struggled against Land Office routine, political stupidity, and wrongheaded points of view. But they struggled in vain.

The tide of crookedness and incompetence in the Land Office was beyond their power to stem.

Good men under bad leadership are fatally handicapped. In disgust and disappointment Roth threw up the job and went to the University of Michigan as head of the new School of Forestry, where he was to make so fine a record. Riley, Allen, Kent, and Tompkins later returned to us. And that was one more proof that the way of the transfer was the only way to get decent handling of the Reserves.

35. *The Fight Continues*

Not long after the Message, the President called to the White House four men, Congressman John F. Lacey of Iowa, chairman of the House Committee on Public Lands, greatly interested in game protection and a strong friend of Forestry and the Bureau of Forestry; my friend Dr. C. Hart Merriam, Chief of the Biological Survey in the Department of Agriculture, whose brilliant work for wild life will long be remembered; his assistant, Dr. Palmer; and myself. Following that conference Major Lacey introduced two bills, both intended "to transfer certain forest reserves to the control of the Department of Agriculture, to authorize game and fish protection in forest reserves, and for other purposes."

H.R. 11536, for which Major Lacey made his fight, provided for the transfer of the Reserves to the Department of Agriculture by Executive Order, one by one, after their permanent boundaries had been established. T.R. being President, that was good enough. What was anything but good, however, although I did not then fully realize what harm it could do, was a provision in the bill as reported from the Committee on Public Lands, that "hereafter no forest reserve in any State shall be created, enlarged, or extended, without the approval or written request of the Governor of such State made prior to the creation, enlargement, or extension thereof."

This nefarious states'-rights provision would have put pretty much the whole Forest Reserve question at the mercy of the Governors of the public-lands states, most of whom were emphatically hostile to the Reserves.

Opposition to the Reserves in parts of the West was still exceedingly vigorous. A year before, in February 1901, the Oregon Legislature had sent a memorial to Congress protesting against a bill because it provided "in effect and in substance that the supervision and control of the U.S. Forest Reserves shall be withdrawn from the Department of the Interior, and placed in the Department of Agriculture."

And again, "your memorialists protest against any law or rule that will withdraw the direct supervision of the Forest Reserves from forest officers, demonstrated to be able, efficient, and practical, and place it in hands unknown and untried and recommended only by their theoretical learning."

Much noise was made, then and later, about the theoretical learning but alleged practical incompetence of Eastern dudes and trained foresters. I must admit that here and there some of it was deserved. While most of our people were far above the Government average, we were only just getting started, and of course there were still some weak spots.

This Oregon memorial was doubtless not unrelated to the fact that Binger Hermann was doing what he could and all he could, in spite of Secretary Hitchcock's approval of the transfer, to keep the Forest Reserves, and hence the appointment of forest officers, in his own hands.

Major Lacey's bill, with amendments, was reported favorably by the Public Lands Committee on March 15, by twelve votes to four. Here, I believed, was our chance. And at once I went to work on the bill. In answer to my call for help, J. A. Holmes wired back, "Will mail fifty letters tomorrow favoring the forest reserve transfers"; Judge Thomas Burke of Seattle wired, "Have sent strong telegrams to our members urging support bill"; and T. J. Grier, of the Homestake Mining Company in the Black Hills, gave a like reply.

When the Lacey Bill came up for consideration and debate, the proceedings supplied an accurate picture of going Congressional opinion on Forestry, and they were anything but dull. Joe Cannon, who held the purse strings as chairman of the Committee on Appropriations, threw his vast influence against the bill. Bell of Colorado declared that the people of his state wanted no buffalo pastures and hunting preserves for rich Easterners. He submitted a letter from the Secretary of the National Livestock Association, who asserted that there was not a livestock association that wasn't opposed to the Reserves, which were usually set aside on petition of the American Forestry Association with headquarters in some codfish district of Massachusetts or Maine. And Shafroth of Colorado backed him up.

The battle was not altogether one-sided. Needham of California, always a strong friend of the forests, McRae of Arkansas, one of the earliest advocates of Forestry in the House, and Williams of Mississippi vigorously supported the transfer. And when Lacey defined Forestry as a great system of tree farming and declared that money spent on Forestry is well spent, that Forestry is of vital importance to the farmers of the United States, the House applauded.

Then came more fireworks. Stephens of Texas charged that "Many of these Forest Reserves embrace lands where over a great many square miles there is not a stick of timber," a favorite argument of the opposition, and sometimes fair enough too, because, as Lacey explained, the boundaries were not yet accurately drawn.

Hill of Kansas wisely opposed, as giving the states a veto power over Federal authority, the provision which required the approval of the Governor before any Forest Reserve in any state could be created, enlarged, or extended.

Mann of Illinois suggested game preservation as the real purpose of the bill. Rodey of New Mexico raised again the buffalo issue and charged that the Gila River Forest Reserve included thousands of acres that would never grow a tree. And many more came in on both sides.

Mondell of Wyoming, afterward Speaker of the House, offered for the record the minority report against the bill. It repeated the usual arguments against the Forest Reserves and the transfer, and praised, in contrast, the great work done by the Interior Department "in developing a national forest policy, in protecting the forests on the reserves, and on the unreserved public lands as well, from destruction by fires and by indiscriminate cutting; in preventing abuses of the privilege of free use of timber by settlers; in providing for the sale of the matured products of the reserves; in controlling the grazing on reserves;" and in much else besides.

During the debate Shafroth, being asked what could be done about forest fires, suggested cutting a half-mile-wide strip through the forest every ten miles—a shopworn, impractical, and thoroughly baneful panacea. Forests are far from fireproof just because trees have been cut down.

Bell also repeated the familiar arguments. The sole purpose of the bill was to build up a lot of English game preserves. There had not been a year since the Reserves were created that we hadn't been flooded with petitions and complaints that the Reserves ruined our entire country.

Out of pure public spirit, Kleberg of Texas spoke for the bill. He could have had no personal motive, for all the public land in Texas belongs to the state.

Perkins of New York stood by the Reserves. He had been in Jackson's Hole, south of Yellowstone Park, and had learned from small cattle owners and other poor men how the great sheep and cattle companies controlled the public range. He had seen with his own eyes poor settlers, small land owners, take their lives in their hands to defend their rights against the big fellows. He would vote for no bill to lessen the usefulness of the Forest Reserves.

John Sharp Williams of Mississippi, my warm friend, afterwards Senator, also strongly supported the bill. On the other side, Shafroth and Jones of Washington tried to pin on me personally the responsibility for including lands unsuitable for growing timber.

Cannon closed the debate with a vitriolic standpat denunciation of scientific men, foresters, reformers, and in general of those who, by the use of their heads, would make progress in the world. Said he: "I hope the Committee of the Whole will take my judgment on this matter, and if they do, they will cut it off right close up behind the ears by striking out the enacting clause."

The Committee of the Whole did take his judgment by a majority of a single vote—37 to 36—which pitifully light vote would go to show that the interest of the House in the forest issue was moderate, to say the least.

However little he may have meant it, Cannon's victory rendered a tremendous service to Forestry in America. Because of it, the President was not required to beg the Governors of the public-land states for permission to set aside Forest Reserves. If he had been, much or most of the National Forests now safe in Federal keeping would not have been reserved at all, or only after most of their best timber had passed into private hands.

"Surely the wrath of man shall praise thee," said the Psalmist. And surely in this case it did.

The final vote was 73 for Lacey's bill, 100 against it. Nineteen voted present, and 159 did not vote at all. The transfer was dead for that year.

Many regular Republicans and other Eastern Representatives voted against the Lacey Bill not because they were against it, but because Joe Cannon was. The powerful chairman of the Committee on Appropriations had made his hostility known, and they went along. The votes of legislators on legislation are apt to be more personal than many people think.

Except for Cannon's opposition, the vote would doubtless have represented the usual attitude of the Eastern Congressmen, who believed in Forestry as a general proposition, were perfectly willing to protect Western forests against the depredations of Western men, but were by no means as vigorously virtuous where Eastern forests were concerned. In the long run it was the votes of Eastern Senators and Representatives that saved the National Forests of the West.

The issue in this debate, as in the great debate of 1897, when the existence of Government Forestry was at stake, was development. The West wanted development—wanted it at any cost. What helped development was good, and what hindered it was bad. All other considerations came behind that.

The West wanted settlers, and wanted them now. It wanted to grow—now. And what might happen or would happen ten years from now, let alone twenty or fifty years later, was clear outside the picture.

Western men had made the West. They proposed to keep on making it along the lines they had laid down. Let the East keep out.

California, however, because of its enormous interest in irrigation, took no such position. And here and there Western Congressmen, for the same reason (like Newlands of Nevada), or because they saw beyond the next decade (like Moody of Oregon), broke out of the corral. But the general statement stands.

The Transfer Bill was by no means the only bill of that session which had to do with the Forest Reserves. The Reserve policy was rapidly becoming important to the West, and the number and character of the bills introduced proved it.

Many of these bills had behind them the general Western opposition to the Forest Reserves. Others sprang from the interests of the great mining and railroad corporations. Others again grew out of the incompetence or the misbegotten thinking of the General Land Office. Fortunately most of them died a-borning.

At that time the whole Forest Reserve policy was still in jeopardy. That year, and for several years to follow, it was in fact less a question of securing good legislation than of preventing bad. The danger was

Future Generation: Did All This Happen Within Your Time, Grandpa?
Present Generation: Yes, My Boy.
Future Generation: What Did You Let 'Em Do It For?

From The St. Paul Pioneer-Press.
1909.

often so acute that the Reserves were saved only by the skin of their teeth. Over and over again their escape seemed almost miraculous.

Many laws affecting the public lands appeared also in 1902. Most of them dealt with the lieu-land law or the grazing policy. A few were good, but more had some special interest behind them. In accordance with its hallowed custom of turning public lands over to private ownership as fast as possible, the Land Office was usually for the bad bills, and against the good. But one conspicuous exception deserves notice.

This bill provided for leasing some 525 million acres of vacant public lands for grazing purposes in lots of various sizes for ten-year periods, subject to renewal. It would have barred leased lands against homestead settlement and would have made it necessary for settlers to fence their homesteads against livestock on leased lands—an unfair and impossible burden—but not the other way round. The lessees need build no fences.

Hermann denounced the bill as "a vast scheme in the interest of a few, by which valuable property of the public is taken for private use without just compensation. It practically amounts to a donation. Some might designate it as a huge graft."

This time Hermann was right. And that was the end of the bill.

The plan for an Appalachian Forest Reserve, suggested by Professor J. A. Holmes ten years before, got as far as the introduction of two bills in the Senate, in both of which, I take it for granted, we had a hand. They got no farther. It was to be a longer fight than we supposed.

36. *Uncle Sam–Forester*

In 1889 Congressman Knute Nelson of Minnesota, afterward Governor and United States Senator, had introduced a bill to give effect to a treaty with the Chippewa Indians of his State, by which they ceded their lands and timber to the United States in return for their net value when sold, plus individual allotments of land.

The Nelson Bill passed. It provided that the timber was to be sold on estimate, not on actual scale, and was to carry the land with it. One reason for this provision appeared when it was found that estimates of the timber made by the Indian Office averaged less than half the actual stand. Considering that the Indian Office was the most political bureau in Washington, there was nothing surprising in that.

Under sloppy Indian Office handling of a later amendment which permitted the logging of dead and down timber, much green timber was cut and paid for as dead and down, or was not paid for at all. One outfit, which included a former Governor of Minnesota, cut and stole more green timber than the dead timber they professed to buy. They were sued and forced to pay nearly $100,000—a story which the newspapers carefully neglected to print. And this case did not stand alone.

Thefts of this character, resentment over robbing the Indians, the protests of an honest Indian Agent named Walker (who was said to have lost his job), together with sentiment for preserving the primeval Pine, aroused vigorous expostulations, among others from the Minnesota Federation of Women's Clubs and the State Medical Society.

Their protests led Secretary of the Interior Hitchcock to suspend a sale of Indian land and timber at public auction, advertised for March 30, 1899, on the Cass Lake, Leech Lake, and Winnibigoshish Reservations, in northern Minnesota.

Dead and down sales continued, nevertheless, under an Indian Agent by the name of Captain Mercer. They were thoroughly exposed during the winter of 1900-1901 by the Minneapolis papers, and in the spring of 1901, under pressure from the Federation of Women's Clubs, Secretary Hitchcock stopped them for good.

The earlier advocates of saving the Indian timberlands wanted a park. So did the members of an expedition to the head waters of the Mississippi, organized and led by Colonel John S. Cooper of Chicago in September 1899. Among them were more than a score of Congressmen, including Joe Cannon and Jim Mann of Illinois, Fordney of Michigan, and Tawney and Morris of Minnesota, with enough presidents of railroads, big lumbermen, merchant princes, newspaper reporters, etc., to make up the best part of a hundred men.

The railroads furnished transportation. The Associated Press gave publicity. The trip blazed into glory for a week of continual receptions, banquets, and speeches, and died, leaving the situation just about where it was before.

Not so with the less flamboyant attack led by the Minnesota Federation of Women's Clubs and notably by Mrs. W. E. Bramhall, the young, modest, but most effective chairman of the Federation's Forestry Committee. She was the first of the park advocates to ask for a

Forest Reserve instead. And to her, more than to any other one person, goes the credit for getting it.

As the result of much agitation, Representative Page Morris of Duluth on December 3, 1901, introduced a bill drawn by himself which did not provide for a Forest Reserve. It was opposed by Mrs. Bramhall and the Federation. H. H. Chapman, then Superintendent of the Minnesota Experiment Farm at Grand Rapids, later professor in the Yale School of Forestry and President of the Society of American Foresters, prepared a draft which did provide for a Forest Reserve, and gave copies to all members of the Minnesota delegation in Congress.

There was much backing and filling about the form the bill should take. Finally, on January 23, 1902, a meeting of the Minnesota delegation was called in Representative Tawney's room, at which were present delegates from the village of Cass Lake and others, including Chapman and Pinchot. At the end of the four-hour meeting the plan for a Forest Reserve was approved, and the bill was turned over to me to be put in shape. This was done, and the bill finally passed in that form.

Its passage was a victory for public opinion and the public interest against local opposition and the fierce hostility of the lumbering interests, who had long ruled the roost in northern Minnesota. Without the farsighted and patriotic support of the Minnesota Federation of Women's Clubs, it would have been impossible. With it the Bureau of Forestry emerged from the period of mere advice to actual control, for the first time, of timber cutting on public land.

Here was the first application of Forestry to Government-owned forests in America. The Minnesota Forest Reserve was still under the Interior Department, but the application of Forestry to its rich Pine forests was in our hands. Brush piling and burning were here made part of the conditions of sale for the first time in a Government forest.

Moreover, this was the first Forest Reserve created by direct Congressional action instead of by Presidential Proclamation. Altogether its establishment amounted to progress of the first importance.

Northern Minnesota was violently against the Reserve, as it had been against the proposed park. Behind its opposition lay three things —the fierce desire for development which marks the frontier, the hunger for profit of land agents and other speculators in land, and the determination of the lumbermen to let no tree escape that would put a dollar in their pockets.

"Land is there to be used," said the pioneers. "Resources are there to be used. And the sooner the better. If in the using they are used up—what has the future done for us, that we should worry about the future?"

"What we want," said the speculators, "is people and business. If the settler we bring in fails to make a go of it—well, we've sold him this and we've sold him that, and he's been a whole lot better for the country than no settler at all."

"This is our bailiwick," said the lumbermen. "This timber is here to be cut, and we are going to cut it, come hell or high water."

There was a lot of that in the Lake States, and indeed all through the West. It was a heartless game, and tough on the victims. Yet in the end, partly because of it and partly in spite of it, the country was settled, the towns grew, conditions changed, and prosperity came to many a region that had seen too much of the bitter struggle to live. Prosperity came also to Cass Lake and the whole neighborhood of the Forest Reserve, and for that the Reserve itself was mainly responsible.

The Morris Bill became the Morris Act on June 27, 1902. It provided that the Forester of the Department of Agriculture, with the approval of the Secretary of the Interior, should select from four Chippewa Indian Reservations in northern Minnesota, 200,000 acres of Pine land and 25,000 acres of "agricultural land" (so-called because it contained not over 1,500 feet of Pine to the acre), to become a National Forest Reserve.

The timber on the 200,000 acres of Pine land was to be cut under rules prescribed by the Forester and approved by the Secretary of the Interior. On these lands, "the purchaser shall be required to leave standing five per centum of the pine timber thereon for the purpose of reforestation" to be selected by the Forester under rules approved by the Secretary. That meant Forestry.

Moreover, "the said Forester shall have power at all times to patrol and protect said lands and forests, and to enforce all rules and regulations made by him as aforesaid." That meant business.

In addition, an area equal to ten sections, 6,400 acres, in the neighborhood of the village of Cass Lake, was to be reserved from sale or settlement, together with certain islands and points in Cass and Leech Lakes, all of which were later (1908) included in the National Forest.

The ten sections, untouched by the ax, were intended to safeguard the beauty of the lake shores. It was an old and a sound device. We had followed the same plan, for example, in the lumbering under Forestry around Lake Lila on Dr. Webb's Ne-Ha-Sa-Ne Park in the Adirondacks. So also at Biltmore Forest in North Carolina, broad strips of uncut forest protected the fringes of important roads ten years before the Morris Bill was passed.

Months before the Morris Bill became law, Overton Price and I had decided, if it did pass, to put Eugene S. Bruce, Lumberman of the Bureau, in charge. He was to examine and select the lands for the proposed National Forest Reserve and park, and prepare rules to govern the sale, cutting, and removal of the timber.

Bruce's long experience as a lumberman and with lumbermen made it clear to him that this would be no pink tea. Nevertheless, after full discussion, and after setting aside his personal inclination, his loyalty to the Bureau led him to accept. Fortunate it was that he did so. We could have made no better choice.

After the bill had passed, Bruce came to Washington from the Adirondacks, where he had been inspecting the Webb and Whitney forests, and tried to secure accurate maps of the territory from the Indian Office; but in vain, which was nothing to be astonished at. From there he went on to northern Minnesota, where he found the people and the local papers bitterly hostile to the coming Forest Reserve.

During that fall (1902) Bruce made himself acquainted with every part of the lands concerned, and incidentally discovered that the War Department had bought from the Indians the right to construct large Government reservoirs within the boundaries of these reservations. The nominal purpose was to regulate navigation on the Mississippi below St. Paul. Later it became evident, as Bruce said, that these dams "had been erected more especially for the benefit of the lumbering interests having timber to drive in the upper Mississippi above St. Paul."

The surveys for the flowage boundaries were not yet completed. Neither had allotments of land to individual Indians, provided for in the Morris Act, been selected.

In the regular course of Land Office procedure, these two different sets of claims on Indian lands would have entailed years of delay. Meantime the local clamor was for opening at once to settlement all "agricultural lands" within the Indian Reservations which would not be included in the Forest Reserve. Bruce accordingly devised and drew what came to be known as the Black Line. It enclosed those parts of the different reservations from which the Forest Reserve and the ten sections would eventually be selected. So far as we were concerned, the rest could then be opened to settlement without delay.

In the spring of 1903, at Bruce's suggestion, I went with Commissioner Richards of the General Land Office, Major George L. Scott, the honest and competent local Indian Agent, and E. L. Warren, Chief Examiner of the Chippewa ceded lands, to look over the area inside the Black Line. Richards agreed with Bruce and approved his plan, and the lands within the Black Line were withdrawn from sale or settlement accordingly.

During the summer of 1903, the ten sections were selected, the boundary lines surveyed and marked, and the rules and regulations were prepared. The rules covered the cutting and removal of 95 per cent of the Pine timber on parts of the Cass Lake and Chippewa Indian Reservations, chosen as the first selection for the Minnesota Forest Reserve.

On October 21, 1903, these rules were formally adopted and prescribed by the said Forester, for the timber to be sold at Cass Lake, Minnesota, on November 17, 1904. They were then approved twice by the Interior Department—which may have been a wise precaution—once by Acting Secretary Ryan on October 24, 1903, and once by Secretary Hitchcock on June 6, 1904.

These rules provided: That the timber to be left standing should be marked instead of the timber to be removed. "No tree shall be cut that is stamped with the letters 'U.S.' ";

That "No white pine or Norway [red] pine 10 inches and under in diameter, 3 feet from the ground, shall be cut for any purpose, except where absolutely unavoidable in necessary logging operations" (and this was what made most of the trouble);

That "All tops and litter from trees cut under these rules must be burned so as to be safe against fire, under the supervision of the Inspector of the Bureau of Forestry, and at such times as he shall select."

The rules contained many additional directions such as: "All merchantable pine timber in felled trees which is 6 inches or over at the small end shall be logged." And any such timber left in the woods must be paid for at double the regular stumpage rate.

All merchantable Pine timber used for booms, dams, camps, or any other purpose, must be paid for at the regular stumpage rate. The Indians were to get their just dues.

On all questions the decision of the Inspector of the Bureau of Forestry was to be final. Persistent violation of any of the rules would be sufficient cause for annulling the contract and canceling the sale.

They were good rules, they were well enforced, and they proved their worth. Under Gene Bruce's intelligent and forceful direction the men responsible for marking the trees and controlling the logging did a good job.

The timber on the first selection of the Minnesota Forest Reserve was to be sold on sealed bids, to be opened publicly on a given day, thereby preventing the customary collusion between bidders. We had to break the old bad habits of the Indian Office or fail.

The regulation which required the piling and burning of the tops was an entirely new departure, and was fiercely denounced as mere theory and nonsense. And likewise as certain to reduce the proceeds to the Indians from the sale of their timber.

The fight on this particular regulation became so violent that certain lumber interests circulated petitions among the Indians, and even sent men among them to stir up trouble. They went so far that Major Scott (who, knowing little about Forestry, was himself against the brush burning) notified me that there was grave danger of an uprising among the Indians, and urged that Bruce and his men should leave the Reservations until after the timber was sold. But Gene Bruce refused to go. He said he knew more about the situation among the Indians than Major Scott, who lived thirty or forty miles away.

When this matter became acute, I happened to be in the West. Price wired me, suggesting that I stop in Minnesota on my way to Washington, and take the matter up directly. That I did.

Gene relates that I jumped on him with both feet for his rashness. He answered quietly that he had been among the Indians for something over a year; that he knew them; and that it would be poor policy to show the white feather. If he had to leave the work now, he would leave it for good. The whole thing was only a part of the game the lumbermen were playing to get the brush-burning clause cut out. Finally I told him I would take his judgment. If he got hurt, it would be his own fault.

But I also was responsible. So on my way to Washington I sent back to Gene from St. Paul a Luger automatic pistol with what he said was "one of the best letters I have ever received from anyone." He certainly deserved it.

Gene wore that gun in a shoulder holster under his coat, but luckily never had to use it for defense. Later he killed with it much big game, including deer, bear, and mountain lion. He was a great hunter and a great shot. Left to me when Gene died, that Luger (no longer serviceable) hangs on my wall today.

The best shot I ever made was on a trip with Gene. In the foothills of the Big Horn Mountains of Wyoming, a whistling marmot stuck its dark head up behind a whitish rock. Only the head was in sight.

So I jumped out of the buckboard, sat down on the ground with my feet together, threw my arms around my knees, pressed them outward to make a steady rest, grasped my .30-caliber Luger pistol with both hands, and concentrated on the shot.

The first bullet missed—struck the rock in perfect line an inch or two low. Down went the head, but was up again in an instant. The second took it in the middle of the throat. Gene and I paced the distance—one hundred and eighty-two paces.

This knee and hand rest is not my invention. I owe it to my friend Speck von Sternburg, a great shot, the youngest colonel on the German side in the War of 1870, and afterward German Ambassador in Washington.

But to come back to Gene's Minnesota problems. When the lumbermen found their agitation was useless, they quit and got ready to bid. The result was that the timber on the 72,856 acres of the first selection for the Minnesota National Forest Reserve, brush burning and all, brought the best price until then ever paid for any considerable body of White or Red Pine in that part of the world. Score one for Forestry.

Soon after this sale, the Interior Department notified us that the State of Minnesota claimed much of the timber on the Indian Reservations under the provisions of the Swamp Land Act of March 12, 1860. This was a blow. The Secretary had already furnished the Bureau with approved lists from which to make our selection for the Forest Reserve. These lists included all the land in the Reservations except that allotted to Indians, whether swampland or not, and we had drawn the Black Line believing that the lists meant what they said.

After the State's claim was set up, I made vigorous protest and furnished the Interior Department with photographic and other proof that the lands in question were not swamplands, but Pine lands. These so-called swamplands ran in some cases to nearly a million feet of stumpage to the forty acres. Major Scott also protested against the injustice of Minnesota's claims, and a convincing legal brief, prepared by A. C. Shaw of the Bureau, was sent in.

In spite of all this evidence, in spite of the fact that these Pine lands had been officially declared to be such, not once but three times, by the Secretary of the Interior and his agents, they were eventually turned over to the State of Minnesota. It was, Gene well said, a travesty on justice, by which the Chippewa Indians were defrauded of hundreds of thousands of dollars' worth of valuable timber and land.

While this difficult and complicated work was being carried on under Bruce's capable supervision, both he and the Bureau of Forestry were under constant hammering from local politicians, local business men, and local newspapers. The Duluth *News-Tribune,* the Cass Lake *Voice,* and the Cass Lake *Times,* all three owned by one G. G. Hartley, led the pack. Hartley was the original purchaser of the townsite for the village of Cass Lake, where Bruce had his headquarters. A. G. Bernard, editor of the Cass Lake *Voice,* was particularly and persistently hostile, because on two separate occasions Gene had refused to recommend his appointment to Government jobs.

In 1904 Bernard and Hartley set out to locate a townsite within the Black Line and on the area selected for the Reserve. They were backed by the political influence of the Minnesota delegation in Congress. Also, for sufficiently obvious reasons, they named the new townsite Richards, in honor of the Commissioner of the General Land Office.

Nevertheless, thanks to Bruce's exposure of false statements, and to my insistence that the Secretary should live up to his agreement of April 23, 1903, "that he would not allow any of the withdrawn area [within the Black Line] to be opened for either sale, homestead entry, or settlement," the town of Richards never came true.

The passage of the Morris Bill by no means ended the fight against the Reserve. A meeting of the American Forestry Association, at that time no appeaser but a fighting friend of Forestry, held in August of 1903, helped to maintain public interest and support. Yet in 1905 the opposition made a new attack which might have succeeded except for the vigorous backing of the Commercial Clubs of St. Paul and Minneapolis.

Hartley headed the assault. With him was Senator Nelson "and the gang of 'skinners' who have been exploiting the northern portion of the state," to quote C. R. Barns, of the editorial staff of the St. Paul *Pioneer Press,* in a letter to me of May 15, 1905.

"As for Nelson," said Mr. Barns, "when I came to Minnesota nine years ago, I had a high opinion of him. That opinion has vanished before abounding proof that he is a treacherous, dishonest, time-serving politician. He will stab Roosevelt at the first opportunity, just as he has joined in stabbing the Foresty movement, so far as it concerns Minnesota."

Nelson will appear again as this story moves along.

Under the pressure of this drive the Legislature asked Congress to repeal the Morris Act. Congress did not repeal it. And that was the last serious threat to the Minnesota (now the Chippewa) National Forest, which has since proved its value beyond dispute. Indeed the Act of May 23, 1908, applicable to additional lands included by the Act in the National Forest, increased the 5 per cent of reserved timber to 10 per cent. That was anything but a criticism of the work the Forest Service had done.

Both because of the inherent difficulties of the job, and because of this constant hammering, Bruce was under heavy strain. So I made it a practice to go and see him as often as possible. Just before one of my visits some of his men had been shot at, by whom we never learned. When Bruce drove me out to the camp where this had happened, we rode in an open wagon with our Lugers ready on our laps. Forestry was not all Forestry in the peaceful and pellucid current of those tranquil days.

In the fall of 1905, Gene was taken suddenly and violently ill at Cass Lake. He believed that he had been poisoned in the hotel where he was stopping. It was owned by Hartley, and Bernard also lived there. Poisoned or not, Bruce was obliged to go home for a long vacation, leaving G. E. Marshall, who had been his assistant, in charge of the work.

Because it was a new thing in the world, and because its establishment was a triumph of intelligent public sentiment over selfish special interest, the Minnesota National Forest was a milestone on the road to better things. That is why I have described its beginnings at some length.

PART VII
MISSION TO THE EAST

37. *Russia*

In April 1900, Captain George P. Ahern had been appointed as head of the Philippine Bureau of Forestry. His task was a very large one. Of the total of seventy-three million acres in the Islands, some forty million acres were forest land, 99 per cent Government owned. These forests were greater in extent and in value than those of British India, but because of the widespread Philippine insurrection, hardly desirable or safe for the peaceful work of a forest officer.

The Spaniards, from whom we took the Islands in 1898, had established a Bureau of Forestry in 1863. The forest laws and regulations, as Ahern said, were excellent, practicable, and in line with the most advanced Forestry legislation of Europe. But these laws and regulations were not enforced. Licensees cut anything and everything. As a matter of fact the forest officials began their work after the trees left the forest and not before.

Ahern's attempt to set matters straight, like many another endeavor to check old habits of waste, was promptly resented. He had reorganized the Bureau, he spoke the language, knew the country and the people, and in general had made good. Nevertheless the attacks kept on.

A year later Ahern wrote me that he wished I would come out to the Islands. I was already deeply interested in forest administration in the Philippines. Yet my fitness for a study of it might well be questioned. Of experience in tropical Forestry I had exactly none. But I had learned something about Forestry in Burma and in British India from Dr. Brandis and his successors and assistants, and was perhaps better prepared than I seemed.

So on August 30, 1902, with Mark Winchester as my secretary, I sailed from New York on the *Lucania* for Liverpool and points east.

This was no vacation. I took my work along, and on the crossing got a good deal done on my annual report.

On September 12 I passed the Russian frontier. I had never been in Russia before. The Russian forests I saw from the train, commonplace as they were, interested me immensely. So did the Russian peasants. They were dreadfully poor—"women, barefoot, working in the fields till absolute dark."

One Russian soldier I noted whom I shall never forget—an officer, engaged in entraining his cheerful-looking men, who seemed to me to represent, more perfectly than any other soldier I have ever seen, one of my boyhood's heroes, D'Artagnan. His hair was white, but the whole impression of vigor, confidence, and capacity was amazing.

In St. Petersburg (now Leningrad) I presented my credentials, saw the head men of the Forest Department, and had the Vice-Inspector of all the Russian forests assigned to look after me. He took me to see the Forest Institute, a "very remarkable forest school near St. Petersburg which graduates from 100 to 125 trained foresters every year. So far as I know this is the largest professional forest school in existence."

The Forest Institute was the highest of three grades of forest schools in Russia. It gave a four-year course, had a nursery, a teaching forest, a practice forest, and a forest museum. It was founded in 1803, nearly a century before the first forest school in America, and was a complete surprise to me, as, indeed, the progress of Russian Forestry was altogether. And no wonder, considering how far behind Russia in Forestry we were then.

From St. Petersburg I went to see the Forest of Lisino, composed mostly of Spruce, Scotch Pine, and Poplar. Lisino was used as the training ground for one of the thirty-two schools for forest rangers. Its 22,000 acres of good forest land netted 89,000 rubles a year, out of about 100,000 gross. Forestry in Russia was obviously good business. By far the larger part of the forests of Russia and nearly the whole forest area of Siberia belonged to the Crown. The success with which these forests were administered was evident from the fact that the net revenue for that year was estimated at 49,000,000 rubles, say $25,000,000.

For forty years many Americans have looked down on Russia. But more than forty years ago the Russians were already far ahead of the point we Americans have reached in Forestry today. In darkest Russia forty years ago practically all forests were safe from devastation by the ax. In progressive America today far more than half of our forests are open to destruction at the will or the whim of the owner, whenever he may happen to choose.

In contrast to the prosperous Russian forests, the typical Russian peasant was poor—poverty-stricken by our standards. His tools were primitive and no mistake. I saw peasants digging with wooden shovels, and their shoes were commonly made of the inner bark of Basswood trees.

But wherever I went, the capacity of Russian workers to co-operate, in the country and in town, was very remarkable. If a house was to be built, or farm land tilled, or whatever work was to the fore, the usual Russian method was to form a co-operative group on the basis of all for one and one for all, and do it that way. In no other land have I seen the tendency so strong to work together on this most democratic plan.

At Moscow my friend George Dudley Seymour turned up. George had come over to make the Philippine trip with me, at my Father's suggestion and to my great delight.

Some forty years afterward, in America, the victim of an accident which prevented him from speaking or writing, George Seymour prepared and published three large books by the laborious device of pointing to letters pasted on a card. Such an achievement under such handicaps by a man over eighty years old was beyond all praise. Small wonder that we of the Yale Class of '89 are glad and proud that years ago we made him, by formal vote, an honorary Eighty-Niner.

From Moscow George and I drove to the Forest School at Petrovsko-Razumovski Academy, now Timiriazev Institute, and there found Nesteroff, then principal professor of Forestry in the Agricultural College, whom I had first known and liked when we were students together at the French Forest School. Nesteroff showed us the school forest, which was a delight, and told us that 90 per cent of the lumber in Russia was sawed by hand.

Much else he showed us—a plantation of Scotch Pine two miles long and half a mile wide; the old road to Siberia, along which companies of exiles traveled in years gone by; and the wretchedness of the peasants.

The latter made a deep impression on me. I went into the home of a forest ranger, which would certainly have been above the average. The entrance, as into another room, was through a lean-to cow stable, completely enclosed, whereby each cow in winter became a furnace to keep the family warm.

Inside there were no chairs, but a bench along the wall, two cradles, one hung to a coiled brass spring, the other to a spring pole, a brick oven in the kitchen, and far fewer cooking utensils than I have ever seen in the poorest cabin at home. Outside was the bathhouse, the cure-all of the peasants. I would have liked to look inside, but somebody else was in there.

The next day, after the fourth straight night unwashed in a second-class day railroad carriage, found us in a wonderfully fertile agricultural country, spotted with woods but inhabited by paupers, and the next, in a region of rich black soil like our own prairies, where gullies formed quickly. The Forest Department had three parties of foresters busy planting up these gullies on private lands, without charge for their services. The owners furnished the labor. Here again Russian Forestry was many decades ahead of us. The Russians had also begun the planting of shelter belts by the government, whereby they beat us again by some forty years.

Nesteroff left us at Kiski on September 24. He had certainly done everything for us. Then, after a kindly Russian lady who spoke French had helped us to find out about trains, George and I caught the Trans-Siberian and found Winchester and the baggage. We were off for Port Arthur at last.

38. *Siberia–Manchuria–China*

The Urals, those smoothly rounded foothills without mountains, separate Europe from Asia. They seemed very inadequate to the task. On September 27 we left them and passed abruptly into the Siberian steppes, "with only occasional patches of Birch and many small and fairly large lakes. There must have been Elm too, for it appeared in the woodpiles." For several days the country was open, of great value for farming or grazing, except for occasional vast areas of swamp.

On the twenty-ninth "At work all morning and part of P.M. on the *Primer* [of Forestry]. Dinner on cold partridge." We were living high.

From the train approaching Irkutsk I wrote my Mother: "I have been in a state of keen enjoyment for the last two days over the unexpected beauty and value of the forests." It was a very pleasant and most enlightening journey. Instead of the dreary wastes filled with equally dreary exiles which the reputation of Siberia would have led one to expect, I was amazed by the immense fertility of the country and the almost total absence of waste land.

As a rule our train was so slow that I could jump off, run alongside, and jump on again at will. So I shifted from our stateroom to the engine many times, watching the country and talking with the engineers, most of whom were German. From them I learned something of the greater freedom and better living in Siberia than in European Russia, and the greater intelligence of the people. "In Siberia every man does what he likes."

At Irkutsk George and I went to the opera and heard an act of *Aïda* very well sung and staged. A sparse but very enthusiastic audience of intelligent-looking men in uniforms and frock coats and of homely women. Opera—Verdi's masterpiece—well presented in Siberia! It was scarcely what I had been led to expect.

Next morning we made the beautiful trip across Lake Baikal, one of the loveliest bodies of water I can recall. We made it in a steamer because the railroad around the shore was not yet built, entrained again on the other side, and had an excellent dinner in a dining car with piano, chairs, and sofa, and seats at table for sixteen. "Best dining car I ever saw, but slow service. The Russians along played and sang charmingly after dinner."

Then a contrast. One freezing evening George and I stepped out on the station platform. A peasant woman, seated, was selling something—I can't remember what. Beside her a little girl, six or eight years of age, patient and quiet, stood on the edge of her mother's skirt to keep her bare feet from the cold stone. It was not much of an incident in our long excursion, but to me it was, and has been ever since, a symbol of the patient, uncomplaining, downtrodden Russian poor of those far-off days.

Beyond Lake Baikal, as I wrote Secretary Wilson, I was "astonished and delighted with the amount and quality of the timber and its admirable reproduction. This is a real forest country apparently of prodigious extent."

From Lake Baikal to the Manchurian boundary, beyond which

began a new phase, not only in the landscape but also in transportation. The good train went no farther.

At a Manchurian railroad station my letters and the good offices of the train conductor enabled me to get grub for several days, some other necessities, and a very rough second-class car, into which I invited several companions of the journey—Dr. Cruzen, Chief Justice of Kiaochow, Dr. Vering of the German firm that was building Kiaochow harbor, Mr. Kawabe, a charming Japanese, a fairly worthless Englishman, and his worse than worthless courier. "We are having a very pleasant social time. We wash dishes in turn. I was orderly for dinner."

Two days later, however, the tune changed. "Flea bitten and constipated," said George, "I despise the hours." Those Manchurian fleas were without doubt the most entirely competent fleas it has ever been my luck to travel with. Having no place where we could undress, we poured flea powder down our necks in quantities, but with very small results.

Manchuria, as I saw it at first from the train, was almost incredibly lovely—"one of the richest," as I wrote the Secretary, "and perhaps the most beautiful country I ever saw, in the highest possible state of cultivation and evidently of enormous value. Walled villages succeeded each other at close intervals, and the whole country was simply teeming with human life." The land was full of little groves, and nearly all the groves were full of graves. They were the cemeteries of the people.

Among the better-to-do Chinese at the railroad stations in Manchuria I noticed a curious nerve appeaser, an ancient oriental equivalent for modern American chewing gum. It consisted of two walnuts, in size and shape like English walnuts, held in one hand and constantly pressed together and revolved about each other until the roughnesses were rubbed off and the shells acquired a remarkable polish. Meanwhile the owner's nerves were soothed and his cares smoothed away.

I tried to buy a pair of these comforting analgesics, but no one would sell. It appeared that the walnuts were most carefully chosen for size and shape, and often descended from father to son.

Two days before reaching Harbin, another change. "From early morning until night of today we have passed through a wild, utterly unpeopled country. Except at the railroad station, I have not seen a house. The only human beings were six or eight mountain herdsmen looking after bands of horses or sheep."

Just before Harbin I wrote to my brother Amos: "There is a mirage outside the window and we have just passed a herd of two-humped camels. Strange lands and no mistake."

At Harbin a completely new town was being born. "New Harbin is manifestly intended for a great railroad center. As elsewhere along the line, everything is built in the most substantial and expensive way." There also we moved into another car, "after nightfall amid wretched confusion, and then had to allow some Russian ladies one of the compartments. The Carls had the coupé."

Mother Carl and daughter Kate were two American women traveling alone over the unfinished Trans-Siberian in the face of probable war between Russia and Japan. "How they ever had the hardihood to undertake it [as I wrote my Mother] I cannot understand. Mrs. Carl is seventy-three years old and rather feeble at that," but because of her beautiful pluck—good American pluck—she finished her journey in fully as good condition as when she started.

Kate was on her way to paint the portrait of Tsi An, once a slave girl, who had become the world-famous Dowager Empress of 400,000,000 Chinese people. And she did it, too.

After leaving Harbin Russian soldiers "became increasingly plentiful as we went south. I noticed many troopers with bayonets attached to the outside of their scabbards and carrying full-length infantry rifles. Towards evening single sentinels patrolling the railroad line with fixed bayonets began to appear. At the stations during the day the mud walls of small forts were common, and at nearly every station was a watchtower."

Two days later: "We have been seeing all day soldiers, who are evidently on campaign, with faded clothes and worn accouterments, but looking clear-eyed and resolute and far more intelligent than I had expected to find them. The men who are detailed as police at the stations beat the Chinese with whips with the utmost freedom. There is still no evidence of any rancor against the Russians."

In ludicrous contrast to the competent Russian soldiers were the Chinese. "A camp of Chinese artillery had the most motley assortment of useless hardware I ever saw. There were even a certain number of old pieces of from one- to two-inch caliber, mounted on poles three or four feet long, stuck in the rear end. In front of headquarters were a number of stacks of muskets, apparently of about one-inch bore, and not less than seven feet long.

"The car we are in is second class, but better than the other. There is, however, no lock to the water closet, and the seats are very hard to sleep on. We live on sardines, canned beef, bread, tea, and preserves.

"We are all feeling pretty ragged. George is tormented with fleas, and we both have some louse bites. A beautiful country, though. Wonderful mountain background.

"As we neared Port Arthur it became increasingly difficult to keep people out of the car, and in the middle of the night I let it fill up. Hard rain. Not much sleep. George and I had a long laugh over the situation in the middle of the night."

When the journey through Russia, Siberia, and Manchuria was done, I sent my impressions to Tama Jim Wilson:

"In European Russia, the emancipation of the serfs, of which we have heard so much, has in reality never taken place. The Russian peasant is tied to the land now as he was before. His material condition is worse than at the date of the emancipation. On that subject I have heard but one opinion.

"While the merchant class may be recruited from the peasants, no peasant can rise to the governing orders. He is practically without mail service, and wholly without newspapers. What little reading he does is confined to the Scriptures and a few storybooks.

"In short, the Russian peasant is still practically a slave. His methods of work are clumsy and wasteful to a degree which I should never have believed without seeing. I do not see how a people so utterly unaccustomed to using their hands in any accurate way can develop into a manufacturing nation in any short space of time."

Whether forty years is a short space of time may be open to question. What is not open is that in the forty-odd years since that sentence was written, the Russians have developed (G.P. to the contrary notwithstanding) an industrial efficiency which was a considerable factor in Hitler's Russian defeat.

My letter went on: "Now the Siberian looks you in the eye, and you feel that there is at least something of the man about him. In European Russia the peasant stands with bowed uncovered head at the side of the road in the rain as you pass, and is so abjectly cowed and so utterly destitute of manliness as to give a decidedly painful cast to a journey in Russia back from the railroad."

About this and other statements I continued: "I know this is strong language and that it is not sustained by recent writings about Russia. But to any man who leaves the railroad at all, the facts are so evident that it would be somewhat difficult to understand the influences which have produced these opinions, except for the charming courtesy and real persuasiveness of the educated Russians. Man after man has gone to Russia and come away filled with the greatness and glory of the Russian Empire."

But there was a reason why I was in better position to judge. No Russian authority had thought it worth while to limit my chance to see, or to tell me only what it was wise to let me know. I went where I pleased, saw what I pleased, and talked with whom I pleased, limited only by language and time.

In consequence my impressions were very different from those of the higher-ups. When I got back to America I told T.R. of my confident belief that if war with Japan should come, as I was sure it would, Russia would lose.

War did come and lose she did. And she lost because her leaders were not equal to making use of the stubborn courage of her rank and file. Carloads of champagne and ballet girls at the front were scarcely to be classed as necessary munitions of war.

On October 13 we reached Port Arthur after nineteen days on the Trans-Siberian, during the last eleven of which I had not had my clothes off. There was no place on the train sufficiently protected to make that civilized custom safe.

"Port Arthur," as I wrote Secretary Wilson, "is naturally by far the strongest naval port I ever saw, and the Russians are sparing neither money nor effort to make it impregnable. The best opinion I can get among thoroughly qualified observers is that northern China must eventually fall into Russian hands."

After four hours in Port Arthur we followed in a steamer the wonderfully picturesque and interesting coast to Dalny (Dairen), "a large town created in two years with no reason beyond what may be perceived by the eye of faith." But I think the Russians knew.

Next Chefoo, where Frank Carl, Commissioner of Customs, made us welcome, and where I squandered $50 gold on certain Chinese jades, said to be part of the loot of Peiping during the Boxer

Rebellion. Also George and I got our clothes off for the first time in twelve days, and had a bath from head to foot. We were yellow with flea powder. I shall always gratefully remember Frank Carl and Chefoo.

We landed at Shanghai on October 16. Everything here seemed to me just out of storybooks. The junks on the river, each with its two eyes, the sampans scattered about, the English settlement, with English roads, Sihk policemen, and perfect order. And then the native walled city: "Streets six to eight feet wide, filth, smells, and crowding. I marvel any human being can live in it. What it must be in summer I can only guess."

In most impressive contrast, at St. John's College George and I attended a service in Chinese. The church was full of Chinese boys and girls. You get a new conception of what missions mean to China when you see that sort of thing.

At Shanghai I went at some length into the question of our consular representation, with T.R. in the back of my head. I never forgot that I belonged to his administration.

We reached Hong Kong on October 22. There we found far more to see than we had expected: "The town is a perfect marvel, built by main force by the English in a way that commands your wonder and respect. New fortifications are everywhere being erected in considerable numbers, I suppose as a reply to the Russians at Port Arthur, and the harbor is full of ships. The monuments in the cemeteries to soldiers and sailors who died in the line of duty show where part of it comes from."

Then off on the *Loong Sang* for Manila, through choppy seas driven by the monsoon, with flying fish to punctuate our progress. During the trip I worked on Ahern's special report, on my Siberian notes, and on the *Primer*. What time I had I tried to use.

On the morning of the twenty-sixth, just a month and a day from the Urals, Luzon was in sight. We passed Subic Bay, where our miniature torpedo boats, forty years later, were to give such brilliant proof of their skill and daring; passed the rock fortress of Corregidor (where Wainwright stayed), whose cliffs rose sheer from the water in which more than one United States soldier has been killed by sharks; passed Mariveles on Bataan Peninsula, made famous forever by General MacArthur's heroic defense; and at last through the marvelous landlocked harbor of Manila to the port.

39. *The Philippines*

At the harbor Ahern met us in a launch and took us up the Pasig River to Malacañan, the official residence of the Governor General. There Will Taft himself met us at the landing and invited George and me to stay with him at the Palace. We were struck at once by the beautiful floors—wide planks of dark narrawood, polished by rubbing with bitter oranges cut in two.

That day I met Ide, Worcester, and other members of the Philippine Commission, talked with the president of the Chamber of Commerce on the price of timber, made calls, and saw sights. Then back to Malacañan. At dinner was General Franklin Bell, for whom I conceived an instant and well-grounded admiration.

After dinner, with Taft and Bell to the Teatro Zonilla to hear *Il Trovatore* and a farce in Tagalog. We went in a diminutive victoria drawn by equally diminutive Filipino horses. As Taft and Bell stepped out at the door of the theater a band struck up, almost under the noses of the ponies. Instantly the little horses ran. The Filipino coachman skillfully held them in the wide circle of the Plaza while I, rather amused, sat quiet in the carriage. As we came around to the theater again, Taft and Bell rushed at the runaways, seized their heads, and stopped them dead. I was too late to be of much use.

My comment at the time: "Taft is splendid."

Next day I saw a bishop (and a fine one, Bishop Brent), a sawmill (of the Philippine Lumber and Development Company), a prison (Bilibid), and much besides. Then once more back to Malacañan, where Taft showed me Roosevelt's cable offering him a seat on the Supreme Court, and his own refusal. I thought it superb. And superb it was, to sidetrack the ambition of his life for the sake of finishing a hard job so far from home.

After which to a dinner given by Ahern at the Army and Navy Club. Present—Judge Taft and about a dozen others. "These are very busy days and very hot."

Next day we were off on the *General Alava,* Captain Jones, a United States gunboat of 1,400 tons, assigned to the Governor General as his official yacht. He had turned it over to me for the trip among the Islands.

Our party included Ahern, George Seymour, Winchester, and Dorsey of the Department of Agriculture. George and I had the captain's cabin. With good reason I wrote my Mother: "This is the proudest way to travel in my experience. A vessel 212 feet long, with a crew of 78 men, to go where you like when you like."

October 30 we landed early at Paluan Bay on the Island of Mindoro, where we found a primitive Filipino settlement—primitive enough so that a young woman wandering about in the dawn was giving a perfect imitation of Lady Godiva without the horse. Here also was the camp of L Company, Thirtieth U.S. Infantry, at whose commissary we got provisions for a hike into the woods.

With an escort and Filipino bearers we started up the Calansan trail, and for five or six hours traveled through almost distressingly interesting tropical forest, where every tree was new and strange, and camped on high ground for the night.

There the "Filipinos built us a shelter, thatched it partly with a palm like nipa, and made a bed of poles (for each of us) about eighteen inches off the ground. Nothing on the poles. About nine o'clock it began to rain, and it rained nearly all night. Roof leaked, part of poles broke down, fire was put out, etc., etc.

"But we had a jovial time, and I had a good think over forest problems. All got more or less wet (in spite of ponchos) and the poles (only three or four to a man) were sinfully hard. Everyone behaved well. Some of the Filipinos shivered and chattered till I thought one would die."

And perhaps he would have died if the sergeant in charge of our escort had not given the poor devil his poncho. But we all got back to Paluan next afternoon, and none the worse.

November 1, at the mouth of the Dioso River, "Spent nearly all day carefully going through the forest" and trying to identify the trees. "Useful day because we went slow." And so on, day after day, from one island to another, sailing past the coasts, going into the deep woods, and writing up the country, the forests, the industries, and the people. Indeed we saw and in most cases landed on practically every island that has got into the news of the war against the Japanese.

Our journey was full of incident. One day, as we tramped and looked and looked and tramped through a tropical high forest so dense that not a green thing grew beneath the shade in the deep bed of dry brown leaves that covered the ground, I suddenly had a feeling that one of my shoes was full of water. And it was full, not of water, however, but of blood. Half a dozen leeches had somehow got inside my leggings. In accordance with their cheerful custom, they had perforated my hide without my knowing it. I carried the scars for a good six months.

At Calbayog on the island of Samar, although the island was commonly called "Bloody Samar" (because there some of the hardest fighting of the Philippine Insurrection took place), "I was struck by the immediate response of the people to courteous or jovial approaches, as well as by the unsympathetic appearance of those to whom we did not speak."

On Samar, and on Leyte, since taken from the Japanese at so heavy a price, we saw Toog trees: "The crown of this tree is so small, and it has a clear length so great, that it can interfere little, if at all, with the field crops over which it grows. I have never seen a tree so thoroughly adapted to the combination of Forestry and agriculture as this one."

At Iloilo, Major Orwig of the Philippine Constabulary gave us all the guns we could carry away and many spears and bolos—weapons captured by his outfit from ladrones—and sent a bundle of them to the President. These captured guns were mainly psychological weapons. The barrel of one I have consists of a length of iron pipe the size of a pick handle. The barrel of another is made of tin cans, beaten flat and then rolled together. The lock of still another, modeled on a Mauser, is all made of wood, while its barrel also is built up of tin cans. Obviously such weapons were intended to frighten and plunder Filipinos and not to fight American troops.

The ladrones are not the only powers that prey in this green paradise. The tree that eats trees, Balete by name, was widely scattered. It grows up from the ground through the branches of its victim, drops runners from above, produces more shoots from below, and gradually envelopes and then extinguishes its host and benefactor, according to the custom of monopolists in more civilized regions. The end of this rapine is a noble-looking forest tree, itself far larger than most of its companions.

These dense timberlands fascinated me. In southern Negros, for example, a trail running inland took us into a forest "the most luxuriant I have yet seen, and in by far the best silvicultural condition. On the lower slopes it consisted of old trees from 130 to 150 feet in height, frequently with from 90 to 100 feet of clear trunk, standing in a selection forest in which all age classes were represented."

On the island of Mindanao, we ran into Santa Maria Bay and went ashore at the mill of the Philippine Lumber and Development Company, whose manager, Mr. Bourns, had much pull at Manila (but not with Taft). We expected to find bad work, and we found it.

"Everywhere we went the untouched forest was in a superb condition. [Yet] I have never seen a more complete slash, because it is impossible to make one. Everything was destroyed as far as logging had gone.

"Unquestionably the kind of logging now going on will lead to erosion of the most serious character on a surface so steep as to be totally unfit for agriculture." Nevertheless the condition of this forest and the grade of labor employed were such as to make conservative methods of logging perfectly feasible.

At the town of Zamboanga was Dato Mandi, a Moro chieftain who was Ahern's forester, his assistant, and one of the inspectors (a Filipino). "Mandi can only just write his name, but his name is useful." Those were times and places where foresters needed friends.

Then to Malabang, on another coast of Mindanao, from which port Ahern, Captain Jones, Dorsey, and I started for Camp Vickers on Lake Lanao, where Pershing had recently taught the Moros a much-needed lesson—a lesson they had not yet fully learned. We took with us an escort of a sergeant and eight men.

On the fine new American road to Mataling Falls, en route to the Lake, we passed several small groups of Moros carrying their campilans on their shoulders—in which sentence there may be more than meets the eye. For a campilan is a long, straight, two-handed sword encased in a scabbard made of two flat pieces of wood lightly tied together with string. If a Moro with his campilan on his shoulder meets someone he does not like, he is all set. His weapon is in perfect position to strike. As the blow falls the string is severed, the blade slips easily out of its obliging sheath, and the victim is no better off than if the sword had never been sheathed at all.

Before our soldiers learned the nature of this little joke, a number of them had their heads split open by ostensibly friendly Moros. After that no Moro with a campilan, friendly or not, was allowed to get within a jump and a blow of our men.

The same type of scabbard was used for the bolo, the big all-purpose knife (or small all-purpose sword) of the Filipinos, all through the Islands. In case of trouble it saved time.

The conquest of the Islands was yet so recent, and the fabric of peace was still so thin, that at the camp at Mataling Falls no one left his tent after dark unless another man stood by with a cocked gun in his hand. Too many men, sentries and others, had been cut up. While we passengers on the *Alava* had not been in the habit of leaving our revolvers aboard when we went ashore, still the road from the Falls to the Lake was distinctly interesting.

When we started for Camp Vickers next morning my poncho slipped off and caught on the saddle, my horse went to bucking on the very brink of a steep arroyo, and the left bridle rein broke at the bit. "But I stayed on him all right." One of the officers asked me where I learned to ride. I was pleased with that.

At Camp Vickers we were welcomed by Captain John J. Pershing (whose name you have heard), saw the Moro fort he and his men had so recently taken, and learned firsthand the story of the fight. Pershing gave me, from the spoils of war, a suit of armor made from carabao horn and several of the long sharpened bamboo stakes the Moros had planted in the ditch before their wall. Armor and stakes I had to pack on my saddle, with much misgiving, for the ride back. But this time nothing happened.

T.R. was, I knew, deeply interested in the fighting in the Philippines. From Manila I wrote him on November 22:

> The first thing that struck me about the military operations in Mindanao was the enormous difficulty of the country in which our troops are at work, and the facility and safety with which a determined enemy could make trouble. Our party, although we had an escort of a sergeant and eight men, might have been fired on with perfect impunity by the Moros every ten minutes for at least fifteen of the twenty-three miles from Malabang to Camp Vickers, yet no one has been molested on the road for about two months.
>
> Captain Pershing struck me as being as good an example of the right man in the right place as I have ever seen. I had a good talk with him about the situation, and was able to gather something of his methods of dealing with the natives, among whom he has already made many strong

friends. When the time comes to settle with the Sultan of Bacolod, who is apparently the only man from whom trouble may come, Captain Pershing will certainly be able to do it with ease.

The fact that Captain Pershing cleaned out the most formidable body of Moros around Lake Lanao just recently, with a total loss to himself of two men wounded, seems to be satisfactory evidence on this point. [Whether the foregoing had anything to do with justifying in T.R.'s mind the promotion of Pershing from Captain to Brigadier General at one step, I do not know. If it did I'm glad of it.]

The thing I chiefly started out to write you is this: A couple of weeks ago two Moros, who had taken oath to die killing Christians, came with eight or ten of their friends to one of the gates of Jolo just as a troop of the 15th Cavalry were saddling up. They attacked two men who were slightly apart from the others, and before they could be killed had severely wounded one of them. Not only did our men, who had seen their comrade attacked and wounded without warning in a friendly place, make no effort to molest the Moros who had accompanied the murderers, but one of the men formally arrested them, and warned everyone to let them alone.

No officers were present. Discipline of this kind on the part of enlisted men seems to me so superb that I wanted you to hear of it if you have not already done so. These are the men whom the Anti-Imperialists are trying to exhibit as bloodthirsty brutes.

Nothing has impressed me more than the quality and bearing of both officers and men wherever I have run across them. The officers are manly, upright, clear-eyed, honest gentlemen, and the men of so high a grade that it makes me proud to be an American every time I see them.

Every camp I have seen was in the pink of order, and the treatment of the natives by the soldiers has been everywhere far better than that by civilians at the same time and place. I never began to appreciate the infamy of the attacks on the Army and Navy until I came to know the men who were being attacked.

From Malabang we steamed to Jolo, where the Moros were particularly subject to the habit of going juramentado, as in the case I wrote T.R. about. Then on to Tawi Tawi, southernmost group of the Philippines, famous for rubber and gutta-percha, and so to the port of Sandakan, in North Borneo.

40. *On the Way Home*

At Sandakan George Seymour, wandering about among the long-legged Dyak huts at the shore, discovered a man of the woods, a young orangutan, in a cage. It occurred to me that it would be nice to possess an orangutan, at least during part of the process of growing up. So I bought this one. He cost me twenty-five pesos, but the distinction of being his proprietor was cheap at the price.

It is more than likely that you have never before come across a man who actually owned a living orang. Is it any wonder that I rejoiced in my own glory?

Later on I presented my treasure to Mrs. Taft at Malacañan, where he built himself a nest in a treetop, after the manner of his kind. Because he was no safe playmate for the children, Mrs. Taft finally gave him to the Manila Zoo, where he lived out a long and highly popular existence as Mrs. Dooley. Why those Filipinos changed his sex remains a mystery.

From Sandakan, with the friendly orang in his flimsy bamboo cage, out of which he broke whenever the whim seized him, and with ten miniature parrots who went to sleep each night hanging by their feet to the top of their cage, we took our way through the Sea of Jolo and past Balabac and Bugsuk to the west coast of Palawan.

Here let me digress a little. I find a note in my diary for November 17, 1902, written as we steamed along the coast of Palawan, two and a half months after sailing from New York: "Loafed all day and read *The Forest Lovers,* the first play, book, or article since I left home." A foolish mistake, for it is not wise to keep the spring too constantly compressed.

So far as my bad eyes would permit, reading has always been to me an enormous relaxation and relief. But I have read for escape far more than for information or improvement, and so have wasted time beyond counting. I have spent much leisure with books, but I have never gained in knowledge from my reading anything approaching what the time expended might easily have yielded. I am not, I am sorry to admit, what is called a well-read man.

The foregoing is addressed to those who still have the chance to form new habits. At eighty it may be too late for me. And besides, I have more books I want to write: the story of my first and perhaps my second term at Harrisburg; another volume of fishing tales; perhaps some hunting stories too; something about the family for my grandchildren; and not a little else. There will scarcely be time for all I have in mind.

Enough of that. Come back with me to Palawan, and Malampaya Bay on that same island, where we ran into real trouble.

The trouble we ran into at full speed was a coral reef on which the *General Alava* hung suspended, with nine feet of water amidships, thirty feet under her bow, and forty under her stern. There being neither telegraph nor telephone on Palawan, nor radios anywhere on earth, outside help was out of the question. Fortunately, after hanging on the reef from early morning till night, after pumping thirty tons of water out of her and throwing much ballast overboard, our anchors and the rising tide took her off, uninjured. Lucky they did, too, for when we steamed into Manila the last coal we had was under the boilers.

Altogether we covered between two and three thousand miles among the Islands, landed at least once on each of the larger ones, and saw an incredible number of smaller islands. I made notes on more than two hundred of them, large and small. We came away, I suppose, with more knowledge of the general forest situation of the Philippines than anyone else had been able to collect. So far as I could learn, no one, except the officials of the Lighthouse Board, had made so comprehensive a journey through the Islands.

On our trips ashore we carried our revolvers. Not seldom a Marine or so went along. It was pleasant to have them, but we found no need for either on this cheerful and peaceful journey. No wild beasts attacked us, nor did anyone make us afraid. I wrote my Father: "This is by far the best trip I ever made and I think it will have the best results."

Back in Manila I worked out my recommendations, set them down in a letter to Taft, and handed them to him on November 24, 1902. The Governor General thereupon called in Worcester, one of the members of the Commission, and read the letter to us both. At the end he said, without comment, that anything that would suit the two of us would suit him.

Of necessity my letter was long, for it embodied the results of the journey you have been following. It was also one of the foundations of Forestry in the Philippines. It began with the cardinal facts of the forest situation as I saw them. Here are some of the more important:

"The internal condition of the forests, the degree of governmental control, the efficiency and spirit of the Insular forest service organized by Captain Ahern, and the general economic situation, combine to present the best opportunity for successful and profitable forest administration of which I have knowledge.

"The regulation of lumbering so as to ensure permanent supplies of the more valuable timbers is impossible at present for lack of a working knowledge of the conditions of natural reproduction.

"A great development of forest industries in the Islands is evidently at hand. If this development is not to be accompanied by serious, extensive, and permanent injury to the forests, preparation by study and experiment must begin at once."

In view of these facts I recommended, among other things:

"That the resources of the forest service be increased as rapidly as men can be found to meet the urgent needs inherent in the present situation.

"That a revision of the forest law and the rules under it be prepared at once, and put in force. Detailed recommendations under this head are in preparation.

"That the work of the timber-testing laboratory be continued, along the general lines adopted by the Bureau of Forestry in the United States.

"That three experimental ranges of not less than five thousand acres each be set aside for the practical study of methods of reproducing the best timbers, for experimental forest planting, and for other silvicultural work.

"That a school for native forest rangers be established in one of the experimental forests as soon as suitable instructors can be found."

Three days later (November 27), "Conference with Taft at palace. He gave me messages for Root and described situation of Islands and measures needed at length. Agreed fully with forest program. Said of law, 'Let me know what you want and we'll pass it.' Said of measures, 'Tell me whatever you want and I'll see that Ahern carries it out.' Situation most hopeful." It was Thanksgiving Day, and I had reason to be thankful.

Cholera was then loose in Manila. The Aherns, with whom George and I were staying, would let us eat no raw fruit without scalding except oranges, whose skin kills the cholera germ.

George Ahern and Filipe Calderon (perhaps the leading Filipino lawyer) took us to see Emilio Aguinaldo, once leader of the Insurrectos, whose capture made Funston famous:

"Aguinaldo is a dapper little man, rather lighter in color than the average Filipino, and showing distinctly, as I think, the mixture of Chinese blood. His head is well shaped, but he makes no impression whatever of unusual capacity and, least of all, of the power which he undoubtedly has in some degree."

I had recommended and Ahern needed a training school for Filipino forest rangers. We went together to look over some available forest land back of Mariveles and Cabcaben on Bataan and found it excellent. You may perhaps be interested in a forester's description of the forest in which MacArthur and his men, with their Filipino friends, made so magnificent a fight.

In places there were more than twenty-five trees over twelve inches in diameter to the acre, some of them of large size and great height. We constantly found Panao trees of a clear length of from eighty to a hundred feet, and Lauan of similar dimensions. Throughout this forest young growth of valuable species was very plentiful. For the most part saplings predominated in the lower story, but there were extensive patches of poles, and it was very common to find all age classes well represented.

We spent the night in the woods. Near our camp my revolver killed the thinnest snake I ever saw, five feet ten inches in length and only one-half to three-quarters of an inch thick. It was a brilliant light yellow-green in color, with a head three times the width of its neck. "The natives said it was deadly poison. Unfortunately, I forgot to see if it would strike." Perhaps that was my good luck.

My business at Manila ended, Ahern, Seymour, Winchester, and I, thanks once more to Will Taft, went aboard the *Alava* again and were off for Japan and home. First we skirted the coast of northern Luzon and landed once in the Province of Cagayan. Then through a very high sea in the Pescadores Channel to the port of Tamsui on the Island of Formosa.

The *Alava* wisely declined the risk of crossing the bar and entering the harbor, so we four went ashore in a lifeboat through very rough water. Our ship put to sea to ride out the storm while we dined on Japanese food, eaten with chopsticks and without a table in a Japanese hotel. We slept on the floor on thick pallets, and had kimonos to sleep in and black velvet quilts for cover. The two maids who brought in the beds insisted on helping us undress for the night. But we all escaped their assistance.

Next day (December 6) "took the 7:30 train for the capital, Taihoku, through a marvelously well-tilled country but not naturally a rich one. First, irrigated rice fields in terraces, then sweet potatoes, sugar cane, pineapple, etc."

We breakfasted and lunched at the American Consulate, called on the acting Japanese Governor, bought camphorwood and not a little else, and then back to Tamsui to find the surf still heavy on the bar and no chance to rejoin the *Alava*.

George and I, in consequence, returned to Taihoku, where two other Japanese maids did their best to wash us at our joint bath in a single huge wooden barrellike hotel bathtub. But we had won against the maids at Tamsui, and once again we defended our modesty with entire success. That incident and a single piece of camphorwood eight feet square made, as you see, a deep impression.

At Tamsui two Scotch Canadian Presbyterian missionaries gave me a most interesting account of their work. I have always been a champion of foreign missions, and the more so the more I learned about them. Dr. Brandis never tired of praising the American medical missionaries in Burma, and he had a chance to judge.

The captain of the port at Tamsui asked me to take his son with us to Nagasaki. The boy was going to study in America. We took young Watanabe, and he was the seasickest human being it has ever been my hard luck to see. It was rough all the way (I lost my own dinner the first night out), and for the three-day trip that young Jap lay on his back in his bunk with his eyes shut, one leg hanging over, dead to the living world.

Next a stop in the Ryukyu Islands (we called them Liu-Kiu then), where our men won so great a glory, and on to Nagasaki and Moji. "Then by train through the beautiful terraced country and along the shores of the Inland Sea all day. Did a good deal of work during the day with Ahern [on our report to Taft, as we did every day we were in Japan] and saw much interesting forest, including planted Pine and planting against erosion on bare granite sand hills."

Somewhere on the route Kyoto-Tokyo-Yokohama (I've forgotten

where) young Watanabe's relations presented me with a sword of honor in token of their gratitude. But their interest in the boy stopped there. He needed more money for his journey, which his relations refused to lend him—a quite customary intra-family distrust, I was told.

December 17 we sailed from Yokohama on the *America Maru.* The second day out we "stopped to send provisions to the *St. David* of Puget Sound, fifty-eight days out of Manila homeward bound, now short of grub, and crew on half rations for the last week." She had run into a typhoon and she looked it.

On the voyage across the Pacific I set myself regular work hours, seven and a half a day. "I hope for some work on the *Primer* before we land, if the weather holds good." It didn't, but the work got done just the same.

At Honolulu, where we stopped for a few hours, I talked all night with my friend George Carter, then Governor of the Islands, saw with him the great cliffs of the Pali, Diamond Head, and Waikiki, and visited the Bishop Museum. It was a busy less-than-a-day.

January 2 we landed in San Francisco, where I found news of the Forest Service and news from home, and then straight across the continent to Washington, which I reached thanks (or no thanks) to a cylinder head that blew out on the locomotive, on January 8, only just in time to go straight from the station to the Capitol for a hearing before the House Committee on Agriculture.

After the hearing, and a glorious lunch with my Father and Mother, I dropped in on Secretary Wilson, who greeted me with "Well, old fellow, I'm glad to see you back." Then to the Bureau: "I do not see that anything except the transfer has suffered, and perhaps not that, because I have been away."

There never was such a body of men and women as those of the Service in Washington and in the field, with Overton Price at their head. I had been away four months and yet nothing had suffered! No wonder I took up work again at the office gladly.

PART VIII

THE GOAL AT LAST

41. *Full Steam Ahead*

Since I could not be sure of getting back from the Philippines in time to be heard by the Committee on Agriculture on our estimates for 1903-04, I had left with Overton Price some notes which summed up very briefly the progress made from 1898 to 1902, and which he presented to the Committee.

In reply to a question in the Committee as to whether the work of the Bureau would be more effective in the Interior Department, Overton made so good an answer (and so timely even today) that I must quote part of it:

"Forestry is a component part of agriculture. Every source of wealth grown from the soil is in the sphere of the Department of Agriculture; hence the forest work rightly belongs to it. The production of timber is as naturally within the scope of the Department of Agriculture as is the production of field crops.

"To take forestry from Agriculture would be to mar the unity and limit the effectiveness of the former. The amount of forest in farms alone is more than four times greater than the whole area of reserves, while the private land now being lumbered under the direction and control of the Bureau of Forestry is many times greater than the area being cut over in all the Forest Reserves together.

"The Department of Agriculture," Overton went on, "is much more familiar with the problems and conditions of the Forest Reserves than is the General Land Office, a fact shown by the request of the Interior Department not only for working plans for practical forestry but for reports on grazing and other subjects. Except for the men loaned by the Department of Agriculture, not a single person now engaged in the Division of Forestry in the General Land Office in Washington has ever been on a Forest Reserve.

"The Interior Department is overloaded and has officially asked to be relieved of its Forest Reserve work; the Department of Agriculture is thoroughly prepared to handle it."

One large piece of work ahead of us for 1902 was a working plan for about a million acres of Longleaf Pine in Texas, owned jointly by the Kirby Lumber Company and the Houston Oil Company. In South Carolina 50,000 acres of Longleaf Pine were waiting, in Georgia 62,000 acres of Pine, and many more cases in many places.

In the Northeast there was work in Maine which we hoped would lead to the adoption of Forestry by the Great Northern Paper Company and many other important organizations.

Furthermore, the Bureau had just undertaken a working plan for 125,000 acres of the Baltimore and Ohio Railroad in West Virginia. The New York Central and the Pennsylvania Railroads had engaged our help in locating timber tracts which under management would furnish a steady supply of ties. The Pennsylvania was the first railroad to appoint a forester. He was John Foley.

Other railroads also were increasingly interested in our work in seasoning and preserving ties and structural timber. They used some 120,000,000 new ties a year besides enormous quantities of construction timber. They owned immense areas in land grants in the West or in lands acquired in the South and East, and their influence on the side of Forestry promised to be of very great importance.

New forest schools began to spring up all over the country. The University of Michigan Forest School was established. The Harvard Forest School was on the way. The University of Nebraska established a Department of Forestry; the Mont Alto Forest Academy was founded in Pennsylvania; and California was hungry for a State Forest School. The University of Maine and several others began to offer courses in Forestry. That summer (1902) about a dozen graduate foresters joined the Division. Another dozen undergraduates from Cornell worked with us. The Division of Forest Management alone had 104 men in the field in addition to packers, choppers, and other helpers.

We used these men to build up the science of American Forestry as we went along. Every piece of field work was aimed (in part) at getting more knowledge of American forest conditions and forest life and of what would happen when specific things were done to the forest. There were then some two hundred commercial species of trees in this country about which there was no previous silvical knowledge whatsoever, and any working plan involved a study of some of them.

Also we had little technical knowledge of actual forest conditions in the different regions. So we pushed as hard as we could the studies of important hardwoods in the Great Smoky Mountains and on the Cumberland Plateau, of second-growth hardwoods in New England, Balsam in Maine, Western Yellow Pine in Arizona, and Sugar Pine in California and Oregon.

Moreover, the states were waking up. Michigan had a small Forest Reserve and was anxious to increase it and to handle it wisely. Pennsylvania had about 400,000 acres already reserved. Maryland was studying her forests in co-operation with the Bureau of Forestry. New York was making a study to justify the repeal of that clause in her constitution which prohibited cutting, and therefore forbade Forestry on State lands. The Bureau was co-operating with Vermont in a preliminary study of her forests. California was thinking of appointing a State forester. Connecticut had done so, and made a small appropriation for a Forest Reserve. And interest also was growing in the forests of Puerto Rico, Hawaii, and especially the Philippines.

Meantime the question of tree planting in the semiarid West was coming to the front. Settlement in the prairies had been followed by a reduction in prairie fires and that by a perceptible spread of natural forest growth, as Professor Charles E. Bessey, distinguished botanist and lifelong friend of Forestry, had early observed. Obviously any trees that were able to extend unaided into treeless areas were good enough to consider for planting, provided they had other desirable qualities. So we undertook to find out what we could.

Beginning in 1900 our investigations were carried on in nearly all the states of the Great Plains. We were not the first in this field. In 1891 some 20,000 tree seedlings had been planted on typical sand hills in western Nebraska under plans made by Dr. Fernow, with the encouragement and assistance of Professor Bessey. The success of this plantation was encouraging. The principal species used were Ponderosa Pine, Jack Pine, Scotch Pine, and Austrian Pine, with Black Locust, Black Cherry, Box Elder, and Hackberry as nurse trees.

Ten years later our study was carried far enough to show that portions of the sand hills heretofore considered almost worthless could be forested with valuable timber at comparatively small expense. As a result, President Theodore Roosevelt in 1902 set aside, at my suggestion, the Dismal River and Niobrara Forest Reserves in Nebraska, mainly to try out our tree-planting plans. It was arranged that the Department of the Interior should ask us to undertake the work, and the first planting was done in 1903.

In time this came to be one of the great successful tree-planting projects of the world, on a par with the reforestation of the Karst in Dalmatia, and of the Landes in southern France. Some 16,000 acres have now been successfully reforested, and cutting, chiefly for firewood, in some of the earlier plantings has actually begun.

Among the pioneers in this early forest planting was Charles R. Scott, who for years was in charge of the Dismal River and Niobrara Reserves, and whose good work should not be forgotten.

The work in Nebraska opened up a vast field for reforestation in other semiarid regions. The great Shelter Belt Plan begun under President Franklin D. Roosevelt, and so brilliantly suggested and successfully directed by Raphael Zon, is its direct lineal descendant.

When this century began it was clear to us that forest planting would grow in importance as time went on. Enormous areas on the Forest Reserves, and on public lands not yet reserved but likely to be, needed planting, and each year new fires enlarged the areas. In southern California, for example, where water was the main consideration, we were confronted with the task of making many trees grow where none grew before. And in the Forest Reserves that was one job which the General Land Office was more than glad to have us take over.

To replace the chaparral of southern California with timber trees turned out to be impossible. But the effort was not wasted. We were learning all the while not only where to plant but where not to plant, and how to select the right trees. And we were training men to grow from seed great quantities of the trees we had chosen.

Nineteenth-century advocates of "Forestry" in the United States had devoted most of their attention to tree planting. Yet they knew little more about how to establish new forests by plantation than they did about how to apply Forestry to existing stands. On this course also we had to break new ground.

While reclamation by tree planting was thus getting its start, the question of a Forest Reserve in the Southern Appalachian Mountains was in the fire. The story begins soon after I went to Biltmore in 1892. There were no Forest Reserves in the East because there were no public lands. The only way to get them would be to buy them.

The first suggestion for the purchase of Eastern Forest Reserves came from Professor Joseph A. Holmes, then State Geologist of North Carolina, and later Director of the United States Bureau of Mines. It was made to me, you may remember, in the little Brick House at Biltmore in 1892 or '93. Holmes's suggestion was never out of my head for long. But in those early days of American Forestry there was comparatively little to be done about it.

In 1898, I understand through the initiative of Dr. George Ambler, the Appalachian National Park Association was started in Asheville. On January 2, 1901, a memorial of the Association was presented to Congress and referred to the Committee on Agriculture, and an investigation was authorized. Accordingly, during the fiscal year 1900-1901 the Division of Forestry, in co-operation with the United States Geological Survey, made a study of the Southern Appalachian forests. An area of 9,600,000 acres was examined and mapped.

The results were set forth in an elaborate report transmitted to Congress with a message on December 19, 1901, by Theodore Roosevelt, and ordered printed as Senate Document No. 84. That document contained reliable information concerning the proposed Appalachian Forest Reserve, and gave exhaustive data on the composition, condition, character, extent, and distribution of the forests of a region then little known.

Early in 1901 the North Carolina Legislature had ceded to the United States authority to acquire title to land for Forest Reserve purposes, with exemption from taxes. For this long step ahead, Joseph Hyde Pratt, lifelong friend of the forests, was largely responsible. Similar measures, also, were passed within three months by Georgia, Alabama, and Tennessee. We were making progress.

In July of the same year, Secretary Wilson had spent ten days in the mountains of North Carolina, making a personal investigation. Very wisely the Secretary took with him Holmes, McGee, Newell, and the local member of Congress. And, of course, I went along.

After all of which nothing happened. One year a bill would pass the Senate, but die in the House. Then another bill would go through the House, but die in the Senate.

Some time later the Society for the Protection of New Hampshire Forests, under the sagacious leadership of Philip Ayres, advocated a Forest Reserve in the White Mountains of New Hampshire, combined with the Southern Appalachian movement, and enlisted the support of the Middle Western states. It was this combined pressure that finally overcame the resistance of the Rules Committee and of that famous idealist, Joe Cannon, Speaker of the House, whose position was "not one cent for scenery."

Nearly twenty years after Holmes's suggestion, which is about the time it usually takes to get a new idea through Congress, in 1911 the Weeks Law was passed. Two facts finally made Federal legislation possible: one, the proof that forests do affect the flow of streams; and the other, that the Federal Government, under the Constitution, has power to deal with the Conservation and improvement of navigable rivers and their tributaries.

Many useful investigations on the relation of forest to climate, erosion, and stream flow were born of this campaign. But the main result was the Weeks law and its 18,000,000 acres of Forest Reserve children.

None of the foregoing made us lose sight for one moment of the transfer, or of the pressing need for new Forest Reserves in the West. With the Reserves it was pretty nearly now or never, for the public timberlands were melting away like ice cream at a Sunday School picnic.

42. *Government Reorganization*

After our frontal attack on the transfer problem had failed in 1901, it occurred to me that a new front might be tied in with another and most desirable objective, a redistribution of the technical work of the Government among the Departments, so long overdue. If it could be brought about, it would greatly increase their efficiency per dollar spent. In addition, the necessary study would unquestionably show that the Forest Reserves were in the wrong place.

Accordingly, in due time, I suggested to T.R. the appointment of a Committee on the Organization of Government Scientific Work. On general principles it was an excellent thing to do. In particular it might serve to bring the Government forests and the Government foresters together in the Department of Agriculture.

T.R. was friendly to the plan on both counts. On March 13, 1903, he appointed a committee to report directly to him "upon the organization, present condition, and needs of the executive Government work, wholly or partly scientific in character, and upon the steps which should be taken, if any, to prevent the duplication of such work, to co-ordinate its various branches, to increase its efficiency and economy, and to promote its usefulness to the Nation at large."

Charles D. Walcott, the exceptionally able and effective Director of the United States Geological Survey, was made Chairman. The members were: Brigadier General William Crozier, in charge of Ordnance and inventor of the disappearing guns in our seacoast fortifications; Admiral Francis T. Bowles, Chief of Construction of the United States Navy; James Rudolph Garfield, head of the Bureau of Corporations, and afterwards Secretary of the Interior in T.R.'s Cabinet; and Gifford Pinchot, who was made Secretary.

The Committee wasted no time. In the four months between its appointment and its preliminary report of July 20, 1903, it held thirty meetings, usually in the library of 1615 Rhode Island Avenue, which for that and other reasons became known as the Hall of Science. There it planned its investigation, heard much testimony, formulated its conclusions, and (speaking for myself) had an exceedingly pleasant and highly instructive time besides.

Some of the facts about the administration of Government bureaus which the Committee uncovered were almost beyond belief. For example: At an Indian agency far in the West the infirmary stove went bad in October. The agent wrote in, as he was required to do, and asked Washington to get him a new stove. The papers went through the regular routine, neither faster nor slower than usual, the stove was bought for $7, and when it reached the agency the agent acknowledged its receipt in these words, "The stove is here and so is spring." Nobody went cold that winter but sick Indians.

The preliminary report of the Committee considered subjects within its field in twenty-five bureaus scattered through six of the nine Departments, and in the Interstate Commerce Commission and the Smithsonian Institution. The Departments of State, Justice, and Post Office were not included. It found only a very small amount of actual duplication. It did find, however, "a lack of efficiency and of co-ordination in the scientific work of the Government," for which it proceeded to recommend remedies.

The conclusions of the Committee were founded, it declared, "upon the theory, which appears to be sustained by the facts, that Government scientific work should be organized upon such a basis that the administrative unit should comprise all the elements necessary for the solution of a distinct scientific problem or a group of closely related scientific problems, the investigation of which is for the benefit of the people in general."

The Committee held "that the individual sciences and arts should not be segregated in the separate bureaus and offices" except in rare cases. It held also that research in pure science was more properly within the scope of private institutions, and that "scientific research on the part of the Government should be limited nearly to utilitarian purposes evidently for the general welfare."

The Committee recommended a number of transfers, three of which could be effected by Executive Order. Others, more numerous, required legislation. Among the latter was this:

"The custody and care of the National Forest Reserves and of the National Parks, now in the Department of the Interior, should be transferred to the Department of Agriculture, and examination of Forest Reserves now in the Geological Survey should be transferred to the Bureau of Forestry in the Department of Agriculture. That Bureau, now engaged in the study of Forestry and the preparation of plans for the care and maintenance of forests, is entirely without authority to carry out the measures necessary to the preservation and proper use of the 62,000,000 acres of forests set aside by authority of Congress as Forest Reserves and those not yet set aside contained in the national domain. The care and administration of the National Parks is work so closely allied to that of the care of the Forest Reserves as to make it evident that they should be subject to the same control."

Everything that had to do with the use of land, including the Geological Survey, the General Land Office, and the Office of Indian Affairs, the Committee recommended foi transfer to the Department of Agriculture. Everything of a statistical nature was recommended for transfer to a statistical office to be organized in the Department of Commerce and Labor.

The report was short and to the point. It recommended not only necessary transfers between Departments, but also changes and reorganizations within Departments. If the Committee's plan could have been carried out the Government at Washington would have been transformed into a far more practical and effective engine for the service of the public than it has ever been, before or since.

But when the time came to ask for the necessary legislation, it became increasingly evident that, thanks to the spoils system, the recommendations of the Committee would stand little chance. Too many Senators and Representatives had too many constituents in office whose salaries might be reduced or whose jobs might be imperiled by the changes we advised.

In those days a much smaller proportion of Government jobs was under the control of the Civil Service Commission than now. Consequently, any reorganization of Government work was far more difficult to bring about then than it would be now. A careful study of the situation made it clear that the changes recommended in our report could never get through Congress.

But if Congressional permission for specific transfers was out of reach, still less would Congress give T.R. blanket authority to make such readjustments as he might choose. It looked as if we were blocked. And we were blocked. Our report was never made public.

The time spent on it, however, for me at least was anything but lost. It gave me a knowledge of Government services, of what to imitate and what to avoid, that was simply priceless in setting up and running the Forest Service; in planning the Roosevelt commissions which were to follow; and in acting, as T.R. put it, as his "counselor and assistant on most of the work connected with the internal affairs of the country."

Not a few of the bureau chiefs, also, gained a new point of view about efficiency and red tape, and some of them applied at least a part of what they learned. The work of the Committee was by no means wasted.

43. *The Public Lands Commission*

The administration of the public-land laws by the General Land Office of the Interior Department is one of the great scandals of American history. At a time when, in the West, the penalty for stealing a horse was death—death without benefit of law—stealing the public land in open defiance of law was generally regarded with tolerance or even with approval. It cast no shadow on the reputation of the thief.

When I was appointed to the Division of Forestry in 1898, the Forestry Reserves were, as you know, still in the Department of the Interior. To get charge of them having become my chief object in life, some acquaintance with the land laws, how they were administered, and how they worked, was hardly less necessary than a knowledge of Forestry itself. Part of that knowledge I personally had already collected. The rest the Division proceeded to acquire.

Even before we were made a Bureau in 1901, our men had examined many of the Western Forest Reserves and public lands. Furthermore, Newell, McGee, Gannett, and others had given me much eyewitness information about them. Moreover, I myself had talked with or had learned about, or both, many of the men who were in charge of the Forest Reserves and Public Domain. My touch with the problem of reclamation also had taught me a lot.

What all this came to was that while many of the public-land laws were more or less defective, their administration by the Interior Department was horrible. And this belief was confirmed and strengthened by the Oregon land-fraud cases, and by much besides.

This being so, something had to be done about it. Accordingly, after much consideration and consultation, I wrote and took to T.R. the form of a letter for his signature, appointing a Public Lands Commission "to report upon the condition, operation, and effect of the present land laws and to recommend such changes as are needed to effect the largest practicable disposition of the public lands to actual settlers who will build permanent homes upon them, and to secure in permanence the fullest and most effective use of the resources of the public lands."

It was a big question. The total extent of the Public Domain, including Forest Reserves and other public reservations, was more than a thousand million acres, or roughly twenty times the size of the State of Pennsylvania. This huge area was spread through more than half the states and territories in amounts varying from 5 to 95 per cent and more of their whole land surfaces, and it offered every variety of topography, mineral content, vegetation, and climate, from eternal snows down through every grade of moisture and productiveness to deserts below sea level, utterly useless without water.

The public lands had been and were being disposed of not only to settlers who would build homes upon them and to miners who would develop them, but also in a multitude of other ways, well calculated to make a few men rich rather than to make many thousands of families comfortable and happy.

The Nation had been giving its lands away with a lavish hand. By June 30, 1904, soon after the Commission was appointed, 2.25 million acres had gone to encourage river improvement; 3.25 million in wagon-road grants; 4.5 million to encourage the construction of canals. The states had received 10 million acres for internal improvement, 69 million acres for common schools, and over 80 million acres of swamplands, not a few of which were dry as a bone.

But the greatest of all the grants were in aid of the construction of railroads. While less than 100 million acres had gone to homesteaders, railroad land grants included more than 150 million acres. In Montana alone the railroads had been given nearly 17.5 million acres of the Public Domain. That number of acres would make five Connecticuts and then some.

The Public Lands Commission, appointed by T.R. on October 2, 1903, did good work, if I say so myself. Its Chairman was former Governor W. A. Richards of Wyoming, who by that time had succeeded Hermann as Commissioner of the General Land Office, and its members F. H. Newell and G. Pinchot, who was Secretary.

Governor Richards was a plainsman turned politician whom it was easy to like and easy to get on with. As a companion he was delightful, and some of his stories were top notch. One, for example, told how Richards himself crept up on an antelope that was lying down with its legs crossed under it, and broke all four of them with a single bullet from his rifle. That is a tall tale, but I believed it when the Governor told it, and I believe it still.

Although he came from Wyoming, where the opposition to T.R.'s public-land strategy was at least as bitter as in any other Western State, as chairman of the Public Lands Commission Richards fell in easily with the T.R. point of view, and in all good fellowship went serenely along with it.

The Public Lands Commission held hearings in Washington and elsewhere, at which Senators, Representatives, state officials, and others gave much testimony. Each member of the Commission also spent much time upon the public lands, making personal investigations on the ground, and discussing public-land questions with Governors, state land boards, public officials, and citizens generally.

Newell and I were together much of the time in the field, to my very great advantage. The statements made to us were illuminating, if not always accurate. In a public meeting in the State Capitol in Cheyenne, for one example, an enthusiastic official praised the Reclamation Service in a fiery speech because it made "two drops of water flow where only one flew before."

The appointment of the Public Lands Commission was thoroughly justified on its merits and in its results. As with the Committee on the Organization of Government Scientific Work, however, I had an ulterior motive, of which I made no secret. In both cases I hoped the investigations would prove the need for transferring the Forest Reserves from the Department of the Interior, where they were thoroughly mishandled, to the Department of Agriculture, where I was confident we could do a good job.

The Public Lands Commission made two partial reports—the first on March 7, 1904, less than six months after its appointment. The changes in public-land laws it suggested had to do mainly with the control, use, and disposal of the forest lands, because they were the most valuable lands still in public ownership. Accordingly, it recommended the repeal of the Timber and Stone Act, under which public timberland could be bought for $2.50 an acre and immediately transferred to a lumber company or a speculative owner.

Instead of the Timber and Stone Act, we recommended that Congress authorize the Secretary of the Interior to sell the timber on any unappropriated, nonmineral, surveyed public lands at public auction to the highest bidder, who would be forbidden to sell it again without the Secretary's permission.

As against $2.50 per acre under the Timber and Stone Act for both land and timber, we cited the public sale of stumpage on the Chippewa lands in northern Minnesota, at which the timber alone brought an average price of $15.06 per acre, and the Government still owned the land. Under the Timber and Stone Act the Government would have received only $438,707 as against $2,650,903 actually realized, and the difference, plus the land, would have gone with the timber to the lumbermen.

We recommended also that lands in Forest Reserves found to be chiefly valuable for agriculture by the Secretary in charge (we had the transfer well in mind) might be opened to homestead entry, but that such lands should not be subject to commutation (purchase after fourteen months' residence) or exchange under the lieu-land law.

The second partial report, transmitted to Congress by the President on February 13, 1905, with his "full sympathy with the general conclusions of the Commission in substance and in essence," turned out to be its last. The enormous pressure which followed the actual transfer of the Forest Reserves to the Forest Service on February 8—five days before—left me small chance for other work, and even if it had, little need remained. We had pretty well covered the ground.

The second report began with a one-page, ten-point summary of conclusions which opened with the statement that "The present laws are not suited to meet the conditions of the remaining public domain," and ended with this assertion of fundamental fact: "The number of patents issued is increasing out of all proportion to the number of homes."

In between the report recommended the purchase of private lands inside Forest Reserves instead of exchange under the lieu-land law; renewed and emphasized its recommendation for the repeal of the Timber and Stone Act; advised the sale of timber from unreserved public lands; advocated three years' residence under the commutation clause of the Homestead Act; and under the Desert Land Act, two years' residence with actual production of a valuable crop.

As to grazing, the Commission's recommendations were based on the long acquaintance of each member with the problem; on careful study of the grazing systems of Texas and Wyoming, the Union Pacific and the Northern Pacific Railroads, and the Indian Office; on a conference with representative stockmen from all the grazing-land states and territories; on 1,400 answers to a circular letter to stockmen throughout the West; on facts and opinions presented at many public meetings; and on innumerable other suggestions.

The report recommended that authority be given to the President to set aside grazing districts (which came to pass a generation later), and to the Secretary of Agriculture ("in whose Department is found the special acquaintance with range conditions and livestock questions which is absolutely necessary for the wise solution of these questions") to regulate and charge a moderate fee for grazing "with the special object of bringing about the largest permanent occupation of the country by actual settlers and home seekers." It was wise enough also to recommend that each locality should be dealt with on its own merits, which was precisely what had not been taking place.

The Commission laid down as its fundamental principle that the public lands should be saved for the homemaker, and based its recommendations squarely upon that undeniable truth. It pointed out that the tendency of the present land laws far too often was "to bring about land monopoly rather than to multiply small holdings by actual settlers. In very many localities, and perhaps in general, a larger proportion of the public land is passing into the hands of speculators and corporations than into those of actual settlers who are making homes."

"Nearly everywhere," said the report, "the large landowner has succeeded in monopolizing the best tracts." And in large holdings, almost without exception, collusion or evasion of the letter and spirit of the land laws was involved.

"Under the present conditions, speaking broadly, the large estate usually remains in a low condition of cultivation, whereas under actual settlement by individual homemakers the same land would have supported many families in comfort and would have yielded far greater returns."

The lieu-land law was, the report pointed out, thoroughly bad. It would have been comparatively harmless if limited to the ostensible object of its interest, the settler. But because under the law not only the "settler" but also the "owner" could make lieu selections, millions of acres of lands in the Forest Reserves, consisting of lava beds, denuded forests, rugged peaks, and other worthless lands, were released to the United States. And in exchange other millions of acres of lands valuable for agriculture, timber, minerals, coal, and oil, surveyed and unsurveyed, were taken up in every state in the Union where there were vacant lands by land-grant corporations, railroads, and lumber companies.

George E. Chamberlain, for eight years Governor of Oregon, and twice elected to the United States Senate, declared in a speech that the lieu-land law originated "not by the fireside of the poor settler, but in the office of a great railroad company in the Middle West"; it was got up, he said, not for the benefit of the small holder but to let the big corporations and railroads profit by exchange. And without doubt he was right.

Representative Fordney of Michigan, himself a lumberman, in a speech on the floor of the House, called it "an absolute fraud. The

Government has lost millions of acres of the most valuable land in this country, and got practically nothing in return." Yet Secretary Hitchcock, in 1899, made it worse by his ruling that lieu selections could be made from unsurveyed lands. That ruling opened the flood-gates wider still.

Political influence was used to get new Forest Reserves established so that the owners of worthless or denuded lands might exchange them, under the lieu-land law, for valuable lands outside. To the credit of the Land Office be it said, it called a halt on the creation of Forest Reserves in order to prevent further such exchanges. In consequence, the area of Forest Reserves increased very little from 1898 to 1902.

Acquisition by the Weyerhaeuser Syndicate of 900,000 acres in Washington and Oregon attracted much public attention in 1900 and powerfully stimulated land speculation. When the people of the West watched the Northern Pacific and other railroads getting immense bodies of valuable land in exchange for worthless tracts in their land grants, and saw huge areas of the finest timberland pass into the ownership of great lumbermen like T. B. Walker, they were naturally indignant. The lieu-land law, therefore, was one of the strongest arguments against additional Forest Reserves.

To remedy the evils of lieu-land selection, in 1901 Congress limited the exchange to surveyed lands open to homestead entry. Two years later agitation for repeal began in earnest, and on March 3, 1905, a month after the transfer, it won out.

But although the law was dead, its consequences were not. The most notable were the Oregon land frauds, for which Senator John H. Mitchell of Oregon was convicted (and died most opportunely of a tooth extraction); another Senator was saved by the statute of limitations.

The appendix to the Public Lands Commission's Report, which the President also transmitted to Congress with a separate message, contained two highly valuable papers on grazing. One, by Albert F. Potter of the Forest Service, included a specific plan for range control. The other was by Frederick V. Coville, Botanist of the Department of Agriculture, whose report on sheep grazing in the Cascade Forest Reserve in Oregon was the first systematic study of the subject.

Another paper, signed by Commissioner Richards, set forth that just before the transfer a force of 505 rangers, assistants, etc., was engaged on the Reserves, together with nearly fifty clerks in Washington. Six or seven years before, "the whole question of forest reserves was disposed of practically by a single employee of this office," with such incidental attention as a limited number of special agents could spare.

Still another, by John H. Hatton of the Forest Service, showed that less than 35 per cent of homestead entries commuted in the Dakotas, Nebraska, Kansas, and New Mexico from 1898 to 1904 were occupied at all, while fully 55 per cent of them were made for pure speculation.

The appendix also contained in 220-odd pages of tables the most accurate accounting ever made of what had been done with the Public Domain. It gave a solid basis of fact for the recommendations of the Commission.

The work of the Public Lands Commission brought its members into direct contact with all the resources of the Public Domain—waters, forests, lands, and minerals. Therefore it may well have had a part in planting and watering the seed which developed into the world-wide policy of Conservation. In any case, whether this guess is right or wrong, the knowledge of the public lands and the laws which governed them, of the Forest Reserves and other problems of the West, which came to me through my work on the Commission was simply invaluable.

44. *The Race for New Reserves*

When the Act of June 4, 1897, appropriated $150,000 for surveys and classification of the lands of the Forest Reserves by the United States Geological Survey, Henry Gannett was put in charge. Gannett was the Geographer of the Survey, a vigorous, forthright, competent man of wide knowledge and varied experience. He had been Topographer of the Hayden Survey in the West, and he knew the terrain of the United States as few men did.

We had become acquainted during the work of the National Forest Commission, and although Gannett was some twenty years older than I, we became fast friends. My interest in his work on the Forest Reserves was hardly less keen than his own. Very generously he gave me a share in it, and especially in that part of it which concerned additions to the Forest Reserves or changes in their boundaries.

Gannett's work, in addition to mapping the Reserves, included descriptions and estimates of the forest stands inside their boundaries and near by, and required expert knowledge of Forestry. Accordingly the Geological Survey asked for our help, and we were more than glad to give it. At first men such as Graves, H. B. Ayres, and J. B. Leiberg were assigned from our force to Gannett's work. Later on, by arrangement with the Geological Survey and the Interior Department, the Bureau of Forestry, beginning in 1902, did the most important boundary work on its own and at its own expense.

The language of our appropriation permitted us to "make and continue investigations on forestry, forest reserves, forest fires, and lumbering." That was enough. The work was done, and the President acted on the facts thus found.

Soon after T.R. became President, he formed the habit of sending to me, for suggestion or approval, Gannett's Forest Reserve boundary recommendations. And I arranged with Gannett that he would not mind if I changed the boundaries he proposed for Forest Reserves when T.R. sent them to me.

Had the country been under a different kind of President than Theodore Roosevelt, the area of National Forests would have been far less than it is today, and so it would if our boundary men had been less enterprising, determined, and effective.

When the boundary work began there was no time to lose. An army of timber cruisers was scouting the forests of the West for the choicest bodies of Government timber. Once discovered and reported, these prizes would be claimed, fairly or fraudulently, under lieu selection or under the Timber and Stone or other public-land laws, and then their forests would be lost to Forestry and the people.

Our independent boundary work began after Dr. Forbes, of the University of Arizona, suggested the establishment of an experimental range reserve in southern Arizona and the Secretary of the Interior asked us for an opinion. Albert F. Potter and R. S. Kellogg of the Bureau were assigned to the work.

Potter and Kellogg were next given four timbered regions in Arizona to examine. And after that Potter went to Utah, where he worked alone and rapidly. His work in the rest of that season led to the creation of the Logan (now Cache), Wasatch, Uinta, Manti, Beaver (now Fillmore), Aquarius (now Powell), and Sevier Forest Reserves.

Other examinations were made during 1902 by other men in other parts of the West. In 1903 the boundary work was systematically organized in districts under the highly competent direction of F. E. Olmsted. Allen was given charge in Colorado, Idaho, and Montana; Potter in California; and H. D. Langille in Oregon and Washington.

The boundary work was not easy. On horseback or on foot, their grub and blankets on pack horses or on their own backs, the boundary men went where their work led them, trail or no trail. And they moved fast. They had to, for they were working against as competent a body of land thieves as ere the sun shone on. The field men covered an average of about a township a day. Some of them even declared that during one field season they could do 3,000,000 acres to the man.

In those early days, moreover, Forest Reserves were not popular, and there was much opposition. Settlers held indignation meetings, and the timberland grabbers neglected none of the tricks of their trade. As one man reported, "It was a mighty unpleasant corner to be in. We had balked several schemes on the part of the 'gang' to obtain valuable timberland, and they were in a mood to give us as much trouble and as many kinds of trouble as they could at every turn."

Sometimes it was a question of locating boundaries in hot haste and beating the grabbers with a wire to Washington recommending withdrawal; at other times of rejecting bribes or refusing to be bluffed. The boundary men needed courage, and they had it.

In some localities, as in the Salmon River Valley in Idaho, in California, and elsewhere, the settlers were in favor of Forest Reserves. But, as usual in public matters, those who were for made far less noise than those who were against.

In 1903 and 1904 we had as many as fifteen boundary men in the field, men like DuBois, Cox, Benedict, and Cohoon, all of them exceptionally good. As a result of their work and that of their successors, and of course of T.R.'s backing, between 1903 and 1909 the area within Forest Reserve boundaries increased from 62,354,965 acres to 194,505,325. The greatest increase in any one year came in 1907.

Most of the boundary work had to be done under pressure, because commonly the penalty for delay was defeat. Under such conditions, the boundaries of the Reserves could not have been perfect. Yet we could well afford to have our work tested by its results.

HEYBURN
TIMBER SYNDICATES
PUBLIC DOMAIN
ROOSEVELT
WASH. RESERVE
MONTANA RESERVE
IDAHO RESERVE
NEW MEXI
NEVADA RESERVE
OREGON RESERVE
WYOMING RESERVE
RESERVE
COLORADO RESERVE
FORESTRY BUREAU
MORRIS
Old Mother Heyburn went to the cupboard,
To get her poor dog a bone,
When she got there, the cupboard was bare.
And so the poor dog had none.
To MR Pinchot - compliments of W-C Morris
Spokane Spokesman-Review

During 1909 all the National Forest boundaries were carefully reviewed. The net result was to cut out about two per cent of the total area within them. The Service could well be proud of that. Indeed more land was found outside the boundaries that should have been taken in than inside that should have been thrown out.

45. *At Last the Transfer*

The final push that drove the transfer through was given by the American Forest Congress, held in Washington, January 2-6, 1905. The American Forestry Association, at that time a powerful agency working wholeheartedly for the advancement of Forestry in America, issued the call, but the meeting was planned, organized, and conducted for the specific purpose of the transfer by the Bureau of Forestry.

The Congress was sponsored by a Committee of Arrangements which included the Secretary of Agriculture, who presided; the Presidents of the Pennsylvania and Northern Pacific Railroads; the Presidents of the National Lumber Manufacturers, Live Stock, and Irrigation Associations; the heads of the United States Geological Survey, the United States Reclamation Service, and the General Land Office; and a number of Senators and Congressmen. Miners, editors, educators, and many other callings also, were well represented.

The American Forest Congress dealt with Forestry as a national policy, but it did not stop there. It considered the forest also in its relation to agriculture and business; to education and to the states; to the railroads, the lumber industry, the livestock industry; and to mining and irrigation. It brought together some four hundred leaders, and for the most part the foremost leaders, in all of these fields. It was a notable gathering, in the fullest sense of the word, and it made a mark on a level with the quality of its personnel.

The Forest Congress was a powerful influence not only toward securing the transfer, but also in spreading sound knowledge and wise conclusions about Forestry throughout the length and breadth of America. For us today it has another value. It supplies a fairly accurate picture—certainly the best available—of public opinion in nearly every section of our people toward Forestry and the forest, some forty years ago.

Furthermore, the Forest Congress provided a rarely valuable measure of the progress made between 1898 and 1905. In 1898 the United States Congress was on the verge of abolishing the old Forestry Division. By 1905 the Bureau of Forestry had won a recognized place as a permanent part of the Government. The question at the Capitol was no longer whether to cut down or to cut out its appropriation, but how much it should be increased.

Among the representatives of industries and occupations, and among citizens generally, the change was just as evident and just as welcome. Nearly every speaker at the Forest Congress made clear his support of the Bureau. To us who had borne the heat and burden of the day it was worth no little to be assured by so wide a public that our work was producing results.

In 1898 the people in general knew little and cared less about Forestry, and regarded the forest, like all other natural resources, as inexhaustible. In 1905 the share of the forest in the life of the Nation was almost everywhere recognized.

It was natural that old friends of Forestry—men like Secretary Wilson, Representative Lacey of Iowa, Walcott, Newell, Ahern, and Fenn—should carry on the fight in the speeches they made. What was important about the Forest Congress was the new recruits whom we had won over to our side. There were James J. Hill, President of the Great Northern Railroad, and Howard Elliott, President of the Northern Pacific. Both recognized that the future prosperity of the West lay in the wise use of land and forest.

The change in attitude of the lumber industry, which furnished by far the largest group of speakers, was even more impressive. It was summed up by the statement of F. E. Weyerhaeuser, son of the head of the great Weyerhaeuser Lumber Company, that "Practical Forestry ought to be of more interest and importance to lumbermen than to any other class of men." Echoing his words were N. W. McLeod, President of the National Lumber Manufacturers Association, the editors of *The American Lumberman* and the *Pacific Lumber Trade Journal,* and T. J. Grier, the Superintendent of the Homestake Mining Co. of South Dakota. They agreed that Forestry was practical, and they praised the work of the Bureau in showing that it was. Even the livestock men, in the person of Francis E. Warren of Wyoming, President of the National Woolgrowers' Association, admitted that the Forest Reserve policy had the endorsement of the people of the Western States.

As to the Resolutions, they were such as you might expect from such a Congress. They favored the transfer, the purchase of Forest Reserves in the East, the repeal of the Timber and Stone Act, the Amendment of the lieu-land law, and much else besides. But it was the character and spirit of the Congress, and not the Resolutions, which gave it its power and its place in the story of American Forestry.

And so at length, thanks to the long struggle we had made for it, and thanks also to the American Forest Congress, H.R. 8460, the Transfer Act, passed easily through both Houses of Congress. It reached the President on February 1, 1905, and was signed by him on that day.

What I had been hoping for and working for, from the moment I came into the old Forestry Division nearly seven long years before, had finally arrived. It had been a long pull, and, as it turned out, a strong pull. Now it had to be a pull all together, if we were to make good use of the chance which perseverance, common sense, T.R., and the American Forest Congress had given us.

Beginning in 1898, the Division of Forestry, and then the Bureau, had pushed its field investigations of forests, forest uses, and forest users all over the West. Our studies of the Reserves had at last come good, as the saying is—studies of their boundaries and their timber; their forage and their mines; their streams, their agricultural land, and their other natural resources; studies of the men who used them and the men who ran them; of the laws which applied to them and the public opinion which controlled their destinies. When our chance came, we were ready to take it.

In my experience, progress in Government work, and doubtless in other work also, commonly comes by fits and starts. Often for months, sometimes for years, hard work for sound objectives gets you exactly nowhere. The solid wall of obstacles is solid still.

Then suddenly comes the break, the dam gives way, what you had hoped and striven for falls into your lap, and your cup is full and brimming over. However mixed these metaphors may be, you have your reward.

As Jacob served seven years for Rachel, so we had labored seven years for the transfer. When at last it came, much else came with it. And whatever else came, you may be well assured, did not just happen. We planned and worked for what we got.

The Transfer Act itself contained a clause without which our handling of the Forest Reserves, soon to be renamed National Forests, would have been badly cramped. Section 5 provided that all money received from the sale of any products or the use of any land or resources of the Forest Reserves should be available for five years from the passage of the Act as a special fund for the protection, administration, improvement, and extension of the Reserves.

That section gave us, in a way, the power to make our own appropriations. We had already, under the Act of June 4, 1897, the right to sell timber, and now we had the timber to sell. But what was even more important, Section 5 was to play the hero's part in getting us, through the Attorney General's opinion of May 31, 1905, the right to make a charge, "in connection with the use and occupation of the National Forests." Which meant revenue from grazing and water power and much besides, as will later appear. The value of that it would be hard to overstate.

Another brimming cup was a clause in the Agricultural Appropriation Act of March 3, 1905, which gave all Forest Service men "authority to make arrests for the violation of laws and regulations relating to the forest reserves and national parks." Without the power this clause gave us our men in the field would have been handicapped indeed. And the same bill gave us a hand "in the enforcement of the laws of the States or Territories in the prevention and extinguishment of forest fires and the protection of fish and game."

Consideration of the Agricultural Appropriation Bill in the Senate, immediately after the Transfer Bill became law, brought to the surface no little opposition to the Forest Reserves and the Bureau of Forestry. Two driving forces were behind it—the states' rights fetish and the Western hunger for development at any cost.

Western Senators like Heyburn of Idaho, Fulton of Oregon, and Teller and Patterson of Colorado, with Southern Senators like Clay of Georgia and Berry of Arkansas, joined together in an attack which was the forerunner of much trouble to come, and which might have had serious results. It did, in fact, kill a provision that would have authorized the Government to accept gifts of land for Forest Reserves.

Teller, who opened the attack upon it, foolishly asserted it had "neither law nor sense behind it."

Heyburn took the occasion to denounce as all theory and misrepresentation the evident fact that forests in the mountains hold back the runoff. Teller declared that the West did not "intend that the Government of the United States shall cover the new states with Forest Reserves where there is not any forest," and he added: "I will venture to say that a two-horse team could cart off every stick of timber that ever grew or will grow on hundreds and hundreds of acres."

These mephitic assaults were, of course, neither the first nor the last. Others which came after were to be far more dangerous.

Senator Proctor of Vermont, Chairman of the Committee on Agriculture, with some help from Hansbrough of South Dakota, defended his appropriation bill, told how greatly he had been impressed by the American Forest Congress, and succeeded in parrying a variety of attacks, especially on that vital clause which authorized us to spend on the Reserves the money we took in for the use of them. What would have happened to the forest work of the Government without his wise and untiring support I shudder to think.

Another useful clause in the Agricultural Appropriation Act of March 3, 1905, extended our markets, and therefore our income, by giving the Secretary authority to permit the export of Forest Reserve timber and other products from any state, territory, or the District of Alaska, except from the Black Hills Forest Reserve or from any Reserve in Idaho.

By still another bill passed on the same day, the pernicious lieu-land exchange was laid away for good and all. That was progress of the first water. All provisions of previous acts were repealed except that selections heretofore made could be perfected, which was fair enough.

One more change gave me great personal satisfaction. I never liked the name "Bureau," and I had had something to do with getting the Reclamation "Service" called by that better name. So when "Bureau of Forestry" disappeared from the Agricultural Appropriation Bill and "Forest Service" took its place, no one was more pleased than I.

For us in the Forest Service the transfer meant a revolutionary change. Before the Forest Reserves came into our hands, all we could say to whoever controlled a forest, public or private, was "Please." That we said it to some effect was proved by the number of applications from timberland owners for forest working plans for millions of acres of their private lands, from the Interior Department for many more millions of Forest Reserves, from the State of New York for lands in the Adirondack State Forest Preserve, from the War Department for military reservations, and more besides.

Before the transfer, we were limited to peaceful penetration. While many still regarded Forestry as pernicious nonsense, comparatively few people were sore at us because nobody was compelled to do as we said.

After the transfer the situation was radically changed. While we could still say nothing but "Please" to private forest owners, on the national Forest Reserves we could say, and we did say, "Do this," and "Don't do that." We had the power, as we had the duty, to protect the Reserves for the use of the people, and that meant stepping on the toes of the biggest interests in the West. From that time on it was fight, fight, fight.

We who took over the Forest Reserves preferred the small man before the big man, because his need was greater. We preferred him in honor and in privilege, in principle and in practice. No wonder we had trouble.

To appreciate what follows you must remember that the Forest Service was the first Government organization not only to assert that the small man had the first right to the natural resources of the West, but actually to make it stick. "Better help a poor man make a living for his family than help a rich man get richer still." That was our battle cry and our rule of life.

It was true, and it was right, and no one could openly attack it. And that was one more reason why it aroused the big men to fury. Because of it came most of the really dangerous opposition to the Service and the National Forests.

At first the small men, for whom we were risking our official necks and the very life of the Service, could not believe that we meant what we said and did. Many of them had lived under Land Office administration or had seen the Indian Office at work, and at first they could not realize that their Government was actually for them. Many settlers fought us in the beginning who afterward became our steadfast friends.

The big men changed more slowly, and small wonder. For in word and deed the Forest Service struck straight at the desire and expectation, the habit and intention, of the special interests to go on creating baronies for themselves out of the resources that belonged to all the people. We denied and opposed their profound conviction that money and profits are all-important and must control, and thereby we hurt both their pockets and their feelings.

But in spite of their vast power, pecuniary and political, in spite of the railroads, the stock interests, mining interests, water-power interests, and most of the big timber interests, in spite of all their proprietary politicians, in the long run our purpose was too obviously right to be defeated. And moreover, T.R. was for it, horse, foot, and dragoons. He said and he believed that the public good comes first, and he practiced his belief. Without T.R. our enemies would have found us easy pickings while the Service was still young.

Now let's get on with the story.

After the transfer, all matters affecting the surveying, prospecting, locating, appropriating, entering, relinquishing, reconveying, certifying, or patenting of lands, and all questions of title and easement remained with the Department of the Interior. All questions of management came to us.

Upon the day of the transfer the Bureau of Forestry, which had never had authority over so much as a square foot of Government land, was given full administrative control of an area about as large as the States of New York, New Jersey, and Pennsylvania combined, 86,000,000 acres of public Forest Reserves, with all the business that went with them.

With the Reserves came the Land Office field force of about 570 and the personnel in the Washington office, except for a few undesirables whom we managed to lose on the way, and also the unexpended appropriation. Our problem was to amalgamate two organizations, one very good and the other very bad.

That, however, was only the beginning. The transfer was made for a far more vital purpose. It was made in order that the national Forest Reserves might be handled under the principles of practical Forestry in the light of local facts and local needs, and so be given their fullest usefulness, now and hereafter.

The guide and charter of the new policy was a letter of instruction from Tama Jim to me, dated the day of the transfer.

That letter, it goes without saying, I had brought to the Secretary for his signature. Being a Departmental letter it had been prepared with care in Departmental style. It began: "The Forester, Forest Service. Sir:" and went on to quote in full the Transfer Act, whose provisions, it said, "will be carried out through the Forest Service, under your immediate supervision."

The letter instructed me to recommend at the earliest practicable date whatever changes might be necessary in the rules and regulations, dealt with the framework of the new job, and quoted the President's recent order which classified under the Civil Service Law all persons employed in the protection and administration of the Forest Reserves.

The Secretary's letter then proceeded to crystallize the purpose and spirit of the new enterprise in terms that are as valid today as they were forty years ago:

> In the administration of the forest reserves it must be clearly borne in mind that all land is to be devoted to its most productive use for the permanent good of the whole people, and not for the temporary benefit of individuals or companies. All the resources of forest reserves are for *use,* and this use must be brought about in a thoroughly prompt and businesslike manner, under such restrictions only as will insure the permanence of these resources. The vital importance of forest reserves to the great industries of the Western States will be largely increased in the near future by the continued steady advance in settlement and development. The permanence of the resources of the reserves is therefore indispensable to continued prosperity, and the policy of this department for their protection and use will invariably be guided by this fact, always bearing in mind that the *conservative use* of these resources in no way conflicts with their permanent value.
>
> You will see to it that the water, wood, and forage of the reserves are conserved and wisely used for the benefit of the home builder first of all, upon whom depends the best permanent use of lands and resources alike. The continued prosperity of the agricultural, lumbering, mining, and livestock interests is directly dependent upon a permanent and accessible supply of water, wood, and forage, as well as upon the present and future use of their resources under businesslike regulations, enforced with promptness, effectiveness, and common sense. In the management of each reserve local questions will be decided upon local grounds; the dominant industry will be considered first, but with as little restriction to minor industries as may be possible; sudden changes in industrial conditions will be avoided by gradual adjustment after due notice; and where conflicting interests must be reconciled the question will always be decided from the standpoint of the greatest good of the greatest number in the long run.
>
> These general principles will govern in the protection and use of the water supply, in the disposal of timber and wood, in the use of the range, and in all other matters connected with the management of the reserves.

They can be successfully applied only when the administration of each reserve is left very largely in the hands of the local officers, under the eye of thoroughly trained and competent inspectors.

Very respectfully,

James Wilson

Secretary

In the four decades between, this letter has set the standard for the Service, and it is still being quoted as the essence of Forest Service policy.

Kenneth D. Swan

PRACTICING THE PREACHING

Gifford Pinchot, Forester, with a group of forestry officials and rangers on a timber marking operation in the Absaroka Division of the Yellowstone Forest Reserve in 1906.

Harvard College Library

T.R. IN THE WOODS

President Roosevelt and a party at the base of a Sequoia in Yosemite National Park in 1903. Third from the right

PART IX
PRACTICING OUR PREACHING

46. *Unlocking the Reserves*

Our first job, after the transfer, was to handle the Forest Reserves wisely and well. The next was to bring the administration of the Reserves close to the people whose wants they served. We must do business not only honestly but promptly, yet without neglecting any of the necessary safeguards.

We had to absorb the obsolete Forest Reserve Service of the General Land Office into the Forest Service of the Department of Agriculture, abolish its bureaucratic habits of dealing with the Reserves, and apply more practical methods of our own.

The Bureau had been steadily training its men to handle the Reserves. It was ready, able, and eager to deal with them, and the people who used them, under broad, effective, and understanding policies—policies that were as sound in theory as they were new in practice.

Promptly upon the transfer, the new methods were applied, and promptly they began to show results. Therefore nearly all the time usually lost in adjustment was time saved. The entire administrative organization of the Forest Reserves and its work was digested by the Forest Service without disturbance and with no violent break—evidence enough of the preparedness of our men and the character and competence of their work.

From the start large executive power was transferred to the field, infuriating delays were avoided, high standards were enforced by frequent inspection on the ground, and the practical usefulness of the Reserves was vastly increased.

Because of these changes, public approval of the Reserve policy throughout the West strengthened from day to day. Attacks upon the Reserves from self-seeking interests continued, of course. So they did from shortsighted persons unable to draw the line between a small immediate advantage and a great permanent good. Nevertheless and notwithstanding, the Forest Service grew rapidly in public esteem.

The steadiness and devotion with which the members of the Service, and many or most of the transplanted Land Office men, accepted and discharged the new duties laid upon them by the transfer were beyond praise. Changes in method, assignment of duty, and point of view brought new and heavy responsibility to many of them. The mass of novel work made demands which could only be met by their giving to it, for months on end, many hours a day beyond the regular schedule. How well they met all demands upon them I shall never forget.

By the end of the fiscal year 1904-05, five months after the transfer, the Forest Service had mainly, if not entirely, replaced the blundering of political Land Office appointees by the skilled and honest judgment and action of trained foresters and experienced Western men. Reserve questions were now settled, so far as was possible, not by the remote control of absentee landlords in Washington, but by local men with local knowledge on the ground.

Secretary Wilson's letter, signed on the very day of the transfer, was proof enough that the Bureau of Forestry had worked out in advance the general principles upon which the administration of the National Forests, to be successful, would have to be based. But to transform those principles into definite, clear, and workable regulations was a horse of an entirely different color.

A *Forest Reserve Manual* had been prepared in the General Land Office under Filibert Roth mainly by E. T. Allen (both of whom were borrowed from the Bureau). It represented an immense improvement over the original Land Office procedure. Approved by the Secretary of the Interior April 12, 1902, there was more than a little to be said for it. Yet it left much to be desired in many directions.

On June 13 the Service presented to the Secretary for his approval, which he gave next day, the manuscript of a completely revised and greatly simplified and humanized set of regulations and instructions to govern the Forest Reserves. They were published in a small pocket volume entitled *The Use of the National Forest Reserves*. This booklet, bound in green cloth with rounded edges, was in the hands of our field men on July 1, 1905, when its contents went into effect.

The Use of the National Forest Reserves, promptly renamed the *Use Book,* contained less than a hundred pages of general information and directions, regulations, and special instructions to forest officers. Extracts from laws and decisions and an index took up forty-odd pages more, and that was all. Its size, however, was no indication whatever of the punch it carried or of the time and trouble that went to its production. It was the formal and detailed statement of our new policy, put together under the immense pressure of reorganization, and well it earned its place in the troubled story of American Forestry.

The *Use Book* marked the beginning of sound, clean, and effective Government forest administration in America. That was a great step forward. Indeed, except for the Act of March 3, 1891, which began the policy of forest reservation, it may well be the greatest step in that field ever taken.

The policies and practices laid down in this little volume were not all new. Many of them I had recommended to Secretary Hitchcock in my letter of October 31, 1901. Others were laid down in the Land Office *Forest Reserve Manual*. But the course the *Use Book* charted had never been followed before in America, and seldom, if ever, anywhere else.

The Land Office *Manual* had marked a real advance. Nevertheless, in the old Land Office tradition, it continued to frown. Take for illustration the first sentences of the *Manual* and the *Use Book* on grazing, which was far and away the bitterest issue of the time.

The Land Office said: "The Secretary of the Interior, in being charged with the proper protection of the forest reserves, has the right to forbid any and all kinds of grazing therein."

The Forest Service said: "The Secretary of Agriculture has authority to permit, regulate, or prohibit grazing in the forest reserves."

Small doubt as to which of the two sentences would beget most good feeling and co-operation in the minds of the stockman and the homesteader.

Fritz Olmsted was in charge of the very difficult and critical task of preparing the *Use Book*, to which fundamental document we all contributed. It represented the best judgment and experience of the whole Service. We finished it at a session at my house which went on all night and to and through breakfast in the morning. Fritz Olmsted, Herbert Smith, Bert Potter, and I were among those present, and who else I can't remember.

The *Use Book* left no room for doubt as to its spirit and purpose. It was prefaced by a statement "To the Public" which declared:

"The timber, water, pasture, mineral, and other resources of the forest reserves are for the use of the people. They may be obtained under reasonable conditions, without delay. Legitimate improvements and business enterprises will be encouraged.

"Forest reserves are open to all persons for all lawful purposes.

"Persons who wish to make any use of the resources of a forest reserve for which a permit is required should consult the nearest forest officer."

Forest Reserves, it continues, "are for the purpose of preserving a perpetual supply of timber for home industries, preventing destruction of the forest cover which regulates the flow of streams, and protecting local residents from unfair competition in the use of forest and range. They are patrolled and protected at Government expense, for the benefit of the community and the home.

"The administration of forest reserves is not for the benefit of the Government, but of the people. The revenue derived from them goes, not into the general fund of the United States, but toward maintaining upon the reserves a force of men organized to serve the public interests. This force has three chief duties: To protect the reserves against fire, to assist the people in their use, and to see that they are properly used.

"Forest officers, therefore, are servants of the people. They must obey instructions and enforce the regulations for the protection of the reserves without fear or favor, and must not allow personal or temporary interests to weigh against the permanent good of the reserves; but it is no less their duty to encourage and assist legitimate enterprises. They must answer all inquiries concerning reserve methods fully and cheerfully, and be at least as prompt and courteous in the conduct of reserve business as they would in private business.

"They must make every effort to prevent the misunderstanding and violation of reserve regulations by giving information fully and freely. The object should be to prevent mistakes rather than to have to punish them. Information should be given tactfully, by advice, and not by offensive warnings.

"Forest officers will be required to be thoroughly familiar with every part of this book, and to instruct the public and assist in making applications for the use of the reserves."

Sound doctrine, and no mistake.

The new regulations made it absolutely clear that the Reserves would be handled in the interests of homemakers and small men first, and that local questions would be decided by local officers and on local grounds. The old Land Office custom of referring pretty much everything to Washington for incubation and ultimate decision was definitely out.

Thenceforth the success or failure of Forest Reserve administration would be almost entirely in the hands of the Supervisor and his Rangers, where it properly belonged. It was radical but it was right, and it worked.

Trespasses and violations of the regulations and of specific Acts of Congress were punishable by fine and imprisonment. As an effective means of preventing them, they were described at some length in the *Use Book*, which pointed out that the United States has also all the civil rights and remedies for trespass possessed by private individuals. We wanted no trouble.

Permission to use or occupy lands, resources, or products in a Forest Reserve must be applied for through the Forest Supervisors. "A reasonable charge may be made for any permit, right, or privilege, so long as such charge is not inconsistent with the purposes for which the reserves were created." In many cases, however, no charge was made. Land for schools and churches was one example.

One result of this new attitude toward the users of the Reserves, and of the prompt and reasonable business methods which went with it, was a large increase in business and revenue. What was far more important, a striking change of feeling toward the Reserves followed throughout the West. When the Western people saw that we understood them and their problems, they began far better to understand us and ours.

Good regulations, as we all know, are of little use without good men to enforce them. While the regulations and instructions were being worked out, the men required to enforce them were partly sifted out from the transferred Land Office force; partly chosen and assigned from our men in the Bureau; partly new men secured by civil service examination; and then all of them trained by practice in their new duties.

Great care was taken to avoid conflict with Federal, State, and Territorial law while protecting the rights and property of the Government. Trails and roads for local settlers; an acre for a school and two for a church; land for stores, stage stations, miners' camps and trappers' cabins; mills, hotels, and summer cabins; grazing and farming; steamboats and ferries were some of the uses.

Among the special privileges and rights of way for which permits might be granted were canals, ditches, flumes, pipe lines, tunnels, dams, tanks, reservoirs; and private railroads, tramroads, telegraph, telephone, or electric-power lines, and the plants or buildings necessary for their use.

These partial lists show clearly how anxious we were to open the Reserves to every legitimate use.

The Reserves contained, of course, in the valleys of streams and in open parks, some agricultural lands. The *Use Book* provided that these lands could be fenced and farmed under permit, but no applicant could occupy more than forty acres, and his permit could be revoked whenever the public interest required it. But these lands could not be taken up by settlers, and that fact naturally led to no little bad feeling.

Alonzo Stewart, Assistant Secretary of the Senate, had suggested to me that these lands ought to be opened to entry and settlement. That was good sense, and I was strongly for it. The Public Lands Commission, in its Partial Report of March 7, 1904, recommended that agricultural lands in the Forest Reserves should be disposed of to actual settlers under the Homestead laws only, and in tracts not exceeding 160 acres.

A bill to that effect was before Congress when the *Use Book* was first printed. A year later, June 11, 1906, the Agricultural Settlement Bill was passed. Its passage brought a notable increase of good will in many parts of the West. Moreover, its effect was to settle settlers on nonforest lands—permanent settlers, with a real interest in helping our men against fire and trespass, to the marked advantage of the National Forests.

47. *Peace on the Range*

In those days grazing was a far more important question on the Reserves than lumbering, and nowhere was the central idea of use better applied. So we'll deal with the range first.

"The Forest Service," said the *Use Book,* "will allow the use of the forage crop of the reserves as fully as the proper care and protection of the forests and the water supply permit. Every effort will be made to assist the stock owners to a satisfactory distribution of stock on the range in order to secure greater harmony among citizens, to reduce the waste of forage by tramping in unnecessary movement of stock, and to obtain a more permanent, judicious, and profitable use of the range.

"On the other hand, the Forest Service expects the full and earnest co-operation of the stock owners to carry out the regulations."

The grazing regulations in the *Use Book* went into much detail, as indeed was essential in organizing the control of a great industry which had hitherto run wild. Permits would be forfeited if transferred. Owners must notify the Supervisor when their stock entered and left the Reserve, and the conditions under which stock would be allowed to cross the Reserve or trail through it to reach private holdings were set forth at length. And much else besides.

From the grazing regulations we wanted three main results: the protection and conservative use of all Forest Reserve land adapted for grazing; the best permanent good of the livestock industry through proper care and improvement of the grazing lands; and the protection of the settler and home builder against unfair competition in the use of the range.

In grazing, as in everything else, the little man and the home owner came first. Small nearby owners who lived in or close to the Reserve, whose stock had regularly grazed on the Reserve range, and who were dependent upon its use, were given preference over all others. Next came all other regular occupants of the Reserve range, and last of all the owners of stock who had not regularly occupied the range.

Much of the range was badly overgrazed, and the number of stock on it had to be reduced. In such cases the small owners were first provided for and the reduction was made on the larger owners. And that reduction had to be made with care.

At the time of the transfer stock wars were common. The cattlemen nearly everywhere had first possession of the range, and they resented deeply, and not without cause, the coming of sheep. Yet sheep had to come, not only because it was fair, but also because the full use of the range required it. Sheep will eat forage that cattle will not.

When we took charge, killing stock, especially sheep, and killing men were still fairly common means for getting and keeping control of the range. Since we took charge, with the possible exception of one case on the Gunnison River in Colorado, so far as I know not a single sheepman or cattleman has been killed in any dispute over the range on any National Forest.

In those days sheep were ten times worse than cattle, although too many cattle can make bad trouble. But when strictly limited and controlled, any kind of grazing, even sheep grazing, can go on without great harm to the forests or the plains.

Special rules for sheep were required. Regulation 20 said: "Sheep must not be bedded more than six nights in succession in the same place, except when bedding bands of ewes during lambing season, and must not be bedded within 500 yards of any running stream or living spring." If you have ever had to drink water where sheep have been, you will know why.

Perhaps I had better confess here that I hate a sheep, and the smell of a sheep, although many sheepmen were my good friends. I have seen too much of the sheep's power to destroy. Yet I recognize (with regret) that sheep are necessary, and (with satisfaction) that good handling can make and keep them harmless. Before my service as Forester was over, I was ready to challenge Senator Warren's title, given him by T.R., as the greatest shepherd since Abraham. For I had under my control on the National Forests sheep and lambs to the number of no less than fourteen million head.

The whole grazing policy of the Service was based on knowledge of the range acquired on the ground. At the end of each season the Forest Supervisor must go over the grazing grounds without delay, examine the effect of grazing on the Reserve, and make a full report to the Forester. Guesswork was out.

With the transfer came the highly controversial question of whether we could or could not charge a fee for grazing on the Forest Reserves. It was just and right that the stockmen should pay for public property used and consumed for their own profit. Eastern farmers paid for their pastures. They grew thei animals on land that had to be bought, and that land cost them taxes every year. Stockmen on the Reserves carried no such load.

The proceeds of a grazing charge, if we could make it, would help us care for and protect the Forest Reserves. The Service was for it, of course. The stockmen, equally of course, were against it. When their stock grazed on Indian reservations, they were paying a fee, although a very inadequate one. But they did not love a charge on the Reserves any the more for that.

We in the Bureau, of course, had seen the charge issue coming, and we had done what we could to prepare for it. During the winter of 1904. George Woodruff had drawn a clause that would have authorized a charge, and I had managed to get it into the transfer legislation of that session. But Mondell spotted it, made his point of order, and out it went.

By that time summer had come, and George was staying at my house. Morning after morning we put our heads together at breakfast. There was no chance for a separate bill with a decision by majority vote. We must get our authority to charge into the Transfer Bill, or not at all.

So George drew another and a different clause, and I succeeded in getting it included in the bill. This time Mondell failed entirely to catch the point, and our plan misfired only for the reason that the whole Transfer went down and out for that year also. Particularly unfortunate, for if the issue of a grazing charge could have been brought before the House, it would have won and won easily.

A new plan had therefore to be made. So, on May 29, 1905, Secretary Wilson signed a letter to the Attorney General (prepared, of course, in the Forest Service under George Woodruff's eye) which set forth that application had been made for a permit to occupy a certain tract of land in the Alexander Archipelago Forest Reserve, at Grace Harbor, Dall Island, Alaska, for a fish saltery, oil, and fertilizer plant, which had already been built there and was of great importance to the locality. Tama Jim's letter continued:

"It is unquestionably best for forest-reserve interests, if it can be done, that leases or permits should at times be granted for a term of years, and also that, when the privilege granted is of actual money value to the permittee, a reasonable compensation should be required from him. I receive many applications of this nature in which the applicant expresses himself as willing to pay a reasonable rental."

He then asked three careful questions:

"1. Have I, as Secretary in charge of forest reserves, legal authority to grant a permit or lease under the Act of June 4, 1897, for the 'use and occupation' of forest-reserve land for the purpose set forth above?

"2. Have I legal authority to grant this permit or lease for a period longer than one year?

"3. Have I legal authority to require a reasonable compensation or rental for such permit or lease within the forest reserve?"

To questions 1 and 2 the answer could only be Yes. That was why they came first. The answer to question 3 was by no means a matter of course. That was why it was asked as to a fish saltery in Alaska rather than about grazing in Wyoming, or Oregon, or Arizona. There was nothing to be gained by arousing opposition. The Capitol was not without direct wires to the Department of Justice.

The result of wise planning was an opinion from the Attorney General, dated May 31, in which, after a long discussion, and after answering questions 1 and 2 in the affirmative, he said:

"In answer to your third question, therefore, I have to advise you that, in my opinion, you are authorized to make a reasonable charge in connection with the use and occupation of these forest reserves, whenever, in your judgment, such a course seems consistent with insuring the objects of the reservation and the protection of the forests thereon from destruction."

The fact that Moody's elaborate opinion was dated only two days after Tama Jim's request might be taken to imply that we had laid the groundwork with due care. We had. Woodruff, in addition to his work on the Secretary's letter, had kept in touch with Moody's assistant who was preparing the reply. Thus he learned that Moody's opinion was likely to be unfavorable. That made it necessary for me to explain the situation to Moody himself. What was more effective, I went also to T.R. and told him exactly what we had in mind. T.R. not only approved our plan with enthusiasm, he also let the Attorney General know just how he felt about it. And so the right to make a charge was won.

When the Western Senators and Representatives learned that a charge for grazing was on the way, they were furious. A strong delegation called on T.R. and protested violently. I was there with some other Forest Service men. We all heard the eruption. But T.R. knew he was right and so did the protestants, and their indignation got them nowhere. So far as I can recall, no dangerous effort was ever made in Congress to abolish the charge.

48. *Timber for Use*

There was no such difficulty about getting payment for Forest Reserve timber. The Act of June 4, 1897, gave us the right to sell the "dead, matured, or large growth of trees" and make a charge for what we sold. You know already some of the abuses which took place when the Land Office sold Forest Reserve timber, as in the Black Hills.

Acting by the authority of Secretary Hitchcock, the Bureau of Forestry had already corrected some of these abuses. We had also gathered valuable experience in the Chippewa Indian lands in Minnesota, and on privately owned timberlands in many other states. The practice of Forestry on the Forest Reserves was the chief purpose of the transfer, and we were ready to go ahead.

The *Use Book* set forth that "All timber on forest reserves which can be cut safely and for which there is actual need is for sale. Applications to purchase are invited. Green timber may be sold except where its removal makes a second crop doubtful, reduces the timber supply below the point of safety, or injures the streams. All dead timber is for sale.

"The prime object of the forest reserves is use. While the forest and its dependent interests must be made permanent and safe by preventing overcutting or injury to young growth, every reasonable effort will be made to satisfy legitimate demands."

Anyone might purchase except trespassers. There was no limit, except the capacity of the forest, to the quantity which might be sold to one purchaser, but monopoly would not be tolerated.

Sales up to $20 (except in California, where all sales had to be advertised) could be made by any Forest Ranger. "No delay is required."

Sales up to $100 could be made by any Forest Supervisor. "The only delay involved is the time required for an estimate and report." Delays in Forest Reserve business, next to dishonesty and incompetence, had been the worst faults of the Land Office days.

Sales over $100 had to be advertised and approved by the Forester. That meant an additional check.

All timber sold must be estimated and paid for before it was cut, and measured before it was moved. All payments must be made direct to Washington. Timber could be cut only on the area designated by the forest officer, and *no green trees could be cut unless they had first been marked for cutting.* We were taking no chances.

Instructions to forest officers for making timber sales needed to be full and clear, for nearly all the men then on the Reserves were without practicing knowledge of Forestry. The first step was to examine the timber and decide whether it could be spared.

"The approving officer must know whether another growth of timber will replace the one removed or whether the land will become waste; whether the water supply will suffer; and whether the timber is more urgently needed for some other purpose. One of the foremost points to be studied is the reproduction of the forest." And the *Use Book* pointed out that the growth on similar areas which have been burned or logged affords the best guide.

Each sale of live timber required a map of the cutting area, an estimate of the stand upon it, and a description of the forest, with specific recommendations and the reasons for them. These must include the effect upon water flow, possible profit in holding the timber for a higher price, the need for it, the possibility or difficulty of getting it elsewhere, the reliability of the applicant, and the price. The latter must be decided by the actual value of the timber as determined by its character, ease of logging, and distance from market, and not by custom or habit. There must be no more sales at half price.

Blank forms to be filled in made all this easier. In addition, a list of a dozen questions concerning live timber was supplied—such as: "To what minimum breast-high diameter should cutting be allowed? Should seed trees be left; and if so, how many to the acre? To what diameter in the tops should trees be utilized? Should the brush be piled, and in what manner? How low should the stumps be [usually not higher than the tree is thick]? During what months should cutting be allowed? [This depends on the danger of destructive insects breeding in freshly cut timber.]"

Because a favorite form of fraud was to cut live timber and pay for it as dead, dead timber was defined as "only timber, standing or down, which is actually dead, and in no case trees which are apparently dying. All evergreen trees having any green leaves are classed as living timber." So were trees dead at the top but green below.

Directions followed for marking the trees to be cut, for cutting them, for piling brush, for scaling the cut, and for reporting it. When the timber to be cut was green, "the supervisor will order the marking of all trees to be cut. This is imperative." Forty years ago we recognized that cutting green timber to a diameter limit without marking is not Forestry but forest butchery.

"Standing timber must be marked with the 'U. S.' marking hammer near the ground, so that every stump will show the mark. Where snow may conceal the marking from the cutters, each tree must also be marked at a point several feet from the ground.

"So far as practicable, all branches of the logging operations must keep pace with each other. Brush piling must never be allowed to fall behind the cutting and removal of logs, ties, and other material. The ground must be cleared as fast as the work proceeds."

The *Use Book's* instructions for logging and scaling the timber cut were based on actual experience in the woods. Indeed most of its highly practical directions for lumbering under Forestry would have been impossible without the work Graves and I had done at Biltmore and in the Adirondacks, or without Gene Bruce's expert advice.

These directions were the work neither of office men nor of amateurs. However much our enemies might describe us as theorists or Eastern dudes, actually we had been through the woods and through the mill.

Under the law of June 4, 1897, the Secretary of the Interior (and since the transfer the Secretary of Agriculture) might "permit, under regulations to be prescribed by him, the use of timber and stone found upon such reservations, free of charge, by bona fide settlers, miners, residents and prospectors for minerals, for firewood, fencing, building, mining, prospecting, and other domestic purposes."

The policy of the Service was to be very liberal, as the *Use Book* said, in granting free use to persons who might not reasonably be required to purchase and who had not enough of their own, to the value of not exceeding $20 in any one year. (Twenty dollars worth of timber would build a small house.) Free use might also be granted to school and road districts, churches, or co-operative organizations of settlers, to an annual value of $100.

The more free use, rightly handled, the better for all concerned. Free use made friends for the Forest Reserves and helped the settlers and the little men whom we wanted most to help.

It was a good plan, and through it we were able to help many small men who needed help, and to assist in the building and maintenance of many homes.

The *Use Book* required all forest officers authorized to grant free use to furnish cheerful assistance to applicants, to act promptly upon all applications, and in general to follow as liberal a policy in the matter of free use as the interests of the reserves and the proper performance of their other work would allow. A settler must not sell free material, nor would the free use privilege be given to any trespasser.

But "Free use of material to be employed in any business will be refused, as, for example, to sawmill proprietors, owners of large establishments or commercial enterprises, and companies and corporations.

"There is no more reason for giving a hotel keeper or a merchant timber without charge, solely to build or warm his hotel or store, than for giving him a stock of goods, yet it need not be refused the proprietor of a small establishment when it will be used chiefly by himself and his family. Prospectors should be assisted to develop their properties, but owners of revenue-producing mines should be required to buy." The small man had the first chance.

In free use, as in timber sales, the welfare of the forest must come first. Living timber must be marked for cutting before it could be cut. Forest officers in charge of cutting would be held responsible if unnecessary damage were done to young growth or standing timber, or if the reproduction of the forest was not properly considered. And we meant just that. Forestry must actually be applied.

49. *Forest Fire Control*

What the little *Use Book* had to say about forest fires was very much to the point. "Probably the greatest single benefit derived by the community and the nation from forest reserves is insurance against the destruction of property, timber resources, and water supply by fire. The direct annual loss reaches many millions of dollars; the indirect loss is beyond all estimate.

"Through its watchful fire patrol the Forest Service guards the property of the resident settler and miner, and preserves the timber and water supply upon which the prosperity of all industries depends. The resident or the traveler in forest regions who takes every precaution not to let fire escape, and who is active in extinguishing fires which he discovers, contributes directly to the development and wealth of the country and to the personal safety and profit of himself and his neighbors. He who does not assumes a great responsibility by endangering not only his own welfare but that of countless others.

"Care with small fires is the best preventive of large ones."

Said the "Instructions to Forest Officers":

"The utmost tact and vigilance should be exercised where settlers are accustomed to use fire in clearing land. Public sentiment is rightly in sympathy with home builders and the control of their operations should give the least possible cause for resentment and impatience with the reserve administration, but it should be exercised firmly none the less. Settlers should be shown the injury to their own interests, as well as to the public, which results from forest fires. But while the aim ought always to be toward co-operation and good will, it is equally important to have it well understood that reserve interests will be protected by every legal means."

The *Use Book* made it perfectly clear that a man who builds a fire and leaves it before it is completely out might go to jail for a year, or pay a thousand dollar fine, or both.

Campfires must not be larger than necessary. Fires must not be built in leaves or rotten wood, against logs, or in other places where they are likely to spread. In windy weather build your fire in a hole or clear the ground around it, and wherever you build it, never leave it, even for a short absence, until it is completely out. Never burn slashings in very dry weather, or without letting the nearest forest officer know.

All permit holders were required to help in fighting fire, and citizen fire brigades were encouraged. The best tools—shovel, mattock, and ax. The best time to work—night or the early morning hours. And remember:

"Protect the valuable timber rather than the brush or waste; never leave a fire, unless driven away, until it is put out; young saplings suffer more than old mature timber; a surface fire in open woods, though not dangerous to old timber, does great harm by killing seedlings.

"A fire rushes uphill, crosses a crest slowly, and is more or less checked in traveling down. Therefore, if possible, use the crest of the ridge and the bottom as lines of attack.

"A good trail, a road, a stream, an open park, check the fire. Use them whenever possible.

"Dry sand or earth thrown on a fire is usually as effective as water and easier to get.

"A little thinking often saves labor and makes work successful. Ill-planned efforts suggested by haste and excitement rarely lead to success.

"In handling back fires great care is needed to avoid useless burning."

All of which is as true now as it was then.

The *Use Book* left no room for doubt that in fire prevention as in everything else, co-operation, not compulsion, was our keynote. We were dealing with men who were peculiarly sensitive about their rights, or what they had come to regard as their rights, and well we knew it. What we wanted from them was willingness based on understanding. It was not an easy road, nor always a short one. In the end we got that willingness, and the Forest Service has it still.

Much work fell to the men on the Forest Reserves besides utilizing their forests and forage and fighting their fires. All forest officers, for instance, were required by the Act of March 3, 1899, to co-operate in enforcing state and game and fish laws, so far as their regular duties would allow. Not a simple thing to do, for the administration of these laws, in many or most of the Western states, was in politics up to its eyes. And if authorized by the Forester and the state game warden, they were to act as wardens, with full power as such. And there was much besides.

Supervisors must use every opportunity to work on a permanent system of roads and trails in their Reserves. The Supervisor was held responsible not only for the work, but for economy in doing it.

Further, all Supervisors must see that the Reserve limits were kept amply marked with at least one boundary notice to each mile where grazing or timber trespass was likely to occur.

Followed lists of field and office equipment, directions for keeping accounts, for records and reports, with which I shall not trouble you, and for correspondence. Letters will be considered in the chapter on administration in the Forest Service. They are far more important than many people think.

50. *Field Organization*

The *Use Book* listed the salaries of a dozen or more grades in the field work of the Service. They ran from top pay of $2,500 a year for Supervisors and $1,400 for Rangers down to $900 for Assistant Forest Rangers and $720 or less for Forest Guards, who worked for not over six months in any year and were not in the classified civil service. Forest Inspectors received $1,500 or more. The lowest pay of all went to Student Assistants at $40 a month in the office and $30 a month plus keep in the field. If the Service did anything like good work, Uncle Sam was certainly getting his money's worth.

This question of pay was always an exceedingly delicate and difficult one, yet most essential. To get good work from his men without good pay is one of the hardest tasks an executive can face. Yet it was literally easier to increase a general item in an appropriation bill by a thousand dollars, or ten thousand, than to raise a salary by five dollars a month.

My own pay was $3,500 a year. Although it was distinctly below the general run for bureau chiefs, I never applied for an increase. In the first place I didn't need it, and moreover I had seen how man after man had injured his standing and held back his work by trying to get more pay. However just his claim, it ran counter to the firm conviction of Congressional committees that all Government servants (except Congressmen) were chiefly interested in boosting their own salaries, and were already getting too much.

Of all forest officers in the field, Inspectors, Supervisors, and Rangers were of first importance. The Inspectors were chosen from men who had gained great familiarity with Reserve problems and unusual efficiency in the conduct of Reserve business. An Inspector could give no orders to any Supervisor, but plenty of suggestions and advice. His duties were to inspect the Reserves in his district, their condition, and the progress, condition, and execution of all work, and to report to the Forester. The Inspectors were the Forester's eyes and ears.

The heads of the Branches into which the Service was divided, each in his own line, directed the work on the ground, through the Supervisors. In this way the best expert knowledge the Service had on grazing was applied through the Branch of Grazing to the use of the Reserves by cattle and horses, sheep and goats. So also the cutting of timber, the control of special uses, etc., were each under the direction of the most capable and experienced men.

All of these specialists, and this is important, worked together in harmonious co-operation, at one end through the authority of the Forester, and at the other through the Supervisors on the ground. It was a good plan: it decentralized the work of the Service, it made full use of local information, of expert skill, and of knowledge of the situation in Washington, and it produced results.

The Supervisors really held the keys of success and failure. They were the responsible business managers of the Reserves and must give their entire time to the Service. They reported directly to the Forester, and through him to the experts in charge of grazing, timber sales, special uses, and so on. They were also public relations men. Their ability to sense public opinion and apply their knowledge, and that of the Rangers under their orders, not seldom made all the difference between local hostility and co-operation.

The Supervisors were either men who had been held over from Land Office days or who had been chosen from the best Rangers and Forest Assistants in the states or territories where their Reserves lay. Each Supervisor must be able to handle men, deal with all kinds of people, and conduct the transactions and correspondence of his office. Knowledge of technical Forestry was desirable but not essential. "Candidates for the position of supervisor are required to furnish the most convincing proof of their moral and business responsibility." Please note that.

As fast as we could find them, Forest Assistants "thoroughly trained in scientific forestry, dendrology, and lumbering" were assigned to the Supervisors as technical assistants. And the Supervisors were held responsible for making good use of them.

Next to the Supervisor in importance, and often on the same level with him, came the Ranger. Like the Supervisors, under the law the Rangers were to be selected "when practicable, from the states in which they are to be employed." And that was usually, but not always, the wise thing. The Ranger was the man who must know, better than anyone else, the details of forest and range, of trespass and use. He was the officer with whom the small men did most of their Forest Reserve business. On how he handled himself and them depended mainly their attitude toward the Reserves and the Service.

Rangers, like Supervisors and Forest Assistants, were required to provide and keep their own saddle and pack horses wherever they were necessary.

Every applicant for a Ranger job "must be, first of all, thoroughly sound and able-bodied, capable of enduring hardships and of performing severe labor under trying conditions. Invalids seeking light out-of-door employment need not apply." (That was a slap at the Land Office, if you like, and certainly it was well deserved.)

The *Use Book* went on: "No one may expect to pass the examination who is not already able to take care of himself and his horses in regions remote from settlement and supplies. He must be able to build trails and cabins and to pack in provisions without assistance. He must know something of surveying, estimating, and scaling timber, lumbering, and the livestock business."

That was no idle talk. "The examination of applicants is along the practical lines indicated above, and actual demonstration, by performance, is required. Experience, not book education, is sought, although ability to make simple maps and write intelligent reports upon ordinary reserve business is essential."

Well I remember a Ranger examination conducted by Fritz Olmsted in the Bitterroot Valley of Montana. It required the candidate to prove by doing that he could run compass lines, chop, pack a horse, and find his way by day or night. It also included two other highly practical tests. The first was: "Cook a meal." And the second: "Eat it."

51. *What Made the Service Click*

The Forest Service was generally recognized as the best Government organization of its day. It set a new standard of efficiency in Washington. That was because it had a great purpose, and knew that it had, and because it was organized on the principle of individual recognition and responsibility.

In setting up any piece of Service work, the first step was to find the right man and see that he understood the scope and limits of his work and just what was expected of him. That was not always easy. Here and there, of course, we made mistakes. But in nearly all cases the man chosen fitted his job and did it well.

The next step was to give him his head and let him use it. Every man in an executive position ran his own show and took pride in it. Just as Secretary Wilson had given me power to choose the policies and personnel of the Division, just as you let a good horse pick his own way over rough ground, so each executive in the Service was put on his own to do the work for which he was responsible.

Each man in executive charge was not only held responsible, but he was given the outward signs of his responsibility. Thus he signed the letters he prepared relating to his own work, instead of sending them up to be signed by his chief, as in many a badly organized Government bureau.

Furthermore, the right man was given the chance to do his work, and the means to do it, to the limit of our power to provide them. What was even more important, he was given the full credit for the good work he did.

The Service assumed, expected, and required complete good will and co-operation on the part of its members, and got it. And what it expected from its leaders, they expected from their men, and they all expected it from me. And of course I required it also from myself. I could not ask for more than I was prepared to give.

The Forest Service was no organization of master and servant. It was a service of mutual effort for a common purpose. We were all working together to the same end. Leaders we had, of course. But there is all the difference in the world between a leader and a boss. It was "Come on, let's do it together"; and not "You go and do it while I sit by and watch you."

The Service, therefore, was not a regiment but a community. Its community life was not based on formal orders, though orders there had to be, but on consultation, co-operation, and general recognition of the dignity and worth of its people and its task.

If for any fault of his, one of our men failed to do his job, he was promptly taken out of it. In that case he went either to another job more suited to his capacity, or out of the Service altogether, according to the quality and character of his default. No man who failed was kicked upstairs, and no failure held a job in the Forest Service.

Nothing destroys morale more certainly or more completely than the bad habit of tolerating known failures and incapables and keeping them on in their jobs or moving them into new ones. Treating incompetents as if they were good men lowers the standards of performance for men who are competent, and good work is made to seem hardly worth while.

On the other hand, the road to promotion was open to everyone in the Service, just as far as each man or woman showed the character, ability, and good will to go. It was the definite and highly productive policy of the Service to fill vacancies by promoting its own people instead of looking for new blood outside. We were fully and rightly convinced that our own strain was the best available, and the results confirmed our conviction.

Half a century of experience in executive work has proved to me that the first condition of success in any job is not brains but character. Over and over again I have seen men of moderate intelligence come to the front because they had courage, integrity, self-respect, steadiness, perseverance, and confidence in themselves, their cause, and their work. Which of these qualities comes first it is not easy to say, but certainly courage, perseverance, and self-respect rank high.

The men and women of the Service earned good pay by their good work, and good pay, by the standards of the time, I was determined they should get. Yet there were many obstacles in the way. One of them was the hatred of promotions in the House Agricultural Committee, which at that time had charge of our appropriations. Another was the Statutory Roll, which pegged certain rates of pay for certain positions and made salary advances in those positions impossible.

One more obstacle was the comparatively low salary of the Forester, which tended to reduce the pay of the men who were closest to him. Fortunately these men, on the average, were younger than men of similar grades and responsibilities in other bureaus. On the basis of age our men were not so badly paid.

Fortunately, moreover, salaries had remarkably little to do with the spirit and efficiency of the Service. The chief driving force which made the Service the best organization under the Government was not the desire to earn good money, but the urge to do good work in a good cause. This was true of the members of the Bureau of Forestry when the transfer was made. In no long time it became true also of most of the Land Office people who were good enough to be kept on.

And fortunate it was that our morale was high, for we had to meet more kinds of opposition, and opposition of higher voltage, than any Government bureau had yet had to meet. The Forest Service stood up for the honest small man and fought the predatory big man as no Government bureau had ever done before, and that was why.

At that time Big Money control in the West was more raw, more violent, and more effective than anything the East could show. The tradition of a land where men were men still lingered. But that merely meant that the Big Money boys had to use methods to fit the times, which they sure did.

In those days men were used to taking chances. The conditions of their life required it. Killings were still common in a land where outside the towns every man packed a gun. When you saw a stranger coming in the trail, it was still the habit to take off your glove.

Therefore concentrated wealth—the great mining, livestock, lumber, and railroad outfits—used force more in the West than in the East, and cunning less. Western bad men were just as easy to buy as crooks back East, and politicians even more so. Big Money was King in the Great Open Spaces, and no mistake.

But in the National Forests Big Money was not King. Every member of the Forest Service in the office and in the field knew that the President was with us. Everyone knew that neither money nor political influence could dictate to the Forest Service or secure or endanger his advancement or his job. Without that knowledge the Service would have been almost as helpless before the spoilsmen as the Land Office itself.

From the day I entered the Division of Forestry under President McKinley till I was dismissed from the Forest Service by President Taft, not one single person in the office or the field was appointed, promoted, demoted, or removed to please any politician, or for any political motive whatsoever.

To appoint public servants for political reasons does two bad things. It selects men and women to do the work of the public for reasons other than their ability to do that work, and it perverts their loyalty. Politics cannot pick the best because the best already have jobs of their own and as a rule refuse to be picked. Furthermore, the first desire of political appointees is not to serve the public but to stand in with the politicians who got them into their jobs and can get them out again.

Public work done by political appointees is not only worse done, but the public pays more for less, and often outrageously more. Accurate comparisons are doubtless impossible, but at a guess the value of public services by political appointees runs from exactly zero (in actual cases I have known) to from 50 to 75 per cent of the same services by honestly chosen civil service appointees. If here and there a political job holder does reach 100 per cent, such cases are seldom found.

To my thinking the essence of sound civil service practice is to make it easy to get rid of an incompetent employee, but through competitive examinations to make it quite impossible for the dismissing power to put in his place the incompetent political friend, or the still more incompetent heeler, of some job-hunting politician. Thus the principal inducement for political dismissals is done away with.

It was so in my time, and the plan worked well. Where it was followed, cases of unjust removal were rare. Every employee should of course be given the opportunity to clear himself of any charges that may be brought against him, but to require legal proof of incompetence before dismissal in my judgment is a serious handicap to good administration. Such proof is often extremely difficult or even impossible to get. The natural result is that many public servants remain in office who, in the public interest, were much better out.

We in the Service followed the Civil Service Law, and it served us well. Moreover, the members of the Service knew that their Chief would back them to the limit in doing their duty, and that if any one of them was fired unjustly, he would go out too.

Of the greatest consequence was this—every member of the Service realized that it was engaged in a great and necessary undertaking in which the whole future of their country was at stake. The Service had a clear understanding of where it was going, it was determined to get there, and it was never afraid to fight for what was right.

Every man and woman in the Service believed in it and its work, and took great pride in belonging to it. And out of this pride grew a strong common interest which made the Service a thoroughly inspiring place to work in.

The Service was doing what had never been done before in America, and within the limits of its job it was constantly building new trails. No wonder its people had the zest of the pioneer. There was only one way for them to go, and that was ahead.

Out of the Service record of doing what to many seemed impossible there grew a strong belief that whatever the Service set out to do, that it could and would accomplish. Among the men who carried on its most difficult work sprang up a slogan not far removed from another which used to hang framed in the office of Admiral Waesche, Commandant of the United States Coast Guard:

Certainly It Can Be Done

Finally the Service was clean. It had nothing to hide. During the dozen years I was a member of it, there was only a single case of financial crookedness, and for that a former member of the General Land Office, transferred with the Forest Reserves, was responsible.

Organized as set forth in the *Use Book* and as I have tried to describe it, the Service got results. Not all at once, of course. To get results we had to revise, common-sensitize, and make alive the whole attitude and action of the men who had learned the Land Office way of handling the Reserves on the ground and in the office. We had to drive out red tape with intelligence, and unite the office and the field.

Next, and this was equally necessary, we had to bring about a fundamental change in the attitude and action of the men who lived in or near the Reserves and used them. We had to get their co-operation by earning their respect.

When the men with political pull, the men who had "fought the Indians and settled the country" and thought they owned it, and the men to whom lawlessness was second nature, undertook to walk on our faces as they had walked on the faces of the Land Office men, we had to make it very clear that the Government held the trumps. And that very thing we did.

Those of the leaders in the Forest Service who were not Western men had seen much of the West and its people. And that was our good luck, for pioneers have a rooted distrust and contempt for office men, city men, tenderfeet of any description. But when we showed them that we could throw the single and the double diamond hitch, carry our own packs, and find our own way by day or night as well as they could, when they found that our men could talk to them, each in his own language about his own business, with good will and understanding, the old rancor began to lose its edge.

Progress on each side was gradual, of course, but far more rapid in fact than we had a right to expect. Considering the area of the Reserves, the number of people affected, and the age, depth, and justice of their hostility, the change came fast. As the idea spread that the Reserves were for use, good will and understanding ceased to be one-sided and grew to be mutual, and the rule rather than the exception.

52. *No Red Tape*

The problem of administration created for us by the transfer was absolutely new. We could not adopt the methods of the Land Office, for both methods and results were thoroughly bad. We had no precedent that we could follow anywhere in the Government service, for no such job as this had ever faced Washington before. We were indeed breaking new ground.

There was just one thing to do—in the light of what we had learned about the Forest Reserves, the people of the West, and the Federal Government—we must go vigorously forward, apply what knowledge and common sense we had to the task ahead, and everywhere and always prefer results to routine.

In other words, our organization and our methods must never be frozen, but always subject to change. Whenever and wherever experience brought better methods or better organization to light, we must be ready to throw off the old and take on the new.

Never change for the sake of change, but change for the sake of betterment the moment we were sure that betterment would follow change. The old battle cry of bureaucracy, "We have always done it this way," meant nothing to the men of the Forest Service.

Our people were constantly on the lookout for short cuts to results. Suggestions for improvement were always welcome, especially from men in the field. Where differences of opinion cropped up between field and office, as of course they did, it was my fixed intention to adopt the field man's recommendations unless there was strong reason against it. That was nothing more than horse sense.

Red tape, which makes routine more important than results, and puts custom ahead of common sense, had few champions in the Service. That was partly because we had seen what the official mind had done to the Land Office and the Indian Office, but mainly because we were on our own, with few tracks in the trail ahead.

No one ever went more penetratingly to the heart of the problem of public administration than St. Paul did when he told the Corinthians that the letter killeth, but the spirit giveth life—even though he was referring to something entirely different at the time.

The Forest Service was alive. Its members were young, on their toes, proud to be engaged in so great an enterprise, ready to meet the future with much the same eagerness for battle that was so evident in T.R. The Service was bound to win, and well our people knew it.

These were no clock watchers. The limit of their service was all they could give. They could be trusted for that. Nobody bothered to see whether or not here and there a man was five minutes late in the morning. Nobody cared, because it was a regular custom of the Service to put in not less but more than the regular Government hours.

So eager were our people that every spring the driving work of the winter was followed by a near-epidemic of sickness, so that I was obliged to shut off work in the office after supper. No one in the whole history of Government administration, I am certain, has ever had a finer collection of men and women to work with than I had. They were simply superb.

The Forestry Division was already under civil service when I joined it. The President's order on December 17, 1904, which applied the Civil Service Act to the whole Forest Reserve Service, finished the old Land Office policy of putting politics first and efficiency second. What we were after now was men of better training and wider experience than the Land Office force, and they must be appointed and promoted on merit alone. In other words, we wanted a body of men as useful to the public which it served as it was possible to make it.

After the transfer, T.R.'s order gave us the chance to get good men by examination, because the Civil Service Commission, through my friend and its President, General John R. Procter, allowed the Forest Service to draw up the examination papers. We wrote them as men who knew the forests and mountains should, with the definite intention of shutting out men who did not know them.

Procter let us do it because he knew we wanted no more incompetents, no more cripples. He knew we wanted experienced men, men who could travel the wilderness, afoot or with horses, by day and by night, and take care of themselves and their stock in the forests and the mountains, winter and summer, alone or in company. We at headquarters in Washington, who set the pace, could do it. Of the field men, who carried out the plans we made, very properly we required no less.

In the office the same point of view prevailed, and nowhere more effectively than in our correspondence. For the form of a letter is far more important than many people think. Few things show the character and purpose of an organization better than its mail, both incoming and outgoing. The outgoing mail carries the message and the quality of its source. The incoming mail brings the proof of failure or success.

It is of the utmost importance that letters should be alive. Dead, dry, formal, official letters, stamped all over with pallid impersonality, are poison.

What the *Use Book* had to say on this crucial subject is worth repeating:

"Use direct, clear-cut language. Avoid unwieldy words where shorter, simpler ones will express the idea equally well. Be concise. Avoid laborious statements, the essence of which might well be expressed in half the space. Never use the substance of the letter received as a preamble to the reply." It was the custom of the Land Office letter writers of my day, who, after addressing the author of an incoming letter as "Sir" instead or by his human name, would acknowledge his communication of such a date "in which you say," and then proceed to recopy the whole of his letter. After which this shining model for genial human intercourse would finish up with "Your request is denied [or granted]. Respectfully yours."

The first object of a letter that does its job is to establish or continue living, moving, productive relations between two persons who are or ought to be interested, and so to get things done. It has to tell somebody something, of course, and do it clearly. But that is only the beginning. It has also to create or maintain good working confidence and co-operation between two individuals or two organizations.

In the Forest Service we held that among the best qualities of a good letter is promptness. The old Roman saying, "He gives twice who gives quickly," is never truer than about the answer to a letter. And close behind promptness comes readability. Short words, short sentences—the kind of language people use when they talk to each other.

You will perhaps remember that something new has been added to that classic of young and old, "Mary Had a Little Lamb." This supplement runs as follows:

"Hurrah for the teacher,
Hurrah for the lamb,
Hurrah for Little Mary
Who didn't give a damn."

That last line is human, and it hits the spot. But the Bureau of Circumlocution might have used, in place of its five short words, some such atrocity as this in characterizing Little Mary:

"Acclamations for Little Mary whose invariable policy it was to maintain a rigid or inflexible attitude of indifference or aloofness to both the remoter and the more immediate consequences of the legitimate or illegitimate results of any action, whether authorized or unauthorized, by any of the participants in any incident with which he, she, or they were directly or indirectly concerned, with regrettable disregard of all those intellectual, moral, and conventional considerations which should always and everywhere animate all persons with proper respect for the accepted formalities of well and duly ordered human intercourse, and which, if official propriety did not forbid, might be alluded to as unfortunate."

To quote St. Paul again: "Except ye utter words that are easy to be understood, how shall it be known what is spoken?"

Many long hours did I spend in rewriting, or showing the authors how to rewrite, letters prepared for my signature. In the end I doubt if any Government organization ever lived up to a higher standard of official correspondence.

53. *Seven Years and After*

The members of the Forest Service, whose rule of faith and conduct I have just laid before you, had no small record of accomplishment behind them when the transfer took place. So far as I am aware, no other bureau, at least in time of peace, had equaled that record.

Secretary Wilson, in his annual report for 1904-05, pointed out that in the seven years from July 1, 1898, when the old ideas went out, to July 1, 1905, when the *Use Book* came in, the progress we had made was nothing to be ashamed of. Between those dates the number of our people had increased 75 times, from 11 in the Division to 821 in the Service, the number of professional foresters 76 times, from 2 to 153.

In the same seven years our appropriation (although the Secretary very wisely did not mention it) had risen from the original $28,520 to $350,000 in 1903-04 and to $439,873 in 1904-05. And with the transfer came to us, of course, what was left of the appropriation for the Forest Reserves for that year.

In the year of the transfer field work was going on in twenty-seven states and territories. Over 900,000 acres of private forest were under management recommended by the Forest Service, and applications for working plans were on file for 2,000,000 acres more.

But the Secretary did not stop with statistics. In a general review of progress by the Forest Service, his report pointed out that in 1898 there existed neither a science nor a literature of American Forestry. An education in Forestry could not be got in America. There were less than ten professional foresters in the United States. Public opinion was partly hostile to Forestry, partly friendly but confused. As the Secretary said, "Forestry was both an evident economic need and an apparent economic impossibility.

"That the whole situation is profoundly altered is directly and chiefly due to the work of the Forest Service. With its offer of practical assistance to forest owners made in the fall of 1898, its field of action shifted from the desk to the woods. The lumberman was met on his own ground."

Furthermore, "Of the exact knowledge concerning our American forests, upon which the practice of scientific forestry depends, vastly more had been gathered during the last seven years than previously from the time Columbus landed." We had made measurements of millions of individual trees of thirty-two important species. We had carried on studies in every state and territory, in Puerto Rico, Alaska, and the Philippines. We had made forest-working plans in twenty-eight states.

Said the Secretary: "Besides creating a science of American forestry, the Forest Service has worked out the methods of operation by which forestry may be put in practice. Had not the Forest Service taken the lead in finding out just how practical rules for conservative lumbering might be laid down and carried out, forestry could not have reached the point at which it now stands in the United States.

"In the field of economic tree planting the same story is repeated and shows definite, important, and permanent results," said Tama Jim. "The Forest Service has made in all 300 separate planting plans for private owners, covering an aggregate area of over 50,000 acres, in 36 States and Territories."

The Service had also made many regional planting studies. It was in a position to exercise great helpfulness in the whole planting movement throughout the United States, including not only individual farms, but also the watersheds of cities, denuded mountains, and regions of little rainfall. It had likewise contributed powerfully to the great work of reclaiming desert lands through water conservation and to the whole irrigation movement.

The Service looked to the Secretary like a good business investment. "In the saving of waste it has enriched the country by many millions of dollars, and in this way alone has added vastly more to the national wealth than its total expenditures for all purposes during its entire history."

Among other things, our timber tests had shown the usability of little used woods; our studies of seasoning and timber preservation had opened the way for an enormous reduction in the drain on our forests, especially for railroad ties; our studies of lumbering had proved that timber formerly wasted in high stumps, tops, and logs left in the woods could be utilized without added expense; and the Herty method of gathering naval stores had produced far larger returns in turpentine without destroying the Southern Pine forests.

The Forest Service, said the Secretary, had rendered a great service by its explorations of forested regions, which had been completed or were under way for every important timber region of the country. And moreover: "In the West, examinations by the Service had been of great value in selecting forest reserves and locating their boundaries. The guiding principle of this policy is, of course, that all land should be put to its best use. This principle the Forest Service has assisted to put into effect by its recommendations as to what lands should not, as well as what should be reserved."

As to the transfer, the Secretary said that its immediate effect was to open the Reserves to much wider use than ever before. That was because we in the Service knew how to use and preserve at the same time. Thus the sales of timber had increased many times since the Service took charge.

Despite the increased responsibility for handling the Forest Reserves, the net cost to the Government of all the work of the Service was less for 1904-05 than that of the Bureau of Forestry alone before the transfer. A property worth in cash not less than $250,000,000 was administered at a cost of less than one-third of 1 per cent of its value, while an increase in that value of not less than 10 per cent per annum was taking place. In two years after the transfer the administration of the Forest Reserves paid for itself from current revenue.

One more clause from the Secretary's report, because it shows that the transfer had not caught us off base: "The administration of these vast forests fell quietly into its place in the Service, and has since been conducted with steadily advancing efficiency. Every office in the Forest Service is actively concerned in their management."

If the Secretary's report was right, and I think it was, we had gone far toward realizing our two main purposes. The first was to practice Forestry instead of merely preaching it. We wanted to prove that Forestry was something more than a subject of conversation. We wanted to demonstrate that Forestry could be taken out of the office into the woods, and made to yield satisfactory returns on the timberland investment—that Forestry was good business and could actually be made to pay.

Our second purpose was to take over the management of the National Forests and handle them as foresters should. Long before my training in Europe was over, it had become my chief ambition, timid at first but determined later on, to tread in the footsteps of Dr. Brandis. Thus I might hope to do for the public forests of the United States some part of what he had done for the forests of Burma and India.

To this original plan in time was added the reservation or acquisition by the Nation under the Weeks Law of other forests whose protection and professional management was necessary in the public interest, and the increase and wise handling of state and community forests.

One more purpose we came to have before my service was finished, and that the most important of all, for it concerned a far greater area and possible productiveness of forest land than all public forests put together. We saw that only Federal control of cutting on private land could assure the Nation the supply of forest products it must have to prosper. We demanded that control, which has long been in effect in the most democratic and the most civilized nations, but in vain.

That the United States will eventually exercise such control is inevitable, because without it the safety of our forests and consequently the prosperity of our people cannot be assured. So far the lumber industry, by its highly organized and very expensive campaign, has succeeded in preventing what the public interest so clearly requires.

On the National Forests the Forest Service has given a practical and successful demonstration of what could and should be done with public timberland. By 1910 their area had tripled, and public opinion had secured their future. State and community forests had made some advance in area and in management, but the practice of Forestry on private land, notwithstanding a beginning that exceeded our highest hopes, still left very much to be desired.

In spite of early promise and later increase, the attempt to introduce the practice of Forestry on private lands by proving that it would pay did not succeed on any general scale. Even in 1910, the peak year, when it had been introduced on about 1,500,000 acres, still less than one-half of 1 per cent of all privately owned forest land at that time was under some form of forest management.

We had been confident in those early days that we could show forest owners how to practice Forestry and make it pay. And we had believed that many or most of them, once they had been shown, would shift permanently from forest butchery to sustained production. On many or most of the private forest tracts for which we had made working plans, the owners gradually lost interest. Actual progress has been so slight that today, nearly half a century after the first offer of assistance in 1898, the percentage of privately owned forest lands under systematic management is still dangerously below the obvious need. It is so small that, together with the production of all the National Forests, it fails dismally to assure anything remotely approaching a sufficient future supply of indispensable forest products.

One thing that had misled us was the lively interest the lumber industry took in our work. As our publicity spread, more and more inquiries kept coming in as to what changes of method would be required, what it would cost, and how much it would pay. And more and more applications followed our preliminary examinations and working plans—applications for practical advice on the ground. Doubtless also some lumbermen saw in our offer a chance to get at small cost a Government estimate of their timber, even though they had no intention of practicing Forestry.

What were the reasons for the setback in private Forestry? There were several. One was that after the transfer the chief attention of the Forest Service inevitably was shifted from private lands to the National Forests, where our first duty lay. Another was the pioneer attitude, bred by the abundance of forest resources, which resisted any change in the old methods of lumbering.

A further cause was the sudden and disastrous change in the value of stumpage. Years of rising prices and increased production had given lumbermen the fullest belief in the future of their business. In 1906 some forty-five billion feet of lumber were produced—an all-time high. Then came the depression of 1907, with its appalling drop in lumber production and prices, followed by other years almost as bad. As an unfortunate result the lumbermen temporarily lost confidence in the future of their business, with a corresponding loss of faith in Forestry.

Still another reason was the Ballinger-Pinchot controversy, which touched off nationwide attacks on the Forest Service in the standpat press. These attacks proclaimed that we supporters of Forestry and the T.R. Conservation policy were fanatics, lawbreakers, and much besides. They gave voice to the hatred and alarm of the Old Line Republicans, who resented our failure to bow down to the overlordship of the special interests, and to the exasperation of Taft's personal followers, who were indignant at the trouble we were making.

But by far the most potent factor in checking the advance of private Forestry in the United States was the end of Theodore Roosevelt's term as President. When T.R. came into office at the end of 1901, Forestry had really begun to find itself. In the wise use of private and public forest lands we were helping the small homemaker as against the big exploiter in insuring future forest supplies for the Nation, in looking beyond tomorrow, and getting ready for the future. We knew where we were headed, and we had learned the road.

On that road T.R. was with us all the way. He knew the forests and he loved them. He understood our problems, and he was able and glad to throw his executive power, his tremendous personality, and his strength with the plain people behind our work and our plans. The result was an opportunity for service such as seldom has opened before any bureau of the Federal Government.

After T.R. came Taft. It was as though a sharp sword had been succeeded by a roll of paper, legal size. It did not take the country long to learn that Forestry and Conservation no longer had a fighting President behind them. That the public good, as T.R. had understood it, no longer came first. That an era had come to an end.

54. *Government Business*

If you have read what goes before, you are aware that the Government which T.R. inherited was anything but a careful and competent business organization. Debased by generations of political control, sunk in the mire of traditional red tape, it was far below the level of decent, or even tolerable, executive administration. Much needed to be done, and the time was at hand when it was possible to do something about it.

Although the morale and production of the Departments had improved enormously under the new spirit of T.R.'s leadership, the old bad habits of previous administrations had by no means disappeared. As I had occasion later on to say of the state government of Pennsylvania under the regular Old Line politicians, it was a mess. The Government machinery needed a thorough overhauling.

I had learned a lot about it in the seven years of my Government service, and I thought I knew what was needed. Accordingly I worked out a plan and a list of the men to carry it out, took it to T.R., and on June 3, 1905, he appointed the Committee on Department Methods, charged to investigate the business methods of the Government and suggest improvements.

We called it the Keep Committee. Charles H. Keep, then Assistant Secretary of the Treasury, was Chairman. The other members were Frank H. Hitchcock, then First Assistant Postmaster General, whose contribution was small; James R. Garfield, then Commissioner of Corporations, whose contribution was by no means small; Lawrence O. Murray, then Assistant Secretary of Commerce and Labor; and myself. Overton Price was its Secretary. To him belongs most of the credit for its good work.

The Keep Committee faced a tough task which had too long been left undone and did it well. Like the rest of the Roosevelt commissions, it was without special funds for the employment of assistants, and its members without relief from their heavy official duties. Nevertheless the Committee on Department Methods tackled the Government's housekeeping with vigor and intelligence, and went a long way toward putting it in order.

Aided by about seventy men chosen for their experience and ability from among the Government's 15,000 civil service employees in Washington (there are about three million now), the Committee made a sustained and successful attack on official red tape and sloppy business methods. I do not mean that it succeeded in doing away with all the going stupidities and wastes of time and money. That would have been too much to expect. But it did bring about many and much-needed savings and improvements.

The Keep Committee made no less than sixteen investigations and reports in the twenty-one months of its active life. The subjects ranged from public printing, crop reports, telephone service, accounts and purchase, to transportation, hours of labor, cost keeping, Treasury bookkeeping, and Government contracts. Each report recommended and was followed by valuable betterments in the particular service examined.

Among the worst examples of waste was getting estimates on the cotton crop from 85,000 people—too many, badly selected, at too much labor and expense.

Another example: the Government was buying 28 different kinds of ink, 278 different kinds of pens, 11 different kinds of typewriter ribbons, and 132 different grades of pencils. One Department was paying $1.70 per dozen quarts of ink; another $4 per dozen quarts. And we uncovered many other cases of inefficiency and waste.

In answer to T.R.'s query, "How much too much is printed by the Government Printing Office?," we found that not only too many but also too large documents were being printed, and that the Government Printing Office had never had a system of cost accounting. We advised keeping scientific treatises out of annual reports, and we recommended the creation of an advisory committee in each Department.

In the reduction of public printing and in improved methods for the testing and purchase of Government supplies, the Keep Committee saved several hundred thousand dollars a year for Uncle Sam. By forcing the adoption of modern business methods instead of the ancient and fishlike routines of the Departments, it also increased their efficiency by many times that amount.

The Keep Committee rendered great service. Never before had the machinery of the Government been inspected so systematically and so thoroughly. Never before had the principle been effectively enforced that the Government is a business, and that it should carry that business on along the best modern business lines. Moreover, the work of the Committee throughout successfully stood the test of examination by the best business experts.

Incidentally, in this analysis of Department methods the Forest Service came out with flying colors and was pointed out as a model for other Government units to follow.

Jim Garfield, then Secretary of the Interior, testifying before the House Committee on Expenditures in the Department of Agriculture, said: "The [Keep] Committee was unanimous in the belief that efficiency in the Forest Service was so much greater than that found in other offices that we used many of the methods we found in vogue there as the basis for recommendations for changes in other branches of the Government service," and he added that if our methods were used generally throughout the Government service, the members of the Keep Committee believed there would be an enormous increase in efficiency in the other offices where they were adopted.

The House Committee itself reported that "The Forest Service has been administered honestly and with great administrative, executive, and business ability."

The fact is that the Forest Service was good. In 1908 the well-known firm of Gunn, Richards and Company of New York City, consultants in business organization and methods, made a thorough investigation of the methods and organization of the Service. Their report said: "We cannot praise too highly the personnel of the Service, and we have much pleasure in stating that, in our rather extended experience in commercial enterprises where the opportunity for financial reward is unlimited, we have rarely, if ever, met a body of men where the average of intelligence was so high or the loyalty to the organization and to the work so great. Without exception, every individual with whom we came in contact was most enthusiastic in regard to the work, and anxious to promote the welfare of the Service in every manner possible.

"The volume of the business transacted, in our opinion, compares most favorably with that in commercial practice, and is worthy of the highest commendation."

The Keep Committee played an important part in creating the unequaled morale and efficiency of the T.R. Administration. Other Roosevelt Commissions had their share also. But first came T.R. himself, his courage, his energy, and his power of leadership. Without T.R. not all these Commissions working together could have brought about even a respectable fraction of the great result. In such matters it is the man at the top that counts.

Lord Bryce, British Ambassador to the United States, wrote of the men under T.R. that in a long life, during which he had studied intimately the governments of many different countries, he had never "in any country seen a more eager, high-minded, and efficient set of public servants—men more useful and creditable to their country—than the men then doing the work of the American Government in Washington and in the field."

55. *Holding the Line*

The management of the Forest Reserves under the Land Office had been as full of abuses as an egg is of meat. These abuses had to be corrected, of course. Obviously any attempt to correct them would have to tread on many powerful toes. And tread on them it did. Hostilities began promptly three days after the transfer, when our appropriation was before the Senate.

The opposition charged that we in Washington were theorists, ignorant of the West; that our local officers were arbitrary and tyrannical; that the National Forests included vast areas of treeless land; that the Service was keeping settlers out of the National Forests; that it was helping big corporations and big stockmen as against the small man; that it was stripping the West of its timber; and so forth and so on. As one illustration, take the remarks of Senator Fulton of Oregon. Said he:

"The truth is, this bureau is composed of dreamers and theorists, but beyond and outside the domain of their theories and their dreams is the everyday, busy, bustling, throbbing world of human endeavor, where real men are at work producing substantial results. While these chiefs of the Bureau of Forestry sit within their marble halls and theorize and dream of waters conserved, forests and streams protected and preserved through the ages and the ages, the lowly pioneer is climbing the mountain side, where he will erect his humble cabin, and within the shadow of the whispering pines and the lofty firs of the western forest engage in the laborious work of carving out for himself and his loved ones a home and dwelling place. It is of him I think and for him I take my stand today."

Senator Fulton it was who introduced an amendment to the Agricultural Bill of 1907 to take away from the President and reserve to Congress the power to create National Forests in the states of Oregon, Washington, Idaho, Montana, Colorado, and Wyoming. The Fulton amendment was passed on February 25. The President had until March 4 to sign the bill.

At once I saw T.R. and got his enthusiastic consent to our plan. Thereupon we set every available man at work drawing proclamations for National Forests in those six states. We knew precisely what we wanted. Our field force had already gathered practically all the facts. Speedily it supplied the rest. Our office force worked straight through, some of them for thirty-six and even forty-eight hours on end, to finish the job. As usual our people were superb.

As the Proclamations were completed, I took them over to the White House. T.R. signed them and sent them to the State Department for safekeeping. And when the job was done some sixteen million acres, or more than there are in any one of half a dozen states, were rescued from passing into the hands of private corporations. Then, and not until then, did T.R. sign the Agricultural Bill.

When the biters who had been bitten learned the facts they were furious. As T.R. said, "The opponents of the Forest Service turned handsprings in their wrath, and dire were the threats against the Executive; but the threats could not be carried out, and were really only a tribute to the efficiency of our action."

An angry delegation led by Senator Tom Carter of Montana came from the Hill to protest. Carter as head of the delegation was hardly a fortunate choice, for his own record left something to be desired. In one of his campaigns, for example, a powerful organization in Montana was bitterly against him. So he bought off the leaders—bought them off with a very considerable check, dated after the election.

Carter won. The check was presented for payment. No funds, said the bank. What? Didn't Senator Carter have that much money in the bank? Sure. But this check was signed Thomas Carter, not Thomas A. Carter, which was the Senator's signature.

This is no fairy story. For years the Thomas Carter check hung framed on the wall of the bank.

T.R. knew that Carter and his delegation was coming, and sent for me. I heard him break into delighted laughter when Carter started his protest. The joke was on them. It was their kind of a joke, and the meeting ended in a highly temporary era of good feeling.

Another enemy of ours, Senator Heyburn of Idaho, made the charge, in his opinion the most grievous of all, that the Service maintained a press bureau to influence public sentiment. We did. Why not give the people the facts?

Heyburn had personal reasons for his hostility. I had published in a bulletin of the Service a long correspondence between Heyburn and myself which by no means brightened his reputation. It was a step without precedent for a mere bureau chief to attack a Senator of the United States in official print, and it did nothing to calm Heyburn's rage.

Not only the big special interests and states' righters were against us, but also politicians who had lost their patronage, old-timers who still longed for the good old abuses under the Land Office, men who rightly resented the wrongs of the lieu-land law, and many more.

The Forest Service had more and more active enemies by far than any other Government bureau. By 1907, said T.R., "the opposition of the servants of the special interests in Congress to the Forest Service had become strongly developed, and more time appeared to be spent upon it during the passage of the appropriation bills than on all other Government bureaus put together."

Quite literally, the Service had to fight for its life. Without constant vigilance, without the generous and effective help of Eastern Senators like Spooner and Beveridge, and above all without the militant backing of T.R., we could not have lasted through a single session of Congress. In both House and Senate it was the men who were free from the pressure of Western interests, men from states that contained no National Forests, who saved our bacon.

But all this might well have failed to carry us through except for the men of the Service itself. The chief responsibility for holding the line fell on four of them.

Overton Westfeldt Price, the son of a Confederate colonel, was a gentleman of the old Southern school—perfectly fearless, completely loyal, extremely able, and with a great capacity for dealing with men. An indefatigable worker, he contributed far more to the building and the success of the Forest Service than he has ever been given credit for. T.R. himself spoke of "the remarkable executive capacity of the Associate Forester, Overton W. Price [removed after I left office]."

Overton had more to do with the organization and reorganization of the Service than I had, and therefore with its efficiency—without equal among Government organizations, then or since. He was far more than my assistant. He was my associate. And his title was made Associate Forester at my request.

His training in technical Forestry was much more thorough than mine, and his knowledge of Service details was likewise much greater. His untiring co-operation made it possible for me, without injury to the Service, to give the immense amount of time required for the thousand and one odd jobs T.R. was in the habit of turning over to me.

Later, after we had both been removed from office for defending the property of the people against Ballinger, he was the mainstay of the National Conservation Association, which carried on the fight, until his deeply lamented death in 1913. I can never be sufficiently grateful to Overton not only for what he did but even more for what he was.

George W. Woodruff was our first law officer. Before the transfer, he and his assistants had carefully watched legislation, and made themselves familiar with the public-land laws and Departmental jurisdictions. Woodruff kept our friends in Congress posted on the pending bills, and furnished them with the facts and arguments they needed to defend our position.

Looking back over a long life which has given me an unusual opportunity to know and estimate many people, I can think of no man of more admirable character than George Woodruff. The first time I ever saw him was at a freshman rush the night before he and I began our four years at Yale. After that George and I never lost touch.

Woodruff was the outstanding football man of his time. As a freshman he made the Yale eleven on the first day of practice, and for four straight years was on the football team, the Mott Haven team, and the crew, which he captained in his senior year.

Physically George was the strongest human being I have ever had my hands on. Al Cowles, captain of the University crew, said to him one day, "Up to your neck, George, you're the best-looking man I ever saw."

In spite of the time and attention he gave to athletics, Woodruff was one of the highest stand men in our class. His power of reasoning was so great that the rest of us speedily learned there was no percentage whatever in arguing with him.

When the Division of Forestry became a Bureau in 1901, George took charge of the legal work. In spite of constant and most bitter attack, from that day until I was removed from the Service in 1910, we were neither reproved nor reversed by either House of Congress, or by any Congressional committee. Nor were we ever defeated or reversed on any legal principle underlying our work by any court or administrative tribunal of last resort. Eleven times George's interpretations of law were taken to the Supreme Court of the United States. Eleven times they were sustained and in every case but one sustained unanimously.

In his *Autobiography** T.R. gives George credit for a great constructive achievement: "The idea that the Executive is the steward of the public welfare was first formulated and given practical effect in the Forest Service by its law officer, George Woodruff." I was proud to have him as Attorney General in my first term as Governor of Pennsylvania, and in my second to appoint him to the Public Service Commission, whose most useful member he speedily became.

His mental energy was such that I have known him to put in thirteen hours a day of intense intellectual application for days on end—thirteen hours of sixty minutes each, mind you, not including time spent at meals or in going to and from the office, or in any other way except actual work. Try it once and see what it means.

Perfect courage, perfect kindness, unending patience, faultless integrity, and at their service a mind of most remarkable power and penetration—all these made George Woodruff, to my thinking, the flawless model of a Christian gentleman, although he did not belong to any church.

* *Theodore Roosevelt—An Autobiography*, p. 420. New York, Charles Scribner's Sons, 1913.

Power and gentleness do not always go together. In George Woodruff ability was balanced by genuine humility. His tolerance was as great as his strength. In him uprightness, forbearance, and capacity were melted and molded together into one of the two or three most admirable and most useful public servants I have ever known.

Two other members of Yale '89 came to work with me in Washington, and each became a pillar of our movement. One of them, Philip Patterson Wells, was one of those quiet, steady, courageous, and effective men whose value grows with the years. He was making a place for himself as an instructor in the Yale Law School when George Woodruff and I agreed that he was the best man in sight for George's assistant.

He came and he made good. When George became Assistant Attorney General for the Interior Department on March 22, 1907, Phil succeeded him in charge of the legal work of the Service, and carried it on without a break. While George was the first authority in America on the law of Conservation, Phil was without a rival in his legal knowledge of water power and utilities in general. Together they formed a pair whom it would have been impossible to duplicate or replace.

After I was removed Phil became Chief Law Officer of the Reclamation Service and counsel of the National Conservation Association. Later he was Deputy Attorney General of Pennsylvania and Chairman of its Giant Power Board. Also he helped me on this book. Phil and I were close friends and fellow-workers until he died. I owe him very much.

When I was at Exeter a long lean youngster by the name of Herbert Augustine Smith was in the class below me. When I got to Yale the same long lean youngster and I were in the same class, for my bad eyes had cost me a year. His classmates called him Dolikoskion, because that was Homer's word to describe a spear that cast a long shadow. Dol Smith certainly did just that.

Like Phil and George, Dol Smith was a high stand man; but while Phil rowed in the class crew, Dol represented Yale in the mile walk. Like Phil also, he became an instructor at Yale—an instructor in English—and I was lucky indeed to get him in 1901 as editor of our Forest Service publications. At first I had edited them myself, but the time came when there were too many publications and too much else to do.

Able, keen, absolutely devoted, and absolutely straight, with a broad view over the whole field, Dol Smith became one of my most intimate and valued advisers. He speedily outgrew his allotted bounds as editor of the Forest Service and took charge of our publicity. He knew the Service from Alpha to Omaha, and to his usefulness there seemed to be no end. Of his work, T.R. in his *Autobiography* had this to say:

"It is doubtful whether there has ever been elsewhere under the Government such effective publicity—publicity purely in the interest of the people—at so low a cost. Before the educational work of the Forest Service was stopped by the Taft Administration, it was securing the publication of facts about forestry in fifty million copies of newspapers a month at a total expense of $6,000 a year. Not one cent has ever been paid by the Forest Service to any publication of any kind for the printing of this material. It was given out freely, and published without cost because it was news. Without this publicity the Forest Service could not have survived the attacks made upon it by the representatives of the great special interests in Congress; nor could forestry in America have made the rapid progress it has."

And for that Herbert Smith was responsible. He it was also who drafted for me my annual reports to the Secretary of Agriculture; for the Secretary the clauses in his annual report to the President which dealt with Forestry; and for the President and many others a long series of sound and effective letters, papers, and speeches on every phase of Forestry and Conservation. Most of his best work appeared under other names.

The extent and value of Herbert Smith's contribution to the Forest Service and the Conservation policy would be hard to overstate. He spent his life in the Service and was the close adviser of forester after forester until he was retired for age.

Dol Smith and I were friends for sixty active years. I can never exaggerate my admiration for his character and intelligence or sufficiently acknowledge and praise the value of his contribution to American Forestry and to the making of this book which, unfortunately, he did not live to see completed.

56. *A New Science—Forestry*

Forty years ago there was in America no science of Forestry, in the true sense of the word. We knew next to nothing about our forest trees, our forest types, their life histories, their enemies, and their friends. Today, while still far from perfection, we have advanced to a fair knowledge of the life of the forest.

Before Forestry came to America, the botanical knowledge of American trees was far advanced, and that was true also of forage plants on the Western ranges. But the practical knowledge of how to use forest and range without destroying them lagged far behind.

The systematic study of American trees, by foresters for foresters, first started in 1896 with the publication of a little book of a hundred pages called *The White Pine,* by Pinchot and Graves. The purpose of *The White Pine* was, as the preface sets forth, "to assist in making clear the real nature of forestry, in exciting an interest in the subjects with which it deals, in stimulating others to similar research, and, above all, in facilitating and hastening the general introduction of right methods of forest management, by which alone our forests can be saved."

In 1898 appeared another diminutive volume, *The Adirondack Spruce,* which, although primarily intended to be of practical assistance to American lumbermen, developed also new knowledge of the behavior of this valuable species in the forest.

Meantime a monograph on the White Pine and a report on its measurements and developments were in preparation by the old Division of Forestry and in press when I joined the Division. From then on the study of commercial trees continued on an increasing scale up to the time of the transfer and after. And so also with the study of the range.

With the transfer the Forest Service became responsible for maintaining and even increasing the permanent production of forest and forest range over tens of millions of acres. For that great task, we needed to know more about how different kinds of trees should be marked for cutting, how best to lumber and dispose of the slash, and especially how to ensure natural reproduction. We needed to know also how the range could best be protected and maintained. And we were short on the underlying facts.

To secure these facts, we brought into the Service skilled men—men able to handle our going problems on the ground, and other men competent to carry on the research essential to really good management.

Our previous studies of commercial trees, and what we knew about Forestry in general, had equipped the Service fairly well to deal with the immediate problems of forest management on the National Forests. That knowledge, fortified by practical experience and common sense, got us by without too many glaring mistakes. On the whole, however, it was still too little and too narrow when compared with the vastness of the field and the complexity of the problems.

After the transfer came storm and stress. The great special interests of the West, whose monopolies we threatened, threw against us their lobbyists and their satellite press. Moreover, our men in the field had to meet the old and ingrained habit of exploitation of the Western pioneer. "This is our country. We drove the Indians out. Now you let us alone." It was to take some little time before the people of the West were won over to the sound new policies of the Service. And the only men who could do it were men of action, who could make quick decisions and yet not stumble too much. There was no time for lengthy observation or the search for precise forest facts.

In addition, the Service was growing, and growing fast. One expansion followed close on the heels of another. New technical problems, new executive tasks had to be taken in our stride. Our best men had to be diverted to boundary work, to recruiting new fieldmen, to working out new policies in timber sales and grazing, and to many other problems of our vast new domain. The respect which the Forest Service commands today from the West bears high testimony to the character, courage, and intelligence of these creators of a new forest administration.

The egg of technical Forestry had been laid, but the chick had hardly more than broken out of its shell. Nevertheless, it had to be converted to the practical uses of forest management. And we were lucky that this was so, that no rigid set of rules was imposed upon our fieldmen from the top. Our technical knowledge was born of necessity, and it grew as the need developed. As everywhere in the

Forest Service, we gave good men their heads, and the results were good.

In those days the research men were not on their own, but were attached to the Forest Supervisors, to help with technical problems. Their presence was often resented on the ground that they were Eastern tenderfeet (which had nothing to do with the case), but more commonly because of their persistent and sometimes unreasonable habit of asking embarrassing professional questions.

In those early days we usually had to split the difference between what was best for the forest and what was practical in logging. The research men and the practical men had to get together on some golden mean before the marking rules could stand the test of good Forestry and good lumbering. And so with slash disposal, range improvement, and many other technical matters. That research in the Forest Service today gives sound and practical results is due to this constant struggle between what is ideally good and what is practically possible.

Since a forest crop takes longer to mature than any other, there is greater need in Forestry for long and carefully recorded observations than in any other field of agriculture. Such observations do not happen by accident. Even before the transfer there was a little hall room in the Atlantic Building where technical forest facts and statistics were assembled. We called it Compilation. Here was the first cradle and treasure house of forest research in America.

Before the transfer also some 450 forest sample plots had been established throughout the East. Here all trees were measured, young growth noted, and other essential facts recorded. Then after five years each plot was measured again.

The idea was good, but it did not work out. The sample plots had to be established on private land, for we had no other. When the time came for the second measurement, many of them had been cut, destroyed by fire, overgrazed, or otherwise disturbed, which made the results of little value.

After the transfer many permanent sample plots were established on the National Forests. But because our research men were few and their load so heavy, many of the plots were neglected. Many others, however, today furnish valuable records of what happens to a forest after it is cut.

On May 6, 1908, a group of research men, under the leadership of Raphael Zon, laid before me a plan for establishing Forest Experiment Stations on the National Forests. The purpose, as set forth in their memorandum, was to carry on "experiments and studies leading to a full and exact knowledge of American silviculture, to the most economic utilization of the products of the forest, and to a fuller appreciation of the indirect benefits of the forest. Each station should be allowed an area sufficient for the proper handling of short-period experiments, for experiments requiring a number of years, and for the maintenance of model forests typical of the silvicultural region.

"These areas will furnish the most valuable, instructive, and convincing object lessons for the public in general, for professional foresters, lumbermen, and owners of forest land, and especially for the technical and administrative officers of the national forests. They should be made the meeting grounds for supervisors, rangers, and guards, where demonstrations may be given for the education of these men, and an active interest stimulated in the technical side of the forest work—an interest which could not be engendered by any amount of literary or oratorical effort."

I had seen forest experiment stations abroad and I knew their value. The plan, therefore, was approved at once.

Here was the beginning of intensive forest investigation in America. In the summer of 1908 the first Forest Experiment Station was established on the Coconino National Forest near Flagstaff, Arizona. Two others followed in Colorado in 1909 and 1910, and others were rapidly established after I left the Forest Service.

Experiment Stations for grazing were carried on, beginning in 1903, outside the Forest Service. As this is written the Service has twelve Forest and Range Experiment Stations working to bring about the best possible management of the forest and the range.

It was in forest planting most of all that the Experiment Stations proved their value. The outstanding success in reforestation was in the Nebraska National Forest, which owes to Carlos G. Bates the major part of its victory. Forest nursery methods, methods of seed collection, seed extraction, and seed storage now used the country over owe their origin to the Forest Experiment Stations.

So also modern working plans, now indispensable in the handling of every National Forest, would not have been possible except for the work of the Experiment Stations in securing essential data on volume, growth, and yield.

Today Forest Research is an independent unit responsible directly to the Chief Forester. High credit for developing research and making it nationwide goes to Earle H. Clapp, first of the Branch of Research, and later for several years Acting Chief Forester. In this position Clapp courageously opposed the transfer of the Forest Service to the Department of the Interior, and incurred the bitter hostility of the lumber interests by advocating Government control of cutting on private lands. I am proud to count him as my friend.

But the greatest contribution of Forest Research is the spirit it has brought into the handling of national resources. Under the pressure of executive work, the technical ideas of the forester at times grow dim. It is Forest Research which has kept the sacred flame burning and has helped to raise Forestry to the level of the leading scientific professions.

The research man must anticipate coming needs. He must of necessity be ahead of his time. That means standing alone, exposed to the skepticism and ridicule of those who live only from day to day.

Because the research man did his job well, forest executives are now eager to turn the results of scientific investigation to practical use. It is only fair to say that, as research takes its rightful place in the vanguard of the forest movement, the early "searchers for forest facts," Raphael Zon foremost among them, will take their places alongside the other pioneers who have helped to build the United States Forest Service.

Hand in hand with the development of scientific Forestry went the study of how to make the best use of the products of the forest.

The beginning of the present-day Forest Products work of the Forest Service dates from 1901. It was planned to support and promote the practice of Forestry in the woods, and not, like the "timber physics" work of the old Division under Dr. Fernow, to substitute for it. That work was ordered discontinued in 1896 by the then Secretary of Agriculture, J. Sterling Morton, as "not germane to the subject of the Division." Its results were printed in three circulars in 1898, and it was dead when I came.

The Forest Products work of the new Division began in a small way. For the first year it was confined to the preparation of a report on the maple sugar industry. But much larger work was already planned. In co-operation with the Bureau of Chemistry we looked forward to important investigations of tanbarks, resins, and gums yielded by some fifty kinds of American and Philippine trees. With the Bureau of Plant Industry we planned an extensive study of the causes and prevention of decay in railroad and other timber.

The Report for my first year as Chief of the new Division pointed out that no systematic attempt had been made to investigate the many serious diseases of American timbers, and announced that, "With a view to obtaining some preliminary data for inaugurating more extensive investigations, an agent has been appointed who will have for his work a study of the more important diseases affecting timber."

Field studies of some of the more destructive diseases were already being made and a preliminary report was planned for the coming year. Dr. Hermann von Schrenck, instructor in the Shaw School of Botany at St. Louis, was put in charge of this preliminary work.

Furthermore, a study of the commercial resins of Southern Pines, and particularly of the Longleaf Pine, and of methods of collecting them, was forecast. It was to have highly important results. Finally, an investigation of the supply of timber for railroad ties available from forest plantations and from natural forests was in mind. It was a good plan, and it made good.

Dr. Harvey W. Wiley, Chief of the Bureau of Chemistry, had a theory, in which he was supported for a time by Secretary Wilson, that all chemical work in the Department of Agriculture, and likewise in any other Department, ought to be handled by his Bureau. Which was just about as reasonable as to confine all typewriting to a single bureau.

So in 1901 a dendro-chemical laboratory was established in the Bureau of Chemistry, to which the Bureau of Forestry contributed about $13,000. It continued for four years, made tests of various species of Southern Pine, and investigated the effect of moisture on the strength of wood. To that end heavy beams were sunk in the Washington Tidal Basin. These pieces had to be fished out, and there was some difficulty about procuring three pairs of official hip boots. But we got them.

The early methods of timber testing were necessarily rough. Today the methods developed by the Forest Service are models for similar investigations throughout the world.

The new laboratory carried on a study of the chemical composition, constituents, and possible uses of a series of tree secretions (gums, etc.) submitted to us by the Philippine Forestry Bureau at Manila, and our own Bureau made a number of independent field studies. In

1902 it began to study and devise improved methods of tapping Longleaf and other Southern Pines for turpentine. The old system for naval stores production was too thriftless to be continued. As far back as the middle of the last century, attempts had been made to provide a workable substitute, but without result.

The old system involved chopping a "box," a sort of bowl in the base of the tree itself, to catch the sap as it trickled down from the scarified trunk. It depreciated the product, weakened the tree, and amounted to a standing invitation to forest fires.

On his own initiative Dr. Charles H. Herty had made, during the spring of 1901, a careful study in the Pine forests of Georgia and carried on a limited experiment in the application of a better method. Dr. Herty had realized that turpentine gathering as then conducted was "needlessly destructive of the forest and needlessly wasteful of the product," and he had devised the cup and gutter system of turpentine orcharding.

The next year the Bureau of Forestry commissioned Dr. Herty to conduct more extensive investigations. As a result of his studies the Bureau published a bulletin in 1903, in which the Herty cup and gutter system was described. Under it two metal gutters guide the sap into a cup fastened to the trunk of the tree. Turpentine operators generally have adopted it as the most economical and practical method, with highly satisfactory results.

In September of 1902 a Division of Forest Products was organized, with Fritz Olmsted, one of our most capable, experienced, and mature men, in charge. Olmsted had graduated as an engineer from Yale, where he had been coxswain of the Yale crew, and had joined the Division on July 1, 1900. Rapidly he developed all-round capacity for leadership. With his background Olmsted was the logical choice for the timber-testing work.

The Division of Forest Products of the Service grew from its small beginning in 1901, until in 1909 the laboratory investigations which formed the most important part of its duties were centered at Madison, Wisconsin. The idea of a central laboratory was largely McGarvey Cline's. Cline and H. S. Betts saw that it was better to bring the wood to the testing machine rather than to take the testing machine to the wood. And it was so ordered.

The University of Wisconsin undertook to provide a laboratory which would "rank among the best wood-testing laboratories of the world." When it was ready for work, the other laboratories of the Service would be closed.

In 1910 the Madison Laboratory moved into the building constructed by the University under plans furnished by the Forest Service. Since 1932 the Laboratory has been housed in a most modern Federal building—next to the State Capitol the largest building in Madison. It has been operated continuously, first under the direction of Cline, followed by Howard Weiss, Carlile P. Winslow, and George M. Hunt, its present Director.

The contributions to the cause of Forestry in America made by the Division of Forest Products and its forebears are highly important. One of the most significant was in opening new sources of raw material and new technical processes to the pulp and paper industry. For instance, prior to 1910 the kraft or sulphate process had been applied only to Spruce. Today, as a result of improved methods developed by the Laboratory, the Southern Pines and Jack Pine also are being used in the manufacture of more than 800,000 tons a year of bond, writing, wrapping, printing, and specialty papers.

The Laboratory also has led the way in the use of wood preservatives. In 1909, 79,000,000 cubic feet of wood was treated. Today the total has grown to nearly 360,000,000.

Again, beginning in the early twenties, the Laboratory pioneered in designing and developing lumber dry kilns. Now more than five thousand commercial kilns in the United States employ the internal fan system invented by the Laboratory. And again, the Laboratory developed the process of glued plywood for wall and floor panels now used in nearly all the prefabricated houses built today.

Another achievement is a fire-retarding chemical formula now used in the commercial treatment of millions of board feet every year. Still another even more spectacular accomplishment is the development of many forms of modified wood—modified through the incorporation of chemicals and the application of heat.

These are but a few of the things done by the Laboratory during its comparatively short existence. Space forbids me to outline more of them. But I should like to repeat that the Madison Laboratory is today, when wood has become the most essential of all raw materials, the greatest and most useful wood research institution in the world.

57. *Life in Washington*

In the early 1900's life in Washington was full of protocol, and calling on your friends was an obligation which had to be met. Thus John R. Procter, chairman of the Civil Service Commission, and I, carefully arrayed in black cutaway coat, striped trousers, and the rest of the regular calling uniform, used to spend nearly every Sunday afternoon together, paying calls on people we liked or who had invited us to dinner or whatever. It was rare that I accepted an invitation, but that made no difference. There was much duty and little pleasure in most of these calls.

In those days many women in Washington official life regularly spent their afternoons calling, which usually consisted in stopping the carriage before a house and sending the coachman or footman to ring the bell and leave cards.

Washington in summer is hot and no mistake. It was my custom to close the windows while the morning coolness—such as it was—still lingered in the air, and keep them closed till evening gave the sweating city some relief. Back from the office, where hard work made a man forget the heat, a shower would change the aspect of my world, and a suit of pajamas made supper welcome and the evening bearable.

It was during one of my Sunday visits to the White House that I first learned how much more Mrs. T.R. had to do with Government business than was commonly supposed. I happened to be present when T.R. was consulting her about a certain appointment, and I heard her suggest Jim Garfield for the place. That was how Jim came into T.R.'s Administration. And his case by no means stood alone.

Life under T.R. was by no means all work. When a new man came to Washington as a member of the Administration inner circle, it was the President's custom, as a part of the testing-out process, to take him on one of his regular walks. More than one soft-muscled, chairwarming Army or Navy officer failed to meet that test.

On these trial walks it was T.R.'s habit to take the new man, as he took me, along what he called The Crack, a sloping fissure in the vertical rock wall of a quarry, on the west bank of Rock Creek, just below the Zoo. If you fell off, you would not be hurt. It was only a few feet above the ground. If you made it, you belonged.

There were other similar places that required a little knowledge of rock scrambling, which was one of T.R.'s favorite amusements. One afternoon, driving in an open wagon, we were on our way to do some scrambling in another quarry along the Potomac. T.R. and (I believe) Leonard Wood were in the back seat, I with the driver in front. Suddenly, as we came opposite the quarry, two sharp explosions sounding like rifle shots rang out. T.R., entirely unheeding, talked on serenely, without the smallest break, and I realized that what we had heard were little blasts in the quarry across the river.

Then we crossed over the Chain Bridge, just below which Ambassador Jusserand's famous remark was made when he and T.R. were about to swim the Potomac in the altogether. Suddenly T.R. observed that Jusserand was wearing gloves.

"Why do you wear gloves?" inquired the President.

"Ah," replied the Ambassador, "we might meet ladies."

It was one of T.R.'s favorite stories.

On his walks and rides T.R. was supposed to be followed by two Secret Service men. It was his delight to get away from them, leaving his safety from a possible assassin in the hands of himself and his companions. He said that the risk he ran was a trade risk, that if you didn't want the risk you shouldn't take the job, and that he would rather trust to Jim and me (for example) than to the Secret Service men, because we walked alongside of him while they followed behind.

At least on some of his rides and tramps, T.R. carried a gun. After my responsibility came home to me, I did so as a regular thing, and I was right. Thank Heaven, I never had to use it.

My days were full days. Jim Garfield usually stopped for me after breakfast, on the way to his office and to mine. That gave us a chance, as we walked, to talk over whatever happened to be on the fire. Then came a crowded morning in the big office room in the Atlantic Building, with Overton Price at one end, Miss Frost in the middle, and G.P. at the other.

Mail, members of the Service, Senators, Congressmen, lumbermen, cattlemen, sheepmen, miners, men and women on the business of some of the T.R. commissions, people who wanted me to intercede for them with the President, all sorts of people who were after what they ought or ought not to get—they all flocked in there until I was driven to keep the room, in the busy winter season, far too cold for comfort. That helped to check the yearning that afflicted most of them to tell me the story of their lives.

Lunch I ate at my desk, or better (when I could) at the geographically named Great Basin Lunch Mess, far down an alley behind the Geological Survey, in the long and narrow office of S. J. Kuebel, who presided over the Mess and lithographed the Survey's maps. There, crowded about the red cotton tablecloth, sat Newell, Gannett, McGee, Gilbert, Hill, Colonel Rizer, and six or eight other distinguished members of the Survey. It was a genial and a jovial crowd, as full of jokes as a squirt is of trouble.

One day Colonel Rizer had invited me to lunch at the Mess. I came, I liked it, and I kept on coming. By the time I discovered, years afterward, that the invitation had been intended for just one meal, I was a fixture—the only outsider, and very proud to belong.

From the Lunch Mess, as likely as not, I went over to the White House to see T.R., as I had occasion to do most days, and sometimes several times a day. The two best chances to get at him were before the rush began in the morning and between one and half past, after the casual visitors had filed through and shaken his hand, and while Delany, the White House barber, was giving him his daily shave. I marveled then and I marvel yet that his face escaped mutilation, for T.R. never ceased talking while the shaving went on.

When I could, I loved to come before the morning rush was quite over and sit in the Cabinet room watching T.R. deal with problems and people. In the early days, before they got to know him, a Senator or Congressman would take him into the embrasure of a window and whisper in his ear. T.R. would listen a moment and then his voice would ring out: "Why, Senator, you know I can't appoint So-and-So to such-and-such a place. You know just as well as I do that he isn't fit for the job." Then you could see the job hunter shrivel up. For the politicians to learn that lesson did not take long.

At other times I watched T.R. throw up his hand in greeting to some ranchman across the room: "Hello, Bill. I haven't seen or heard of you for twenty years." But with that marvelous memory of his, T.R. knew him and all about him the instant he came in sight.

When my business with T.R. was done, then back to the office, with mail to be signed, perhaps a "Service Meeting" and the daily grist of Service questions to be decided. After that, exercise. Perhaps a ride on my old horse Jim, alone or with Overton Price, perhaps jujitsu with T.R. at the White House, from which I often came back too tired to eat.

But not T.R. I have seen many men who could keep pace with him physically, and a few who could endure as much high pressure mental strain. But I have never seen another man who could combine as much mental and physical exertion day after day as he could.

Or else my day's exercise might be tetherball on the roof of our house with Coville, or passing football or medicine ball with George Woodruff in the cellar, where an iron plate fastened on the wall made it possible also to practice with a revolver. Or it might be a cross-country walk, or tennis on the White House court with T.R., Jim Garfield, Jusserand, Herbert Knox Smith, or Lawrence Murray, followed by tea in T.R.'s office, which Mrs. T.R. sometimes came to pour. Meantime T.R. would sign mail or put his signature, often abbreviated to T. Roosevelt, on Army or Navy commissions, which he never blotted but scattered to dry over the desk and the floor.

One walk with T.R. I shall never forget. At the time set, I turned up at the White House in old clothes, for I knew what might be ahead. There I found Robert Bacon, recently appointed Assistant Secretary of State, whose walks with T.R. had obviously been fewer than mine, for he wore a cutaway coat, striped trousers, patent leather shoes, an expensive silk necktie, and carried in his hand a beautifully rolled silk umbrella.

On this particular occasion we headed into the swamp which has since been reclaimed and is now a part of the park on the bank of the Potomac. After sloshing through mud and water for the better part of an hour, we reached the bank of an inlet which has since disappeared, perhaps a couple of hundred feet wide. There T.R. had expected to find a boat. But the boat was on the other shore.

For a moment we stood in silence on the bank. Then T.R. took off his hat, reached into his pockets, put his watch and their other contents into his hat, and set it back carefully on his head. Bacon and I, watching him, did the same. After which, without a word, T.R. started down into the water. Bacon and I were not far behind.

The time was late in November. The sun had set. It was freezing. Halfway across Bacon raised his umbrella, shook it, and sang out, "A lot of good this is doing me now."

Our dripping tracks could have been followed easily to the White

House, where we left T.R., and then to Bacon's home and mine. As I ran up the stairs to my room, my old Irish nurse, Mary McCadden, who had been with me since I was eleven weeks old, was standing with her hand on the newel post. I rubbed my wet sleeve across it. She turned like a flash, pointed her finger at me in reproof, and exclaimed, "You've been out with that President." She knew her Roosevelt.

Exercise over, at home again, I always stopped, of course, to see the Mouse (my Mother) in her room, and then to mine, where I read (often for a complete change of scene, and because I loved it, Dr. Holder's *Big Game at Sea,* or *Huckleberry Finn,* or the *Oxford Book of English Verse,* or whatever) till dinner.

After dinner came sometimes the rare treat of a quiet evening. But most often work or meetings, as of the Society of American Foresters, which met in our house every Thursday, or one of the Roosevelt Commissions, or a reception to some public or scientific body such as the National Academy of Sciences or the Conference of Governors. Indeed our library was so often occupied in some such way that my Father was driven to build an addition to the house where he could withdraw from its continual pursuit of knowledge.

PART X

A WORLD MOVEMENT IS BORN

58. *The Birth of Conservation*

At the beginning of 1905, when the Forest Service was created, the twenty-odd Government organizations in Washington which had to do with natural resources, as I have said before, were all in separate and distinct watertight compartments.

In the Department of Agriculture the Weather Bureau dealt with the rain that makes erosion, with the measurement of stream flow, and with floods. The War Department, through the Corps of Engineers, had to do with the control of floods, the effects of erosion on the navigability of rivers, the measurement of stream flow, and inland navigation.

Another bureau in Agriculture made soil surveys and dealt with soil management, partly from the point of view of erosion, and partly from that of agricultural crops. This was the feeble forerunner of the present Soil Conservation Service.

In the Interior Department the Geological Survey also was concerned with soils, and the erosion of soils, as geological phenomena. Likewise it measured the streams in flood and drought, and made forest descriptions and recommended and corrected the boundaries of new and old National Forests. The Survey also mapped the surface of the earth; studied its geological structure; explored and recorded the development of coal, oil, iron, gold, and other mineral resources; and did all this and much more under the able and forceful leadership of Charles D. Walcott.

Under Agriculture again the Bureau of Plant Industry dealt with Western dry-land farming, which later turned out to be one of the daddies of dust storms. In the Interior Department the Reclamation Service also dealt with the arid lands of the West. Under Newell's wise and effective leadership, it measured the Western streams, studied their possibilities in relation to the deserts, and, with the invaluable support of George H. Maxwell and the National Irrigation Congress, was admirably advancing the irrigation of arid lands in the West. It had created and brought to its assistance a body of public sentiment hardly second to that which stood behind the Forest Service.

The General Land Office, also a bureau of Interior, from which, with T.R.'s help, we had succeeded in taking the National Forests and which deeply resented the efforts of the Chief Forester to change its dearly treasured traditions of inefficiency and political favoritism, was as hostile as it dared be.

Much against its will, the Land Office had been driven, by the Public Lands Commission and T.R.'s insistence, to abandon some of the worst of its shortsighted wrongheadedness in dealing with the immense resources of the public lands, and to go at least through the motions of setting the public interest, instead of private interests, in the first place. But its heart still clung to the ancient ways.

The Interior Department handled the National Parks, and by turning them over to profiteering concessionaires, in general did it very badly. One of its bureaus, the Indian Office, even more corrupt and inefficient than the Land Office, had control of farms, forests, and all other natural resources on Indian reservations.

The Bureau of Animal Industry (in Agriculture) resented the control over grazing in the National Forests exercised by the Forest Service (also in Agriculture), while the Service regarded with no pleasure at all the mostly ineffective efforts of the Land Office to prevent removal of any more public lands from its jurisdiction by the creation of National Forests.

Finally (to make the picture fairly complete), the Department of Agriculture kept watch over game and the Department of Commerce over fish.

To put it in a sentence, there were three separate Government organizations which dealt with mineral resources, four or five concerned with streams, half a dozen with authority over forests, and a dozen or so with supervision over wild life, soils, soil erosion, and other questions of the land.

It was a mess, a mess which could be cured only by realizing that these unrelated and overlapping bureaus were all tied up together, like the people in a town. The one and only way to bring order out of this chaos was to supply a common ground on which each could take its proper place, and do its proper work, in co-operation with all the rest.

It had never occurred to us that we were all parts one of another. And the fact that the Federal Government had taken up the protection of the various natural resources individually and at intervals during more than half a century doubtless confirmed our bureaucratic nationalism.

Moreover, every separate Government agency having to do with natural resources was riding its own hobby in its own direction. Instead of being, as we should have been, like a squadron of cavalry, all acting together for a single purpose, we were like loose horses in a field, each one following his own nose.

Every bureau chief was for himself and his own work, and the devil take all the others. Everyone operated inside his own fence, and few were big enough to see over it. They were all fighting each other for place and credit and funds and jurisdiction. What little co-operation there was between them was an accidental, voluntary, and personal matter between men who happened to be friends.

While the Forest Service, as the newest of them all, and by far the most rapid in growth, had rather more than its full share of hostility from other bureaus, it did more co-operating also. I suppose the best example of mutual assistance in those days was between the Geological Survey and the Forest Service, between Henry Gannett and Gifford Pinchot, in the matter of revising the boundaries of existing National Forests and recommending new ones, of which the Geological Survey had charge.

Yet how loose it was appeared when the Geological Survey, in my absence and without my knowledge, consented to and put through the elimination from the Olympic National Forest of some of the heaviest timberland in America, on the utterly imaginary ground that it was more valuable for agriculture than for Forestry. Nearly every acre of it passed promptly and fraudulently into the hands of lumbermen.

In another case the Forest Service asked the Reclamation Service not to practice destructive lumbering in cutting the timber it needed from the public lands. That would seem like a reasonable request, but the latter refused on what seemed to it the sufficient ground that to devastate the forest would cost it less than to practice the simple measures of Forestry we asked for.

It was my great good luck that I had more to do with the work of more bureaus than any other man in Washington. This was partly because the Forest Service was dealing not only with trees but with public lands, mining, agriculture, irrigation, stream flow, soil erosion, fish, game, animal industry, and a host of other matters with which other bureaus also were concerned. The main reason, however, was that much of T.R.'s business with the natural resources bureaus was conducted through me.

It was therefore the most natural thing in the world that the relations of forests, waters, lands, and minerals, each to each, should be brought strongly to my mind. But for a long time my mind stopped there. Then at last I woke up. And this is how it happened:

In the gathering gloom of an expiring day, in the moody month of February, some forty years ago, a solitary horseman might have been observed pursuing his silent way above a precipitous gorge in the vicinity of the capital city of America. Or so an early Victorian three-volume novelist might have expressed it.

In plain words, a man by the name of Pinchot was riding a horse by the name of Jim on the Ridge Road in Rock Creek Park near Washington. And while he rode, he thought. He was a forester, and he was taking his problems with him, on that winter's day of 1907, when he meant to leave them behind.

The forest and its relation to streams and inland navigation, to water power and flood control; to the soil and its erosion; to coal and oil and other minerals; to fish and game; and many another possible use or waste of natural resources—these questions would not let him be. What had all these to do with Forestry? And what had Forestry to do with them?

Here were not isolated and separate problems. My work had brought me into touch with all of them. But what was the basic link between them?

Suddenly the idea flashed through my head that there was a unity in this complication—that the relation of one resource to another was not the end of the story. Here were no longer a lot of different, independent, and often antagonistic questions, each on its own separate little island, as we had been in the habit of thinking. In place of them, here was one single question with many parts. Seen in this new light, all these separate questions fitted into and made up the one great central problem of the use of the earth for the good of man.

To me it was a good deal like coming out of a dark tunnel. I had been seeing one spot of light ahead. Here, all of a sudden, was a whole landscape. Or it was like lifting the curtain on a great new stage.

There was too much of it for me to take it all in at once. As always, my mind worked slowly. From the first I thought I had stumbled on something really worth while, but that day in Rock Creek Park I was far from grasping the full reach and swing of the new idea.

It took time for me to appreciate that here were the makings of a new policy, not merely nationwide but world-wide in its scope—fundamentally important because it involved not only the welfare but the very existence of men on the earth. I did see, however, that something ought to be done about it.

But, you may say, hadn't plenty of people before that day seen the value of Forestry, of irrigation, of developing our streams, and much besides? Hadn't plenty pointed out the threat of erosion, the shame and pity of the destruction of wild life, and the reasons against man's vandalism of many kinds? Hadn't plenty pointed out that forests, for example, affect floods, and many other cases in which one natural resource reacts upon another?

Certainly they had. But so far as I knew then or have since been able to find out, it had occurred to nobody, in this country or abroad, that here was one question instead of many, one gigantic single problem that must be solved if the generations, as they came and went, were to live civilized, happy, useful lives in the lands which the Lord their God had given them.

But, you might go on, after the new idea was born, wasn't the situation just as it had been before? Shouldn't each Government bureau go on dealing with its same old subject in its same old way?

Not by a jugful, as they say in the backwoods.

The ancient classic simile of the bundle of twigs, which the Fascists have perverted and made known throughout the world, might point the moral and adorn the tale I am trying to tell. In union there is strength. But perhaps we can find a better illustration in the birth of our own Government.

The American colonies, like the Government bureaus which have to do with the various natural resources, were founded at different times, for different reasons, and by different kinds of people. Each colony, from Georgia to New Hampshire, dealt with nature in a somewhat different form. Each had to face a problem unlike the problems of all the others, and each was itself unlike all the other colonies.

Before the Declaration of Independence they were so many weak and separate twigs. Could we have become what we are today if the thirteen colonies had remained independent, self-sufficient little nationlets, quarreling among themselves over rights, boundaries, jurisdictions, instead of merging into a single nation with a single federal purpose?

The mere fact of union produced something different and unknown before. Here were new purpose and new power, and a future infinitely greater than anything thirteen separated colonies could ever have lived to see. Union did not wipe out the thirteen separate characters of the thirteen separate states, but it did bind them together into the strength of the new nation.

E Pluribus Unum is the fundamental fact in our political affairs. *E Pluribus Unum* is and always must be the basis in dealing with the natural resources. Many problems fuse into one great policy, just as many states fuse into one great Union. When the use of all the natural resources for the general good is seen to be a common policy with a common purpose, the chance for the wise use of each of them becomes infinitely greater than it had ever been before.

The Conservation of natural resources is the key to the future. It is the key to the safety and prosperity of the American people, and all the people of the world, for all time to come. The very existence of our Nation, and of all the rest, depends on conserving the resources which are the foundations of its life. That is why Conservation is the greatest material question of all.

Moreover, Conservation is a foundation of permanent peace among the nations, and the most important foundation of all. But more of that in another place.

It is not easy for us moderns to realize our dependence on the earth. As civilization progresses, as cities grow, as the mechanical aids to human life increase, we are more and more removed from the raw materials of human existence, and we forget more easily that natural resources must be about us from our infancy or we cannot live at all.

What do you eat, morning, noon, and night? Natural resources, transformed and processed for your use. What do you wear, day in and day out—your coat, your hat, your shoes, your watch, the penny in your pocket, the filling in your tooth? Natural resources changed and adapted to your necessity.

What do you work with, no matter what your work may be? What are the desk you sit at, the book you read, the shovel you dig with, the machine you operate, the car you drive, and the light you see by when the sunlight fails? Natural resources in one form or another.

What do you live in and work in, but in natural resources made into dwellings and shops and offices? Wood, iron, rock, clay, sand, in a thousand different shapes, but always natural resources. What are the living you earn, the medicine you take, the movie you watch, but things derived from nature?

What are railroads and good roads, ocean liners and birch canoes, cities and summer camps, but natural resources in other shapes?

What does agriculture produce? Natural resources. What does industry manufacture? What does commerce deal in? What is science concerned with? Natural resources.

What is your own body but natural resources constantly renewed —your body, which would cease to be yours to command if the natural resources which keep it in health were cut off for so short a time as 1 or 2 per cent of a single year?

There are just two things on this material earth—people and natural resources.

From all of which I hope you have gathered, if you did not realize it before, that a constant and sufficient supply of natural resources is the basic human problem.

But to return to the newborn idea. The first man I carried it to was Overton Price. Within a few days I told him the story as we rode our horses together on the Virginia side of the Potomac, and asked what he thought of it. He saw it as I did. I was glad of that, for my reliance on his judgment was very great.

After Overton, I discussed my brain child not only with my Father and Mother, whose interest in my work never flagged, but with McGee, Newell, Gannett, Shipp, Beveridge, and others. It was McGee who grasped it best. He sensed its full implication even more quickly than I had done, and saw its future more clearly.

McGee became the scientific brains of the new movement. With his wide general knowledge and highly original mind we developed, as I never could have done alone, the breadth and depth of meaning which lay in the new idea. McGee had constructive imagination.

It was McGee, for example, who defined the new policy as the use of the natural resources for the greatest good of the greatest number for the longest time. It was McGee who made me see, at long last and after much argument, that monopoly of natural resources was only less dangerous to the public welfare than their actual destruction.

Very soon after my own mind was clear enough to state my proposition with confidence, I took it to T.R. And T.R., as I expected, understood, accepted, and adopted it without the smallest hesitation. It was directly in line with everything he had been thinking and doing. It became the heart of his Administration.

Launching the Conservation movement was the most significant achievement of the T.R. Administration, as he himself believed. It seems altogether probable that it will also be the achievement for which he will be longest and most gratefully remembered.

Having just been born, the new arrival was still without a name. There had to be a name to call it by before we could even attempt to make it known, much less give it a permanent place in the public mind. What should we call it?

Both Overton and I knew that large organized areas of Government forest lands in British India were named Conservancies, and the foresters in charge of them Conservators. After many other suggestions and long discussions, either Price or I (I'm not sure which and it doesn't matter) proposed that we apply a new meaning to a word already in the dictionary, and christen the new policy Conservation.

During one of our rides I put that name up to T.R., and he approved it instantly. So the child was named, and that bridge was behind us.

Today, when it would be hard to find an intelligent man in the United States who hasn't at least some conception of what Conservation means, it seems incredible that the very word, in the sense in which we use it now, was unknown less than forty years ago.

59. *Inland Waterways*

The United States is fortunate in many ways, but not least in this, that we have the finest natural system of inland waterways on the globe. When the Nation was still young these waterways played a great part in its progress and prosperity. Where they were improved, in those early days, it was for actual use.

But for many decades, before T.R. became President, the improvement of navigable streams under Federal appropriations had become a racket and a farce. Huge sums were spent here, there, and anywhere, without order and without plan, not to provide water-borne transportation, but to secure the re-election of office-holding politicians. As a result, a smaller and smaller percentage of the Nation's inland freight went by water, until the railroads were no longer able to meet the demand.

While this was going on, but with little attention from the public, long-distance transmission of electric power (100 to 200 miles) had begun to be commercially practicable. The electric companies, with an eye to the future, were grabbing water-power sites wherever they could find them, sometimes for present use, often to hold them for future development, and not seldom merely to keep them out of the hands of somebody else.

Gradually the Nation began to wake up. The damming of navigable rivers without a license from Congress was forbidden in 1899. Thereafter such licenses were issued by special acts which gave away enormously valuable power sites forever and for nothing—without a charge and without a time limit. The first sign of change came when T.R., on March 3, 1903, vetoed a bill to make a present of the now famous Muscle Shoals power to private interests, and thereby kept the door open for the Tennessee Valley Authority.

In 1906 the General Dams Act fixed, in part, the terms of all future licenses. Under it the War Department, acting through the Corps of Engineers, did as little regulating as it could—which was to be expected. In my time at least, the War Department has always had a soft spot for Big Business, High Society, and the Overrich. I suspect that soft spot is with it still.

Whether W J McGee or G. Pinchot originated (1906) the idea of an Inland Waterways Commission, I do not remember, and it does not matter. The chances are McGee did. In any case it was a joint undertaking in which together we worked out the plan, and later selected the members to be recommended for appointment. In the end, his contribution was far greater than mine.

After submitting the plan to T.R. and getting his prompt and vigorous approval, the next step was to create a public demand that would support the President in creating such a Commission. That was easy. Business men interested in water transportation, and in other uses of the most usable system of rivers on any continent, had already organized numerous promoting associations, of which the Lakes-to-the-Gulf Deep Waterway Association, with headquarters in St. Louis, was the most important. The appointment of a national commission would be water on their wheels, and the petitions for it which they sent to the President were vigorous and effective.

The letter by which T.R. created the Inland Waterways Commission bore far greater internal evidence of McGee's handiwork than it did of mine. It pointed out that "the time has come for merging local projects and uses of the inland waters in a comprehensive plan designed for the benefit of the entire country. Such a plan should consider and include all the uses to which streams may be put, and should bring together and co-ordinate the points of view of all users of water."

The Commission's task was not light. Said T.R. on March 14, 1907:

"The questions which will come before the Inland Waterways Commission must necessarily relate to every part of the United States and affect every interest within its borders. Its plans should be considered in the light of the widest knowledge of the country and its people, and from the most diverse points of view."

This letter gave the first official recognition to the newly formulated policy of Conservation:

"It is not possible to properly frame so large a plan as this for the control of our rivers without taking account of the orderly development of other natural resources. Therefore, I ask that the Inland Waterways Commission shall consider the relations of the streams to the use of all the great permanent natural resources and their conservation for the making and maintenance of prosperous homes."

The membership of the Commission was important. Representative Theodore E. Burton of Ohio, Chairman by the President's appointment, was also Chairman of the House Rivers and Harbors Committee.

Senator Francis G. Newlands, elected Vice-Chairman by the Commission, author of the bill which created the Reclamation Service, was Chairman of the Senate Committee on Interstate Commerce.

Senator William Warner of Missouri, once Mayor of Kansas City, was afterwards Commander-in-Chief of the Grand Army of the Republic.

Representative John Hollis Bankhead of Alabama, elected United States Senator while a member of the Commission, was the father of a son of the same name who was to be a United States Senator in his turn.

General Alexander Mackenzie, head of the Corps of Engineers of the United States Army, was a Union veteran of the Civil War.

The other members were McGee, Newell, Pinchot, and Herbert Knox Smith, head of the Federal Bureau of Corporations, whose contribution to the work of the Commission was outstanding. Under his eye were prepared most of the 664 pages of appendix to the Commission's report.

The Inland Waterways Commission, like all the rest of the Roosevelt commissions to which I belonged, did its work without Congressional appropriation or special staff, and did it in less than a year, between March 14, 1907, the date of its creation, and February 3, 1908, the date of its report. Its most important inspection trips were on the Mississippi, one from St. Louis to New Orleans and the Passes, the other from St. Paul to Memphis; and one on the Missouri from Kansas City to St. Louis.

Action is the best advertisement. The most effective way to get your cause before the public is to do something the papers will have to tell about. So when the Inland Waterways Commission wanted to impress the need for inland waterway improvement on the whole United States, the Commission asked T.R. to sail down the Mississippi River with it and the Mississippi Valley Improvement Association on river steamers provided by the latter.

The trip was a huge success. Members of the Inland Waterways Commission met the President at Keokuk, Iowa, on October 1, 1907. There the Governors of twelve states joined the party, and ten more Governors at St. Louis. On October 4 the flotilla reached Memphis, where the President spoke to a convention of the Lakes-to-the-Gulf Deep Waterway Association, and announced his intention to call a conference on Conservation. Next day he left us.

Throughout his trip down the river, T.R. was given such a reception as I doubt has ever been equaled before or since along the Mississippi. Great crowds assembled to greet him wherever his steamer stopped. Where he could not stop, at numberless places along the banks, at towns and villages where no houses were, throngs gathered from daylight to dark.

At night the people built bonfires and waited patiently through the hours, although they knew they could not see the President, just to watch his steamer go by. T.R. himself, as he told us, would gladly have stayed awake all night to greet them if the demands of the daylight hours had been less exacting.

During the river trip T.R. and I were one day photographed as we were talking on deck. This particular picture was so unusual that it was reproduced all over the United States. Here is the story that goes with it.

Once upon a time Harry Stimson and I were on a hunting trip in the Sun River country of Montana, in the main range of the Rockies. During the course of one day's hunting, we found ourselves on a high and very narrow ridge, with a great cliff on one side. We were resting and looking the country over for what we could find.

Suddenly a mother Rocky Mountain goat and her kid came round a corner and walked quietly toward us along the ridge. We kept still and let them come. They had arrived within a few tens of yards of us when all at once a great golden eagle appeared out of nowhere, flew over mother and child, wheeled, and dived straight at the kid. Evidently the eagle was trying to drive the youngster over the cliff. Once at the bottom, killed by the fall, it could and would have been eaten at leisure.

It was a good plan, not seldom practiced, I understand, by hungry eagles. But this particular mother goat had a different idea. Each time the eagle dived, she rose on her hind legs, struck upward with her horns, and drove the eagle off, while the kid cowered behind her. Again and again the great eagle swooped, and each time the mother struck back. It was one of the most touching examples of maternal devotion that ever came my way. And, thank Heaven, it won out.

Harry and I kept perfectly quiet until the eagle admitted defeat and took itself off. Then the mother and kid passed us within three or four yards, so close we could almost have touched them, and went on about their business.

That was the story I was telling T.R., and the explanation of my curious attitude. You can see that he was interested. But why on earth I was wearing a cutaway coat and striped pants I do not know, except that in those days we used to do it on the slightest provocation.

The proceedings, findings, and recommendations of the Inland Waterways Commission, written by McGee, covered hardly more than a dozen pages, which was very much as it should be. Its report was based on two fundamentally important principles, for whose formulation McGee was responsible—that every river system is a unit from its source to its mouth and should be treated as such; and that "Hereafter plans for the improvement of navigation in inland waterways, or for any use of these waterways in connection with interstate commerce, shall take account of the purification of the waters, the development of power, the control of floods, the reclamation of lands by irrigation and drainage, and all other uses of the waters or benefits to be derived from their control."

TVA is the direct descendant of these two principles.

The Inland Waterways Commission was nationally minded. Accordingly it insisted that local questions of waterway control should be treated as general questions of national concern, which was far from the prevailing policy of the time. It found that the United States had 25,000 miles of navigated rivers; at least 25,000 more miles actually or potentially navigable; and some 2,500 miles of navigable canals. It found also that every state in the Union was directly interested.

It pointed out that the annual loss of fertile soil from erosion was about one billion tons; that three times the ten million acres then irrigated were irrigable; and that swamp and overflow land enough to support ten million people could be reclaimed. Furthermore, McGee told me that in those days the Mississippi alone carried yearly to the sea a cubic mile of the richest portions of our richest farms. By now one-third of our top soil, the soil which feeds us all, has been lost for good.

As to Conservation, the Commission had this to say: "The immediate use of natural resources in the rapid development of the country is often allowed to stand in the way of more beneficent and permanent utilization. Steps should be taken without delay to outline and initiate the more pressing projects of conservation, and to apply practically the principle of conservation before it is too late."

The Commission also recommended a National Waterways Commission to go on with the work and to frame specific plans. Such a Commission was created by the Rivers and Harbors Act of March 3, 1909, with Representative Burton as its Chairman. In 1912 it submitted its final report, which contained as an appendix a paper by Raphael

Zon of the Forest Service entitled "Forests and Water in the Light of Scientific Investigation." This paper, since reprinted several times and translated into several foreign languages, remains today the most comprehensive and authoritative statement on the relation of forests to water.

The Commission repeatedly warned against monopolistic control over forests, waters, lands, and minerals. It said that an excessive share of our natural resources "has been diverted to the enrichment of the few rather than preserved for the equitable benefit of the many."

The most important of the Commission's recommendations was that any plans for the use of inland waterways "shall regard the streams of the country as an asset of the people, shall take full account of the conservation of all resources connected with running waters, and shall look to the protection of these resources from monopoly and to their administration in the interests of the people."

But the greatest service of the Commission lay in suggesting to the President a Conference of Governors on the conservation of natural resources, of which more later.

T.R. promptly transmitted the report of the Inland Waterways Commission to Congress with a message not less important than the report itself. This report, said he, "is thorough, conservative, sane, and just."

Of our river systems T.R. rightly asserted that they "are better adapted to the needs of the people than those of any other country. In extent, distribution, navigability, and ease of use, they stand first. Yet the rivers of no other civilized country are so poorly developed, so little used, or play so small a part in the industrial life of the nation as those of the United States.

"The Commission finds," T.R. went on, "that it was unregulated railroad competition which prevented or destroyed the development of commerce on our inland waterways. The Mississippi, our greatest natural highway, is a case in point. At one time the traffic upon it was without a rival in any country. The report shows that commerce was driven from the Mississippi by the railroads. Later they prevented the restoration of river traffic by keeping down their rates along the rivers, recouping themselves by higher charges elsewhere."

It was Herbert Knox Smith whose good work uncovered the facts on which this statement was based.

The message contained this very definite and striking declaration:

"While we delay our rivers remain unused, our traffic is periodically congested, and the material wealth and natural resources of the country related to waterways are being steadily absorbed by great monopolies.

"Among these monopolies, as the report of the Commission points out, there is no other which threatens, or has ever threatened, such intolerable interference with the daily life of the people as the consolidation of companies controlling water power. I call your special attention to the attempt of the power corporations, through bills introduced at the present session, to escape from the possibility of Government regulation in the interests of the people. These bills are intended to enable the corporations to take possession in perpetuity of national forest lands for the purposes of their business, where and as they please, wholly without compensation to the public."

The message continued: "No rights involving water power should be granted to any corporations in perpetuity, but only for a length of time sufficient to allow them to conduct their business profitably. A reasonable charge should of course be made for valuable rights and privileges which they obtain from the National Government."

The Report of the Inland Waterways Commission and T.R.'s message to Congress together form one of the great Conservation documents of American history. To McGee and to T.R. himself belongs most of the credit.

60. *Water Power Control Begins*

The first and simplest form of mechanical power to be harnessed by the human race was water power. Today, with electricity to give it reach and scope, it is one of the most essential sources of the good life among men, and also, unless atomic energy shall move into first place, more dangerously subject to the evils of monopoly than any other. Here, if anywhere, public control is indispensable.

When the transfer took place in 1905 it was the established custom of Congress, in exercising its constitutional control over navigable streams, to give away the extremely valuable rights to erect power dams upon them, without compensation to the public and without a time limit—in other words, forever and for nothing. This habit of

Congress to make presents of the public property was wholly unnecessary and wholly without excuse, barring the ancient bureaucratic shibboleth, We have always done it that way.

When responsibility for the Forest Reserves was transferred to the Forest Service, most of the undeveloped water power of the Nation was still in the hands of the Government. Undoubtedly more than half of the grand total was on the Forest Reserves and the Public Domain. Nowhere, however, was the Government taking effective steps to protect the public interest.

Under the Transfer Act, as mutually interpreted by the Departments of Agriculture and Interior, all grants of rights or privileges within Forest Reserves which did not affect the title to the land or cloud the fee were under the jurisdiction of Agriculture. All those which did remained under Interior. But still the men who profited by these rights and privileges were not required to pay for what they got.

Meantime, many corporations had realized how vast was the future of electric power. They spied out the best power sites on navigable streams, and on the Forest Reserves and the public lands, and they were as busy as bees in taking them over.

By hook or crook, through every workable use or misuse of the public-land laws and the laws relating to navigable rivers, they were rapidly sewing up the best sites, either to develop them at once, to hold them undeveloped for future use, or to keep them out of the hands of possible rivals.

The Government's problem, as we saw it, was to ensure the fullest possible development of water power and its sale to the consumer at the cheapest possible price. That meant the prevention of monopoly where we could, and effective regulation of it where we couldn't. It was no easy task.

In dealing with the vast possibilities in water power which had come under its control, through the transfer, the Forest Service could follow one of three paths. It could continue the indefensible policy of Congress by giving away these powers forever and for nothing; it could conform to the policy of the Interior Department, which in 1901 had been given a limited power of control in the public interest but made little or no use of it; or it could develop a water-power policy of its own.

There was no question which course to adopt. We must make our

HYDRO
ELECTRIC
POWER
TRUST
THE CONSUMER
PACIFIC
SLOPE
WATER-POWER
SITES
BARNETT
in Los Angeles Herald
Aug 17th 1909

own policy, and above all keep the title to the power sites in the public hands.

The *Use Book* declared definitely for a reasonable charge "for any permit, right or privilege." The report of the Forester for the fiscal year 1905-06 went into detail. After noting the collection for the first time of fees for grazing on the Forest Reserves under the Moody decision already described, it set forth as an underlying principle that a reasonable charge should be made for all permits which involved the withdrawal of the particular resource or land from use by the people in general, and definitely determined the basis upon which charges connected with the use of water should be calculated, as follows:

"(1) A charge per mile for the length of the ditches, conduits, pipe lines, transmission lines, etc. This applies when no greater width is allowed than that actually necessary at any one point for the enjoyment of the privilege.

"(2) A charge per acre for land actually granted for occupancy, as areas flooded by reservoirs, land for power houses, residences, hotels, fenced pastures, etc.

"(3) A charge for the conservation of water supply and the use of advantageous locations and other privileges. The water supply itself is granted by the State, not by the United States.

"Thus, in a permit for a project to develop electricity the charge would be based upon: First, the length of the conduits, transmission lines, etc.; second, the area occupied by the power houses, reservoirs, etc.; third, the conservation of the water supply and the advantageous location which makes it possible to obtain a fall to turn the water-wheel."

Here was the beginning of the present Federal water-power policy. It was deeply resented and bitterly fought, of course, by the power interests and their followers in Congress. Nevertheless and notwithstanding, in all essentials it is in force today, both on lands owned by the Government and on navigable streams.

The Forest Service held that the amount of water used was a proper measure of its Conservation by the Forest Reserves, and that the horse-power developed at the wheel, since it resulted from the water conserved and from the fall furnished, was a proper measure of the entire Conservation supplied by the Service to the permittee.

The Service was wise, I think, in not attempting to enforce the new charge at once. In the spring and summer of 1905, a few permits were issued for electric development without compensation, but terminable at the discretion of the Forester. We wanted not only a fair return in due time but also good will and co-operation.

Later in the same year the charge began. John S. Eastwood, for example, in August renewed his power permit on the Sierra Reserve in California (now the Sequoia) with a new annual charge of $100. The Shasta Power Company, on the Lassen Forest, California, and the Nevada Power Mining and Milling Company agreed to pay smaller sums. Thus for the first time the principle was established in actual operation.

But what was far less simple than the charge was the duration of the permit. The Edison Electric Company of Southern California had secured, with the consent and approval of the Service, a bill granting it a permit in the San Bernardino, San Gabriel, and Sierra Forest Reserves, for a period of 99 years. I had personally approved the 99 years, and I recommended to Secretary Wilson that permits issued by the Forest Service should run for an even century. In that I was thoroughly and completely wrong.

The Secretary's judgment was better than mine. He cut my suggestion in two, and he was right. I had been too easily convinced by the power people that they needed so much time to recover their investments. Fifty years was long enough, as experience has since fully proved. Fifty years is the limit today.

But the permits were still revocable at the will of the Secretary. That was obviously unfair to the permit holder and of no advantage to the public. In the end, working with the power men, we persuaded Congress to set that right.

From the beginning the power companies had protested violently against paying any charge. Early in 1907, in order to avoid lawsuits and soothe the feelings of the companies, I agreed to refer the question of the charge once more to Attorney General Bonaparte, meantime, with T.R.'s entire approval, requiring payment as before. In October of that year Bonaparte sustained our position. Only a single lawsuit followed, and that was decided in our favor in 1908. The next year the War Department was authorized to make a charge for power on navigable streams.

The Forest Service plan for handling water-power development on the National Forests not only was the beginning of effective water-power regulation by the Government, but also beyond question it was fair and reasonable. As such it should have been accepted by the water-power interests. But a fair and reasonable plan was not what they were after. Their purpose was to get all they could from the public, and give as little as they could to the public in return. And that purpose remains unchanged until this day.

Men in such a frame of mind were naturally unwilling to accept the fair terms the Forest Service offered, and (naturally also) they left nothing undone to force the Service back to "the good old days." When personal appeals failed, and false arguments to show that the companies could not stay in business under the new plan, they turned to their friends in Congress.

The main object of their attack was the Conservation charge. All the resources of the subsidized press and of a highly effective lobby were turned loose upon us. Although the Service won, and won, and won again from 1906 on, the fight of the water-power interests against reasonable Government control continued without a break.

Numerous bills, too, were introduced in Congress. For one example, Senator Teller's bill of April 14, 1908, would have opened the National Forests to condemnation by state courts. Even worse was the Mondell-Crane Bill which would have granted perpetual rights for hydro-electric purposes to any and all applicants.

Without T.R.'s support all reasonable regulation of the development of water power on the National Forests would have been broken down. But with his backing and especially by reason of his vetoes of the Rainy River and James River bills in 1908 and 1909, the new plan won out.

In the James River veto T.R. announced that he would approve no power bill which did not contain provision for a charge and a time limit. Said he: "The great corporations are acting with foresight, singleness of purpose and vigor to control the water powers of the country." And he concluded: "I esteem it my duty to use every endeavor to prevent the growing [power] monopoly, the most threatening which has ever appeared, from being fastened upon the people of the Nation." And so the basis for a reasonable regulation of the development of water power on navigable streams and on the Government's lands was firmly laid.

The general attitude of the water-power interests described above was not without exception. Here and there a fair-minded citizen realized the justness of the new plan, accepted it, and operated under it in a decent co-operative spirit. But these as a rule were the little men and the exceptions.

The most specious and least-expected argument of the power people was the old states' rights argument, dead as Hector since the Civil War. They hung it on the fact that water rights belonged to the states, which was true enough, and they have clung to it ever since. The special interests find it far easier to control a State Legislature than the Congress of the United States. Federal regulation of power on public lands, be it noted, is not now and never was based on ownership of the water, but on ownership of the land.

In those critical days we took every possible chance to get favorable publicity for the Forest Service plan. The *Outlook* was for us. So was *Collier's Weekly*. The report of the National Conservation Commission was of real help, and so was Garfield's annual report as Secretary of the Interior, in which he advocated the temporary withdrawal of power sites as a means of saving them for the people.

The end of T.R.'s presidency was close at hand, but the end of the water-power fight was by no means in sight. It continued not only during the rest of my time in the Service, but throughout the long and bitter battle between the power interests and the National Conservation Association (of which I happened to be President).

Overton Price, George Woodruff, Phil Wells, Harry Slattery, afterwards Under Secretary of the Interior and head of the Rural Electrification Administration, and Tom Shipp, Secretary of the Conservation Association, pulled the laboring oars in that long contest. The water-power fight resulted in 1920 in the passage of the Act which created the Federal Power Commission. The story of that struggle and victory is a long one, and there is no space for it here. The essential fact is that the people won.

T.R. told the truth when he said that there was no other monopoly which threatened or had ever threatened such intolerable interference with the daily life of the people as the consolidation of companies controlling water power. Yet the power monopolies, while far less dangerous now than they once were, nevertheless are with us still.

61. *Calling All Farmers*

When this century began, the Department of Agriculture was deeply concerned with better crops on American farms, but little interested in better living among American farmers. That T.R. was awake to this unfortunate limitation was made clear in his Annual Message to Congress in 1904, in which he said: "Nearly half of the people in this country devote their energies to growing things from the soil. Until a recent date little has been done to prepare these millions for their life work."

As his *Autobiography* sets forth, T.R. discussed the improvement of country life on the land with many agricultural authorities. One man from whose advice he profited especially was not an American, but an Irishman, Sir Horace Plunkett. It was Horace Plunkett who gave to the Irish co-operatives their great objective—better farming, better business, and better living on the farm. And what he aimed for he achieved.

Plunkett had gone into the cattle-raising business in Montana at the time when T.R. was ranching on the Little Missouri, and thereafter often came back to the United States. He was slight in figure and soft spoken, but of an iron determination. It was only after addressing some fifty public meetings that Plunkett succeeded in putting over his admirable plan for co-operation among the Irish farmers. I recall also that he took up aviation after his seventieth year, and was in the habit of flying solo at the age of seventy-four.

T.R.'s *Autobiography* relates: "In the spring of 1908, at my request, Plunkett conferred on the subject with Garfield and Pinchot, and the latter suggested to him the appointment of a Commission on Country Life as a means for directing the attention of the Nation to the problems of the farmer, and for securing the necessary knowledge of the actual conditions of life in the open country."

My work in Forestry had brought me into contact with life on the farm in many parts of the United States. I had seen no little of its hardships, and especially of the hardships of farm women, and I was more than glad to be of help.

After much planning the Country Life Commission was created in August of 1908. Said T.R. in his letter of appointment:

"It is at least as important that the farmer should get the largest possible return in money, comfort, and social advantages from the crops he grows, as that he should get the largest possible return in crops from the land he farms. Agriculture is not the whole of country life. The great rural interests are human interests, and good crops are of little value to the farmer unless they open the door to a good kind of life on the farm."

The Country Life Commission, like the other five Roosevelt Commissions herein described, cost the Government not a dollar. Like them, it was composed of men of consequence, but not exclusively of farmers. Liberty Hyde Bailey of Cornell, one of the great agricultural authorities of the United States, was its Chairman, and its members were:

Henry Wallace, founder and editor of *Wallace's Farmer,* father of a Secretary of Agriculture, and grandfather of a Vice-President of the United States;

Kenyon L. Butterfield, President of the Massachusetts Agricultural College, who shed much honor on that office;

Walter Hines Page, editor of the *World's Work,* and afterwards Ambassador to Great Britain;

And three more—Charles S. Barrett, President of the Farmers' Cooperative and Educational Union of America, a man of real influence among farmers; W. A. Beard of the *Great Western Magazine,* Sacramento, California; and Gifford Pinchot, whom you know about already.

No member was paid for his work on the Commission. Its very moderate expenses were met not by the Government, but by the Trustees of the Russell Sage Foundation. The Commission made a trip through the East, South, and West, which other work forbade me to share; it held thirty public hearings to which came farmers and farmers' wives from forty states and territories; and it sent out, in cooperation with the Department of Agriculture, printed questions to which it received 120,000 answers. It secured, as T.R. said, a most valuable body of first-hand information, and laid the foundation for the remarkable awakening of interest in country life which has since taken place.

The Commission found that the general level of American country life was high compared with any preceding time or with any other land, but that nevertheless farming did not yield either the profit or the satisfaction that it ought to yield. We must measure our agricultural efficiency rather by what it could be than by comparison with what it actually was. The absence of a highly organized rural society was due mainly to a lack of good training for country life in the schools, the disadvantage of the farmer as against established business, lack of good roads, widespread soil erosion, and the absence of new and active leadership.

The remedies suggested by the Commission included better organization among farmers, greater influence by farmers on legislation, and above all a more creative social life. It declared that, while the question of better life in the country intimately concerns both the state and national Governments, the farmers themselves must decide whether or not country life is to become more dignified, better thought of, with larger rewards in comfort, income, and social advantages.

Most important of all, for it includes all the others, if the farmer decides that he will himself put an end to his own isolation and work in co-operation with his fellows for all the great objects common to the farmers of each farm neighborhood, then the beginning of great things will have arrived. The co-operative spirit was the most important spirit of the age, and the farmer had been the last to follow its influence and respond. Our farmers as a whole were largely unorganized for their own benefit.

Organization among farmers, the Commission asserted, means better farming, for many heads are better than one. It means better business, for if anything is clear in modern business life, it is that the man who stands alone is at a disadvantage. And most of all, it means better living on the farm, better social and educational advantages for the farmer, his wife, and their children—more comfort, greater satisfaction, and less desire to leave the farm.

When more of the things that make life worth living are found in the country than in the towns, then country life will take its rightful place. The way to reach that place is along the road of co-operation.

The United States Department of Agriculture and the state agricultural colleges and experiment stations had established a broad foundation of available knowledge. Now, said the Commission, was the time to apply this knowledge to the fundamental farm problem, which was this: How can the farmer and his family realize the best home life, the best business life, and the best social life on the farm? The great problem of the country was not a problem of crops, but of human lives.

In his message of February 8, 1909, transmitting the report of the Commission to Congress, the President said:

"The object of the Commission on Country Life is not to help the farmer raise better crops, but to call his attention to the opportunities for better business and better living on the farm." And he added that the farmers of every progressive European country have found in the co-operative system exactly the form of business combination they need.

The report of the Commission met venomous hostility from the reactionaries, as was to be expected. In his message the President asked for $25,000 to print and distribute it. Congress refused even to print the report, which would have remained unpublished except for the public-spirited, farsighted action of the Spokane Chamber of Commerce. In addition, Congress passed the Tawney Amendment to the Sundry Civil Appropriation Bill, which forbade the President to appoint any commission of inquiry unless Congress gave him specific authority.

The Tawney Amendment was pure spite, and pure foolishness besides. If it had been passed earlier and obeyed by the President, it would have prevented the appointment of all the six Roosevelt commissions I have described. But T.R. would not have obeyed it. As his *Autobiography* puts it, "As almost my last official act, I replied to Congress that if I did not believe the Tawney Amendment to be unconstitutional, I would veto the Sundry Civil Bill which contained it, and that if I remained in office I would refuse to obey it."

Most certainly he would have done just that, for it is obvious that any President can rightly ask anybody to advise him on any subject on which he wants information, no matter what Congress may say about it.

The Report of the Country Life Commission was the first effective step ever taken in America toward the solution of the rural-life problem. Although President Taft did not press the matter, many recommendations of the Commission have now come to pass. Advances have been made in farm organization and co-operation, in better roads, better rural schools and sanitation. In particular, rural electrification has made rapid progress. The farmer heard the Commission's call and his demands are now given a respectful hearing on Capitol Hill and in State Legislatures.

62. The Conference of Governors

Minerva, you will recall, was born full-armed from the head of Jove. Unlike the Goddess of Wisdom, the Conference of Governors, unquestionably Wisdom's child, was a gradual growth. It began in a suggestion made to other members of the Inland Waterways Commission by F. H. Newell on board the river steamer *Mississippi*, during the Commission's high-water trip down the Father of Waters in May of 1907. Newell proposed that the Commission should hold a conference on natural resources during the coming winter in Washington. His idea was approved by the Commission, was made public by Chairman Burton, and Burton and Pinchot were appointed a committee to bring the matter to the President's attention "as an expression of the view of the Commission, leaving him to decide how the call shall issue."

During the following summer Newlands, McGee, Newell, and I prepared the draft of a program for the proposed conference. They, but not I, also attended a meeting of the National Irrigation Congress, at Sacramento, where they learned that the Lakes-to-the-Gulf Deep Waterway Association expected to bring together at its coming Memphis convention a score or more of Governors.

Accordingly it was decided that the Conference ought to be primarily a conference of Governors, with such experts and others as might be desirable.

To that T.R. agreed. And the draft of his coming Memphis address announced that the Inland Waterways Commission would, with his approval, call a Conference of Governors and experts on the conservation of natural resources in Washington during the coming winter. But it did not happen that way.

On the President's trip down the Mississippi in the autumn of 1907, the Commission, after consulting the twenty-odd Governors present, asked the President, in a formal letter, to call the Conference himself. The letter, which was written by McGee, gave these as among the reasons for such a Conference:

"Hitherto our National policy has been one of almost unrestricted disposal of natural resources, and this in more lavish measure than in any other nation in the world's history; and this policy of the Federal Government has been shared by the constituent States. Three consequences have ensued: First, unprecedented consumption of natural resources; second, exhaustion of these resources, to the extent that a large part of our available public lands have passed into great estates or corporate interests, our forests are so far depleted as to multiply the cost of forest products, and our supplies of coal and iron ore are so far reduced as to enhance prices; and third, unequaled opportunity for private monopoly, to the extent that both the Federal and the States sovereignties have been compelled to enact laws for the protection of the People."

Later in the same day, October 4, 1907, T.R., with his usual prompt decision, made the announcement in his Memphis address:

"As I have said elsewhere, the conservation of natural resources is the fundamental problem. Unless we solve that problem it will avail us little to solve all others. To solve it, the whole nation must undertake the task through their organizations and associations, through the men whom they have made especially responsible for the welfare of the several states, and finally through Congress and the Executive. As a preliminary step, the Inland Waterways Commission has asked me to call a conference on the conservation of natural resources, including, of course, the streams, to meet in Washington during the coming winter. I shall accordingly call such a conference. It ought to be among the most important gatherings in our history, for none have had a more vital question to consider."

The Conference was all that T.R. foresaw. Not only did it bring together, for the first time in our history, the Governors of the states and territories to consider a great common problem with each other and with the President, but it was undoubtedly the most distinguished gathering on the most important issue ever to meet in the White House, or indeed, with one or two exceptions, anywhere in the United States.

In November T.R. invited the Governors, each with three advisers, to attend the Conference. All the Governors accepted. In December the great national organizations concerned with natural resources, some three score and ten in number, were asked to be represented by their presidents, and half a hundred general guests were added. Earlier invitations had been sent to all Senators and Representatives of the Sixtieth Congress, Justices of the Supreme Court, and members of the Cabinet. The Inland Waterways Commission, of course, was included.

Five outstanding citizens were chosen to represent the people of the United States. They were William Jennings Bryan, thrice candidate for President; Andrew Carnegie, foremost steel magnate of his time; John Mitchell, foremost labor leader of his day; James J. Hill, builder of the Great Northern Railroad; and ex-President Cleveland, whom illness kept away.

Responsibility for the details of the Governors' Conference fell to a Conference Committee (appointed October 5) consisting of McGee, who pulled the laboring oar, Newell, and me, to which we added Tom Shipp, whom we had chosen to be Secretary of the Conference. Throughout the winter and into the spring, the Committee met almost daily in an upper room in the Cosmos Club.

Together we prepared the Syllabus for the Conference, under the three main heads of mineral resources, land resources, and water resources. Yet for the Syllabus, as for choosing the experts to speak and for much besides, McGee was mainly responsible.

The four special guests were anxious for help in preparing their speeches. So were other speakers. We were equally anxious that they should say what needed to be said. Accordingly McGee wrote how many speeches for how many speakers I can no longer recall. But it was an astonishing number, and every one of them clicked.

What was far more important, a draft of T.R.'s opening speech had to be made. For that again, McGee was chiefly responsible. But as so often happened, T.R. declined to be bound by what others wrote, and added no little by his own hand.

The most essential thing our steering committee had to do, however, was none of these things. Its main purpose and responsibility was to see that the Conference put Conservation before the American people as what it was, and is, and always will be, the central and most vital material problem of the human race.

One special danger faced the Conference. Speechmaking Governors are notoriously short of terminal facilities. Here would be not only Governors by the dozen, but also leaders in every walk of life, men with the habit of having their say and saying it out. Three days would be nothing like time enough for all of them to talk as much as they would want to talk. Therefore a limit had to be set and a plan devised to confine each speaker to the time allotted him.

The plan we hit upon was this. In the East Room of the White House, behind the stage from which the speakers spoke, were hidden a bell and a man to ring it. T.R. announced, after his opening statement, that twenty minutes would be the time allowed to each, and that the bell ringer would ring his bell three times when only three minutes of the allotted twenty remained, and again twice when the time was up. Throughout the Conference the only man who disregarded the ringing and talked beyond the rule was Jim Hill. He took no orders from any bell.

On the morning of May 13, 1908, the Conference opened with prayer by the Reverend Edward Everett Hale, Chaplain of the Senate. Then the President spoke. What follows is condensed:

"So vital is this question [of Conservation], that for the first time in our history the chief executive officers of the states separately, and of the states together forming the Nation, have met to consider it. It is the chief material question that confronts us, second only—and second always—to the great fundamental question of morality.

"The occasion for the meeting lies in the fact that the natural resources of our country are in danger of exhaustion if we permit the old wasteful methods of exploiting them longer to continue. In the development, the use, and therefore the exhaustion of certain of the natural resources, the progress has been more rapid in the past century and a quarter than during all preceding time of which we have record.

"Nature has supplied us, and still supplies us, more kinds of resources in a more lavish degree than has ever been the case at any other time or with any other people. Our position in the world has been attained by the extent and thoroughness of the control we have achieved over nature; but we are more, not less, dependent upon what she furnishes than at any previous time of history since the days of primitive man.

"All these various uses of our natural resources are so closely connected that they should be co-ordinated, and should be treated as part of one coherent plan and not in haphazard and piecemeal fashion.

"No wise use of a farm exhausts its fertility. So with the forests. We are over the verge of a timber famine in this country, and it is unpardonable for the Nation or the states to permit any further cutting of our timber save in accordance with a system which will provide

— WASHINGTON D.C, AND THE CHERRY TREE. —

that the next generation shall see the timber increased instead of diminished.

Then, after quoting the United States Supreme Court to show that the people have the right he claimed for them, the President concluded with this expression of the highest statesmanship:

"Finally, let us remember that the conservation of our natural resources, though the gravest problem of today, is yet but part of another and greater problem to which this Nation is not yet awake, but to which it will awake in time, and with which it must hereafter grapple if it is to live—the problem of national efficiency, the patriotic duty of insuring the safety and continuance of the Nation.

"I wish to take this opportunity to express in heartiest fashion my acknowledgment to all the members of the Commission. At great personal sacrifice of time and effort they have rendered a service to the public for which we cannot be too grateful. Especial credit is due to the initiative, the energy, the devotion to duty, and the farsightedness of Gifford Pinchot, to whom we owe so much of the progress we have already made in handling this matter of the co-ordination and conservation of natural resources. If it had not been for him this convention neither would nor could have been called." (I hope you will agree that it would have taken superhuman fortitude on my part to leave that last sentence out.)

The President went on: "We are coming to recognize as never before the right of the Nation to guard its own future in the essential matter of natural resources. In the past we have admitted the right of the individual to injure the future of the Republic for his own present profit. The time has come for a change. As a people we have the right and the duty, second to none other but the right and duty of obeying the moral law, of requiring and doing justice, to protect ourselves and our children against the wasteful development of our natural resources, whether that waste is caused by the actual destruction of such resources or by making them impossible of development hereafter."

T.R.'s epochal declaration fits like a glove the situation in which we and all other nations find ourselves today. In this atomic age it is even truer than it was when he made it, nearly forty years ago.

Having thus for the first time introduced the policy of Conservation to the Nation and the world, T.R. suggested the appointment of the five Governors whom McGee, Newell, and I had recommended for the Committee on Resolutions, with Governor Blanchard of Louisiana at their head. They were elected unanimously. And so ended the first session which had assured the success of the Conference.

The second began with a paper by Andrew Carnegie, who spoke of iron, and included discussion by John Mitchell, who spoke of coal, John Hayes Hammond, Elihu Root, then Secretary of State, and several Governors.

The third dealt with the natural wealth of the land. James J. Hill opened the discussion. R. A. Long, an outstanding lumberman, entered a plea in confession and avoidance. And the rest of the session was mainly devoted to forest conservation.

The fourth session began with an address by ex-Governor George C. Pardee of California, one of the best friends Conservation ever had. He spoke on irrigation and Forestry and was followed by H. A. Jastrow, President of the National Livestock Association, who discussed the grazing of sheep and cattle on the public lands, and described the handling of the National Forests by the Forest Service as "a splendid example of successful and practical management."

In such a meeting on such a subject as Conservation, dissent on some details was inevitable. Devotion to the doctrine of states' rights, which is still the darling of the great special interests, was voiced by Governor Brooks of Wyoming, by Governor Gooding of Idaho, who demanded the transfer of the National Forests to the states, and by Governor Norris of Montana, who protested against the charge for grazing on the National Forests and called it "the levying of tribute." Jim Garfield answered him in a firm but conciliatory statement, which completely disposed of Norris's argument, although probably not to Norris's satisfaction.

The general tone, however, was of overwhelming approval. Far more was well and wisely said than I can report here. Governor Folk of Missouri expressed the evident conviction of the Conference when he declared, "This meeting is world-wide in its influence."

Next to the President's address, which set the pace, the high point of the Conference was the Declaration of the Governors. Its wisdom in policy and clearness of statement were due mainly to Governor Blanchard and to Dr. McGee, who, as Recording Secretary of the Conference, sat with the Committee on Resolutions and was very largely responsible for its admirable report.

The Declaration said:

"We, the Governors of the States and Territories of the United States of America, in Conference assembled, do hereby declare the conviction that the great prosperity of our country rests upon the abundant resources of the land.

"We look upon these resources as a heritage to be made use of in establishing and promoting the comfort, prosperity, and happiness of the American people, but not to be wasted, deteriorated, or needlessly destroyed.

"We agree that the great natural resources supply the material basis on which our civilization must continue to depend, and on which the perpetuity of the Nation itself rests.

"We agree that this material basis is threatened with exhaustion. We recognize as a high duty the adoption of measures for the conservation of the natural wealth of the country.

"We declare our firm conviction that this conservation of our natural resources is a subject of transcendent importance, which should engage unremittingly the attention of the Nation, the States, and the People in earnest co-operation."

And the Declaration added this pregnant sentence:

"We agree that the sources of national wealth exist for the benefit of the People, and that monopoly thereof should not be tolerated."

It continued: "We declare the conviction that in the use of the natural resources our independent States are interdependent and bound together by ties of mutual benefits, responsibilities, and duties." And it advocated similar Conferences on Conservation in the future.

"We agree that further action is advisable to ascertain the present condition of our natural resources and to promote the conservation of the same; and to that end we recommend the appointment by each State of a Commission on the Conservation of Natural Resources, to co-operate with each other and with any similar commission of the Federal Government.

"We urge the continuation and extension of forest policies adopted to secure the husbanding and renewal of our diminishing timber supply, the prevention of soil erosion, the protection of headwaters, and the maintenance of the purity and navigability of our streams. We recognize that the private ownership of forest lands entails responsibilities in the interests of all the People, and we favor the enactment of laws looking to the protection and replacement of privately owned forests.

"We recognize in our waters a most valuable asset of the People of the United States. We especially urge on the Federal Congress the immediate adoption of a wise, active, and thorough waterway policy, providing for the prompt improvement of our streams and the conservation of their watersheds.

"We recommend the enactment of laws looking to the prevention of waste in the mining and extraction of coal, oil, gas, and other minerals with a view to their wise conservation for the use of the People, and to the protection of human life in the mines."

The Declaration ended with this memorable sentence: "Let us conserve the foundations of our prosperity."

There were no evening sessions. In addition to a dinner at the White House on May 12, the Governors were guests of the Washington Board of Trade at dinner on the thirteenth, at a reception to them and the Inland Waterways Commission at my home, where something like a thousand guests were received by my Mother on the fourteenth, and at a garden party given by Mrs. Roosevelt to the members of the Conference and their ladies at the White House on the afternoon of the fifteenth.

The Conference gave its members a conception of the land they lived in that was brand new to nearly all of them. The impression it made upon them was profound. The Governors especially came away with a conviction of national unity that had never dawned on most of them before. Governor Willson of Kentucky expressed the general attitude when he said: "There is not a man here, either Governor or advisor, who will not go away from here a good deal better man than he came. No, not one of them."

The Governors' Conference on Conservation was the first of its kind—the first not only in America, but in the world. It may well be regarded by future historians as a turning point in human history. Because it introduced to mankind the newly formulated policy of the Conservation of Natural Resources, it exerted and continues to exert a vital influence on the United States, on the other nations of the Americas, and on the peoples of the whole earth.

The Conference set forth in impressive fashion, and it was the first national meeting in any country to set forth, the idea that the protection, preservation, and wise use of the natural resources is not a series of separate and independent tasks, but one single problem.

It spread far and wide the new proposition that the purpose of

Conservation is the greatest good of the greatest number for the longest time.

It asserted that the conservation of natural resources is the one most fundamentally important material problem of all, and it drove home the basic truth that the planned and orderly development of the earth and all it contains is indispensable to the permanent prosperity of the human race. That great truth was never so true as now.

The Governors' Conference put Conservation in a firm place in the knowledge and thinking of the people. From that moment it became an inseparable part of the national policy of the United States.

It is worth mention that this brilliant example of national foresight occurred not in a time of scarcity, not in a depression, but in a time of general abundance and well-being.

One concrete result of the Conference was its Declaration, so simple, sound, and fine that the President himself, and not a few of the rest of us, believed it should be posted in every schoolhouse in the United States.

A second consequence was that suddenly, almost in the twinkling of an eye, as the direct result of the Conference, Conservation became the characteristic and outstanding policy of T.R.'s Administration, and has been more and more generally accepted as such ever since.

The third consequence, vastly more important, was that the policy of Conservation was so well and wisely presented that it was instantly and universally accepted and approved by the people of the United States. I doubt whether any great policy, except perhaps in time of war, has ever been so effectively set forth and so generally adopted in so short a time as the Conservation policy, when it was presented to the American people in the spring of 1908.

A fourth consequence, not yet generally realized or fully understood, but destined in time to become perhaps the most vital of all, is this: the Conservation policy, if internationally applied, provides a basic foundation for permanent world peace.

The Governors' Conference made front-page news all over the United States, as was natural, and in many other parts of the world also, while it was in session. Afterward followed a flood of friendly editorials and magazine articles, with only here and there a touch of opposition in some trade paper or from an unusually alert and acrimonious political opponent. The general tone was of unstinted praise. Conservation became the commonplace of the time.

Teddy's Newest School

Minneapolis *News*, May 13, 1908

That is, Conservation was universally accepted until it began to be applied. From the principle of Conservation there has never been, because there could not be, any serious open dissent. Even when applied in practice to the other fellow, it was unattackable. But when it began to interfere with the profits of powerful men and great special interests, the reign of peace came to a sudden end.

From that day to this, men and interests who had a money reason for doing so have fought Conservation with bitterness, and in many cases with success. That war is raging still, and it is yet very far from being won.

63. *The National Conservation Commission*

The recommendation of the Conference of Governors for the creation of state and national commissions on Conservation was carried out by some forty of the states (at that time there were only forty-six), and by T.R. for the Federal Government. Moreover, by the end of the year, no less than forty-one Conservation committees had been appointed by national organizations.

The National Conservation Commission was created by the President in a letter dated June 8, 1908. In it he said that because the action of the Governors in recommending it could not be disregarded, "I have decided to appoint a Commission to inquire into and advise me as to the condition of our natural resources, and to co-operate with other bodies created for a similar purpose by the States.

"The Commission on the Conservation of Natural Resources will be organized in four Sections to consider the four great classes of Water Resources, Forest Resources, Resources of the Land, and Mineral Resources. I am asking the members of the Inland Waterways Commission to form the Section of Waters of the National Conservation Commission."

The President then referred to the basic fact that the life of the Nation depends absolutely on the material resources which have already made the Nation great and declared: "We intend to use these resources; but to so use them as to conserve them." And he added this:

"The recent conference of the Governors was notable in many respects; in none more than in this, that the dignity, the autonomy, and yet the interdependence and mutual dependence of the several States were all emphasized and brought into clear relief, as rarely before in our history. There is no break between the interests of State and Nation; these interests are essentially one. Hearty co-operation between the State and the National agencies is essential to the permanent welfare of the people. You [members of the Commission] on behalf of the Federal Government, will do your part to bring about this co-operation."

Each section of the Commission had twelve members. It was a distinguished company, full of Senators and Representatives, the heads of Government bureaus and of professional schools, and other leaders in their lines.

The Section of Waters, with Representative Theodore E. Burton of Ohio as its Chairman, included, among its dozen, four Senators and three heads of Federal bureaus.

The Section of Forests, with Senator Reed Smoot of Utah as its head, counted three lumbermen, two economists, one Governor, and the head of the Yale Forest School.

The Section of Lands, under Senator Knute Nelson of Minnesota, had two Governors, one in being and one ex, and James J. Hill, the foremost railroad man of his time.

The Section of Minerals, whose Chairman was Representative Dalzell of Pennsylvania, head of the powerful House Committee on Ways and Means, included John Mitchell, John Hayes Hammond, and Andrew Carnegie.

The Executive Committee consisted of the Chairmen and Secretaries of the four sections, with Tom Shipp as its Secretary and myself as Chairman of the Commission. It met in Chicago within two weeks after the Commission was appointed and set December 1 as the date for the first full meeting of the Commission. Also it undertook to prepare and submit a report for discussion at that time, and authorized the Chairman to invite Governors of States and others to a Joint Conference on Conservation early in December.

The work of preparing the inventory was done or directed by the Secretaries of Sections, each of them an outstanding expert in his field —W J McGee for Waters, Overton W. Price for Forests, George W. Woodruff for Lands, and Joseph A. Holmes for Minerals. In addition, Henry Gannett, Geographer of the United States Geological Survey, was assigned by the President to supervise the compilation of material.

Under the vigilant eyes of these competent and devoted men, with what Tom Shipp, Harry Slattery, and I could do to help, the first inventory of natural resources ever made for any nation was begun and completed in less than six months.

Every assistance from all the Government was opened to the Commission by an Executive Order which directed the heads of Departments, Bureaus, and other Government establishments to "secure, compile, and furnish to the said Commission all such information and data relevant to its work as the Commision may from time to time request, and as may be respectively within the lawful powers of such Departments, Bureaus, and Government establishments to secure, compile, or furnish, and not inconsistent with express provisions of law."

The last seven words carried T.R.'s own brand.

All the Government organizations concerned co-operated superbly. The rapid appointment of friendly State Conservation Commissions was also of great assistance, and many national organizations, through their Conservation committees, gave us valuable help.

Each of the four sections had completed its task before the first general meeting of the Commission. It was held in the Library of Congress and lasted from December 1 to December 7, 1908. At that meeting the men mainly responsible for the inventory discussed their work before the full Commission, the completed inventory was submitted, considered, and approved, and the Commission's report to the President was prepared and unanimously adopted. It was a document whose influence extended not only throughout the United States, but all over the world, for it set a fashion which has since been widely copied by other nations.

Like the other T.R. Commissions, the National Conservation Commission had no appropriation. Its inventory of the natural resources of three million square miles of the richest continent on earth cost the Government not one red cent. Thanks to the highly remarkable and most willing assistance of hundreds of individuals, and especially thanks to the members of the Executive and Legislative branches of the Government, already with full-time jobs, and to the experts, the work was done. And it was well done. Except for the spirit which T.R. inspired, so outstanding an achievement would have been utterly impossible.

Under the inspiration of his example, unselfish devotion to the public interest was characteristic both of the men T.R. brought into the

Government service, and of the great body of public servants already there. Indeed, during a long experience in official life, I have always found it true that the great majority of public servants, even political job holders, were more than glad to give the best that was in them to the public service if and when they were well led.

In my experience men and women who pull the laboring oar in public work usually would rather do good work than bad work—would rather work hard than waste their time—provided only they have been shown, and have understood, that the work they are doing is worth while, and that they are themselves a part of a great public movement whose purpose is the public good.

Loafers in public office I have seen in plenty. Political appointees who drew their salaries and literally did nothing else have not been to me unknown. But the vast majority need only really good leadership to make the public service fully as efficient as private business at its best.

I hope I have made it sufficiently plain that the Conservation policy originated in the Administration of Theodore Roosevelt, that it was presented to the American people by him, and that it was accepted by the American people while he was President and largely because of him. Since that time it has become customary for each succeeding President to "discover" the Conservation policy for himself, reintroduce it to the people with some minor change of emphasis, and thereupon be acclaimed by his acclaimers as the man who has done most for Conservation since the world began.

To this proceeding I have no objection. It is a relatively innocent amusement, it seems to please each President in turn, it recognizes the standing Conservation has with the people, and it has the very real advantage of committing each President to the Conservation policy. For that reason I hope an unbroken succession of Presidential Columbuses will continue to discover the continent of Conservation, and call upon successive generations of the American people to admire their achievement. At the same time I think a summary of the facts about the original landfall and what it included should be somewhere accessible. That is what I have been trying to provide.

Here let me say a word about a man whose service to the United States through Conservation was outstanding. I refer to W J McGee, anthropologist, geologist, hydrologist—a fountain of almost universal knowledge.

So far as such a thing can ever be said of any one man in a movement so extensive, W J McGee was the scientific brains of the Conservation movement all through its early critical stages. Since from the first, the distinguishing fact about that movement was its joint consideration of all the natural resources as the working capital of humanity, McGee's wide and balanced knowledge of this continent and its resources gave him very special fitness to deal with this wide and weighty problem.

McGee, at least as much as any one man, was responsible for formulating the plan for T.R.'s Inland Waterways Commission, which for the first time considered the wise handling of all the natural resources of the continent as a single problem. Of all his services to the Conservation movement, this was the one which carried most clearly the mark of his personality and in which his contribution was most effective.

McGee was always ready to put his knowledge and his ideas at the service of his friends. Almost alone among the scientific men of Washington, he cared nothing about credit. It was enough for him to be useful.

The fertility of McGee's mind was as amazing as his generosity. He was ready to speak to any audience on almost any subject at a moment's notice, and he always spoke with effect.

I have never met a man whose imaginative suggestiveness in scientific work, and in the application of scientific results to human problems, could equal his. It was always the *application* of knowledge that appealed to him. His mind passed easily across the details of scientific problems to their bearing on matters that would count for the welfare of the people.

Out of the Conference of Governors grew, as you know, the National Conservation Commission. Officially McGee was merely Secretary of one of its four sections. Practically he was the trusted and effective adviser in every branch of the Commission's work. Without him its historic report could scarcely have been brought together.

For many years I was in effect his pupil. It was McGee who first pointed out to me that the wise Conservation and use of natural resources for the benefit of the people involved the whole question of monopoly. At first the idea seemed to me fantastic. Gradually I came to see that McGee was right, that the concentration of natural wealth in the hands of monopolists is one of the greatest of Conservation problems.

Although McGee lived much of his life among rough men in the roughest parts of this continent, I never heard him utter a word that could not have been spoken in the presence of ladies. He was one of the most kindly and genial of men, a lover of his neighbor as himself, and full of that finest courtesy which is never out of fashion.

I have never seen another man whose appearance at first sight so completely belied his real character. McGee was of a soft and cherubic countenance, and in his later years his girth matched his face. Yet I have known few men who were his equals in physical endurance, and none of more perfect courage. He began life as a blacksmith; turned, self-educated, to science; and made in the State of Iowa the most extensive geological and topographic survey ever executed in America without public aid. He made it on foot at the rate of forty miles a day, and the reason he made it on foot was because he could not find a horse that would carry him so far and keep it up.

It was McGee who headed the first exploration of Tiburón Island in the Gulf of California, whose Indian inhabitants were killers as notorious as the sharks for which their island was named. He gave me, I am proud to say, the .50-caliber Winchester rifle he carried on that dangerous mission. I have it still.

W J McGee died of cancer. The certainty that his days were numbered, that they would end in prolonged agony, unrelieved by the companionship of his wife and children, nevertheless left him cheerful, clear-eyed, wholly without self-pity, calm and sane, and as keenly and unselfishly interested in the affairs of his friends as he had been in the days of his greatest vigor. Until pain robbed him of consciousness just before death, he kept notes of the progress of the disease in the hope that they might be of use to others. He was a great gentleman and a great American.

Now back to my story. The Joint Conservation Conference, called by the National Conservation Commission, met in Washington December 8, 1908. By it the report of the National Commission was considered and unanimously approved. And altogether the Conference made Conservation history. More about it further on.

64. *North American Conservation Conference*

Following the appointment and organization of the National Conservation Commission, I suggested to T.R. (whether the original idea was mine or somebody else's I cannot now recall) that he should bring together a North American Conservation Conference. Such a conference would be of great value in itself, and moreover could be made to lead to a similar conference of all the nations of the world. T.R. approved the idea, promptly, as was his wont. At his direction, I carried his personal invitation to Lord Grey, Governor General of Canada, and to President Diaz in the City of Mexico.

In his letter of December 24, 1908, to Lord Grey (who must not be confused with Sir Edward Grey, T.R.'s warm friend and the friend of fishermen the world over), T.R. said:

"It is evident that natural resources are not limited to the boundary lines which separate nations, and that the need for conserving them upon this continent is as wide as the area upon which they exist. The purpose of the conference I have the honor to propose is to consider mutual interests involved in the conservation of natural resources, and in this great field deliberate upon the practicability of preparing a general plan adapted to promote the welfare of the Nations concerned.

"As my representative to convey to you this letter and invitation, and at your desire to consult with you concerning the proposed conference, I have selected an officer of this Government, Chief of the United States Forest Service and Chairman of the National Conservation Commission, whom I commend to your kind offices."

In one of my Canadian talks I said:

"You will perhaps remember that Mark Twain, in his book called *Pudd'nhead Wilson,* prefaced each chapter with a maxim. One of these was 'Don't put your eggs in separate baskets; put all your eggs in one basket, and then watch that basket.' That is what we are doing with Conservation; we are trying to stop putting our eggs into the forest basket, the waterways basket, the coal basket, the oil basket. We are grouping all that we want to do under the one title, and making one attempt to save what we have.

"If the nations of the North American continent can approach these questions from a common point of view, and each within its own sphere take such action as will lead to the best results for its own citizens, then unquestionably these results will lead to the best good of the whole continent."

In his reply, the Governor General conferred on me a title to which at that time I had scant claim. Said he:

"Mr. Chairman and Gentlemen: I rise to express my thanks and your thanks to Dr. Pinchot, not only for the letter which he has handed to me from the President of the United States, but for the illuminating, impressive, and warning address to which we have just listened. I do not remember that I have ever listened to any address more replete with points of the greatest personal interest to the audience to whom it was addressed. I hope, Dr. Pinchot, that your appeal to us to treat with common sense, common problems for the common good will not be forgotten in Canada. I may say to Dr. Pinchot that there is no subject in which Canada will more heartily co-operate with the United States of America. I am happy to be able to inform Dr. Pinchot that this invitation is gladly accepted by His Majesty's Canadian Government."

Sir Wilfrid Laurier, Premier of Canada, then rose "to say that his Excellency, the Governor General, has told you of the action that his advisers intend to take," and Mr. R. L. Borden, leader of the Opposition, amid laughter and applause, remarked that "the Opposition, contrary to what may be regarded as ordinary usage, will have no amendment whatever to offer."

T.R.'s letter to Diaz, in addition to covering the same ground as his letter to Grey, made the definite statement that in his opinion Diaz had done more for his people than any other living ruler had done for any nation.

The North American Conservation Conference included, as Commissioners from Canada, Sidney Fisher, Clifford Sifton, and Henri S. Beland, and, from the independent colony of Newfoundland, E. H. Outerbridge. Mexico was represented by Romulo Escobar, Miguel A. de Quévedo, and Carlos Sellerier. Gifford Pinchot, Robert Bacon, and James Rudolph Garfield were the Commissioners of the United States.

On the morning of February 18, 1909, the Conference assembled in the White House, where T.R. spoke. Its meetings were held in the Diplomatic Room of the State Department. A supper and a luncheon at the White House, a dinner by the Secretary of State, and another by the Chairman of the Conference (meaning me) were among the distractions offered to its members.

The Conference was marked throughout by a most cordial spirit of mutual respect and co-operation, and all its actions were taken without a dissenting voice. Considering the forthright character of its Declaration, that is worth keeping in mind.

At the opening of the Conference the President made this highly significant statement: "In international relations the great feature of the growth of the last century has been the gradual recognition of the fact that instead of its being normally to the interest of one nation to see another depressed, it is normally to the interest of each nation to see the others elevated." And he added: "I believe that the movement that you this day initiate is one of the utmost importance to this hemisphere and may become of the utmost importance to the world at large."

T.R. was right. Read in the light of the world-situation of 1946, the Declaration of Principles of the North American Conservation Conference points out an essential to a prosperous world and a permanent peace. For without the conservation of natural resources on a world-wide basis, we can have neither the one nor the other.

Much of that Declaration is so pat to the moment that I offer no apology for quoting it here. If its principles can be given effect, they may indeed become of the utmost importance to the world at large. (I have put in parentheses in three places words which would limit the application of these principles to North America alone.)

From the Declaration of Principles, North American Conservation Conference, February 23, 1909:

"We recognize the mutual interests of the Nations (which occupy the Continent of North America) and the dependence of the welfare of each upon its natural resources. We agree that the conservation of these resources is indispensable for the continued prosperity of each Nation.

"Natural resources are not confined by the boundary lines that separate Nations. We agree that no Nation acting alone can adequately conserve them, and we recommend the adoption of concurrent measures for conserving the material foundations of the welfare of all the Nations (concerned), and for ascertaining their location and extent.

"We recognize as natural resources all materials available for the use of man as means of life and welfare. We agree that these resources should be developed, used, and conserved for the future, in the interests of mankind, whose rights and duties to guard and control the natural sources of life and welfare are inherent, perpetual, and indefeasible. We agree that those resources which are necessaries of life should be regarded as public utilities, that their ownership entails specific duties to the public, and that as far as possible effective measures should be adopted to guard against monopoly.

"*Public Health.* Believing that the Conservation movement tends strongly to develop national efficiency in the highest possible degree (in our respective countries), we recognize that to accomplish such an object with success, the maintenance and improvement of public health is a first essential.

"*Forests.* We recognize the forests as indispensable to civilization and public welfare. We regard the wise use, effective protection, especially from fire, and prompt renewal of the forests on land best adapted to such use, as a public necessity and hence a public duty devolving upon all forest owners alike, whether public, corporate, or individual.

"Such lands should be protected with equal effectiveness, whether under public or private ownership. It is therefore of the first importance that all lumbering operations should be carried on under a system of rigid regulation.

"*Waters.* We favor the development of inland navigation under general plans adapted to secure the fullest use of the streams for all purposes. All waterways so developed should be retained under exclusive public ownership and control.

"We regard the monopoly of waters, and especially the monopoly of water power, as peculiarly threatening. No rights to the use of water powers in streams should hereafter be granted in perpetuity. Each grant should be conditioned upon prompt development, continued beneficial use, and the payment of proper compensation to the public for the rights enjoyed; and should be for a definite period only.

"*Lands.* The possession of the land by the men who live upon it not only promotes productivity, but is also the best guarantee of good citizenship. In the interest of the homemaker, we favor regulation of grazing on public land, the disposal of public lands to actual settlers in areas each sufficient to support a family, and the subdivision of excessive holdings of agricultural or grazing land, thereby preventing monopoly.

"*Minerals.* The mineral fuels play an indispensable part in our modern civilization. Such fuels should hereafter be disposed of by lease under such restrictions or regulations as will prevent waste and monopolistic or speculative holding, and supply the public at reasonable prices.

"We believe that the surface rights and underground mineral rights in lands should be separately dealt with so as to permit the surface of the land to be utilized to the fullest extent, while preserving Government control over the minerals."

Two highly important recommendations, important then and more important now, closed the Declaration:

"*Conservation Commissions.* To derive the greatest possible benefit from the work which has already been done, and to provide proper and effective machinery for future work, there should be established in each country a permanent Conservation Commission.

"When such Conservation Commissions have been established, a system of intercommunication should be inaugurated, whereby, at stated intervals, all discoveries, inventions, processes, inventories of natural resources, information of a new and specially important character, and seeds, seedlings, new or improved varieties, and other productions which are of value in conserving or improving any natural resource shall be transmitted by each Commission to all of the others, to the end that they may be adopted and utilized as widely as possible."

The Declaration of the North American Conservation Conference is as pat to the moment in 1946 as the day it was written. If its recommendations had been given effect a generation ago, no timber famine would face our country now—as it does.

Millions upon millions of acres of soil, once fertile, would not be exhausted—as they are.

Vast quantities of coal and oil and other most necessary minerals would not have been wasted—as they have been.

And monopolies in land, electricity, and other indispensable materials and services would not oppress our people—as they do today.

If the recommendations of the North American Conference had been followed, our people would today be living freer, happier, and more productive lives. Furthermore, the chance of war would have been vastly reduced. International cartels, those dangerous promoters of injustice within nations and quarrels between nations, would have been abolished. And the world would have come to understand that the Conservation of natural resources is an indispensable basis of permanent peace.

All this being true, one other recommendation of the North American Conference is so vital that it requires a separate chapter.

65. *World Conservation Conference*

The weightiest recommendation of the North American Conservation Conference was this:

"The conference of delegates, representatives of the United States, Mexico, Canada, and Newfoundland, having exchanged views and considered the information supplied from the respective countries, is convinced of the importance of the movement for the conservation of natural resources on the continent of North America, and believes that it is of such a nature and of such general importance that it should become world-wide in its scope, and therefore suggests to the President of the United States of America that all Nations should be invited to join together in conference on the subject of world resources and their inventory, conservation, and wise utilization."

In his message to Congress transmitting the Declaration of the Conference the President warmly approved the proposal for an international conference. "I have deemed it my duty," said he, "to welcome and act upon the far-seeing suggestion of the conference, and have accordingly addressed such an invitation to the nations of the world, in the confident belief that such a meeting, will foster the interests of every nation, will injure those of none, and will confirm and strengthen in us all the belief that the good of each is likewise the common good of all."

What the Declaration recommended was, however, already under way. The President and his advisers had foreseen that the North American Conference would be the precursor of a world conference. Already, to quote Elihu Root, then Secretary of State: "By an *aide-mémoire* in January last [1909], before the North American Conference had met, the principal governments were informally sounded to ascertain whether they would look with favor upon an invitation to send delegates to such a conference. The responses have so far been uniformly favorable."

"The people of the whole world," said the preliminary *aide-mémoire,* "are interested in the natural resources of the whole world, benefited by their conservation, and injured by their destruction. The people of every country are interested in the supply of food and of material for manufacture in every other country, not only because these are interchangeable through processes of trade but because a knowledge of the total supply is necessary to the intelligent treatment of each nation's share of the supply."

And this significant sentence followed. "Reading the lessons of the past aright it would be for such a conference to look beyond the present to the future."

These statements made it evident that the President and the men in whose minds the plan for a world inventory was born regarded the proposed conference only as a first step. They believed that international co-operation between nations for the conservation of natural resources and for fair access to necessary raw materials would greatly reduce the danger of war and work powerfully for permanent peace. Such a result, as well I know, was a definite part of their plan.

With the concurrence of the Netherlands, invitations were sent to fifty-eight nations to meet at the Peace Palace in The Hague in September 1909. Thirty of the nations, including Great Britain, France, Germany, Canada, and Mexico, had already accepted when President Taft, who succeeded Theodore Roosevelt on March 4, 1909, killed the plan.

Two unsuccessful attempts (at my initiative) were made to revive it. At the end of World War I, President Wilson, by the suggestion of Colonel House, took steps toward securing world-wide co-operation in the conservation and distribution of natural resources. Unfortunately nothing came of it.

Again, during Hoover's Administration, a group of nearly two hundred leading citizens from all parts of this country urged the President, in a public petition, to take action along the same general line. Once more, nothing came of it.

This book was planned to end in 1910, after my removal from the Forest Service. But because permanent peace, as this is written, is so clearly and so urgently the basic question before the nations, and because it cannot be solved without world-wide conservation of natural resources, I have broken my own rule. On this one subject I have attempted to bring this book more nearly down to date.

Here, I offer you my apologies for the number of quotations which follow in this chapter. They are, I believe, necessary parts of the story I am trying to tell. And they are also from documents which ought to appear in their original form.

In May 1940, I brought up the conservation of natural resources as an essential foundation for permanent peace before the Eighth American Scientific Congress at Washington:

"National life everywhere is built on the foundation of natural resources. Throughout human history the exhaustion of these resources and the need for new supplies have been among the greatest causes of war.

"A just and permanent world peace is vital to the best interests of all nations. When the terms which will end the present war [World War II] are considered, the neutral nations should be in position to assist in finding the way to such a peace. That being so, it would be wise to prepare in time.

"The proposal is that the nations of the Americas prepare now for an endeavor to bring all nations together, at the right moment, in a common effort for conserving the natural resources of the earth, and for assuring to each nation access to the raw materials it needs, without recourse to war.

"In all countries some natural resources are being depleted or destroyed. Needless waste or destruction of necessary resources anywhere threatens or will threaten, sooner or later, the welfare and security of peoples everywhere. Conservation is clearly a world necessity, not only for enduring prosperity, but also for permanent peace.

"No nation is self-sufficient in essential raw materials. The welfare of every nation depends on access to natural resources which it lacks. Fair access to natural resources from other nations is therefore an indispensable condition of permanent peace.

"War is still an instrument of national policy for the safeguarding of natural resources or for securing them from other nations. Hence international co-operation in conserving, utilizing, and distributing natural resources to the mutual advantage of all nations might well remove one of the most dangerous of all obstacles to a just and permanent world peace."

The problem of permanent peace includes, of course, great factors which the foregoing proposal does not cover, but it does cover that factor which is certainly, in the long run, the most potent of them all.

As an immediate step toward permanent peace, I suggested that the Scientific Congress recommend to the Governments of the American nations the creation of a commission, representing all of them, to assemble the necessary basic facts. That could well be done without further original investigation. Then would follow, I said, "formulation by the Commission of a plan and of recommendations to the American Governments for a general policy and a specific program of action, including the presentation of the plan when prepared to neutral and belligerent nations.

"Such a Commission would be of immense and lasting value to the American nations. It could not but advance their intersts, both individual and mutual, in addition to opening a road toward a workable basis for permanent peace.

"Finally, the situation in Europe and in Asia suggests that action for the purpose outlined above was never more necessary than at present." Which statement, because of the atomic bomb, is far truer and more timely today than it was when I made it.

The resolution passed by the Eighth American Scientific Congress, without a dissenting vote, for the appointment of an Inter-American Conservation Commission, was as follows:

"WHEREAS: Needless waste and destruction of necessary natural resources everywhere threatens or will threaten, sooner or later, the welfare and security of peoples;

"Throughout human history the exhaustion of these resources and the need for a new supply have been among the greatest causes of war;

"The welfare of every nation requires natural resources which it lacks, and fair access to such resources from other nations is an indispensable condition of national welfare and permanent peace;

"Conservation of natural resources and fair access to needed raw materials are steps toward the common good to which all nations must in principle agree;

"International co-operation to inventory, conserve, and wisely utilize natural resources to the mutual advantage of all nations might well remove one of the most dangerous obstacles to all nations to a just and permanent world peace; and

"An Inter-American Conservation Commission representing all the American nations would be of great and lasting value to the Americas, and through them, to all the nations of the world by advancing the knowledge of the natural resources of the earth, by promoting mutual access to necessary natural resources, and by bringing nearer the permanent removal of one of the greatest causes of war;

"The Eighth American Scientific Congress

"*Resolves:* To recommend to the governments of the American Republics the appointment of an Inter-American Conservation Commission co-operating with the Pan American Union and representing all the Americas.

"That this Commission be charged with the duty of preparing an inventory of world natural resources, and of formulating a general policy and specific program of action to promote the mutual conservation and prudent utilization of natural resources for the welfare of all nations, in the interest of permanent peace."

Since the resolution of the Scientific Congress was adopted six years ago the United States and two or three other North American nations have appointed members of the proposed Commission, but so far they have not come together. For that the war may be in part responsible.

Resolutions alone, however wise and right, without action to follow, get us exactly nowhere.

On July 26, 1944, I saw the President and laid the idea of an International Conservation Conference before him. Roosevelt, unlike Taft, Wilson, and Hoover, grasped the full implications of the idea at once, received it with immense enthusiasm, and expressed the desire for rapid action, even to the possibility of launching the movement in the autumn. After some discussion I felt that there should be more work done to bring the idea up to date—the President then authorized me to call upon any individual in any Department for any technical help that I needed.

During the summer of 1944 I kept in touch with the President on the subject, and on August 29 sent him a "Proposal for an International Conference on Conservation." This asserted that "We cannot safely ignore any course that may assist in abolishing war. Therefore I believe that it would be wise for the United Nations, through their appointed delegates, to meet and consider the conservation of natural resources, and fair access to them among the nations, as a vital step toward permanent peace."

On October 24 the President wrote me this note:

Dear Gifford:—

Remember that I have not forgotten that conservation is a basis of permanent peace, and I have sent the enclosed to Cordell Hull. I think something will happen soon.

You must, of course, be on the American Delegation.

This blankety blank campaign [for the Presidency] is nearly over.

My best to you.

As ever yours,

F.D.R.

Franklin Roosevelt's letter to Cordell Hull said in part:

In our meetings with other nations I have a feeling that too little attention is being paid to the subject of the conservation and use of natural resources.

I am surprised that the world knows so little about itself.

Conservation is a basis of permanent peace. Many different kinds of natural resources are being wasted; other kinds are being ignored; still other kinds can be put to more practical use for humanity if more is known about them. Some nations are deeply interested in the subject of conservation and use and other nations are not at all interested.

It occurs to me, therefore, that even before the United Nations meet for the comprehensive program which has been proposed, it could do no harm—and it might do much good—for us to hold a meeting in the United States of all of the united and associated nations for what is really the first step toward conservation and use of natural resources—i.e., a gathering for the purpose of a world-wide study of the whole subject.

The machinery at least could be put into effect to carry it through.

I repeat again that I am more and more convinced that conservation is a basis of permanent peace.

Would you let me have your thought on this?

I think the time is ripe.

Always sincerely,

Franklin D. Roosevelt

On January 21, 1945, I wrote to the President:

"When you told me at luncheon on Friday [the day before his inauguration] that you are going to take up the proposed Conference on conservation as a basis of permanent peace with Churchill and Stalin, I saw great things ahead and was more delighted than I can easily say. In view of that decision, would it be a good plan to make for you a rough preliminary list of subjects to be considered and get together some applicable facts about natural resources?

"If you think it might be helpful, shall I go ahead, quietly and informally, and of course without publicity, and ask a few Government experts for needed assistance? For I am very far from knowing it all."

Next day, at his suggestion, made through his daughter, Mrs. Boettiger, I sent to the President a brief preliminary statement of the proposed World Conservation Conference to take with him on his trip abroad, and received his authority to prepare a more detailed draft still with the help of any Government experts I needed. This I did during his absence at the Yalta Conference. Because of his untimely death, however, it was never presented to him. It remains an unfinished part of Franklin Roosevelt's plan for the work of his Administration.

After some months I saw President Truman, who told me he was familiar with the plan, had heard it discussed in Cabinet meetings, and proposed to prosecute the idea as vigorously as Mr. Roosevelt.

Editor's Note: A few days before Mr. Pinchot's death, President Truman sent to the Economic and Social Council of the United Nations, the American Plan embodying the idea of a World Conservation Conference, and in March 1947, the United Nations accepted the plan and put it on the Agenda for 1948.

PART XI
END OF AN ERA

66. *Desertion Under Fire*

Theodore Roosevelt was going out of office on March 4, 1909. One question overshadowed the work and play of T.R. and his close advisers: Would the incoming Administration protect and maintain the progress made in seven strenuous years, or would it not? Would the T.R. policies flourish or decay, survive or perish? That must depend on the man who came after him.

In the choice and election of his successor everything that T.R. stood for was at stake. And that would have been so even if the President's own enemies and the enemies of his policies had not been more and more active and effective as the end of his term drew near.

Among the possible choices for the man to take up T.R.'s burden and continue his work, two stood head and shoulders above the rest. One of them was Elihu Root, easily the ablest thinking machine then in public life, and one of the most useful men that had ever sat in T.R.'s Cabinet.

Root was a lawyer and an advocate. As such the interests of his client were his interests. During his service in the Cabinet, both as Secretary of War and as Secretary of State, the President was his client. Consequently Root devoted himself faithfully and with extraordinary ability to the promotion of the T.R. policies.

But Root was no longer in the Cabinet. He was now a United States Senator, hand-picked by the New York Republican machine and the Wall Street interests who were behind it. These men were now his clients, rather than the President and the people of the United States as heretofore.

In his Senatorial incarnation Root was anti-Conservation and pro-privilege. It was clear he could not be trusted to carry on the T.R. policies. Root would not do.

The other possibility was William Howard Taft. As Secretary of

War, Taft was highly efficient and devoted. He stuck to the lines laid down by his Chief, he backed up the T.R. policies. In particular he had been of great use in certain important matters of foreign policy, where he acted as an ideal ambassador.

In the walks and talks which Jim Garfield and I were constantly having with T.R., the subject of his successor came oftener to the fore as the winter of 1907-08 wore on and the opposition in Congress grew worse. And T.R. repeated over and over again how lucky we should be if it were possible to get Will Taft into the Presidency. If only that could be done, the T.R. policies would be safe, Conservation would be assured of intelligent and enthusiastic backing from the White House, he was confident, and everything that had been won for the general good during the seven strenuous years would be vigorously defended and advanced under the new Administration.

To T.R. and his little group of intimates Will Taft was "the substance of things hoped for, the evidence of things not seen." None of us questioned that Taft would stand by the ship. So T.R. threw all his own force and the whole force of his Administration behind Taft, and brought about his nomination. Then came the campaign.

So far, in the main, Will Taft had successfully followed and chuckled his way through life. But this was a new situation. However much he shone as an after-dinner speaker, however well he met people, however great his personal charm, as a campaigner he lacked the fighting edge. In that respect William Jennings Bryan, his Democratic opponent, outclassed him completely.

Almost before it was well under way, the Taft campaign began to bog down. T.R. saw the situation, saw that it needed the fire and iron Taft could not supply, jumped in, gave life and snap to the fight, and put it over. It was Theodore Roosevelt, not William Howard Taft, who won the election of 1908.

Until after the election was over it never occurred to me, and I am certain it never occurred to T.R., that Will Taft could fail to carry on the T.R. policies. That he would carry those policies not on but out—out on a shutter, as the newspapers afterwards put it—was beyond my imagination.

But the ballots had hardly been counted before things began to happen that were hard to understand. Although he was under every possible obligation to do so, Taft promptly ceased to consult with the man who had made him President. Instead he avoided the White

House. In place of T.R.'s friends, he gathered around him such men as Jim Tawney and Adam Bede, both of Minnesota, who were T.R.'s open enemies. And in other ways he raised the question whether the new President really was what we would have bet our bottom dollar he would be. It was a sickening doubt.

We of the Tennis Cabinet had been doing the very best we knew to bring the T.R. Administration to a triumphant end. We had given all there was in us to put over the T.R. policies, and Conservation in particular, with the generous and enthusiastic help of men and women all through the Government Departments, and we were succeeding far beyond anything we had reason to expect. In Taft's nomination and election T.R. had brought about the one thing necessary to keep the good work going. We were walking on air until suddenly the whole situation threatened to blow up in our faces.

We couldn't believe it, we couldn't let ourselves believe it. Hadn't Taft made a speech during his campaign (not such a bad speech either—I wrote it myself) in which he defined Conservation as the use of intelligent common sense and ordinary business foresight in dealing with our natural resources which are the foundations of our prosperity, and went on to speak of the "great policy of Conservation on which our whole future depends." That would seem to make assurance doubly sure . . . and yet . . . and yet . . . It couldn't be true that he was going back on Conservation. Or could it? We had doubts, but much or most of the time we doubted our own doubts. And that was natural, for what we were afraid of was the last thing on earth we wanted to believe.

Our reluctant dread that something was wrong with Taft gradually crystallized into the fear that, under pressure, he might go back on his salt. T.R. was most concerned about the Conservation policy. In order to make sure there would be no hitch about that, he called Will Taft and me to the White House one night shortly after the election.

We three spent the whole evening together in the old Cabinet Room upstairs, which had become T.R.'s study. Then and there Taft pledged himself to T.R., and incidentally to me, to stand by and carry on the Conservation fight. I was there and I heard him do it.

It was no perfunctory promise. We went over the essential Conservation questions in detail, and water power in particular. T.R. asked Will to call me in if ever there was any trouble about Conservation. He gave his word that he would. And in general he bound himself, as completely as one man can to another, to stand by and go forward with the T.R. Conservation policy.

That should have clinched the matter for good. But before the election was a month old, we were almost convinced that the fat was in the fire—that the Taft Administration was not going to carry on the Roosevelt policies, but rather going to carry them out on a shutter.

Since its introduction to the people through the Conference of Governors less than a year before, the Conservation policy had accumulated behind it an extraordinary body of public support. But it had also accumulated an extraordinary body of private opposition. To the exploiting special interests, in their greed for the people's resources, Conservation was like the ring on the neck of a cormorant—like the muzzle on the jaws of a hungry dog. And they were not taking it lying down.

Therefore the incoming President, if he stood by his word, would have to fight even to hold T.R.'s gains. And if he refused to fight, it was quite on the cards that public property worth literally billions of dollars would pass into grasping private hands.

But were we justified in our questioning? Had Taft really gone over to the enemy, as the evidence seemed to indicate? We thought there was a way to find out. The Joint Conservation Conference of Governors and representatives of organizations interested in Conservation (the successor to the Governors' Conference of the previous May) was to meet in Washington on December 8, 1908. T.R. was to address it. We arranged to have Taft invited to serve as Chairman.

The first words Taft spoke after I called the meeting to order and introduced him as its presiding officer gave us the clue. He said:

"Mr. President, Ladies and Gentlemen: There is one difficulty about the conservation of natural resources. It is that the imagination of those who are pressing it may outrun the practical facts."

Some of us (I suppose I had a hand in it) had written for Taft a speech which took the T.R. position on Conservation. He had it with him but declined to read it. His only reference to it, made with his infectious chuckle, was this: "How many parts of the speeches that have been delivered Mr. Pinchot has written I am unable to testify for others."

True, Taft did assert his deep sympathy with the Conservation movement and his purpose "to do everything I can do to carry on the work so admirably begun and so wonderfully shown forth by President Roosevelt." But that merely repeated what he had said before. To us on the firing line of a fight that was far from won, the first words were what told the real story and set the real pace. This was notice of the coming of a new and darker day.

Of T.R.'s address to the Joint Conservation Conference, I quote only two fragments: "Your task is to make the Nation's future as great as its present," and he added that Conservation "is the largest national task of today." He also took strong ground against wanton forest destruction, and for securing without delay the Appalachian and White Mountain National Forests.

Two days later, my Mother, as was her custom, received the members of the Joint Conservation Conference at our home at 1615 Rhode Island Avenue. It was a good custom, for it gave me far-flung contacts that would otherwise have been difficult or impossible.

But no reception, nor any other thing whatsoever, could blanket the great central problem of the moment. I shall never forget how this one question walked with me by day and kept me awake at night: Would Taft stand by his promise? Or would he turn our great Conservation victory into defeat?

During the last months of T.R.'s presidency the walks which Jim Garfield, Lawrence Murray, H. K. Smith, and I were in the habit of taking with him changed vitally in character. Until then, we had talked of our work, of cabbages and kings, and all sorts of cheerful matters. Now the talk ran mainly to the coming Administration, and what we could possibly do to protect the T.R. policies. We were angry and indignant, and no wonder.

There was, indeed, grave reason for anxiety about the public resources. At the end of T.R.'s Administration large numbers of immensely valuable water-power sites on navigable streams, on streams useful for irrigation, and in the National Forests, had been withdrawn by his order from threatened appropriation by private interests, but they were not yet permanently safe. A President who chose could still turn them over to the water-power grabbers.

That was true also of rich coal lands, oil lands, iron-ore lands, and phosphate lands, millions of acres of them, and even of the National Forests themselves. The latter, having been created by Presidential Proclamation, could be destroyed by the same road. Taken altogether,

A BIG JOB FOR THE PLUMBER

what Taft himself had called "the foundations of our prosperity" were at stake.

Obviously there was just one thing to be done. Every acre of the Public Domain that would serve the people better in public than in private ownership must immediately be withdrawn from entry and set aside so that the incoming Executive would have to act affirmatively to give them away. We must make it as difficult as possible to hand the public property over to the grabbers, to turn T.R.'s great Conservation victory into defeat. Every step that could be taken to protect the public interest must be taken. And it was taken.

At once after the Joint Conference, Price, Woodruff, Garfield, Newell, and I set to work. In the ten weeks before T.R. went out of office, with the President's eager support and all the help we could otherwise command, we left nothing undone that we could do to safeguard and secure every natural resource that belonged to and ought to remain in the hands of the people of the United States. Our first business was to sew up every opening, tie down every loose end, make every possible public resource safe against anything less than an open attack on T.R.'s Conservation policy.

Those were great days, days of the intensest action, and in them I did the hardest work of my life. And so, I believe, did every other man in T.R.'s inner circle.

Perhaps this is as good a place as any to repeat that, as I see it, the greatest of all luxuries is to work yourself to your very limit in a cause in which you believe with your whole soul. If that be true, the last three months of T.R.'s term was one time I lived the life of Riley.

67. *The Last Days*

When March 4 arrived everybody was used up but T.R. His iron endurance was untouched.

When that day came vast quantities of public resources had been put where they were safe unless positive action should be taken to deconserve them. For the same power that had saved them—the power of the President—could also undo them. That was the weak spot—the inevitable weak spot—in the defenses we did all we knew to set up.

During his last days as President, T.R. was carrying not only the normal burden of his great office (which, as he personally handled it, was enormous), not only the heartbreaking work of trying to save the Roosevelt policies, and Conservation in particular, from the man of all men who should have been the first to defend them, but very much else besides. His coming African trip, for one example, was on his hands. At the overcrowded end of his term he must choose his party, decide on his route, select and assemble his weapons, and pick out the famous "Pigskin Library" to take along, for T.R. could not be happy without books.

And for another example, since he was coming home through Europe, speeches would have to be made. Some of them he wrote before he started. He showed me and I read in Washington, long before his term was out, the lecture he was to deliver at the Sorbonne in Paris after his return from Africa.

Yet in the midst of that tornado of work, T.R. and Mrs. Roosevelt forgot none of the men and women who had worked and played closely with them. Letters of appreciation were written, little presents were sent, and there was even a meeting of the Tennis Cabinet at the Garfields' house at which printed diplomas of appointment, signed by T.R., were presented to each of us by T.R. himself.

Each diploma gave individual reasons for the appointment. In my case these alleged reasons were "loyalty, agility, courtliness, tennisity, Forest Service, and contortion returns" and because of them I was admitted to "all the rights, indignities, emoluments, detractions, and delights" appertaining to membership in that celebrated organization.

At whatever risk to my modesty, and however little I may have deserved it, I cannot refrain from reproducing here a letter from T.R. written two days before he left the White House.

Dear Gifford:

I have written you about others; I have written you about many public matters; now, just a line about yourself. As long as I live I shall feel for you a mixture of respect and admiration and of affectionate regard. I am a better man for having known you. I feel that to have been with you will make my children better men and women in after life; and I cannot think of a man in the country whose loss would be a more real misfortune to the Nation than yours would be. For seven and a half years we have worked together, and now and then played together—and have been altogether better able to work because we have played; and I owe to you a peculiar debt of obligation for a very large part of the achievement of this Administration.

With love to your dear mother, I am,

Ever faithfully your friend,

Theodore Roosevelt

The night before inauguration I went to an enthusiastic meeting of Yale men at the New Willard Hotel. The next day a Yale man would be President of the United States. Taft dropped in and made a talk. That talk was curiously full of hesitation and foreboding. I cannot remember a single confident note in the whole of it.

To me, steeped in T.R.'s gallant acceptance of every hazard, his spirited delight in the daily struggle, it was shocking to find that Taft was approaching his new task with doubt and dread. I had learned that the use of power to good ends is one of the greatest of all pleasures. But Taft spoke like a man whose job had got him down even before he tackled it. He had set the stage for his own defeat.

T.R., in striking contrast, lost nothing of his high spirit at the end. I was with him in his office in the White House during the whole of his last morning there, and I ought to know. He wrote for me (except for signing certain bills at the Capitol) his last signature as President of the United States.

It would not have been a busy morning, as T.R.'s mornings went, for the crowd was looking to the rising sun, except for his determination to leave nothing behind for Taft to handle. Every item of business was brought to him the moment it reached his office. Every report was disposed of, every last-minute letter answered. When T.R. left the White House as President for the last time his desk was clear. It was a remarkable achievement.

As it came time to start for the inauguration, T.R., Will Loeb, and I went over to the main building where Taft, Mrs. Taft, and Mrs. Roosevelt were waiting. The two Presidents rode to the Capitol in an open carriage, drawn by horses of course, with the Secret Service men all about them. Will Loeb and I were in a covered landau next behind. You may well believe me when I say that to us it was a melancholy ride.

After the new President had taken his oath of office I went with others of the Tennis Cabinet and the formal Cabinet to see T.R. off at the Union Station. He was by far the most cheerful of the lot. And no wonder, for he could look back upon his work and see that it was good.

For the rest of us it was a dreadful day. Not because of the storm and the snow, inches deep in the streets, but because the leader we loved was leaving us, because we should never know such days again.

It was the end of one era and the beginning of another. The plain people, whom T.R. loved and who loved him, to whom he gave the best there was in him, were no longer to come first. From then on for many a year they were to get the short end of the stick.

The blizzard of Inauguration Day delayed T.R.'s train so that he did not reach Sagamore Hill till the early hours of the following morning. Yet his vitality was such that by eight o'clock he was up and out, and ready for the next adventure, which was Africa.

We who were to remain behind were anxious and uneasy. It was not pretty, but it was true, that during T.R.'s absence in Africa and Europe his policies were going to need defense against the man who was most fully pledged and most deeply obligated to maintain them. We had seen the battle coming, and we were set to make the fight—the best fight we could with the best of all fighters away. We were not happy, and again no wonder.

68. *T.R.'s Service to America*

As T.R. prepared to leave office, he had every right to look back upon his Administration with head erect. His service to the Nation was colossal. To mention only a few—a very few—of the things done, things with which I had some connection:

T.R.'s Administration originated, formulated, and laid before the American people and the world the Conservation idea—the greatest good for the greatest number for the longest time, the development and use of the earth and all its resources for the enduring good of men—both on a national and international scale. And not only the idea, but its practical and successful application in many fields.

The T.R. Administration held the first National Conference on Conservation ever held in any country, prepared the first inventory of natural resources ever made for any nation, initiated and held the first international conference on Conservation. It issued the first call for a world-wide inventory of natural resources and received the acceptance of practically all of the great nations, and a majority of all of them, great and small.

When the Roosevelt Administration went out of office the Conservation policy, to which it had given birth, had been everywhere publicly approved in America, and had been introduced to the whole civilized world. It was on the way to being recognized for what it is, the fundamental material policy in human civilization.

Moreover, there was strong hope that the Conservation policy, once accepted by the nations, would serve as the most effectual of all defenses against the danger of war and the most dependable of all the bulwarks of permanent peace. At last, long years after T.R.'s death, that hope may indeed be realized.

The T.R. Administration reorganized and consolidated the forest work of the Government, took it out of politics and out of mere talk, rescued the National Forests from incompetence and corruption, and started Forestry in actual practice in the woods on an area larger than the thirteen original states.

For the first time, it handled the great forests on Indian Reservations in the interest of the Indians instead of as spoils for politicians and their friends. And it began the practice of Forestry on Army reservations.

It created the Reclamation Service, and through irrigation it was changing huge areas of worthless deserts into productive fields. The good movement then begun continues its vast usefulness to this day.

It found the public lands everywhere mishandled and misappropriated by corrupt politicians and their supporters for their own private profit, and it converted the Public Domain from private spoils into a great instrumentality for the public good. It convicted two United States Senators for public-land frauds, and stopped the looting of the property of the people. Best of all, it set the Homestead Act in the highest place, established the making and maintenance of prosperous homes as the central purpose of our public-land policy, and made all the natural resources in public hands serve that great objective.

It saved to the American people their greatest deposits of phosphate rock, that most essential fertilizer, and prevented its exportation abroad. It stopped the sale of vast areas of coal lands still in public hands for a fraction of their true value. And for the first time it protected effectively from theft and monopoly the oil lands both on the Public Domain and on Indian Reservations.

For the first time in American history, it did away with political pork-barrel waterway development on navigable streams and public lands and made it into an intelligent, scientific, and effective enterprise for the public good.

For the first time it recognized the enormous value of the public water power to the people, safeguarded the public water-power sites against the grabbing of private monopolistic interests, checked the misuse of the land laws for that evil purpose, regulated through Government permits the development of public power by private capital, set a time limit on the permits, and required the power interests to pay the public for the use of public property.

In his Administration generally, and especially in the public enterprises which came to be grouped under the Conservation policy, T.R. set and enforced standards of personal and civic honesty, capacity, and efficiency never approached by anv administration since the early days of the Republic.

It was one of T.R.'s greatest services that his Administration established the fact (which none then believed possible, and hardly any now) that Government servants, freed from politics and well led, can be as loyal and devoted, and their work as effective per dollar spent, as the workers and the work of the best-managed private corporations. That it could be done was proved by actually doing it.

Countless other great and notable services rendered by T.R. might well be mentioned, such as the Panama Canal and the fleet's voyage around the world. They belong, however, rather in the province of formal history than in such a book as this. Therefore I pass them by.

T.R.'s influence with the politicians was far less than with the people, which was as it should be. But the power he had he used. Before he became President the Republican Party had become the conservative party—the party of the special interests. For a time at least, T.R. put an end to that. Under his leadership, to quote his words, "the Republican Party became once more the progressive, and indeed the fairly radical progressive party of the Nation." Unfortunately it did not stay so.

Before T.R. left the White House, Jim Garfield and I decided to write the story of his Administration. We had T.R.'s own blessing on the project in the form of an introduction, written before the book was even begun. The work was started, but Jim's legal practice, the Ballinger case, and the long fight for Conservation headed us off, and the book is unfinished to this day.

Lest you may think I have given myself too large a share in T.R.'s great service to America, let me set the matter right.

Among lesser people the allotment of credit for decisions made or work done is often complicated and difficult. In the case of any authority of last resort, such as the President, the rule is simple. The President is personally responsible for every decision he makes, every order he gives, every speech he delivers. Who wrote the speech, who advised the order, who suggested the decision has nothing to do with the price of butter.

Which assistant or adviser first formulated what the President said or did is of no moment—what counts is that the President took action. To the President, and to the President alone, belongs the praise or the blame. No one can tell him what he must do or say. Good or bad, success or failure, the outcome is his and nobody else's, no matter what were the steps by which the end was reached.

I speak with conviction because (for one reason) I suppose I have written more speeches for more Presidents and candidates for President than most of my fellow-Americans. Whether they were good or bad, wise or foolish, the moment the President made them his own they ceased to be mine, and the President alone became responsible.

I wrote many speeches for T.R., either by myself or in co-operation with others, and suggested many plans, but the decision to use them was his. He could have thrown them out if and when he chose. Once he adopted them, the credit or the blame was his. For example, I wrote for him while he was Governor a message to the New York Legislature on Forestry. Newell and I, with the help of Maxwell, McGee, and doubtless others, drew up for him, as you know, those clauses in his first message to Congress which started the ball in Forestry and irrigation.

In my brother's office at 120 Broadway, shortly before it was delivered, I wrote, at T.R.'s request, a draft of his Ossawattomie speech on human rights, a first draft of which, by another hand, had already been prepared and discarded. Beveridge, who had seen it, told me it was nothing but a historical essay, wholly unfit for a platform of the Progressive movement, which was the purpose in hand. I went at once to Oyster Bay, told T.R. what Beveridge had said and that I agreed, and was promptly authorized by the President, to make a new draft.

But does that make the Ossawattomie speech my speech? Most emphatically it does not. T.R., if he had chosen, could have done with my draft what he did with the other one. His acceptance of it made it his own.

So also I suggested and wrote for T.R. his message on "Equality of Opportunity," which summed up and interpreted the achievements of his two Administrations. But I repeat that this speech, and many others in which I had a hand, were T.R.'s own after he had once adopted them.

In the case of a Governor, the captain of a ship at sea, and other authorities of last resort, the rule is just the same. But not in the case of lesser powers and dignitaries. For in their cases authority is divided, and they get credit for work which is by no means all their own. Take my own case for example.

When T.R., or anybody else, spoke approvingly of my part in advancing Forestry and Conservation, he was necessarily speaking not only of me but also of many others whose names he did not mention but whose work was the occasion and justification for what he said.

If praise was due, it was due just as much to these men and women whose representative and mouthpiece I happened to be as it was to me. Many of the best ideas and plans which we worked out had been suggested to me by somebody else. The good organization of the Forest Service, as I have already told you, was due far more to Overton W. Price than it was to me.

Its impregnable legal position against attacks in Congress and the courts sprang from the wisdom and knowledge of George W. Woodruff and Philip P. Wells.

Its success in educating the public, which far surpassed that of any other Government bureau, stemmed from the rare common sense and untiring diligence of Herbert A. Smith, and from the skill as a newspaperman of Thomas R. Shipp, who gave our handouts the necessary professional touch.

The credit for its sound, workable, and productive grazing policy belonged mainly to Albert F. Potter. Price, Woodruff, Smith, and many others did most of the thinking and deserved most of the credit. The case of Conservation was different. That was my own pigeon, yet even there I would have been in serious difficulties without the encyclopedic scientific knowledge of W J McGee.

Because all this was true, and much more, I have not hesitated to quote in this book letters and statements which, had they referred to me alone, might well be charged to bragging. But since they do not, to omit them would be to deprive of their just mead of praise the men whose names I have mentioned and many, many others.

The men, and the women too, who laid the foundations of the Forest Service and made it what it was—far and away the best bureau under the Government of the United States—were a magnificent group, and nothing that T.R. said then, or that I can say now, is too good for them.

69. *The Public Good Comes First*

Under the T.R. policies, which Taft had pledged himself to continue and enforce, the Government's business was admirably handled, with little waste, little political and big business plundering, and great benefit to the Nation and its people. Take, for example, the case of the public lands, which under T.R. were far safer from spoilers than they had ever been before.

T.R.'s vigorous offensive against the land thieves had at last made the theft of public land dangerous. Frank Heney's successful prosecution of Senator Mitchell of Oregon was notice that high public office was no sufficient protection, and Garfield's vigilant defense of the public lands was more water on the same wheel.

Undoubtedly, also, the example of the Forest Service helped to force on the General Land Office the revolutionary innovation of examining each claim on the ground to see whether the law had been complied with, instead, as was the established custom, of merely looking over the papers to find out whether perjury had been made plausible enough to get by, and letting it go at that.

These things had combined to drive some of the older officials of the Interior Department into unwilling activity in defense of the public rights. The opportunity had been eagerly seized by some of the younger officials as a welcome chance to do good work. But most of the alleged guardians of the Public Domain still loved to tread the ancient round and would have welcomed with delight a return to what they thought of as the good old days.

Before T.R.'s time, under the tradition and the practice of the General Land Office and the Indian Office, the public good came last. Here were the happy hunting grounds of predatory Western interests and their trainbearers in the Senate and House.

To protect the public interest and checkmate the land grabbers, beginning (I believe) in 1907, large areas of phosphate lands had been withdrawn from entry by T.R., lest the indispensable fertilizer they contained should be wasted, monopolized, or shipped abroad. But would Taft continue the withdrawals? The executive authority which had withdrawn these lands could also be used to open them to the resource grabbers.

The same was true of oil-bearing lands, great tracts of which had been protected in the same way. Vast tracts of coal lands also, in many parts of the West and in Alaska, had likewise been withdrawn. By the time Taft came in the total of coal-land withdrawals amounted to no less than 68,000,000 acres, or more than twice the area of Pennsylvania.

Garfield, after he became Secretary of the Interior in 1907, had broken up the bad old custom of selling public coal lands at the lowest price permitted by law, and those which had not been withdrawn were bringing something in the neighborhood of their actual value. This change was so obviously right that no administration could return to the old plan.

Large numbers of dam sites on public lands, in National Forests, and on navigable streams, valuable for water power or irrigation or both, were still unappropriated. There was no law under which they could be taken up as power sites, but under Land Office custom that was no obstacle. In spite of the fact that perjury was often involved, through homestead and desert-land claims power sites were passing into corporate hands in ways both legal and illegal.

Many such dam sites the power and irrigation interests had already acquired. Some they had developed, some they held dormant in order to keep them out of the hands of competitors, or until they themselves should be ready to use them. Before Taft's tergiversation, T.R. had already begun to withdraw sites from entry to keep them safe until Congress could act to protect them. This work he now pushed forward with redoubled vigor through the Geological Survey, the

Reclamation Service, and the Forest Service until the total area of such sites withdrawn along sixteen Western rivers amounted to a million and a half acres. Because of the tremendous final rush, some of them were doubtless larger than necessary. Better that, however, than none at all.

Forest Ranger stations also required attention. The National Forests could neither be protected nor utilized without Rangers, and the Rangers could neither live near their work nor maintain their saddle and pack horses unless Ranger stations, which must include pasture for the stock, were reserved for their use.

Accordingly, orders from Washington withdrew such stations from entry in or near the National Forests all over the West. But they had to be surveyed before they could be withdrawn, and although we did our best we couldn't secure anything like all the Ranger stations we needed before T.R. went out of office. Some of these Ranger stations we located deliberately on water-power sites, in order to ensure some form of Government control until regular power-site withdrawals could take their place, which they did in practically all cases before March 4, the day of Taft's inauguration.

T.R. did not have, and could not get from Congress, specific authority of law for these withdrawals. But neither was there specific authority of law for the Louisiana Purchase by Jefferson, or for freeing the slaves by Lincoln, or for the acquisition of the Panama Canal by T.R. himself.

There were, however, precedents in plenty. President after President had withdrawn public lands from private acquisition, with no more and no less legal authority than T.R., just because the public interest required it. For that definite reason, and to give Congress the time to legislate in the public interest, T.R. followed their example.

But there was also another reason. If our suspicions were correct, it must be made as difficult as possible for Taft to let the Conservation policy down. Matters must be so arranged that not mere neglect, but positive hostile action, would be required. And so vast areas of public lands were put where only a direct Presidential Order would throw them open again to the grabbers.

In all this not only natural resources were at stake, but the very integrity and efficiency of the Government service. If Taft should forsake the T.R. policies, his desertion would naturally carry over into the Department and take the starch out of them.

There is nothing that permeates any group of human beings, any body of workers, any regiment, any business, any service, as fast and as far as the spirit of the man at the top. During T.R.'s presidency, his gallant contagious courage and marvelous executive effectiveness filtered down to the last messenger boy in the smallest Government division.

T.R.'s service to the Nation came both from what he was and what he did—from the citizen and man, as well as the statesman and executive. "He was the leader of the people because his courage and his soundness made him so. His ideals, his purposes, his points of view, his hostilities, and his enthusiasms were such as every right-thinking man could entertain and understand. He rose to greatness in his practical application of them."

It was my immense good fortune to have known him at work and at play, to watch him as he directed the affairs of the government, both in Albany and Washington. I was with him in his hours of relaxation as well as in his hours of work.

"What explains his power? Life is the answer. Life at its warmest, and fullest and freest, at its utmost in vigor, at its sanest in purpose, at its cleanest and clearest—life tremendous in volume, unbounded in scope, yet controlled and guided with a disciplined power that made him, as few men have ever been, the captain of his soul." *

Under T.R., the Government service was on its toes, alive and awake. The men and women of the Departments did their work without watching the clock. Whoever was called by the President for extra service, above and beyond the ordinary call of duty, was eager, glad, and proud. It was worth while to be a member of an Administration that had T.R. at the head of it.

Never before or since in my working life has the Government service operated under such high standards of integrity, efficiency, and accomplishment. I make that statement with confidence, for I have been in working contact with every Administration in Washington for a full half century.

* Quoted from a great memorial meeting in Philadelphia.

PART XII
THE PAY-OFF

70. *And Then Came Taft*

When Taft came into office, with his joviality and his fondness for the easier way, it was unlikely that the vigor and snap which the Government service took from T.R. would last. But I was certainly unprepared for the promptness with which Taft imposed his slipshod nature on the Departments. When I got back to Washington from the West a month or so after T.R. had left, the place was scarcely recognizable. Listlessness pervaded it. Hardly anybody seemed to care about anything any more.

I suppose I had as good a chance to judge as anyone, for I was the only man who had served on all six of the T.R. Commissions which I have already described. And if I knew anything about the Government, I knew that the fire had gone out of it.

The Government service, under its new, easy-going head, was slumped down on its heels. The only people I found who were thinking about anything much but quitting time were in the Reclamation Service, the Geological Survey, the Forest Service, and in two or three other bureaus whose leaders had been permanently converted to the T.R. point of view, all of whom were still eager to carry on the work and live up to the standards he had set them.

Washington was a dead town. Its leader was gone, and in his place a man whose fundamental desire was to keep out of trouble. Which, in my experience is the surest way to bring trouble about.

Actually Taft was much less good natured than his famous chuckle would give one to think. It was a bid for approval, and usually an effective one. What he wanted was the good opinion of those who happened to be about him at the moment.

He was self-indulgent in many ways. He hated to pull against the stream. For him the Indian Heaven where rivers ran uphill on one side and downhill on the other, so that one could always travel with the current, would have been Heaven indeed.

Taft, like many another failure in high places, was an admirable lieutenant but a poor captain. Under T.R.'s eyes and orders he was a fine public servant, very able, quick and willing to catch the tone and temper of his leader. After he became President, however, we learned to our sorrow what none of us had hitherto suspected, that his strength was not his own but T.R.'s—that, when put to the test, he would weaken. The thing he was worst at was paddling his own canoe. A fatal tendency to be swayed by the last man who talked to him was an added source of weakness, in which connection I am reminded of Senator Dolliver's apt description of him as "that ponderous and pleasant person entirely surrounded by men who know exactly what they want."

Taft's so-called judicial temperament, much lauded during his campaign, leading as it did to an insistence on limiting his defense of the public interest in terms of precedent and strictly-construed legal mandates, was one of the most important lines of demarcation between himself and Roosevelt.

The latter, as I have tried to make clear, held that under all circumstances the public good comes first. He saw himself as the active and aggressive champion of the public welfare who looked upon impartiality between right and wrong, between the people and the plunderers, as little better than treachery. Taft, on the other hand, regarded himself as an impartial judge acting under the letter of the law, without bias for or against the public interest, and curiously indifferent about the way his action affected the public welfare.

I want to be fair. Taft was a man of real intelligence, great working power, abundant physical courage, high legal attainments and immense personal charm. Weak rather than wicked, he was one of those genial men who are everything that fancy paints until a showdown comes along that demands real toughness of moral fiber.

It is no more than just to say that Taft may really have believed his general position to be right. However that may be, the stand he deliberately assumed was water on the wheel of every predatory interest seeking to gobble up natural resources or otherwise oppress the people. It made him the accomplice and the refuge of land grabbers, water-power grabbers, grabbers of timber and oil—all the swarm of big and little thieves and near-thieves, who, inside or outside of the law, were doing everything they knew to get possession of natural resources which belonged to the people and should have been conserved in the public interest.

It is certainly fair to say that, had Taft not been brought up with a round turn and forced to reverse his anti-conservation policies, as he had to do as the result of the revelations of the Pinchot-Ballinger hearings, many of the remaining natural resources on the Public Domain would have been lost to the people by the end of his four years.

Now, as to the question of Taft's relation to Roosevelt—in a letter to T.R., written soon after he became President, he said: "I can never forget that the power that I now exercise was a voluntary transfer from you to me, and that I am under obligation to you to see to it that your judgment in selecting me as your successor and bringing about the succession shall be vindicated according to the standards which you and I in conversation have always formulated."

In the political sense Taft was "made" by Roosevelt who put him in the Cabinet and was directly responsible not only for his availability as presidential candidate, but for the nomination and election. Both before and after his election, Taft pledged himself over and over again to carry out the Roosevelt policies. These were not only personal pledges to T.R. They were public pledges, publicly made to the American people.

Taft's desertion of the Conservation policies, his later support of the Payne-Aldrich tariff bill, his general swing to the right, were fundamental causes for the break between him and T.R. America was progressive minded—it is practically certain that, had Taft lived up to his progressive promises, he would have been reelected. The loss of every state outside of Vermont and Utah in 1912 is a clear indication of how the people felt.

I did not break with the President because I wanted to but because, as one of the originators of the Conservation policy, it was obviously my duty to make the fight for its protection. That fight forced me to choose between my early friendship for Taft and my public duty to the people of the United States. To that there could be only one answer.

But Going the Wrong Way

La Follette's Weekly Magazine, March 19, 1910

71. *Commissioner Ballinger*

When Jim Garfield became Secretary of the Interior (on March 5, 1907) he chose, as Commissioner of the General Land Office to succeed Governor Richards, a college mate of his at Williams, Richard Achilles Ballinger by name, a Seattle lawyer, once Mayor of that town.

Mr. Ballinger was a stocky, square-headed little man, of no inconsiderable energy and no little executive punch. In spite of being easily influenced, he had made a fairly good Mayor, as Mayors go. And like nearly all Western lawyers of his day, he believed in turning all public resources as freely and rapidly as possible over to private ownership. For the T.R. public-land policy, now firmly established, he had little or no use.

As Commissioner of the General Land Office, Ballinger became Chairman of the Public Lands Commission in place of Richards. His attitude would determine the Commission's future action on the one major subject upon which it had not yet reported—mineral lands, and especially coal.

In order to feel Ballinger out, Newell, Richards, and I held a meeting with him, and I had a separate talk with him alone. These conferences made it clear that Ballinger was against our public-land policy so far as coal lands were concerned. We were for leasing them. Ballinger was for selling them outright into private hands. It was obvious that no good could come from further meetings of the Commission; Ballinger called none; and no more meetings were held.

You will recall that Achilles, Mr. Ballinger's middle-namesake, had a vulnerable spot which became his undoing. With the Homeric hero that spot lay in his heel; with Mr. Ballinger it lay in coal—coal in the public lands of Alaska.

The incident that upset the apple cart was this. Beginning in 1902 one Clarence Cunningham had located (staked out) in his own name and in the names of dummy entrymen (afterward changed to the names of friends) a group of thirty-three coal claims of 160 acres each, or a total of 5,280 acres, in the Bering River coal field, about twenty-five miles back of Controller Bay in the Territory of Alaska.

But before the Cunningham claims were entered (recorded and paid for at the legal rate of $10 per acre) the law of 1904 was passed. Under that law each claimant had to swear that his entry was made "in good faith for his own benefit, and not directly or indirectly, in whole or in part, in behalf of any person or persons whomsoever," and that he had no intention of consolidating his claim with other claims.

The law also provided that four men could form an association and together locate four claims of a total of 640 acres. The Cunningham claimants formed no such association.

It was a poor law, for the cost of development was such that nobody could reasonably hope to work a single claim by itself and make it pay. But it was the law nevertheless. Under it the Cunningham claims were obviously fraudulent, because from the beginning the claimants had intended to consolidate. They had even located and paid for four claims which had no coal but did have timber needed to operate the rest.

In 1905, two years before Ballinger became Commissioner, the General Land Office was notified of the attempted Cunningham fraud by the special agent responsible and by letters from residents of Alaska. In 1907 the fraudulent character of these claims was recognized by the Land Office. It was common knowledge throughout the Northwest, and particularly in Seattle. That was inevitable, because large numbers of Seattle residents had invested money and filed coal claims in Alaska. The prosperity of Seattle was tied up with the development of the Territory.

Of about 900 coal claims that had been located in Alaska, perhaps a third were by people from Seattle. Out of 460 Alaska coal claimants whose addresses Special Agent Horace T. Jones had secured, 250 were residents of the State of Washington, and 164 were registered as from the City of Seattle, Mr. Ballinger's own home town.

The actual value of the Cunningham claims was estimated all the way from twenty or thirty to two or three hundred million dollars. The claimants' own expert said they contained sixty-three million tons of coal. Coal from the State of Washington delivered in Alaska was worth from $12 to $15 a ton, and poor coal at that.

The Cunningham claims were well known not only for their intrinsic and strategic value, but also because the claimants, far from being obscure Alaskan sourdoughs, were well-to-do business men, residents of Spokane, Seattle, and other towns in Washington, and of the States of Idaho and Ohio. One of them, Miles C. Moore, had been

THE STORM ON THE CONSERVATION CANAL
"TRUST IN BALLINGER HE WILL FETCH YOU THROUGH"

From The St. Paul Pioneer Press
August, 1909

Governor of Ballinger's own state. Another, like Ballinger, had been Mayor of Ballinger's own town. Another, Charles Sweeney, was publicly credited by United States Senator Piles with having made him Senator. Others were prominent politicians, "able capitalists and financiers who together controlled their party and, through it, the State." Many or most of them were Ballinger's personal friends.

Under all these circumstances, it is altogether incredible that Ballinger could have escaped knowledge of the Cunningham claims, their importance, and their fraudulent character. Unquestionably he brought that knowledge with him to Washington when he became Commissioner.

But if by some miracle he did not know what everyone else knew, the evidence was not slow in reaching him. Both in writing and by word of mouth, the new Commissioner was notified over and over again by two Special Agents of the Land Office, Horace T. Jones and Louis R. Glavis, that the claims were bad, and by another, H. K. Love, that they were doubtful. During July and August 1907, Ballinger, who had come out to Seattle, had no less than six interviews with Love or Jones or both.

The facts were already so well known to the Land Office that Ballinger's Assistant Commissioner, Fred Dennett, had written on June 21, 1907, to Jones that the Cunningham claimants "were engaged in a criminal conspiracy" and had ordered him to make "a thorough, complete, and energetic investigation" of Alaska coal claims, and to do it "to the exclusion of any other business."

On July 20, a month after Dennett wrote his "criminal conspiracy" letter, the Morgan-Guggenheim Syndicate was given an option on the Cunningham claims, and on December 7, 1907, it took up the option, which provided for the organization of a $5,000,000 corporation with $250,000 of working capital contributed by the Syndicate. The Cunningham claimants were to have half the stock.

The Alaska, or Morgan-Guggenheim, Syndicate belonged to J. P. Morgan & Co. and the Guggenheim-controlled American Smelting and Refining Co. Kuhn, Loeb & Co., H. O. Havemeyer, and other New York banking firms also had an interest in it. Behind it was one of the most powerful combinations of capital in America.

The Alaska Syndicate already owned the great copper mines at Kennecott, it controlled the only two railroads then capable of being operated in Alaska, it ran the biggest line of Alaska steamships, and it had gone into the fisheries business. A monopoly of coal, in addition, would round out and sew up the Syndicate's control of the natural wealth of the Territory.

But if the Cunningham claims should be proved to be fraudulent and therefore invalid, the whole Morgan-Guggenheim Alaska monopoly was likely to die a-borning. Very great interests were at stake.

A few days after the Morgan-Guggenheim option was signed, the "thorough, complete, and energetic investigation" Dennett had ordered Jones to make was called off. Instead Ballinger personally ordered Jones to make his investigations partial and rapid, instead of thorough and complete. Nevertheless, on August 10, Jones made a report in which he recommended a further strict investigation of each and every claim. Two days afterward he was ordered to different duty at Salt Lake City.

Within the week Clarence Cunningham reported to Daniel Guggenheim that "We understand the Commissioner of the General Land Office [Ballinger] has stated that everything will be cleared up within ninety days."

In addition to his talks with Ballinger in Seattle, Jones promptly made a second official report in which he recommended "that these entries be carefully investigated by an experienced and fearless agent," on the ground that "the disposal of the lands all tends toward one direction, and that is the Guggenheim companies."

For family reasons, Jones asked a delay in removing to Salt Lake, and he was still in Portland when, about October 1, 1907, Louis R. Glavis, a young man with large experience in coal-land cases and a firm intention to see the law enforced, was made chief of the Portland field division.

Glavis and Jones put their heads together. At the suggestion of Glavis, Jones made a third report. In it he said that "few, if any, of the applicants [claimants] were complying with the requirements of the law." This report Glavis sent on to Ballinger with his endorsement, and asked to be put in charge of the Alaska coal cases.

No reply. That worried Glavis. On November 22 he wrote again to Washington, asking to be called in for consultation. In granting his request Dennett made this curious comment: "The situation you write about is, of course, a vexed one, and we all feel it needs skillful treatment." Or was it so curious, if Dennett knew that Ballinger was trying to patent claims known to be fraudulent?

Glavis then came to Washington, saw Ballinger, and was ordered by him (as Jones had been ordered by Dennett) to make a thorough investigation and examination of all the Alaska coal cases—a matter not of days but of months.

On December 19, 1907, Glavis left Washington to make the thorough investigation Ballinger had ordered. Seven days later ex-Governor Moore saw Ballinger in the interest of the Cunningham claims. Thereupon Ballinger, although the investigation he had ordered could barely have begun, although he had been repeatedly notified by his own agents that the claims were fraudulent, directed the clear-listing of the claims.

To clear-list a claim is to order it to patent. It is the last step before turning the title over to the claimant. Ballinger's order to clear-list the Cunningham claims was his decision that the claims were not fraudulent, but legal and valid. Thus the Glavis investigation was decided by Ballinger in favor of the claimants before it began. Like the Jones investigation, Ballinger cut it off in the bud.

If Glavis had been no more than the usual political special agent, that would have settled the matter, and the Cunningham claims would have passed into Morgan-Guggenheim hands. But Glavis was something more—something entirely different. When he heard of Ballinger's action, on January 22, 1908, he wired his protest to the Commissioner, and Ballinger immediately suspended the clear-listing order. In the face of that protest, it would have been too dangerous to go ahead.

Glavis was just, and only just, in time. When his wire came, the Cunningham patents were all ready to be signed. And this was interesting, because usually the shortest time between clear-listing and patent was three months. Indeed it often ran to two or three years.

The Cunningham claims, however, suffered no such delay. Although these were the first Alaska coal patents, and although a new form had to be worked out, the Cunningham patents went through the mill in three weeks.

Ballinger not only personally ordered the claims clear-listed when the Glavis investigation he had personally ordered had hardly begun, not only rushed the patents through in a fraction of the usual time, but he also, to quote a letter from Clarence Cunningham dated January 15, 1908, furnished the claimants "with copies of all the correspondence and telegrams relating to our entries between the various special agents and also with your office."

This was in direct defiance of Land Office regulations, but it was worse than that. On that point I quote Louis D. Brandeis, who was to become one of the most distinguished of the Justices of the United States Supreme Court. At the time of his death he held the respect of the American people to a degree probably not surpassed by any other living man. His opinion of the professional conduct of any lawyer is beyond dispute.

Brandeis said: "It is hardly necessary to comment on the grave impropriety of Mr. Ballinger's communications to the Cunningham claimants. These claimants were suspected of having entered into a conspiracy to defraud the United States. The agents of the Government were trying to uncover evidence of the fraud. As in all other detective work, secrecy was important. Yet, while the special agents were at work, their Chief, Mr. Ballinger, maintained confidential relations with the suspected claimants and let them know what evidence the agents had secured and what they proposed to do. The statement of such conduct is more impressive than a denunciation of it could be."

On February 28, 1908, Commissioner Ballinger telegraphed ex-Governor Moore: "Temporary delay caused by report of field agent." His intention to hand the Cunningham claims over to the claimants remained clear as crystal, but by this time the accumulation of protests had made it unsafe. There remained, however, one other way—new legislation.

So Ballinger himself drew a bill—the Cale Bill—which would have validated the Cunningham claims, and on March 3, 1908, next to his last day in office as Commissioner, appeared to support it before the Public Lands Committee of the House. It provided, as he testified, "for the consolidation of existing entries, and does not call for proof of good faith of the original entrymen."

Cunningham himself wrote that the Cale Bill "seems all that Katalla interests [meaning the Alaska Syndicate] could possibly wish." The Cunningham claimants, Ballinger wrote Dennett on March 31, "are in hearty accord with the main features of the Cale Bill and would like to see the same enacted into a law."

Ballinger recommended also that coal claims thereafter located in Alaska should be paid for on the basis of their actual value, but that this provision should not apply to claims which had been entered before the withdrawals. The pending claims would thus be the only coal claims in Alaska to which the $10 per acre limit of the going law would apply, to the great advantage of the Morgan-Guggenheim Syndicate.

Garfield was against the Cale Bill, and it failed to pass. The Heyburn Bill, which also dealt with coal and which Garfield likewise opposed, did pass, but in a form later found to be unsatisfactory to the Cunningham claimants.

Through all this maneuvering of Ballinger's ran the persistent attempt to help his friends by patenting claims which he knew to be fraudulent. But while there might be nothing legally criminal or even personally corrupt about this, it certainly amounted to a continuous betrayal of the public interest. It was simply the working out of what Ballinger had to the nth degree, the traditional Land Office point of view. In the eyes of his precedent-ridden subordinates, therefore, he was an excellent Commissioner.

But even as part of the Roosevelt Administration, whose views he knew before he joined it, Ballinger's determination to follow the old Land Office way was anything but dead. Frustrated by Garfield's insistence on following the T.R. way—Ballinger did his disloyal best to carry his own will through, to put private interests ahead of the interests of the common people. Thus, while Garfield was away in the summer of 1907, George Woodruff found himself, as Acting Secretary, in a constant struggle to keep the Land Office practice in line with the Administration's policy.

Instead of subsiding after Garfield's return to Washington from a Western inspection trip, Ballinger's antagonism grew, and it grew so fast that before he had been in office twelve months he came to Garfield and told him that he, Ballinger, was out of sympathy with the public-land policies of the Interior Department, which were, of course, T.R.'s. For that reason he proposed to resign.

Garfield agreed that he should resign, and so Ballinger went out of office on March 4, 1908, after serving just a year under a President to whose fundamental land policies he was, by his own statement, so much opposed that he could not work under them. It was a fitting introduction to what followed.

Although Garfield understood, it should be noted here that T.R. had been in complete ignorance of Ballinger's position in public-land matters and was still unaware of it when, expressing his regret that

Ballinger was leaving the public service, he said: "I thank you heartily for the admirable work you have done." History is full of similar misunderstandings.

72. *Attorney Ballinger*

Immediately after his resignation Ballinger went back to Seattle, and promptly became attorney for the Cunningham claimants, whose claims he had tried his best as Commissioner to hand over, fraud or no fraud. And not only for them, but also for members of at least four of the most powerful groups of coal locators in Alaska. In addition he incorporated two Alaska coal companies; he represented clients in prosecuting against the Government land claims, timber and stone claims, and water-power claims; and he worked and overworked his influence with Dennett, his former subordinate and now his successor, in favor of a variety of claimants.

On March 6, 1908, two days after Ballinger's resignation, Glavis and Jones saw and copied Clarence Cunningham's journal, which disclosed in the entry of February 1, 1903, that after title was secured "each subscriber [claimant] agrees to deed his interest to a company to be formed for the purpose of developing and marketing said coal, and receive stock in said company in payment for the same." Practically all the other claimants corroborated Cunningham's journal. And, furthermore, the accounts obtained from Cunningham by Glavis and Jones showed that from the date of filing all entrymen were assessed equally, and that the claims were developed as a unit.

On the same day (February 1, 1903) Cunningham had made an affidavit which declared: "We have an understanding that when the patents had been secured we would form a company for the development of the coal fields. . . . We have always proceeded with this end in view. . . ."

That was proof enough that each claimant was not making his entry "in good faith for his own benefit, and not directly or indirectly, in whole or in part, in behalf of any person or persons whatsoever" as the law required.

Taken in connection with the Morgan-Guggenheim option, this affidavit of Cunningham's clearly admitted the fraud. It had to be disposed of. Accordingly Ballinger personally drew another Cunningham affidavit, intended to show the good faith of the claimants. In it Cunningham swore that he knew "of no individual entryman in said group of entries that has any contractual obligation of any nature whatsoever with the Guggenheim syndicate, or any other syndicate or corporation whatsoever."

As attorney for the claimants, Ballinger knew about the Morgan-Guggenheim option, and he knew this statement to be false. Nevertheless, he himself made a trip from Seattle, for which he was paid by the claimants, and put the affidavit before Dennett in Washington and Jim Garfield in Mentor, Ohio. Garfield, of course, turned him down.

Section 190, United States Revised Statutes, forbade any person who had been an officer, clerk, or employee in any of the Departments to act as "counsel, attorney, or agent for prosecuting any claim against the United States which was pending" while he was in office, "nor in any manner nor by any means, to aid in the prosecution of any such claims," within two years after his separation from the service.

Although it had been interpreted by Secretary Lamar, afterward a Justice of the United States Supreme Court, to cover all cases, including land claims, and by Secretary Hoke Smith not to include land claims, the intention of the statute is perfectly clear. To use against the Government connections made and confidential information acquired as a Government official is a betrayal of the public interest and morally indefensible.

What Ballinger was willing to do for the influential Cunningham claimants he was not willing to do in a less important case. After his resignation as Commissioner he became attorney for a man named Bales in the matter of an entry in the Siletz country in Oregon. On November 4, 1908, Assistant Secretary Pierce called his attention to Section 190 and to a Department circular of July 15, 1901, to the same effect. Thereupon, from the Bales case, and from that case only, Ballinger immediately withdrew.

Of Ballinger's conduct in accepting employment from the Cunningham claimants immediately after he left the Government service, in drawing the perjured affidavit of September 4, and in using his personal influence to get that affidavit accepted by Garfield and Dennett, Brandeis said this:

"Mr. Ballinger's conduct in acting as attorney for the Cunningham claimants was absolutely improper and must meet with the condemnation of every lawyer. This is the kind of thing for which attorneys in practice are and always have been disbarred."

Ballinger had been out of office just a year when on March 4, 1909, he was appointed by Taft to succeed Garfield as Secretary of the Interior. What led Taft to make the appointment I cannot definitely say. The common explanation was that Hitchcock, Taft's campaign manager, had promised to certain large Western interests a Secretary of the Interior with his sting drawn, and so Ballinger was produced out of their hat.

If Taft had reappointed Garfield, the Ballinger scandal would never have shown its ugly head. Why then was Garfield not continued in the Cabinet, as were Wilson and Meyer? Taft's own explanation was that he knew Garfield—the very reason why Garfield should have been retained.

A different explanation came from D. A. McKenzie of Seattle, an Alaska coal claimant, while he was making an affidavit before Special Agents Horace T. Jones and L. R. Glavis at Seattle in June 1909. In a joint statement the two Special Agents certified that: "During his statement he [McKenzie] said: 'Now, this is confidential and I don't want it to go down in the affidavit.' He then said in substance that when he was in Washington endeavoring to get legislation by Congress to enable the Alaska coal claimants to secure title to their lands that he on several occasions conferred with Mr. James R. Garfield, then Secretary of the Interior; that Mr. Garfield's demeanor toward these Alaska cases was such that they brought pressure to bear on Senators and Representatives to prevent his remaining in the Cabinet. Mr. McKenzie also stated that Mr. Garfield's attitude toward the Alaska coal cases was the real reason for his not being in Mr. Taft's Cabinet; that the Alaska coal claimants wanted somebody as Secretary of the Interior who recognized the needs of Alaska."

McKenzie's statement, said Jones and Glavis, "is very fresh in our minds, for the reason that we both thought of it a number of times, because it impressed us very much, as we commented at the time that if the Alaska coal claimants had sufficient influence to remove a Cabinet officer, that we would be removed from office whenever they desired, if our reports did not suit."

Two days later McKenzie brought S. W. Eccles, of the Guggenheim Syndicate, to see Jones and Glavis, who reported that: "During the interview Mr. Eccles stated that the railroad to the Alaska coal fields would cost them about $2,500,000; that they were prepared to build this railroad, but would not do so until the Government passed on the titles to the coal lands; that unless the claims were patented they would not build the railroad, and that this coal was very necessary for the operation of their Copper River Railroad and the proposed smelter."

Whether or not Taft was aware that he was appointing the lawyer for the Cunningham claimants, and for other claimants against the Government, when he made Ballinger Secretary of the Interior, I do not know. Nor do I know how much Taft knew about Ballinger's hostility to Conservation. In any case his personal pledge to protect T.R.'s outstanding policy should have made him raise that momentous question.

The Conservation movement had grown from a series of disjointed efforts into the most vital single public question before the American people. It had been planted and watered, and was just ready to blossom and bear fruit. But it was still too young to be safe.

That was why Taft's attitude was so vital. That was why any attack by Ballinger on the T.R. Conservation policy, if and when it came, would have to be met head on. It did come, it was met, and it was stopped in its tracks. But reputations not a few, even the presidency itself, were lost in the struggle.

The split between the T.R. policies according to T.R. and the T.R. policies according to Taft began to show itself in practical form immediately after the latter's inauguration.

On March 6, Governor Pardee of California, one of the pillars of the Conservation movement, and W. K. Kavanaugh of St. Louis, President of the Lakes-to-the-Gulf Deep Waterway Association, called on Mr. Taft to discuss the Tawney Amendment and urge him to continue the National Conservation Commission in spite of it. No luck.

The Tawney Amendment, as may be recalled, forbade the President to appoint any Commission without authority from Congress. T.R. had notified Congress that if he had continued in office he would have refused to obey it.

As Chairman of the National Conservation Commission, I also had a duty in the premises. Two days later I went to see the new President at the White House and asked him to let the Commission go ahead with its work in spite of the Tawney Amendment. I had no better luck.

Next day I tried again, with exactly the same result. So I had to notify the members of the Conservation Commission, and several other T.R. Commissions, that there was nothing further for them to do at present. The Joint Conservation Commission, appointed by the Joint Conference in December, would have to carry on the work, so far as it was able.

Taft did undertake to ask Congress to continue and support the National Conservation Commission. But nothing ever came of it, as was to be expected, and the "fundamentally important" work of the Commission was allowed to die.

Another of the T.R. plans, this time of world-wide consequence, was allowed to die also. Thirty nations had promptly accepted T.R.'s invitation to meet in conference at The Hague and prepare for an inventory of the natural resources of the earth. Only five nations, all of them small, had declined.

The thirty nations which accepted controlled among them by far the greater part of the world's forests, waters, lands, and minerals. Nevertheless Taft killed the plan, and no such conference was held. If the conference had been held, and if it had been followed up, as we intended, by further conferences to work out and assure to each of the nations fair access to raw materials in accordance with its needs, I for one am persuaded that the first World War might never have taken place, and that the dreadful cost of the second World War could have been avoided.

In the face of the threatening situation which Taft's attitude forced us to look in the eye, there was one perfectly obvious thing to do. We who believed in them must call public attention to Conservation and the Forest Service at every possible opportunity.

I had already addressed the Legislature of Pennsylvania, at its invitation, on February 3, 1909, and laid the Conservation question before it. But that was only a beginning.

Right after seeing the President I left Washington, spoke to the Legislature of New Mexico, in Colorado debated the National Forest question before a crowded meeting with State Senator (afterwards Governor) Ammons, and made a score of other talks.

The Conservation issue was so much in the public mind that they ran excursion trains to the meeting at Delta, and my Denver talk was published at length in the Boston *Herald*. After that I spoke in the Mormon Temple in Ogden, Utah, and on March 29 addressed the Legislature of Iowa.

Then more talks, and on April 4 an interview with Taft, at which he authorized me to say for publication that the President "is in entire sympathy with the forest policy, and the Conservation policy, and stands behind them."

Then a lot more talks, including one to the Rhode Island Legislature, two more interviews with the President, conferences in New York and Cleveland, and one more talk in New Orleans. After that I went fishing.

73. *Secretary Ballinger*

It was, as we have seen, his personal hostility to the T.R. land policies that had led Ballinger to resign as Commissioner of the Land Office. But now, as head of the Department of the Interior, the door was wide open for him to put his own policies into effect.

The new Secretary was hardly warm in his seat before he moved against Conservation on several fronts. He continued, directly and through subordinates, his effort to turn the Cunningham claims over to the Morgan-Guggenheim outfit. And he undertook to reverse several of T.R.'s most important natural resource policies.

Ballinger's opening attack was against the T.R. plan of saving the water-power sites on public lands for the people, and from the grabbers. T.R. himself, in his veto of the James River Dam Bill, January 15, 1909, warned the whole nation that "the great corporations are acting with foresight, singleness of purpose, and vigor to control the water powers of the country."

Prompt action was obviously imperative. There was no time to make detailed surveys. Without them, the only safe plan was to make sure that the withdrawals were large enough to cover the power sites. Accordingly Newell selected and Garfield withdrew from all forms of entry some 3,928,780 acres along the courses of sixteen rivers in seven Western states, the last on March 2, 1909, two days before the end of his term.

These withdrawals were necessary not alone to check the growing water-power monopoly. They were necessary also, and necessary at once, as a part of our effort to protect the natural resources of the Nation after we came to fear that Taft could not be trusted to protect them himself.

Ballinger, acting on the Taft theory that he must have specific authority of law for everything he did, and in accordance also with his fixed desire to turn all public resources over to private ownership, decided to decide that the water-power withdrawals were unjustified. He sent for Director Newell and Chief Engineer A. P. Davis of the Reclamation Service, told them that the withdrawals were illegal, and acted, as Davis testified, "as though a great crime had been committed in making the withdrawals." And although he had abundant authority to act on his own motion, he ordered them to recommend that the withdrawals be canceled and the lands restored to private entry.

Newell and Davis protested by word of mouth against this assault on the public interest. When that brought no result they protested also in writing, and Davis even submitted a brief. Finally, however, they were obliged to yield, and the first restorations of lands withdrawn to prevent the gobbling and cold storage of water-power sites were made on March 30, 1909.

Between March 30 and April 16 all the power sites on fourteen large tracts of public land were restored to entry. When I got back to Washington, early in April, I learned what was going on. Garfield and I talked it all over. Here was the confirmation of our fears.

So on April 19 and again on the twentieth I saw the President, pointed out the danger to the public interest, and protested as vigorously as I knew how against Ballinger's action. To his honor be it said, Taft promised to see Ballinger, did so on April 23, and directed that such of the lands as were actually valuable for water-power purposes should be withdrawn again. I was, of course, profoundly pleased.

On May 4 the rewithdrawals began. The second withdrawals covered much less acreage than the first, which were intentionally generous where surveys were lacking, in order to be sure to cover the necessary ground.

No question of legality was raised. The second power withdrawals were made under precisely the same authority that Ballinger had denied before. And so the power sites were saved.

Shortly before he became Secretary, Ballinger had declared, in a newspaper interview in Seattle, that "Reclamation is a phase of our national development which is commanding more and more attention —one of the big things in fact. There is nothing that the Government has undertaken which has accomplished so much good in so short a time."

All of that good had been accomplished under Newell's direction. The Reclamation Service had twenty-seven projects under way, upon which it had spent, honestly and effectively, some fifty million dollars.

Nevertheless, reclamation also was in danger. Moved in part, I imagine, by the opposition of Newell and Davis to his water-power restorations, and in part perhaps by the rewithdrawals, Ballinger was openly hostile to the Reclamation Service, T.R.'s first great achievement for the protection and development of natural resources, and to Newell in particular. For Newell, of course, vigorously supported T.R.'s point of view.

The news began to spread that Newell was doomed. And Ballinger in fact did his best to force out Newell, who had T.R.'s confidence in the highest degree, and put a Seattle politician in his place.

Ballinger refused to let Newell dismiss a man who was taking graft from certain railroads; on the same old false plea of illegality (with the assistance of Attorney General Wickersham) he prevented settlers who had taken up land under a reclamation project from paying for it with work instead of with dollars; and he made his bias against the Service so clear that some of its engineers resigned, and others considered resigning in a body, in protest.

Already in April I had protested to the President against Ballinger's hostility to the Reclamation Service, and he had assured me that the Service would be protected. And so, for whatever reason, Newell was retained.

This again was water on the wheel of my desire. I was eager, of course, to believe that after all we might have been mistaken about Taft, still eager to give him the benefit of every doubt.

Soon after Ballinger became Secretary, several hundred applications for Forest Ranger stations were pending—requests from Secretary Wilson for setting aside a hundred or two hundred acres in a place where a Ranger's cabin and fences could be built, and where a Ranger could live and pasture his horses. To do his work the Ranger must live near it. That is why Ranger stations were and are indispensable. But National Forest lands are subject to mineral entry, so that unless it is withdrawn, any land on which Ranger stations had been established might be located, patented, and lost to the Forest Service, with all its improvements.

A certain number of Ranger stations were applied for which were needed less for Rangers than to give the Government a temporary hold on some power site and prevent the power octopus from sucking it in. I took special steps to learn where such withdrawals should be made, and I have no apology whatever to offer. These Ranger stations, I repeat, were withdrawn again as power sites before T.R. went out of office.

Requests for Ranger station withdrawals had always been granted by previous Secretaries of the Interior. Secretary Ballinger, however, discovered certain legal reasons why they could not be withdrawn. In three letters written on April 13 he not only refused to withdraw them, but demanded of Secretary Wilson that applications for Ranger stations outside National Forests should be accompanied by a statement "showing clearly the necessity for the appropriation of the lands proposed to be withdrawn for the purpose indicated, the quantity of land required, and that it is unoccupied, and non-mineral."

That demand not only was unprecedented, but also, as between members of the same Cabinet, it amounted to a slap in the face.

Another Ballinger attack on Conservation in which the Forest Service was concerned had to do with forests on Indian Reservations. Of all the Government bureaus in Washington the Indian Office was unquestionably the worst. For years it had been rotten with politics; the Indian Agents in the field were, for the most part, men of low grade, often dishonest; and the execution of its work was hampered and held up by more complicated provisions of law, and rules and regulations under them, than afflicted any other Government organization.

There were on Indian Reservations about 12,000,000 acres of forest containing timber worth in the neighborhood of $75,000,000. No one in the Indian Office or on the ground was capable of handling these forests. The result was what you might expect.

The Indians were being cheated right and left by contracts unduly favorable to the purchasers of Indian timber; by the failure of Indian Agents to enforce such contracts as they had; by the complete absence of provisions for reforestation; by the waste of timber that had been cut; and by the sale of timber which should not have been cut. I remember that one Indian Agent sold for lumber the sugar bush upon which his Indians depended for their maple sugar. And there was no organization for forest fire control.

Indian Commissioner Francis E. Leupp and his secretary, R. G. Valentine, were both excellent men, doing their best under an impossible legal setup. We three put our heads together, and on January 22, 1908, after full consideration of its legality, a co-operative agreement was signed by the Secretaries of Agriculture and the Interior which provided for the management and protection of forests on Indian Reservations by the skilled men of the Forest Service, the cost to be paid from Indian Office appropriations.

The agreement was in complete accord with T.R.'s often expressed desire for the fullest co-operation between the two Departments, and was fully approved by him. It continued in effect for a year and a half. During that time the Forest Service conducted what was probably the largest single lumbering operation in America up to that time (170 million feet), organized systematic cutting under the principles of Forestry on thirteen reservations, established fire control on six reservations, and conducted studies to determine the best possible use of the lands on eleven reservations. At one time on a single operation we had 900 men busy piling brush for burning.

In those eighteen months we saved large sums of money to the Indians, gave many of them profitable employment, and by the introduction of Forestry promised to make that employment permanent.

The co-operative agreement worked admirably so long as Garfield was in office. After Ballinger came in we began to have trouble, and in July 1909, it was abrogated by the Interior Department on the same old plea of illegality, although its own auditor had approved the accounts, thereby certifying that the agreement was legal.

It was a pity. The Forest Service had done a job of which it had no reason to be ashamed, and the Indians' forests, for the first time, were being handled not for the profit of political contractors, but for the lasting benefit of the Indians and all the rest of us.

One trouble with Ballinger was that he did not wait for the courts to declare illegal any action, such as the power-site withdrawals, which was plainly in the public interest, but did it himself, off his own bat, when nothing but good would have come from letting the sleeping dog lie.

In all these attacks on the Conservation policy, Ballinger was butting his nose against stubborn facts, like a polliwog in a bottle. Yet wrong as he was, he had the power, and therefore he was dangerous.

On the other hand, Taft's sound and prompt action in the vital matters of water power and reclamation was greatly to his credit. It cheered me up immensely. From the first I had balanced my fear that Taft had gone wrong against my fervent hope that he would prove he hadn't.

At that time we T.R. men were all doing our best to hope for the best and making for Taft every excuse that we could. And for a while I thought I had solid reason for my hope. As I look back, however, it seems inconceivable that Ballinger could have acted in such open hostility to the T.R. Conservation policy without first getting the consent of his chief, who was so fully committed to it.

74. *The Rift*

Taft's wise action in requiring at least a part of the water-power sites to be rewithdrawn was widely and wishfully accepted as public notice that he was still on the T.R. track. Before the first of May, nevertheless, the question of whether or not he would carry on the T.R. Conservation policies was being openly discussed in the newspapers, and there was real public concern about it. This was the more remarkable because the tendency of the people to think well of every new administration, unless and until it has proved itself unworthy, is one of the salient facts in our democracy.

And so definite were Taft's pledges, and so strong the general belief that he would stand by the Conservation policy, that many newspapers reported the conflict as between the President and his Secretary of the Interior.

On April 28 the Des Moines *Register and Leader's* headlines said "Taft May Remove Secy. Ballinger. Latter's Reversal of Conservation Policy Cause." "Pres. Taft and Ballinger in a Serious Clash," said the Detroit *News*. "Taft for Conservation," said the Boston *Transcript* on April 29, and continued with an explanation which might have come straight from the President himself:

"President Taft is unwilling that the law shall be strained or that the members of his Administration shall exceed their constitutional

THE BLAZED TRAIL

and statutory powers in the effort to prevent the monopolization of water-power sites. It is this consistent determination to act solely within the law which has given rise to the impression that the Administration is hostile to the conservation policy."

"Taft Calls Ballinger Down," said the Tacoma *Times* at the head of a Washington dispatch. The Seattle *Times* saw the matter otherwise: "Mr. Ballinger to Enforce the Law. No Foundation for Story that Cabinet Member Has Difference with President."

The best and most enlightening press statement of the change in policy was made by Gilson Gardner of the Newspaper Enterprise Association, one of the ablest correspondents in Washington. The copy I have is from the Berkeley, California, *Independent* under date of May 4, 1909:

"The original disagreement took place when Mr. Ballinger was commissioner of the land office and Garfield was secretary of the interior. Mr. Ballinger claimed that there was no authority in law for the action taken by President Roosevelt and Secretary Garfield, in the withdrawal of public lands valuable for power-site purposes, and for other reasons.

"President Roosevelt said he would take a chance on the law. So he withdrew the lands and asked Congress for a law to govern their ultimate disposition.

"Congress failed to act.

"It is a habit which Congress has.

"Under Roosevelt's policies lands were withdrawn and examined afterwards.

"Under the present policies such lands are restored and an examination ordered.

"Under the previous administration the public wealth was put beyond the reach of predatory interests pending legislation at the hands of congress.

"Under the present administration the public wealth is restored to the reach of the predatory interests, pending legislation at the hands of Congress.

"Under the previous administration any doubt as to the power of the chief executive to make withdrawals of public lands was resolved in favor of the people.

"Under the present administration any doubt as to the right of the president of the United States to make executive orders withdrawing public lands, is resolved in favor of the doubt—that is in favor of the predatory interests.

"The previous administration had a high regard for the public's interests in seeing that the public domain be conserved.

"The present administration has a high regard for the technicalities of law.

"The previous administration was bitterly condemned by railroad corporations, corporate land thieves, and members of congress who represented interests of this character.

"The present administration is cordially endorsed by these same people."

By this time the Administration's attitude toward Conservation was becoming first-page news from California to New York. Said the Meriden, Connecticut, *Journal:*

"Probably for the first time since the Civil War the cabinet at its meeting today listened to a discussion of serious differences of opinion between two of its members. The President's official family sat practically as a court. It was really the Roosevelt policy of Conservation that was on trial."

In the face of much damaging publicity, more and more Republican papers made headline news of the President's intention to carry out his predecessor's policies. "Taft Promotes Roosevelt Idea," said the headlines of the St. Louis *Times.* "Makes Conservation One of Taft's Issues," said the Chicago *Post.* "Taft to the Rescue," said the Washington *Times.*

As the summer came on, the fight about Conservation was reported more and more as a quarrel between Ballinger and Pinchot. Headlines in the Salt Lake *Herald,* for example, declared "Forest Service Rule in Doubt"; in the Denver *Times* "Pinchot Gets Slap from Ballinger"; in the Cheyenne *Leader* "To Curtail Mr. Pinchot. No More Wyoming Lands Under His Power." There was so much of it that on July 13 Ballinger gave an interview quoted in the Seattle *Post-Intelligencer* as follows:

"The idea seems to have gone forth that I have clashed with Secretary of Agriculture Wilson over the forest reserves, but such is not the case. I have no quarrel with Secretary Wilson. My views and those of Gifford Pinchot, head of the forestry bureau, which is a part of the department of agriculture, diverged in the matter of forest reserves. I maintained that the law should be enforced and it is now up to the attorney general for a decision.

"The department of the interior has charge of all public lands and does not intend that the forestry bureau, a part of another department, shall run the department of the interior."

Which pronouncement, as you may well imagine, did nothing to quiet the quarrel. From then on the Ballinger-Pinchot issue made many a headline. "Ballinger on Scene to Stay," said the Seattle *Times,* and the Oakland, California, *Inquirer* editorially demanded that Ballinger should resign. The St. Paul *Pioneer Press* said that Ballinger's "retention in office, after his real attitude toward forestry, irrigation, and other matters on that program has become evident, has done not a little to weaken the present administration in the confidence of a great many who were inclined to give it loyal support." "Conservation of natural resources is an unwieldy phrase but a live wire," said *Collier's Weekly,* and told the truth.

Obviously the newspapers and their readers were fully alive to the Conservation situation, which was given weight and point by the more immediate and personal question to which it led: Had Taft gone back on T.R.?

Would Taft carry out the T.R. policies on the level, or would he carry them out on the traditional shutter? Had he gone over to the Old Guard? How about the reactionary Payne-Aldrich Tariff Bill? How serious was Taft's split with the Insurgents in Congress, and other friends of T.R.? What was the trouble between Ballinger and Pinchot? Was Conservation really in danger? All these questions and many others like them were being widely and constantly discussed all over the shop.

Ballinger and I were to speak before the National Irrigation Congress at Spokane early in August. The issue between us had become nationwide. Both of us were very much in the limelight, and both were on guard.

Mine was only a ten-minute speech, but I think it went to the heart of the matter. It began by asserting that the purpose of the Conservation movement is to make our country a permanent and prosperous home for ourselves and for our children, and for our children's children.

Nobody could quarrel with that, but the next paragraph threw down the gauntlet: "An institution or a law is a means, not an end, a means to be used for the public good, to be modified for the public good, and to be interpreted for the public good."

A generation later Harlan F. Stone, Chief Justice of the United States, said this at the Harvard Tercentenary celebration:

"We are coming to realize that law is not an end but a means to an end and that end is to be attained through reasonable accommodation of law to changing economic and social needs."

My talk went on: "Strict construction necessarily favors the great interests as against the people, and in the long run cannot do otherwise. Wise execution of the law must consider what the law ought to accomplish for the general good."

That was reasonably straight talk, considering the issue between Ballinger and me, but there was more to come: "The great oppressive trusts exist because of subservient lawmakers and adroit legal constructions. Here is the central stronghold of the money power in the everlasting conflict of the few to grab, and the many to win or keep, the rights they were born with. The people, not the law, should have the benefit of every doubt."

Every man at the Irrigation Congress knew that Ballinger had been charged with practicing the very opposite.

The final clause left small doubt of my position:

"I stand for the Roosevelt policies because they set the common good of all of us above the private gain of some of us; because they recognize the livelihood of the small man as more important to the Nation than the benefit of the big man; because they oppose all useless waste at present at the cost of robbing the future; because they demand the complete, sane, and orderly development of all our natural resources, not forgetting our rivers; because they insist on equality of opportunity and denounce monopoly and special privilege; because discarding false issues, they deal directly with the vital questions that really make a difference with the welfare of all of us—and most of all, because in them the plain American always and everywhere holds the first place. And I propose to stand for them while I have the strength to stand for anything."

It was not a bad speech, if I do say it. Anyhow it was my own speech. I wrote it myself.

You may find it a little difficult, at this distance of time and circumstance, to realize why my talk at Spokane should have made the first page all over the United States. The reason lay neither in

Ballinger nor in Pinchot, but in the fact that Taft was on trial before the jury of the people as to whether or not the T.R. policies were safe in his hands.

Ballinger's reply was awaited by the meeting with almost breathless interest. But when it came it was no reply at all. It was only a typical, colorless, Secretary of the Interior routine dissertation on public-land matters, and would have been just as pat to the moment if the conflict between us had never been born.

As to the present issue, there was nothing more direct than this: "The Nation is, therefore, to be congratulated that, even if not seasonably undertaken, we have now entered upon a period of rational protection and of saving of its resources in the Public Domain. You may be assured, my fellow-citizens, that all the energies of the Government will be put forward to make effective the means necessary to accomplish this result."

As soon as he had delivered his banalities, Ballinger went out of the hall, and thereby escaped many a question. In his absence, ex-Governor George C. Pardee of California, one of the ablest, most fearless, and most useful public servants of his generation, a strong defender of the T.R. Conservation policy, rose to reply. He minced no words.

"Is it not about time," said Pardee, "that the plain, ordinary, everyday, God-fearing, law-abiding, patriotic people of this country should receive some little attention in the disposal of these things [water powers]? And is it not time that if, by any possibility, there can be any doubt, that doubt should be resolved once in a while to the benefit of the people of the country?"

Roosevelt, Pardee went on, never hesitated under those circumstances. His motto was "Go, do it, and talk about it afterward."

On which side the National Irrigation Congress stood its resolutions left no doubt. "We approve," it declared, "of the honest, intelligent, and efficient manner in which the work of the Forest Service and Reclamation Service has been carried on, and we are convinced that the work of these bureaus has been to the interests of the small landowner and settler."

That was good, for it was being freely predicted that both Newell and I were on the way out.

75. *After Spokane*

The controversy at Spokane had its repercussions across the continent. Said the Boston *Christian Science Monitor* on August 13: "Gifford Pinchot, chief of the forestry bureau, has opened one of the liveliest public questions of the day through his speech at the national irrigation congress at Spokane. President Taft will have no more important question facing him next winter."

The Washington *Post* of August 14 announced "Pinchot-Ballinger War Likely to Reach Congress," and asserted that the issue "precipitated by the forester's defiant speech at Spokane is squarely joined between the Roosevelt policies of conservation and the strict construction methods of Secretary Ballinger."

"Official Washington," said a dispatch in the Seattle *Times* of the same date, "is stirred by the Pinchot-Ballinger controversy as it has not been since the 'embalmed beef' scandal," which dated back to the Spanish War.

Obviously the T.R. Conservation policy generally was in for a tough fight, and so was the Forest Service. It was my business to defend them both. One way to do that was to continue speaking as often and as widely as possible. So after Spokane came a series of talks in which I discussed and explained Conservation, but carefully avoided any reference to Ballinger.

At Denver I said to the Trans-Mississippi Commercial Congress that the Conservation movement, more than any other movement of our time, promotes business stability. "Its object is so to handle the great natural resources upon which the prosperity of all business rests that steady supplies of raw materials may be continuously available to meet the needs of trade."

And I added: "The Forest Service is a public servant—your servant in the work of preserving our forests. It asks, I think it deserves, and I know it desires and expects, your admonition, counsel, and assistance in the work the American people have given it to do."

Then to the Black Hills, where the big sheepmen were of opinion that the routine thing to do with small men and settlers was to run over them and drive them out. Next, a talk to the Missoula Chamber of Commerce, and an inspection of the District Office, and after that to the First National Conservation Congress, held during the Alaska-Yukon-Pacific Exposition in Seattle.

From Connecticut to California and from Canada to Carolina came a distinguished list of delegates who made that Congress national in fact as well as in name. To it the President sent a characteristically strict-constructionist message. Said he:

"You can count upon the earnest support of this Administration of the policy of conservation of natural resources by every reasonable means properly within the Federal Executive jurisdiction, and such recommendations to Congress as may be best adapted to secure useful legislation toward the same end." Which was right down Ballinger's alley.

To the Congress I repeated what I said at Spokane and Denver, that we may congratulate ourselves that "the author of these Roosevelt policies which are summed up in Conservation has for his successor another great President whose Administration is most solemnly pledged to support them."

"Solemnly pledged to support them." Everywhere I went that was the burden of my song.

At the end of the National Conservation Congress Ballinger arrived and spoke briefly. He commended the purpose of the Congress, endorsed the President's telegram, and said that he would "prefer that my acts in connection with my official conduct shall speak rather than my words." Frank Heney, who was present, took him up. "I am glad also to assure Secretary Ballinger that we intend to judge him by his acts and not by his declarations."

To the members of the Congress Heney added this: "I say to you that your children and your children's children will have the right to denounce you as a set of fools who knew nothing about self-government or the preservation or conservation of equal opportunities if you permit that [the monopoly of water power] to happen."

That was right down my alley, and I came in behind Frank. "Mr. Heney is absolutely right when he says that this water-power problem is the largest problem that confronts any body of people interested in Conservation right now. There is nothing else that begins to compare with it, because in no other possible way can a few men achieve such control over a whole body of men as by owning the one great stable source of power."

In its resolutions the Conservation Congress, like many another body that summer, vigorously supported the Forest and Reclamation Services, but its strongest emphasis was on the danger of monopoly: "We hold that all natural resources belong primarily to the whole people and should not be alienated by municipal, state, or national grants or franchises to individuals or corporations except for a limited period."

The Congress voted down unanimously and vociferously a resolution to turn minerals, timber, and water power over to private ownership, and generally took my side against Ballinger. It was worth something to get such support in Ballinger's own home town.

And there was more to come. Also at Seattle, according to the Washington *Star:* "Mr. Pinchot met the members of the Pacific Coast Lumber Association for the first time, and was the subject of eulogy by every speaker. The change in public sentiment concerning the forest reserve system and the general conservation policy of the administration in this section is one of the most remarkable that ever occurred in the history of any country. Gifford Pinchot is today the most popular member of the administration in this part of the country. As the Secretary of the Pacific Coast Lumber Association remarked, 'He can have anything he wants.'"

Secretary Wilson's part in this remarkable change in public sentiment should not be overlooked. He made an inspection trip that summer through a number of the Western National Forests, and wherever he went he made friends. It is also worth noting that a committee representing the railroads, of which A. S. Baldwin, chief engineer of the Illinois Central, was Chairman, was appointed to co-operate with the Forest Service in advancing the Conservation movement.

As I told a San Francisco *Bulletin* reporter, "the growth of the conservation feeling among the Western people during the last year has been very remarkable. I believe that the West is now more actively in favor of conservation than the East."

On September 6 I wrote my Mother, who had a natural interest in the future of her son:

"Really, I seem to be getting to be a person. People are most kind. At San Diego just now I was met at the train by Lyman Gage, John Spreckels, Colonel S. S. McClure, E. W. Scripps [second largest owner of newspapers in the United States], the Mayor, and a lot more."

(For your information, since a whole generation has gone by, Lyman Gage was Secretary of the Treasury under two Presidents, Spreckels one of the big sugar family, and Sam McClure head of the McClure Newspaper Syndicate and *McClure's Magazine.*)

My letter went on: "I don't quite see how anyone can touch the Service or me, and strength with the people generally seems to grow by leaps and bounds. So I don't think I am the one to walk the floor."

Which would go to show either that I was trying to promote my Mother's peace of mind, or that I had a whole lot still to learn about Bill Taft and the power of Big Money in government. Take your choice.

I would not have you imagine that this Western trip was devoted solely to counteracting Ballinger. This was also one of my regular Forest Service inspection trips. At Spokane, Seattle, Portland, San Francisco, Santa Barbara, Los Angeles, San Diego there were Forest Service offices to be looked over, problems to be discussed, personnel to be talked to and with, and not seldom difficulties to be ironed out.

The change in Western public opinion concerning Forestry was well illustrated by William E. Smythe (incidentally a personal friend of mine) in the *Western Empire* of Los Angeles, who pointed out that three years before, when I spoke in San Diego, about twenty-five citizens came to the meeting, whereas this year, at a few hours' notice, the biggest theater "was filled with a large and brilliant audience, and the appearance of the Forester upon the platform was greeted by loud and long-continued applause."

In quoting descriptions of the highly significant change of public sentiment in the West, I have included certain friendly or over-friendly references to myself. That is because some such references are necessary for a true picture of the extent of that change, and because they applied to me only as a representative of certain definite policies and purposes.

Yet throughout this Western trip the comments of the friendly papers, and that was most of them, on G. Pinchot were so very friendly that I decline to copy any more of them. As usual I was being given credit that rightly belonged to others. It was the Forest Service that deserved the praise, and sometimes it was given its due.

Thus George H. Maxwell's *Talisman,* the organ of the irrigation movement, in that October's issue, called attention to the small National Forest loss from fires in a disastrous fire season and had this to say of the Service:

"The reliability of the Forest Service is rooted in its personnel and in its *esprit de corps.* This service is recruited from the flower of our young American manhood. It is an army of peace engaged in saving the nation's forests. The young foresters of the service are fired by a zeal that matches the old-time ardor of war, and that is on an infinitely higher plane."

The Forest Service had never stood so well with lumbermen, irrigators, miners, stockmen, and the public generally as it did that summer.

76. *The Clean Bill of Health*

The story I have been trying to tell about Ballinger's attack against the Conservation policy after he became Secretary of the Interior has had, up to this point, but little to do with Ballinger's Achilles heel. So now let's get back to the Alaska coal claims.

Ballinger's first action as Secretary bearing on the claims was an order, promptly given, to expedite all Alaska cases. That done, he announced that having been counsel for the Cunningham claimants, he would have nothing to do with Alaska matters. "But when he accepted the office," as Brandeis well said, "he became responsible to the people for the administration of a great trust, and he could not properly delegate the responsibility to a subordinate.

"What an amazing ethical distinction it was that Mr. Ballinger drew! When he left the Government service, he thought it right to use against the Government on behalf of his private clients the knowledge and influence he had acquired while in the Government's employ; but, when he returned to the Government service, he thought it wrong to use his knowledge on behalf of the Government and against his former clients."

With the position held by Brandeis ex-Governor Moore did not agree. In a letter to Ballinger he expressed his chagrin:

"We had all felt that when you were named to the position of

Secretary of the Interior, with your full and complete knowledge and your sense of justice, that our long-delayed patents would be forthcoming." And he added, "This letter is not intended for your official files but simply to express the feeling of disappointment felt by myself and many of your former friends."

But in spite of Ballinger's alleged aloofness, within a week after the new Secretary took office Dennett ordered Glavis by wire to "submit at once complete reports on present status investigation within sixty days"—which, in view of their location and extent, was obviously impossible. Other hurry-up orders followed these first two.

A little later Glavis came again to Washington and asked Ballinger to get from the Attorney General a legal interpretation of the Heyburn Bill as affecting the claims. Ballinger promised to do so. Within three days Edward C. Finney, formerly of the Land Office, then Assistant to the Secretary, who was developing into Ballinger's hatchet man, turned the question over instead to Ballinger's Assistant Secretary, Frank Pierce, who on May 19, 1909, rendered an opinion which would have admitted the Cunningham claims to patent.

Glavis, then only twenty-six years old, whose courage, persistence, and devotion to the public interest deserve the highest praise, still refused to quit. He took his troubles to Henry M. Hoyt, a man of high ability and standing, Attorney General of Puerto Rico, and through him succeeded in seeing Attorney General Wickersham and laying the case before him. The effect of Wickersham's opinion was to reverse Pierce, sustain Glavis, and for a time hold Ballinger in check.

The pressure for patenting the Cunningham claims, however, did not let up. Neither did Glavis. He held that "The question at issue in these cases is of such importance to the people of the Pacific Coast, and the difficulties in the presentation of the Government's testimony are of such a nature, as to make the fullest preparation essential." On July 16, 1909, Glavis asked Ballinger in Seattle to give him more time for investigation, so that field examinations could be made before hearings were held. Ballinger refused.

On the same day Glavis, at the end of his rope, in desperation appealed to the Forest Service. Within a week Secretary Wilson asked Ballinger for time to examine the claims. Since most of them lay within a National Forest, he could not turn Wilson down, and so the hearings were postponed.

Quite obviously, Glavis was in the way and had to be got out of it.

On the very next day after his appeal the Cunningham claims were taken out of his hands and turned over to Special Agent James M. Sheridan. It was a poor choice so far as the claims were concerned, as Sheridan, though he had little experience, was honest and able. After investigation he also, like Jones and Glavis, reported against them.

Later on Dennett, acting at Pierce's direction, cut out the proposed local hearings at Juneau, Alaska, where the facts were known, and transferred the case to Washington to be heard before Dennett himself, who, forgetting that the Cunningham claims represented, in his own words, a "criminal conspiracy," had become friendly to the claimants. Dennett's action was directly contrary to the regulations of the Department and was without known precedent.

Dennett, by this time Commissioner of the General Land Office, was much disturbed, as you know, by the failure of Glavis to be "good." He wrote to Schwartz, one of his men, on July 20 and again on July 22, complaining bitterly:

"Glavis has these coal cases on the brain. I have told him how it looks to us and have reminded him of everything we have done for him and that it looks as if he were returning our favors by not standing by us as he ought to. He has not acted as you or I would act under similar circumstances. It looks a little treacherous to me, this calling in the Forestry."

Which is also a valuable commentary on the superiority of favors over facts in the code of the General Land Office in those days.

Now that the claims were no longer in his bailiwick, a less resolute man than Glavis would have called it a day. But not Glavis. The day before I made my talk at Spokane, Glavis came to me with a letter from Frank Heney, and laid his case before me. The Cunningham claims were, most of them, in the Chugach National Forest. Therefore I had an official right to be concerned about them.

It is worth recalling here that when the Secretary of Agriculture, in 1907, recommended the creation of the Chugach, with boundaries which took in twenty-one out of the thirty-three Cunningham claims, Ballinger as Commissioner opposed it vigorously. Nevertheless the Chugach was created, and later on was extended so that it included all the thirty-three.

I had met Glavis first in 1903, at Cass Lake and in the woods, in Minnesota. He was estimating timber and classifying lands on the Chippewa Indian Reservations for the Land Office. Gene Bruce and

I were there on similar business for the Bureau of Forestry. Afterward Bruce had brought Glavis to see me in Washington, because he wanted him in our work.

I believed Glavis was honest, and when he had told me his story I believed he was right. The material he submitted satisfied me completely that the Cunningham claims were fraudulent. I wanted that fraud stopped.

It was not only bad morals to let these claims go to patent, but extremely bad politics as well. The facts were known not only to the Interior Department and the Forest Service, but also to many persons in private life. Sooner or later they were bound to come out, and when they did, the dickens would be to pay.

Obviously this was a matter of the gravest importance. Through the Guggenheim Syndicate the natural resources of Alaska were in danger of monopoly. Coal and the Cunningham claims were the key. And moreover the good name of the Taft Administration was at stake.

There was no use appealing further to the Secretary of the Interior. Ballinger's position had been taken for good and all. There was only one thing to do, and that was to carry the case to the President of the United States. It was the last chance.

I advised Glavis accordingly; he agreed; and I gave him a letter of introduction to Taft. Also I wrote the latter an additional letter in which I pointed out the danger of a public scandal. That letter concluded: "This is clearly a matter for your personal attention, and my function ends with seeing that it reaches you." And so it would have ended, if Taft had been T.R.

At Glavis's request I sent a member of the legal staff of the Forest Service, A. C. Shaw, a man of courage, public spirit, and great experience in public-land matters, formerly in the General Land Office, to meet him in Chicago on his way East and help him prepare his statement for Taft.

On August 18, 1909, Glavis saw the President at Beverly, Massachusetts, where he was spending the summer, and laid the case (which involved not only Ballinger but also Pierce, Dennett, and Schwartz) before him in a restrained and moderate statement of about fifty pages, composed almost entirely of copies of official documents, which the President read then and there. Glavis was told to go to Boston and wait. A few days later he was notified that the President would not see him again and that he might return to Seattle.

The President forwarded the Glavis report to Ballinger at Seattle, and Ballinger came back to Washington to prepare his reply. There he announced that he proposed to "kill some snakes."

On the evening of September 6, Ballinger, with his close friend and assistant, Oscar Lawler, brought to Beverly his written answer to Glavis, and the answers of Pierce, Dennett, and Schwartz, together with over one thousand typewritten pages of documents relating to the Glavis charges, largely letter-press copies on tissue paper, and put them all in Taft's hands. The documents turned over to the President by Ballinger formed a bundle "large enough to fill an ordinary suitcase." Other material, including Land Office files on water-power site withdrawals and restorations, amounted to about as much more.

The matter was discussed between the three of them for half the night, as Ballinger later testified. Then Taft, to quote his letter of September 13, "sat up until three o'clock that night reading the answers and the exhibits; so that at my next conference I was advised of the contents of the entire record and had made up my mind that there was nothing in the charges upon which Mr. Ballinger or the other accused could be found guilty of either incompetency, inefficiency, disloyalty to the interests of the Government, or dishonesty."

This mass of material was neither indexed nor arranged for reading. Later on "the entire record" was printed. It covers over seven hundred large and closely printed pages, not counting maps and diagrams. Obviously, therefore, the President could not possibly have become acquainted with it in the time at his disposal. It took Louis D. Brandeis, counsel for Glavis, more than ten days to do what Mr. Taft alleged himself to have done in certainly less than half as many hours.

The next evening the President saw Ballinger and Lawler again. Having reached the conclusion that there was nothing against Ballinger, "I, therefore," Taft himself admitted later, "requested Mr. Lawler to prepare an opinion as if he were President." This opinion, in the form of a letter addressed to Ballinger for Taft's signature, was brought to him at Beverly on September 12 by Lawler and Wickersham, the Attorney General. It covered thirty typewritten pages.

Whether Taft, when he asked Lawler to write his decision for him in the Glavis case, knew that Lawler was Ballinger's friend and an enemy of Glavis, who had preferred charges against Lawler in a California land-fraud case, I do not know. Whatever the fact, a man like Lawler must have regarded Taft's request as a Heaven-sent chance to get even.

The same evening Taft went over and revised the Lawler opinion and cut it down, but kept some of its actual language and many of its ideas. The rewritten letter contained a defense of Ballinger against charges concerning water-power sites and the Indian co-operative agreement with the Forest Service, a defense which was not in the Lawler draft.

The Taft letter of September 13, which came to be called the Whitewash Letter, is too long to quote here in full. It dealt first with the Glavis charges.

"I have examined the whole record most carefully and have reached a very definite conclusion. It is impossible for me, in announcing this conclusion, to accompany it with a review of the charges and the evidence on both sides. It is sufficient to say that the case attempted to be made by Mr. Glavis embraces only shreds of suspicions without any substantial evidence to sustain his attack.

"The whole record shows that Mr. Glavis was honestly convinced of the illegal character of the claims in the Cunningham Group and that he was seeking evidence to defeat the claims."

Of Glavis the President said: "The reading of the whole record leaves no doubt that in his zeal to convict yourself, Acting Secretary Pierce, Commissioner Dennett, and Mr. Schwartz he did not give me the benefit of information which he had that would have thrown light on the transactions, showing them to be consistent with an impartial attitude on your part toward the claims in question."

The President then gave Ballinger a strong certificate of character, using the exact language of the Lawler opinion.

"The great responsibility of Cabinet positions demands the selection therefor of men of the highest character and integrity. Possession of these qualities, as well as an ability and experience which especially fitted you to direct the affairs of the Department of the Interior, warranted your appointment as Secretary."

As to Ballinger's use of official information acquired as Commissioner to help the Cunningham claimants defeat the Government, the President said: "I find the fact to be that as commissioner you acquired no knowledge in respect to the claims except that of the most formal character, and nothing which was not properly known to your clients when they consulted you."

If Ballinger's knowledge of the Cunningham claims was of the most formal character the question naturally arises, Who really knew anything about them?

Concerning the highly important question of the restoration of water-power sites, the letter went on to say that "the persons responsible for the circulation of these charges have done you cruel injustice," and proceeded to clear Ballinger also of any wrongdoing in stopping the reclamation certificates and in killing the Indian cooperative agreement. It ended with this blanket endorsement:

"In my judgment, he is the best friend of the policy of conservation of natural resources who insists that every step taken in that direction should be within the law and buttressed by legal authority. Insistence on this is not inconsistent with a wholehearted and bona fide interest and enthusiasm in favor of the conservation policy. From my conference with you and from everything I know in respect to the conduct of your department I am able to say that you are fully in sympathy with the attitude of this administration in favor of the conservation of natural resources."

(But most emphatically not in sympathy with the Administration of T.R., as you have already seen.)

Taft's letter authorized Ballinger "to dismiss L. R. Glavis from the service of the Government for filing a disingenuous statement, unjustly impeaching the official integrity of his superior officers."

On the same day the President wrote me a most considerate and friendly letter, enclosing a copy of his letter to Ballinger. Said he:

"I wish you to know that I have the utmost confidence in your conscientious desire to serve the Government and the public, in the intensity of your purpose to achieve success in the matter of conservation of natural resources, and in the immense value of what you have done and propose to do with reference to forestry and kindred methods of conservation; and that I am thoroughly in sympathy with all of these policies and propose to do everything that I can to maintain them, insisting only that the action for which I become responsible, or for which my administration becomes responsible, shall be within the law. I write this letter in order to prevent hasty action on your part in taking up Glavis's cause, or in objecting to my sustaining Ballinger and his subordinates within the Interior Department, as a reason for your withdrawing from the public service.

"I should consider it one of the greatest losses that my administration could sustain if you were to leave it, and I sincerely hope that you will not think that my action in writing the inclosed letter to Secretary Ballinger is reason for your taking a step of this character."

On its face this was a courteous and friendly letter, but later it appeared that Taft's opinion of G. Pinchot as expressed to G. Pinchot was subject to a considerable discount. In a letter to his brother Horace, written three months before, Will Taft had this to say: "I do regard Gifford as a good deal of a radical and a good deal of a crank, but I am glad to have him in the government." And to his daughter Helen early in October he wrote that Pinchot "and Roosevelt sympathized much more than he [Pinchot] and I can, for they both have more of a Socialist tendency." *

All this may seem to you like unessential details of an issue long since dead. As a matter of fact they are highly essential as first links in the chain of events which ended in Taft's defeat for a second term, turned the national Administration in Washington from Republican to Democratic, put Woodrow Wilson in the White House, and therefore largely determined the action of the United States in World War I, and in the crucial peace which followed it.

Taft's letter exonerating Ballinger was made public on September 13. Its effect upon the country was convincing in the East at least and for the moment. Great publicity had been given to the Alaska controversy by the press of the whole nation, involving as it did a member of the President's official family, an exceptionally powerful and well-known group of capitalists, public coal fields of great value, monopoly of the natural resources of Alaska, and, largest of all in the public mind, the question whether the Taft Administration was or was not standing by the T.R. Conservation policy. The case was almost unparalleled in real importance as well as in dramatic interest. Not since the days of Grant had a national Administration faced a situation so dangerous.

Perhaps as good an example of the attitude as any of the conservative Eastern papers was an editorial in the New York *Sun* of September 17:

"Mr. Forester PINCHOT is an honest and excellent gentleman, of elevated aspirations, unimpeachable sincerity and consuming energy.

* *Taft to Horace D. Taft,* June 6, 1909, quoted by Pringle, Henry F., *The Life and Times of William Howard Taft,* New York, Farrar and Rinehart, 1939, p. 480.

Taft to Helen H. Taft, October 3, 1909, quoted by Pringle, *loc. cit.* p. 492.

He has committed the error of assuming that he had inherited from Mr. ROOSEVELT the privilege of disregarding the statutes of his country at convenience; and it had not occurred to him that it were better that his zeal were tempered with discretion. His example, though painful, will be useful. Mr. TAFT's letter to Mr. BALLINGER is admirable and will be a desirable intimation to Mr. ROOSEVELT's surviving acolytes that they will, one and all, have to reckon with the law as it is written."

77. *Salt Lake*

Meanwhile, after my speechmaking trip along the coast, I had gone to San Clemente Island, out of reach of mail and newspapers, with nothing to do but fish. It was there the news reached me that Taft had decided for Ballinger and that Glavis had been fired. The very friendly and conciliatory letter to me from the President, written on the same day as his exoneration of Ballinger, was brought to the Island by a big revenue cutter.

My vacation over, I spoke to the Women's Club at Los Angeles, and then met President Taft at Salt Lake City on September 24, where he had come on the Western speaking trip for which he had been preparing at Beverly. (Ballinger was with him, but he passed me by without speaking—a fact which did not escape the newspapers.)

Our first talk took place at the Knutsford Hotel that same night, from 11:40 to about 12:50. It might fairly be called unusual, as between the President and a mere bureau chief; and it would, of course, have been impossible except for the old friendship between us.

This talk seemed to me so important that I wrote down careful notes of it the same night. Here follow the essential parts of these notes, just as they were written, except that abbreviations are spelled out, and here and there a word in brackets added for clearness. After some discussion of water power, for which he favored fifty-year permits, and a general plan of waterway development, which he was for, the President:

"Said he wanted my advice on Conservation matters and as to specific reasons why things were necessary, etc.

"Said he was sure Ballinger would be found most careful not to do anything to hamper Forest Service, but would bring such questions to him. Repeatedly said he was sure it would work out all right.

"He said that he must have unity of action in his administration. That if he did not get it he must take necessary action.

"I said I fully understood that and that it might be necessary to fight.

"I said I was not going to resign. He said he was greatly relieved, and said it with emphasis.

"I said I might find it necessary to attack Ballinger, because I was afraid of what he would do. Used simile of wolf guarding sheep. Taft said he was going to study the whole Conservation problem. He said it was most confused and uncertain, meaning the legal side of it. I begged him to study not only the legal side, but the whole problem—what we need as well as what we have.

"[He] thought our press bureau responsible for fuss about this fight. I told him we gave out nothing whatever but *information* on forestry and nothing controversial ever.

"Thought he had no law to impose conditions on navigable streams. I told him of his letter on the Newlands bill. He could not believe it.

"Said my idea of construction of the law in Spokane speech was wrong. Said he believed in assuming that Congress had good intent, and carrying out what Congress ordered. In case of reasonable doubt give the people the benefit. Did not believe in assuming he was last remaining hope of the people. Said he wanted to get this water power matter 'settled one way or the other' by Congress. I said I wanted it settled one way only.

"[I] said I did not believe he realized importance of the stake. He insisted he did [water power matter] but that I exaggerated it. Then we discussed coal supply.

"Throughout [Taft] looked at the whole question from legal standpoint. [He] said I wanted to have him set aside will of Congress and make law. I said I had never done anything I did not have direct law or opinion of Attorney General for, because I realized we should have Congressional investigation some day.

"I told him of Ballinger's action as Commissioner of the Land Office—concerning Alaska National Forest and Public Lands Committee. Then as Secretary—concerning water power withdrawals, Ranger stations, Indian co-operation [attempts to find reason for stopping it, and failure to supply funds to fight fires]. I explained fully that I have no confidence in Ballinger. He said my zeal was so great I tended to think any man who differed as to method was corrupt. I denied and said I had not accused Ballinger of being corrupt.

"I said I would not make trouble if I could avoid it, but might be forced to, and he might be forced to fire me.

"He said, replying to me, that he was not thinking much about this second-term business—he would do what he thought was right whether the people liked it or not—he was going to be President during these four years anyway."

The next day (September 25) our talk was continued on a train to Saltair, a bathing beach on Great Salt Lake. My notes of the conversations on the twenty-fifth were written on the twenty-seventh.

The newspapermen had been after me, as usual, for a statement on the Ballinger matter, and especially on the question of whether or not I proposed to resign. I told the President (here my notes begin) that "I must make some answer to newspapermen. Taft suggested I say simply that I was going to stay. I said No, because people generally thought that he, Taft, had decided against me. I must say something more. T. then suggested that he give out a statement and that I could make parts of his letter [of September 13] public—I could go as far as I liked in committing him to conservation within the law. I agreed, and said I believed he had been deceived and I would write stating the facts about the Ballinger matter. He said that was good—perfectly proper I should answer his letter, and he could then come back if he desired. He said it was a good plan to have it all in writing now, when memories were fresh, and not have to depend on recollection later. I said I could then make the correspondence public if I found it necessary. He said, There is one thing I want to ask you. Don't make it public unless you find it really necessary. I said I would not unless, etc.

"On the train returning, Mr. Wagner [Presidential secretary] brought me a pencil copy of the statement given out by the President that same day and asked me if it was O.K. I showed it to John Hays Hammond, who liked it very much, and I kept it till I had written my own statement. Showed the President's to Albert F. Potter and Senator Borah, also Clyde Leavitt.

"At the Country Club same day about 2:45 P.M. showed the President my statement and he said it was all right. Then we parted on the friendliest terms and I went back with Wagner, who wrote out the two statements and gave them to the press. Senator Smoot saw them [word illegible in notes] at the Country Club, and seemed to think them O.K."

What Wagner gave out for the President was kindly and conciliatory to the last degree.

"In view of the published statements that the letter of the President to Secretary Ballinger was to be considered in some way a reflection on Mr. Pinchot, the President today authorized the publication of the following: That at the time he wrote the letter to Secretary Ballinger he also wrote a letter to Mr. Pinchot assuring him that the conclusions stated therein were not intended in any way to reflect on him; that the President deemed Mr. Pinchot's continuance in the public service as of the utmost value; that he expected to continue the Roosevelt policies as to the conservation of resources, including the reclamation of arid lands and preservation of our forests and the proper restrictions in respect to the use of coal lands and water sites as well as the improvement of our waterways and to ask Congress for such confirmatory and enabling legislation as would put the execution of these policies on the firmest basis, and that he would deem it a great loss if, in respect to the matters with which Mr. Pinchot had been concerned, the Administration should be denied the benefit of his further service."

My statement was friendly too, but of course I had to stick to my guns.

"At the suggestion of the President, I make public the following extracts from his letter to me mentioned in the statement he has just authorized:

" 'I wish you to know that I have the utmost confidence in your conscientious desire to serve the Government and the public, in the intensity of your purpose to achieve success in the matter of conservation of natural resources and in the immense value of what you have done and propose to do with reference to forestry and kindred methods of conservation; and that I am thoroughly in sympathy with all of these policies and propose to do everything I can to maintain them, insisting only that the action for which I become responsible, or for which my administration becomes responsible, shall be within the law.

" 'I should consider it one of the greatest losses that my administration could sustain if you were to leave it, and I sincerely hope you will not think my action in writing the inclosed letter to Secretary Ballinger is reason for your taking a step of this character.'

"These expressions by the President, which are most kind toward me and most favorable toward my work, as well as the statement authorized by him, define his attitude toward the conservation policies with convincing clearness.

"I shall not resign, but shall remain in the Government service. I shall give my best efforts in the future, as in the past, to promote the conservation and development of our forests, waters, lands, and minerals, and to defend the conservation policies whenever the need arises. Especially I shall continue to advocate the control of water power monopoly in the public interest, and the use of our institutions, laws, and natural resources for the benefit of the plain people. I believe in equality of opportunity and the Roosevelt policies, and I propose to stand for them as long as I have the strength to stand for anything."

The comments in the papers after Salt Lake were highly favorable. It appeared that a sort of honeymoon was expected to follow, to the general satisfaction of everybody. But I knew better.

My situation was simple. One way was open to me, and only one. No one else in public office in Washington was in so good a position to keep up the fight for the policy of Conservation as I was. And even if there had been, there was no one else whose relation to that policy, or whose responsibility for it, was as close and binding as mine.

That policy I was in honor and in duty bound to defend. If in defending it I lost my job—that was all in the day's work. It had happened to others before me.

Moreover, I was filled with deep and proper indignation that the President and his judicial temperament should suffer the Ballinger attack on Conservation to go on. And I proposed to stop that attack if there was any way to do it. It never occurred to me that there was any other course I could follow.

During my interviews with President Taft at Salt Lake City it had been agreed between us that I should write him a letter describing the facts of Secretary Ballinger's opposition to the T.R. Conservation policies, as I understood them. That letter, written with great care after my return to Washington, was dated November 4. It said:

"The conservation policies extend far beyond my province as Chief of the Forest Service. But since your inauguration I have come to you freely upon questions concerning them, because of your expressed

DISGUISED AS THE FAITHFUL SHEPHERD DOG, A WOLF IS FOUND WITHIN THE CORRAL

FEBRUARY, 1910

desire that I should do so, and because I remain by your wish chairman of the National Conservation Commission. The same reasons justify this letter. I realize that without your willingness that I should write it, this letter would have been a serious official impropriety."

If you have read so far you are already familiar with the story my letter told. There is no need to repeat it here. My letter concluded: "These examples leave no doubt in my mind that Secretary Ballinger has shown himself actively hostile to the conservation policies. Unless he is vigorously friendly to the conservation policies and prompt to defend our natural resources against the unending aggression of private interests, the public interest must suffer. If he does not defend it in certain matters, no one else can. In these matters indifference and hostility differ little in their final results.

"The effect of Secretary Ballinger's action in the instances cited was actively harmful to the public interest in the most critical and far-reaching problem this Nation has faced since the Civil War. Both because of his attitude and of what he did, I am forced to regard him as the most effective opponent the conservation policies have yet had."

Taft's answer, dated November 24, was still friendly, but it showed the growing tension. I was no longer "Dear Gifford" but "My dear Mr. Pinchot." Said the President:

> . . . I am bound to add that you have not by anything that you have suggested in your letter shaken in the slightest my confidence in Secretary Ballinger's good faith, and in his earnest and hearty cooperation in carrying out the policy of the conservation of our resources, insofar as that policy lies within the jurisdiction of his department. . . .
>
> I do not ask any further correspondence on this subject, unless you insist on it. I wish to renew my earnest desire that you remain as Chief Forester and continue the work which you have been doing, and that you assist me by using your influence to prevent further conflict between the departments by published criticisms in the newspapers. I believe it to be entirely possible that Secretary Ballinger should pursue, as I have no doubt he will pursue, a consistent course in his department in support of the Government's policy of conserving natural resources, and I know you will do the same in the Forestry Department. . . .
>
> With the hope that you will regard this letter as written in an entirely friendly spirit, and in the anxiety to compose all differences and make the work go on in all departments, believe me,
>
> Sincerely yours,
>
> Wm. H. Taft.

What the President was asking me to do was to forget what I knew about Ballinger, accept him as a convinced advocate and supporter of Conservation, and work in hearty co-operation with him. Perhaps the Angel Gabriel could have done it, but it was beyond me. And if the President had been even a moderately good executive, he would have known it couldn't be done.

78. *The Coming Storm*

The President's statement, in his letter of September 13, that he had "examined the whole record most carefully" and had "reached a very definite conclusion" had been generally accepted as conclusive, at least in the East. Glavis was beaten, discredited, and dismissed, and the incident seemed to be closed.

The New York *Times,* for example, vigorously approved Taft's letter. "The country is indebted to Mr. Taft for this thoroughgoing exposure of the methods of the muck-rakers. During the chief part of his predecessor's Administration they kept the Nation in a ferment by their indiscriminate, ill-judged, and baseless attacks upon public and private character. President Taft's letter calls a halt upon their proceedings."

But in the West it was otherwise. The San Francisco *Call* spoke for much of the West when it said:

"The effect of Glavis's summary dismissal will not convince the West or convert it to Ballingerism. The West knows Ballinger too well. It knows his associations. The West knows Pinchot and his work. The vindication of yesterday is not conclusive of the West's interest in this matter. The West is willing, even anxious, to be convinced. It will wait to see who gets that Alaska coal, and whether Ballinger or his friends share in the profits.

"There is no regularly constituted court of law to which Pinchot can appeal. He can, however, appeal to the highest of all courts—that of public opinion—and public opinion has not yet turned against Pinchot."

In spite of Taft's letter and the general approval by the powers that were, Glavis refused to stay beaten. On September 20 this determined young man wrote to the President in effect that he was not through—that he refused to accept defeat.

"I deemed it my duty," said he, "to submit the facts to you and I cannot regret my action. Since there may be now even greater danger that the title to these coal lands will be fraudulently secured by the syndicate, it is no less my duty to my country to make public these facts in my possession, concerning which I firmly believe that you have been misled. This I shall do in the near future, with a full sense of the seriousness of my action and with a deep and abiding respect for your great office."

Gradually it became known that men like Francis J. Heney of San Francisco, famous for his prosecution of the Oregon land-frauds cases; Walter L. Fisher of Chicago, head of the National Conservation League, who later succeeded Ballinger as Secretary of the Interior; Henry M. Hoyt, Attorney General of Puerto Rico; Henry L. Stimson of New York, former partner of Elihu Root and afterward Secretary of War in two Administrations and Secretary of State in one; Joseph P. Cotton, Jr., afterward Under Secretary of State; and other lawyers of standing had seen Glavis's report and found it convincing.

It also became known that Glavis had been given no chance to defend himself against the charges made in the President's letter, but had been dismissed without a hearing. The fat was beginning to drip into the fire again. And when *Collier's Weekly* on November 13 published an article by Glavis under the title of "The Whitewash of Ballinger," the said fat actually began to burn.

Glavis had been offered $3,000 for this article by another publication. It speaks well for his high-mindedness that he refused to take pay for his defense of the public interest and gave his article to *Collier's* for nothing.

Many people, nevertheless, were reluctant to concede that Taft had gone wrong. They still believed in him as T.R.'s personal representative. As one Westerner put it, "They didn't like to look T.R.'s gift horse in the mouth." But that did not apply to Ballinger.

Back in Washington on October 1, I refused to talk about Ballinger, but I did tell the newspapermen that I had never seen the work of the Forest Service in as good condition as it was then. Its morale was admirable, as always. Secretary Wilson's recent trip in the National Forests had been a real help.

The men and women of the Service knew, of course, that there was trouble in the wind, but they were not upset. Their spirit remained as high and fine as ever. That I was able to be away from Washington, on my campaign for Conservation, for more than two-thirds of October and November without risk to the Service is proof of Overton Price's leadership.

On October 25 Taft left St. Louis on his famous trip down the Mississippi, and he did not leave alone. With him went Vice-President Sherman and twenty-five Governors; Cabinet officers, Senators and Congressmen to the number of 112; many delegates to the Lakes-to-the-Gulf Deep Waterway Convention at New Orleans; and one lone Forester. It was an obvious imitation on a larger scale of T.R.'s trip of two years before.

The fleet which carried this distinguished company down the river for 1,165 miles numbered ten vessels. It met at New Orleans another fleet of one battleship, three cruisers, and four torpedo boats, gathered to do the President honor.

At New Orleans I had two speeches to make. To the Lakes-to-the-Gulf Deep Waterway Convention I said that "the connection between forests and rivers is like that between father and son. No forests, no rivers," and I went on to defend the Service against the charge of illegality, which our enemies were spreading around.

"I hold it to be the first duty of a public officer to obey the law. But I hold it to be his second duty, and a close second, to do everything the law will let him do for the public good, and not merely what the law compels or directs him to do.

"Let the public officer take every lawful chance to use the law for the public good. The better use he makes of it the better public servant he becomes.

"The Forest Service proposes to use the tools—obey the law—made by the representatives of the people. But the law cannot give specific direction in advance to meet every need and detail of administration. The law cannot make brains or supply conscience. Therefore, the Forest Service proposes also to serve the people by the intelligent and purposeful use of the law and every lawful means at its command for the public good. And for that intention it makes no apology."

For what followed I was, of course, held up to scorn by the beneficiaries of the evil I denounced.

"The present economic order, with its face turned away from equality of opportunity, involves a bitter moral wrong, which must be corrected for moral reasons and along moral lines. It must be corrected with justness and firmness, but not bitterly, for that would be to lower the Nation to the moral level of the evil which we have set ourselves to fight.

"This is the doctrine of the Square Deal. It contains the germ of industrial liberty. Its partisans are the many, its opponents are the few. I am firm in the faith that the great majority of our people are Square Dealers."

The Ballinger-Pinchot controversy had not been very long under way before I was convinced that it would result in a Congressional investigation. Almost from the beginning of my work in the Forest Service the likelihood of such an investigation had been clearly before me. And that was fortunate. Even at that stage of the game I understood that a Government officer must not only be right—he must also seem right. And that, as I found later on, is just as true of a Governor as it is of a Forester.

Taft's personal letter to Ballinger of September 13 had referred to a Congressional investigation as "not unlikely." By the time I got back to Washington from the West after Salt Lake a Congressional investigation was practically certain. If it came, I would need counsel, and counsel of the very best. The man to whom I naturally turned first was my brother Amos. He could not, of course, appear as my formal representative. Nevertheless his advice and his help were invaluable.

Next I turned to Henry L. Stimson. Stimson was a hunting partner of mine, and far and away the best friend I had in the class next ahead at Yale. With him I talked over the situation and asked him to be my counsel. He took the matter under consideration; and finally wrote me a letter accepting the job, and mailed it. But before the letter left the New York Post Office, Stimson, persuaded thereto, I believe, by Elihu Root, withdrew on the ground that he was counsel for the Government in another case.

Nevertheless Harry continued to take an intense and active interest in the case, and gave me much good advice. For his place as counsel he recommended George Wharton Pepper of Philadelphia. And Pepper, to my immediate satisfaction and ultimate regret, accepted. Later on Amos suggested Nathan A. Smyth, his classmate at Yale, who as Pepper's assistant did far better work than his chief.

The campaign of *Collier's Weekly* against Ballinger, conducted with great intelligence and effectiveness by Norman Hapgood, was helping powerfully to build up public interest. The people wanted to know all the facts.

But when *Collier's* published the Glavis article of November 13, it exposed itself to a suit for libel. Before long word came to Norman Hapgood that Ballinger proposed to sue for a million dollars, no less. Thereupon a conference was held at Stimson's house which brought together Stimson, Hapgood, Pepper, Amos, and me. It resulted, most fortunately, in the determination of *Collier's* to retain Louis D. Brandeis who would also serve as acting counsel for Glavis in the coming investigation. If Glavis was justified, *Collier's* would be cleared also. That, however, was only the first step.

79. *The Storm Breaks*

In those days Congress met on the first Monday in December, a month earlier than it does now. Public interest in Taft's dismissal of Glavis for his charges against Ballinger had become so great that a number of resolutions were introduced asking for information. Finally on December 21, 1909, the Senate passed a resolution asking the President "if in his opinion not incompatible with the public interest, to transmit to Congress any reports, statements, papers, or documents upon which he acted in reaching his conclusions with reference to the said charges."

On the same day Senator Jones of Washington, who introduced the resolution, read on the floor a letter from Ballinger written after conferences at the White House with the President, Cabinet officers, and party leaders. In this letter Ballinger courted the fullest inquiry and urged that "Any investigation of the Interior Department should embrace the Forest Service, since I have reason to believe that the pernicious activity of certain of its officers has been the inspiration of these charges and involve in part the common administration of the public domain."

As the year 1909 drew to its close, the Ballinger-Pinchot controversy and the coming Congressional investigation absorbed more and more public attention. Consultations to prepare for it were held between the President and his leaders in House and Senate, and the make-up of the investigating committee was widely discussed.

It was decided that the investigation should be authorized by a joint resolution of House and Senate, as befitted the importance of the case. In its Washington correspondence the New York *Journal of Commerce* told its readers that "Practically the whole attention in political circles is now centered upon the proposed Congressional investigation of the doings of Secretary Ballinger. With but few exceptions members of Congress still in the city regard this investigation as of unusual significance because they think it is practically an investigation of the President himself."

The *Journal* rather let the cat out of the bag when it said, "it is also understood throughout the Congressional circles that none but eligible men need apply for places on the committees of inquiry." And it added that "it will be difficult to get many Pinchot sympathizers" appointed.

The papers carried detailed accounts of the line of attack which would be followed. Said the Brooklyn, New York, *Citizen:*

"In addition to attempting to prove that Chief Forester Pinchot and his assistants have interfered with the work of the Interior Department, and have inspired the attacks in the public prints against the Secretary of the Interior, Ballinger will endeavor to show that Pinchot has disregarded the law in the administration of his bureau."

Some papers regarded the whole trouble as a "tilt between Taft and Ted." That idea was always in the background, when it was not out in front. Many papers carried stories of Taft's displeasure. And a speech of mine deliberately offered no appeasement.

I was to speak on Conservation and Equal Opportunity at New Rochelle, New York, on December 27, and had given my speech to the papers. But a blizzard came along, and I had to deliver my talk, not to a Forum with Horace Plunkett as chairman, but to half a dozen friends in the University Club in New York. And to them I read it only by title. Nevertheless it was more widely printed than any speech I had ever made.

My talk said that "there is no other question before us that begins to be so important, or that will be so difficult to straddle, as the great question between special interest and equal opportunity, between the privileges of the few and the rights of the many, between government by men for human welfare and government by money for profit, between the men who stand for the Roosevelt policies and the men who stand against them. This is the heart of the Conservation problem today."

It went straight to the kernel of a question that is not yet solved when it declared that the Conservation issue is a moral issue—that when a few men get possession of one of the necessaries of life, and use that control to extort undue profits, they injure the average man without good reasons, and they are guilty of a moral wrong.

"Is it fair that thousands of families should have less than they need in order that a few families should have swollen fortunes at their expense? Let him who dares deny that there is wickedness in grinding the faces of the poor, or assert that these are not moral questions which strike the very homes of our people. If these are not moral questions, there are no moral questions. Too often we have seemed to forget that a man in public life can no more serve both the special interests and the people than he can serve God and Mammon."

There are many men, I said, who believe, and who will always believe, in the divine right of money to rule. With such men argument, compromise, or conciliation is useless or worse. The only thing to do with them is to fight them and beat them. It has been done, and it can be done again. All of which is just as true today as it was when I said it, and even more pertinent and essential. And then I went straight to the essence of the fight against the Forest Service.

"It is the honorable distinction of the Forest Service that it has been more constantly, more violently, and more bitterly attacked by the representatives of the special interests in recent years than any other Government bureau. These attacks have increased in violence and bitterness just in proportion as the Service has offered effective opposition to predatory wealth.

"The more successful we have been in preventing land grabbing and the absorption of water power by the special interests, the more ingenious, the more devious, and the more dangerous these attacks have become."

A favorite charge was that the Forest Service, in its zeal for the public welfare, had played ducks and drakes with the acts of Congress. The fact, on the contrary, was that:

"Not once since it was created has any charge of illegality, despite the most searching investigation and the bitterest attack, ever led to reversal or reproof by either House of Congress or by any Congressional committee. Not once has the Forest Service been defeated or reversed as to any vital legal principle underlying its work in any court or administrative tribunal of last resort."

Ballinger's demand that the coming investigation should include the Forest Service was reasonable enough. For while I was doing all I knew for the T.R. policies at Spokane, Seattle, down the coast to Los Angeles and San Clemente, and at Salt Lake, Overton W. Price and Alexander C. Shaw had been holding the fort back in Washington. They were holding it by making known to *Collier's Weekly* and other magazines and newspapers the truth about the Cunningham claims and what Ballinger had been doing. And they had done it with remarkable effect.

Technically, Price and Shaw were wrong. Without question they had instigated attacks on the Secretary of another Department and furnished the ammunition. But also without question they had taken their official lives in their hands in defense of the public interest. What they did was to endanger and finally sacrifice themselves and their future for the public good. Actually they deserved well of the Republic.

When I came back, I talked it all over with them. We agreed that they should write me a joint letter giving all the facts, and that they had better take a reprimand from me lest worse befall.

The Price-Shaw letter of January 5, 1910, to the Forester was a remarkable document. I doubt if the records of the Government contain its parallel—not because of the manner of its writing, but because of the matter it contained. The story it told was of the rarest and most intelligent devotion and courage, above and beyond all ordinary calls of duty, in defense of the public resources and the public interest.

With no attempt to conceal or gloss over any fact, without apology or plea for mercy, with steadiness and self-respect, Price and Shaw told just what they had done, and why, when they gave information to the press. "In so doing," they said, "we acted upon the theory that there are no facts which the people of the United States are not entitled to know respecting the source, nature, and progress of the claims of individuals seeking to acquire for themselves large portions of the public domain except those facts a general knowledge of which would be prejudicial to the Government's case."

"We believe," said they, "that our activities have been pernicious only from the point of view of those who have been hampered in urging fraudulent claims to the public domain. In all that we have said and done we have been animated by a desire to safeguard the public interest. We have nothing to conceal."

The letter concluded with this fine, straightforward statement:

"We are of course aware that, from the point of view of comity between the departments, our conduct has been irregular. As employees of subordinate rank in the Department of Agriculture, we have violated official precedents in directing public attention to the conduct of public business in the Department of the Interior. But nothing that we have either said or done has been for any other purpose than the protection of the property of the people and Government of the United States against claims which we believe were fraudulent, and in respect to which there was grave and immediate danger of public loss."

I was proud of them—more proud than I could begin to say, and in that I was dead right.

After the letter reached me, and when Tama Jim sent for me to discuss what should be done to Price and Shaw, my reprimand had already been delivered. In my opinion, as I told the Secretary, nothing further was necessary.

80. *The Dolliver Letter*

The reprimand disposed of, what to do next was the question. The investigation would, of course, develop everything the Forest Service had done. In the usual run of things, Price and Shaw would be questioned and then hauled over the coals for their share in our attack, and it would probably go hard with them. Both of them depended on their salaries for a living. The fact that, since their fight was part of my fight, it might also go hard with me, was far less important. What I was thinking about was the future of Conservation and the Forest Service. That was the heart of the matter.

Much experience in testifying before committees of Congress had shown me the immense difference in effect between a fact told voluntarily and the same fact proved on a witness against his will. There was, I thought, but one thing to do—lay all our cards on the table, of our own motion tell the whole truth, admit that Price and Shaw had been wrong, and so give no one a chance to uncover anything that could be held against us.

Even if you are in the wrong, there is all the difference on earth between telling your story yourself, with your head up, and having the same thing brought out against you by somebody else. We had nothing to hide and nothing to take back. Morally everything that had been done was right because it was in defense of the public interest.

As the new year approached and the situation grew more tense, Price feared more and more that what he and Shaw had done might get me into serious trouble. Accordingly, and with the utmost generosity, he went to Secretary Wilson on December 28, took upon himself the whole blame for promoting publicity against Ballinger, and offered to resign.

Next day the Secretary wrote and asked me for a recommendation concerning Price and Shaw. I was in New York at the time. On my return to Washington on December 30 I had two conversations with Secretary Wilson when he came to my home to address a meeting of instructors in Forestry. When I met him at the front door, we both expressed sympathy with Price for his frank and manly attitude in taking the blame on his own shoulders. Both repeated our sympathy in another conversation when the Secretary left. I told him then of the reprimand, and that I would not recommend dismissal.

Again on the morning of January 3, in the Secretary's office, we spoke of Price and Shaw. I told the Secretary then that Senator Dolliver, chairman of the Committee on Agriculture and Forestry and the Secretary's lifelong personal and political friend, had asked me, voluntarily and without suggestion from me, to write him a letter on this subject, and that I intended to do so. The Secretary made no objection.

We discussed the President's order forbidding any official to apply to Congress for action of any kind, or to respond to any request for information from any committee or any Member of Congress, "except through, or as authorized by, the head of his department." The Secretary told me definitely that we would have no trouble about that.

As I testified later before the Investigating Committee, "I was convinced when I left the Secretary that morning that he was in favor of my effort to defend Price and Shaw, although probably not in favor of the method I desired to adopt of getting publicity at the same time that the other side got publicity, but I also left his office with the firm conviction that I had secured his permission to write the letter to Dolliver."

Moreover, it was only fair that the case for Price and Shaw should be presented to Congress at the same time as Wickersham's defense of Ballinger. As for me, it seemed about an even chance whether or not I would be removed. That, however, was all in the day's work.

Senator Dolliver was my friend. He approved my letter and undertook to read it in the Senate, as Senator Jones had read Ballinger's letter of December 21. And he did read it on January 6, the same day Taft transmitted to Congress the Glavis papers, including the Wickersham report.

Dolliver was the man whose description of Taft became a classic—"that ponderous and pleasant person, entirely surrounded by men who know exactly what they want." He was one of the foremost leaders of the Republican Party, and much discussed as a presidential possibility.

My letter to Dolliver vigorously defended everything that Price and Shaw had done. It set forth that they had made public certain official information concerning the Cunningham claims and that this information "was properly within the knowledge of the Forest Service, because these claims lie chiefly within a National Forest. This information, also, was of a nature proper to be made public unless there are secrets which the people of the United States are not entitled to know concerning the source, nature, and progress of claims made for portions of the public lands.

"Messrs. Price and Shaw were confronted by an extraordinary situation. Information had come to them which convinced them that the public interests in a matter within the line of their official duties were in grave danger at the hands of fraudulent claimants to these coal lands.

"It is abundantly evident," my letter went on, "that the action of Price and Shaw was taken with the single object of protecting the property of the people of the United States. It is clear not only that they acted from a high and unselfish sense of public duty, but that they deliberately chose to risk their official positions rather than permit what they believed to be the wrongful loss of public property.

"You asked me what recommendation I would make to Secretary Wilson as to Price and Shaw. Without hesitation I shall take the position that their action violated a rule of propriety as between the departments. It deserved a reprimand and has received one. But I shall recommend, likewise without hesitation, that no further action in their case is required.

"Price and Shaw concede that what they did transgressed propriety.

But measured by the emergency which faced them, by the purity of their motives and the results which they accomplished, their breach of propriety sinks well-nigh to insignificance.

"I disclaim any intention or desire to shirk any part of my own legitimate responsibility for what was done by Price and Shaw, who were selected by me and trained in the Forest Service. If they appealed too readily to public opinion, it must be remembered that they belong to a Service which has been and is now almost wholly dependent upon enlightened public approval.

"What Price and Shaw did raises a question of principle which should not be obscured either by personal considerations or possible mistakes on their part. This question relates to the duty of a public officer. It may be answered thus: A public officer is bound first to obey the law and keep within it. But he is also bound, at any personal risk, to do everything the law will let him do for the public good.

"In taking unusual steps under this principle of public duty the faithful public servant may risk reprimand or dismissal. So may any man who does his duty under difficulties." And I quoted Jefferson's defense of his action in the Louisiana Purchase, that he had done for the people "unauthorized, what we know they would have done for themselves had they been in a situation to do it."

Price and Shaw, my letter concluded, broke no law but "without question, they did for the people of this country what the people would have done for themselves had they been in a situation to do it."

Price and Shaw were good citizens, in the finest meaning of the words. Again I say, I was proud of them.

Before the Investigating Committee I maintained stoutly, and I believe rightly, that I was justified in writing the Dolliver letter. From the narrowly official angle, however, it was doubtless insubordinate, and to that extent without excuse. It condemned the action of another Department, and even criticized publicly an official decision of the President of the United States. On that basis Taft was perfectly justified in firing me. I had asked for it, I could not complain when I got it, and as a matter of fact I never did. Officially we were quits.

But from every other angle I was right and Taft was wrong. As an executive he should never have let the issue reach any such point. Since he was supporting Ballinger, he should have told me long before to shut up or get out. As President he should never have approved my aggressive and defiant statement at Salt Lake. And as a man he was in honor and in duty bound to stick to his word, given to T.R. in my presence, and call off Ballinger's attack on T.R. Conservation policy.

Both at the time and since I have been credited (or discredited) with a political motive in writing the letter to Dolliver. I had no such motive. My reason, and my only reason, has already been given in this chapter.

On the day after my letter to Dolliver was read in the Senate there were two Cabinet meetings—one regular meeting and another later, lasting four hours, to consider the letter. The result was not long in reaching me.

81. *Fired!*

On the evening of the same day, January 7, 1910, I was going out to dinner—I have forgotten where. As I was about to leave the house I ran into General Crozier, who had just come in to dine with my Mother. While we were greeting each other the doorbell rang. I opened the door, and a messenger from the White House handed me an envelope. I looked into the envelope, found the letter I half expected, walked upstairs with the General, waved the letter at my Mother as we entered the dining room, and said, "I'm fired."

My Mother's eyes flashed, she threw back her head, flung one hand high above it, and answered with one word: "Hurrah!"

That was the stuff my Mother was made of. We talked for a few moments, and then I went on to my dinner.

82. *The Morning After*

The President's letter to me of January 7 first reviewed the facts as he saw them (but emphatically not as I saw them), and then went on:

> These facts understood, the plain intimations in your letter are, first, that I had reached a wrong conclusion as to the good faith of Secretary Ballinger and the officers of the Land Office, although you and your subordinates had only seen the evidence of Glavis, the accuser, and had never

EXPECTING A ROAR FROM THE JUNGLE. —By De Mar.

Philadelphia *Record,* January 10, 1910

seen or read the evidence of those accused or the records that they disclosed, which were submitted to me; and second, that under these circumstances, without the exploitation by Messrs. Shaw and Price in the daily, weekly, and monthly press of the charges of Glavis, the Administration, including the President and the officers of the Interior Department and Land Office, would have allowed certain fraudulent claims to be patented on coal lands in Alaska, although the matter had been specifically brought to the attention of the President by the Glavis charges.

Both of these points were well taken. My letter to Dolliver did just what Taft said. The President's letter continued:

You solicited the opportunity to make such a declaration in Congress for the purpose of offsetting, if possible, in the public mind the President's decision in the Glavis case supported by the opinion of the Attorney-General, after a full examination by both, of the evidence adduced by the accuser and the evidence on behalf of the accused, while the latter evidence you and your subordinates had never seen. You did this against the advice of the Secretary of Agriculture, without notifying him that you intended to do so, and without conferring with me at all.

Certainly I did not confer with the President. Just as certainly I did notify the Secretary. Furthermore I did not solicit the Dolliver letter. That was written at his request. Taft's letter proceeded:

Your letter was in effect an improper appeal to Congress and the public to excuse in advance the guilt of your subordinates before I could act, and against my decision in the Glavis case before the whole evidence on which that was based could be considered. I should be glad to regard what has happened only as a personal reflection, so that I could pass it over and take no official cognizance of it. But other and higher considerations must govern me. When the people of the United States elected me President, they placed me in an office of the highest dignity and charged me with the duty of maintaining that dignity and proper respect for the office on the part of my subordinates. Moreover, if I were to pass over this matter in silence, it would be most demoralizing to the discipline of the executive branch of the Government.

By your own conduct you have destroyed your usefulness as a helpful subordinate of the Government, and it therefore now becomes my duty to direct the Secretary of Agriculture to remove you from your office as the Forester.

Very sincerely yours,

Wm. H. Taft.

Hon. Gifford Pinchot, The Forester.

Considering the false information Ballinger had given the President, and considering the President's strict-constructionist judicial temperament, his letter was about what might have been expected. So far as I personally was concerned, I had no complaint to make. The public interest was a horse of a different color.

As for me, here was the end of a chapter. But not in the least the end of the book and most emphatically not the end of Conservation. As a matter of history, this was the end of Taft's opposition to Conservation.

On the morning of January 8 I went down to the Service to say good-bye. It would be foolish to deny that I was sorry—very deeply sorry—to be cut off from the Service in which and the people with whom I had expected to spend my life. But it would be just as wide of the mark to say that I repented, in any slightest degree, of what I had done. I had taken the only course I could have taken, and I have never regretted it.

Nevertheless the break wasn't easy, and in particular it was far from easy to say good-bye to the Service. There was only one way to do that, and I tried to follow it.

First I spoke to a little group of the leaders—Overton Price, A. C. Shaw, Herbert Smith, Phil Wells, Lee Kneipp, Gene Bruce, Cox, Sudworth, and some others, and then to all the members of the Service who were in Washington. Someone must have taken it down, for it was printed in the paper. To the leaders I said:

"I want every man here to stay in the Service. I do not want any of you to do anything whatever that will let this Service fall, or even droop, from the high standard that we have built up for it together. That is first. Never forget that the fight in which you are engaged for the safe and decent handling of our timberlands is infinitely larger than any man's personal presence or personal fortunes. We have had here together the kind of association that I do not believe any set of men in the Government service ever had before.

"Never allow yourselves to forget that you are serving a much greater master than the Department of Agriculture or even the Administration. You are serving the people of the United States. You are engaged in a piece of work that lies at the foundation of the new patriotism of Conservation and equal opportunity. You are creating a point of view that will in the end control this and all other nations.

"The best service you can do me, the best testimonial I can get from you, is for you men to stick to this work. I want you men to stay by it with the same point of view, the same spirit, the same energy, the same devotion that have made the Forest Service the best body of men under the Government.

"This is not good-bye, because there isn't going to be any. We are still in the same work—different parts of it, but always the same work. My interest, my loyalty, and my affection belong to it and to you, and they always will."

Then I spoke to all the members of the Service in Washington. I shall never forget their kindness on that difficult day.

"You are engaged in one of the best pieces of public service that has ever been done in this country, and you have been doing it with a finer spirit than any other body of Government people have ever had to my knowledge, unless in time of war. I have always been able to count on the loyalty and devotion of this Service to the uttermost. Continue that loyalty to the cause. The work is the big thing.

"Don't let the spirit of this Service decline one-half inch. Stay in the Service. Stick to the work. You are servants of the people of the United States.

"I shall esteem it the highest compliment that you can pay me, and the highest evidence of the spirit in which we have been working together, if you stand by the ship.

"Conservation is my lifework, in the Government service or out of it. And this is the most important piece of Conservation work there is. Go ahead with it, exactly as if I were still here."

For Price and Shaw I felt far more deeply than I did for myself. I spoke of Shaw's long and honorable service, and of his carrying with him as he left the affection and respect of my hearers.

Of Price I said that he had had a closer relation to this Service and was more responsible for the growth of it and its achievements than any other man. "I have never known a more high-minded, more earnest, efficient, loyal, clean, or finer man than Overton W. Price."

Finally, "I want you to feel, every one of you, that my interest in you is just as keen as it ever was, and that whenever you want to see me I want to see you. I want to thank you with all my heart for a better support, a finer loyalty, a more generous co-operation, as I think, than any public servant has ever had before.

"The best of good luck to every one of you."

What I said I meant, and no wonder. For this was the very finest group of public servants I have ever known.

To the men in the field I wrote in effect what you have just been reading. To the papers I said nothing, which was far and away the wisest thing I could have said.

Senators and Congressmen generally refused to comment on my removal. Not so the newspapers. The morning editions of January 8 carried the story of my dismissal and the afternoon papers of the same day gave some chance to estimate the public reaction. The Washington *Evening Star* in its leading editorial said that the President's letter left no possible question of the propriety of the Chief Forester's dismissal. And then it went on: "He is a high type of citizen, whose devotion to the public welfare is an inspiration. In his own line he is an expert, qualified by a lifelong study, and there is no estimating the worth of his services during the years of his official activity."

I apologize for quoting a passage so unduly complimentary to myself, but it is perhaps the least offensive way to describe with accuracy the general public attitude.

In its news columns the *Star* reported: "With the rounding of the week-end political Washington has stirring in its midst probably a greater tempest than it has had at any other period in recent history. It has all grown out of the summary dismissal by President Taft of Forester Gifford Pinchot.

"One point seems certain, namely, that a great fight is imminent within the ranks of the Republican party."

The *Times,* the other Washington evening paper, under a four-column front-page head referred to me as the stormy petrel of the Administration, mentioned the controversies aroused in House and Senate by the Ballinger-Pinchot feud; and added that "the Ballinger-Pinchot conservation quarrel has in a single day precipitated the whole national political and legislative situation into chaos, and what some extreme people call anarchy."

The *Times* account went on: "Forester Pinchot's big outer office was crowded by 10 o'clock with friends calling, not to condole, but to extend their earnest congratulations. Mr. Pinchot was the most cheerful man present. He expressed regret at leaving the Service, but none whatever at the manner of his leaving.

"Telegrams began early to come in from all over the country, and these, likewise, were couched in terms of congratulation. In short, the friends and supporters of the defeated forester seemed utterly unable to recognize the outcome as a defeat."

That statement goes to the heart of the matter. There was no slightest feeling of defeat in my office, either on that day or on any later one. Very much the contrary. Also, and fortunately, I had no papers to hide, no correspondence to destroy, as has happened to more than one public man whom I might name.

When it became known that I had been fired, letters as well as telegrams of approval, congratulation, and support began to pour in. Many indignant citizens were so strongly moved that they both wired and wrote. Their letters varied all the way from a single sentence to pages and pages—from "Bully for you" to "I hasten to express my great regret and indignation, etc., etc." But I think about the most welcome word of all was this: "The people have faith in you, by the million."

Some letters were typed on embossed letterheads. Many more were handwritten on lined paper. Those were the letters I liked best. "Get ready for a big fight with the big thieves," said one. "Stand by your guns and we will stand by you," said another. And they surely did.

Here and there a letter denounced me, but they were few. Many more denounced the President. One who signed himself "Voter of the Republican ticket thirty-one times" was against the Republican Administration none the less. Some discussed politics, some equal opportunity. Not a few used the occasion to descant at length upon whatever cause they loved best—a human tendency I have noticed also in other times and places.

I did what I could to handle the flood of correspondence, but the letters and telegrams still unanswered at the end of January amounted, according to my diary, to about two thousand. The few hundred I can still lay my hands on came from every state in the Union except North Dakota, and from far separated lands—from Rome, Italy, and Rome, New York.

The head of the National Lumber Manufacturers Association wanted me to run for President, if T.R. wouldn't. So did some thirty editors polled by the *Chicago Tribune*. How many more didn't I do not know. "Marse" Henry Watterson of the Louisville *Courier Journal,* the most famous editor in the South, discovered that once upon a time I had voted the Democratic ticket and nominated me for President on that ticket in 1912. But all that was just excitement and foolishness.

The newspapers generally approved of what Taft had done. Even my friends among them did not see what other course he could have followed. And for that they could scarcely be blamed.

Before long it began to appear that letters coming into my office had been opened before they were delivered—steamed open and resealed. You can almost always tell if you look closely. It was evident that the opening was done in the United States Post Office. And it was altogether likely that my own outgoing letters were being opened in the same way, and especially my letters to T.R. in Africa.

So I wrote a fierce letter to Frank H. Hitchcock, Chairman of Taft's campaign committee and then Postmaster General. But it did little good. Hitchcock denied the soft impeachment, but agreed to have William J. Burns, the famous detective, make an investigation. The opening of letters, nevertheless, went right on. Wrong as it was, however, it made small difference to me. I had other things to think about.

Secretary Wilson had very wisely chosen Albert F. Potter, Chief of Grazing, one of the very best men in the Service, as Acting Forester in my place. But Potter was away in the West, and so Tama Jim selected McCabe, Solicitor of the Department, as a temporary replacement.

McCabe was no friend of the Service, as we had good reason to know. Although he was Acting Forester for less than a week, he managed to do the Service a serious injury by shutting off the money for our newly established Ranger training schools, although it was highly necessary and clearly authorized by the language of our appropriation.

Nearly two hundred of the best young men in the Service had been ordered to these schools and were officially in attendance. They were low-salaried men, working at from $900 to $1,300 a year. McCabe's vicious action cost them not only their pay for the time they were learning to do their work better, but also money advanced for traveling and other expenses. Yet so fine was the loyalty of these men to the Service that about half of them, at their own expense, stayed on in the schools, the better to learn their public duties.

At the same time the legal work of the Service, which George Woodruff and Phil Wells had headed so brilliantly, was transferred to McCabe, and its accounts were taken over by the Department. The good old days were over.

PART XIII
LET THE PEOPLE JUDGE

83. *The Work Goes On*

The old days were over, but the Service was not over. New days were ahead, and they were full of questions. In those new days, who would be the new Forester? Who would guide the future of the Forest Service? And whoever did would have no small influence also on the future of the great cause the Service had embodied and led.

To every man and woman in the Forest Service this was, of course, Question No. 1. And hardly less so to me, whose interest in the Service was anything but dead.

On the hectic day after I was dismissed, Herbert Smith, of whom you know already, heard that A. P. Davis of the Reclamation Service, a first-rate man but without training in Forestry, was likely to be made Forester in my place. On his way home that afternoon he stopped to see me and lay down two propositions—that my successor ought to be a forester, and that Harry Graves was the best man in sight. With both these statements I was in the heartiest accord.

Between us we worked out a benevolent conspiracy. It involved, first, a telegram from Herbert to Harry, urging him to accept the position if offered; and second, a telegram from our friend Lee McClung, then Treasurer of the United States, but formerly Treasurer of Yale University, to Anson Phelps Stokes, Secretary of Yale, urging the latter to suggest Graves to the President. As a result Taft sent for Graves and saw him at the White House on the morning of January 11.

Albert Potter, to Wilson's credit, was Secretary Wilson's candidate. He had arrived in Washington that same morning, had been taken by Wilson to the White House, and the President had seen him just before he saw Graves. It was then that Potter did a fine and generous thing. He stepped aside and urged that Graves be appointed Forester instead of himself. And so, by Taft's decision, it was done. And Potter became Associate Forester.

Things being as they were, and Overton Price unavailable, the appointment of Harry Graves as Forester was the very best possible. A man of the highest character, the best-trained forester in America, with no little executive experience, Graves had in addition friendly relations with the President which promised extremely well.

Harry's appointment gave me keen satisfaction at a time when subjects for rejoicing were scarce. But I had no time and no desire for moping. To say that I was keyed up, after the break, would be a good deal of an understatement. In those days, when I did not take the stairs two steps at a time, I took them three at a jump. My hands were full and overfull. Family and friends were vigorously on my side. Things were happening, life had purpose, and I was on the right track.

Now that I had lost my job there was more to do than ever—a new office to be opened at 1615 Rhode Island Avenue and an enormous mail to be handled; consultations to be held with counsel and with friends about the coming Congressional investigation; and my forthcoming testimony to be gone over. Most immediate was the preparation of a statement to be made public, and then the inevitable speeches.

In dealing with the newspapers and in preparing what I had to say, my friend John F. Bass—famous war correspondent and brother of Robert P. Bass, afterward Governor of New Hampshire—was of the greatest use. He insisted that nothing I said should even be capable of interpretation as an attack on the President. That was of the essence of wisdom, and carefully I followed his advice.

John Bass did great service to Conservation in many ways. He was a powerful supporter of the National Conservation Commission and its inventory of our natural resources; he was the main organizer of the Joint Conservation Commission, of which Walter L. Fisher, Ballinger's successor, was Chairman; he was actively against Ballinger's attacks on the Conservation policy; and the help he gave me I shall not easily forget.

For several days after my dismissal, in spite of great pressure, I refused to talk for publication. That too was good sense, but it could not go on forever. On January 13 I gave a release to the papers which said that at the time I had no comment to make on recent events. Whether in or out of the Government service, I proposed to stay in the fight for Conservation and equal opportunity. "The supreme test of movements and measures is the welfare of the plain people. I am as ready to support the Administration when it moves toward this paramount end as I am to oppose it when it moves away.

"I leave the Forest Service with profound regret."

Then, after bearing eager testimony to the character, capacity, and devotion of the members of the Forest Service I pointed out that the recommendations of the National Conservation Commission still waited for action; and that "unless Congress acts, the water powers will pass into the hands of special interests without charge and without limit of time. So with the phosphate deposits on public lands, when the withdrawals which now protect them are removed. So with the enormously valuable coal deposits in Alaska, which the present law would sell for $10 per acre.

"Those who steal public lands steal homes from men and women who need them. Congress can stop the pillage, or Congress can let it go on."

And I ended by declaring that the great issue between the special interests and the rest of us "is whether this country shall be managed by men for human welfare, or by money for profit. It is a tremendous moral issue, far greater than any man's personal feelings or personal fortunes. I repeat that the supreme test is the welfare of the plain people. It is time to apply it."

Four days after my public statement I spoke to the Conference on Uniform State Legislation in Washington. Referring to Taft's recent message on Conservation made necessary by the coming investigation, I said:

"Most of the recommendations which the message contains are well known to the friends of Conservation and well approved. If it has omissions or passages with which I disagree, I have no concern with them today.

"Today the first consideration is this—that the friends of Conservation must not be divided. The issues at stake far transcend every personal question. The plain duty of all the friends of Conservation is to sink their differences, to unite on essentials, and to demand with a unanimous voice that Congress shall act on the President's recommendations, and act wisely and without delay.

"The President urges that the measures he recommends shall be taken up and disposed of promptly without awaiting the investigation which has been determined upon. I echo his desire. In the face of this great opportunity, let us go farther. Let us disregard the controversy altogether in a general effort to secure what every good citizen earnestly desires. Now is the time for all good men to come to the help of the Conservation movement without regard to party, or prejudice, or any personal consideration whatsoever. The public good comes first."

The which, I am sorry to say, turned out to be far easier said than done.

84. *The Joint Committee*

The documents which Taft, in answer to the Senate Resolution of December 21, transmitted to Congress on January 6 did little to quiet the controversy. On January 19 a Joint Resolution of the Senate and House provided for the creation of a Joint Committee of both Houses, six members to be appointed by the President of the Senate and six members to be elected, not appointed, by the House, empowered and directed to make a thorough and complete investigation of the Interior Department and of the Bureau of Forestry (meaning the Forest Service) "touching, relating to, or bearing upon the reclamation, conservation, management, and disposal of the lands of the United States, or any lands held in trust by the United States for any purpose, including all the resources and appurtenances of such lands."

The Joint Resolution of January 19, in its original form, provided for the appointment of the House members by the Speaker. Their election instead was a milestone in the story of progressive politics in America. It was the first time the Insurgents in Congress succeeded in defeating Speaker Cannon and the regular Republican organization, and it came about in this way.

When the Joint Resolution was introduced in the Senate by Senator Wesley L. Jones, from Ballinger's own state, and before it was voted on, the names of the Senate Republicans and Democrats who were to be appointed were announced in the Washington papers. In the same way, before the Resolution, introduced by Humphreys, also of Washington, which provided for the appointment of the House members by the Speaker, was voted on in the House, the names of the members to be so appointed were published in the press.

Vice-President Sherman and Speaker Cannon were, of course, strongly pro-Taft and pro-Ballinger. The signs of a coming whitewash were clearly evident. And that whitewash would undoubtedly have been delivered according to plan had it not been for an astute move by George W. Norris of Nebraska, then leader of the Insurgent Republicans in the House.

The Insurgents were Progressives, T.R. men, opposed in most things to the Regular Old Line Republicans. It occurred to Norris that it might be possible to defeat the slate prepared by the Regulars by amending the Resolution so that the House members of the Committee would not be appointed by the Speaker but elected by the House.

When the Resolution reached the House, the Rules Committee provided for twenty minutes debate on each side. Dalzell of Pennsylvania, Chairman of that Committee and a seasoned reactionary, was asked by Champ Clark, leader of the Democrats, whether he would be willing to extend the debate to three hours. Dalzell agreed. Then Champ Clark asked whether the rule could be modified to provide that amendments might be offered. Again Dalzell agreed, and the rule was unanimously approved on that basis.

That opened the way for Norris. In his own language (somewhat condensed), taken from a letter to Alfred Lief, a copy of which Norris himself gave me:

"I was in the House all of this time, watching proceedings. With the idea that Dalzell, who had charge of the time on the Republican side, would soon go to lunch and that he would probably leave Mr. Smith of Iowa, who was next to him on the Rules Committee, in charge of the time on the Republican side, I waited my opportunity.

"About one o'clock, I observed that Mr. Dalzell left the Chamber. As soon as he was out, I went to Mr. Smith and told him I wanted to speak, and asked him if he would yield me some time.

"Smith yielded me two minutes. I took the floor, and in substance said that if this committee was to make a real investigation, one that would have the confidence of the people at large, the committee must be appointed by some person other than the Speaker of the House. I therefore moved to strike out of the Resolution the words 'appointed by the Speaker,' and to insert in lieu thereof the words 'elected by the House,' and then sat down.

"Immediately there was excitement in the House; everybody saw that if my motion prevailed there would be a real investigation, instead of a whitewash. There was a scurry at once to get everybody into the House to answer to roll call at the close of the general debate which occurred later in the day."

The Democrats and the Insurgents voted solidly (with one exception) for the Norris Amendment, and it was agreed to. Following its adoption the Republican machine held a caucus, the Democrats did likewise, and so did the Insurgents.

"At this meeting of the insurgents," said Norris, "it was decided that the insurgents would insist on naming one member of the Committee from the House, that the Democrats could name two, and the regular Republicans the other three, but we also decided that several members belonging to the Administration wing should not be members of the Committee. The Democrats in caucus agreed to our proposition."

Norris was unanimously tendered the one Insurgent place. Modestly he declined, and suggested Judge Madison of Kansas instead. Then the whole proposition was put before and accepted by the Administration forces. There was nothing else they could do, for Democrats and Insurgents together controlled the House.

And that is how, thanks to George Norris, Cannon went down to his first defeat, the Progressive movement scored its first victory, and the projected Ballinger whitewash was changed into a real investigation. The two (and also too) complacent Democratic members of the Committee from the Senate were forced to go along with their two (but not too) belligerent colleagues from the House, as many a vote of seven to five was to prove. And five votes, plus publicity, plus Brandeis, plus Glavis, plus Kerby, turned out to be enough.

This first Progressive victory was won in a fight to prevent the monopoly of natural resources, and it is one of the proofs of my contention that Conservation is the heart of the Progressive movement. You ask why? Because, for one thing, Conservation is the most effective weapon against monopoly of natural resources, and monopoly of resources is the basis for the concentration of wealth in the hands of the few. In a democracy that is the fundamental evil. That is what Progressives fight. Under T.R. and later under Taft the Conservation issue brought more Progressives together than any other issue—more even than the Payne-Aldrich tariff.

Please forgive this digression, if it is a digression. It is hard for a man to keep from talking about the object of his lifework.

In addition to Norris's history-making amendment to the House

Resolution, two others were accepted. One gave every official or ex-official involved the right to appear and be heard in person or by counsel. Without it the Committee could have silenced our side almost completely. The other opened to the public all meetings of the Committee or its subcommittees.

The vote on the Norris Amendment took place on January 7, the day I was fired. It was carried by 149 to 145, with 26 Republicans voting for it—5 more Insurgents than in any previous vote. Among them were Charles A. Lindbergh of Minnesota, friend of the Forest Service, father of the flyer, and a genuine American (I am speaking of the father only), and Herbert Parsons of New York.

The vote was followed, according to the Baltimore *Sun,* by "a demonstration of enthusiasm such as seldom has been seen in the House." The same paper reported that "political observers in Washington say the situation created by today's developments is the most tense in many years. What the outcome will be no one is willing to prophesy."

The political possibilities, according to the Washington *Times,* had become "unlimited and fraught with concern to the dominant party in a year when a Congressional election is pending." As a matter of fact they included a presidential election as well.

The Joint Committee of Congress to Investigate the Interior Department and the Bureau of Forestry consisted of six Senators and six Representatives—seven regular Republicans, four Democrats, and one Insurgent Republican. Measured by the standing of its members among their colleagues, it was a distinguished body.

Senator Knute Nelson of Minnesota, Chairman of the Committee, was a hardboiled, tobacco-chewing, short and powerful squarehead Norwegian who had fought in the Civil War. He was also Chairman of the Senate Committee on Public Lands. As such he had been friendly to the Forest Service, but times had changed. As Chairman of the Joint Committee he showed himself to be bitterly and openly partisan, Old Guard to the finger tips, and relentlessly determined to carry out the whitewashing of Ballinger according to plan.

Senator Frank P. Flint of California was a Southern Pacific man. As a member of the Committee he was steadily and vigorously pro-Ballinger and anti-Pinchot.

Senator George Sutherland of Utah, bitter enemy of the National Forests, was one of the most consistent reactionaries it has ever been my ill fortune to meet. Both as a member of the Joint Committee and later as a Justice of the Supreme Court of the United States, Sutherland was uniformly, one might almost say viciously, for the people of property and the powers that be. His vote could always be predicted in advance.

Senator Elihu Root of New York, in my opinion easily the ablest man in either House of Congress, was keen, cool, and consistently on the Taft side. Although willing at times to be fair when fairness cost nothing, Root acted, in effect, as one of counsel for the Administration. With his hair banged and his rather dapper clothes, it never seemed to me that Root looked his part and his power.

Of Senator Thomas H. Paynter of Kentucky I remember little. His part in the investigation was not important. Early in the proceedings he was replaced by Senator William E. Purcell of North Dakota, who became deeply and intelligently interested in the issues at stake. Appointed on February 1, 1910, he voted, I believe by honest conviction, with the other Democrats on the Committee.

Senator Duncan U. Fletcher of Florida, Democrat, was one of the men picked with the enthusiastic approval of the Senate Republican machine for the proposed Ballinger whitewash. Nevertheless he followed the leadership of James and Graham, Democrats from the House, refused to take Administration orders, and used his head. His contribution toward bringing out the truth was of genuine importance. Long after the hearings were over he remained my friend.

On the House side, Representative Samuel W. McCall of Massachusetts, born in Pennsylvania, Vice-Chairman of the Committee, was an educated man whose historical perspective was no obstacle to his intense standpat Republican regularity. Member of the powerful Committee on Ways and Means, he was a leader of the Regulars in the House. Also he was another highly dependable rubber stamp. In 1916 he became Governor of Massachusetts.

Representative Marlin E. Olmsted of Pennsylvania, a typical member of the Old Guard Pennsylvania machine, was uniformly and consistently with the Chairman and for the Administration. He was a leader in the power crowd. His action, like that of Sutherland, could always be predicted in advance.

Representative Edwin Denby of Michigan was the man who later on, as Secretary of the Navy under President Harding, was to turn the Navy's oil reserves in California over to Secretary Fall of the Interior Department and thus open the door to the Teapot Dome steal, the greatest Government scandal of the time. Denby, as might be expected, was with the Administration, right or wrong.

Representative Ollie M. James, Democrat of Kentucky, afterward elected United States Senator, was so huge in body that a special chair had to be provided. He had seconded the nomination of Bryan for President in 1908. Honest and powerful, he had the courage of his convictions. Nobody put anything over on him.

Representative James M. Graham of Illinois, the other House Democrat, was conscientious, able, and fearless, and generally respected. His determination to get at the truth, whoever might be hit, was his most conspicuous characteristic. All in all he was, I think, the best member of the Committee.

From my point of view, however, the most important member of the Committee was Judge E. H. Madison of Kansas. He, you will remember, was selected by the House Insurgents as their representative. No better man could have been chosen. He was quiet, able, fair, and unafraid, and his minority report, which he alone signed, gives, at least as I think, one of the very best statements of the case.

Before the Committee began its hearings, Senator Nelson wrote to me asking what subjects I thought should be covered by the investigation. After consultation with Brandeis and others, I replied that in my opinion the Committee should consider "what has actually been done and is being done with our coal and timberlands and with our water-power sites under existing law, with a view to the framing of such a body of new legislation as will prevent the abuses that exist or are threatened."

And I suggested in substance these three questions:

"Have the Alaska coal lands been passing into the hands of those who needed them or into monopolistic control?"

"What should be done to guard against the future concentration of water power in a few hands?"

"Are the laws governing disposal of timber on Indian lands leading to their destruction by fire and unskilled management?"

And I respectfully suggested that the investigation might be made of great practical value to immediate legislation and right administrative practice. Not Ballinger's scalp but good government was what I was after.

My letter added that "I neither withdraw nor modify views heretofore expressed by me respecting the inadequate protection which the public interest had been receiving, but I am willing to subordinate all personal considerations to the advancement of the cause to which I am devoted." And it ended with the statement that Brandeis endorsed my suggestions.

Most of the questions proposed in my letter to Nelson were answered in substance as I would have answered them myself in the final majority report of the Committee. You will see if you read on.

Just what line the investigation should follow was the subject of a good deal of discussion in the Committee. Root wanted it to take a line which would result in constructive Conservation legislation—very much the line advocated in my letter to Nelson. But Nelson's eye was fixed on the intended whitewash, not on constructive legislation. And so Root's statesmanlike suggestion was brushed aside.

85. *The Counsel*

On January 26, 1910, at half-past two in the afternoon, the Joint Committee to investigate the Interior Department and the Forest Service held its first public session in Room 207 of the Senate Office Building.

The members of the Committee sat on either side of a long table with the Chairman at one end and the witness at the other. At one side was the press table where the reporters, most of them personally friendly to Glavis and me, wrote what they were required to write by the policy of their employers. The Associated Press, for example, was strongly pro-Administration, as usual, but the United Press was with us. The lawyers and their clients and the waiting witnesses were scattered about.

My Mother attended almost all of the hearings, usually accompanied by some of her friends. I shall never forget her dignity and beauty as she sat listening with keen understanding and appreciation to everything that went on. The attendants soon came to know her and to reserve certain seats for her and her party. And so they did for Mrs. Ballinger and her friends. I had genuine sympathy for Mrs. Ballinger, and real regret. She was a fine woman.

It was not, as I remember it, a very impressive setting, but what went on there was another matter. For the man who was on trial before the Committee, the listeners, and the Nation was neither Glavis, nor Pinchot, nor even Ballinger, but the President of the United States. And that was true even before Brandeis uncovered the Wickersham misdating and the Lawler memorandum.

Brandeis, counsel for Glavis, went to the bottom of things; and when he got to the bottom, he made the results unmistakably clear—clear not only to the Committee but also, through the newspapers, to the people of the United States.

Just as later in the Supreme Court of the United States, Brandeis showed himself to be a most exceptionally able, fearless, patient, indomitable, farsighted, and socially minded lawyer and citizen, whose grasp reached every side of the question at issue and also its remoter consequences. Brandeis was a wonder. He it was who won our case.

That is to say, it was Brandeis, plus Glavis, plus Kerby. Above all these, it was Taft himself without whose—insert your own term—in deliberately sending to Congress a document which he knew to be misdated, we would have been lost indeed. So far as I know, Taft was the only President in our history against whom such a charge could be made.

Brandeis was distinguished by a very remarkable dignity and gentleness of character and manner, combined with unyielding tenacity and inflexible resolution. Throughout the investigation he showed extraordinary penetration and equally extraordinary freedom from the shackles of conventional thinking; wherein he shone in marked contrast to George Wharton Pepper. His mind was alert and eager, always ready for new expedients, to meet new situations. His poise was unbreakable, and his temper almost incredibly under control.

Pepper himself, in his autobiography entitled *Philadelphia Lawyer,* has this to say:

"One day, when the latter [Brandeis] was on his feet the Colonel [Vertrees, Ballinger's counsel] suddenly rose from his chair and addressing the Chairman said with emphasis and deliberation, 'The gentleman says what is untrue and what he knows to be untrue.' Brandeis gave him a beaming smile and waited. 'The gentleman,' repeated the Colonel, 'states an untruth, and he states it knowing it to be an untruth.' This time surely there would be an explosion, perhaps a challenge and possibly an old-fashioned free-for-all. Not a bit of it. Brandeis, with arms folded and wearing an indulgent smile, looked silently at the old gentleman for a few seconds and then asked with an air of deference: 'Anything further, Mr. Vertrees?' The Colonel, literally speechless with rage, sank into his chair, and Brandeis resumed his argument at the point at which he had been interrupted."

Brandeis' industry was amazing. Commonly, during the heat of the investigation, he was at work at four o'clock in the morning in his hotel room, preparing his day's work before the Committee. And his work was the essential work. Brandeis was the backbone of the fight against Ballinger. Without him our cause would have been hopelessly lost.

Brandeis' assistants were worthy of such a leader. One of them, George Rublee, had already won a distinguished place at the bar, and his subsequent honors are too numerous to relate. I mention only that he was a member of the Federal Trade Commission and legal adviser to the American Delegation to the London Naval Conference, and that he was decorated by both France and Italy.

The other, Joe P. Cotton, in addition to much else, did fine work in the United States Food Administration in World War I, was a member of the Interallied Finance Council, and served with distinction in the Hoover Administration as Under Secretary of State.

In addition, my brother Amos, who had been in the case from the very beginning, and who remained a most valuable member of our legal staff till the end, brought in his Yale classmate, Nathan A. Smyth, for whose effective assistance I was and I remain most grateful. Amos was indispensable, and was especially useful in getting the facts to the public before and after the hearings were over and the verdict rendered.

My own counsel, George Wharton Pepper, was highly impressive in size and bearing—a big man, tall, broad-shouldered, powerful. When he stood up, spread his legs apart, clasped his hands behind him, and began to speak, he seemed immovable. It was almost as though you were being addressed by the Colossus of Rhodes.

Pepper became my counsel while I was still in the Forest Service. In a passage of his autobiography Pepper makes manifest his disapproval of my letter to Dolliver and his sympathy with Taft's action in removing me:

"Pinchot in his eagerness for effective publicity wanted to get an immediate statement of his case before the country. With this in mind he insisted upon writing an open letter to the Secretary of Agriculture and much time was spent in drafting it. The letter was finally put into a form which Stimson and I approved. To our dismay Pinchot subsequently and without our knowledge changed it both in substance and form and, instead of sending it to his Chief, addressed it to Senator Dolliver and contrived to have it read in the Senate at about the time that a message upon a phase of the pending controversy was received from President Taft. The President interpreted Pinchot's letter as a reflection on the President's own conduct and an attempt to excuse in advance an alleged serious breach of discipline by two of Pinchot's subordinates in the Bureau of Forestry. The President therefore immediately directed the Secretary of Agriculture to remove Pinchot from the office of Forester. This was done; and I thus found myself no longer the adviser of an important officer of the federal government but merely the attorney for a private citizen whose own conduct had brought about his summary dismissal. I seriously considered withdrawal from the case but as this would have seemed like deserting a client under fire I decided to stand by him." *

Pepper's reminiscence does not click with his record. I sent him a copy of the Dolliver letter of January 6, saying that "it embodies, as I understand it, completely the point of view and policy which you and Harry Stimson gave it, and for which none of us can ever be too thankful.

"I am sure you will not feel that any deviation from your advice was made in any respect, for there was no intention of that kind. We were only too glad to have the chance to follow it. Certain additions were made for reasons which I am sure you would have approved, if we had been able to reach you with them."

To which, on January 7, Pepper made reply:

"I am duly in receipt of yours of Jan. 6th with enclosures as stated. I need hardly say that I am very much obliged to you for the cordial expressions in your letter, which I most heartily reciprocate. I wish that I could have been of more service to you than was in fact the case.

"I infer from the newspapers that the plan of addressing yourself to the Secretary of Agriculture was modified, and that you wrote direct to Senator Dolliver. I suppose there was some good reason for this course."

Pepper's *Philadelphia Lawyer* records that "Of all the difficult and disagreeable duties I have ever performed this was the most arduous and nerve-racking" and he declares that the case "was a constant and

* Pepper, George Wharton, *Philadelphia Lawyer*, Philadelphia and New York, Lippincott, 1944, p. 83.

grievous anxiety." His exclamatory statement is in thorough accord with my estimate of him.

"My effort," says Pepper, "uniformly was to present Pinchot's case to the Committee in such a way as to win for him their respect and if possible their verdict." But on the next page he remarks that "the judicial atmosphere was wholly wanting. The Committee was a political body, governed by political considerations. Even on questions of admitting or rejecting evidence the vote was a party vote."

George Pepper was really able, unusually able, within his limitations, and in an ordinary case would doubtless have done an excellent job. But this was not an ordinary case, and George couldn't adjust himself to the central fact that the judge before whom this issue was being tried was not the Committee, with Knute Nelson at its head, but the whole people of the United States.

The newspapermen at the press table were never part of the audience to which George spoke. After he had made an important point and got it in the record, it never occurred to him that a minute or two would be well spent in getting that point to the general public through the press.

Again and again I had to supplement George's failure to connect with the larger audience by making a public statement of my own, and again and again George, horror-stricken, threatened to resign. From his point of view that wasn't cricket. From my point of view it was the indispensable essence of the whole affair.

The trouble with George was that he had lived too much with courts and lawyers, and not enough with the world of men.

All the rest of us knew that the majority of the Committee, with its carefully selected standpat membership, would report in favor of Ballinger (and according to his reminiscences, Pepper knew it too). What we were after, therefore, was the verdict of a larger jury, and that, in spite of Pepper, in the end we got.

There could have been no greater contrast than between Brandeis' view of what this whole conflict was about, and George Pepper's. And it was never more clearly shown than when Brandeis, by almost incredible skill and persistence, and with the courageous and patriotic help of young Kerby, as will later appear, uncovered the Lawler letter and the Wickersham misdating. To Pepper it was lese majesty of the deepest dye, and he couldn't stand it.

After Brandeis had brought Taft into the case, Pepper evaporated.

He didn't resign; he just simply, for all practical purposes, wasn't there any more. His rigid conformist mind was out of its depth in water in which it couldn't swim—and if that is a mixed metaphor, you'll get what I mean anyhow.

Perhaps a conversation I had with Pepper at Milford in later years, while he was in the United States Senate by the choice and grace of the Mellon Pennsylvania Republican machine, may help you to realize his fundamental inability to go up against the powers that be. In this talk George told me that he had grave doubt whether he, as United States Senator, could properly refuse to support for appointment men recommended to him by local political leaders, although he knew or suspected that the men so recommended were unfit.

Which was the perfect machine politician's position, and scarcely in harmony with T.R.'s preached and practiced doctrine that he would follow the recommendation of a political leader when, and only when, the man recommended measured up to the requirements of the job. And of that T.R. himself would be the final judge.

Personally I like Pepper. Also I liked a magnificent Great Dane dog we had in the family, in spite of the fact that he was afraid of a gun. Call it a Big Gun, and I think you will get the idea. As you may have gathered, no one should pick Pepper to lead a forlorn hope —if the constituted authorities were on the other side.

After George Pepper's soul had quit marching on, my brother Amos, for whose support in the Ballinger case I can never be sufficiently grateful, and Nat Smyth took over, pressed forward, and carried through their admirable work. But Pepper might as well have been in the Land of Nod.

Three other men rendered inestimable service. To John Foster Bass, distinguished war correspondent, I owe more than I can tell for his advice in my relation to public opinion, both before and after I was fired. Thomas R. Shipp, keen and experienced in politics and publicity, helped no end; and so did Harry Slattery. I was more than fortunate in my friends.

Ballinger's lawyer, John J. Vertrees, was a more or less fire-eating Southerner, a long lank Colonel from Tennessee. Colonel Vertrees, we were given to understand, was the President's personal friend and personal choice. If so, the choice was scarcely fortunate, for the Colonel, who came into the investigation after it was well started, showed little knowledge of the questions at issue and none at all of Government organization. Moreover, his conduct of the case was about on the level of the usual police-court lawyer.

It was rumored that Vertrees was only a second choice—that Taft had first invited former Senator Spooner of Wisconsin to take Ballinger's case. Spooner had everything that Vertrees lacked. And so, very nearly, had Carl Rasch, former United States District Attorney for Montana, and afterward on the United States bench, who started as Vertrees' assistant and left in disgust before the end.

Vertrees, like Brandeis when he came into the case, knew little about the public lands of the United States or the laws and practices thereunto appertaining. But Vertrees, unlike Brandeis, who promptly mastered the legal and administrative situation, never succeeded in learning many things that he very much needed to know. More than once on the stand I had to point out the limits of his knowledge, as the record shows.

Vertrees' methods of cross-examination were at times so unfair that more than once they brought protests from his own friends on the Committee. His favorite device was an attempt to trick the witness into some admission by questions on the order of the old joke: When did you stop beating your wife? The criminal lawyer was always to the front.

86. *The Hearings*

It would be useless, and there is no space, to review the enormous mass of testimony from many witnesses in forty-six days of hearings spread over four months. What it established you know already, if you have read the Ballinger story hereinbefore set down.

The first witness called was Louis R. Glavis. No sooner did he take the stand than the Chairman started out to browbeat and confuse him. Nelson was promptly joined by Olmsted and Sutherland. Glavis's testimony was thereby so disrupted that Brandeis was asked to make a statement of what he expected to prove. To that, also, there was constant interruption by the Chairman, Olmsted, Denby, McCall, and Flint. Thus at the very outset the bias of the Administration forces was clearly exhibited.

The truth is that their politics had overcome their consciences—a phenomenon common alike among Regular Republicans and Regular Democrats. I have had occasion to observe it many times. But this time the open-minded Democrats were on our side.

Glavis as a witness was a marvel. The obvious honesty of his intention, the accuracy of his memory, the clearness and moderation of his statements, and the inability of hostile members of the Committee to confuse him, together made up a record of which he has every reason to be proud. Judge Madison said of him in his minority report:

"It is doubtful if a more remarkable exhibition was ever given on the witness stand in this country than was given by Glavis during these hearings. He was for days upon the stand and every question that was put to him received a concise and clear-cut answer. His recollection of past events was remarkable, his sincerity and earnestness of purpose were apparent. He evaded no issue and in but few respects has it been proven that he was incorrect in his relation of the facts.

"There is no evidence anywhere in the record that he sought any advantage for himself through his conduct, but only desired that the wrong which he thought was about to be consummated, should be prevented."

These words of praise have not a syllable too much. Glavis deserved them all.

I, the only witness from the Forest Service, was on the stand little more than three days out of the forty-six. Price and Shaw were not called. Their story—the worst that could be said about the Service—had been admitted in advance in the Dolliver letter. Thanks to that fact we were on the offensive from start to finish.

My own testimony was less impressively accurate than Glavis's. One very shabby trick my memory played me. When I was questioned about the letter I gave Glavis to the President, and my statement that I had known Glavis for several years was brought up, I could not remember that I had in fact known him since 1903, and mistakenly stated that my letter was wrong.

Otherwise what I had to say was, I think, reasonably effective, and neither Mr. Vertrees nor the hostile members of the Committee were able to shake it. The former must have gained little comfort from his cross-examination. At any rate, the Forest Service emerged from his attack totally unscathed.

My testimony began, before I was sworn, with what is called an offer of proof. It was carefully prepared in co-operation with counsel, and the hearings made it good. By it I desired to lay three principal matters before the Committee.

The first two dealt with Ballinger's sins of omission and commission concerning water-power sites, the Cunningham coal claims, and his willful deception of the President—all matters established by the record, as you have read in previous chapters.

"The third principal matter is concerned with the attitude of this Government in law and administrative practice toward the conservation of the natural resources belonging to the people. I shall show you that under our present law and practice the more difficult task falls on those who would protect the public property, and not on those who would despoil it; and that under the present system the betrayal into monopolistic control of what belongs to all of us is made easy and monopoly often in practice inevitable.

"The imperative duty before this country is not merely to get rid of an unfaithful public servant. A far more important duty is to bring about a fundamental change in the law and the practice toward conservation, to prevent for the future what has been in the past, the useless sacrifice of the public welfare, and to make possible hereafter the utilization of the natural resources and the natural advantages for the benefit of all the people instead of merely for the profit of a few.

"When this story has been told, and the witnesses whom I shall ask you to call have been heard, you will realize that the interests of the people are not safe in Mr. Ballinger's hands, and that the country will demand of this committee a verdict in harmony with the general conviction that the Secretary of the Interior has been unfaithful both to the public, whose property he has endangered, and to the President, whom he has deceived."

The letter to Dolliver had deprived the opposition of its most effective line of attack on the Forest Service. Next came my alleged insubordination. It had, as you know, played a very large part in justifying my dismissal, and it gave the Administration papers a strong peg to hang their condemnation on.

My examination on the point of insubordination was postponed, at Secretary Wilson's request, to allow him to be present. After he came, I asserted, and told the truth, that I had not been insubordinate, "but

PINCHOT
TESTIMONY
PUBLICITY
ALASKA
LAND THIEVES
LAND
GRABBERS
LAND GRABBERS
Bushnell 1910

I have no desire as a matter of mere personal vindication to go into that question."

Pepper asked, "Why not?"

"Because," I said, "it does not seem to me to be very important whether I was insubordinate or not. And, furthermore, I should regret the necessity of bringing out a difference of opinion between Secretary Wilson and myself. I have served under the Secretary for about twelve years. All I have said about him [in praise] in my various letters, in the letter that was read not long ago, expressed my real conviction in the matter, and it would be a painful thing under all the circumstances to go into a controversy with him, and for that reason I have kept still."

I refused to answer the Chairman's question, "Did you consult the Secretary about sending that letter [to Dolliver]?" until it was made a Committee question, as I had a right to do. Then I answered, "I did."

More than once I had given Secretary Wilson the facts concerning the actions of Ballinger and his subordinates. Price also went over the matter with the Secretary very fully on several occasions.

But perhaps the best way to give you the story, if you should be interested enough to read it, is to quote a few passages from a letter of January 20, 1910, before the hearings began, to my friend W. K. Kavanaugh, head of the Lakes-to-the-Gulf Deep Waterway Association, who wrote me that he was worried about charges of insubordination in the newspapers. After apologizing for my delay because I had been "simply buried in letters of congratulation and support—I never knew I had so many friends," my letter said:

"On Monday, January 3, I told Secretary Wilson of Senator Dolliver's voluntary, unsolicited request to me to write him, and of my intention to do so. We discussed briefly the right of the Senator, as Chairman of the Committee on Agriculture, to ask for such information, and referred to my uniform practice in the past of giving it direct when asked.

"Neither during the conversation nor at any other time did Secretary Wilson express or imply any prohibition against my writing to Senator Dolliver. Later in our talk, referring to the Executive Order of November, he said that he and I would 'have no trouble about the President's order.' From the foregoing I could not do otherwise than believe that I had his consent to write to Senator Dolliver.

"During the same conversation I told him that, in my judgment, it was wiser for every reason to lay our hand on the table, tell in advance all the facts, and assign the exact reasons for everything that had been done. The whole interview was on the basis of confidence and co-operation for the defense of the Forest Service against an attack we both foresaw.

"As a matter of fact, I was not insubordinate, and did not break the President's regulation. But if I could not have done my part toward assuring even justice to Price and Shaw without breaking the Executive Order of November 29, I would have been obliged to break it. The question at issue in this whole affair is too large to be governed by considerations of this kind. I believed at the time that I had complied with the provisions of the order, and I believe so now. But it must be clearly understood that I am not trying to lay any blame or responsibility on Secretary Wilson. Whatever blame there may be is mine, and I do not propose to let him or anyone else carry a pound of it."

On January 6 I handed to the Secretary, with my report on Price and Shaw, a copy of my letter already sent to Senator Dolliver. My letter of transmittal concluded as follows: "In reply to a request from the Chairman of the Senate Committee on Agriculture and Forestry, I addressed to him a letter of which I transmit a copy for your information."

Now back to my letter to Kavanaugh: "Our previous conversation had apparently slipped from the Secretary's mind, for he read the letter of transmittal and asked me to what that clause referred. I replied that this was the letter I had written to Senator Dolliver at his [Dolliver's] request, as I had already told him [Wilson] I was going to do. To this statement he made no reply of any kind. He then suggested the omission of the clause [of transmittal] just quoted, to which I assented, adding that I would have the letter rewritten and send it to him. He directed me to have it rewritten at once in his office, to which I observed that it would not then be upon the letterhead of the Forest Service. He said that would make no difference."

Accordingly the letter was at once rewritten in his office on his letterhead without the clause in question, and I signed in his presence. At his suggestion I did not leave with him a copy of my letter to Senator Dolliver, which I had brought for that purpose.

Later on my letter transmitting the Price and Shaw report to the

Secretary was submitted in evidence, with the clause about enclosing the Dolliver letter struck through, as I had said.

The Kavanaugh letter once more: "From my last talk with him before sending my letter to Senator Dolliver I was entirely certain that I had the Secretary's consent to write it. From the same talk, I understood clearly that he sympathized with me in my intention to see, if I could, that my subordinates had fair play, and in my effort to prevent the charges against them from being used to divert the investigation from its real object. That was why I wrote."

When Secretary Wilson offered me the position of Chief of the old Forestry Division in 1898, he agreed that I should be responsible to him for results, and that I should choose my own methods and subordinates. "It is part of my debt to him that this agreement was scrupulously kept. During the latter part of my service our relations became intimate and confidential. I had already high respect for his work as Secretary of Agriculture, but his attitude toward me gave rise, in addition, to warm personal affection. This I expressed many times, in conversation with him and others, and in public addresses.

"So I have kept still. I would rather take my medicine if I have to. Furthermore, I do not want to sink the issue to the level of a mere personal squabble. It is too fine and high for that. As long as I can I intend to keep this whole matter free from personal considerations."

Robert Wickliffe Woolley told the story as he understood it in *Van Norden's Magazine* for March 1910, under the title "What Pinchot Did Not Tell." I admit in advance that what Woolley wrote was very much more than I deserved. Nevertheless it does throw light on the situation.

"Gifford Pinchot has long been the leading curiosity in human form to the politicians—professional and otherwise—at Washington, but when he took his 'medicine' in silence a few weeks ago and allowed the charge of insubordination to stick, the hundreds who knew the real facts proclaimed him their own particular eighth wonder of the world.

"In fact, if it were left to Pinchot, the whole truth about his retirement from the position of Chief Forester of the United States never would be known. He doesn't do business that way. When he was preparing his statement to the public, following his discharge, his friends importuned him to spare no one; instead, he referred all too little to himself and appealed to the patriotism of the American people, saying that the cause of conservation was bigger than any man or set of men, and that the fight for the masses as opposed to a certain grasping and favored class had to continue."

Secretary Wilson's testimony, when it came, was generally recognized as pitiful. Under examination by Vertrees he asserted, "I never saw it [my letter to Dolliver] and never heard of it." A few minutes later, in answer to a question from Pepper about that same letter the Secretary said: "We had quite a vigorous and lengthy discussion about that. I protested against it. I tried to show that he [Pinchot] was doing a foolish thing to try to get anything of that kind into the Senate."

The Secretary was uncertain about my letter to him which had been rewritten on the Secretary's letterhead, and then found it among papers he had with him. He testified that he objected to my sending a letter to blanket the President's message, and then said that he did not know what the President's message was about. Altogether it was most distressing, and I am glad to say no more about it.

The effect of the Dolliver letter, so far as the Forest Service was concerned, was precisely what I had hoped. The joint resolution had authorized an investigation of the "Bureau of Forestry," but my letter had told in advance the worst the enemy could hope to prove against us. Consequently, as Representative Madison said in his minority report, "no specific charges were made against that bureau or any official or ex-official of it, or anything connected with its administration."

Toward the end of my examination, questions from Senator Fletcher gave me the chance to point out that the Service encouraged homesteading instead of opposing it; that it wanted all agricultural land used for agricultural purposes; that it regarded settlers as our best safeguards against fire; and that the settlers themselves wanted more National Forests instead of less.

Opposition to the National Forests, I testified, came mostly from the big cattlemen and sheepmen; we never made any charge for water to the power people, but only for the use of Government land; our forest plantations represented probably the largest piece of reforestation ever undertaken; and the yearly cost of National Forest administration ran to about two cents per acre.

After the hearings were over I learned that the Administration had sent men to examine the accounts of the Forest Service at regional headquarters in the West, with the hope of discovering irregularities. To the high credit of the Service be it recorded that their search was so completely in vain that this part of the planned attack was never even begun.

When my testimony was finished, Garfield, Davis, Newell, and others of my friends were examined at length on the T.R. policies. Space is lacking to follow their testimony or Vertrees' futile efforts to break it down. It showed them to be high-minded, energetic, and efficient public servants who knew their business and had done it well.

Speaking of T.R.'s stewardship theory, Garfield said this: "It is like an engineer on a track. A man can keep on the track and do nothing, or he can move ahead and carry the load of the train behind him. In either case he is on the track. So a man may be within the law and do nothing, or he may be within the law and do much for the public good." That is worth remembering.

When Ballinger took the witness chair, his testimony under Brandeis' wise and keen, patient and penetrating cross-examination should have been sufficient in itself to destroy his case and wreck his reputation. It would serve no useful purpose at this distance of time and circumstance to point out in detail his contradictions and evasions, "allowing the truth to be dragged out of him by slow degrees rather after the fashion of a witness in a case of petty larceny," to quote A. T. Mason, Professor of Politics in Princeton University, in his book on the Ballinger case, *Bureaucracy Convicts Itself.*

Professor Mason goes on: "Little wonder that his testimony tended to reveal him as a man of unparalleled credulity and obtuseness, capable of defending himself by twisting into some meaning at variance with common sense and common English every statement of his own with which the 'prosecution' confronted him. As a witness, he gave a pitiable exhibition of shiftiness, evasion, and—to call things by their right names—untruthfulness. To deny a thing but almost in the next breath, when cornered, admit it; to say that he knew nothing about a matter and then, after a little prodding, to show that he remembered it quite accurately; in short, to present the appearance of one willing to lie, and yet afraid to stick—such a performance was doubly significant as bearing on his credibility as a witness and on his fitness to continue in charge of our natural resources. 'Slippery Dick' was a name well earned."

Contrast this estimate by a man with no ax to grind with a eulogy pronounced by Frank Hitchcock in Ballinger's own state at a meeting at which Taft himself was present: "Richard Ballinger's character is as unsullied as the snow of your mountain ranges. As well attempt to shake the foundations of the great Mt. Rainier as to assail the character of the Secretary." And then take your choice.

87. *The Lawler Memorandum*

One of the many things in which it is practically impossible to interest the general public is public administration—good administration or bad administration. If a public servant steals a dollar—that is real news, and everybody understands and resents it. But if a public servant is charged with wasting a dollar, or a hundred or a thousand, that leaves the people, except when politics comes in or is dragged in, entirely calm. They have few standards to judge by, and maybe it's true and maybe it isn't. And anyhow everybody is too busy to bother.

Ballinger was not charged with stealing or even with corruption, but only with bad administration—with failing to protect the public interest as a good administrator should. And if Ballinger had taken the stand when the hearings began, our side might have been in trouble, for Brandeis did not then have all the facts he needed to check Ballinger's misstatements.

But it was not alone the proof that Ballinger was lying that brought us victory. The false date on Wickersham's report to Taft—the date of September 11 when in fact the report was finished six weeks later—had far more to do with it. And so did the Lawler memorandum.

Congress had asked the President for "any reports, statements, or documents upon which he acted in reaching his conclusions" on the Glavis charges against Ballinger. In reply to that request, on January 6 Taft sent to Congress, among other papers, the Wickersham report and summary. But the Wickersham report and summary were not in existence until long after Glavis was dismissed. Therefore they could not have been among the documents upon which the President acted in dismissing him. Hence Taft, when he included them, made himself the only President in our history, so far as I know, who, over his own signature, ever deliberately transmitted to Congress information which he knew to be false. It is a melancholy distinction.

Brandeis, as he said, read the Wickersham report "ten, fifteen, twenty times," and saw that it was no patchwork, hastily thrown together, but a carefully prepared consecutive unit. It could not possibly have been worked up and put together in the few days between the time Taft gave the huge mass of documents into Wickersham's hands and its alleged date of September 11.

Brandeis was sure of it, but he had yet to prove it. Finally he found the proof in Wickersham's refutation of an assertion by Glavis that was not contained in his original statement to Taft in August, but was contained in his article published in *Collier's* in November.

So Brandeis wired Hapgood, editor of *Collier's,* to come to Washington, and asked him to watch Edward C. Finney, Assistant to Ballinger, on the stand while Brandeis asked him questions which Finney would understand meant that Brandeis had discovered the pre-dating. The questions were asked, Finney's face gave him away, and both Hapgood and Brandeis were completely satisfied that the date was false and that Finney knew it. That changed the whole picture.

If they were right, Taft's decision of September 13 for Ballinger and against Glavis could not have been based on the Wickersham report. Then it must have been based on some other document. For Brandeis had established, by careful checking of the President's work and play, that no human being could have had time to review the evidence and form a conclusion upon it in what few spare moments Taft had during the busy week before he started West. There must have been something else.

You will perhaps remember that when Ballinger came to Beverly to answer the Glavis charges, he brought with him Oscar W. Lawler, Assistant Attorney General assigned to the Department of the Interior. You will remember, also, that Taft had told Lawler to write a letter disposing of these charges "as if he were President." But that was very far from publicly known.

When the hearings began neither Brandeis, nor Pepper, nor any of the rest of us had any knowledge or intimation that the President had turned the drafting of his decision against Glavis over to a man who was the friend and subordinate of Ballinger, and also, because of an old quarrel, the bitter enemy of Glavis. We knew nothing of the Lawler memorandum, for it was not included in the papers Taft had sent to Congress on January 6. And Brandeis' repeated requests for all the material on file in the Interior Department bearing upon the Ballinger case had failed to produce it.

Ballinger, who had helped to prepare the Lawler memorandum, as the testimony abundantly proved, at first denied on the stand that he knew anything about it. Then under questioning by Brandeis he admitted that Lawler had brought with him to Beverly "a sort of résumé of the case." At once the majority members, who doubtless understood what was at stake, rushed in to prevent further exposure.

That door being blocked, Brandeis, through the Committee, made calls upon Ballinger, Lawler, Wickersham, Dennett, and Schwartz for information on the résumé that Lawler had brought to Beverly. All of them denied that any such document was in their possession. Did any of them have any knowledge of such a document? No. And again the majority members of the Committee intervened to shut off further search.

Meantime one of Ballinger's secretaries, Frederick M. Kerby, a youngster of twenty-four, was in a tight place. Kerby knew about the missing document because he had been one of the stenographers who worked on it in Ballinger's own office. He had been present when, to ensure secrecy, the rough drafts and the extra copies were burned. And he knew that a copy of the memorandum for which Brandeis was seeking was in a file behind his chair, within reach of his hand as he sat at his desk.

Kerby, now a distinguished newspaperman, was one of the young men Garfield took with him from the Bureau of Corporations to the Interior Department. Hugh Brown, Kerby's close personal friend, was another. When Taft's letter exonerating Ballinger was made public, Brown asked Kerby what he thought of it.

"Just between you, me, and the gatepost," Kerby told Brown, "we wrote that letter in Ballinger's office." Whereupon Brown wrote Garfield that "the Taft letter was rough-drafted in Ballinger's own office."

Garfield, thus made aware of the truth, grew more and more anxious, as the case proceeded, that the truth should come out. Finally, through Brown, he made an appointment to meet Kerby at my house in mid-February, and got the story straight from him.

Kerby, who had a wife, a baby, and a mother to support, realized that if he told what he knew it would mean his dismissal from the public service. Nevertheless, after talking it over with his wife, he determined to go through with it. And this decision of Kerby's, added to Brandeis' acumen and persistence, was at the heart of the outcome of the Ballinger-Pinchot case.

At my house Kerby also saw Brandeis, to whom he repeated his willingness to testify to the facts unless the truth could be brought out in some other way. In all this difficult matter Kerby showed an exceedingly fine and high sense of his obligation to the public, without forgetting his duty to his family.

Garfield and Brandeis had taken the position, with which I thoroughly agreed, that every attempt must be made to develop the facts about the Lawler memorandum without calling upon Kerby for the sacrifice he was patriotically willing to make. That was to happen only as a last resort.

"With that understanding," to quote Kerby's own statement, "I said good-bye and went back to await what might befall, hoping against hope, it must be confessed, that I would never be called upon to play the patriot—or traitor—according to the viewpoint."

Brandeis made every possible effort to uncover the truth about the Lawler memorandum without involving Kerby. His repeated calls would have produced what he was after except for consistent lying. And when that lying defeated his efforts to get the information from the men whose clear duty it was to give it, still Brandeis, as the months went by, applied no pressure to Kerby. Although the facts would never appear unless the latter made a public statement, Kerby himself must decide.

William B. Colver, Gilson Gardner, Robert Wilson, and other members of the Newspaper Enterprise Association, to which Kerby had agreed to give his story if and when it was printed, were equally considerate. Eager as they were for the great newspaper beat Kerby's disclosure would mean to them, they were careful, as Kerby himself testified, to bring no pressure upon him. They left the yes or no to Kerby and his wife, whom he consulted from first to last.

Says Kerby, "I won't attempt to describe that week of hell I had coming to a decision." But he came to it, and on Saturday, May 14, 1910, the afternoon papers carried Kerby's own story of the Lawler memorandum.

"The [Interior] Department went wild. Secretary Ballinger hurried at once to the White House. Lawler rushed to the Department of Justice to see the Attorney General. President Taft was on the Chevy

Chase golf links. His secretary, Carpenter, telephoned frantically while Ballinger stood by. The President, busy with his game, was informed that an employee of the Interior Department in Ballinger's office had publicly charged that the President's letter of exoneration of September had been largely prepared by Ballinger's subordinate and Ballinger himself in his private office.

Still I quote from Kerby's account:

"'Deny it absolutely; state that there is not a word of truth in it!' came the order from the President. And all over the country that afternoon I was branded as a liar by the official word of the White House itself—unconditionally and absolutely a liar.

"But—Lawler had gone to the Attorney General. The Attorney General had a copy of the Lawler memorandum in his office. Shortly before, he had written the committee saying there was no such animal in existence. They conferred. And, evidently panic-stricken, they reached the decision that the best thing to be done was to rush a copy of the Lawler memorandum to the committee room as soon as possible, with a statement that it had been 'found,' having been 'inadvertently overlooked.' At any rate that is what they did.

"And so on Saturday night President Taft returned from his golf game to the White House to find this situation confronting him:

"(1) He had denied the existence of the Lawler memorandum.

"(2) He had stated that he had prepared every word of the Ballinger exoneration himself.

"(3) And that in spite of all these denials the Attorney General had that afternoon, before his [Taft's] golf-course denial had been made, sent the 'nonexistent' document to the Congressional Committee.

"I certainly had spilled the beans—a whole freight car of them."

Kerby's revelation got action, and no mistake. A conference of Republican Senators sat late Saturday night at the White House. Sunday papers carried no statement. But on Monday morning appeared a long letter from the President to Senator Nelson—a letter in confession and avoidance—in which the President not only admitted the existence of the Lawler memorandum but said specifically, "I therefore requested Mr. Lawler to prepare an opinion as if he were President."

The President's letter to Nelson said of Lawler's opinion: "It contained references to the evidence which were useful, but its criticism of Mr. Pinchot and Mr. Glavis I did not think it proper or wise to adopt. I only used a few paragraphs from it containing merely general statements."

As to the Attorney General's summary and conclusions the President's confession was no less clear. Said his letter:

"I, therefore, directed him to embody in a written statement such analysis and conclusions as he had given me, file it with the record, and date it prior to the date of my opinion so as to show that my decision was fortified by his summary of the evidence and his conclusions therefrom."

Having spilled the beans, Kerby was, of course, promptly dismissed. As he says, "I was dismissed on account of 'treason.' It was treason—to Ballinger. But to the people of the United States and the Government I served, I believe it was loyalty."

High loyalty it was, and courage, and devotion to the right. And it was also the decisive blow. Kerby's testimony closed our side of the case. Unless he could be discredited the case, so far as public opinion went, was lost to Ballinger and Taft for good and all. So Kerby was put on the stand, and Vertrees set out to browbeat the young stenographer and destroy the effect of his revelation.

And when it became obvious that Vertrees was getting nowhere, the Regular Republicans came swiftly to his aid. If there had been before the slightest pretense of impartiality on their part, it was now thrown completely to the winds. Nelson, Root, Sutherland, Denby, Olmsted joined in using their legal knowledge and experience in a discreditable effort to confuse and break down this youngster who so obviously was doing what he thought was right, and just as obviously telling the truth.

It is a high compliment to Kerby that not even Root made the slightest progress.

Kerby's testimony led to an acrimonious debate among the members of the Committee in which Root took a leading part. "This so-called Lawler memorandum," said he, "which has been inquired into with such great particularity, with all the indicia of suspicion, has no place whatever in the investigation of the affairs of the Interior Department. It is a paper which relates solely to the action of the President of the United States, and it is a paper of the most ordinary and common character.

". . . There is regarding this Lawler memorandum no element of suspicion whatever and no ground of criticism whatever, and the testimony regarding it has no bearing whatever upon the conduct of the Interior Department. The whole line of testimony is an attempt on the part of counsel [Brandeis] to make use of this committee and, in my judgment, to abuse the privilege which has been given to him by this committee for the purpose of a covert attack on the President, over whom we have no jurisdiction."

All of which, in the light of Lawler's relation to Taft, Ballinger, and Glavis, I think you will agree was going some.

When Lawler was called to the stand, his testimony showed him to be evasive, bombastic, abusive, and ridiculous. He was obviously suffering from an illusion of persecution. Said he (I quote from the record):

"For some months previous thereto [before Lawler's trip to Beverly] I had been confident that gumshoe men had been on my own trail; that parties had been following me hither and thither in the city of Washington and elsewhere. I knew that there was absolutely no depth of degradation to which these despicable scoundrels who were on my trail would not stoop. The record has demonstrated absolutely that my suspicions were more than well founded."

Asked who these scoundrels were, Lawler went on:

"There is one [indicating Mr. Brandeis]. The man Hapgood, who has been sitting next to him for weeks, is another one. A man named Connelly, who stood on the deck of a steamboat and trampled down women and children in an attempt to get to a lifeboat, is another."

Incidentally, it turned out that Lawler had the wrong Connelly in mind. And he added that Brandeis "is simply the flower of this foul flock," which is good competent abuse, whatever else you may think of it.

Asked why these men were following him before September 9, before any investigation was even ordered, Lawler replied:

"I cannot imagine why they did it, except upon the general proposition that they were carrying on a constant campaign against everyone in the Interior Department.

"I was satisfied that I had been gumshoed ever since I came to Washington."

But that wasn't all. Graham asked: "Do you really mean—you realize that you are sworn—when you say that Kerby was corrupted, do you mean deliberately to say that as a part of your testimony?"

And when Graham asked Lawler to tell the Committee whom he knew to be the corrupter, Lawler's answer was: "I do not know, but I believe that James R. Garfield and Mr. Gifford Pinchot and Mr. Brandeis are the parties."

This remark provoked hisses from the audience, as the official record shows. A little later Lawler charged Brandeis with falsehood in such a way that even Denby protested that "the witness was using uncalled-for heat."

Much argument followed. Brandeis, when pressed with questions by Republican members, remarked, according to the record: "Unfortunately one would have to be a triple-headed cerebus to answer all questions at one time." Nature of a cerebus not stated, but I think you will be able to guess what Brandeis actually meant.

Madison grew weary of delays. Said he: "Well, let us proceed. It is getting hot in Washington and I weigh 250 pounds!"

Lawler was the last important witness before the Committee. Final arguments of counsel were made on May 27 and 28. The majority and minority reports of the Committee would come months later. While the investigation was not yet officially over, the popular verdict had already been rendered. There was no question about that.

88. *Three Verdicts*

The hearings covered four full months, from January 26 to May 28, 1910. The Committee heard testimony on forty-six days, and arguments on two additional days. In all, thirty-three witnesses were heard. The record of the hearings fills nearly five thousand closely printed octavo pages.

There were three sets of findings, each of them voluminous. The Republican majority report, as we knew it would, in words at least exonerated Ballinger completely. "Neither any fact proved nor all the facts put together exhibit Mr. Ballinger as being anything but a competent and honorable gentleman, honestly and faithfully performing the duties of his high office with an eye single to the public interest."

The majority found also that Ballinger "is not an enemy of, nor hostile to, a reasonable and judicious policy of conservation, and that no ground whatever has been shown justifying the opinion that he is not a faithful and efficient public officer."

Technically the majority reported against us. But in its recommendations—its action—it was as strongly with us as its words were with Ballinger. In words the majority completely exonerated Ballinger. But they did not propose to trust him with the decision on the Cunningham claims.

"Your committee find no reason to doubt that those officers [of the Interior Department] would decide these cases fairly and impartially; but the nature and wide publication of the charges and imputations referred to in this report would inevitably impair the confidence, both of the claimants and of the public, in the impartiality of such a decision. For that reason your committee recommend the enactment of a law for the transfer of these and any other cases involving claims to Alaska coal lands to an appropriate court of the United States for hearing and decision."

That meant, I repeat, taking the Cunningham claims out of Ballinger's hands, which was precisely what Glavis and I had set out to do when we took them to Taft.

And the final clause of the majority report was a strong endorsement for the position Glavis and I, with Garfield, Newell, Davis, and the rest, had taken all along. Glavis and I, Price and Shaw and Kerby, had lost our jobs, but even on the basis of the majority report, we had won our case. Listen:

"Your committee believe that it would be the height of unwisdom to permit these great coal fields to be monopolized, or gathered into the private ownership of a few for speculative purposes. As they increase in value, the increment should inure to the benefit of all the people. To bring about this result, and at the same time put an end to the unreasonable condition now existing, your committee recommend that the Government refuse to sell these lands, but that, retaining their ownership, it shall grant leases at fair royalties for periods limited, but long enough, and covering areas large enough, to justify the necessary investments upon sound business principles, and thus secure the opening and operation of sufficient mines to meet the necessities of Alaskan consumption, afford relief from the present outrageous prices paid by consumers, and at the same time afford some revenue to the Government. We recommend legislation to that end, and that, pending such legislation, the existing withdrawal from entry of the Alaska coal lands be continued."

You will note that the majority report denounced monopoly in Alaska coal lands, recommended keeping them in public ownership, advocated the passage of a law to lease them for development, and urged meantime that the existing withdrawals be maintained. We had won the war—in spite of the fact that technically we had lost the verdict.

The report of the four Democratic members was penetrating and intelligent. Of the thirty-three witnesses who testified before the Committee, says the Democratic report, "about one-half were connected with the Interior Department in one way or another, and many of those who were most familiar with the workings of the department were the personal adherents and loyal supporters of the Secretary." The Democratic report then proceeded to prove it by giving a list of their names, after which it discussed their testimony.

"Of every one of these witnesses," the Democrats went on, "it can be said his interest was on the side of the Secretary. Most of them showed bias, some of them strong bias, and in some instances, there were apparent evasion and an absence of frankness and directness which often amounted to a want of candor.

"On the other side, with the possible exception of Mr. Garfield, Mr. Pinchot, and Mr. Glavis, the witnesses gave testimony against their apparent interest.

"It can hardly be said that Kerby, or Newell, or Davis, or Hoyt, or Kennedy, or Jones was personally interested in opposing Mr. Ballinger or the administration, or anxious to lose the positions they held.

"Even Mr. Vertrees' fine ingenuity could only account for their action by conceiving a conspiracy against Mr. Ballinger on the part of Garfield, Pinchot, Newell, and perhaps others, and that these induced the other witnesses in some way or other to testify against their own interest.

"However that may be, their conduct on the witness stand was in marked contrast with many of the other witnesses. Their answers were direct and clear, meeting the questions fairly and responsively, in a manly, frank, candid way."

The Democratic members gave Kerby the credit he so amply deserved. He had, they said, "been denounced as a traitor, and as issuing 'a treasonable publication,' and as unworthy of belief. To us he ap-

THE REAL-STORM CENTER.

Evansville, Illinois, *Journal,* January 23, 1910

peared to be a very bright, conscientious, and truthful young man, who, whether rightly or wrongly, believed a great wrong was being done by giving the public misinformation on an important matter about which he knew the truth, and that he believed it to be his duty to make the truth known to the public."

The Democrats then proceeded to demolish the Vertrees theory that Kerby owed a greater allegiance to Ballinger than he did to the people of the United States.

Of Glavis their report said: "Mr. Glavis is a central figure in this drama. A young man, only 26, with but a common-school education, a plain matter-of-fact American citizen, with very little imagination, seeing only the facts which confront him; with splendid recollection, with aggressive integrity, and courage such as very few men possess, a courage which stood out against the whole Interior Department in his fight for the public interest and the performance of his official duty. Indeed, before it became necessary to discredit him, this was the view entertained of him by his superior officers."

They then quoted from the record high praise of Glavis contained in letters from Dennett and Schwartz, written in 1908 and 1909 before the Cunningham case had become acute.

The report of the four Democrats concluded "that Mr. Ballinger has not been true to the trust reposed in him as Secretary of the Interior; that he is not deserving of public confidence, and that he should be requested by the proper authority to resign his office as Secretary of the Interior."

Judge Madison's report was undoubtedly the least partisan as well as the ablest of the three. George Norris confirmed his opinion. In a letter to Alfred Lief he said: "After the evidence was all in, I met Mr. Madison at Minneapolis, Minnesota, and went over with him fully the independent report which he made. This tells the true story of the legislative history of the Ballinger-Pinchot investigation."

Early in his report Madison defined his position. Said he: "The duty to be performed by the Committee is judicial in its nature. We are, in arriving at and forming our conclusions, the judges of the law applicable to the questions involved and also of the facts and what the facts prove. The burden of proving the things charged against Mr. Ballinger is fairly cast upon his accusers, and before an officer of such exalted rank should be discredited by the report of this committee the evidence should not only point to the truth of the charges, but should clearly and unmistakably prove it."

Madison first made an exceedingly thorough and enlightening summary of the charges and the evidence, and then set forth his conclusions. Of Glavis he said:

"Whether right or wrong, he honestly entertained the opinion that the Interior Department was not protecting the people's interests. His actions toward his superior officers cannot justly be accounted for upon any other ground except that of a high and patriotic motive. There is no evidence anywhere in the record that he sought any advantage for himself through his conduct, but only desire that the wrong which he thought was about to be consummated, should be prevented."

Madison's summing up of Glavis and his conduct was just and right. "He did his duty and his whole duty, as he understood it, toward the Government and the people of the United States."

Judge Madison ended his report with a clear and definite verdict which fairly represented, I think, the opinion of the people of the United States:

"First. That the charges made by L. R. Glavis against Secretary Ballinger should be sustained; that in the matter of the disposition of the Cunningham coal lands Mr. Ballinger was not a faithful trustee of the interests of the people and did not perform his duty in such a manner as to properly protect such interests.

"Second. That the charges made by Mr. Pinchot should be sustained; that Mr. Ballinger's course in the administration of the General Land Office and the Department of the Interior has been characterized by a lack of fidelity to the public interests; that this has been shown in his treatment of the Cunningham coal claims, the restoration of the water-power sites to entry without intention to rewithdraw, and in his administration of the Reclamation Service, the latter resulting in unnecessary humiliation to the director and tending toward the disintegration of the service.

"He has not shown himself to be that character of friend to the policy of conservation of our natural resources that the man should be who occupies the important post of Secretary of the Interior in our Government, and he should not be retained in that office."

The Washington *Times* of June 26, 1911, carried this two-column head on its front page: "Coal Land Claims in Alaska Lost by the

"The Return from Elba"

Cleveland *Press*, January 14, 1910

Guggenheims. Repudiation of Ballinger and Victory for Pinchot." Under it was printed this forthright statement which may be taken as fairly representing the public opinion of the time:

"Pinchot-Ballinger feud ends with a complete vindication for former Forester Pinchot.

"Guggenheim effort to grab dominating section of Alaska's greatest coal field is defeated.

"The thirty-three Cunningham claims, containing $500,000,000 [sic] worth of coal, are restored to the public domain.

"Long fight of the Administration to sustain the former Secretary of the Interior ends in complete repudiation of his policy.

"Pinchot, Glavis, Price, Shaw, and Kerby, who were dismissed for making the fight against Ballinger, are sustained by the ruling."

All of which, except as to the value of the Cunningham claims, was not far from the truth.

As I write this the Cunningham coal claims are still in the hands of the Government. Under Walter L. Fisher, chosen by President Taft to succeed Mr. Ballinger, they were canceled. They were canceled by Commissioner Dennett of the General Land Office—the same man who had, under Ballinger, done his best to hand them over to the Cunningham claimants. For that Walter Fisher, of course, deserves the credit.

In conclusion, it might be said that Taft and Ballinger won, because the majority of the Committee went their way. Practically, the people of the United States were so definitely against them that Ballinger resigned from his office in less than a year after his exoneration, and Taft lost his re-election as President. And that was that.

89. *Porto Maurizio*

While all this was going on T.R. was either in Africa or in Europe on his way home. The news that Taft had dismissed me reached him very promptly nevertheless. On January 17, 1910, in a letter to me dated "In the Lado," he wrote, "We have just heard by special runner that you have been removed. I cannot believe it. I do not know any man in public life who has rendered quite the service you have rendered; and it seems to me absolutely impossible that there can be any truth in this statement. But of course it makes me very uneasy. Do write me, care of the American Embassy at Paris, just what the real situation is. I have only been able to follow things very imperfectly while out here."

T.R. would not reach Paris for many days. But before his letter reached me I had already sent him a letter to Khartum which may not be without value as showing how much larger issues were at stake than anything that could happen to Ballinger or Pinchot. Here it is:

Washington, D. C.
December 31, 1909.

Dear Theodore:

You may have wondered why I have not written you since you left America. Several times I have set out to do so, but on the whole thought you would be glad to be altogether free for a time from the echoes of trouble. So I let it go until now.

In my judgment the tendency of the Administration thus far, taken as a whole, has been directly away from the Roosevelt policies. It is not yet certain, however, that the final attitude of the Taft Administration toward these policies has been reached.

In so large a matter as this, snap judgment has no place and full conviction supplies the only reasonable basis for action. I am not yet convinced that it is too late to hope for real support of the interests of the people by the present Administration, and as long as I can I intend to give it the benefit of every doubt.

On the other hand, it would be utterly foolish to be blind to obvious and well-known facts and tendencies. We have fallen back down the hill you led us up, and there is a general belief that the special interests are once more substantially in full control of both Congress and Administration. In that belief I share.

I do not attribute the present conditions to deliberate bad faith on the part of Mr. Taft, but to a most surprising weakness and indecision, and to his desire to act as a judge, dealing with issues only when they are brought to him and not as, what the President really is, the advocate and active guardian of the general welfare. The Reactionaries evidently believe that Mr. Taft has a strong tendency to follow the advice of the last man who talks to him as against all others, for they have built a fence round him with their own men.

It may help you to understand the present situation if I write down briefly some of the principal reasons for thinking, as I do, that Mr. Taft has gone far toward a complete abandonment of the Roosevelt policies. It is true that he has repeatedly professed his intentions to carry out these policies, but we can no longer rely on professions in the face of actions which continually contradict them.

1—He permitted himself, as soon as he was elected, to be surrounded by a circle of Trust attorneys and other Reactionaries, from which he has never broken away.

2—He allowed the attacks upon yourself in Congress during the last session of your term to continue unchecked when a word from the incoming President would have ended them.

3—He surrendered to Congress in its attack upon the Executive's power to appoint advisory commissions, thereby abandoning the strong position taken in your memorandum upon the last Sundry Civil Bill. Thus he allowed the work of the National Conservation Commission to be stopped, prevented the Commission from formulating the specific measures on Conservation which it would otherwise have laid before him, and seriously retarded the practical progress of the Conservation movement.

4—He surrounded himself in his cabinet by corporation lawyers who were necessarily in opposition to the Roosevelt policies.

5—He affiliated himself in Congress with the leaders of the opposition to the Roosevelt policies and the makers of personal attacks upon yourself. I refer to Cannon, Aldrich, Hale, Tawney, and others whom he has chosen as his advisers.

6—By the appointment of Secretary Ballinger he brought about the most dangerous attack yet made upon the Conservation policies—an attack now happily checked, at least for the time.

7—He established, by his appointment and support of Hitchcock (Chairman of the Republican National Committee, and Taft's Postmaster General), a vicious political atmosphere in his Administration, and revived the spoils system of political appointment in some of its worst forms.

8—He failed during the course of the tariff debate to support the Insurgent Republicans in the House and Senate who were honestly trying to fulfill the party pledges and reduce the tariff, and intervened before the Conference Committee only when it was practically too late.

9—He signed and now defends a tariff bill made by and for the special interests, following the passage of which the cost of living rose beyond all precedent.

10—He indorsed, in his Boston speech, in the person of Senator Aldrich, the most conspicuous representative of reaction and special interests in the Senate.

11—He indorsed, in his Winona speech, in the person of Mr. Tawney, your bitterest enemy in the House of Representatives, and next to the Speaker himself perhaps the most conspicuous advocate of Cannonism and reaction.

12—In the same speech at Winona he tried to read out of the Republican Party Senators Nelson, Beveridge, Cummins and other Republicans whose fight was made for equality of opportunity and a square deal, and the honest redemption of our party pledges.

13—He has repeatedly set party solidarity above the public welfare, and has yielded to political expediency of the lowest type, as in the case of the reported offer, first of a Federal Judgeship and later of a diplomatic post, to ex-Senator Fulton, and the appointment of R. C. Kerens as Minister to Austria.

14—He has apparently impaired or abandoned, through a decision of his Attorney General, the principles which you established of Federal regulation and control, in the public interest, of water powers on navigable streams.

15—He is placing or has placed himself in a position such that the only alliance open to him is with the special interests.

16—He has allowed the great mass of the people to lose confidence in the President.

The general tendency shown in these examples cannot be mistaken. It is away from the Roosevelt policies and the people, and in favor of the special interests and the few. Nevertheless, I want to say again that while the whole trend of the Administration has been opposed to the purposes and ideals of the last seven years, I have not yet lost all hope.

The issue is so tremendously important to the public welfare that a man's duty is clear to describe the facts as he sees them. I have known, and admired, Mr. Taft since my boyhood; I have been anxious to give him the benefit of every doubt. I have reached the point of view herein stated as the result of a period of disappointment through which I would not willingly pass again. If my fears should turn out to be justified I realize that your disappointment will be even keener than mine. I regret intensely that it is necessary to write this letter, but I can see no proper way to avoid it.

I have supported Mr. Taft and I shall continue to support him up to the point where my loyalty to the people of this country requires me to break with the Administration.

Just a final word. The hold of your policies on the plain people is stronger than ever. Many of your former enemies are now your friends. The line between the friends of special privilege and the friends of an equal chance is daily growing sharper. The issue has become immeasurably larger than politics or any man's political fortunes. It is a straight fight for human rights. That is how it looks to me on the last day of 1909.

Looking back over almost forty years I find no reason to quarrel with that estimate of Taft and the situation created by his weakness.

We had fallen back down the hill T.R. led us up. The special interests were once more in full control. The whole trend of the Administration had indeed been opposed to the purposes and ideals of the last seven years. It was too bad.

This was T.R.'s reply:

Upper White Nile
March 1st, 1910.

Dear Gifford:

At Gondokoro I received your letter and also the definite news that you had been removed. The appointment in your place of a man of high character, a noted forestry expert [Henry S. Graves], in no way, not in the very least degree, lightens the blow; for besides being the chief of the forest bureau you were the leader among all the men in public office—and the aggressive, hard-hitting leader—of all the forces which were struggling for conservation, which were fighting for the general interest as against special privilege.

It is a very ungracious thing for an ex-President to criticize his successor; and yet I cannot as an honest man cease to battle for the principles for which you and I and Jim [Garfield] and [Herbert Knox] Smith and [Attorney General] Moody and the rest of our close associates stood. I shall of course say nothing at present. But I do wish I could see you. Is there any chance of your meeting me in Europe? If not, will you not meet me on the steamer on my return? I wish to see you before I in even the smallest degree commit myself.

Our trip has been a real success; Kermit has developed in remarkable fashion.

With love to your mother.

Ever faithfully yours,
Theodore Roosevelt.

However well I realize that it is overgenerous, I am proud of that letter. That is one of the reasons why it is printed here.

T.R. wanted to see me no more than I wanted to see him. So on March 29, after the lawyers and the Committee had asked their questions, and after the witnesses on my side had said their say, quietly I left Washington. Under the assumed name of Gaylord Smith, I sailed to Hamburg on the liner *President Grant.*

At Copenhagen I spent a week with my sister, where her husband was British Minister, stopped to see Lady Brandis at Bonn, reached Porto Maurizio in the Italian Riviera the next night, and at the hotel there had a fine talk with Cal O'Laughlin and Gilson Gardner, who had met T.R. in Africa.

The next day, April 11, 1910, I had, says my diary, "One of the best and most satisfactory talks with T.R. I ever had. Lasted nearly all day, and till about 10:30 at night."

It was a good talk. I brought him up to date—told him the facts. We discussed them, and he understood them. They left him in a very embarrassing position, but that could not be helped.

T.R. had lost none of his interest in the Conservation policy, and showed it by agreeing to speak at the National Conservation Congress (at St. Paul) after he got home. That was Associated Press front-page news, and it had its effect.

After Porto Maurizio (the suitcase with which I made that trip has traveled with me many thousands of miles since then, but the hotel label is visible still) I began to relive old times. At Zurich, says my diary, "Forstmeister Meister came while I was at breakfast. We spent the morning in the city forests near by, and after a very pleasant lunch at his apartment with Mrs. Meister [over the offices of the *Neue Zuercher Zeitung* which he owns] we went to the Sihlwald by train."

The dear old gentleman came expressly from Berne to see me, took me through the forest I loved so well, and wouldn't even let me pay my fare on the train. That I enjoyed it all immensely goes without saying.

Next to Nancy, where I found Joseph Hulot at the station, almost dissolved in tears. He had had a hard time. We called first on his mother and met his two children—girl thirteen, boy twelve. Then on Guyot, who had resigned as Director. He showed us all over the Forest School. Then we saw Hueffel, and after that had a fine talk with Henry.

Next we took train to Pont-à-Mousson and drove to Dombasle, Joseph's farm. He had a huge house and enormous farm buildings, with 500 acres of land, and he rented all but the house for about 6,700 francs a year net. He lived with excessive simplicity—we should call it hardship in America. It did me no end of good to see Joseph again.

From Nancy to Paris, where for two days I revisited the scenes of my childhood and youth in many miles on foot, talked with Bob Bacon, Mrs. T.R. and Ethel, saw the Jusserands, heard "most interesting reports from home. Taft losing steadily," and left for London

"BY GEOEGE, PINCHOT, I'M GLAD TO SEE YOU!"

Southern Lumberman, April, 1910

and Horace Plunkett's house near Dublin, where I rejoiced in the superlative greenness of the Irish spring, and nearly froze in its chilliness.

But there was nothing chilly about the welcome of Horace and his friends. I got to know G. W. Russell (famous as A.E.), Dr. Mahaffy, and many more, went up the Hill of Tara, learned that "no stoves are used—cooking hereabouts by the rank and file all on open peat fires."

Best of all, Plunkett took me to Mt. Charles, the birthplace of my dear old Irish nurse, Mary McCadden, who looked after me, baby, boy, and man, for almost fifty-nine years. I wrote her from there.

After that I went to see Sir William Schlich, who had been so kind to me when I was getting started, and in due time sailed for home.

The *Arabic* reached New York on May 30. Amos and Tom Shipp met her at Quarantine, and there was much eager talk and many questions. Next day to Washington, where I discussed the situation that same evening with Senator Dolliver. The Ballinger-Pinchot investigation might be over, but the fight for Conservation and the rest of the T.R. policies most certainly was not—was not then, is not now, and will not be until in actual fact the public interest moves into first place.

90. *What It All Means*

I have come to the end of my story—the story of how Forestry in America was born and how American Forestry in turn gave birth to the Conservation policy. It is the outline also of how the conservation of natural resources, and of human resources as well, began to spread from America to all the world as the firm basis of permanent prosperity among men and of lasting peace among nations. But what does it all mean?

I believe, and I have made no secret of my belief, that a good forester must also be a good citizen. I have tried to be both, with what success it is not for me to say. But at least I am not without experience.

What I have learned in more than half a century of active life, whatever else it may be, is not mere book theory. The conclusions I have reached are based on what I myself have lived, and seen, and known, and had to fight. They are the direct results of responsible work in Forestry and Conservation; in public administration, national and state; in politics, national, state, and local; in city, farm, and frontier; in college and church; in many other phases of American life; and on personal acquaintance with every state in the Union.

Through all my working days, a part of my job, in office and out, and a most essential part, has been to estimate and understand public opinion, and to arouse, create, guide and apply it.

What then, as I see it, is the conclusion of the whole matter?

This: The earth and its resources belong of right to its people.

Without natural resources life itself is impossible. From birth to death, natural resources, transformed for human use, feed, clothe, shelter, and transport us. Upon them we depend for every material necessity, comfort, convenience, and protection in our lives. Without abundant resources prosperity is out of reach.

Therefore the conservation of natural resources is the fundamental material problem. It is the open door to economic and political progress. That was never so true as now.

The first duty of the human race on the material side is to control the use of the earth and all that therein is. Conservation means the wise use of the earth and its resources for the lasting good of men. Conservation is the foresighted utilization, preservation, and/or renewal of forests, waters, lands, and minerals, for the greatest good of the greatest number for the longest time.

Since Conservation has become a household word, it has come to mean many things to many men. To me it means, everywhere and always, that the public good comes first.

To the use of the natural resources, renewable or nonrenewable, each generation has the first right. Nevertheless no generation can be allowed needlessly to damage or reduce the future general wealth and welfare by the way it uses or misuses any natural resource.

Nationally, the outgrowth and result of Conservation is efficiency. In the old world that is passing, in the new world that is coming, national efficiency has been and will be a controlling factor in national safety and welfare.

Internationally, the central purpose of Conservation is permanent peace. No nation, not even the United States, is self-sufficient in all the resources it requires. Throughout human history one of the commonest causes of war has been the demand for land. Land (agricultural land, forest land, coal, iron, oil, uranium, and other mineral-producing land) means natural resources.

Therefore, world-wide practice of Conservation and fair and continued access by all nations to the resources they need are the two indispensable foundations of continuous plenty and of permanent peace.

Conservation is the application of common sense to the common problems for the common good. Since its objective is the ownership, control, development, processing, distribution, and use of the natural resources for the benefit of the people, it is by its very nature the antithesis of monopoly. So long as people are oppressed by the lack of such ownership and control, so long will they continue to be cheated of their right to life, liberty, and the pursuit of happiness, cheated out of their enjoyment of the earth and all that it contains. It is obvious, therefore, that the principles of Conservation must apply to human beings as well as to natural resources.

The Conservation policy then has three great purposes.

First: wisely to use, protect, preserve, and renew the natural resources of the earth.

Second: to control the use of the natural resources and their products in the common interest, and to secure their distribution to the people at fair and reasonable charges for goods and services.

Third: to see to it that the rights of the people to govern themselves shall not be controlled by great monopolies through their power over natural resources.

Two of the principal ways in which lack of Conservation works out in damage to the general welfare are: (A) by destruction of forests, erosion of soils, injury of waterways, and waste of nonrenewable mineral resources. Here is strong reason for Government control. (B) by monopoly of natural and human resources, their products and application, and of the instruments by which these are made available.

Monopoly means power—power not only over the supply of natural resources, but also power to fix prices, and to exact unfair profits which lead to higher living costs for the people. It is the very essence of democracy that the greatest advantage of each of us is best reached through common prosperity of all of us. Monopoly is the denial of that great truth.

Monopoly of resources which prevents, limits, or destroys equality of opportunity is one of the most effective of all ways to control and limit human rights, especially the right of self-government.

Monopoly on the loose is a source of many of the economic, political, and social evils which afflict the sons of men. Its abolition or regulation is an inseparable part of the Conservation policy.

And that is far from the whole story. What the people are forced to pay for Concentrated Wealth and its monopolies is by no means confined to an unjustly high cost of living. A moral and intellectual price, a price in knowledge and understanding, in education, in degradation of standards, and in limited freedom of thought and action, must be paid also. Here may well be the heaviest cost of all.

Said Louis D. Brandeis in an opinion from the Supreme Court bench: "Those who won our independence believed that the final end of the State was to make men free to develop their faculties. They valued liberty both as an end and as a means. They believed liberty to be the secret of happiness, and courage to be the secret of liberty. They believed that freedom to think as you will and to speak as you think are means indispensable to the discovery and spread of political truth; that the greatest menace to freedom is an inert people; that public discussion is a political duty; and that this should be a fundamental principle of the American government."

How far Concentrated Wealth is willing to go in pursuit of profit has been clearly shown in this war and the last. In both wars profit was put before patriotism by certain great concentrations of capital which traded, through international cartels, with similar concentrations in the enemy's country, even to the extent of furnishing military supplies for hostile armies. To them profit justified anything.

(When I speak of Concentrated Wealth I refer to the many forms of concentration of economic power by which greedy men have sought domination. I mean the monopoly power of great corporations, of banks and insurance companies, of utilities and power companies, as well as individual fortunes. The devices by which Concentrated Wealth controls men and resources are many, complicated and devious. The financial manipulations, control of prices, interlocking directorates, monopolization of patents and materials, and last but not least, the concentration of ownership of newspapers and radio broadcasting networks, are all part of the far-reaching web of Concentrated Wealth.)

Concentrated Wealth attributes the prosperity and progress of the

United States to what it calls free enterprise. To it free enterprise means freedom to take, keep, and control all the resources, services, and opportunities it can, and charge for them the last possible cent. It overlooks the three main factors in our progress: first, our incomparable natural resources, some of them still in the hands of the people; second, government by the people, so far as we have actually had it; and third, the drive and stimulus of mixed races adventuring in a new land.

Concentrated Wealth can only maintain its strangle hold over the general welfare if it can get the people to accept its exactions, and especially the methods by which it gets its power, as normal and natural. For the people can destroy monopoly at any time they choose to exert themselves.

The monopolists must accustom people to their tyranny by a constant stream of praise for great corporations and of free enterprise according to their own interpretation, as well as discrediting of liberal movements and leaders—all of which is facilitated by their ever increasing control of the press, the radio, and other news outlets.

They are infinitely resourceful in their campaigns. On the highly controversial issue of state or national regulation of natural resources and public utilities, the Economic Royalists, as F.D.R. called them, are for whichever is the least effective. Thus, when certain of the states began to enforce effective regulation, they were all out against state control. But when T.R. used the power of the Federal government to limit exploitation, Concentrated Wealth made an about-face and became the foremost advocate and defender of states' rights. It is so still today.

In many states huge sums are poured out for the upkeep of political machines and the financing of primary and general elections, for the purpose of controlling legislation and also executive action and judicial decisions. It is far more prevalent than the general public has any idea of. This is not mere theory. It is based on evidence secured by personal experience over many years and in many parts of the country.

Because so much of my work has been done in public office, I have had the need and the opportunity to understand what makes politics tick. For many years I have known and had to fight the political servants of the great special interests, who were never more dangerous than they are today.

But in the hearts of the American people democracy has not been denied. The Four Freedoms of Franklin Roosevelt—Freedom of Speech, Freedom of Worship, Freedom from Want, and Freedom from Fear—have, I am confident, been accepted by those whom Abraham Lincoln called the plain people, accepted as their right, and no more than their right. If that is true, we have come to a turning point.

At each turning point in human history two great human forces have fought for control. One demanded a greater share of prosperity and freedom for the many. The other strove for the concentration of power, privilege, and wealth in the hands of the few. One wanted to go forward to better things. The other strove to go back to what it called "the good old days."

Just as Feudalism, with its tyranny, finally made itself intolerable, so too plutocracy, with its rule over the man by the dollar, with its hardships for the many and its luxury for the few, with its greed and its injustice, must be made to travel the same road. It is time for America and the world to move on from a social order in which unregulated profit is the driving force. It is time to move up to a social order in which equality of opportunity will cease to be a dream and actually come to pass.

I do not pretend to foretell just what that order will be or by what steps it will be reached. When it comes, I want it to come by development and not by revolution.

When it comes, I hope and believe the new order will be based on co-operation instead of monopoly, on sharing instead of grasping, and that mutual helpfulness will replace the law of the jungle. When it comes, I hope and believe that great unregulated concentrations of wealth, with their enormous power for evil, will no longer be allowed to exist.

I believe in free enterprise—freedom for the common man to think and work and rise to the limit of his ability, with due regard to the rights of others. But in what Concentrated Wealth means by free enterprise—freedom to use and abuse the common man—I do not believe. I object to the law of the jungle.

The earth, I repeat, belongs of right to all its people, and not to a minority, insignificant in numbers but tremendous in wealth and power. The public good must come first.

The rightful use and purpose of our natural resources is to make all the people strong and well, able and wise, well-taught, well-fed, well-clothed, well-housed, full of knowledge and initiative, with equal opportunity for all and special privilege for none.

Whatsoever ye would that men should do to you, do ye even so to them.

That is the answer.

Index

About Island Press

Island Press, a nonprofit organization, publishes, markets, and distributes the most advanced thinking on the conservation of our natural resources—books about soil, land, water, forests, wildlife, and hazardous and toxic wastes. These books are practical tools used by public officials, business and industry leaders, natural resource managers, and concerned citizens working to solve both local and global resource problems.

Founded in 1978, Island Press reorganized in 1984 to meet the increasing demand for substantive books on all resource-related issues. Island Press publishes and distributes under its own imprint and offers these services to other nonprofit organizations.

Funding to support Island Press is provided by The Mary Reynolds Babcock Foundation, The William H. Donner Foundation, Inc., The Ford Foundation, The George Gund Foundation, The William and Flora Hewlett Foundation, The Joyce Foundation, The Andrew W. Mellon Foundation, Northwest Area Foundation, The J.N. Pew, Jr. Charitable Trust, Rockefeller Brothers Fund, and The Tides Foundation.

Island Press Board of Directors